A HISTORY OF

JUDAISM

IN TWO VOLUMES

DANIEL JEREMY SILVER

BERNARD MARTIN

A HISTORY

OF

Judaism

VOLUME I

From ABRAHAM *to*

MAIMONIDES

DANIEL JEREMY SILVER

Basic Books, Inc., Publishers

NEW YORK

296.09
H673
1974
V. 1

Copyright © 1974 by Basic Books, Inc.
Library of Congress Catalog Card Number: 73–90131
Volume I SBN: 465–03006–8
Volume II SBN: 465–03007–6
Set SBN: 465–03008–4
Printed in the United States of America
DESIGNED BY VINCENT TORRE
74 75 76 77 78   10 9 8 7 6 5 4 3 2 1

To Adele

A good wife means a good life.
She is one of the gifts of God to those who fear Him.

Ben Sira 26:3

CONTENTS

PREFACE   ix

ACKNOWLEDGMENTS   xiii

TRANSLITERATION OF HEBREW TERMS   xvii

I	The Fathers and Their Way	3
II	The Covenant Relationship	19
III	God's Freedom and God's Bondage	34
IV	Land	50
V	Power	67
VI	The Way and the Wayward	77
VII	This Was Believed	106
VIII	Judah Is Judged	125
IX	Defeat, Dispersion, and Exile	140
X	From the Exile to Alexander	155
XI	The Age of Variety	172
XII	A Change in Cultural Style	197
XIII	Torah in the Age of Variety	215
XIV	Angels, Devils, and Judgment Day	239
XV	After the Fall	255
XVI	Talmudic Judaism	279
XVII	The Rabbinic Mind	300
XVIII	Judaism and Islam	320
XIX	Dar al Islam—West	352
XX	The Other Moses	390

Contents

APPENDIX I   Books of the Apocrypha and
the Pseudepigrapha   417

APPENDIX II   The Dead Sea Scrolls   418

APPENDIX III   Chronology of *Midrashim*   419

APPENDIX IV   The *Talmud*   422

APPENDIX V   Tables of Abbreviations   426

NOTES   429

GLOSSARY OF HEBREW TERMS   436

BIBLIOGRAPHY   442

INDEX   465

ILLUSTRATIONS FOLLOW   238

PREFACE

THESE VOLUMES are an attempt to give a historical account of Judaism—a way of life, thought, and faith in which we believe deeply and which nourishes our spirits as it has sustained and inspired countless men and women for more than a hundred generations. Our story begins three and a half millennia ago, on the outer fringes of the settled lands of Bronze Age western Asia, and continues to the present day, when communities of Jews are to be found in virtually every country of the world. Jews have been on the historical scene for a very long time, and their religion, Judaism, has played a major cultural role in almost all civilizations except those of eastern Asia. Hence, our story is inevitably long and complex.

We have written for an understanding but not necessarily technically trained audience and have sought to avoid the esoteric terminology and discussion of subtle and refined points that would delight only the professional scholar. We have written to provide Jews with self-understanding and to suggest to others the contributions of Judaism to the creative development of world civilization. Many questions of faith and philosophy suggest themselves, many problems of truth and value arise. But perhaps the most intriguing question of all is that of definition: What was/is Judaism? If Moses, or David, or Jeremiah were to come into a modern synagogue, however "traditional," they would shake their heads in bewilderment, wondering what this building was, who these persons called rabbi and cantor might be, and whence the chanting and prayers came. Moses would not even recognize the Hebrew letters in the Torah and Prayer Book. What then is Judaism? Belief in God? But is the God of Abraham, Isaac, and Jacob the God of Mordecai Kaplan? Is Judaism the Ten Commandments? Certainly honoring father and mother meant one thing to the polygamous family in an autocratic tribal setting and means quite another in an Israeli kibbutz today. Are we entitled to say: *Toujours ça change, toujours c'est la même chose?* Perhaps. But can a community that bases its life on a revealed law undergo endless change? What were/are the enduring elements of Judaism that may be defined in terms of doctrine, of calendar and ceremony, of moral values and imperatives? Or is it a case of each generation simply labeling its adaptation, "tradition"? The reader will make up his own mind. We have made up ours. Our studies confirm our preconception that, despite all the changes, there has been no age which has not listened reverently to the divine voice of Sinai, no generation without a gripping tension between the word of God and the palpable realities of the present day. The Jew has always looked back, and his historical past has always informed his present.

What we have attempted here is an account of the spiritual odyssey of the Jewish people from its beginnings to the present day. We have refused to restrict our understanding of Judaism to a creed, code of conduct, or cultic system. Judaism is all of these and more. It also includes the entire intellectual culture of the Jewish people and the phenomena that have significantly molded its inner life.

The story of Judaism cannot be told without reference to the story of the Jewish people—its living bearers. We have, where necessary, sketched elements of the social and political history of the Jewish people that are essential to an understanding of the evolving forms of its faith and spiritual culture. A good deal of our discussion revolves around literature. "The Jews," Mohammed said long ago, "are the people of the Book." It is on the Book of Books that Judaism is founded, and it is almost exclusively in the written word that Jews throughout the ages have expressed the ideas, values, and insights that are uniquely Jewish.

Rejecting as historically untrue the notion that Judaism is a monolithic, unchanging, closed system, we have attempted to indicate the richness, diversity, and complexity that have characterized it in virtually every one of its great ages. We have sought to deal meaningfully with what we regard as the major phenomena, and we have resisted the temptation to discuss minor details that would only divert the reader's attention.

Since this book is written for a general audience, we have kept the scholarly apparatus to a minimum and provided only those aids which we believe may be useful in orienting the reader when he might not be quite sure of his location.

We are more than conscious of the presumptuous scope of this undertaking, and of our own limitations. Given the vastness and complexity of the sources on which such a study must be based, no two persons can hope to have complete mastery of all of them. Neither is it possible for them to achieve a full understanding of the perhaps twenty separate host cultures in which Jews have lived and to which they have necessarily related. Yet the task we have here undertaken is worth working on and stumbling over. Surely others will refine and expand what we have begun.

While we collaborated in the planning of this study, in the actual execution Volume I was written by Daniel Jeremy Silver and Volume II by Bernard Martin. We have read and criticized each other's work and profited from many discussions; nevertheless, each of us is responsible only for his individual volume.

A final word about our prejudices. The authors are products of the Western intellectual tradition, now in their middle years, liberal and critical in their orientation toward the Jewish tradition, but nonetheless committed Jews. We were trained to respect intellectual honesty, to strive for truth, and to avoid twisting facts to fit preconceived ideologies. These pages were written in the spirit of love, but not as apologetics.

DANIEL JEREMY SILVER
BERNARD MARTIN

ACKNOWLEDGMENTS

THANKS are due to the following for permission to quote from their material:

The Jewish Publication Society of America, Philadelphia, for quotations from *The Torah* © 1962; *The Book of Isaiah* © 1973; *The Book of Psalms* © 1972; *Mekilta de-Rabbi Ishmael*, edited and translated by Jacob Z. Lauterbach, copyright © 1935; *Selected Poems of Judah Halevi*, edited and translated by Nina Salaman, copyright © 1924; *Selected Poems of Moses Ibn Ezra*, edited by Heinrich Brody and translated by Solomon Solis-Cohen, copyright © 1934; and *The Book of Tradition* (*Sefer Ha-Qabbalah*) by Abraham Ibn Daud, a critical edition with a translation and notes by Gerson D. Cohen, © 1967.

Quotations from the *Tanach* excepting The Five Books of Moses, Isaiah, and Psalms from *The New English Bible*. © The Delegates of the Oxford University Press and The Syndics of the Cambridge University Press 1961, 1970. Reprinted by permission.

References from *The Revised Standard Version of the Apocrypha* copyrighted © 1957 are by permission of the Division of Christian Education of the National Council of Churches of Christ in the U.S.A.

Bloch Publishing Company, New York, for quotations from *The Authorized Daily Prayer Book* by Joseph H. Hertz, rev. ed., copyright © 1948 by Ruth Hecht; *Solomon Ibn Gabirol's Choice of Pearls*, translated by A. Cohen, copyright © 1925; *The Commentary to Mishnah Aboth* by Moses Maimonides, translated with an introduction and notes by Arthur David, © 1968 by Arthur David.

Harvard University Press, Cambridge, for quotations from Josephus, *The Jewish War, Jewish Antiquities*, and *Against Apion*, with an English translation by H. St. J. Thackeray and Ralph Marcus, 9 vols., copyright © 1926–1965; Philo, *De Confusione Linguarum, De Somniis, Legum Allegoria, De Praemiis et Poenis, De Specialibus Legibus, Questiones et Solutiones in Genesin, De Vita Moyesis*, and *De Opificio*

Acknowledgments

Mundi, with an English translation by F. H. Colson and G. H. Whitaker, 13 vols., copyright © 1929–1953. Both of these sets are in The Loeb Classical Library.

Yale University Press, New Haven, for selections from *Karaite Anthology*, translated with notes by Leon Nemoy, copyright © 1952; *Saadia Gaon: The Book of Beliefs and Opinions*, translated by Samuel Rosenblatt, copyright © 1948; *The Code of Maimonides—Book Three— The Book of Seasons*, translated by Solomon Gandz and Hyman Klein, © 1961; *The Midrash on Psalms*, translated by William G. Braude, © 1959; *The Fathers According to Rabbi Nathan*, translated by Judah Goldin, copyright © 1955.

Raphael Haim Cohen's Press, Ltd., Jerusalem, for selections from *The Tahkemoni of Judah Al-Harizi*, translated by Victor Emanuel Reichert, © 1965 by V. E. Reichert.

Harper & Row, Publishers, Inc., New York, for selections from *The Third and Fourth Books of Maccabees*, edited and translated by Moses Hadas, copyright © 1953.

East and West Library, London, for selections from Jehuda Halevi, *Kuzari*, abridged edition with an Introduction and a commentary by Isaak Heinemann, copyright © 1947.

Reprinted by permission of Routledge & Kegan Paul Ltd. and Schocken Books Inc., New York, from *The Meditation of the Sad Soul* by Abraham Bar Hayya, translated and with an Introduction by Geoffrey Wigoder. Copyright © 1968 by Geoffrey Wigoder.

Vallentine, Mitchell & Co. Ltd., London, for quotations from *The Kingly Crown* by Solomon Ibn Gabirol, translated and with an introduction by Bernard Lewis, © 1961 by Bernard Lewis. Published by Vallentine, Mitchell & Co. Ltd., London, 1961.

Ancient Near Eastern Texts Relating to the Old Testament, ed. by James B. Pritchard, 3rd. rev. edn., with Supplement (copyright © 1969 by Princeton University Press): Selections from "Egyptian Myths, Tales, and Mortuary Texts," transl. John A. Wilson, pp. 19 and 378; "Akkadian Myths and Epics," transl. E. A. Speiser, p. 90; "Collections of Laws from Mesopotamia and Asia Minor," transl. S. N. Kramer, p. 165; and "Ugaritic Myths, Epics, and Legends," transl. H. L. Ginsberg, p. 153. Reprinted by permission of Princeton University Press.

The Soncino Press, London, for quotations from *The Babylonian Talmud*, translated under the editorship of I. Epstein, copyright © 1935–1948.

The Clarendon Press, Oxford, for quotations from *The*

Acknowledgments

Mishnah, translated by Herbert Danby, copyright © 1933.

American Academy for Jewish Research, New York, for quotations from Boaz Cohen, trans., *Epistle to Yemen*, in Abraham Halkin, *Iggeret Teman*. Copyright © 1952 by American Academy of Jewish Research.

Oxford University Press for quotations from *The Apocrypha and Pseudepigrapha of the Old Testament*, edited by R. H. Charles, copyright © 1913, The Clarendon Press, Oxford.

I am also grateful to the following sources for permission to use the illustrations:

The earliest representation of the *menorah* courtesy of N. Avigad and The Israel Exploration Society. Originally published in *Israel Exploration Journal*, Vol. 20, Numbers 1–2, 1970.

The silver tetradrachm courtesy of the Israel Department of Antiquities and Museums, Jerusalem.

Two pieces of gold glass courtesy of the Israel Department of Antiquities and Museums, Jerusalem.

Bronze oil lamp courtesy of the Israel Department of Antiquities and Museums, Jerusalem. Collection of Mrs. M. Schloessinger, New York. Photograph © David Harris, Jerusalem.

Mosaic pavement from Bet Shean courtesy of the Israel Department of Antiquities and Museums, Jerusalem. Photograph © David Harris, Jerusalem.

Carpet page from the *Second Leningrad Bible* courtesy of *Encyclopaedia Judaica* Photo Archive, Jerusalem.

The Dead Sea Scrolls copyright by E. L. Sukenik, *The Dead Sea Scrolls of the Hebrew University* (Jerusalem: Magnes Press, 1955).

The photograph of Qumran courtesy *Encyclopaedia Judaica* Photo Archive, Jerusalem. Photograph by W. Braun, Jerusalem.

Bet Alpha mosaic, Susiya synagogue, and model of the Second Temple in Herodian times, photographs © David Harris, Jerusalem.

The photographs of the Temple in Arad, the model of the First Temple, the mosaic floor at Maon, and the carved wood panels from the Ben Ezra synagogue are reprinted by permission of the Israel Museum.

I am grateful to Miriam Leikind, Librarian of The Temple, Cleveland, Ohio, who provided me with invaluable bibliographic assistance, and to a dear friend, L. Y. Rahmani of the Department of Antiquities of the State of Israel, who made ancient Israel live as we walked

Acknowledgments

in the new State, and who made available the photographs that grace the text. My students at Case Western Reserve University and at The Temple asked the questions which I have tried to answer and suggested what background information could not be taken for granted. Marie Pluth and Lillian Abramovitz carefully typed the manuscript during each of its revisions.

TRANSLITERATION OF
HEBREW TERMS

א is not transliterated

ב = b

בּ = v

ג ,גּ = g

ד ,דּ = d

ה = h

ו = v (where not a vowel)

ז = z

ח = ḥ

ט = t

י = y

כּ = k

כ = ch

ל = l

מ = m

נ = n

ס = s

ע is not transliterated

פּ = p

פ = f

צ = tz

ק = k

ר = r

שׁ = sh

שׂ = s

ת ,תּ = t

ָ = a

ַ = a

ֹ ,ו = o

ֻ ,וּ = u

short ָ = o

י ֵ = ei

ֶ = e

ִ = i

ֵ = ei

ְ = e

ָ: = o

ַ: = a

vocal *sheva* = e

silent *sheva* is not transliterated

[xvii]

VOLUME I

From ABRAHAM to

MAIMONIDES

❧ I ❧

The Fathers and Their Way

I<small>N</small> the beginning they were called Hebrews. In dress and custom they could not be distinguished from other groups of seminomads who infiltrated the western horn of the Fertile Crescent during the first half of the second millennium B.C.E. Organized by tribes, they traveled on donkeys in rather large paramilitary groups. They spoke a West Semitic dialect, a close relative to Aramaic. They treasured their chronicles in spoken sagas, some of which, edited by their descendants, form the nucleus of the book of Genesis (chapters 11–50). They traded in grain, wine, and wool; pastured flocks of sheep and goats on unclaimed land outside the boundary stones of local city-states; hired themselves out as smiths, musicians, and field hands, and their young men as mercenaries. If the local feudal lord was weak, the Hebrews were not above engaging in attack and plunder.

Their families were patriarchal and polygamous, and inheritance passed according to a fixed schedule among the children of the first or breeding wife. Within the tribe justice was determined by the tribal chief or a Council of Elders, and the entire tribe was responsible for the actions of its members toward outsiders. The principle of monetary compensation for injury was known. Slavery was taken for granted, although the purchase of a slave was rarely within the tribe's means, and the tribe was under heavy obligation to ransom any of its members who were captured and enslaved. There was always danger when someone traveled outside the reach of his tribe's protection. Hospitality to the stranger was, therefore, a much-prized virtue and definite rules governed a host's obligation, as Lot well knew.

Genesis presents the history of the Hebrews in the form of biographies of the direct descendants of a single clan head, Abraham. The accuracy of the events described has often been challenged, and few critical scholars confidently defend the historicity of Abraham's sacrifice of Isaac or Joseph's coat of many colors. Some see the patriarchs as tribal chiefs, not necessarily directly related, around whose persons popular legends grew and clustered, later to be simplified and edited into a single narrative. Others prefer to consider Abraham, Isaac, and Jacob, not to speak of Ishmael, Esau, and the twelve brothers, as tribal epigones. There are many theories, none provable, since these men appear nowhere except in the biblical narrative; whatever the particular theory, it is now certain that these stories are not later Israelite fancies woven out of imaginative cloth, but contain authentic descriptions of what Hebrew life must have been in the early second millennium.

Modern research enables us to understand details of various Genesis stories which the biblical editors reported faithfully but obviously no longer understood. When Rachel and Jacob fled her father's home, Laban zealously pursued the pair, and on catching up bitterly accused them of the theft of his household gods. No explanation is offered why the theft of these small, inexpensive figures should have caused such a sensation. Over the centuries commentators have exhausted their ingenuity trying to explain the situation, but without solving the mystery. Then, a generation ago, archeologists uncovered the archives of the city of Nuzi on the upper Tigris. These cuneiform records date from the fifteenth or fourteenth centuries B.C.E., but reflect a much earlier Hurrian or West Semitic culture. They record, *inter alia*, that a son-in-law could, on behalf of his wife, claim a share in the family inheritance if he could produce the family idols as proof that the testator had decided to make such a transfer of property. Similar discoveries "explain" why Abraham and Isaac describe their wives as sisters (sisterhood involved a higher degree of honor and protection), and why Abraham allowed Sarah to choose Hagar as his wife (the right to choose a concubine for breeding purposes was sometimes vested with the barren first wife).

[4]

The Fathers and Their Way

Authenticity of detail does not prove the historicity of an entire episode, or even the existence of the named protagonists. The Genesis heroes may not have lived, and if they lived, their lives may not have included the episodes attributed to them. But the wealth of culturally and chronologically appropriate detail suggests that the sagas were formed in the period which they describe, and reliably transmitted over many generations. The events so described can no longer be summarily dismissed as fanciful inventions.

The most important of these events was the break made by Abraham and the fathers away from conventional religious forms. The saga describes how Abraham was ordered by God to leave the ancestral home in Ur, and how, when he arrived in the west, a special covenant was struck with his Patron. Without exception, the various strands and traditions which make up the Bible emphasize that Abraham moved away, not only from his birthplace, but from his religious background, and that his move westward coincided with the formation of a new basis for his clan's spiritual life. The precise nature of the new bonds cannot be described; what was originally distinctive may have been no more than a sense of being bound to a patron deity different from those which Terah and Abraham's other ancestors had worshipped. Outwardly Hebrew practice probably changed little, if at all, but there had been a change of loyalties, a new beginning, and this time would be revered as the constitutive moment in Israel's life. The myth of origins grew quickly and was quickly ritualized. "Long ago your forefathers, Terah and his sons Abraham and Nahor, lived beside the Euphrates and they worshipped other gods. I took your Father Abraham from beside the Euphrates . . ." (Josh. 24:2–3).

Possibly the Hebrews believed no more than that their headman had a patron God who protected their travels. Probably they were only dimly aware of anything distinctive about their relationship with this God; they certainly were unaware that they and their sagas were destined for immortality. But their descendants cherished these sagas as all peoples do their beginnings, and would insist that these events had established and confirmed the close and special relations of the people and its God, and represented the initial moment of God's inexplicable but wonderful special love for a special people.

The term "Hebrew" is appellative, not generic. It may derive from an Akkadian root *apiru* (Heb. *ivri*), which meant caravaneer and was applied by the settled folk of Syria-Palestine to the motley of landless tribes who came from beyond the boundaries. It is not certain that the various tribes called Hebrews were conscious of any racial unity or common ancestry. Those dull genealogies in Genesis, generally skipped over by the reader, relate Abraham and his descendants not only to other West Semites but to North and South Arabian tribes as well. When, a millennium later, the Israelites talked about their progenitors, they claimed for them neither noble birth nor purity of blood. Typically during the Sukkot, the autumn harvest festival, as the Israelites presented their thanksgiving offerings in the Temple, they recited a ritual formula which proclaimed simply, "My father was a fugitive Aramean . . ." (Deut. 26:5). The sixth-century prophet Ezekiel mocked the social pretensions of some of his contemporaries by reminding the prideful that their ancestors had been both quite ordinary and a mixed breed: "Canaan is the land of your ancestry and there you were born; the Amorite was your father and a Hittite your mother" (Ezek. 16:3). Not only had they been ordinary and mixed, but also peasant:

This is how you were treated at birth: when you were born, your navel-string was not tied, you were not bathed in water ready for the rubbing, you were not salted as you should have been nor wrapped in swaddling clothes. No one cared for you enough to do any of these things or, indeed, to have any pity for you; you were thrown out on the bare ground in your own filth on the day of your birth (16:4–5).

Hebrew traditions did not provide the stuff out of which national arrogance and ambition might easily sculpt racial myths, and such vanities remained largely foreign to the Jewish tradition.

The epic of Hebrew beginnings is remarkably unpretentious. Sunday School texts sententiously label these progenitors "patriarchs," a word redolent of age, dignity, and wisdom. The synagogue called them simply *avot*—the fathers. The Bible does not claim for them a divine lineage. They are not offspring of the gods, nor are they described as godlike men or as saints. Their lives, described boldly and without shame, indicate that they shared in all the normal human frailties. The fathers and mothers were ordinary folk. When the Israelites later affirmed that they had been chosen by God, they knew that they had not been chosen because of any natural superiority. The reasons for their election were God's, and whatever His reasons they were not ordinary. "It was not because you are the most numerous of peoples that the Lord set His heart on you and chose you—indeed, you are the smallest of peoples; but it was because the Lord loved you . . ." (Deut. 7:7–8).

The Fathers and Their Way

These early Hebrews had little sense of being set apart. Unaware that they were destined for a central role in history, they moved back and forth along the edges of the Fertile Crescent, herding, smithing, and trading, the general drift of their migration west and south—that is, from northern Mesopotamia across Syria to Palestine and Egypt. The exact route and time of these migrations and what set these peoples in motion are not known. Their trek may be related to a large-scale movement of Semitic tribes from Mesopotamia to the west and south which took place during the early years of the second millennium, probably impelled by the descent of various Indo-European peoples from the mountains north and west of Mesopotamia into that well-cultivated plain. Another factor may have been the enclosure of farm land which accompanied the expansion of settled kingdoms in the middle Euphrates area and in Syria at this time. The landless move on when the landed build fences. But we do not know the real impetus. They felt God had set them on the way.

Canaan, the land which attracted them, was not as densely populated as Syria and northern Mesopotamia. The hills which separated its various small city-states were forested and still largely unsettled and uncultivated. Canaan was not a kingdom but an agglomeration of culturally related but politically competitive, feudally organized principalities. The local nobility had constant need of mercenaries, servants, and harvest hands. Canaan's reputation at this time was not unlike its later biblical designation as "a land flowing with milk and honey." An Egyptian adventurer of the twentieth century B.C.E., Sinhue, described its attractions:

Figs were in it and grapes. It had more wine than water, plentiful was its honey, abundant were its olives. Every (kind of) fruit was on its trees. Barley was there and emmer. There was no limit to any (kind of) cattle.[1]

Sinhue's description is neatly complemented by the biblical text:

Lot looked about him and saw how well watered was the whole plain of Jordan, all of it—this was before the Lord had destroyed Sodom and Gomorrah—all the way to Zoar, like the garden of the Lord, like the land of Egypt (Gen. 13:10).

Canaan would remain an attractive area for immigrants until the fourteenth and thirteenth centuries, when its prosperity faltered and then failed under continuous Egyptian misrule.

The biblical account imposes literary unity and a four-generation span on what was obviously a far more complex and lengthy history. It suggests that during the first stage of their migration the Hebrews settled near established cities and remained on relatively good terms with local inhabitants, who allowed them water rights, pasture, trading privileges, and even certain land purchase agreements which the Hebrews later cited as validation of their presumptive rights in the land. The first Hebrew identified with Canaan, Abraham, purchased land near Hebron as a burial place for Sarah (Gen. 22:1–19), that she might not lie unprotected outside the clan's territory and consequently be denied its protection. Identification of Canaan-Palestine-Israel as the land which God had promised them was from the first a central element in Israel's awareness. According to this people's cherished tradition, the promise of this land and a guarantee of permanent title to it had been made to Abraham and sealed by the original covenant. "I am the Lord who brought you out of Ur of the Chaldeans to give you this land as a possession" (Gen. 15:7–17). This promise was renewed to Isaac and Jacob. Though the Hebrews never controlled any significant area in Canaan, the Exodus saga generally assumes that Moses is leading a people returning to their ancestral home.

Why God chose this particular land is never explained. It is only stated that it was a blessed choice. For what purpose did God promise this people this land? He offered it as a place to settle, to build homes, and to plant farms and vineyards. The Hebrews looked toward the land with the land hunger of pioneers, not the spiritual thirst of pilgrims. There is no theology and little folklore which ascribes miraculous or magical potency to this particular land. Canaan was a promised and a promising land, not a holy land. The descendants of these patriarchs never worshipped the land as land. In their Temple during Shavuot, the spring barley harvest festival, Israelites blessed God's gracious providence, not the earth's magical fertility: "All the bounty that the Lord your God has bestowed upon you and your household" (Deut. 26:11). The promised land was a gift of God. A good harvest was due to God's grace, not to the land's miraculous fertility, and it followed that the bounty of the land could and would cease, that the harvest would be meager, if God came to feel that the people merited punishment. Being in Zion was never natural. It was always a privilege which the donor could revoke. Israel could feel secure in the land only when the people were righteous, that is, right in their relations with God. When they were defeated and exiled they knew that God had driven them out for disobedience to His will.

The Hebrews were not bedouin. They came from the fringes of the settled and sown, not the depths of the wilderness. They arrived on the stage of history aware of, and to a certain degree conditioned by, the dominant Mesopotamian culture. Mesopotamia, of course, did not produce a monolithic culture. There were significant variations between Sumer, the thronging capital of Sargon's empire, and the provincial city-states of Syria. The Hebrews were traveling folk who lived on the outskirts of this civilization, receiving a blurred version of Mesopotamian culture at third hand. Yet Mesopotamia profoundly influenced the life of the Hebrews by providing the raw material from which their descendants fashioned their special ethos.

The diffused Mesopotamian culture set the forms and often the norms of life for many peoples from Babylon to Syria and Palestine. Tradition associates Abraham with Ur, an important city-state of the lower Tigris-Euphrates delta. Abraham's family is more intimately associated with Haran and Nahor, two important cities in the Balikh Valley in northwestern Mesopotamia. Abraham's nephew Lot was in semipermanent residence in the Dead Sea area in Sodom. Hebrew chiefs must have mingled freely with folk of many different cities, and their business dealings necessarily were registered in the accepted commercial form by local scribes familiar with that area's laws and requirements.

The common calendar was lunar, and to this day Jewish religious life is governed by a similar system updated only by sophisticated astronomical computations which have obviated the need to declare each new moon by actual observation. The practice of intercalation (insertion) of leap months, by which the familiar calendar is adjusted to the solar year, already existed in Mesopotamian astronomy. The Babylonians were passionate astrologers. Widespread interest in astrology has pervaded the unofficial regions of Jewish life down to modern times, and surfaces even today in the familiar congratulation *mazzal tov*—literally, "a good planet."

Mesopotamian legends familiar to the early Hebrews were recast and edited by later Israelites to illustrate sacred teachings; the classic examples are the biblical stories of Creation, the Garden of Eden, the Flood, and the Tower (ziggurat) of Babel. Perhaps no Hebrew ever heard a sanctuary priest recite the Gilgamesh epic exactly as it was ceremonially inscribed on clay tablets in the temple library of Nineveh, but Hebrew merchants and smiths had gathered around itinerant storytellers and minstrels as they recited folk versions of these epics in provincial market places for the edification and pleasure of the yokels. These myths were in the air, and the Hebrews and their descendants used their themes, much as Shakespeare used the story forms of his day, as raw material out of which to construct a special literature. One example will suffice. The Gilgamesh epic, which was known from Canaan to southern Mesopotamia, contains a story within a story. After an arduous journey undertaken to discover the secret of eternal life, the hero, Gilgamesh, has reached Utnapishtim, the one human ever to gain immortality. Gilgamesh has been led to believe that this man can reveal to him the knowledge he has been desperately seeking. Utnapishtim confesses that, though the gods have made him immortal, he is ignorant of the secret. He seeks to console Gilgamesh for the failure of his mission by telling him a tale of his youth—of a flood which the grand council of the gods brought upon the world because they were annoyed by mankind's general boisterousness. Mankind had been too noisy and had disturbed the gods' slumber; moreover, the gods were angry with men for having become lax and miserly in their service at the various temples. Utnapishtim had been warned of the impending catastrophe by the goddess Ea, of whom he was a favorite. She had advised him to build an ark, and in it he had escaped drowning. It had poured for six days. On the seventh day, Utnapishtim looked out and saw that all the clay buildings had been reduced to mud and all life had ceased; only he and his family survived. The ark finally grounded and he let fly a dove which returned because she could find no resting place. Later he sent out a swallow which also returned, and finally a raven which flew away and did not come back. She had found a perch. Descent was now safe. Utnapishtim had disembarked and offered an appropriate sacrifice.

The basic outline of this story was known across the length and breadth of the Fertile Crescent as early as the third millennium B.C.E. Parallel elements to the Noah saga, as recorded in the Bible, are striking. There are also obvious changes; in the biblical story a West Semitic hero, Noah, is acclaimed, rather than a Babylonian hero, Utnapishtim; a Syrian mountain, Ararat, replaces the Iranian mountain Nisir as the place where the ark came to ground; and the Semitic preference for forty (days) replaces the Babylonian emphasis on six and seven. Dependence on the Mesopotamian myth is beyond question, yet the Hebrew story reflects an entirely different theology. God alone and not a council of gods decides on a flood. Mankind is to be punished for its violence, not merely for making a nuisance of itself or not spending enough money on sacrifices. The hero is saved because he is righteous and merits salvation, not because a goddess takes pity on him. The animal world is preserved along with humankind. The Babylonian saga warns man that the secret of immortality will never be his. The Hebrew story assures man that he need never be terrified by the caprice of God. The Babylonian myth simply ends, while the Noah episode concludes with the creation of a "covenant between Me and the earth" (Gen. 9:13)—the pledge that God will never again willfully or spitefully destroy terrestrial life. In the Babylonian world, as in the Greek, men saw themselves at the mercy of the gods; their anxiety reverberates in every myth they told. In the Israelite world order replaces fear and trembling. The rainbow rises high after each storm. "So long as the earth endures, seedtime and harvest, cold and heat, summer and winter, day and night, shall not cease" (Gen. 7:22).

Hebrew history does not begin in the vast emptiness of the wilderness among ignorant and illiterate peoples, but in the trading outposts of the Mesopotamian cultural empire. The Hebrews had an indigenous tribal culture. They learned much from their betters, and refashioned what they learned to suit their tastes and needs. Judaism did not spring out of nothing and from nowhere.

The Bible associates all law with Sinai, but the customary laws and forms of the West Asian world are reflected in the Genesis narrative, and various parallels to the laws of this time appear in the codes which later tradition associated with the revelation at Sinai. The very idea of a code is Mesopotamian. Nowhere among the many writings which remain from Egypt has a law code been deciphered. The concept of a written and published legal code is Babylonian, and there are innumerable examples, such as Lipit-Ishtar, Eshnunna, and Hammurabi. Law can be promulgated in many forms. Babylonian law tends to adopt the casuistic form, that is, it sets out in specific detail a model case and then prescribes how it must be handled (if this happens, then this must follow). Many rules in perhaps the earliest biblical code, the so-called Book of the Covenant (Ex. 21–23), are set out in precisely such formulas. The procedure of inscribing the law on stone stelae is also Babylonian. The two stone tablets on which, according to the book of Exodus, Moses carved the Ten

Commandments are obviously related to this stele form.

Formal parallels abound. The biblical law code closes with a series of curses and blessings that will inexorably follow violation or obedience; certain Mesopotamian covenants conclude with similar horrendous imprecations. The Hebrew term for a contract or legal document, *sefer*, turns up in earlier Babylonian legal texts, and was obviously appropriated from such sources.

There are similar procedures and formulas. As already indicated, it is only as a result of the discovery of the legal practices of Nuzi, Alalakh, and Ugarit that a number of biblical episodes can now be adequately explained. One further example must suffice. In the biblical story of Judah and Tamar (Gen. 38), Tamar proves that Judah has been with her because she holds Judah's pledge, "your sealcord and the staff you carry." The use of the cylinder seal as a means of personal identification spread from Babylon throughout the Middle East. The staff harks back to the Babylonian *bukanum*, an object something like a military officer's swagger stick, which was exchanged at the end of bargaining to symbolize that agreement had been reached, much like our handshake.

There are, of course, original elements in Hebrew-Israelite law. Mesopotamian law was class law. There was a separate and much more severe set of penalties for crimes committed against persons of noble class than for crimes committed against peasants or slaves—an arrogance of caste absent from biblical regulation. Mesopotamian codes promised the obedient a just social order, prosperity, security, and the favor of the gods. The biblical code promised a just social order, prosperity, security, God's favor, and sanctification, that through obedience men not only please God but become godlike.

Biblical law defines itself not only as rules for the public good, but as an exact statement of God's will. Certain underlying assumptions are crucial. Babylonian legal theory, far from being tyrannical, had developed in an embryonic way the concept of a social contract. It acknowledged that there existed a cosmic, universal, unalterable law (*kittum*) of which the gods were custodians. A god—Shamash or Marduk—inspired the king with some notion of *kittum* and exhorted the ruler to promulgate just laws in accordance with these ultimate principles. Ideally, royal legislation gave concrete expression to the cosmic principle of justice. In practice, of course, a ruler's power was circumscribed only by the reach of his control over the ambitions of his nobles. There was no way to appeal the king's rule against the *kittum*. But a pregnant idea had been launched, leading toward the limitation of absolute power and a theory that law must somehow translate abstract but immutable principles of justice into specific social terms.

On his stelae Hammurabi's laws are "my words." [2] Biblical law begins "God spoke all these words, saying" (Ex. 20:1). In biblical legal theory, law has no source independent of God's will, of which it is always an exact statement. The natural phrasing of biblical law is the simple imperative "you shall" or "you shall not." Apodictic rules appear more frequently in the Bible than in other contemporary codes. The Torah contains the law of God, not the law of Moses. Its editors took pains to make clear that Moses had no role save that of messenger in the legislative process. He is to judge according to the law, not make law. There is no historical record to indicate that a king of Israel or Judah promulgated fundamental law on his own authority. The law is God's, administered by the king, and kings as well as commoners must obey its inviolable terms. Marduk may have made Hammurabi aware of the *kittum*. God had revealed not only general principles of justice, but its specific requirements and forms; moreover, His law was not revealed privately to the king to do with as he willed, but to the leader, with the express command to transmit it fully and exactly to the people. "The Lord spoke to Moses, saying: 'Tell the Israelite people . . .'" (Ex. 25:1). In Babylon and Assyria the king personified the nation. As clan chief Abraham could bind his clan to the covenant in the conventional way, but Israel's spirit was more democratic than royal. At Sinai Moses "went and repeated to the people all the commandments of the Lord," and the entire assembly vowed to keep God's law (Ex. 24:3–4). Israel would have priests, representatives of the people before God, but also a tradition that God does not mediate His favors through priest or prince, but broadcasts His word: there are no reserved priestly secrets, and God accepts the service of any member of this kingdom of priests and holy nation.

⋙⋘

The precise nature of early Hebrew faith is much debated. Genesis assumes that the fathers were monotheists, but is this skillful editing or fact? The text contains many names of God (gods?); conservative readers tend to elide these names as if they represented different titles for the one God of later times, but those who are more critical insist that such names designated distinct and different gods,

[13]

and spend a good deal of energy trying to establish precisely what deities are being referred to and in what specific context. A list of theophoric names of undoubted antiquity but uncertain origin or power emerges from such a reading, including some apparently special designations of the West Semitic high God El, others which apparently designated the patron deity of a particular chief, and still others which referred to, or are relics of, popular deities who personified natural forces.

Despite this multiplicity of names, suggesting a pantheon of some sort, there are those who argue that Hebrew piety centered on the worship of one high God—a supreme creator deity known as El Elyon (God Most High), or El Shaddai (God Almighty). These scholars accept the essential validity of the biblical narrative which portrays Abraham as worshipping the one God even before he leaves Haran for Canaan. They argue that there is no explicit statement in the sagas which would indicate that God shares His sovereignty with other gods or goddesses, that the altars and memorial stones raised by the Hebrews in their travels always were dedicated to the one God of heaven and earth, and that Moses summoned the Children of Israel in the name of the God of Abraham, Isaac, and Jacob, and insisted on the identity of the patriarchal God with YHWH. They further suggest that tribal religion among the West Semites during the second millennium tended to develop around some concept of a high God, known in a variety of local manifestations and by a variety of names, but believed to be behind and above all lesser gods. Presumedly each tribal chief made a personal profession, entered into a private compact with El, and ever after spoke of El in relation to himself (for example, the El of Abraham, the El of Isaac). El was the God of the patriarchal tribes; their only God, but not yet *the* only God. These scholars agree that the Hebrews were not idol breakers, did not denounce the gods of other tribes and peoples, set store by tutelary deities like the *terafim* (Gen. 31:19) and believed in spirits and demons. Even so, they argue, monotheism was in the air. Certainly such a religious environment was assumed by the biblical editors, and there is no compelling reason to dispute their contention.

Other scholars find little evidence of even rudimentary monotheism at this period. They hold that El Shaddai, El Roi, El Olam, and El Elyon are not various manifestations of a single high God El, but separate and distinctive deities, and that the presence of these names testifies to an active polytheism which later, more "orthodox," editors deliberately smudged and obliterated. Each of the patriarchs, it is claimed, established a private covenant with his own special God: the El of Abraham (Gen. 28:13, 31:42, 53); the Paḥad (kinsman) of Isaac (Gen. 31:42, 53); and the Abir (champion) of Jacob (Gen. 49:24). Such writers point out that some of the names of the various tribes are obviously theomorphic, which would indicate worship by that clan of its own protective deity—Gad (possibly the god of fortune), Asher (a masculine counterpart of Asherah), and so on. These scholars remind us that there is no evidence in Genesis of any religious tension between the Hebrews and their polytheistic neighbors. Therefore, even if the tribes had brought an El-centered religion with them, El was quickly associated with the local gods of the major cultic sites, and worship at such shrines inevitably introduced El into the pantheon previously worshipped there.

The issue may never be resolved, but at least one critical observation commands general agreement and is of prime importance: most Mesopotamian and West Semitic pantheons contained gods who represented spirits dwelling within natural phenomena (storms, the bull, light), while the God/gods of the Hebrews generally are represented in a relation of kinship with the chief and his people. It would seem that, from the beginning, the Hebrew God is personal, father, patron, "God of Abraham, Isaac, and Jacob," "God of your fathers," bound to His own by ties of obligation and love. Such kinship gods were not unknown among other West Semitic groups, but apparently the Hebrews were unique in emphasizing these attributes. Although we cannot validate the later piety that assumed that Abraham was the original monotheist, it seems probable that, from the first, Hebrew faith emphasized a personal God and personal ties to that God/gods. Other West Asian faiths emphasized the miraculous powers within nature which animate life. Hebrew faith emphasized the miraculous power within the covenant which bound God and man. To use a much later vocabulary, the Hebrews saw God primarily in history, while others saw God principally in nature.

Man is alternately blessed and buffeted by nature. An animistic world view designs powerful myths to explain the caprices of natural phenomena. In saga and myth the gods were described anthropomorphically—an idiom which the Bible editors did not easily shake. Since man has no real hope of controlling the natural forces, an animistic culture tends to involve itself with carefully elaborated ritual designed to please the gods. Hebrew ritual, in contrast, was strikingly uncomplicated and free of formal routine.

The Bible alone of the literatures of antiquity is almost devoid of myth. Perhaps because they did not share their neighbors' tense anxiety before the various powers which animate nature, the Hebrews do not seem to have been deeply impressed by the elaborate cosmological myths of the area which allotted various senior gods specific roles in nature and creation. There are those who insist that the text of Genesis reveals the worship not only of El, but also of his consort Anath and a son god, Shaddai, who is associated with mountains and probably is connected with Hadad, the storm god of the Syrians. Perhaps some Hebrews did worship some nature gods, but the absence in the biblical literature of any extensive mythology is striking, particularly when contrasted with Canaanite and Mesopotamian elaboration. Vestigial elements of Babylonian myth can be discovered in the texts by careful linguistic study, and testify to the deep impression these stories made on the idiom and thought pattern of the times. However, they are more an indication of the conservative force of language than of any sacralization of these myths. In Genesis 1, the Hebrew word *tehom* (depths) is linguistically similar to the name of the Assyrian goddess Tiamat, from whose slain body the cosmos was formed; but *tehom* does not designate this goddess, but simply the deep on whose face darkness lay before the creation of light.

Seeing God in a kinship relationship, the original faith did not require an elaborate cult. There were no temples or separate priest class. The headmen offered appropriate sacrifices on altars raised on a nearby high place. The Hebrews seem not even to have established a specific religious calendar. God was not associated with any single place, but made Himself manifest in various places. The headman had sensed or heard God on certain heights, under specific trees, or by certain fountains, and monuments or altars were erected to commemorate the event, but this God went wherever the chief and his people chanced to go. Men called upon the name of the Lord whenever there was need or opportunity. The cult was simple and portable, and its holiest moments probably centered on fairly regular rites which confirmed the relationship between the tribe and its tutelary deity.

The Hebrews seem to have thought of salvation primarily in terms of mundane needs: security, land, pasture, rain, and protection from the enemy. Salvation was not the promise of life eternal. These were children of a Mesopotamian world which lacked the overriding Egyptian concern with death rites and personal immortality. In the

Gilgamesh epic the hero is moved by a morbid fear of death to seek the secret of immortality, but despite strenuous efforts he does not win this boon and is advised instead to make the most of each day.

> When the Gods created mankind,
> Death for mankind they set aside,
> Life in their own lands retaining,
> Thou, Gilgamesh, let full be Thy belly,
> Make thou merry by day and by night.
> On each day make thou a feast of rejoicing
> Day and night dance thou and play!
> Let thy garments be sparkling fresh,
> Thy head be washed; bathe thou in water.
> Pay heed to the little one that holds on to thy hand
> Let thy spouse delight in thy bosom!
> For this is the task of (mankind).[3]

Similarly, the Hebrews seem not to have held any certain promise of immortality. Salvation was security in the here and now; Sheol was a shadowy, undefined place where a man went when he was gathered to his fathers. Faiths whose expectations center on the present must inevitably face the question of theodicy (Why do the obedient suffer?), and this problem will bedevil biblical faith throughout its history.

Hebrew religion was simple, and does not seem to have taken over the more complex myths and sympathetic magical rites of the fertility cults of West Asia. The Hebrews were shepherds and traders, not farmers. They were largely landless. The power they needed of God was protective—to shield and guide them in their wanderings. The seasonal death and rebirth of the earth was not as crucial as the shield—the covenant—provided by a tutelary deity against the terrors of landlessness and the danger of constant attack. Not unexpectedly, it was their loyalty to a God who was not tied to a particular place and who promised them their place which preoccupied their thought. The transformation of the separate Hebrew tribes into a self-conscious and unique community (Israel) awaited the Exodus and Sinai. Still, the attitudes which the tribes brought to Sinai are significant because they provided the raw material out of which later generations molded a distinctive way of life.

Others would call the Jew "the seed of Abraham." There is to the term a sense of inbreeding, of race, which is inaccurate. From the "first Jew" to the present generation of Jews, conversion and inter-marriage have brought men and women of every color and race into this covenanted community. But these first Hebrews, their ways and their saga, are the seed from which a colorful and sturdy faith community emerged. In that beginning all was not empty and void; there was a life style, a land, a way of addressing God, a sense of divine order which marked off this people and made them unique.

CHAPTER

❧ II ☙

The Covenant Relationship

HERE are constitutive forms in this people's history which must be discussed apart from a strict chronological scheme, because their emergence simply cannot be described with any confidence. Perhaps a hundred recent volumes debate whether monotheism first appeared among the Hebrews of the patriarchal age, the Israelites of Moses' time, or the prophets of the Babylonian exiles. The time variance spans more than a thousand years, because scholars can argue with equal logic that the biblical evidence, which is all that we have, faithfully reports the early beginnings or piously projects much later ideas back upon the founders.

Biblical history assumes that the conscious religious life of this people was organized from the beginning around a covenant between God and the fathers, between God and the people. The sacred histories tell of such a covenant being confirmed with each of the fathers, with the tribes and Moses at Mt. Sinai and again at Kadesh Barnea, with the tribes and Joshua at Shechem, and hint at an annual covenant ceremony celebrated by the tribal league during the period of the conquest (1200–1000 B.C.E.). We do not know whether all or any of these covenants was actually "cut." No archeological dig has yielded a stele bearing covenant terms, but it is certain that the Israelites believed that their faith was governed and empowered by a covenant with God, and that the covenant relationship could be traced back to the first of the fathers, Abraham. So central was covenant to their faith that this people's rite of initiation, the surgical act of circumcision, mirrored the form of a covenanting ceremony—each man-child was "cut" as a sign that he had entered into this relationship.

When a man is circumcised, part or all of the foreskin of the male organ is cut away. According to chapter 17 of the book of Genesis, Abraham, as an old man, entered into a covenant with God by circumcising himself and the males of his household in obedience to God's express command. The text is quite precise, suggesting that circumcision was not a familiar ritual among the settled peoples of West Asia, but special to the Hebrews. But the Bible also suggests that circumcision was practiced by all who were descended of either Abraham or Lot, that is, those tribes who moved west and south, including the Ishmaelites, Moabites, Edomites, and the children of Amon, and by men of an entirely different stock, the Egyptians (Jer. 9:23–25).

In Egypt we find that such surgery was occasionally, though not universally, carried out. A sixth-dynasty (late third millennium) tomb painting from Sakkarah portrays priests cutting a group of boys. Egyptian boys seem to have been circumcised just before or during puberty, and the rite had unmistakable sexual purposes—perhaps to inhibit, perhaps to stimulate, or perhaps to propitiate, as if the gift to the god of part of the sex organ might please him and win the boon of male issue. About fifteen hundred years later, the inquisitive Greek traveler and historian Herodotus reported that those Egyptians who practiced circumcision did so "for the sake of cleanliness," [1] but one feels that a sophisticated guide had offered him a somewhat expurgated explanation.

When practiced as a rite, circumcision can never be innocent of sexual overtones, and it was not among the Jews. Traditional commentaries never explain circumcision as a stimulant, the key to greater physical pleasure; for all its vaunted this-worldliness, Judaism was never indulgent. Still the sex theme is there and a reader will find in Hellenistic Jewish apologetics, in medieval *midrash*, and in the rather proper manuals of the nineteenth-century enlightenment, among more theological explanations, the suggestion that cutting away the foreskin actually limits sensation or serves as a valuable reminder to a male that he should curb excess and not squander his strength in bestial lust, but be restrained and disciplined.

Hebrew practice differed in surgical procedure, schedule, and apparent purpose from the Egyptian pattern. An Israelite baby was circumcised eight days after birth, not during puberty, and, unlike the Egyptian custom, the foreskin was completely removed. Circumcision was the universal rite of initiation. Whether the Abraham story is accepted as history or pious invention, it indicates that the first surgery was performed on a male long past his sexual prime. In Abraham's mind, or at least in the minds of those who told and retold the story, circumcision was consciously related to covenant, not sex, and was accepted as tangible evidence of initiation into the covenant's field of force, a physical and ineradicable proof of belonging.

For the Hebrews, the emphasis on infant circumcision centered on its efficacy as the rite of initiation. They were eager to bring the man-child as quickly as possible under the protection of the covenant. Possibly they wished to mute the sexual overtones of the ceremony; certainly they wished to avoid the pain of adult surgery. What had been for Abraham a painful test of his loyalty was transformed into a painless routine process as each generation of fathers enrolled their infant sons in God's service.

In later times, when a father presented his son for the simple operation he thanked God for the privilege of allowing the child "to enter into the covenant of Abraham our father." Circumcision was known as the permanent and visible seal of the eternal bond with Israel's God. Since medieval times, a chair has been set at the circumcision for the prophet Elijah. Why Elijah? The historical Elijah had complained that Israel neglected the covenant. Let him come and see!

The early sagas abound in paradox. Circumcision is known and valued by the biblical writers as the rite of initiation into the covenant and a physical sign identifying one who belongs. Abraham, the primal ancestor, was circumcised at God's command at the original covenant making. Strangely, circumcision is not associated by these sagas with the covenant at Sinai. It might be argued that by the time of Sinai all Israelites were circumcised as a matter of course, but the book of Joshua describes at length how Joshua organized a mass rite of circumcision before leading the troops into the Promised Land, to make sure that they would be protected by the covenant's power during the dangerous battles ahead (Josh. 5:2–8).

Circumcision among the Hebrews may have been, like so much

else in their religious lives, an occasional ritual undertaken before battle or when God's protection was of particular concern. There are frequent references to circumcision in both infants and adults. Moses apparently felt no need to circumcise his infant son (Ex. 4:25). Constant warfare with the uncircumcised, first the Canaanites and then the Philistines, may have been the catalyst which drove home the urgency of early protection under the covenant through infant circumcision. Certainly Israel was conscious that the enemy was *arel*, uncircumcised.

Circumcision brought the Jewish child within the magnetic field of the covenant, where he was safeguarded and protected. Such surgery no doubt stirred complicated and deep emotions, some certainly sexual, but the primary historical purpose, reinforced in law, liturgy, and legend, was related to initiation into the covenant. The covenant between God and Israel was not viewed as an abstract theological construct or as a social compact, but as a powerful and protective relationship entered into by God and the ancestors, confirmed at Sinai, and reconfirmed by each male member as he was physically identified as a member of the fellowship. God was bound by the covenant to protect the armies and soldiers of Israel. Simple folk came to look upon circumcision as a sacrament, an essential rite on the way to salvation. When, in the second century B.C.E., a Syrian Greek emperor (Antiochus IV) and, in the second century C.E., a Roman Caesar (Hadrian) banned circumcision, the Jews rose in revolt. Circumcision, the physical proof of being covenanted, had become a protection Jews would not do without. To be uncircumcised was not to be a Jew. Jews gave way on many things, but never on this. We touch here visceral emotions which can be described but never satisfactorily explained. The earliest Israelite chroniclers were so awed by this rite's power that we find in Exodus (4:24–26) a brief episode about Moses which suggests that God was prepared to kill the future leader because he had not circumcised his son, and desisted only when Moses' wife, Zipporah, managed to have emergency surgery performed.

Those prophets who insisted that ritual and rite were means, not ends, never challenged the objective value of circumcision, mute testimony, if any is needed, of its redemptive force in the people's consciousness. *Arel*, one who is uncircumcised, became a popular term of opprobrium, describing a no-good as well as a non-Jew. The literary prophets used *arel* as a synonym for the unrighteous and venal, but they pointedly suggested, or at least Jeremiah did, that, more than the cutting away of the foreskin, God requires the cutting away of ethical insensitivity and spiritual callousness, the so-called circumcision of the heart (Jer. 9:25).

Judaism has looked upon circumcision and covenant as inseparable. Male conversion requires *berit milah*, the covenant of circumcision, a proud and stubborn requirement which cost Judaism dear during the centuries when it competed with Mithraism and Christianity for the allegiance of a Roman world weary of paganism. In the city of Rome many a noblewoman accepted Judaism while her husband found reasons to avoid what would have been for him a painful conversion.

Early Christianity recognized the inseparability of covenant and circumcision in the Jewish mind, and argued against circumcision on the grounds that continuation of this practice was an assertion that the old covenant was still efficacious. The church could not do otherwise. To have adopted the practice would have been to accept the ongoing power of the old covenant, and would have weakened the church's claim that a new covenant, confirmed in the blood of Christ, superseded the old covenant, confirmed with a drop of the blood of each male child.

In one version of covenant making, the tutelary God appears, usually in a vision, and promises protection for the tribe and its descendants and, that most precious of hopes for a nomadic people, a homeland. God's expectation of obedience is implied or broadly stipulated. The whole is sealed with a sacrifice, and a memorial altar is raised on the spot. A covenant was accepted, not negotiated; the terms of the divine announcement were not subject to bargaining. Conventional piety would declare particularly praiseworthy those who accept God's terms without hearing them out; men should know that God would decree only that which is for their good. The Sinai episode is told so as to praise Israel for having assented before asking to hear God's terms.

An eight-day-old child enters the covenant in the same trusting way as the children of Israel at Mt. Sinai. Such was the people's faith in God's beneficent concern that the literature records no protest that the child was marked for a relationship he might not later want to share. Covenant represents a blessed election, an inexplicably, blessed intrusion by God into the affairs of men. Covenant testified to God's active concern and mercy. Why would anyone reject God's special kinship and kindness? Israel's covenant was a compact with life, a statement of hope and promise.

The power of the covenant was both sensed and seen. The first ceremonial object to be associated with the worship of the Israelite tribes seems to have been the Ark of the Covenant (*Aron ha-Berit*). It was an acacia wood chest containing two stone tablets on which the terms of the covenant, God's commandments, had been chiseled. The Ark was carried on a litter. When the tribe camped it was placed within the Tent of Meeting. During most of the conquest the Ark was carefully kept in the shrine at Shiloh. When David brought the Ark of the Covenant to Jerusalem and Solomon fixed it permanently in his royal chapel, its presence made Jerusalem the nation's religious capital.

The Ark of the Covenant represented the visible presence of God in the midst of this people. During the period of the Judges, Levites carried the Ark of the Covenant into battle in the confidence that God's presence would shield the army and guarantee victory. After the crushing defeat at Ebenezer, the Ark fell into Philistine hands and suicidal despair took hold among the tribes, but, so the legends piously insisted, the Ark retained its power and on its own created such havoc among the Philistines that it was quickly returned by an enemy eager to be rid of it. Divine power was so closely associated with the Ark that carelessness with it could have deadly consequences. "Tell your brother, Aaron, that he is not to come at will into the Shrine behind the curtain; in front of the cover that is upon the Ark, lest he die; for I appear in the cloud over the cover" (Lev. 16:2). In the popular imagination the Ark became the seat or throne of God, so the Ark of the Covenant becomes "the Ark of the Lord." Its appearance in the Israelite camp leads the Philistines to say, "A God has come into their camp. We are lost!" (I Sam. 4:6–7).

The Hebrew noun, *berit*, has yet to be derived etymologically to the satisfaction of most scholars. It is often suggested that it is cognate to the Akkadian *beritu*, "fetter," and it may be; certainly under the covenant the parties are tied with special bonds. "Now then, if you will obey Me faithfully and keep My covenant (*berit*), you shall be My treasured possession among all the peoples" (Ex. 19:5).

God offered and stipulated, but the covenant was not activated until Abraham or the people assented, even though, like Caesar's soldiers, they could only acclaim and not bargain. Israel was offered the privilege of service and there is no suggestion that they were impressed against their will. But the covenant must not be confused with an agreement between equals. In the covenant relationship God is *melech*, king, at His most potent, and Israel is *eved*, servant. The divine tone is peremptory. The covenant rules are curt: you shall, you shall not. A *berit* was not lightly entered into. A covenant was ceremoniously and impressively adopted by oath at a sacred feast or during special sacrifices, at which the blood of the covenant offering was sprinkled on the oath takers. You "cut" a covenant. In one ritual an animal was slaughtered and the parties passed between the two halves of the corpse, apparently by this act accepting the penalty of death, being cut in pieces, if they violated the terms. There are also indications that a list of grand blessings and fearsome curses was read out, as the stipulated rewards and penalties for steadfastness or disobedience. The covenant was not a modern business contract which is honored as long as it is not cheaper to violate it. It was binding, eternal, without a release clause; default would be harshly punished by God, and obedience correspondingly rewarded. Entering this covenant with their God made a palpable change in the status of the tribes and established a powerful new relationship between the deity and the people.

From Israel's vantage the covenant was a contract of exclusive fealty to God. "I will be your God, and you shall be My people" (Lev. 26:12). Modern research has shown that covenant-associated idioms and forms reported in the Torah follow patterns known from various Near Eastern treaties, particularly Hittite and Neo-Assyrian, between the sovereign and his major vassals in which, *inter alia*, the vassal promised exclusive fealty. "You shall have no other liege" becomes "You shall have no other gods beside Me" (Ex. 20:3). Following other gods is always a cardinal sin under the covenant. Given such a frame of reference, it is a tribute to the loving spirit of Israel's faith that, when speaking of the covenant, her prophets and poets supplemented images derived from the world of power (master-slave, lord-vassal) with those which saw the covenant relationship as between husband and wife or father and son. To obey the covenant is to evidence toward God the steadfast love (*hesed*) a wife owes her husband and a son his father. To violate the covenant is adultery or rebellion.

Israel's willing acceptance of a covenant has been explained in psychological terms. Men live surrounded by frightening evidence of the raw power of God. One perfectly natural response to existential anxiety is to project some control device onto the world. By "knowing" and doing what is required, man gains peace of mind. He can take proper care of his obligations to God. The covenant transmutes confusion into a program and gives assurance that specific deeds will protect man and his family because they have been stipulated by God Himself. But Israel's involvement in a covenant cannot be fully explained on psychic grounds. Israel alone of the peoples of the area invested such intense psychic energy in a covenant. Why? Possibly for no better reason than that there had been a covenant with Abraham, and this covenant had been renewed at Sinai and periodically thereafter. Covenant may be a primary datum. Great spiritual moments are the original happenings.

Reports of the early covenants tend to detail only the various pledges made by God to man. God promises Noah that He will maintain the natural cycle of the seasons and set limits to His anger. God promises the patriarchs that He will multiply their numbers, cause their descendants to prosper, and establish the wanderers in a land of their own. These covenant pledges are made specifically to this people, but in spirit they were certainly not unique. Most peoples of West Asia believed that their national gods would look after their welfare if the gods were loyally served.

The covenant of Sinai, as the descendants of those who had been there understood it, was unique because it detailed in extended and specific terms not only what Israel could expect of God, but what God expected of Israel. Vague words like fealty, trust, and loyalty, which sound noble but are easily trivialized, are avoided for lists of *mitzvot*, specific, detailed, divine commandments.

Much of the Torah consists of the successive paragraphs of the contract God had drawn up for His people. Commandment follows commandment. There are stipulations concerning sacrifices and festivals and long lists of rules dealing with righteous living and crime, personal hygiene, marriage, divorce, inheritance, court procedures, and agricultural practices. God's words regulate many areas of life. In time rabbinic piety would draw out the implications of these Torah laws until every aspect of daily living was seen as regulated by covenant requirement. Biblical law does not derive from revelation; it *is* the revelation. Laws of leprosy and sexual impurity are as much part of revelation as are the Ten Commandments. Revelation deals with specifics of conduct rather than with metaphysics, myth, or even moral theory. Hence Torah is law, Torah is revelation, and Torah is teaching. Biblical Judaism's truths are its laws.

Jews eventually came to believe that all the laws now in the Torah were stipulated to Moses on Mt. Sinai or as he sat before the Tabernacle. This assumption permeates the Torah, but it cannot be critically verified. Linguistic and structural analysis as well as many redundancies and discrepancies point to the composite nature of this material. Torah law as we have it is an anthology of *devarim*, words believed to be of divine origin, coming from various sources and periods. Some became consecrated because they were read out and affirmed as *berit* at a ceremony of covenant renewal. Others represent customary practice which became venerated. Other words represent oracular teachings delivered under inspiration by shrine priests. Other laws, particularly those dealing with cult, represent the priestly regulations of various shrines which, by age, familiarity, and common consent, became accepted as God-given. At an early period such oracular teachings seem to have been called *torot*, from which is derived the word "Torah," a treasured word which came to describe the Five Books of Moses, the general obligation of religious study, and, in time, the entirety of Jewish religious thought.

Torah law is a conglomeration of rules from various sources and periods, unified only by the post-exilic assumption that every phrase had been revealed by God to Moses. How did all these codes come into being? Joshua compiled a collection of *torot* and enshrined them in the Ark at Shechem (Josh. 24). Samuel wrote out God's words which dealt with the king's power and prerogatives (I Sam. 10:25). Hilkiah, the High Priest (seventh century B.C.E.), "found" a scroll of the law during a purification rite in the Temple in Jerusalem. These became Torah. These laws were not concocted by some power group which forged God's words in order to sanctify their privileges. Such an act was inconceivable in that believing day and age. The word of God came frequently enough, and man's awareness of the numinous was powerful enough, for all these laws originally to have been spoken under the spirit. If Israel's law had been consciously invented, the extant code would certainly be far more consistent and complete. Law requires precision. Yet the editors made no attempt to eliminate patent discrepancies between texts, even though the resulting disparities can only have been stumbling blocks to judges and others concerned with legal process. Men at this time would not have dared to invent the word of God.

Exactly what happened at Sinai? The question cannot be answered. One wants to say that at least the Ten Commandments were revealed and affirmed, but doubts can be raised even to this seemingly modest claim. There are two slightly variant versions of the

Ten Commandments; would the founding document have been tampered with? Other decalogues seem to be buried in the biblical text. One such can be culled from an old legal code, Exodus 33–34, and since it is primarily cultic in content, some have argued that it is older than the Ten Commandments and more likely to represent the original covenant.

All that can confidently be said about Sinai is that the moment was seared into the Israelite consciousness. As piety retold it, nature itself was awed by the significance of that day. The moment was holy, full of God's power. God gave Moses specific and exact instruction as to where he was to bring the tribes and where they might not go. The mountain was full of the presence of God, dangerous and taboo; the people were to hear, but not to approach. Moses could approach only in a state of ritual purity. There was fasting, fear, and a background of thunder and lightning. Moses ascended; the word descended. "I the Lord am God" (Ex. 20:1). The words multiply.

Israel was bound.

The various covenants with the fathers had been personal to each. Sinai covenanted the whole people. It was the first, not the last, national covenant ceremony. Another may have been confirmed while the tribes were at Kadesh Barnea. Joshua 24 describes another such ceremony at Shechem, when Moses' successor was about to relinquish his authority. Many scholars believe that until monarchy was established there were annual ceremonies of covenant renewal. Such a ceremony would have encouraged the sense of unity among the various tribes, and have provided an appropriate occasion to listen to and affirm God's words. The last such ceremony, and already a stylized one, was organized in the fifth century B.C.E. by Ezra, at which he read out "the book of the Torah" to those who had returned to Jerusalem from Babylonia (Neh. 8:1).

The issue of which specific "words" Israel accepted as covenant at any period of its early history exceeds the grasp of even the most assiduous researchers. Our evidence is too meager. There is more benefit in discussing the broad implications of the existence of a covenant, of Israel's acceptance of covenant, and of its experience as a people who looked to the direct word of God for the regulation of their lives.

Covenant establishes kinship. A covenanted community acknowledges God's transcendent power but is preoccupied by His close and tender concern. A covenant God has spoken to men, can speak again, is patently concerned with their behavior, and will reward them when they are steadfast to the covenant's terms.

A covenant faith begins with an act that proclaims God's grace. There is no indication that Abraham merited or sought the choice. God's decision to enter the life of the people is seen as a wonderful and unmerited blessing—a miracle, if you will. The covenant God may be imperious, but He is always a benevolent chief ready to welcome the petitioner into His presence.

Covenant implies election. God chose Abraham; God initiated His relationship with Israel. Why was Israel chosen? At the beginning, men simply accepted gratefully. Later it was suggested that Israel was chosen precisely because she was the least significant of the nations and the impact and success of such an improbable choice would present to the world impressive evidence of God's power. He could take the least likely and raise them on high (cf. Deut. 7:6–8). Another tradition suggested that God had not at first chosen Israel, but that the more auspicious candidates had disqualified themselves when they found God's stipulations too demanding. Israel was ever conscious that election was both a special advantage/privilege and a special obligation/burden.

Confidence in election could easily lead the people into an attitude of smug satisfaction. God promises Abraham so much—a bountiful homeland, many and successful descendants—that it would be easy to expect too much of such a Patron. When Jacob finally settled his long and bitter quarrel with his father-in-law, he is joyous that his expectations have been confirmed. "Had not the God of my father . . . been with me, you would have sent me away empty-handed" (Gen. 31:42). There were always those who relied on God's special concern for Israel to protect them and make them prosper and who depended on it as on a talisman. The more thoughtful rejoiced in God's intimacy but knew that love always imposes obligations: "You specially have I known, therefore . . ." (Amos 3:2).

Covenant establishes responsibilities for both parties. God's special care is guaranteed only if the people obey. If the people fail to obey God's express will, they merit special punishment. The existence of the covenant testifies to a vigorous faith in divine providence. Actions under the covenant must inevitably be judged, and God will be a fair judge. Sometimes in the later writings obedience seems calculated, and duty will sometimes be discussed as if it were first a matter of prudence and only then a matter of principle. So be it. A realistic view of human nature must accept the fact that at times men need to be goaded as well as coaxed along. Moreover, acts have consequences which are independent of the actor's motivation. I would not stop a man from feeding and clothing the poor because he seeks the approval of his neighbors for those acts.

God's law relates to a wide spectrum of human affairs. There is no boundary between sacred and profane. Thus there is no failing which is merely a crime, punishable only by man. Similarly, there is no boundary between ethical statement and legal enactment. The covenant states the right and in so doing defines righteousness. The covenant God does not exhort—He requires. *Mitzvah* means both specific duty and good deed.

God wills what man must do; since He is righteous, what He wills must be right, and to violate His will is to sin. Failure to obey the covenant wrongs God, and therefore God must punish the wrongdoer. This attitude marks off Israelite law from other contemporary codes. Among other peoples the king could pardon a man convicted of murder. Not so in Israel; God had been wronged, life was of God, and men were not allowed to interpose themselves. "You may not accept a ransom for the life of a murderer who is guilty of a capital crime, he must be put to death" (Num. 35:31). Other codes permitted an aggrieved husband to cancel the death sentence of his wife's paramour. Not the Torah; the sin was against God, and it was not up to the husband to determine the punishment (Lev. 20:10). Both outcomes seem harsh, but what was lost in flexibility was regained in moral certainty. Man cannot shape God's will to suit his convenience. Strict discipline strictly enforced helped to raise these families and communities above the area's commonness. What appeared to outsiders as stiff-necked discipline was not stubbornness or hardness of heart, for this people was as loving and forgiving as any. However, they were obligated to the will of a determined God who was just, demanding, and fair, who was no respecter of persons or circumstances, and who knew that men were capable of better than they customarily admitted.

Man is God's creation. Adultery and murder harm His creatures and are an affront to Him who made man and fashioned him in His own image. Crimes against persons were therefore severely punished, while crimes against property were not as severely punished, for God is not as severely aggrieved by them. The law insisted on just weights and measures. Theft was punishable by restitution and fine, as were willful damages, but, unlike other codes of the period, no property offense was punishable by death.

The Covenant Relationship

Torah law is specific, since it expresses God's will for a definite situation. The law wastes no time developing general moral principles for an abstract entity called mankind. It is national law established by the nation's God. God addresses "the tribes of Israel" and regulates relationships with "your brother," "your neighbor," "your people." God punishes the sinner by cutting him off "from his people," "from Israel," or "from the midst of the assembly." In this respect the *devarim* are similar to the nation-bound rules found in Canaanite and other Mesopotamian legislation. Torah law was God's law for Israel, in the specific context of Israel's social order. There is one rule for Israelite slaves and another for all others who are enslaved. There is one rule covering interest to a fellow Israelite, another governing loans to outsiders. Israel was forbidden to make idols, bend the knee at shrines, consult sorcerers or necromancers, participate in orgiastic rites, or eat the wild boar or any other totemic animal; the non-Israelite was not so enjoined. It is not suggested that the list of rules regulating Israel's sacrifices and festivals is universally obligatory; at most the rules apply to the stranger who is within your gates. Generally the early prophetic literature, despite its harsh attacks on idolatry, does not hold the idolatry of other nations to be a crime. "Let all people walk each one in the name of its god, but we will walk in the name of the Lord our God forever and ever" (Micah 4:5). Later moralists would seek with great skill and benefit to universalize the Torah's implicit principles, but the Hebrews' world was a small place and their law dealt with them in their place.

There was no excuse for disobedience. Disobedience is simply, awfully, sin. Swift punishment awaits those who sin. The law was not only operative in an ordinary way, and provided with all the necessary and familiar provisions for courts and fines, but also operative on a divine plane since God is party to every proceeding. The image of God as judge is one of the most common in the Bible. The implication is that God not only reviews the activities of men and nations, but carries out the sentence suggested by His findings. Israel's hymns were filled with this theme "for God is judge; He puts one man down and raises up another" (Ps. 75:8). The balance of justice was not left to human agency alone. It is God who ultimately rewards the good and requites the evil. "God judges the people with equity" (Ps. 96:10). Man is always under the judgment of God, and the tragic yet glorious tension of his life flows from the fact that he is mortal, by nature unable to meet these absolute demands, yet bound to them by divine fiat and his own sense of their rightness.

Such a faith forced Judaism to confront the problem of justifying the obvious cruelties of the world. Divine providence inevitably became the central issue of self-conscious apologetics. Since the law was the word of God and the word of God must be true, it was assumed that law and justice were synonymous. "The Rock!—His deeds are perfect, Yea, all His ways are just; A faithful God, never false, True and upright is He" (Deut. 32:4). And this faith was stubbornly upheld despite all evidence to the contrary.

God ruled; people obeyed. God was omnipotent but never careless or unjust. At times He explained His will to men. "Do not take bribes, for bribes blind the clear-sighted and upset the pleas of the just" (Ex. 23:8). "He may be given up to forty lashes, but not more, lest being flogged further, to excess, your brother be degraded before your eyes" (Deut. 25:3). Most times God offered no explanation. Explanations were edifying, but not deemed necessary. It was reason enough that God had so willed.

The God of Israel was royal, but also *El raḥum veḥanun*, "God merciful and gracious" (Ex. 34:6). His law was never capricious, spiteful, or vindictive. Even the laws which seem to deal with cultic minutiae were to Israel a sign of God's favor, and obedience to them was a way of proving oneself to God. Israel rejoiced: "What great nation has laws and norms as perfect as all this Teaching that I set before you this day?" (Deut. 4:8).

The law had the advantage of being specific. God's words were pointed and unmistakably clear, and through them Israel's life developed a unique pattern. Torah law set Israel apart and established for her an identity born of obedience. The reasoning was that this is the way God wills us to go. It is a different way and we must obey, for God has His reasons.

Righteousness, *tzedakah*, was understood as obedience to the covenant stipulations. When Israel obeyed these laws, the nation had a claim on God's favor. When they failed to obey, God had a legal case against them; the denunciations of the prophets are often cast as lawsuits, with the original witnesses, heaven and earth, called upon to testify to God's faithfulness to His side of the bargain (cf. Micah 6:1 ff.).

The law was venerated as the word of God, and the terms of God's covenant were cited as evidence of God's wisdom and of His concern. Later men would turn each law over and over, flesh it out, find its unsuspected consequences, and argue over the normative philosophy it expressed. With these laws as their yarn, generations of Jews wove an all-encompassing way of life and quite naturally declared the whole to have been divinely ordained.

Judaism evolved, but these laws remained fixed, enshrined in the Torah as they had been revealed. There was no tampering with the word of God. God's word could be interpreted, but men felt constrained to be faithful to both its spirit and its letter. Unrestrained allegory was rarely the "Jewish" way. These original prescriptions represent the given of Jewish life—its distinctiveness and its limitation. They explain why the Sabbath is observed, why pork is forbidden, and why in traditional Jewish life, even today, women cannot initiate a divorce proceeding. In Judaism God's words are constitutive.

CHAPTER

❦ III ❧

God's Freedom
and God's Bondage

THE Hebrews appeared on the field of history early in the second millennium B.C.E., only to disappear a century or two later. They did not cease, they simply ceased to have a history. Some tribes remained in or near the hill country of central and southern Canaan; related groups went south for food and opportunity and ended as numbers on an Egyptian slavemaster's roll. When the mists part again at the beginning of the thirteenth century, the Hebrews have a new identity. They are now the *benei Yisrael*, the tribes of Israel.

The etymology of the name "Israel" is uncertain. It may be theophoric: "may El preserve." Genesis introduces the name in connection with an event in the life of Jacob. Greedy for the elder's share of the family inheritance, Jacob had tricked his father and bilked his brother. The wrong was grievous, and when, after some years, Jacob sought to be reconciled with those he had wronged, he sent apologies and gifts. But his presents were not acknowledged and he could not be certain he would be forgiven. According to the epic, Jacob spent the night before his reunion with Esau wrestling with an anonymous adversary.

[34]

God's Freedom and God's Bondage

That same night he arose, and taking his two wives, his two maidservants, and his eleven children, he crossed the ford of the Jabbok. After taking them across the stream, he sent across all his possessions. Jacob was left alone. And a man wrestled with him until the break of dawn. When he saw that he had not prevailed against him, he wrenched Jacob's hip at its socket, so that the socket of his hip was strained as he wrestled with him. Then he said, "Let me go, for dawn is breaking." But he answered, "I will not let you go, unless you bless me." Said the other, "What is your name?" He replied, "Jacob." Said he, "Your name shall no longer be Jacob, but Israel, for you have striven with beings divine and human, and have prevailed." Jacob asked, "Pray tell me your name." But he said, "You must not ask my name!" And he took leave of him there (Gen. 32:23–30).

The indicated etymology, "he who strives with God," is linguistically unacceptable, but certainly it was the cherished belief of that biblical editor and remained a central theme of later piety. To struggle with one's duty and fears and to persevere whatever the cost were traits highly respected by those who called themselves by Israel's name.

The earliest known specific extrabiblical reference to Israel appears on a triumphal stele set up by the Pharaoh Mer-ne-Ptah to record certain victories by his armies in Syria-Palestine (ca. 1230 B.C.E.). "Israel is laid waste, his seed is not. Hurru [Canaan] has become a widow for Egypt!" [1] Many a son of Israel has smiled wryly as he read this epitaph to his people, written before Jewish history had actually begun.

How did the Hebrews become the Israelites? The answer probably lies in the desire of collaterally related Semitic tribes (the *benei Yisrael*) to unite in common cause, possibly the conquest of Canaan. An existing saga of common ancestry through Jacob (Israel), father of twelve, was used as the mythic bond of this new league.

To understand Israel's emergence, we need to retrace our steps. Palestine subsists, for the most part, on marginal rainfall. In the days of prescientific agriculture, famine and drought were constant threats. Directly south lay Egypt, where the harvest depends not on rainfall but on the annual riverine gift of water and soil. Egypt often had grain when Canaan had none. Around 1750 B.C.E., Semitic tribesmen, the Hyksos (literally, rulers of foreign countries), conquered Egypt and established an outsider's regime which lasted for about a century and a half. During this period many Semitic tribes came for trade, for pasture, to escape famine, and for the advancement of their bright young men, needed by a colonial adminstration which did not trust the natives. The famine which brought Jacob's sons to Egypt, Joseph's rise to high position in the Egyptian bureaucracy, and his decision to resettle his family in Goshen near the Hyksos capital of Avaris represent events which are historically plausible.

The Bible indicates that, after a period of relative well-being, "a new king arose over Egypt who did not know Joseph" (Ex. 1:8), and the status of the Hebrews deteriorated precipitously. About 1550 B.C.E., a native general, Ah-mose I, overthrew the foreigners, founded the eighteenth dynasty, and launched Egypt on an ethnically assertive period of conquest and power which is known as the New Kingdom. Harsh revenge was meted out to the erstwhile conquerors. The ruling elite was slaughtered. Hangers-on were driven out or made into slaves. The book of Exodus indicates that the descendants of those Hebrews who came with Joseph were enslaved and remained in bondage for a period of several generations. The cruelty of that bondage seared itself into the people's soul. Twenty-four times, whenever the Torah deals with the rights of persons, protection for the "stranger that is within your gates" is insisted on. Why? "Because you were strangers in the land of Egypt" (Ex. 22:20, 23:9, etc.). In most aspects the Israelite law of persons corresponds to what we know of the class structure and family relationships of neighboring peoples, but no other law of the time and area shows a similar concern for the resident alien. He enjoyed the same rights as Israelites before the courts (Deut. 1:16). He could own land, share in the produce of the sabbatical year (Lev. 25:6), and even participate in the festivals (Deut. 16:1 ff.); indeed, "you shall love him as yourself, for you were strangers in the land of Egypt" (Lev. 19:34).

Biblical laws concerning slavery are tinged with memories of Egyptian bondage. By necessity these were slave economies; productive methods were crude and money exchange rudimentary. There is a direct reference to slaves as chattel (Ex. 21:21); fines for bodily harm to another's slave were to be paid to the beaten man's owner, but a remarkable law protects the runaway slave from extradition.

> You shall not turn over to his master a slave who seeks refuge with you from his master. He shall live with you in any place he may choose among the settlements in your midst, wherever he pleases; you must not ill-treat him (Deut. 23:16–17).

Mesopotamian laws universally required the slave's return, prescribed severe fines or death for aiding and abetting a runaway, and considered the slave under the category of property. Israelite law viewed the slave as a person rather than as a tool. Punishment for killing a slave was the same as for killing a free man, even if the act was committed by the slave's master (Ex. 21:20). A slave who has been badly mauled must be set free (Ex. 21:26–27). A master had proprietary rights over the slave, even to the extent of choosing his wife, but an Israelite slave was to be treated as a hired domestic and household familiar, not as a beast of burden. "You shall not rule over him ruthlessly" (Lev. 25:43). If an Israelite was taken captive and enslaved, he must be ransomed. A slave of foreign birth was "property," but no Israelite could be held by another Israelite in perpetual bondage. When, after six years of service, an Israelite slave was released, "You shall not let him go empty-handed: Furnish him out of the flock, threshing floor, and vat, with which the Lord your God has blessed you. Always remember that you were slaves in the land of Egypt" (Deut. 15:14–15). The master-slave relationship had interesting theological overtones: the man who redeems a slave from his owner becomes his owner; by extension, since God had redeemed Israel from bondage, Israel was now in bondage to God. The Sabbath was a weekly reminder of this condition of spiritual fealty. "Remember that you were a slave in the land of Egypt and the Lord freed you from there . . . ; therefore the Lord your God has commanded you to observe the Sabbath day" (Deut. 5:15).

The tribes came under Egyptian influence in many places and ways. During most of the second half of the second millennium Egypt held real or nominal control of Canaan, and even of some city-states east of the Jordan, so there must have been contact between local garrisons and the Hebrew caravaneers. However, the classic confrontation took place in Egypt, and biblical man never forgot his beginning in Egyptian slave pens.

A good bit of superficial acculturation took place. Many who left with Moses had been given Egyptian names; Moses himself bore an Egyptian name which means simply "offspring" or "born of." On balance, Israel seems to have been repelled rather than seduced by Egyptian example. Work gangs who sweat and die to build great monuments for the privileged few rarely sing the building's architectural praise. Simple folk retain their trust in various primitive healing and mimetic arts, having neither the opportunity nor the funds to consult the sophisticated priests and physicians who cater to their hated masters. The Bible makes a point of insisting that Moses discomfited all the sorcerers of Egypt, and their magical and prophetic powers are vilified. The Hebrew slaves found much to scorn.

Thus Israel saw not the magnificence of the pyramids but the ugliness of a civilization which spent its surplus capital to provide lavish entombment and expensive perpetual care for upper-class corpses, while the bodies of slaves were tossed to the crocodiles or into a common grave. They saw the elaborate and vain rites designed to guarantee immortality to the nobility; it must have enhanced their self-respect to mock the superstitious fears which required the building of such pretentious mausoleums.

After the Egyptian experience Israel sought to eliminate any funeral practice which might develop into a death cult. Although there is some evidence of embalming in the patriarchal age, there is none in the Israelite period, and later Jewish law prohibited the practice. Israelite faith is remarkably free of myth dealing with the grave and beyond. The spirits of the dead descend to the pit, Sheol, a place of dark shadows and no return which is not further defined. In the early strata of the Bible, as in the prevailing Mesopotamian world view, physical resurrection is not much considered. To be sure, care was lavished on the dead. The required burial was simple, prompt, and designed to prevent any indignity to the corpse. Taboos associated with a corpse were limited to prohibition of direct contact with it. The corpse of a criminal was not to be left hanging overnight on the gibbet. The bodies of soldiers had to be brought home for burial. One had to be buried with one's family, and preferably in one's own land. The protection of one's clan so necessary in this world was felt to be equally essential in the next. Clans had their own burial caves. United in the cave, the spirits protected each other (Gen. 23, I Sam. 4:2 ff.). The dead must be left undisturbed; exhumation was considered a punishment (Jer. 8:1 ff.).

On the folk level people no doubt believed in ghosts and disembodied spirits, and employed sacred rites to handle the danger. But the religious tendency was basically unsympathetic to a death cult and related customs. No pyramids and few, if any, mausoleums were built. Embalming was proscribed. The dead were buried without pomp and without expensive provisions of food, drink, and utensils. Archeologists have found that the number and value of personal belongings and funeral offerings left beside the corpse diminished rapidly during pre-exilic times. Israelite literature did not produce a

Book of the Dead which set out a sophisticated magical art intended to placate and appease the spirit world. Priests were specifically prohibited from any role in the funeral rite. A son buried his father. No particular death rite was established within the official cult. The grief-associated need to punish oneself for assumed guilt, which led in many cultures to the custom of actual physical scarring, was recognized but proscribed. "You shall not make gashes in your flesh for the dead, or incise any marks on yourselves" (Lev. 19:28). The tearing of a garment was substituted, but even then the more sensitive spirits insisted "rend your hearts and not your garments" (Joel 2:13).

Burial was not a time to rejoice that the dead had passed to a better life, but was a time for fasting, wearing sackcloth, and lamentation. It is worth noting how reticent the Bible is on subjects which preoccupied other faiths and later concerned Judaism: resurrection, immortality, the hereafter, heaven, and hell. "A live dog is better than a dead lion" (Ecc. 9:4). The law is given not as a preparation for the afterlife but as a guide for this life, so that "you will be doing what is good and right in the sight of the Lord your God" (Deut. 12:28).

Having seen Egyptian society as the urban poor see American affluence—from the perspective of the exploited and unnoticed—the Israelites remembered its indulgence and its class-ridden cruelty rather than its art and high culture. The palaces and pyramids were not described or praised, but much was said of the "diseases of Egypt" (Deut. 28:60). A set of commandments which deal with sexual discipline have as a preface, "You shall not copy the practices of the land of Egypt where you dwelt" (Lev. 18:3). Egypt became a symbol of the rottenness and insensitivity of a powerful nation and a caste society. But in later years, on an everyday level, there was a paradoxical bond between the peoples. "You shall not abhor an Egyptian, for you were a stranger in his land" (Deut. 23:8).

❧❧

Sometime around 1300 B.C.E. the Exodus took place. The Exodus is not recorded in any known Egyptian chronicle. The breakout of a band of slaves, however small, would hardly do honor to any pharaoh or senior officer in charge of public works, and so was unlikely to be included in his triumphal tomb list. Successful breakouts simply do not take place in slave-owning societies. The event is probably beyond reconstruction, but the impact of the Exodus was volcanic and reverberates in Jewish life to this day. Israel was humbled, awed, and led to God by this manifestation of the power of God's right hand to deliver. Israel was overwhelmed by God's unexpected concern for a slave people of no particular distinction. The events associated with this deliverance became the paradigms and recurrent symbols of Israel's faith. The Exodus expressed God's will to save, the urgency of freedom, the possibility of escaping tyranny, and God's anger with every form of social abuse. Sinai was the divine law, revelation, covenant, objective truth, a reproach to anarchy, and the wellspring of righteousness. The wilderness trek bespoke suffering, the hard realities, the high cost of lofty ambition, and the obduracy of human nature. Moses' death restated man's frailty, every man's fate to die with his hopes not fully accomplished. Finally, the Promised Land was a statement of possibility, of hopes that come true; a denial of black pessimism, a hard place to conquer and to settle, a harder place in which to hold fast to high ideals and strict disciplines, the home of which men must constantly prove themselves worthy. Though the Jewish tradition titled this history simply *yetziat mitzrayim*, the going out from Egypt, these moments were hallowed in psalm and poem, cited repeatedly in Scripture, rehearsed annually during the Passover Seder, and evoked daily in the liturgy.

Interestingly, Israel never piously retraced its freedom trail. The tradition was not even clear as to where the great revelation of God's word had taken place and where the covenant had been sealed. Was it at Mt. Sinai or Mt. Horeb? Or were these simply two names for the same height? In any case, where was Mt. Sinai-Horeb? Only one biblical figure, Elijah, is reported to have returned to the mountain of revelation. Buddha first spoke in the Deer Park at Sarnath, Mohammed at Mecca, and Christianity began at Bethlehem, and those places ever since have drawn pilgrims. Israel's freedom began in the will of God. The Exodus affirmed God's place in history and, since He is God and not man, to touch the original freedom it was only necessary to worship God; one did not have to climb reverentially up some rocky hillside or walk reflectively along some wilderness trail where once Moses and the tribes of Israel dragged their weary feet.

There are many truths. One truth describes exactly what happened ca. 1300 B.C.E. Another truth defines what centuries of Jews believed to have happened. These truths are not the same, but neither are they as divergent as they once seemed. In the first flush of critical scholarship, many assumed that the Exodus and Sinai were literary inventions created to backdate the constitution of the Jewish people and enhance its sanctity. In the light of current knowledge, such a radical disparagement of tradition is not necessary. Of course, not all the related Hebrew tribes went to Egypt. The biblical text indicates that some joined Moses at Kadesh Barnea, while others joined Joshua after the conquest began. The miraculous legends of the plagues which brought Egypt to its knees, of the hands which turned leprous and then became healthy again, and of staves which turned to snakes, represent the inevitable literalization of radical amazement. How else does one shape the incredible into words? It is doubtful that the mountain of revelation is the rugged peak in the southern part of the Sinai Peninsula where St. Catherine's Monastery now sits and which, since the Middle Ages, has been labeled Sinai on world maps. The Bible, read with the aid of our century's linguistic and archeological capacity, seems to indicate a march far to the north: first eastward through the bullrush bayous of the Nile delta, then across a narrow sandspit which runs along the Mediterranean coast from near Port Said east toward El Arish, forming Lake Bardawil, and finally a southeastern passage just below a line of Egyptian fortifications guarding the coastal highway, the famous Via Maris of Roman times, to a rallying point at Kadesh Barnea, where the tribes settled for a time and from which they apparently launched an abortive attack on southern Canaan.

Not all or even most of the Torah laws were given to Moses at Sinai or during the forty years of wandering, but this is the crucial point: the memories of an exodus and of a mountaintop revelation are as old as the Israelite faith, and are central to that faith (Ps. 106:7–12). The faith of Israel begins in a response of fear and trembling to the unexpected intrusion of the right hand of God into their history. This awe already reverberates in perhaps the oldest verse of biblical song, which may, in fact, be contemporary with the event. "Sing to the Lord, for He has triumphed gloriously; Horse and driver He has hurled into the sea" (Ex. 15:21). Israel relished its sense of God's special care and took pains to sensitize each succeeding generation to it. The Passover holiday resurrected this mood annually and made it palpable. Each segment of the miracle was separated out and elaborated. God had heard the cries of the Hebrews. God had compelled Pharaoh to free the slaves. God had sent each of ten plagues and, finally, slaughtered the first-born. God had split the Red Sea and sunk the pursuing chariots and riders in the returning waters. God had fed the tribes in the barren wilderness. God had guided the people with a pillar of cloud by day and a pillar of fire by night. Baalam was hired to curse Israel, but God put words of blessing into his mouth. God defeated the armies which sought to prevent the people's advance.

The magnificence of God's grace confirmed in Israel so strong a feeling of God's special protection that the Exodus is cited continuously by prophets and psalmists as incontrovertible proof of God's power and continuing concern. The prophets of the Babylonian Exile recalled this first return to reassure their generation of exiles that they, too, would be redeemed (cf. Isa. 43:18–21). Three millennia later, the national anthem of the State of Israel reminds the singer that Israel is the living proof that "our hope is not lost." When the Jewish people rehearse these classic events during the Passover festival, they declare this story not to be ancient history but their own ongoing narrative: "that which the Lord did for me when I went free from Egypt" (Ex. 13:8), with Egypt of course representing Germany, Poland, or the Soviet Union.

The Exodus is deliverance, and God is the deliverer. "I am the Lord your God who brought you out of the land of Egypt, the house of bondage" (Ex. 20:2). Protected by such a God, this little people knew it would survive the abrasions of time; perhaps this "knowledge," if not God's protection, made survival possible.

The Exodus was deliverance and a revelation. God had acted within historical time. The Exodus history was written by "the finger of God." "The Lord freed us from Egypt by a mighty hand, by an outstretched arm and awesome power, and by signs and portents" (Deut. 26:8). Revelation describes God become manifest. God revealed Himself to Israel with mighty deeds, and the Bible lingers lovingly over the various miracles, recounts with astonishment the thrust of God's power, and blesses "the Lord God, the God of Israel who alone does marvelous things" (Ps. 72:18).

The Exodus established God's claim upon Israel. Other Near Eastern sagas which proclaim national origins assume some special merit upon the part of that race or nation. The Bible goes out of its way to underscore the unworthiness of the Hebrews: they are riffraff, sullen-eyed, stiff-necked men who had no faith in Moses' promise; once freed, they caviled against the rigors of wilderness life and any and all authority. At the first chance they worshipped false gods. There was open revolt in the camp. With good reason their descendants sang of those years, "Not unto us, O Lord, not to us, but unto Thy name ascribe the glory" (Ps. 115:1). Israel's only real virtue lay in her willingness to respond to God's imperious claim.

God's Freedom and God's Bondage

≈§≈

What was Moses' role?

In Judaism Moses is a key figure, revered principally in his role as classic prophet and messenger of God's word. The biblical eulogy established his precedence: "Never again did there arise in Israel a prophet like Moses, whom the Lord singled out, face to face" (Deut. 34:10).

The Law is known as the *Torat Mosheh*. The Pentateuch is called the Five Books of Moses. Though the word of God came by way of visions and dreams to a number of prophets, Moses received the revelation directly from God's mouth (Num. 12:6–8). The Bible endows Moses' infancy with miraculous elements—the watertight cradle plucked out of the Nile by, of all people, Pharaoh's daughter. In later folk literature Moses became even more of a *wunderkind:* a peculiar and brilliant light filled the house of his parents at the time of his birth; he was able to walk and talk to his parents at birth; he began prophesying at the age of three. This exaltation of the man was due not only to the natural elaboration of hero worship but to a conscious need to exalt the validity of the Torah, which he had mediated. Since all men know from sad experiences that their memories lapse and their minds sometimes play tricks, Moses' hearing and memory had to be exceptional. For the law to be a faithful transcription of God's word, Moses had to be absolutely trustworthy, his perception faultless.

Paradox lies at the heart of many religious phenomena. There is in Judaism, beginning in biblical days, a demythologizing tradition which not only insists that Moses was heir to all infirmities of the flesh, but seems determined to diminish his historical importance. Biblical law differs from Mesopotamian law, not in assuming that God promulgates law, but in its conscious insistence that the leader, Moses, is only a messenger. Compare the preamble of Hammurabi's code:

> When Marduk commissioned me to guide the people aright, to direct the land,
> I established law and justice in the language of the land thereby promoting the welfare of the people.
> At that time [I decreed]: [2]

with the ordinary preamble of a biblical section:

[43]

And the Lord spoke unto Moses saying: Speak unto the Children of Israel and say unto them . . . (Ex. 25:1 et passim).

The words are God's and the power His. Moses is only a spokesman; Israel is responsible to God, not to Moses. Further, Moses is anything but a perfect physical specimen; he stammers. Moses is no saint; he can be irascible, he is cold to his family, and on at least one occasion he willfully disobeys God. Textual criticism has generally shown that the later a particular portion of the Torah, the more the text limits Moses' role. In the Hallel Psalms of Ascent and Thanksgiving, which were sung as the people came up to Jerusalem on their pilgrimage festivals, songs which glorify the Exodus events, no mention is made of Moses. Much later the Haggadah actually retold the Exodus story for the Seder fellowship on the first night of Passover without once mentioning Moses. In postbiblical times, Moses was spoken of familiarly as *Mosheh Rabbenu*, Moses our rabbi (teacher). Rabbis are commentators on the text, not oracular figures.

The biblical account of Moses' death, with its emphasis on his burial in an unmarked and consequently unvisited grave, clearly seeks to underscore his humanity. Moses has no role in heaven. He does not sit at God's right hand to relay the prayers of the faithful. There are no shrines dedicated to his name. Careful theology thus made the point that God alone makes history, but the memory of the great leader was so powerful that it could not completely be held in check. "The people feared the Lord: they had faith in the Lord, and in His servant Moses" (Ex. 14:31).

Moses' actual biography is beyond any but a purely impressionistic reconstruction, but the inconsistencies of the chronicles and the tradition mattered little to Israel. Reverence does not pay much attention to scholarly footnotes. Moses was the faithful servant of God, the throneless monarch of a spiritual kingdom.

❦

The Exodus God was not a hidden God—a *deus absconditus*—or a creator God who retires within nature after setting the world in motion, but a God who cares, conscious of and near to His people, who does not hesitate to interfere on their behalf when justice is perverted. The Exodus took place because I, God, "have marked well the plight of My people in Egypt and have heeded their outcry because of their taskmasters; yes, I am mindful of their sufferings. I have come down to rescue them . . ." (Ex. 3:7–8). God is purposefully involved in history and obviously has a plan for Israel and for the world. The nature gods of Canaan and Mesopotamia also were active and involved. Their favor or displeasure determined the outcome of battle and the fertility of the land. All these gods worked miracles. The activity of Israel's God is distinguished by a self-imposed ethical standard. Like other Semitic gods, God protects the army, assures fertility, and insures fecundity; the difference is that Israel's God acts out of His own sense of justice, and not arbitrarily out of a bursting sense of power.

The image and impact of a God who responds to injustice is radically different from the impression of gods who simply personify the awesome powers of nature. Near Eastern myths captured in telling images the creation of cosmos out of chaos, the struggle of day and night, and the annual rebirth of seed in the womb of the earth. These stories are the grand myths of the race, echoes of which can be found in the first chapters of Genesis, but they are not central to Israel's view. God transcends nature. He reveals Himself symbolically in a bush that burns but is not consumed, and existentially in a deliverance which could not take place but did. All gods are powerful, but there is a vast difference between divine power which is the surge of nature and divine power which imposes its will on nature and parts the seas so that an oppressed people can go free. Such a God is not only an active and vigorous force within human history, a God who works wonders, but a force for good who "lifts the weak out of the dust" (I Sam. 2:7). He not only controls the destiny of nations, but judges the nations in righteousness. History ceases to be equivocal and becomes hopeful; divine power is no longer indifferent to humanity; and the Exodus is read as a paradigm for all human history. God will help man escape from every shackle and fetter. " 'Because of the groans of the plundered poor and needy, I will now act,' says the Lord; 'I will give help' " (Ps. 12:6). Faith in a God who will not close His ears to human suffering, and who will deliver the downtrodden, chained Israel to hope (to use the phrase of a postexilic prophet) and allowed Israel to exalt God's righteousness. God's ways are never fully revealed but the faithful knew, on the evidence of the Exodus, that God's actions are for man's ultimate benefit.

The Exodus faith finds and affirms God's beneficence, but never loses sight of His awesomeness. God turns the Nile into a river of blood, summarily executes the first-born of Egypt, and strikes down any who touch the Ark of the Covenant. Though God is known as beneficent, His power is without limits. Since God is the source of all power and ancient men had noted the irrational and compulsive side of human activity, the Bible often speaks quite awkwardly of what we could call man's more perverse and self-destructive actions. God hardens Pharaoh's heart (Ex. 4:21). He induces Absalom to reject Ahitophel's sage counsel (II Sam. 15). He leads David on so that the king begins a forbidden census (I Sam. 26:19). The inexplicable must have some divine explanation. However, what began as innocent piety became a theological embarrassment. Men began to ask: "Does God entice men to sin?" "How can we speak of retribution if God Himself speeds the sin?" Piety persistently denied man's ability to judge God's actions. God's reasons are just and right even when we do not understand them. Israel not only loved but feared the Lord its God. Biblical man knew that God's power was untrammeled. Yet there is a rather constant theme in Israel's faith that insists that all God's actions are prompted by His will to save, and that His anger is never capricious. Misfortune represents either merited punishment or necessary instruction. After all, God's first identification in history is with and for the subjugated and powerless. His first act is one of deliverance—He is the Savior.

So real is Israel's awareness of God's presence, so personal is God to Israel, that the literature is full of disingenuous expressions which transfer human emotions to God. Those who quake in their boots when the earth swallows up Korah and his rebels, or who lose control of their emotions once the sea is safely forded, know that God can be angry or glorious in act. God had not yet become a God-head or a God-idea; He was naturally perceived, though not necessarily conceived in anthropopathic terms. Perception and conception in this context must be carefully distinguished. God is "seen" by men who simply and artlessly express their perception, but conceptually "God is not man . . . or mortal . . ." (Num. 23:19).

Early biblical texts associate God with control of the seasons (Jud. 5:4), the gift of fecundity (Deut. 33:13 ff.), and certain shrines and heights; but He is never identified as nature or personified as any aspect of this physical universe. There are no myths in which the forces of nature are deified. There are no consort gods or lesser gods. God is immanent, yet His powers are broad. He can bring the children of Israel out of Egypt, protect their tribes on the way, and reduce for them the high-walled cities of Canaan. His use of power is neither willful nor capricious.

God's Freedom and God's Bondage

Iconoclasm came much later. Israel's faith in the high God and the faith of Israel's neighbors in various gods coexisted with less rather than more friction. What is crucial is that Israel's awe before the reality of God's deliverance must have included some awareness that God's powers extended beyond the tribe. The Exodus, lying at the heart of Israel's collective memory, was always attributed to the far reaching power of God. But of which God?

As we have seen, the patriarchal stories contain a number of names for God: YHWH, Baal, Adon, El, and a variety of combinations with El. Some texts which report the Exodus saga say in effect that the God of the patriarchs is now properly to be known as YHWH. The Ten Words begin: "I am YHWH your God." The Deuteronomic watchword is technically translated "Hear O Israel! YHWH is our God, YHWH alone" (6:6). Who is YHWH? Some have assumed that Moses covenanted the tribes to the god of his Midianite (Kenite) father-in-law, and simply insisted that this YHWH and the God of the fathers were one and the same. This argument is based on a single text in which Jethro officiates at a sacrifice to YHWH and at a communion meal (Ex. 18:12–30). There is, however, a contradictory text which has Jethro exclaim after the deliverance: "Now I know that YHWH is greater than all gods" (Ex. 18:11). Archeology has not provided any evidence that YHWH was the Midianite high God. Other theories are that YHWH was a divine name which Moses heard at his moment of summons, or a name known in earlier time to certain Hebrew tribes which Moses simply confirmed as the name of the God who had commissioned him.

An early text embedded in the much-edited story of the "burning bush" suggests yet a different name for the God who delivers.

Moses said to God, "When I come to the Israelites and say to them, 'The God of your fathers has sent me to you,' and they ask me, 'What is His name?' what shall I say to them?" And God said to Moses, "Ehyeh-Asher-Ehyeh." He continued, "Thus shall you say to the Israelites, 'Ehyeh sent me to you' " (Ex. 3:13–14).

Some have suggested that *Ehyeh-Asher-Ehyeh* is to be understood as an expansion of the causative forms of the verb "to be," which might be read, "I shall be what I shall be." The argument is that YHWH took unto Himself all the powers and protective attributes of the patriarchal high God (El, El Elyon, El Shaddai) and added an attribute implying the power to be and to bring into being. God is immediately present and active. The emphasis is on divine power within history. This argument, although theologically appropriate, is philologically suspect. Other suggested translations, "I am that I am," "I will be what I will be," are equally uncertain. There is no etymological proof that YHWH comes from the root "to be." The shortened forms of YHWH (Yah, Yahu, Yo) which appear in early theophoric names and as names of God in such extrabiblical documents as the sixth-century Elephantine papyri would seem to derive from some other root. *Ehyeh-Asher-Ehyeh* simply does not yield an acceptable translation.

Did Moses bind Israel to a new God, or to an old God under a new name, or did he simply know God under one of His older names, since YHWH frequently appears in the patriarchal stories? Given the limitations on our information, this question presently is unanswerable, although it is the scholarly consensus that YHWH appears for the first time in the Israelite period. But we must appreciate why the question has so often been raised. In West Asia's cultural ethos names were more than convenient means of identification. A name embodied the essence of personality. To name a god, or for that matter a man, was to describe and reveal his basic nature. Presumably a change in the nature of man's awareness and thinking about God would be reflected in a change of divine name. But the name of God remains as much a mystery as His essence.

The name of God had unique holiness. To be able to name God was to gain certain power over Him, for the name was part of God, and to know the name was to know God. His name sealed oaths and pledges; it assured the effectiveness of curses. The name of God was spiritually potent and consequently taboo. The Decalogue includes the requirement that God's name not be part of common speech (Ex. 20:7). God's special name was at first spoken freely, but by post-exilic times there were prohibitions against YHWH's name being spoken at all. The High Priest alone pronounced God's name, and then only once a year when he entered the Holy of Holies on the Day of Atonement. The community adopted a variety of euphemisms, and to this day Jews read the name YHWH as *Adonai* or *Adoshem;* sometimes the pious carry this taboo into the vernacular and leave out a letter when they write G–d in English.

A word should be said about "Jehovah," which is found in so many texts. Jehovah is a coined word made up of the consonants Y, H, W, H, of the biblical Tetragrammaton, and the vowels of the rabbinic substitution *Adonai.* The result is a graceless and pointless artificiality. Scholars tend to use the original consonants YHWH to name the biblical God, but YHWH, usually pronounced Yahveh, represents no more than a calculated guess as to how the Tetragrammaton was sacrally pronounced. There are some good reasons not to use YHWH consistently in reading and discussing the biblical faith. YHWH is a proper name, not a descriptive title, and implies one god among many. The use of YHWH after the earliest history tends to misrepresent the reality of Israel's monotheistic development. Somehow YHWH suggests that the prophets and wise men of Israel worshipped a deity who was more tribal and less universal than the God of contemporary speech, which is simply not the case.

Sinai and the covenant were central and critical in Israel's spiritual life. The exaltation of God's deliverance was tied to an emphatic requirement of obedience to God's words. Salvation had entered history, and Jewish history has become a record of Israel's struggle to be worthy of God's deliverance and, as God's covenanted people, to abide God's way. As told in the Pentateuch, it is a history which must give an optimist pause. Despite having seen with their own eyes God's power to save, the people remain remarkably obdurate. For a brief moment Israel rises to exalt God for His deliverance. But thirst, hunger, and plain truculence soon dampen the ardor, and Israel proves a remarkably unlikable lot—stiff-necked, a motley band without grace, complaining constantly about rations and exhaustion. They berate Moses and even question the value of their freedom. Their attitude toward God is, "What did He do for me today?" "Is the Lord present among us or not?" (Ex. 17:7).

A saga which begins in exultation ends in the weariness of the wilderness trek, with the sad need to bury a whole generation so brutalized by slavery that they could not cope with freedom. Though propelled by faith, the Israelite spirit was remarkably realistic. This world was a harsh place. One should not count on miracles, but somehow a new force had entered history. Israel became an organic unity, a people, and not just any people, but God's. This thought pressed and would not let them go. Individually the people were quite ordinary, but collectively they had a new identity, a covenanted discipline, a proud awareness that they were no longer anonymous, a conscience which drove them on to obey the will of God.

CHAPTER

ɛ§ IV ﻉﻩ

Land

Dᴜʀɪɴɢ their migrations, the Hebrews had camped along the Jordan river valley and in the Judean hill country; apparently they made no attempt to conquer any of the city-states which controlled most of the area. It was reported of the fathers that they had bought small parcels of land, Abraham in Hebron, Jacob at Shechem (Gen. 33:18), but their legal status remained that of resident alien (Gen. 23:4). Only centuries later, after a protracted period of incursion and conquest during the era of the judges (1250–1020) and the early kings, Saul and David (1020–965), was physical control of the Promised Land wrested from its inhabitants. Nevertheless, biblical documents insist that possession of this land was pledged to the Hebrews by God when He cut the covenant with Abraham (Gen. 15:18 ff.); whether this is pious hindsight or self-fulfilling prophecy, it cannot be doubted that Canaan was identified as the homeland quite early in this people's spiritual self-consciousness.

Actually, there never was a nation named Canaan. The Canaanites were one of the several ethnic leagues of city-states in West Asia during the second millennium. A report given to Moses by his spies described these various confederations "Amalekites dwell in the Negeb region; Hittites, Jebusites, and Amorites inhabit the hill country; and Canaanites dwell by the Sea and along the Jordan" (Num. 13:29). The physical center of the Canaanites lay along the Lebanese coast (Tyre, Sidon, Byblos), reaching eastward into Galilee. Though

Land

Canaan is often used as a synonym for the entire Promised Land, the actual territory of the Canaanites represented only a part of the area which the tribes looked upon as covenanted to them; in fact, Israel never succeeded in conquering some of the Canaanite city-states, specifically those in Phoenicia. Canaan is more accurately used as a shorthand term for a cultural milieu rather than a political entity, and will so be used here. Canaanite customs extended far beyond Canaanite power, and left a lasting cultural imprint on the Israelite invaders.

According to Israel's national saga, the tribes under Moses headed directly for the hill country west of the Jordan; they did not consider any alternative home, such as Moab or Edom. Even when their initial attacks from the south were repulsed, the tribes prepared for a prolonged delay rather than settle in another locale. They looked on this land as theirs. It had been promised to the fathers by God, who had determined it as their proper residence. At Shechem, after Jericho and some of the cities of the hill country had been taken, when God confirmed the covenant with Joshua, He names Himself as He who "gave you a land on which you had not labored, cities which you had never built; you have lived in those cities and you eat the produce of vineyards and olive groves which you did not plant" (Josh. 24:13). Israel's founding covenants bracketed the gift of freedom with the gift of land as proof of God's mighty acts on behalf of His people.

This land was a constant sign to those fortunate enough to settle in it of God's mercy to their fathers, His faithfulness to His pledged word, and His irresistible power. God accomplished what the spies had suggested would be an impossible feat. He had conquered for His people a land whose soldiers were fierce and of great size and whose cities were well fortified and seemingly impregnable (Num. 13:25 ff.). From Egypt God had redeemed His people. In Canaan He had established them in the land which He had promised would be their home and their passport to identity. The landless of the world are the overlooked, the outsiders. Land is not only the most precious of possessions, but psychologically the most necessary. The landed have always looked down on the landless. It is the settled who build civilization, not the gypsies.

Precisely what were the boundaries of the land which God promised to Israel? Biblical evidence is not consistent on this point. Compare the greater Israel, running from the Euphrates to the Wadi El-Arish, which is pledged to Abraham (Gen. 15:18–19), with the more circumscribed national perimeter described in Numbers (34:2–12), which includes most of the Negev, Palestine, northern Lebanon, and Syria. Neither description tallies with the known settlements of the tribes or the imperial conquests of the kings, so we cannot assume that these descriptions are late insertions designed to make the original promise conform to existing conditions. The traditional division of land gave the tribes of Reuben, Gad, and Manasseh territory east of the Jordan, and in the tenth century Solomon controlled most of Trans-Jordan and reduced Moab to a vassal state; yet the eastern boundary of the Promised Land south of the Sea of Galilee stops in both surveys at the Jordan River. It has been suggested that the concept of a Promised Land developed on the authority of oracular prophecy, and events simply never conformed with the early oracles. However we explain these inconsistencies, awareness of the discrepancies is not a recent discovery. At least one biblical writer wrestled with the question of why Israel had never conquered the whole of the promised territory, particularly areas in modern Lebanon and Syria, and offered an answer which could be understood by this covenant-bound people: God had not allowed the full conquest because the nation had not deserved it, for almost from their first incursion the invaders had disobeyed the terms of their compact with God (Jud. 2:20–23).

The actual course of the conquest is beyond final historical reconstruction, but the tribes came at a propitious time. Pharaohs of the eighteenth and nineteenth dynasties had bled this land of much of its wealth and natural resource, and had exhausted themselves and their Hittite enemies in a continuing struggle for imperial control. Beginning about 1200 B.C.E., sea peoples, much like the Normans of a later time, attacked all along the eastern Mediterranean coast from Cilicia to Egypt, and, with iron-tipped weapons and iron will, pillaged, conquered, and ultimately controlled the city-states of the coastal plain, the valley of Jezreel, and of Beth-Shean. Egypt no longer effectively ruled in Canaan, and Philistines from the coast and Israelites from the wilderness raced to fill the power vacuum.

The first chapters of the book of Joshua speak of a major settlement by the Israelites in Gilead east of the Jordan, and of a direct attack from across the Jordan which reduced Jericho, Ai, and most of the cities of the central highlands. Other records in Joshua and Judges, in addition to archeological evidence, indicate a protracted and complicated period of incursion and settlement.

Some tribes, who later joined the Israelite confederation, apparently had been in and around the Promised Land during the entire period of Egyptian slavery. Some never took to the field, but entered into feudal compacts with local princes and seized on each display of deteriorating local power to wrest some advantage. Some simply moved into the well-forested but sparsely settled highlands and asserted squatters' rights, while others tried direct military attack. One result of this protracted and sizable incursion was that, for the first time, "this land of hills and valleys" (Deut. 11:11) became fully populated, utilized, and, consequently, a unified region. During most of the second millennium the Promised Land had been an agglomeration of disparate and loosely linked city-states separated from each other by mountains and the forests. The Israelite tribes filled in the interstitial areas, farmed the heights, and for the first time this area developed as an economically integrated region.

During the two centuries of conquest (1200–1000) a growing awareness of unity emerged among the tribes. The fraternal relationship was symbolized in the persons of Jacob's twelve sons. Those who joined the confederation later did so by participating in the covenant at one of the occasions at which it was renewed. Since the covenant was not simply a mutual defense pact, but a divine compact in which the parties who joined pledged fealty to the will of God, proclaimed a litany of YHWH's mighty acts and joined in an oath of fealty, a sense that all had shared a common history naturally emerged among those who now considered themselves "of the congregation of Jacob" (Deut. 33:4).

Historians can find evidence in nooks and crannies of the Bible of various changes in the composition of this confederation. Caleb, once a member, disappears; Benjamin, not originally a member, appears. But through it all God's covenant operated as a unifying vehicle through which a gaggle of tribes become confederated and develop a shared history and faith. The pressures of the conquests made community advisable; the sense that the God of the fathers (plural) sponsored the conquest made for a community of faith; the power of the covenant which bound tribe to God and all God's servants to each other made confederation legally and structurally feasible.

On the way the tribal league had shared a covenanted relationship, the Ark, God; they were the people (*am*) of God. To the wanderers God had promised: "I will make of you a great nation" (Gen. 12:2). A nation is a people rooted to their land. This people became a nation when they were settled in their land. The people had been covenanted to a God and a discipline; the nation was covenanted to

God, a discipline, and a land. Forever after, landlessness and exile, whenever endured, would be a void crying out to be filled. Life is possible for a people in the wilderness; once the people has become a nation, not to live in the land is to be an outcast and to suffer a sense of incompleteness.

The tribes were invaders, but in their eyes the conquest was justified. God had willed Israel to have this place and legally had covenanted it to them. The conquest was carried out with the usual bloody excess and patriotic gore, but it was not a case of royal chaplains sermonizing that God was on their side; this was God's war. The advancing troops were the "armies of the living God" (I Sam. 17:26). They fought the *arel*, the uncircumcised, those not covenanted to God. Those who defended a city's walls against them were the "enemies of God," with the list of victories duly recorded in "The Book of the Wars of God" (Num. 21:14). God was consulted on strategy and He marched before the host. When the Holy Ark was carried before the troops, men cried out: "Advance, O Lord! May Your enemies be scattered, and may Your foes flee before You" (Num. 10:35). God waged the war and God's army felt assured of the outcome before the battle was engaged.

Later editors described the conquest as a *milḥemet ḥovah*, a war of obligation, from which comes the term "holy war." The term needs precise definition, for this was not a crusade against unbelievers and heretics. Unlike the later concept of *Djihād* in Islam, a war of obligation never was declared to spread the faith. Land was at issue, not souls. After the conquest had been achieved, only response to attack could be declared a war of obligation. The conquest was not a *Kulturkampf*. It was not YHWH against Baal. Canaanite shrines were not molested. Iconoclasm comes later. The war of obligation represents the urgency of settlement and then simply self-defense.

Israel did not fight for God—God fought for Israel. Israel fought successfully only as long as God willed the fight to last. When Israel became greedy and went off on its own, defeat was swift and terrible. The image of God casting stones on an enemy host or holding back the dusk so that an enemy's decimation may be completed is disconcerting to those conditioned to think of God in terms of divine gentleness and unbounded love, but in those days God was feared as well as romanticized. The Israelites' ease in conceiving of God as warrior, as God of the hosts, simply testifies to the simplicity and thoroughness of their identification of power and God. It also testifies to the fullness of their faith. After all, the covenant was God's, it was He who had promised the land; the war had been launched on His word. However, God is never a swirling sword hacking murderously on all sides killing indiscriminately. He fights for Israel only the battles of necessity, settlement, and self-defense. God does not cry out for blood. The sacrifice of captured soldiers is unknown. There are no kamikaze cults whose votaries are assured of salvation if they die for God in holy battle, nor did God hesitate to war against His own people when they were wantonly cruel or continued to war against cities that had offered to surrender.

Since the war was God's and God was the chief warrior, the spoils were in the first instance His. On His order whole cities were reserved and came under the *ḥerem* (taboo). The *ḥerem* was not easy to enforce. Soldiers pick up things, and the Bible records a number of cases of summary punishment for looting. The holocaust of a captured town was a not uncommon Semitic military ritual, but the sacrifice of the *ḥerem* seems rarely to have been practiced. God conquered but did not slaughter. There are no records of forced conversions and, surprisingly, no record of mass enslavement of the indigenous population.

The national home was private property, God's: "The land is Mine" (Lev. 25:23). Israel was simply God's chosen cultivator. As tenants, the tribes paid annual rent in the form of tithes and made further payment in the form of the return to God of the first-born. They were carefully instructed by the Master of the place to obey His strict and specific rules of cultivation and conservation. The land was to lie fallow each seventh year. Trees were not to be cut down even for the battering rams and scaling ladders required to besiege and conquer an enemy town. No field was to be planted with mixed seeds. These rules obviously represent an early understanding of conservation. However it is not for their practical value, but because they represented God's specific orders, that they were to be obeyed.

The rule that the land remain fallow during the seventh year was not presented as a conservation measure, but because that year is "a sabbath of the Lord" (Lev. 25:4). The prescribed rest preserved the land's holiness, not its fertility. Since the land belonged to God, no land could be held in perpetuity. On the Jubilee, every fifty years, "each of you shall return to his holding" (25:13). Why? Simply because God wills it. "For it is a jubilee. It shall be holy to you . . ." (25:12). In an environment where most peoples said "The land is mine," Israel said "The land is Thine," and willingly obeyed the terms its owner, God, had stipulated in the lease. To be sure, boundary stones were carefully raised, but these established only a conditional title. God had allotted the land among the tribes of Israel, and the law protected each family's rights to that plot which God had designated for it. Those who sought to aggrandize or monopolize land violated God's homestead program and would be punished not only for the common sin of greed, but for the covenant sin of disobedience.

Since the land was God's and consequently holy, its state of purity was a constant concern. "You shall not defile the land in which you live, in which I Myself abide, for I the Lord abide among the Israelite people" (Num. 35:33–34). The belief grew that the land might actually, on God's orders, vomit out Israel if the Israelites indulged in idolatry, sexual license, or public contempt of God's law (Lev. 18:28). Innocent blood spilt on the earth defiled the land (Gen. 4:11–12, Num. 35:33). In the Canaanite *Tale of Aqhat*, after the hero suffers a particularly scandalous and bloody death, "the fruits of summer are withered, the ear in its husks." [1] Israelite law prescribed a number of elaborate expiatory rites designed to free the land of such defilement, but the tradition added two specifically Israelite touches. In the Canaanite myth the earth is personified, and on her own authority closes up her powers of fertility when she comes into contact with innocent blood. In Scripture, God orders the land to become infertile to punish Cain for fratricide (Gen. 4:11–12). In the Canaanite myth the hero's father tries to revive nature by practicing various acts of sympathetic magic; he goes to the field, chants incantations, and lays his hands on the corn. [2] In Israel one offered a sacrifice and asked God's forgiveness.

The people came to recognize that land as such is neither pure nor defiled. A land is pure when those who dwell on it are obedient to the will of God; it is defiled when they are not. Sinful citizens suggest to God that He should close off the land's fertility, while a righteous nation is rewarded with a bountiful harvest. Various exorcistic rites associated with the spilling of blood seem to have been practiced, but the prophets would teach that to be pure the land must have inhabitants who are obedient to the covenant, that if the rains come in their season it is because men merit the harvest, not because the land has been kept in a state of ritual purity.

The land of Israel is praised in the Bible far beyond its real merit.

For the Lord your God is bringing you unto a good land, a land with streams and springs and lakes issuing from plain and hill, a land of wheat and barley, of vines, figs, and pomegranates, a land of olive oil and of honey; a land where you may eat food without stint, where you will lack nothing; a land whose rocks are iron and from whose hills you can mine copper. When you have eaten your fill, give thanks to the Lord your God for the good land which He has given you (Deut. 8:7–10).

This place is "a patrimony fairer than that of any other nation" (Jer. 3:19). But this blessed condition is not intrinsic to the land. It is God who places fertility here. The land remains green only so long as God wills it. When the people displease God, "ten acres of vineyard shall yield but one *bath*, and a field sown with a *homer* of seed shall yield a mere *epah*" (Isa. 5:10). Such an emphasis on God's providential control of nature turns agriculture into a moral art and precludes any concept of an inexorable natural law. Still the seasons and planets have their observable cycles. In His concern for man, God had established a covenant that guaranteed that "so long as the earth endures, seedtime and harvest, cold and heat, summer and winter, day and night, shall not cease" (Gen. 8:22). If the children of Israel looked to God for a good harvest, they did not cease to labor in their fields. In this land's long history, only the farms of modern Israel would match the productivity of the first farmers of Israel.

Some passages seem to personify the land. "You must not cause the land to sin, which the Lord God gives you for inheritance" (Deut. 24:4). The idiom is poetic and probably was so intended, since biblical theology was enthusiastic. Because God had chosen this place it was holier than other places. Of course, piety inevitably literalized such poetry. Amos threatens Amaziah that he will die in an "impure land," that is, outside of Israel (Amos 7:17). The Lord's presence was felt uniquely in Israel. Understandably, for many the Promised Land became God's place and God became like a Baal, divine lord of a territory. Some had reservations about the efficacy of cultic acts performed outside God's land. Absalom, hoping for a safe passage home, does not sacrifice to God in Aram but pledges a sacrifice upon his return (II Sam. 15). The non-Israelite Naaman, convinced of God's power by Elisha's successful use of it to cure his leprosy, takes home some of the land's good earth so that he can set up a proper and efficacious altar (II Kings 5:7). To this day a pious Jew may have a small bag of the sod of Israel placed in his coffin, in the belief that resurrection will begin there. This same man has acknowledged all his life in his liturgy that it is God alone who revives the dead. Israel never worshipped Mother Earth: "The earth is the Lord's and all that it holds" (Ps. 24:1).

The land was God's and holy; God was uniquely in this land.

Exile is described as God's "banishing them [Israel] from His sight" (II Kings 13:23; 17:20; 24:24). This identification of land and God had become so much a part of the people's awareness that Jeremiah instinctively uses it in the very message in which he attacks those who have so identified God and Temple that they believe that God always will protect the Temple simply because it is His shrine:

> Therefore what I did to Shiloh I will do to this house which bears my name, the house in which you put your trust, the place I gave to you and to your forefathers; I will fling you away out of my sight, as I flung away all your kinsfolk, the whole brood of Ephraim (7:14–15).

Much later, in rabbinic times, some of the pious said that it was possible to obey the law of God fully only in the land of Israel. Travel to Israel became and is *aliyah*, going up, a rising toward God. God was uniquely in this land, but not limited to it. There was the tradition that the Promised Land was God's place, and there was also the Exodus tradition which described God's power over Egypt. God had "come down" on Sinai. God had led the tribes for forty years in the wilderness east of the Jordan, and during that trek God had stopped the sun in its track so that He might complete the discomfiture of Amalek. In religious belief logically inconsistent concepts can be held simultaneously. The same Deuteronomic historian who looked on exile as banishment from God's presence tells how Elijah, using God's name, performed wondrous cures in Phoenicia. God had His place, but place had many labels (Sinai, Promised Land, Jerusalem— "the whole earth is full of His glory" [Isa. 6:3]). A consistent theology of God's universal power was first developed by the literary prophets, but its roots are old and go deep. After all, God's original dwelling was a portable tent and His throne a movable ark. The tension between "surely God is present in this place" (Gen. 28:16) and "the heavens is My throne, and the Earth is My footstool: Where could you build a house for Me" (Isa. 66:1) was to remain vital in Jewish life, and to this day underlies all discussions, halachic and theological, of the legitimacy of life in the Diaspora.

Neither the land nor the earth which composed it was God. Among the Canaanites the productivity of the earth and the power of the gods were mysteriously one. The earth was literally a mother goddess whose fecundity gave the earth its fertility. Each fall the rain god, Baal, had to impregnate Mother Earth for the land to blossom forth in the spring. The nature cults assumed the interdependence of all that is: man, earth, and the spirit which animates both. Sophisticated nature cults such as those that flourished in Canaan transformed these relationships into myth. The myths in turn suggested that, by sacrifice and mimetic magic, men could please the gods, drive away evil spirits, and even stimulate nature. The Baal rite which is most famous (only because it seems so shocking) involved cult prostitution. In theory, the impregnation of a consecrated maiden set up harmonies which reminded the gods of their duty and stimulated them to it. The Bible does not contain a single overt reference to a female deity. Prostitution is prostitution and sacred prostitution was "abhorrent to the Lord" (Deut. 24:4).

The Canaanite myths grew out of man's natural amazement at the powers which animate nature. The people knew the various natural forces and their myths spoke of various powers and did not limit each god to a single function. Flux and change are at the very center of their perception. Nothing in the universe was immutable or fixed. Their gods are as capricious as the weather or the winds. Rain can be gentle, torrential, life-giving, life-destroying, essential to the earth's fertility, or the flood which washes away the topsoil. Thus, Baal among the Canaanites was a cosmic hero, the storm, the annual victor in a battle with the dragon Mot, impregnator of Mother Earth, a bull according to strength, and a champion of life who wrestles the god of the underworld into submission. In the Canaanite myths the powers which animate nature can and do act on their own initiative. Baal is not limited to thunder or the storm; he is brother to Anath, a cosmic adventurer. The gods often change their masks, and one never can truly know which is their essential nature; all that can be said is that they are never wholly separate from whatever power of nature they describe at the moment.

The Canaanite gods are at times human, at times animal, at times composite and hybrid forms. Man has not yet become fully conscious of the gap between himself and the phenomena of nature. The god Baal is sometimes pictured as a young prince from whose forehead grow the horns of a bull. Nobility, strength, virility, and youth are expressed without any sense of distinction between the virility of a bull and the virility of a youth, or the nobility of man and the nobility of a beast.

Israel's descriptions of God are sometimes anthropomorphic, but never zoomorphic. God has separated Himself out of the flux of life. A gulf opens between God and nature and between man and the animal kingdom. Man sees both his God and himself with new respect. Whereas heretofore man has seen himself and his species as part of the stream of life, now he comes to know himself as distinct from all else. Adam names the animals. It is as if he had said to himself, "If there is only one guiding will, all phenomena are distinct, and so then am I." Soon men will define that distinction: man is specifically created to subdue and dominate the animal kingdom and to husband God's earth for Him. In his own mind man becomes a unique creation, unique among all species in his relations to God and in his relation to all other beings.

Israel withdrew personality from nature. There is no power in nature save such power as God places there.

> Of old You established the earth;
>   The heavens are the work of Your hands.
> They shall perish, but You shall endure;
>   They shall all wear out like a garment;
>   You change them like clothing and they pass away.
> But You are He whose years are without end.
>
> (Ps. 102:26–28)

In the Ras Shamra version of the Canaanite myths (14th cent. B.C.E.), the high God El is browbeaten by his daughter, and many gods refuse to do his bidding. In Israel God is the only power and incontestable. Nothing exists outside His knowledge or acts independently of His will. He is the transcendent creator, not limited by or to His creation. In a later period, when Israel elaborated a creation story, the world was not pictured as evolving naturally and inevitably from God; rather, God determined to create a world and ordered "let there be," and there was! Myth presumes that natural forces act out their own reality, and can therefore be personified. The elemental interplay of sun, rain, and earth fascinates, for men are the beneficiaries and victims of that drama. The Bible is largely without myth because the powers of nature are no longer independent: all obey God's will. "The earth is the Lord's and all that it holds" (Ps. 24:1). God brings the winds, sends the rain, moves the sun, and causes the earth to give harvest and the seasons to run their appointed course (Ps. 104). Monotheism displaces myth; all depends on one will. Such faith contains an unresolved question: Does God direct nature with any specific concern for each man's welfare? Within that is yet another question that asks whether the way men behave has any effect on God's governance: Will God shut up the heavens to punish a sinful people? Many, perhaps most, in ancient Israel believed He would, as the covenant explicitly stipulated. In Israel's understanding nature was not a physical universe operating according to the laws of cause and effect, but His handiwork, His creation, operating according to God's will.

Israelite thought turned the Canaanite view inside out. Instead of men being dependent upon nature and the gods who animate and personify its movements, nature depends, in the last analysis, upon men. The equation seems to be that man's obedience to the covenant places God under a self-imposed obligation to abide by the covenant—to have the earth yield an abundant harvest—whereas man's sin leads God to invoke the penalty clauses of the covenant—to dry up the springs and shut off the rain. Israel came to understand that a good harvest depended upon obedience to the covenant of God, and not upon divine caprice or the willingness of nature to yield her produce. Nature ceased to be a complex of willful forces and became man's God-given and God-regulated environment. To be sure many hedged their bets, and for some centuries Israelite farmers visited the Baal altars. Archeologists routinely find small clay figures of the Canaanite goddess of fertility in Israelite homes. On the popular level, the sense of nature's independent power died slowly, if it can be said to have died at all.

Obviously the period of settlement was a time of cultural shock for the Israelites. In the arts and in technology the Canaanites were superior to the invaders. Their cities were larger and better defended than any that the Israelites would be able to build for some generations. The corbelled redoubt, the *migdol*, of Canaanite design, became a feature of Israelite battlements. Ivory-banded furniture and the expensive gold, silver, and alabaster utensils of the Canaanite nobility became objects of Israelite greed and subjects of prophetic denunciation. Such was the reputation of Canaanite craftsmen that King Solomon sent to King Hiram of Tyre for skilled craftsmen to build the royal chapel—the so-called First Temple in Jerusalem. The Canaanites taught the Hebrews to use an alphabet, and Israel was conscious of speaking "the language of Canaan" (Isa. 19:18). The Canaanite peoples had developed what was probably the world's first true alphabet, a consonantal system which Israel adopted and used until the end of the monarchy (6th cent. B.C.E.). The unrhymed doublets and carefully phrased parallelisms of Canaanite poetry set the style for Israel's psalmody. Israelite temple music reached back through Canaan to Mesopotamia. A square earth floating on the seas and crowned by the bowl of heaven was Israel's cosmic model, and that of Canaan and of the Semitic world generally.

There had been no elaborate sacrificial cult in patriarchal times, and the literary prophets of the eighth and seventh centuries insisted that there had been none in Moses' day. "Did you bring me sacrifices and gifts, you people of Israel, those forty years in the wilderness?" (Amos 5:25). "When I brought your forefathers out of Egypt, I gave them no commands about whole offerings and sacrifice. I said not a word about them" (Jer. 7:22). But if Amos doubted the antiquity of sacrifices, the Torah editors did not. Torah law is full of sacrificial regulation. It seems likely that Canaanite influence led to an elaboration of cultic ceremony, particularly to many ramifications in the role of the priest. The Hebrews had had no priestly caste, whereas Canaan was Temple-oriented. Priests and sacrifices were part of every city's routine, and the tribes of Israel obviously enjoyed the spectacles. Solomon's Temple and probably the temples at Beth-El and Shechem were built in Syrian style and oriented eastward, after the Canaanite manner. The Ras Shamra tablets include terms which are etymologically identical to various technical terms which Israel came to use to designate her various sacrifices. However, Israelite ritual differed in one significant detail from the Canaanite model. The Canaanite priests were members of the ruling class and among a city's major landholders. In Israel the priests were not allowed to own land, but were to be supported by the rest of the population (Deut. 18:2). This people had no caste tradition and evidenced what amounts to an inherited fear of caste power.

There were three great pilgrimage holidays in ancient Israel, during which the people went up to a shrine and later to the royal Temple in Jerusalem to offer sacrifice, hymn, and prayer to God. Two of these, Shavuot and Sukkot, the spring and fall harvest festivals, seem to have been Canaanite agricultural festivals which the Israelites appropriated and reshaped. Seed time and harvest did not change simply because the area had new rulers.

The Pesaḥ holiday may have native Israelite roots. The paschal sacrifice suggests a shepherd's world, but Pesaḥ too was integrated with elements of the Canaanite agricultural year, as its role as the Feast of Unleavened Bread (the early grain) suggests. Israel borrowed selectively and shaped what it borrowed to fit Israel's specific needs. Israel's God was Lord of freedom; Passover became a time to relive the exultation of the Exodus. Israel's God had established a covenant with His people; Shavuot was a time to renew the acceptance pledged at Sinai. Israel's God was Lord of nature; Sukkot was a time to bring an offering of first fruits to the altar and to dwell in booths such as those Israel had pitched in the wilderness when God had shielded them on the way (Lev. 23:43).

Acculturation is a complicated exchange. Israel took over many practices, adopting some whole, like the alphabet, but stamping others with her peculiar identity. Thus the so-called peace offering, the communion sacrifice, was offered in Canaan long before the Israelite settlement. Sharing a meal with God reestablished the close ties which bound community and deity. In that world those who ate together assumed specific responsibilities toward each other. Canaanite practice assumed that God shared the meal with the worshipper, and therefore included an element of actual physical union, like Christianity's Eucharist. The sacrifice somehow became God, and man digested part of God and became more godly. There is no such theme in the biblical literature, where men eat of the offering but remain "before," never "with," God.

Why did men offer sacrifices? In Israel sacrifice seems to have had three basic purposes. It was a free-will offering through which men returned to God that which was of God: "For everything comes from Thee, and it is only of Thy gifts that we give to Thee" (I Ch. 29:14). It was a communion tie reestablishing bonds of kinship, and it was an expiation offered to relieve the community or the individual from a burden of guilt or sin. The concept of sacrifice can be spiritually sterile, as prophetic denunciations make quite evident, but it must not be parodied. The Bible contains no evidence that Israel conceived of the sacrifices as God's lunch. Nor were their sacrifices extravagant. Few were actually burnt up. Most of that which was offered was retained as the priest's due, providing maintenance for the sanctuary and support for its officials. In addition, a "poor" tithe was required to provide the shrine with food to disburse to the indigent (Deut. 12:28–29). Sacrifice permits men to give something of what they have to the powers whom they love and fear. It is an acknowledgment of dependence, the bringing of tribute by a vassal to his king, a pledge of loyalty, a gift of love. Sacrifice was deemed an essential way of maintaining the ties between God and man. The tradition was not satisfied with perfunctory rites; rather, it valued honest motivation rather than mechanical performance, denied the efficacy of hypocritical devotion, but accepted the need for cult.

Canaan gave Israel Shavuot and Sukkot (although not their particular content), temples, the paraphernalia of an elaborate priest class and a ramified sacrificial cult, language, and hymn forms. So much was accepted gratefully and even sanctified that it is clear that the law of separation, "You shall not follow the practices of the nation that I am driving out before you" (Lev. 20:23), was applied selectively to those customs, like sacred prostitution, which the Israelite leaders considered abominations.

The word Canaan derives from *Kinaḫni.* a Mesopotamian term which described the Lebanese Syrian coast and was derived in turn from the *kinaḫḫu,* a much-prized purple dye extracted from mollusks trapped in these coastal waters. The Israelites stipulated that the fringes which God's law required them to wear on their garments (*tzitzit*) must be colored with the tint of this deep purple dye. Though the use of such fringes probably derives from the common practice of wearing cloth talismans as a shield against evil spirits, coupled with the practical need of a uniform for clan identification, the Bible justifies the wearing of the purple as a reminder of one's obligation to serve God. A native Canaanite color comes to signify Israel's commitment, and the custom seems to say: Appropriate what you will, but make it your own.

To the poor, the challenge of prosperity seems no challenge at all. Wealth is to be taken, not wondered about. The tribes readily exchanged the life of resident aliens, gypsy merchants, and wanderers for that of farmers and settled folk with status as a proprietary class. In Gideon's dream in which his victory over Midian is foretold, Israel is symbolized by a cake of barley bread and Midian by the nomad's tent. Economic and occupational change seem to have been effected with relative ease. There were, however, critical areas in which the covenant ruled out cultural assimilation. Israel was not to make graven images, pour out libations to Baal, or offer sacrifices to strange gods. Religious eclecticism was a clear and present danger. But such was the tug of Canaan that at times even the most elemental distinctions were forgotten. According to one history, during the reign of Ahab (9th cent. B.C.E.) it was discovered that only seven thousand men in the northern kingdom had not bowed the knee to Baal or kissed his image (I Kings 19:18). Religious assimilation raised the specter not only of idolatry but of immorality. The prohibition against following the customs of the Canaanite comes as a postscript to a long series of rules prohibiting incest, child sacrifice, and licentiousness (Lev. 20:1–21). When Amnon incestuously raped his sister, the historian editorialized "we do not do such things in Israel" (II Sam. 13:12). Canaan faced Israel with a challenge to many of the Hebrews' most venerated decencies. Biblical rules against commingling are motivated as much by an ethical gap as by purely cultic concerns.

The issue of intermarriage became a focus for much of this tension. In his valedictory, Joshua told the tribes not to make marriages "with the peoples that still remain among you." His reasons were political. "They will be snares to entrap you, whips for your backs and barbed hooks in your eyes" (Josh. 23:12–13). There was danger that the large Canaanite population might overcome its inertia and harass the Israelites militarily and diplomatically. Torah law prohibits intermarriage with any of the nations that inhabit Canaan, using in explanation the same "snare and trap" phraseology, but there the context is clearly protection of the faith and the faithful. Alien wives "will cause your sons to lust after their gods" (Ex. 34:16). In the Semitic world, wives brought with them household gods and, of course, a particular conditioning. According to the prevailing custom, the wife came into her husband's clan but did not have to adopt her husband's faith. She remained free to worship familiar gods. Many Canaanite women who married Israelites gave their children theophoric names ending in Baal. As late as the eighth century the prophet Hosea looked forward to a time when little Israelites would no longer be called the Canaanite equivalent of Isidore or Christopher (Hos. 2:16–17).

By their very nature such rules lock the barn door after the horse is out. Whether or not the book of Ruth actually reflects the period of the Judges, it certainly reflects the ease with which intermarriages were undertaken during that period. There were many intermarriages, they were officially frowned on, but even when they were most bitterly opposed the basis of the objection was religious, not racial.

Canaan proved a mixed blessing. Prosperity and power led to the loosening of tribal ties and of the strict sexual code. The prevalence and popularity of several luxuriant, colorful, and attractive cults enticed many Israelites, and so the Israelite cult became more and more opulent. The royal shrine often was filled with idolatrous totems, some brought by foreign queens, some raised there by Israel's own kings. The rich behaved as callously as the rich generally do. Religious reaction set in. The Deuteronomic histories (Joshua, Judges,

Samuel, and Kings) are essentially moralizing chronicles in which pious judgments are set down against innumerable royal acts which involved religious syncretism. The more traditionalist elements became increasingly passionate in their opposition to Canaanite abominations and cultural assimilation.

We hear of Rechabite and Nazirite bands who left the city, took vows of poverty, wore the meanest garments, eschewed wine, and lived in the open as they felt true servants of God were meant to do. There was protest, but it was limited. Had there not been a second burst of vital spiritual energy, leading to the prophetic movement, the uniqueness of this people's history and spirit might have been submerged.

CHAPTER

V

Power

Power, absolute, ultimate power, belongs to God; "God reigns; let the people tremble" (Ps. 99:1). All human power is delegated and contingent. Those who invest great expectations in men of power are blind. "Oh, disloyal sons!—declares the Lord—making plans against My wishes . . . thereby piling guilt on guilt" (Isa. 30:1). Those who do not acknowledge man's political impotence are atheists. "A curse on the man who trusts in man, and leans for support on humankind while his heart is far from the Lord" (Jer. 17:5). It follows that the use of power by any save God is always suspect. "One thing God has spoken; two things have I heard: that might belongs to God . . ." (Ps. 62:12).

Today power is suspect because it is routinely abused; we agree with Lord Acton that power corrupts. The biblical suspicion of power was more radical: Not only do men inevitably abuse power, but they hold mistaken notions about its effectiveness. Man cannot accomplish his purposes through power. The power broker "walked after things that do not profit" (Jer. 2:5). Carrying out his policies, the king decides to send his troops against one country, make a treaty with another, and arrange a secret agreement with a third, all to no avail. "Put not your trust in the great, in mortal man who cannot save" (Ps. 146:3). Only what God proposes will happen. "Unless the Lord builds the house, its builders labor on it in vain; unless the Lord watches over the city, the watchmen keep vigil in vain" (Ps. 127:1).

[67]

The biblical outlook is power conscious, but not in the sense of realpolitik. "His sovereign rule is over all" (Ps. 103:19). God does not need armies, a vast host. The ancient sagas told an incredible story: On the eve of a great battle against the Midianites, God had ordered Gideon to cut back the size of Israel's army from twenty-two thousand to three hundred, lest "Israel will claim the glory for themselves and say that it is their own strength that has given them the victory" (Jud. 7:3). Such faith is a scandal to realistic men of affairs, who ask not whether your cause is just, but if your army is fully equipped and battle-ready. Biblical faith was scandalized by the almost endemic state of war perpetuated by the art of statesmanship. Bitter experience taught those who were not blinded by power that "it is better to take refuge in the Lord than to trust in mortals . . . or in the great" (Ps. 118:8–9). Put not your trust in armies or alliances, but expend your energies obeying and pleasing God, and perhaps He will have mercy. "Not by power nor by might, but by My spirit, says the Lord" (Zech. 4:6).

Bittaḥon, trust, patient submission to God, is what the Bible means by faith: "Leave all to the Lord: trust in Him; He will do it" (Ps. 37:5). "Be patient and wait for the Lord, do not be vexed by the prospering man who carries out his schemes" (Ps. 37:7). "Put all your trust in the Lord and do not lean upon your own understanding" (Prov. 3:5).

Bittaḥon begins in confidence and hopeful reliance. "He will bring it to pass" (Ps. 37:5). Israel's faith despaired of kings but not of the King of kings, and therefore it did not disparage life. The stance was not one of indifferent passivity but of joyous expectation. If Israel were faithful to God, He would be faithful to the promise of His covenant.

Bittaḥon operates within the field of force of the covenant, which may explain why this faith in God's omnipotence did not exalt monastic withdrawal or stoic resignation, but encouraged men "to establish justice in the gates" (Amos 5:15).

God's law imposed social restrictions—you shall not steal, murder, or commit adultery—and required the proper organization of the community—you shall appoint judges, provide cities of refuge, and avoid charging interest of your brother. The specifics of Israel's covenant dealt with courts, just weights and measures, marriage and family, and the treatment of a hired hand. Torah law not only assumed the legitimacy of government and prescribed many of its forms, but assumed that proper government helps organize and en-

[68]

force God's will. "You shall appoint magistrates and clerks for your tribes . . . and they shall govern the people with due justice . . . that you may thrive . . ." (Deut. 16:18–19). The covenant can be fully obeyed only by those who remain in the community. Anyone who drops out the better to serve God is a sinner, not a saint. It is not a sin to be politically active or even to exercise power, but it is a sin to be morally inert—"devote yourself to justice" (Isa. 1:17)—and it is a sin to divorce activity and authority from the will of God. "Thus says the Lord: for three transgressions of Judah, yes for four, I will not pardon them; because they rejected the law [Torah] of the Lord and have not kept His statutes" (Amos 2:4).

Community activity which conforms to the will of God is legitimate; even more, it is meritorious. Community implies some power structure, but obviously to believe in community is not to authorize any and all systems of authority. What was biblical Israel's attitude toward government? The Hebrew clans were patriarchal and democratic. There was a clan chief who had certain prerogatives, but among the clan elders there seems to have been a rude egalitarianism. No one was allowed unrestricted power. The Exodus story, which provided so many of the symbolic elements around which Israel formed its historical self-consciousness, contains two incidents which tell of an attack on untrammeled authority. At one point Korah and some followers protested unsuccessfully at certain claims being pressed on behalf of Aaron and the priest caste. Korah's rebellion was not an impulsive act by disenchanted youth, but the action of "chieftains of the community, elected in the assembly, men of repute" (Num. 16:2), against what they felt were the arbitrary actions of Moses and Aaron. Their indictment against Moses claimed: "You have gone too far! For all the community are holy, all of them, and the Lord is in their midst. Why then do you raise yourselves above the Lord's congregation?" (16:3). The second episode involved the prophets' guild, which sought to bar outsiders from competing in their trade. In this case it was Moses who ordered the cult prophets to cease acting in restraint of trade. Two nonprofessionals, Eldad and Medad, had begun to prophesy. Joshua had sought to silence them, but Moses stopped him: "Would that all the Lord's people were prophets, that the Lord put His spirit upon them" (11:29).

The tribal confederation was governed by God's words, but ruled through an assembly of tribal heads. Authority was conferred, not inherited. Moses was chosen by God. We hear that Moses had sons but that is all we hear of the lads; there is no talk of succession. At

God's command, Moses invests Joshua, the son of Nun, no relation, with leadership of the tribes. Again, Joshua did not pass his authority to a son. During the next two centuries the tribes maintained only a loose alliance and drew together only under threat of enemy attack, when a war chief, a *shofet* (inadequately translated "judge," hence the book of Judges), would be acclaimed. The *shofet* held both military and judicial authority for an emergency period. He lacked authority to raise troops on his own, impose forced labor or taxes on the tribes, or appoint his son to his place.

Despite the strong traditions of loose alliance and circumscribed authority, within two centuries the tribal confederation became a monarchy. David was anointed in 1005 B.C.E., and thereafter kings were anointed over Israel and Judah as long as these kingdoms survived (720 and 586 B.C.E., respectively). The messianic hope, which blossomed during the Babylonian Exile and was cherished thereafter, looked to a reconstituted and sovereign nation justly ruled by a descendant of the royal house of David. An oracle had promised: "The scepter shall not depart from Judah" (Gen. 49:10). The prophetic word read, "And a shoot shall grow out of the stump of Jesse" (Isa. 11:1).

How did it happen that the tribes of Israel accepted the rule of a king, and why was the exilic vision of national deliverance royalist in its image? Monarchy was an institution of necessity. The sea peoples who had planted themselves along the coast during the twelfth century expanded their territory rapidly and with notable success in the eleventh century. Philistine spirit was high and their iron-edged weapons technically superior. Their pressure was unremitting. By 1020 B.C.E. they had overrun the main Israelite defenses in the valley of Jezreel and threatened the hill citadels. The Ark had been captured, the shrine at Shiloh had been razed, and a majority of the Israelite tribes were paying tribute. The familiar system of acclaimed war chiefs armed with limited powers obviously was not equal to the emergency. A more centralized, efficient, and continuous authority was needed, and the tribal council seems to have approached the seer Samuel with the request that he ask God to name a king for them, a king "like all the other nations" (II Sam. 8:5). Monarchy came to Israel as an emergency measure.

Samuel anointed Saul and Saul held power longer than any *shofet* before him (ca. 1020–1000). He died still in command but without having effectively modified the power situation to establish the principle of dynastic succession. At his death the tribal assembly convened to name the next chief. The practice of dynastic succession begins with David (1000–962), a glamorous and charismatic adventurer who recognized weakness and confusion and exploited it. Unwilling to wait for the acclamation of the assembly, David, the chief of a hired band, put an effective army in the field against the Philistines, grabbed power, and eliminated those whom the tribal assembly might have proposed in his stead. True, early in his career David was anointed by Samuel, but Samuel may simply have been empowering the only general still able to continue operations. The tribal chiefs seem to have come under David's authority unwillingly, under the irresistible pressure of his growing military success. Their chronicles indicate that they delayed seven years before they formally nominated him (II Sam. 5:3).

Jerusalem today is a city holy to three faiths. In David's day it was a small Jebusite citadel whose value in David's eyes was that it stood astride the major trade route across the Judean hills and belonged to no tribe. David conquered Jerusalem and made it his own. Its tolls paid his mercenaries. Its walls made him independent. To make Jerusalem an effective center of power, a capital in the true sense, became the active policy of his dynasty. David designed a revolutionary new power structure based on a mercenary army financed by booty, the proceeds of a royal domain, and the taxes and tariffs of his city-state (*Kiryat David*). It is not known why mercenaries were not a feature of political life before David. Possibly the small tribal landholdings had not produced sufficient surplus capital for any tribal chief to pay their wages. What is clear is that a conscript army, fighting between harvests, could no more withstand the discipline and training of David's bands than they could the Philistine legions. David triumphed, the Philistines were defeated, and monarchy became the order of the state.

David viewed himself as a king. He was eager to centralize power and arrogate the symbols of authority. He brought various cult objects, specifically the Ark, to Jerusalem, and sought to centralize cultic worship. His son Solomon built in Jerusalem a royal chapel, and as long as David's heirs sat on his throne it was their firm intention to turn this chapel into the nation's central and ultimately its sole shrine, "*The* Temple of the Lord" (Jer. 7:4). Solomon continued David's royalist policies. He sought to break down tribal autonomy by imposing new administrative districts (I Kings 4:7 ff.). Power and pageantry were the substance and show of his power. The tribal assembly, which was controlled by the powerful northern tribes, never fully accepted the theology of monarchy but could do little against Solomon's unceasing success. However, at Solomon's death, his son Rehoboam was rejected. The tribal chiefs might have dismantled the monarchy if it had been feasible, but the advantages of a centralized authority were inescapable and the northern assembly contented itself with secession from the Davidic dynasty. These "men of Israel" felt no need to choose someone of imperial blood (12). "What share do we have in David?" (12:16). Their choice, Jeroboam, was an officer from the tribe of Ephraim. In Israel, that is the northern kingdom, the older traditions prevailed. Jeroboam did not invest himself as king but was acclaimed by the assembly. Kingship was by election of one's peers, dynastic succession was not deemed crucial, and the king ruled with the consent of the tribal council. In the century and a half of its existence, Israel was ruled by ten different and unrelated dynasties. In the south, in the kingdom called Judah, the case was altogether different, and rule by a sacrosanct royal dynasty was fully accepted. In Judah's two and one half centuries of existence, no one but a member of the house of David sat on the throne and the tribal council disappeared from the political scene.

How shall we account for Judah's acceptance of what Israel rejected? Judah was a latecomer to the tribal league and may have had a different political tradition. Judah constantly felt threatened by the dominance of the more powerful northern tribes. Could it be that whatever northern scruples were felt at this radical political departure were silenced by obvious success? Or by a convenient oracle? Were Nathan's prophecies of Solomon's succession (II Sam. 7:12 ff.) and Solomon's dream that God had granted him special endowments (I Kings 3:5 ff.) disingenuous after-the-fact legitimizations of what had already proven successful? Did the Israelite tribal assembly and Judahite confederation possess diametrically opposed oracles? These questions cannot be confidently answered. Two versions of the original request made to Samuel by the tribal assembly, asking for God's consent to the appointment of a king, appear in the book of Samuel (I Sam. 8:1–23 and 10:17–24). In one God tells the seer to accede, shows him whom to choose, and has Saul properly anointed to indicate that God has poured His grace and offered His protection to the king (9:15–17). The other suggests that, despite the emergency, God was displeased by this request, taking it as an indication of the people's lack of faith in Him: "They have rejected Me that I should not be King over them" (10:18). The questions are intriguing; the answers are open. It is clear that David established the monarchy and that hereditary monarchy gained legitimacy in the southern kingdom, while monarchy, but not the hereditary principle, was accepted in the north. Israel, the north, retained much of the older antiroyalist spirit. Hosea, the only northern literary prophet, was also the only prophet to denounce "the burden of kings and princes" (Hos. 5:10), and indeed to decry in God's name the whole institution.

> Where now is your King that he may save you,
>   or the rulers in all your cities
> For whom you asked me,
> Begging for king and princes?
> I gave you a king in my anger
> And in my fury took him away.
>
> (13:10–11)

No king ever ruled Israel by divine right; at best he ruled by divine tolerance. Northern reservations about monarchy were based on ancient traditions, if not on God's word, and could not be discounted completely even in the royalist south. Despite the panoply of office, and general acceptance of the authority of David's house, Judah's kings were by and large judged quite severely by their Judean biographers. We can still read these judgments in the Deuteronomic histories. Isaiah was no more reticent than Hosea when it came to condemning the specific sins of individual rulers. Jeremiah was quite explicit about Jehoiakim's and Zedekiah's faults.

> Shame on the man who builds his house by unjust means
>   and completes its roof-chambers by fraud,
>   making his countrymen work without payment,
>   giving them no wage for their labour!
> Shame on the man who says, "I will build a spacious house
>   with airy roof-chambers,
>   set windows in it, panel it with cedar
>   and paint it with vermilion"!
> If your cedar is more splendid,
>   does that prove you a king?
> Think of your father: he ate and drank,
>   dealt justly and fairly; all went well with him.
> He dispensed justice to the lowly and poor;
>   did not this show he knew me? says the Lord.
> But you have no eyes, no thought for anything but gain,

[73]

set only on the innocent blood you can shed,
on cruel acts of tyranny.

Therefore these are the words of the Lord concerning Jehoiakim of Josiah, king of Judah:

For him no mourner shall say, "Alas, brother, dear brother!"
no one say, "Alas, lord and master!"
He shall be buried like a dead ass,
   dragged along and flung out
   beyond the gates of Jerusalem.

(22:13–19)

Even in Judah royal power was circumscribed. The Judean king lacked the authority to promulgate fundamental law. The sacred scroll which sparked the Deuteronomic reformation was "found" and the king, Josiah, had it read aloud as God's word and confirmed by acclamation of the people. Though in fact their powers may have been broad, in theory the kings of Judah were subject to God's law.

When he is seated on his royal throne, he shall have a copy of this Teaching written for him by the levitical priests. Let it remain with him and let him read in it all his life, so that he may learn to revere the Lord his God, to observe faithfully every word of this Teaching as well as these laws. Thus he will not act haughty toward his fellows or deviate from the Instruction to the right or to the left, to the end that he and his descendants may reign long in the midst of Israel (Deut. 17:18–20).

In theory the king was not above the law, and on occasion he was charged with violation of God's law by his own officials. When David committed adultery with Bathsheba and conspired to murder her husband, it was Nathan, his court prophet, who brought God's accusation and made public both the sin and God's sentence. Prophet after prophet hammered home the theme that the king is under the law and must obey the Torah like any other man. There is some indication of a written Magna Carta: "Then Samuel told the people the terms of authority (*Mishpat ha-Meluchah*) and wrote it in a book and placed it before the Lord" (I Sam. 10:25). When Deuteronomy states unequivocally, "Be sure to set as king over yourself one of your own people" (Deut. 17:15), we might expect that the following sentences would enumerate the royal prerogatives; instead we find a list of what the king may not do: conflate his army,

[74]

enlarge his harem, overtax the populace, and so on. These were published *devarim*, divine words, against which a king's actions could be judged and in reference to which the prophets brought God's judgment.

Even the royal messianic dream was shaped with built-in restraints. The king of messianic political theory was in effect not a king at all. Law allowed him certain personal privileges but limited power. A summary of traditions found in the *Mishnah* concerning this king-to-be's authority lists the prerogatives of the royal office in four brief paragraphs. No one may ride the king's horse, sit on his throne, compel him to act as a litigant or witness in court, marry his widow, view him while he is having his hair cut, and so on. The king enjoys certain presumptive rights in the booty taken from enemies. He is enjoined to lead the troops in battle. He has the right of eminent domain for his armies, but he may not declare war, for that authority is vested with the high court of seventy-one, and he may not initiate fundamental law.[1]

Some modern scholars, heavily influenced by the cultural interdependence of the various West Asian cultures, find allusions in the Bible to a theology involving the sacred character of the king's person, his divine adoption upon coronation, and his crucial role in the cult; some even find glimpses of the king as a god incarnate. Such suggestions rely heavily on highly literal interpretation of some scattered and probably metaphoric phrases, such as "The Lord said to me, You are My son. I have fathered you this day . . ." (Ps. 2:7); "You are a priest forever after the manner of Melchizedek" (Ps. 110:4); or, in reference to Saul, "Then the spirit of the Lord will suddenly take possession of you, and you will be rapt like a prophet and become another man" (I Sam. 10:6). In most cases the context does not support a purely literal reading, and Assyriologists like E. A. Speiser have shown that only rarely did a Mesopotamian community deify its rulers. Consequently, the various parallels adduced to Mesopotamian practice do not stand inspection.

Unlike the Pharaohs, who were literally gods incarnate, the kings of the east were not deified, and no one has advanced the claim that Israelite jurisprudence was modeled after Pharaonic absolutism. Egyptian political theory insisted on the divine will of the Pharaoh. No law was valid without his approval. Mesopotamian political theory tended toward what would later be called constitutional monarchy. The king was subject to the advice of his council and the authority of the gods whose justice he and his people must obey.

Israelite political theory emphasized and defined the obligations of all men (including the king) under God's law. Israel's God was "the King of kings." The glory of the Davidic king became a powerful messianic image, but the real kings were never adored. The Jewish community understood itself as organized under God's law. Therefore, no one who violated the covenant could have authority over it. Biblical thought deals with law rather than with persons: the rule, not the ruler, was consecrated. Court prophets may have received royalist oracles, but there were other words, too: "They have rejected Me, that I should be king over them" (I Sam. 8:9). "I will not rule over you, neither shall my son rule over you. The Lord shall rule over you" (Jud. 8:23).

We deal here with the unglamorous exigencies of history. David's victories gave the small southern kingdom glory and authority it had never enjoyed before. Under Solomon, Jerusalem was the center of a sizable empire whose attendant activity brought prestige and income. It became an important capital, and the empire's wealth allowed fortification so that it could not be easily taken. When, after three centuries, Judah and Jerusalem fell, it was by then natural that the oracles of Judahite restoration should look forward to a revival of the first days of Jerusalem's glory. But even the oracles of restoration were not purely royalist. Deutero-Isaiah was a Judean, yet his vision does not reflect monarchic presuppositions. The Davidic house is never mentioned. When, around 536 B.C.E., the Judahites were allowed to return to Jerusalem, a scion of David's house came with them, but he quickly disappeared. It is significant that during the next half millennium there is no record of any political attempt to place a Davidite king on a throne in Judah. The faithful wept few tears when the post-exilic monarchy could not be sustained. Royalist hopes expressed in the prayers for national restoration were conventional, not specific.

Only the power of God was fully legitimate. Man and nation can confidently trust God's power, for He is faithful to the covenant. God's power cannot and need not be restricted. "Our God is in the heavens, and all that He wills He accomplishes" (Ps. 115:3). Biblical thought sanctified God's will and knew that His will had been made specific in published *devarim*, which prescribed the rule for God's community. Israel did not need anointed leaders who could legislate a consecrated way of life. Israel never sanctified any particular political institution. It had the Torah. There was no "right" political form, only a revealed way to live.

CHAPTER

❧ VI ❧

The Way and the Wayward

I N ancient Israel the word of God was close and available; not to everyone, of course, but certainly to various diviners, priests who rendered oracular judgments at the various shrines, the guilds of ecstatics who trained themselves in the mantic arts, and also ordinary men and women unexpectedly seized by the word of God. Beyond these were a unique series of individuals who "heard" or "saw" the word of God and felt compelled to deliver that word to the people—the men whom we know as the biblical prophets.

The Bible contains fifteen prophetic books, each of which purports to present the words delivered by one of these messengers. These books must be handled with caution since most are composite anthologies in which material from various men and times has been brought together, usually without any editorial warning. Texts that can confidently be credited to the particular prophet are scattered in uncertain order and include jumbled paragraphs and phrases which have been garbled by scribal error. Some chapters which purport to be historical are clearly legendary. Jonah is a short story about a fictitious prophet. Malachi may not have been a prophet at all, but an invented label (*malachi*, my messenger) for a short collection of messages by an anonymous bearer of the word.

Nevertheless, these fifteen books represent the entire literary remains of a truly remarkable group of men, who brought the words of God to His people at a time when the nation's religious vitality was at low ebb, sapped by the high culture and high living in Canaan. The prophets were alive to God; the power of the words they brought and the impact of their witness gave many in Israel strength to reject the blandishments of the pagan world and later to remain steadfast, despite the trauma of defeat and exile. The prophets in their day revived the ancient faith and deepened it with their teachings, so that it developed that clarity and power which has so significantly informed the spiritual life of Western man.

A prophet delivers the word of God. Israel had many prophets, over many centuries. Most were of little consequence and remain anonymous; some of obvious consequence we know dimly from legendary descriptions of their actions and words (Nathan, Elijah, Elisha); others, and these are for us the "classic" prophets, emerge from the mists of history because the Bible includes some written record of their testimony.

Israel did not invent the prophet. The spirit rested upon many individuals in many countries of the ancient Middle East. The Mari Tablets (18th cent. B.C.E., Middle Euphrates) tell of a man who, while in a trance, spoke in the name of the god Dagon: "Go now, I send thee to Zimri-lim, the king, you shall speak to him these words. . . ." Another Mari prophet began his message: "The god Dagon has sent me." [1] During the twelfth century B.C.E., an Egyptian adventurer, Wen-Amon, found himself stranded in the Canaanite port of Byblos. Quite a furor developed over his presence there without residence papers until one day "the god seized one of the king's youths and made him possessed," and the youth spoke instructions on how to handle the case of the unwanted traveler. [2] The Bible mentions the four hundred and fifty prophets of Melkart whom the princess of Tyre, Jezebel, brought with her to Samaria, and the four hundred prophets of Asherah who ate at King Ahab's table (I Kings 18). The most famous biblical reference to a non-Israelite prophet is to the seer Baalam, hired by a king of Moab to curse Israel, who found that the word which came to his lips was an unexpected, unbidden, and unwanted word of blessing. In those days people ascribed real power to the word of God. Once spoken, such words would take effect and could not be unsaid. Presumably, had Baalam cursed Israel, the tribes would have stood accursed and suffered the fate his words indicated.

The Way and the Wayward

Israelite prophecy grew in an environment familiar with all kinds of ecstatic and mantic activity. However, the classic prophets are anything but frenzied in speech or act. Classic Hebrew prophecy is not a phenomenon of compulsive babbling or talking with tongues, but of powerful inspiration and deliberate speech. The prophets "received" or "saw" or "heard" the divine word, and formed the vision into appropriate and effective phrases. Some were poets and stylists of substantial skill. Their prophecy was both revelation and art; their skill turned the divine afflatus into divine sentences.

In West Asia men went often to consult the man of God. Saul asked the prophet Samuel to find his father's lost donkeys. Prophets were consulted about military decisions, business, names for children, marriages, even about the plans for a sanctuary. It is the special mark of Israel's literary prophets that these men brought a word which had not been asked. They were sent forth (apostles), not sent for (diviners). They did not predict the future on a client's request, but declared on God's demand His judgment on their contemporaries.

The prophet is one upon whom the spirit of God rests or has rested so that he can speak words which clarify God's will. Some prophets were significant, some merely loud; what they shared was a sense of being possessed, which is the root meaning of *navi*, one who has a call or vocation (from God).

There was no unified, all-embracing prophetic theology. Prophecy describes speech believed by the speaker to have been inspired by God; the subject matter of such speech might include any topic of God's interest. Obviously different prophets might bring different, even contradictory, words. One diviner told the king to open hostilities on the second day of the month, while another told the same ruler not to commit his armies that whole year. Amos has little patience with Temple or cult; Ezekiel draws out God's plans for the Temple that must be rebuilt and the service which will be celebrated there. Each prophet must be discussed in his particularity. Still, we need to identify the various types of phenomena we are discussing. I use "diviner" or "ecstatic" to describe the mantic and the speaker with tongues; "court prophet" to describe those paid to bring specific words to help decide specific issues of policy; *navi* to describe the Israelite seers who by their words stimulated a nationalist and reformist revival; and "classic" or "literary prophet" to describe those who heard the words that men still find good reason to hear.

Today, if a man rose at a public meeting and announced: "Thus says the Lord . . . ," someone would summon a psychiatrist. Were the ancients naive and easily deceived? Not at all; they simply had no psychiatric labels to dispel the sense of mystery which rises when one hears the hidden voices of the mind. Biblical man knew nothing of the operations of the unconscious, but he did dream, and those dreams had to have some source—if not in his mind, then in the mind of another, and what other mind was there but God's? Inspiration, *déjà vu*, clairvoyance, all the psychological mechanisms of the unconscious represented to him communication from another plane of reality, from God. It could only be assumed that the divine or supernatural world was always breaking into this lower plane of reality. The reality of dreams, words, and intuition was beyond question. What other explanation was acceptable but that God put words in the prophet's mouth and visions in his mind?

Prophecy is revelation: "The Lord came unto me and said; go and say. . . ." Revelation was not something unique which could occur only once, say at Sinai, but an open and available, if intermittent, source of truth. Theoretically, prophecy posed a threat to the immutability of the Torah tradition; God's next word might nullify one of the *devarim*. But no such words came. An arresting feature of biblical prophecy, and one not yet fully explained, is the absence of any message commanding new laws or abrogating existing ones. Prophecy assumes the Torah covenant and does not seek to reshape its specific regulations. Biblical prophecy is never antinomian. When a prophet argues against laws which appear in the Pentateuch, as in the case of Isaiah's and Micah's denigration of the cult, "That you come to appear before Me—Who asked that of you? Trample my courts no more" (Isa. 1:12), it is probable that such rules had not yet been universally accepted as Torah. The Torah, after all, is a much-edited code which assumed its present form only after the Babylonian Exile.

Most prophetic words must be considered as conservative rather than revolutionary, calling men back to an older obedience rather than breaking new religious ground: "These are the words of the Lord, stop at the cross-roads; look for the ancient paths; ask, 'Where is the way that leads to what is good?' Then take that way, and you will find rest for yourselves" (Jer. 6:16). When the prophets denounce the religious spirit of their day, they do not attack earlier teachings as inadequate; they insist that the people have been inadequate in fulfilling their duties and have applied these rules indifferently to their lives. God's complaint is that "I reared children and brought them up—and they have rebelled against Me! Israel does not know, My people takes no thought" (Isa. 1:2–3).

How does Torah differ from prophecy? Torah is prescriptive, prophecy is hortatory. Torah is timeless, prophecy is existential and deals with the struggles of frail men to meet the unbending demands of the covenant. Torah is formal, prophecy argues against the insensitivity of those who carelessly or mechanically carry out the prescribed forms. Torah legislates, prophecy reproves and consoles.

These messengers of God came with a particular word for a particular time. The word came to each man privately, and each spoke what he had heard; he spoke it as the truth, and sometimes his truth conflicted with another prophet's message. Some prophets heard words which promised security for the nation, others heard the sentence of national doom. Inevitably prophets bearing dissimilar or opposing words came into direct conflict, each attacking the authenticity of the other's inspiration (Jer. 28). A wise man may at times be full of insight and at other times be banal or irrelevant; even some of his significant statements may need qualification. Prophecy must be either true or false, since one cannot mediate between opposing revelations. Who would dare correct God? Or qualify His expressed will? A prophet speaks God's word or he speaks lies, there is no middle ground. No problem troubled this believing world more than the question of whether God spoke through a particular prophet or whether that prophet had been deluded. There was no infallible test. Both true and false prophets sometimes accompanied their message with impressive quasi-magical feats, and it was generally agreed that too much credence ought not be put in such signs. The most obvious test for separating genuine from ersatz "words" was to wait and see if events bore the prophet out (Deut. 18:21–27).

But the best of the prophets predicted events which did not occur. Elijah spoke words which condemned Ahab and Jezebel to die in a specific manner at a specific place; they died elsewhere and in far less gory fashion. Nathan foretold David's death, the swift end of David's dynasty, and the death of Bathsheba's unborn child; David died in old age, his dynasty lasted nearly four centuries, and Bathsheba's unborn son we know as Solomon. Hosea heard that the kingdom of Israel and Israel's royal house would fall on the same day, a prophecy which proved false in Hosea's own lifetime; the kingdom of Israel outlasted the reigning dynasty by some forty years. Jeremiah's record is particularly telling, because he so readily attacked the "false" prophets. Neither defeat nor exile arrived with the speed he

[81]

had predicted. He prophesied that King Zedekiah would be exiled but die in peace; in fact, he was exiled, his sons were slain in front of him, and he was then immediately blinded that this carnage might be his last sight.

Classic prophecy did not always pass the test of verifiability; indeed, it could not. Prophecy does not fit naturally into a covenant faith. For the prophetic message to be prophetic as opposed to merely sermonic, it must pronounce God's final judgment. The words of a God whose power is untrammeled and whose knowledge is omniscient reverberate with the somber tones of inevitability: this is what will happen, no ifs, ands, or buts. But the God of the prophets had bound Himself to a covenant and His words must take into account the covenant's conditionality: this will happen unless you amend your ways and your doings. God did not speak merely to prove that He knew the future, He spoke to prove His power and to change the ways of men. The best of the biblical prophets found their reputations as prophets threatened if the nation mended its ways and God relented on His sentence, or if God simply had a change of heart. No wonder Jonah fled his commission and, after Nineveh had been reprieved, lodged a serious complaint against God for having exposed him to ridicule. The prophet is forever being compromised. His is a miserable, pathos-ridden role. If the people do not repent, he shares with them the nation's fate and must live with the bitter recognition that all this might have been avoided. If they repent and their fate is rescinded, he is mocked. The tension between the unconditional nature of the prophetic announcement and the conditional nature of covenant thought was never resolved, and when, centuries later, prophecy took the road to apocalypse and became thoroughly determinist, the faith did not fully welcome the new certainties. With happy inconsistency the biblical spirit affirmed both man's moral responsibility and God's absolute control over history, themes as logically inconsistent as life, and as natural.

As time went on there were so many conflicting words that the more sophisticated outgrew the once pervasive sense of awe and taboo which had surrounded the prophet and made his person inviolate. At Jeremiah's trial for high treason, evidence was introduced indicating that an earlier prophet had been executed on the king's order with no apparent harm to king or nation. Paradoxically, this growing skepticism may have saved Jeremiah's life. He was being tried for having prophesied against Jerusalem, and consequently for having brought harm to Jerusalem. Those who were still credulous demanded his life, but the liberated prevailed by showing that the earlier prophet's words of doom had not brought defeat. Why fear such words or the annoying men who bring them?

Since the accuracy of his predictions was not a particularly useful test of the merit of a prophet's message, other standards were offered. In his attacks on the "false" prophets, Jeremiah suggested that integrity was the mark of a true prophet and disingenuousness the mark of a charlatan. False prophets, he said, put together a pastiche of prophecy-associated phrases to counterfeit the real thing. They speak what they have not heard (Jer. 23:30–32). But how does one look into a charlatan's mind? Certainly among those whom Jeremiah stigmatized there were men who honestly felt that they had heard God's words. In sum, no adequate test was ever devised.

The "false" prophets were not so much charlatans as trivial. They told their audiences what they wanted to hear, and their words, designed for the moment, offer little to men of another age or situation. It was the originality and objective worth of a prophet's ideas, not any test of predictive accuracy or authenticity of inspiration, which led men to become his disciples and encourage us to read his speeches.

If classic prophecy during pre-exilic days can be said to have any central theme, it was that God was made heartsick by an age which misinterpreted and disobeyed its covenant obligation, which looked upon the covenant as essentially a series of cultic and institutional requirements, but was blind to its basic obligation—the law of righteousness.

These are the words of the Lord of Hosts the God of Israel; Add whole-offerings to sacrifices and eat the flesh if you will. But when I brought your forefathers out of Egypt I gave them no command about whole-offering and sacrifice; I said not a word about them. What I did command them was this: If you obey me I will be your God and you shall be my people (Jer. 7:21–23).

Micah asks rhetorically what specific service God requires of Israel (6:6–8). Is it sacrifice? No. "It has been told you, O man, what is good and what the Lord requires of you: specifically to do justice, to love mercy and to walk humbly with your God" (6:8). The classic prophets not only insist on the primacy of the law of righteousness, but, with that peculiar Jewish instinct for the specific, define the general term "righteousness" both positively—relieve the fatherless, deliver the prisoner—and negatively, by pillorying the greed, indulgence, and cruelties which respectable people tolerate, but which are in truth intolerable—adding field to field, and filling one's home with costly items of furniture and jewelry while the hungry beg at the door.

Moved by their impressive damnations of the specific social and private sins of the privileged, a reader tends to picture the prophets as radical activists. This impression is misleading in one basic respect. The prophets condemned injustice in all its forms, but they lacked the peculiarly modern notion that men can engineer a better social order. The prophets had no faith in man's capacity to solve social problems or legislate progress. In the prophet's world men do not make history, only God does. The messianic elements in this literature are visionary, not blueprints from which men can piece by piece construct utopia. The messianic age will come in God's good time, or, as Jeremiah put it, when God gives men a new heart, that is, when God changes human nature. Today the supreme virtue is commitment, to be involved in some significant crusade; then the supreme virtue was *hesed*, steadiness, patience, obedience, and perhaps God will be moved to be merciful. Social crusaders have felt themselves inspired by the prophets whose anger at injustice is holy and awesome. However, the prophets did not seek to send men to the barricades or to bureaus where they can program revolutionary five-year plans. They sought to summon the individual to repentance and obedience.

The word of God as spoken by the prophets is judgmental, often freighted with an awful sentence. But God as royal judge is not the only image of God evident in the prophet's language. Hosea saw God as a forgiving Father who will welcome the prodigal whenever he returns (Hos. 21:20). Hosea, Micah, and Jeremiah use the shepherd image, with its associations of care, vigilant protection, and warmth. God's mercy is always implicit in His justice (Jer. 25:4–5). God will reduce the sentence if the nation will repent: "If you return to Me, I will return to you" (Mal. 3:7). Several prophets saw themselves as a watchman who sounds the warning which alerts the city to present danger and summons men to make appropriate security measures. Their warning is not of an enemy without, but of the enemy within: to warn the wicked "to give up his wicked ways and so save his life" (Ezek. 3:17–18). The response God sought was not that men should rush out to reform the world, but that each man should energetically reform himself and walk a straight path.

The prophetic paradox lies in the fact that God's word is dependable, but that it is His nature to be merciful. God's word is final, but somehow there is room for the conditional "if." If Israel repents, God will pardon. If men turn from their evil ways, they will be forgiven, even after God has spoken their doom. God's word was His bond, but He will not be bound to His words, particularly when there exists the possibility of human benefit. David committed adultery, a capital offense, a covenant violation, but his contrition was honest; God forgave him and the death sentence was annulled (II Sam. 12). Ahab confessed, fasted, and sat in ashes, and his sentence of execution was not carried out (I Kings 21).

The promise of divine forgiveness is held out. Men thirst for the word of hope, the possibility implicit in the command "return." But God is God and not an indulgent parent. God's words are powerful and will have their effect. God's threats are not really revocable, so we often find in the prophets a rather bleak conclusion. The possibility for reform exists—but men will not take it. They hear but do not understand; their souls are fat and insensitive. Despite the theme of repentance, a current of fatalism runs through pre-exilic prophecy. But God's love of the people ran deep. We hear of sin, callousness, and spiritual deafness, and of condign and final judgment, and at the same time we hear of an "original" love which God will not deny, much as parents cannot deny their feelings toward a prodigal, and of "the merits of the fathers," an inherited virtue which somehow still protects a weak generation. "I remember the unfailing devotion of your youth. . . . Israel then was holy to God, the first fruits of His harvest; no one who devoured her went unpunished, evil always overtook them. This is the very word of the Lord" (Jer. 2:1–2).

Having been summoned by God, the prophets shared a particular awareness of Him. God was person, alive, conscious of men's actions, concerned with the nation, intimately involved in man's struggle with himself, near. They spoke for a God who was vital and forceful and not merely an intellectual postulate or a vague universal force. Their God noticed and judged man's every act. The prophets felt that if others knew God as fully as they did, they would not, could not, sin. When American blacks say "Keep the faith!" they speak of faith as the prophets knew it—absolute, active, proven within the context of human relationships, and tested in the streets.

Given the prophet's sensitivity to God's power and program, how could the nation continue so careless in its obedience? Because they are "foolish and senseless people, who have eyes but they see nothing, ears and hear nothing" (Jer. 5:21). They have not seen what the prophet has seen. The average man has not been overwhelmed by God, and so can speak of God and even worship Him without any real sense of His awesome power. The prophet hopes against hope that his witness may impress even the deaf and blind. Ezekiel is told: "They will know that they have a prophet among them, whether they listen or whether they refuse to listen" (Ezek. 2:5).

Why are men deaf and blind to God? Because they are self-important. They have eyes and time only for themselves. Pride, wealth, the sense of power enjoyed by men of wealth and station preoccupy their thoughts to the exclusion of any awareness of God. Faith begins when a man strips himself of pretensions. There is an inverse relationship between one's sense of self and one's sense of God. You will not find in the prophets' words any talk about a healthy ego. Faith and righteousness begin in humility, not in pride.

The prophet seeks to shatter pride in the hope that consciousness of God's power will cause men to cast aside all sense of competence, the illusion that they can bend circumstance to their will, the foolish notion that by diplomacy and military force they can enlarge or secure territory and wealth. Only what God wills, will be. These men are political quietists. Again and again God's words underscore the "truth" that every political event—and even the so-called natural phenomena, such as drought or rain—are not natural at all, but the result of a conscious decision by God, a display of His power.

"For the Lord God does nothing without giving to His servants the prophets knowledge of His plans" (Amos 3:7). Why is God eager to describe through prophetic words the future course of events? There must be no doubt that what is and will be was made to happen by Him. God believes, or so the prophets suggest, that only men overawed by God can accomplish the radical change of heart and habit which the covenant requires. Unlike the classic Greek philosophers, the prophets did not assume that logical demonstration and reason could convince men to be righteous; unlike the Christian fathers, they set little store on the lasting value of spontaneous and impulsive displays of human sympathy. They believed that men act out of awe and fear, and that only those who truly fear God will abide His covenant.

Pride is the enemy of faith. Pride shuts out the prophetic word: "You are no more . . . than a singer of fine songs with a lovely voice, or a clever harpist; they will listen to what you say but will certainly not do it" (Ezek. 33:32). How to be really heard is the prophet's constant burden; how to break through the layers of insensitivity is the prophet's constant preoccupation. Sometimes he can point a finger and say "I told you so," but then it is already too late. If God's punishment is delayed or not exacted, the prophet is reviled for having given everyone a scare. If the people repent, these new resolutions will fade as the crisis abates, and the prophet finds himself repeating his jeremiad to a jaded and mocking audience. Frustration shadowed his every move.

◈

There were significant prophets before the appearance of Amos, Hosea, Isaiah, and Micah in the eighth century. Their names are familiar—Samuel, Nathan, Elijah, Elisha—but their actual careers are so encrusted with legend that we can barely, if at all, recover the real man and his actual words. Each is called a *navi*. Of each it is said that he was summoned by God to speak and perform specific prophetic acts—to publicize a king's carefully hidden sin or to contest with the priests of the false gods in ways which would expose the folly of idolatry and reveal the untrammeled power of the true God. These men can be distinguished from the classic prophets by the absence of any extended record of their words. They are distinguishable in other ways. They were closely involved with the courts and the apparatus of power, whereas the classic prophets, for the most part, had no official role in the establishment. Nathan and at least two minor prophets, Gad and Iddo, were courtiers. Elijah broke with King Ahab and Queen Jezebel, but he had been a member of the royal entourage. Elisha was deeply involved in the intrigues that led to the fall of the poweful Omri dynasty. The first of these men in point of time, Samuel, anointed the first king after a period of some years during which he had exercised de facto authority over the hard-pressed tribes of Israel.

The *navi* was in the king's court, but not always subservient to it. Nathan served David in the dual role of royal diviner and trusted courtier. Later he played a role in the intrigues which led to Solomon's succession. Yet in the last analysis Nathan was God's man, not David's. When God sent Nathan to condemn David for his adultery with Bathsheba and his murder of Uriah, he went and spoke out. Still, the *navi's* court role contained within it the seeds of his spiritual failure. How often did a *navi* tell the king what he felt the king might wish to hear? How often did the *navi* consciously or unconsciously manipulate words in order to manipulate power? Jeremiah's battle with the court prophet Hananiah, who promised the king the victory he sought, has fixed in our minds the association of "false" prophecy with wishful thinking about dynastic ambitions and foreign alliances. Court prophets inevitably brought a word which was entangled with politics. Their word was patriotic, expedient, and, precisely for this reason, inadequate as a tool for exploring the full implications of God's sovereignty and man's servitude and obedience.

Naviism involved both individuals and fraternities of prophets. Samuel and Elisha are separately described as the head of a prophetic band. There are numerous references to roving guilds of ecstatics, closely related to the shrines, who acted as clairvoyants and messengers of God's word, and accompanied their activity with stylized forms of dance, songs, and words. These groups were more or less associated with the court, but seem also to have wandered about serving the ordinary folk by casting spells, curing sickness, finding lost articles, and speaking God's words.

Naviism is not an erratic parapsychic phenomenon. A clear political and a religious message emerges from the record. The spirit of God spoke strongly through the *neviim*, calling man and nation away from the sins of the city, wealth, religious syncretism, and moral permissiveness, and back to the simpler, more clearly delineated ways of the past. These men associated God's spirit with the values of an austere time, when the tribes had been lean wanderers in search of the promised home. Their protest was against the new sophistication. Idolatry, the cardinal sin, described not only paganism, but all the weaknesses and allurements of Canaan.

The message these men brought was a call back to an older, stricter faith: a protest against settlement, class divisions, arbitrary power, the growing secularization of much of life, and urban laxity; a renewed declaration that God alone is King, that the king is as bound to Torah law as his humblest subject; and a passionate protest against the reduction of the covenant faith to a series of ceremonies patterned after the sacrifices and agricultural rites of the Canaanites. *Naviism* was intensely patriotic, devoted to the nation and to the nation's past, but not so narrow or parochial as later prophets declared.

The classic prophets sometimes treat the *neviim* cruelly, accusing them of selling prophecies as if they were merchandise, of inventing words, of walking in lies, and of being a source of pollution to the whole land. The suggestion is offered by Jeremiah that these men preach what the court and Temple want to hear, not what God has said. Kings consulted them for their sure knowledge of the future; many were fed and maintained by the court; some undoubtedly were mere sycophants, but the best of them were strong and served God well. They fought hard to save the nation from itself by forcing it to purge itself of foreign gods, foreign habits, and foreign wives. The classic prophets would not fully share the *navi's* instinctive patriotism or his faith in political solutions, but their denunciation was over-drawn and tendentious when applied to the best of the *neviim*, such men as Samuel, Nathan, and Elijah.

Samuel appears as a transitional figure who combines in his person the ancient functions of the seer, who finds things like lost donkeys and future kings, and the emerging role of a rhapsodic bearer of God's word. His charisma depended on the aura of fear and veneration which traditionally surrounded a prophet, but his significance derived from his successful role as catalyst of a renewal of the na-tional spirit during one of Israel's bleakest hours, when the enemy seemed irresistible, when the great shrine at Shiloh had been razed, and even the Holy Ark had been captured.

In Samuel's career we glimpse some themes which will be devel-oped in prophetic thought. Nothing happens by chance. Every event has a "why." Samuel had been raised by the High Priest Eli in the Israelite sanctuary of Shiloh. According to the received test, while Samuel was yet a stripling, God made known to him in a dream that the authority of Eli's house would soon be ended because of certain sinful acts on the part of Eli's sons and the father's tolerance of their misdeeds. What happens to man or nation, for weal or woe, is never the result of chance. Long life, health, national prosperity, and secu-rity are signs of God's favor, which is granted only when it is de-served. Death, illness, defeat, and drought are signs of His anger, and since His anger is never capricious, they are responses to the peo-ple's sinfulness.

Samuel explained the Philistine success to his generation. Many felt that God had deserted His people. Others believed He had been defeated by the gods of the Philistines. But Samuel said that it was God's will that Israel be defeated. Israel had been indifferent to the covenant, flaunting and misrepresenting it. They had taken to them-selves foreign gods. Was Israel's sin purely that of religious syncre-tism? The Canaanite cults were not only polytheistic, but often orgiastic, and their rites were heavy with crude forms of sympathetic magic, even sacred prostitution. Religion can be immoral as well as untrue.

If our texts report faithfully, Samuel taught that rites are not efficacious unless they are practiced by men who obey the law of righteousness. "Does the Lord desire offerings and sacrifices as He desires obedience? Obedience is better than sacrifice, and to listen to Him [is better] than the fat of rams" (I Sam. 15:22), remarkable words for a man who was trained in his youth for the priesthood and officiated all his life as a priest.

Samuel spoke God's words and did God's bidding in ways which illumined the speech. With the prophet word and act are one. When Saul violated a specific command of God and did not burn certain booty which God had declared *ḥerem* (taboo), Samuel was ordered to condemn the king publicly, and promptly did so (I Sam. 15). God commanded His prophets both to "say" and to "go and do." Other prophets shamed kings publicly and scandalized cities by their demonstrations. In speaking God's word and doing His will, the prophet was protected only by the fear of the people for a holy man. In this case Saul was abashed and repented, but when Elijah slew the prophets of Melkart, Queen Jezebel was not abashed and pursued her tormentor. Amos was denounced to the king. The prophet Uriah was extradited from Egypt and killed at the king's specific command. Jeremiah stood trial for his life. The prophets fought the wars of God without being protected by any Geneva Convention.

W. F. Albright's research has made it seem likely that the priest-prophet, Samuel, was the man most responsible for the rise and spread of *naviism*. Samuel seems to have drawn about him several prophetic groups eager to restore Israelite faith to its pristine form and free it of Canaanite horrors. These bands included ecstatics whose simple dress, a hairy mantle, and strict ascetic regimen forcefully reminded their audiences of simpler times, the wilderness, and of a faith not yet infected by the luxuries and abominations of Canaan. In that time of military defeat and great danger, many must have felt that God had deserted them, but these prophets said no, it was only that He had to punish the nation. What was Israel's guilt? The people had not directed their hearts toward God, which translates to mean: They had committed idolatry, had lost the open honesty and tight loyalties of tribal relationships, and failed to be righteous.

The prophetic message rejects all geopolitical explanations of history. It was not land hunger which brought the Philistines up against Israel; it was God's will. It was not Israel's unpreparedness or lack of iron-edged weapons which led to defeat, but God's anger at the tribes' repeated violation of the covenant. We children of a secular age often are disturbed in our readings when a prophet seemingly shifts gears from tangible social and political concerns, where we can follow his warnings, to recommendations of spiritual obedience and loyal patience which seem irrelevant to the problem he describes. The confusion is ours. God's word is never to a secular world, but to a world where ultimate power is God's alone: "For the Lord of Hosts has planned. Who then can foil it? It is His arm that is poised, and who can stay it?" (Isa. 14:27).

For over half a century Samuel played a pivotal political role. Although he was deeply involved in the selection and anointing of both Saul and David, he would have denied that he was a statesman. What he attempted, or what biblical history says he attempted, was to explain God's decision to his compatriots. Samuel did not choose, the choice was God's. God alone brought men to the throne and sustained them there. God alone determined the nation's fate. Security was not to be found in defense budgets or international alliances, indeed not in power at all, but in obedience to the word of God. Thus the disconcerting political quiescence of God's forgiving but fateful words through Samuel as He accedes to the people's demand for the protection of a king: "Give them a solemn warning and tell them what sort of king will govern them" (I Sam.8:8).

Toward the end of his career Samuel anointed David (1005–965), who blunted the Philistine threat and created the basis of a small but strong and centralized kingdom. David's son, Solomon (965–925), took advantage of the temporary weakness of the superpowers, Egypt and Babylonia, to establish an imperial Israel. This empire, which at its apogee stretched from the Euphrates to Akaba, did not survive the wars of succession which followed Solomon's death. The tribal alliance become a miniempire quickly lost its colonies and broke into two small kingdoms. From the royal city of Jerusalem the house of David maintained its hold over the smaller part, Judah, the south. In Israel, the north, various tribal alliances put various dynasties on the throne. Egypt and Babylonia revived, and during the ninth century Israel and Judah frequently paid tribute to one or another of the two great powers.

The most effective strategy for the small states of West Asia was to establish alliances among themselves for power and safety; such arrangements were sealed by royal marriages and solemn treaties. Such treaty queens brought to their husbands' courts their own gods, priests, and values. It was such an occasion that brought Jezebel, daughter of the King of Tyre, to Samaria to marry Ahab, King of Israel (874–853), and with her hundreds of priests and prophets of Melkart, the Baal of Tyre, she entered that royal city. These priests continued to perform their rainmaking rites in Israel when suddenly, without announcement, the prophet Elijah appeared at court and proclaimed on God's authority a more or less permanent drought. For three years the Baal priests vainly performed their incantations, but the heavens stayed shut until Elijah, who had fled the royal wrath, allowed himself to be found. Ahab had him brought to the palace and accused Elijah of the drought, calling him "the troubler of Israel." Ahab spoke with the voice of conventional wisdom: the drought existed because Elijah had pronounced fateful words. Elijah answered with divine wisdom: "It is not I who have troubled Israel; but you and your father's family, by forsaking the commandments of the Lord, and following Baal" (I Kings 18:18). Ahab would have agreed that God controlled nature, but he probably felt that if the Temple ceremonies were properly offered (and he had seen to that), what he did and how he lived had nothing to do with God's meteorological decisions. Elijah knew that the drought, like everything else, was divinely instigated, and that God's decision represented His judgment of the king's actions. The words are words of doom, but they were spoken not to curse or doom a people, as Baalam had sought to speak, but to make clear that the nation's infidelity to the covenant left God no other choice. The king has a choice: repent, and perhaps He will pardon.

Elijah is a theophoric name which means "YHWH is my God." So many legends cluster about his career that some scholars doubt that a real man can be disentangled from the fable; these legends, even if pure invention, reveal significant elements in Israel's understanding of prophecy. Elijah overpowers the prophet-priests of Baal in a test of the power of their respective gods; he performs miracle cures, there is a miraculous provisioning of a poor family, the prophet himself is miraculously hidden and fed, and he is told by God precisely where to intercept a messenger sent by Israel's king to secure a magical Philistine potion. The legends deal with the untrammeled power of God and God's absolute demand that Israel abide the terms of the covenant, and ascribe divine power to the man of spirit.

The Elijah stories revel in God's awesome power. Elijah's response is one of awe, fear, and submission, yet for all its awesomeness, the divine force which Elijah serves is not a blind and irresistible surge, but the thrust of divine justice. A commoner, Naboth, had a small vineyard near the king's summer palace. The king coveted these acres but Naboth would not sell. Ahab complained about Naboth's refusal but acknowledged Naboth's right under Torah law to hold onto his land. Not so his Canaanite wife Jezebel. Conditioned by a different and unabashedly authoritarian ethos, Jezebel read Naboth's refusal as an unforgivable affront to the king's honor. The king must have his royal way, so she hired men to accuse Naboth of treason and fabricated incriminating proof. Naboth was convicted and executed, whereupon his lands reverted to the crown. The word of God thundered through Elijah: "Have you killed your man and taken his land as well?" (I Kings 21:19). Swift punishment was pronounced on the royal pair. When he does "that which is evil in the sight of the Lord," the king is accountable to God. What is evil in the sight of God? Arbitrary power, perjury, contempt for covenant law. Ahab is denounced for permitting Jezebel to introduce her priest-prophets and a Baal shrine into Samaria.

Elisha, Elijah's prophet disciple and spiritual heir, is an even more shadowed figure than his master. He emerges as a doughty foe of Baal worship and prophet champion of the house of Jehu, which had overthrown and succeeded Ahab's heirs. The Elisha "histories" detail the humbler sides of *naviism*. Elisha purifies polluted water, effectively curses those who mock him so that they are torn apart by wild animals, conjures up food for the penniless widow of a God-fearing man, blesses a barren woman who proceeds to conceive, and later revives her mortally ill son. Elisha is, as it were, filled with God's own power. His prophetic role is constructed of the stuff of folk piety, and in this respect has little in common with that of the classic prophets, who never appear as miracle workers or faith healers. Yet the folk hold on to their miracles! Centuries later Elijah reemerges in the rabbinic tradition as the herald of the Messiah and as a wandering good wizard of many disguises whose occupation is to succor ordinary Jews enmeshed in the extraordinary problems of the Diaspora. In Christian tradition Elisha's "miracles" provided the pattern which editors of the New Testament traced as they cut and shaped the wonder-working legends of Jesus' life.

The *navi* stories are found in the Deuteronomic histories, Joshua, Judges, Samuel, and Kings, which were compiled and edited from chronicles of the conquest and various dynastic records by men deeply influenced by *naviism's* perspective. A continuous history of the nation from Joshua to the Babylonian Exile was compiled to prove that the fate of Israel depends on obedience to the covenant. Each royal career is assessed by a single standard: whether or not the incumbent did what was right in the eyes of God. If so, the nation prospered. If not, various calamities were the result of his sins.

These histories were edited by several hands, but the standard *navi*-istic judgments and phrases fairly leap out of the pages: "and the Israelites did that which was evil in the sight of God, and forgot the Lord their God and served the Baalim and the Asheroth. Therefore, the anger of God was kindled against Israel and . . ." (Jud. 3:7). Of those kings who tore down the offensive high places, we hear that their "heart was perfect with God all His days" (I Kings 15:14). Of a king who worshipped God at the high places or brought some totem of Baal into a shrine, we are told that "he did that which was evil in the sight of the Lord" (15:26) and "his sin made Israel to sin" (16:13).

These chronicles are, of course, sacred history, in the sense that they affirm that all that happens is ordained by God. God supports the nation when it is steadfast under the covenant and punishes when it is not. The decision is always God's, but He does not act capriciously. God is steady, dependable, and covenant-bound, the God who made His covenant not alone with those who had gathered at Sinai, but "with those who are not with us here this day" (Deut. 29:13–17), the God who specified "all His laws and commandments that it may go well with you" (6:2–3), and who set before Israel the "blessing and the curse" (30:1). This spirit was and always remained the conventional religious pattern for biblical man.

⋘⋙

Amos is the earliest of the classical prophets, and he is quite conscious that his way is different from those prophets who came before. "I am no *navi* nor a member of a fraternity of *neviim*" (Amos 7:14). Amos is a solitary, not associated with any guild. His vision was private and overwhelming, but he took special care to form what he saw and heard into effective phrases. He was possessed, but he did not speak as one possessed. *Naviism* was powerful but artless; classical prophecy derives some of its power from the literary skill of the prophet. Amos was not trained for prophecy—he had nothing professionally to do with court or shrine—but was unexpectedly summoned from his ordinary employment. He goes to Beth-el because he has been sent there by God with God's message. He goes because God must be heard. "The Lord God has spoken, who will not prophesy?" (3:8).

The mid-eighth century represented a short-lived period of prosperity and ascendance for the northern kingdom. Israel's kings sent their armies into Syria, took Damascus, and brought Judah under nominal control. Tolls and tribute increased the affluence and arrogance of the Israelite upper class, and the voice of God was "seen" by a shepherd of Tekoa (1:1). God offered the vision, and Amos fit words to it. To Amos God is not divine mystery, but a disclosed will who "declares to man what is His thought" (4:13). God's judgments determine the fate of men and nations, including nations which do not acknowledge Him. In the first two chapters of the received text, God accuses in turn each of Israel's neighbors of specific crimes and pronounces a heavy sentence on each. They are judged, but apparently not by the same standards as Israel. They are accused of brutality, killing women and children, being pitiless, a long list of cruel and blatant vices (1:1–15). Israel is accused of selling debtors into slavery, miserliness, sexual promiscuity, indifference to human suffering, and expropriation of consecrated offerings (2:6–8). Obviously more is expected of Judah and Israel. Judah is condemned for not abiding the law of the Lord (2:4). Israel has "rejected the Torah of the Lord and has not kept His statutes" (2:4). Amos did not know the Torah as we have it, bound and edited in one scroll. His Torah was covenant law, the law of righteousness, the will of God to "set justice on her feet again" (5:14). God has known the children of Israel uniquely and has, therefore, obligated them uniquely. Amos assumes Israel's and Judah's election, but let no one misjudge God's purpose; chosenness guarantees not the special privileges of a favorite but special duties: "You specially have I known of all the families of the earth, therefore will I punish you for all your iniquities" (3:2). And lest anyone think that special burdens deserve special rewards, God reminds Israel forcefully that His ties with her are no different from His ties with other races, even the black of Ethiopia or such perennial enemies as Egypt, Philistia, and Syria.

God controls both natural and historical events and reveals His plans. Man is powerless except to be obedient: "Flight shall not save the swift, the strong man shall not rally his strength, the warrior shall not save himself, the archer shall not stand his ground; the swift of foot shall not be saved nor the horseman escape" (2:14–15). God has given men a law of righteousness involving specific duties, and God determines men's fate according to whether they are obedient or willful. God stands ready to reward obedience, but He must have proof in deeds, not words. God is an honest and fair judge, but obedience is a strict and demanding measure and the nation is inconstant. Despite the hope implicit in the covenant equation, the prophet's song is a funeral dirge: "She has fallen to rise no more, prostrate on her own soil, with no one to lift her up" (5:2).

Why are the prophet's words a lament? Israel has heard the words of the covenant, but has not obeyed them. Perhaps the nation no longer cares. Amos speaks God's judgment on the beautiful people who are nevertheless ugly within, who pervert justice, oppress the poor, sell their fellow into slavery for debt, and "are not grieved at the ruin of Joseph" (6:7). Amos literally trembles before God's anger at those who violate the law by trampling the poor into the dust. "The Lord has sworn by the pride of Jacob: I will never forget any of their doings" (8:7). Amos has heard God "roaring" an irrevocable and irreversible sentence. The conventional faith confidently expected a day of God when its enemies would be defeated and joy reign, but Amos paints the day of God in nightmare colors—the sun will go down at noon, men will put on mourning dress, and a great lamentation will rise. The day of God will be "a bitter day" (8:9–10).

To the modern reader comfortable in his chair, Amos' language seems excessive. The wealthy are denounced as swine, callous and venal. There is no opportunity to explain, to introduce evidence in mitigation. There are no grays, no kind word for mother love, respectability, or occasional acts of charity. Such words shake the deepest reaches of the soul and leave man staggering. They set standards which so-called reasonable men cannot reasonably match. What is demanded of man is a complete transformation, not minor repairs; he must turn his life around. God's law is clear and uncompromising; no one can ask to be excused from its rigors or plead for time. Justice is not rooted in sentiment or empathy, but in an imperative that requires a response of total obedience. Amos does not talk of the United Appeal or Brotherhood Week. He does not suggest visits to the slums of Beth-el, where the sight and smell of misery may move the rich to impulsive generosity. Amos does not deal in sympathy but in justice, which is the fundamental requirement of the covenant: "Hate evil and love good, and enthrone justice in the courts" (5:15).

God had ordered Amos to the grandest sanctuary of his day, Beth-el, where the senior priest Amaziah was a well-respected functionary; their confrontation allows the reader to contrast the prophetic and conventional religious views. Amaziah understood man's need for concrete symbols and reassuring rites. He too valued justice as the basic obligation of the covenant. Much of the money and food brought to the shrine was turned over to the poor. Most sacrifices were not burnt and dissipated, but deposited with the tithes in warehouses to provide sustenance for teachers, attendants, hospitals, and hospices. Amos swept such consideration aside. Charity is no virtue if it only mitigates injustice. The shrine does not exist to safeguard the nation. The shrine does not draw God closer to the nation; only righteousness can do that. The shrine's various societal functions do not validate its existence.

> When you present your sacrifices and offerings
>   I will not accept them,
> Nor look on the fat beasts of your shared-offerings.
> Spare me the sound of your songs;
> I can not endure the music of your lutes.
> Let justice roll on like a river
> And righteousness like an ever-flowing stream.
>
>   (5:22–24)

It is not that God denies all efficacy to such rites, or the possibility of salvation; rather, such rites and attitudes misrepresent the covenant and seem to validate a technique for gaining salvation which God has not guaranteed.

No obedience is sufficient if it is not total and all-embracing. God's words mock those who offer the Sabbath sacrifices with their minds already on their next day's opening bid in the grain market or on some particularly noble bit of commercial trickery (8:4–6). In addition, cult-associated hopes are mistaken. The king Jeroboam (782–753) came often to Beth-el for divine reassurance, and its priests blessed his person. In deliberate contrast, Amos at Beth-el prophesies Jeroboam's untimely death (7:11) and his nation's doom (7:16). Furthermore, all of the nation's conventional hopes are empty of substance. The long-expected deliverance, "the day of the Lord," will be the reverse of men's expectations, not a dream come true but a nightmare: "A day of darkness and not light" (5:18). His images are not those of green trees and bright sun but of omnivorous swarms of locusts, fires burning out of control, the Temple mouldering on its foundations. What is the way to salvation? "Seek Him and live" (5:4). What does it mean to seek God? Was Amos a mystic? Would he have understood Martin Buber's advice to search for God in the context of human relationships? No, in Amos' view to "seek God" is to "seek good" (5:14). The only hope for the nation is a full and unflagging obedience to the full law of God: righteousness. Has not the covenant promised God's favor to the obedient? Yes, but there is no real basis for optimism, since human nature is obdurate and offers little realistic expectation of change. Amos is a powerful but gloomy prophet and his words of hope, when they do come, relate to a far distant time.

Modern political activists find it hard to understand that sense of resignation which allows men to know their doom and not move heaven and earth to avoid it. Yet there it is. There is no indication that Amos led any social crusade after his Temple sermon. Amos appealed to the spirit of man, not to national planning commissions. God alone could change the world, and He would do it only if men changed their hearts and their ways.

⚜

The third quarter of the eighth century was a perilous time for the northern kingdom. Israel struggled desperately to maintain her political power and her independence against the armies of a truly fearsome Assyria. Six kings came to the throne in rapid succession as desperate scheme followed desperate scheme, all to no avail. In 732 B.C.E. Tiglath-Pileser III ravaged much of Israel and exacted a crushing tribute. Ten years later his successor, Sargon, destroyed Samaria, exiled the upper classes, who were to be immortalized as the lost ten tribes (in fact they simply assimilated into their new environment), and resettled the land with colonists from other parts of his empire.

During these anxious and dangerous years God revealed to Hosea thoughts which desperate politicians could only dismiss as irrelevant. They did not doubt that God would send word, but this messenger, Hosea, brought words that were not pertinent: "the prophet is a fool" (Hos. 9:7). For realistic men there were only two alternatives: take arms from Egypt or pay tribute to Assyria. But according to Hosea, God had said to those who advised paying tribute to Assyria, "He [Assyria] is not able to heal you" (5:13), and to those who counseled an arms purchase agreement with Egypt, "Memphis shall bury you" (9:6). If the prophet was no fool, he was certainly no help.

According to Hosea's message, no practical strategy could be effective. The frantic diplomacy of king and court dealt with appearances and ignored reality. Deliverance depended solely on God, and

[98]

God was not interested in treaties but in a spiritual turning. To statesmen, God's word must have seemed pure defeatism. What was God's program? It was simplicity itself: "Return." Israel had abandoned the worship of God for an elaborate cult full of vulgar forms and ethical compromises. Israel had abandoned the principles of mercy and truth in favor of false oaths, lies, adultery, theft, sexual perversion, and murder (4:2). God defined return as a turning back from moral and cultic wanderings to the straight way, and this meaning has remained the classic Jewish definition of repentance (*teshuvah*). God's word approached national survival from the viewpoint of national integrity rather than national defense. God's word is radically irrelevant, inspiring but impractical, appealing to the best in us, and apalling to the caution in us.

We must watch terms carefully here. God did not speak as a moralist, but as God. God spoke not of a return to some set of ethical principles but of a return unto Me. When Hosea challenged Israel, "let us eagerly strive to know the Lord" (6:2), he was talking not of gnosis, some secret knowledge of God's being, but of understanding God's nature as it is revealed by His actions. When God said "My people are ruined for lack of knowledge" (4:6), He meant the knowledge that men can learn from revelation and from God's self-revelation, from His mighty acts in history.

Like Amos', Hosea's words insisted on God's righteous power. God's will is untrammeled but always just. Rather than exalt divinity as a thing unto itself, Israel exalted God in relation to His creatures. God had created the universe for man's benefit, brought exiles from slavery unto freedom, revealed His will and a proper way, and sent His prophets as messengers of His will to offer men another chance. Such talk is embarrassing to the theologically precise, who feel compelled to describe a pristine God above the confusions of life, but neither Amos nor Hosea was disturbed in the least. Their God was alive to them, spoke to them, overwhelmed them, and they did not worry about the analytic problems of a theory of attributes.

Whereas Amos dwelt on the image of God as righteous judge, the images Hosea invoked are more complex. God is a judge-prosecutor "who has a charge to bring against the people: There is no good faith or mutual trust, no knowledge of God in the land" (4:1), and God is a tender father who cannot help but see the smiling infant whom He once taught to walk in the gawking figure of the delinquent son who no longer accepts reproof (2:1–4). The theme of God's mercy is personified through Hosea's relationship with a harlot whom he seems to have taken as his wife. God had said, "Go take an unfaithful wife," and after Gomer had lived up to her advance billing, God ordered, "go yet love a woman who was beloved of another, and a wanton" (3:1). Why? Because God wanted Hosea to understand the illogic of love, for love at this point remained the only basis of God's continuing relationship with Israel. Hosea endures, on the scale of human frustration, God's frustration with Israel. God is the ever-patient husband, tied to Israel "with bands of love" (2:3). Gomer is an Israel which sins and sins again. Hosea finds he cannot free himself by force of will from Gomer; despite all her transgressions, he suffers for her and with her. He senses that he will take her back, and he does. Hosea's suffering love is the reality of God's patient grace. The covenant is not only a business contract with penalty clauses, but a marriage contract between lovers. God expects obedience, and Israel proves disobedient; God could turn His back and walk out of Israel's life, but is restrained by compassion and love. God finds Himself saying, "I will have compassion upon her who has not merited compassion and I will say to them that were not My people: You are My people" (2:23).

Gomer is received back under Hosea's roof but not into his bed. Israel is to be punished and the punishment will be severe, but in time God's love will induce Him to send the spring rains after a long winter. Israel will be scourged but not slaughtered. "Come, let us return unto the Lord; for He has torn us and will heal us, He has struck us and He will bind up our wounds" (6:1). The need to be just is basic to God's nature, but greater yet is the need to be generous—to be God: "My heart is changed within Me, I will not let loose My fury . . . for I am God and not a man . . . and I will not turn around to destroy Ephraim" (11:8–9). God is both just and compassionate. Later biblical editors will add a line of promise when a scroll happens to end on a black note. Israel's catechists will admit that the Messiah is long delayed, but still affirm his coming. Why? Because it is God's nature to love man and to forgive. God does not protect the sinner from being whipped, but as in the Israelite law, which is a reflex of His will, the beating is held within tolerable limits. In the end God safeguards a culprit Israel to make sure that Israel is neither permanently maimed nor totally destroyed.

When Sargon defeated Israel, the king of Judah paid a heavy tribute to Assyria to spare his country and his capital. His cities were not molested but Assyrian rule was iron-booted and extortionate. In the decades after 722 B.C.E., whenever Assyria was preoccupied with the uncertainties of royal succession, the little states of Asia showed signs of restiveness. In 705 B.C.E. King Hezekiah of Judah renounced his allegiance to the emperor Sennacherib, only to be shut up in Jerusalem "like a bird in a cage," to endure a potentially disastrous siege from which Judah was miraculously saved by the emperor's unexpected recall to his capital, an event which contributed heavily to the folk belief in Jerusalem's inviolability.

To this age of political turmoil and overheated political activity the Judean prophet Isaiah brought words which insisted on the futility of power politics. "Be firm and be calm. Do not be afraid and do not lose heart" (Isa. 7:4). God is king, majestic and royal (6:4). What men call policy is actually pointless activity. The future will be decided not by kings and battles, but by the nation's righteousness and God's judgment of the people's obedience. Those who play at politics are "disloyal sons making plans against My wishes" (30:1).

The facts are that the children of Israel have rebelled against God. They are a sinful nation (1:4) and God has decided "to turn My hand against you" (1:24). There is no staying the hard sentence "till towns lie waste without inhabitants" (6:11). Why? Because of widespread violation of the covenant as evidenced by acts of exploitation, violence, venality, and greed. The terms of God's law are clear: "Devote yourself to justice, aid the wronged, uphold the rights of the orphan, defend the cause of the widow" (1:17), yet in Judah and Israel men have tyrannized weaker neighbors (3:5), ground the face of the poor (3:9), perverted justice through bribery (5:23), and scoffed at all decency (28:14). God's law is clear, and the sins of Israel and Judah are equally clear.

God excoriates the greedy, the indulgent, those who pervert justice, the dissembler, the ambitious, the calculating, and the cruel, but He proposes neither legal remedy nor social reforms. The changes God proposes will come when the nation will know God and be faithful and steadfast to Him. Such hope as exists depends on the nation becoming responsive to the true nature of God—His ethical person—and in the flowering of its will to be obedient and righteous.

One who denies the efficacy of political solutions is not likely to offer practical suggestions. Prophets who speak of spiritual reorientation to men burdened with hard and unyielding practical problems find that their words fall on deaf ears. In Isaiah one senses the full pathos of the prophetic task and vision; he speaks as he has been told, but even before he speaks he knows no one will listen. "And

He said: 'Go and tell this people: You may hear, but you will not understand, you may look and look again, but you will never comprehend' " (6:9). Nevertheless, God wills His word to be spoken. God has no patience with the prophet's sense of frustration. In some distress Isaiah asks, How long must I do my thing? God answers, "until Israel has been plowed under" (6:11–12).

The reformer can organize legislative remedy; the visionary can only dramatize his brave new world. His remedy is utopian, *u-topos*, not of this world; instead of a teacher or city planner he becomes a demonstrator, a gadfly. He has turned away from the wordly, but still hopes to turn the world around. Isaiah sang his vision and his criticism with a zither across his shoulder. He wore the outlandish costume of a prisoner of war to suggest the fate of those who lead Judah into the snares of political alignments. He used his sons in a Children's March for Peace and gave them names which proclaimed the fallibility of human pretensions. Isaiah did not demonstrate for any group or party—but for God. He was interested in reaching the hearts of men rather than in organizing a peace movement or building low-cost housing.

Why did God send these words? What did God want the remnant of the nation to see and admit? He wanted an admission that they did not serve Him properly, that ceremonies were not the central religious enterprise. Worshippers were not lacking at the Temple, but justice and righteousness were in short supply in the cities. God thunders, "I cannot endure iniquity along with solemn assembly . . . I will not listen, your hands are full of blood" (1:13–15). Faith is a category of deed rather than a category of cult. If ritual does not lead to radical change in the hearts of men, it is at the very least irrelevant and at its worst misbegotten, because it misrepresents the way of salvation by assuring simple folk that God will be gracious to them in return for routine appearances at ceremonies.

Did Isaiah see any hope for Judah? In the short term and in the political realm, no. "There shall be none to deliver" (5:29). In the contemporary world the nation would pay for its real sins. The destruction which Judah will suffer will be as devastating as that which had swept over Israel. In one dramatic image Judah is pictured as a vineyard carefully planted and tended by God. The grapes ripen, but grow into wild, sour grapes, and God has no alternative but to plow the whole vineyard under. Nor does the prophet add an optimistic afterword, to the effect that the next season's planting was successful. For the moment the die is cast. But today's world is not the only reality. Isaiah has heard of a world in which men acknowledge fully that God is king. This world is both a hope for tomorrow and a standard for judging today. Here matters are different: "God will be a sanctuary" (8:14). A child who is not yet born bears the symbolic name Immanuel (God is with us). Human nature will be transformed and the new breed of men will be instinctively obedient to the will of God.

A group of perhaps overly systematic scholars has pictured the first generation of classical prophets as messengers of doom whose words are devoid of any hope. Prophecies of a happy end of days do occur in these scrolls, but are dismissed as later oracles added by pious editors who sought to tone down the finality of the despairing word. Those who insist that Isaiah's message is unrelieved mistake the import of his condemnation. Isaiah had no real hope for his generation, though he did believe that a "saving remnant" would somehow survive the Assyrian devastation; more to the point, Isaiah's thought is God's thought, not a private opinion. God controls and determines all that we call history, and it is not beyond reason that God should postulate an "impractical" hope of a time when what we call human nature will be transformed. The arrogance and self-assertion which blind man and limit his full acknowledgment of God and heartfelt obedience to God's law will no longer be a stumbling block. "In all of my sacred mount nothing evil or vile shall be done; for the land shall be filled with devotion to the Lord as water covers the sea" (11:9). Various visions describe a beautiful and new world where "men shall beat their swords into plowshares and their spears into pruning hooks: nation shall not take up war against nation; they shall never again know war" (2:4). God has promised such a world—but not necessarily soon. Yet such hopes did sustain Israel's spirit and provided encouragement as the nation struggled to maintain its spirit and integrity during terribly difficult days.

Micah, a contemporary of Isaiah's, completes the quartet of eighth-century greats. The main political event remains Assyria's progressive reduction of the states of West Asia. Aram and Israel were taken in 733; Israel was finally and decisively beaten in 722; the Philistine city-states fell in 711; and finally in 701 Sennacherib invaded Judah. The shadow of defeat hangs heavy over Judah as God seeks to explain the meaning of His actions.

The words are heavy and unwelcome. The danger is real—disaster will come and be full blown. Samaria's defeat is final (Micah 1:9), and Judah will not be spared. "Disaster has come down . . . to the very gate of Jerusalem" (1:12). The capital will be taken and the Temple will be razed (3:12). God's interest is not to forestall but to foretell, that men may understand that it is His doing and know why these awful events have happened. The nation deserves its fate, since there has been a fatal moral decay: "Loyal men have vanished from the earth, there is not one upright man" (7:2).

The prophet's role is to declare the unhappy bill of particulars (3:8). The rich conspire to rob the poor of their paltry possessions, strip the impoverished of their land, and reduce them to a serfdom which is little better than slavery. Employers treat laborers like pack animals, withhold their pay, and abuse them as if they were brutes. Justice can be bought, and all the while the legitimizers of virtue, the priests and many prophets, encourage the illusion of the wealthy that their mask of respectability is really their true face (3:5). The nation practices witchery, visits sorcerers, and worships other Gods (5:11 ff.).

God not only reveals the nation's impending punishment, but defends His decision. He wishes to have Judah appear with Him in a court where the justness of His actions can be tested. The silent mountains which have witnessed all history shall serve as judges. God speaks in His own behalf. Has He misled the nation? Has He taxed her beyond a nation's strength? Did He not more than fulfill His obligations under the covenant? Had He not performed mighty acts for the people, brought them out of Egypt, and protected them from powerful neighbors? What else could have been done to impress them with His steadfastness? Yet they continued to mistake what God demanded of them. The nation perceived the covenant as a way of holiness centered on ritual and regimen, while God's law requires sacrificial and sensitive living outside the sanctuary. Sacrifice cannot atone for the sins of a man's soul (6:6–7). What does God require? The words are so well known that they sometimes seem vapid: "To do justly, to love mercy and to walk humbly with your God" (6:8). They were meant quite specifically. Turn around the denunciations which list the nobility's sins and you have a definition of righteousness.

In the last analysis, the prophetic word appeals to the heart rather than to the head. The words of God are words of command rather than counsel. They condemn evils rather than propose specific national reforms. Reasonable men will question words which seem to begin and end in outrage. It is not enough to damn a callous society. Steps must be taken, a nation must build homes and schools—but this common sense attitude is not that of the classic prophets. Indeed, it is explicitly rejected. Conferences and five-year plans will not delay the coming of the day of wrath. There will be no muddling through, not even with blood, sweat, and tears. But this slice of time is not the fullness of time. There is now no real hope, yet "though I dwell in darkness, the Lord is my light" (7:8).

The surviving literature is remarkably radical in spirit and theology, often subversive of cult and establishment, a fact worth underscoring for many reasons, not least as a caution against glib generalization. The survival of prophetic materials and their ultimate canonization must have been carried out largely by establishment figures, probably scribes and priests associated with the Temple and the court. In this light, what shall we make of the many facile distinctions made between priests (establishment people, dispensers of conventional wisdom, conservative, institution-bound) and prophets (antiestablishment, institutionally subversive, politically radical)? Nathan was a courtier; Samuel, Elijah, and Elisha prophesied for hire. Amos went to the royal shrine and was heard out. Jeremiah was saved from death by the high nobility, specifically those who no longer feared (believed in) the prophetic word. Post-exilic theocrats canonized texts in which God wondered aloud: "Why do you trample My courts?" (Isa. 1:12). The impression of an Israel which rejected its prophets is both true and false. They were feared and rebuffed, but never fully rejected.

CHAPTER

⸎ VII ⸎

This Was Believed

After the devastation of Israel (722 B.C.E.) and the submission of Judah (701 B.C.E.), the voice of God would not be heard in the land for nearly a century. God punishes, but He does not gloat. The word of God never began: "I told you so."

Diviners must have plied their trade. Court prophets certainly consulted God for their masters. But no prophet emerged with words of towering significance. In one way the classic prophets are not unlike sunspots; when they are visible you can be sure that violent storms are raging underneath. Their voice was heard before the Assyrian terror; it would be heard again just before Judah was conquered and broken by the armies of Babylonia.

The first three-quarters of the seventh century, however, was a period of political slack water between raging floods. Instead of the voice of God rising above the clatter of war chariots, one heard the voices of men teaching their children, singing hymns, and puzzling out the meaning of God's will and the strange bafflements of human destiny. It was the quiet before a storm. Men taught, sang, improvised, and debated the meaning of life, and much of their concern involved the operation of the covenant. Men quietly analyzed what their predecessors had enthusiastically assumed. The covenant as it was presented was a discipline and an equation: If you obeyed, it would be well with you; if not, you would properly be punished. So went the promise; but where was the proof?

That God's ways are just and dependable is the underlying assumption of biblical faith. God had freely declared that He would not exercise His power willfully, but would be governed, as a judge must be, by the facts. What made the covenant attractive to men was its implicit divine promise: If they are obedient to these terms, God would arrange their destiny to fit their merit. Man felt that he had something to say about his destiny.

God need not have made such a covenant with men, but since He had, man knew God as not only omnipotent but also just and kind. But had the extinction of Israel been a just sentence, or had it been excessive? Was it just that Assyria, iron-booted slave master of millions, be raised so high, and that Israel be crushed and Judah brought low? Certainly Israel's fate was not kind.

Retribution had been meted out to the nation. Biblical men were conditioned to think largely in corporate terms. In the tribal past the clan's needs had been paramount. Men and women were totally dependent on their clan for survival. Their personalities were so submerged in the group that even in death they felt secure only if "they slept with their fathers" (Gen. 47:30). Jacob had died in Egypt, his last wish being that his body not lie forever alone and exposed in foreign soil, but be brought back to the security of the burial cave of his ancestors in Hebron. According to the law, a father might have a stubborn and contumacious son put to death (Deut. 18:18–21); we shudder at the establishment of such authoritarian power, but it was essential to clan survival. Survival depended on numbers and solidarity. The son who challenged his father's authority shattered the unity on which all else depended. If he took off with his wives, tents, and children, the parent clan was not only poorer but that much less capable of survival.

The conquest of Canaan had led to an attenuation of tribal ties and attitudes. Israelites began to live in villages and cities. Families no longer needed to be totally self-sufficient. Occupational specialization grew apace with urban development, and men began to be conscious of themselves as individuals. Clan law, in which all were responsible for all, was replaced by Torah law, where the man alone and not his kinsmen were involved in the consequences of an act. No master could send a slave and no clan head could send a dependent to be punished in place of the real offender. Torah law seems to have been the first Near Eastern code to prohibit vicarious punishment. During the first stages of the conquest a man had pilfered from the booty taken after the capture of Jericho. The booty had been devoted to God and was consequently taboo, and he and his entire clan had been put to death (Josh. 7), a punishment deemed fitting. Now God's law required that: "Parents shall not be put to death for children, nor children be put to death for parents: a person shall be put to death only for his own crime" (Deut. 24:16).

As man began to emerge from clan, the individual began to apply the terms of the covenant promise to himself. If the wicked nation is punished, must not also the wicked individual, even if his community is otherwise righteous? Similarly, must not a righteous man be rewarded, whatever the character of his community? But is he? What of the pious elder in the next town who was afflicted with leprosy and spent his last years an outcast? What of the greedy trader in our town who blatantly violates Torah law when he charges interest to fellow Judeans and keeps the only cloak of a poor man as pledge? He seems in good health, has fine sons, and much money.

How retribution worked and how one could tally what one saw with the covenant's unqualified promise of just rewards and punishments were questions that began to preoccupy men's minds. In pre-exilic times faith was the statement: God cares, God judges, God acts within the terms of the covenant. But where was the proof of this claim? The prophets had warned the nation that they deserved a hard fate, but how can one explain the fate of those within the nation who had not whored after other gods or been unrighteous? Where are all the Israelites gone? Into extinction, every one. Yet some among them certainly deserved a better fate. Look at the prophets themselves, obedient servants of God whose reward has been calumny. It was a difficult age. Men suffered and wondered whether God's management of the world was providential or careless, just or simply awesome. What survives of the literature of the age deals with many themes and reflects many moods, but invariably it returns to the question of God's justice.

❦

The book of Proverbs presents wisdom, not the radical wisdom of Amos or Isaiah, but the common sense of thoughtful and experienced men of affairs. Wisdom is both a synonym for learning and the label for a literary genre familiar among the cultivated classes of many Near Eastern nations. Wisdom describes the proverbs, parables, riddles, legends, didactic poetry, fictional dialogues, fables, and fancies in which the upper classes summed up their experience, formed their clichés, and devised the lessons by which they trained their children.

Egypt had been an early center of wisdom literature. Collections of proverbs, riddles, and animal parables of Egyptian provenance can be traced well back into the third millennium B.C.E. The impact of Egyptian wisdom literature on biblical thought can be seen in the close parallels between Proverbs 22:1–24:27 and the tenth-century *Instructions of Amen-Em-Opet*.[1] Wisdom literature was also a feature of Babylonian life, although there the wise man was more a Merlin, a sorcerer-diviner, than the tutor, scholar, and mentor of princes and kings. The book of Proverbs reflects wisdom's international scope. Chapter 30 and most of 31 of Proverbs are credited to Agur and Lemuel, non-Israelite wise men. Kings were prepared to take wisdom wherever it could be found. Solomon had at his court a counselor-secretary, *sofer*, or master of books, of Egyptian name; Daniel of lion's den fame is described as a member of the court of the Babylonian emperor Nebuchadnezzar. Wise men manned the royal secretariats and wrote what today would be called political position papers. It was said of Ahitophel, adviser to David and Absalom, that the "counsel which he counselled in those days was as if a man inquired of the word of God" (II Sam. 16:23). Wisdom was the basis of sound policy: "Through me [wisdom] kings are sovereign and governors make just laws" (Prov. 8:15).

The primary meaning of wisdom, *ḥochmah*, is a talent, grasp of a particular skill. Bezalel was a *ḥacham*, a wise man, because he possessed the skill to build the Holy Ark. Skills in magic, choral singing, government, medicine, and war are at various times called wisdom. Wisdom literature was often quite prosaic, sometimes little more than a few simple, easy to memorize verses which reminded men of essential agricultural or medical information. One such bit of practical advice on the planting of wheat and threshing of various grains somehow was included in the text of Isaiah (28:23–29).

Wisdom at its most prosaic included popular sayings redolent with an ageless folk skepticism: "Can the Nubian change his skin, or the leopard its spots?" (Jer. 13:23). There were riddles not unlike the one Samson put before his wedding guests: "Out of the eater came something to eat; out of the strong came something sweet." Answer: A honeycomb in a lion's skin (Jud. 14:10 ff.). There were fables in which animals or trees came alive and spoke: Baalam's talking ass (Num. 23 ff.), Jothan's story of the trees who seek to elect a king and find that only the most worthless among them will accept the office

(Jud. 9:7 ff.), and Jehoash's fable of the lowly thistle who wanted to marry the daugher of the most princely tree of them all, the cedar of Lebanon (II Kings 14:9 ff.).

There was a good bit of such popular wisdom, but biblical wisdom literature grew primarily out of the concerns of formal education—"To give prudence to the simple, to the young man knowledge and discretion" (Prov. 1:4) —and specifically out of the educational curriculum offered to the sons of wealth. Wisdom tends to be calm where the prophets are indignant; wisdom, like prophecy, often lists the sins of the rich—kept women, self-indulgence, sloth, gluttony, insatiable lust for things—but stresses these as failings of the individual rather than evidence of the injustice of the social order. Wisdom moralized about the vices of wealth against which an audience of young men born into opportunity and temptation needed to be warned, rather than about the immorality of a class society.

Israelite wisdom was associated with the court and the better classes. Wisdom first flourished under Solomon, who is described as the composer of three thousand proverbs and a thousand and five songs (I Kings 4:32 ff.). He organized Temple choristers according to the musical theory of the day, which was largely Mesopotamian, and organized the palace bureaucracy according to a scribal wisdom which was largely of Egyptian origin. It was perhaps inevitable that later tradition should ascribe the book of Proverbs to this royal patron of the learned. The association of wisdom and the court continued under King Hezekiah of Judah (729–686), whose "men" are said to have edited a section of Proverbs (chapters 25–29).

The book of Proverbs makes no attempt to disguise its composite nature. The opening section, chapters 1–9, is certainly post-exilic and represents a glorification of wisdom as the constitutive element of the universe, a metaphysical notion which bears the impress of late intellectualist theories popular in Persia and Greece. Wisdom is "the beginning of His works, before all else that He made long ago" (Prov. 8:22), the tool by which God created earth and life (3:19). We are offered a poetic image which says that wisdom is implicit in every act of creation, a hopeful fact, since it suggests that man has only to understand this wisdom to know truth, be happy, find life, and obtain God's favor (8:32 ff.)—that is, to be in tune with the universe. He who begins to understand wisdom begins to understand the meaning of life. But even in these rather academic chapters the search for wisdom is not conceived of as a purely academic or logical enterprise. The search for wisdom begins in the fear of the Lord (1:7) and requires a strict avoidance of sin (1:10).

The long central portion of the book presents such wisdom as was taught in seventh-century Judah. The text is a filigree of short couplets and slightly longer verses, each a discrete comment on what constitutes the good life and how to achieve it. In form these proverbs are usually consecutive sentences or clauses which modify or support a central thought. We know these proverbs only in their nakedness, as couplets which delineate a single thought in what often seems a simplistic manner. In the schools each proverb probably represented a chapter heading evoking a whole series of illustrations and inferences with which pedagogues were familiar.

The general tone is didactic, the basic moral standard utilitarian: "A double standard in weights is an abomination to the Lord" (20:23). "If your enemy is hungry, give him bread to eat; if he is thirsty, give him water to drink" (25:21). "Do not move the ancient boundary-stone or encroach on the land of orphans" (23:10–11). Wisdom is the key to a good life, and these proverbs indicate how the good life can be achieved in many relationships: marriage, family, schools, government, and community. Much of the advice is hard-nosed. One ought not act as surety for a pledge or interfere in a quarrel to which one is not a party (26:17). Often it is a matter of maintaining your balance and keeping your nose clean. "My son, fear the Lord and grow rich, but have nothing to do with men of rank" (24:21). These proverbs represent the wisdom of men who had few illusions about human nature. Fools, innocents, sluggards, contentious women, and the venal are lampooned in one illustration after another. Human nature is in no way romanticized. "Who can say: I have a clear conscience; I am pure from my sin?" (20:9). This world is not perfect or really perfectible. What we call progress—man's making for himself a better future—is not even contemplated. Proverbs does not talk of better times or describe visions of a glorious end of days. The operative assumption, if unstated, seems to be that human nature cannot be changed and society will remain pretty much as it is. The wise learn to expect reversals, take care of themselves, meet their responsibilities, limit their risks, value only that which is truly valuable, control their emotions, and find what pleasure they can in the moment. They learn to expect little and so avoid bitter disappointment. It is assumed that men are capable of great folly and stupidity, that none are saints, but that it is possible to live with a certain measure of dignity and discipline. Wisdom is the key to graceful self-control.

Wisdom teaches those willing to be taught to take life as it is and not roil it further with inordinate ambition or appetite. Proverbs accepts the propriety of happiness, sex, and possessions. Moderation "yes," asceticism "no." "Hope deferred makes the heart sick; but desire fulfilled is a tree of life" (13:12).

One is tempted to call this wisdom secular, but it is not. In this time and place it could not be. Though concepts such as the priesthood, the sacrificial cult, and Zion rarely appear, Proverbs assumes throughout God's moral government to which everyone is accountable (11:2). God champions the cause of the poor (23:11) and sees that the fortune of the wicked ultimately falls into good hands (28:8). Retribution is treated almost as a natural law (11:6), the inevitable working of an order that takes away ill-gotten gain and punishes for illicit pleasures. At times it seems puzzling to hear such hard-headed realistic men, who knew that wealth sticks to greedy fingers and that the rich man is seldom a righteous paragon, and who even advised up-and-coming young men to pay deference to those who have no other recommendation than great wealth (18:5), voice, as they did, the conventional phrases about God's providence.

How did providence operate? Proverbs emphasizes that wealth and position, all the accoutrements of success, do not guarantee happiness. "Better a dry crust and concord with it than a house full of feasting and strife!" (17:1). "The heart knows its own bitterness; and a stranger has no part in its joy" (14:10). What may satisfy one man may bring bitterness and frustration to another who wants still more (13:25). Misfortune may be a blessing in disguise, for it may shock us into greater sensitivity and, like a father's whipping of his son, be a sign not of God's disinterest but of His great love (13:12). Do not expect instant retribution. Retribution comes in its own good time. The wicked penalize their children, the righteous lay up a store of blessings (13:22). A shroud has no pockets, but the righteous need not worry, for their deeds protect them: "The righteous shall be requited on earth, how much more the wicked and the sinner" (11:31). And, just when the reader loses patience with such self-righteous pieties, he stumbles on the startling suggestion that God is all-powerful, human freedom only a human conceit, and man presumably not responsible or accountable: "It is the Lord who directs a man's steps; how can mortal man understand the road he travels?" (20:24). "The king's heart is under the Lord's hand; like runnels of water, He turns it wherever He will" (21:1). Here is a fresh, if dangerous, idea: God's power is unrestricted, hence man's sense of freedom is an illusion. We wish this literature were not so episodic and the ideas so undeveloped. It is suggested that man's fate depends entirely on the grace of God, even though such ideas undermine covenant thinking, for they imply that man is not free, and that it is pointless to imagine that he will be rewarded or punished for his actions. Others, such as Paul, Augustine, and Calvin, would pursue these concepts, but in Judaism these ideas would not flourish. However, they had been thought, and would be thought about again, within this faith in which the concept of accountability for one's deed is central and normative.

❧

The psalms represent the poet and the sanctuary. The Psalter is an anthology of pre-exilic pieces (pre-586 B.C.E.) to which have been added songs composed and sung during the Babylonian Exile and the period of the Second Temple (536 B.C.E.–70 C.E.). The use of song and orchestra to accompany Temple ritual was common in West Asia, and the biblical psalms owe much to the poetic styles and rhythms of the area; formal parallels have been found in the cult literature of Ugarit. Considering the overblown exuberance of exaltation and despair which delighted this world and affected, or afflicted, all its poetry, it is a tribute to the vigor and honesty of many of these pieces that they have remained so central to the worship and spirit of Western man.

Most of the psalms were written to be sung liturgically and are still published with a superscription indicating mode and orchestration. I often suspect that, as in opera, the texts were secondary to performance and setting. It is best not to read some of the psalms too carefully. Their faith is sometimes so full as to be fulsome. What is one to make of "I have been young and am now old, but have yet to see a righteous man abandoned, or his children seeking bread" (37:25), or "Though the misfortunes of the righteous be many, the Lord will save him from them all" (34:20)? Some of the psalms exhibit the limitations of having been composed for a particular antiphonal sound desired at a Temple ceremony (136). Yet, on reading the less stylized pieces, I am struck by the immediacy of the poet's feeling, a rare accomplishment in oriental literature, and by the anguish, urgency, and faith with which he confronts the turmoil of his life, and the honesty with which he contrasts his experience with the familiar teachings about the justice of God's ways.

The one hundred and fifty psalms which were finally canonized reflect almost every spiritual mood from calm assurance to desperate need, from conventional expressions of amazement and awe over the wonders God had performed for Israel to ecstatic happiness with personal or national good fortune. The more lyric of these songs represent perhaps the first unselfconscious introspective poetry written by anyone, in this case by one whose "soul thirsts for God, the living God" (42:2).

God is judge. His justice is so often praised that the reader suspects repressed doubts and is not surprised to find the poet reassuring himself that judgment will come speedily (7:9–17). The poet alternately badgers God: "Lord, how long shall the wicked exult?" (94:3) and summons God to do His duty: "Rise up, Judge of the earth, give the arrogant their deserts!" (94:2). I know of no other early liturgy which is as remarkably candid about the many who doubt that God cares what men do, who say in their hearts: "God is not mindful, He hides His face; He never looks" (10:11; cf. 94:4–6), or who feel that God is tardy in making good on His promise (13:2–5). These are hymns, so in the end faith triumphs over the tragic. "But, I trust in Your faithfulness [hesed]; my heart will exult in Your deliverance" (13:6). This faith generally is full—but not blind.

The first of the psalms ascribed to a certain Asaph (73) is that rare achievement, a successful piece of philosophizing in poetic form. What does it philosophize about? The common faith—"God is truly good to Israel, to those whose heart is pure" (73:1)—and the obvious discrepancy between the decent man's burdens and the rather attractive wages of sin:

> Such are the wicked;
>> Ever tranquil, they amass wealth.
> It was for nothing that I kept my heart pure
>> And washed my hands in innocence,
> Seeing that I have been constantly afflicted
>> That each morning brings new punishments.
>>> (73:12–14)

But typically, for he is of the faithful of that day, Asaph pronounces himself satisfied when, seeing the wicked, "he reflected on their fate" (73:17). He has confidence in God's promise of a distant retribution (73:18) and finds comfort in admitting that his earlier uncertainty was a measure of his emotional frailty, not of God's failure. "My body and mind fail; But God is the stay of my mind, my portion forever" (73:26).

[114]

Many of Israel's hymns are innocently nationalist in spirit, full of praise for God's wondrous care of His people, and hope that Israel may be worthy of future benevolence (2:10 ff.). The justice of God's ways is praised, the list of His delivering acts for Israel is rehearsed with loving care. These were Temple hymns chosen for the service of the national shrine. We expect a proud sense of Israel's particular history and confidence that the Guardian of Israel neither slumbers nor sleeps, but we must not overlook the many expressions of gratitude for the powerful, redemptive privilege of belonging to this people.

Salvation is both national and private, and no real attempt is made to keep these two categories separate. "I" and "we" interchange easily in psalm language. The hymns restate the national faith, but surging private need constantly spills over the stated boundaries of doctrine. We say, "Happy is the man who has not followed the council of the wicked. . . . The wicked are like chaff that wind blows away" (1:1, 4). But I pray, "Deliver me, O God; for the waters have reached my neck" (69:1–2). The psalmists answer variously the question of why men suffer, and the reality of suffering is profoundly vivid in these hymns. One poet justifies God by adopting a mood of self-criticism verging on self-debasement. Evidencing what another age would label the virtue of humility, he finds that God is always in the right and just, for man is always in the wrong. "There is no soundness in my flesh because of Your rage, no wholeness in my bones because of my sin. For my iniquities have overwhelmed me; they are like a heavy burden, more than I can bear" (38:4–5). Another pious answer looks beyond God's judgment to God's grace. The psalmist accepts patiently, confident of the blessing that awaits. "Weeping may linger for the night, but at dawn there are shouts of joy" (30:6).

Under the covenant Israel has a claim on God's faithfulness; the psalms express Israel's longing for more than justice, for assurance that God will comfort, console, encourage, sustain, and shield. It is this surge from judgment to blessing, from criticism to consolation, from failing to forgiveness, which gives the psalms their continuing appeal. They provide the covenant faith with its tenderest face. Forgiveness is seen as a special proof of God's power. "Yours is the power to forgive so that You may be held in awe" (130:4). The psalms enlarge man's awareness of the benevolence of the covenant God. God is Father, Shepherd, and Redeemer, and men invoke God's mercy. The strictness of covenant thinking gives way to a statement of the soul's need; Israel has no claim on God, but rejoices in the knowledge that God cares and that it is His nature to be gracious and merciful. "For Your name's sake" translates to: I have no basis for an appeal on the facts, but I throw myself confidently on Your mercy. Exalting God's power, the psalms consistently label it a power to save.

But good men of Israel had vanished into the Assyrian shadows and good men died young every day; for all the encouragement of the psalms, all their song, there remained the need for hard reflection, for Job. The book of Job presents wisdom as dialogue. The dialogue form is more than a matter of style. Dialogue represents an exchange or contrast of ideas, a search for meaning rather than its confident statement. God's government of the universe is closely examined. That He governs the universe is never denied, but His involvement with the details of an individual's fate is seriously questioned. "He passes by me, and I do not see Him; He moves on His way undiscerned by me; if He hurries on, who can bring Him back? Who will ask Him what He does?" (Job 9:11–12). When one of Job's comforters offers a hymn to God's power, he exults in its beneficence: "God gives rain to the earth and sends water on the fields; He raises the lowly to the heights . . ." (5:10–11). When Job offers his hymn to God's power, he invokes a power which is dark and cold: "It is God who moves mountains, giving them no rest, turning them over in His wrath. Who makes the earth start from its place so that its pillars are convulsed; who commands the sun's orb not to rise and shuts up the stars under His seal . . ." (9:5–7).

Job knows that in the end he must submit to God's incomprehensible power. What he denies is that any theology can comprehend God's ways. To man the terms of divine providence remain unsearchable and unknowable. The conclusion of Job represents Job's emotional response to a display of God's power. Out of the whirlwind God describes the vastness of His authority. Somehow in the vision of eagles soaring in the air and a crocodile moving majestically in the river, in the image of nature's wild beauty, Job is able to feel that the Creator does care. Job never admits that God's power is especially directed toward the good of any individual, but he has shaken the feeling that God's power may be raw and indifferent.

The book of Job is sometimes described as presenting in its hero the classic Promethean spirit, man at his noblest and strongest. Job is possessed of an indomitable spirit, but the book of Job hardly glorifies man. In the creation story as told in Genesis, man is the climax of creation. In Job man is one of many powerful and beautiful creatures in God's powerful and beautiful universe, no better or dearer to God than any of the others. A psalmist had hymned the tradition which saw man as almost God-like, created in God's own image:

> What is man that You are mindful of him,
> Mortal man that You have taken note of him,
> That You have made him little less than divine,
> And adorned him with glory and majesty.
> You have made him master over Your handiwork,
> Laying the world at his feet,
> Sheep and oxen, all of them,
> And wild beasts, too,
> The birds of the heavens, the fish of the sea,
> Whatever travels the paths of the seas.
>
> (Ps. 8:5–9)

The author of Job may have had this exuberant anthropology in mind when he wrote these sharply contrasting lines: "What is man that Thou makest much of him, and turnest Thy thoughts towards him, only to punish him morning by morning and to test him every hour of the day?" (Job 7:17–18). The birds in the air and the fish in the sea are not under man's authority. Far from being God-like, "Man born of woman is short-lived and full of disquiet" (14:1). He is a driven leaf, dry chaff (13:25). "His days are like those of a hired laborer, like those of a slave longing for the shade, or a servant kept waiting for his wages" (7:1–2). The world is a bruising and frightening place. Man stumbles about and does the best he can, while Job longs for the quiet and peace of the grave.

Job can be read as an early protest against the smugness of those devotees of wisdom who assumed that all can be known and all life responsibly regulated. The dialogues of Job explore without clear resolution. There is thesis and antithesis, but no synthesis. The issue is not the cruelty of Job's suffering, but its irrationality. The comforters, all model wise men, insist on the conventional wisdom: "Where have you seen the upright destroyed? This I know, that those who plough mischief and sow trouble reap as they have sown" (4:7–8). Job sets his own experience against such broadly held and cherished ideas. "I am innocent—therefore I say: 'He destroys blameless and wicked alike' " (9:21–22). Job tells it without embellishment; he has discovered that beyond the assumptions of the familiar covenant teachings is a power, vast, immanent, and unknowable, which dwarfs man and shatters all his pretensions to wisdom.

There is an Akkadian text from the last half of the second millennium B.C.E. in which the hero falls ill, suffers great pain, feels forsaken, and questions why no God came to his rescue. His question, "Whence come the evil things everywhere?" [2] is the same as Job's theme. Theodicy was already a familiar issue in Job's day. Though there has been a tendency to date Job in the post-exilic period, Job raises questions which were current much earlier. The central theme is classic, that of a wise man trying to explain what he has seen, using the familiar categories of wisdom and finding them inadequate to the problem of retribution.

The opening fiction (1–2) and the conclusion (42:7 ff.) are separate from the dialogue in form and purpose; either this little stage business was fitted around the dialogues to give them form and a conclusion, or the dialogues were inserted into it. It presents Job not as a wise man but as a righteous man, "whole-hearted and upright." God and the accuser angel (*satan* with a small "s," not the Devil of much greater subsequent fame) debate the human condition. The angel claims that man does not serve God without hope of a payoff. The issue is put to the test, and Job meets the test. He holds fast to his integrity. The righteous Job is stubborn. To him the issue is quite clear and not profoundly complicated. "If we accept good from God, shall we not accept evil?" (2:10). The test concluded, Job is returned to mint condition and lives out his days surrounded by the good things of life. This Job is prepared to affirm God and bless Him, come what may. No holocaust can shake his faith.

The Job of the dialogues is not such a sturdy paragon, but a suffering man, introspective, probing, and aware. There is a good bit of self-pity in him. "Why should the sufferer be born to see the light? Why is life given to men who find it so bitter? They wait for death but it does not come . . ." (3:20–21). Trouble had come, and with it three comforters who presented themselves formally to console Job and, this social duty met, to vindicate God to him. They offer conventional justifications of God. Suffering is always merited—it is the result of sin. Suffering is a blessing in disguise, for suffering increases sensitivity. You cannot cry for someone until you have been hurt yourself. Suffering tempers and hardens the will, and purges good men of their few transgressions so they can face death confident of reward.

Job, the clear-eyed, refuses such consolation. He is prepared to affirm God's power, but not the justice of His ways. "One man, I tell you, dies crowned with success, lapped in security and comfort. . . . . Another dies in bitterness of soul and never tastes prosperity; side by side they are laid in earth and worms are the shroud of both" (21:22–26). Job knows what he knows; he refuses explanations whose only proof is that they are widely believed, and dismisses pietistic mumblings that mask the problem by promising that the scales are balanced in some future existence, a life after death in which he does not believe. "So mortal man lies down, never to rise until the very sky splits open. If a man dies, can he live again? He shall never be roused from his sleep" (14:12).

Job affirms God's power, but it is raw and elemental, not the benevolent power the faithful like to consider. Chapter 24 says it succinctly: Look about the world at those who remove the landmarks, at those who take pledges from the widow and the weak and do not return them, and at those who drive the poor of the earth into hiding and abject destitution. They are the powerful. Hear the poor. They groan and cry from the city of the wounded. "But God pays no heed to their prayer" (24:12).

A fourth comforter, Elihu, appears in chapter 32 and reopens the question of the moral government of the universe. The text here is garbled, but Elihu seems to be saying three things: Man's wisdom is so inferior to that of God that he would not recognize God's justice if he should see it in operation. As proof that God is solicitous of men, note how He warns and advises men through visions, dreams, and the flash of insight (32). Furthermore, there is evidence of the sudden destruction of the proud and the disdainful (36).

Elihu's arguments are not met by Job. God interrupts and answers Job out of the whirlwind with a great paean to His own majesty— What is man compared to Him? Where was man when He created the world? How is man's puny power to be compared to His cosmic power? Because all is God's creation, God cannot and will not allow any of His creatures to boast themselves over Him (41:4), and, implicitly, to get out of line. There is a line, even if man does not see it.

Job is overwhelmed, silenced, and responsive: "I knew of Thee then only by report, but now I see Thee with mine own eyes. Therefore I despise myself; I repent in dust and ashes" (42:5–6). Job seems to be saying that he had dismissed as questionable what his friends had claimed earlier, and now he understands that what was said was somehow true. No proof of God's justice is given. God's praise of His creative might establishes His majesty and power, but not necessarily the justice of His purposes. A valid justification of unmerited suffering has not really been offered, unless we assume Job had a conventional Judean mind which could not separate God's power from His goodness. Furthermore, if God is omnipotent and if He is free to act at will and does so, He is no longer covenant-bound. Man's fate is no longer bound up with his obedience. Thus, there is no reason for men to abide God's law, or any law. Logically we have no resolution to Job's dilemma; Job's acceptance is presented as a spiritual act, an act of faith.

In the resolution of these dialogues we have more than logic. We have affirmation, and faith is, after all, what we affirm despite uncertainty. All the questions have been clearly stated, and we have discovered not Job, but man. Moses, Amos, and Isaiah were heroes of God's spirit, strong, courageous, determined men who obeyed God's will. Job is the first biblical man to hold fast to his human spirit, to set his experience against the familiar deposit of accepted truths. Job represents a faith not totally conditioned by the cultural norms of covenant theology. In that sense Job is not a Jewish book, and the author, I believe wisely, chose as his protagonist not a Judean hero, but one of a trio of heroes of West Asia (the others are Noah and Daniel) who "had delivered their own souls by their own righteousness" (Ezek. 14:14).

❧❧

Before the Exile, the central themes of the biblical faith had been established. God is King, all powerful. He controls the actions of men and nations. He has a special relation to Israel, whom He adopted as a nation unto Himself and to whom He granted freedom and gave a homeland. By such gracious deeds, God revealed His most important attribute—gracious concern (ḥesed). He is dependable.

The special relationship between God and Israel has a quasi-legal base, the covenant. The basic terms of this compact had been suggested to the fathers and defined at Sinai. The covenant required many forms of obedience, and Israel's security was contingent upon this obedience. Under prophetic influence the covenant terms were defined as essentially ethical obligations, and its central term, righteousness, is seen as obligatory for all men and all nations. God's moral government is extended to include mankind.

This covenant faith finds its classic expression in the book of Deuteronomy. In 621 B.C.E., during an extensive refurbishment of the Temple, a scroll of law was found by workers and brought to the High Priest, Hilkiah. There is general agreement, though the fact is never specifically stated in the Bible, that this scroll contained at least the central part of the book we call Deuteronomy. Some writers have assumed that this scroll was a pious fraud, a pastiche of *torot* edited on order of king and High Priest to legitimatize a calculated plan to close down the local shrines and center all pilgrimage and sacrifice in Jerusalem. Certainly the discovery came at an opportune time, during a royal reform initiated by Josiah (640–609) designed to reassert the royal prerogatives after several generations of royal weakness. But the history of this reform as told in II Kings indicates that it had begun before the scroll was found, and careful analysis of the legal materials in Deuteronomy has vindicated the antiquity of much of its legislation, which is closer to that of the book of the Covenant (Ex. 20:23–23:19) than to any other biblical code. Besides, biblical man did not invent God's words.

Deuteronomy is more than another list of covenant stipulations. The laws are explained to a degree not otherwise found in Scripture, and have been integrated into a review of the Exodus and the wilderness period which emphasizes election as the miraculous gift of God's grace, obedience to God's law as the obligation of the chosen, and the blessings and curses which state the consequences of Israel's obedience or sin. Deuteronomy retells these events according to a consistent scheme of history: God chose, Israel accepted; God set down stipulations, a covenant, Israel accepted the covenant; consequently God will give Israel the Promised Land and, sadly, Israel will fail God. God will perforce punish Israel. In time Israel will see the error of her ways, take hold of herself, and God will provide her with a period of happiness and glory.

Deuteronomy is fully confident of the justice of God's ways. As an explanation of apparent injustices, Deuteronomy insists that sin and righteousness are lingering realities which affect not only the sinner and the righteous but also their descendants. God visits the guilt of the parents upon the children for three or four generations, but shows mercy for a thousand generations to those who love Him and keep His commandments. Ill fortune could be blamed on one's predecessors, and a righteous father was comforted by the thought that he was storing up blessings for his sons. Here theology veered away from legal practice. The law prohibited courts from imposing collective sentences: "Parents shall not be put to death for their children" (Deut. 24:16). This separation of attitudes is realistic and prudent. Law can protect the innocent son from the penalty which should be imposed on his father, but it cannot protect him from the gossip and social consequences of his father's crime. David's descendants could be kings because David was king; others, perhaps better suited but less well-blooded, could not. Cities have long memories, particularly in fairly stable societies, and this age wisely taught its young that the legacy of a good name was the most precious of all.

In its final form, Deuteronomy is best seen as the first *midrash*, the first fully developed commentary on the founding law. Old laws are rationalized. The rule against self-mutilation and facial scarring as acts of mourning is explained on the basis of Israel's status as a holy people (14:1–2). The Amonites and Moabites are excluded from the tribal assembly, it is said, because these nations were inhospitable to the children of Israel and hired Balaam to curse Israel (23:4–7). A man who has intercourse with a young woman who is free to marry him must marry her if the matter becomes known "because he has violated her and he can never have the right to divorce her" (22:28–29). Generally, the reasons offered appeal either to the people's sense of spiritual otherness—"For you are a people consecrated to the Lord" (14:21) — or to their ethical sensitivity. Rules requiring care for the poor and sabbatical release are explained on the basis that poverty is endemic in society, and God holds the cry of the poor against those who do not respond to His appeal (15:9–11). The rule against a judge accepting even the most trivial and innocent gift is based on the fact that a gift "blinds the eyes of the discerning and upsets the plea of the just" (16:19). Gleanings are to be left for the poor, and justice is due the stranger because Israel had experienced want and tyranny in Egypt and knew the virtue of compassion (24:19 ff.).

Such explanations are not unique to Deuteronomy, but are far more frequent here than in Exodus, Leviticus, or Numbers. What is unique is a rather consistent hortatory and didactic tone. The three addresses by Moses which constitute the bulk of the book are set out as if they represented an extended valedictory by the great leader before he gives over the reins of office. They are his comments on the events of his day, the covenant, and the law. Some statements are self-justifying: a population explosion forced him to establish the court system (1:9 ff.). Some are explanatory: the people sulked in their tents when the spies brought their report of the size and power of the Canaanite army. This reaction caused God to declare them unfit to attempt the conquest and necessitated the long stay in the wilderness (1:14 ff.), which suggests to Moses a sermonic peroration to the effect that, with God on their side, the people have no reason to fear: "None other than the Lord, your God, who goes before you, will fight for you" (1:30). Some of Moses' comments lay bare the terms of covenant theology and the operation of reward and punishment. God chose Israel from among many peoples and graced Israel with His law; when the children of Israel abide by the law, they will be blessed; when Israel violates the law, they will suffer. In Deuteronomy the blessings and the curses are vividly spelled out (27:12–28:18). Obedience to the law "is proof of your wisdom and discernment" (4:6) and the key to your good fortune, "that it may go well with you and with your children after you" (5:26). Obedience should not be grudging. A reverent love of God should be Israel's motivation. The Deuteronomist, an enthusiast who lovingly detailed the many wonders God had performed for Israel, has every hope that, when Israel seeks God, "you will find Him" (4:29).

We cannot reconstruct how these speeches came to be so edited or how the scroll came to be placed in the sanctuary, although we are certain that it was used as a document of covenant renewal. The decalogue is reviewed and renewed, not only with our fathers, "but with us, the living, every one of us who is here today" (5:3). The final text gives the appearance of having been edited in some school which emphasized the centrality of the covenant and the divine meaning of history. Why do I suggest a school? Because there is a heavy emphasis on teaching. Heretofore, the *torot* had been known only to the priests. The prophets had taught by word and deed, and their words had been cherished by small groups of disciples. The decalogue had been kept in stone, as a testimony, and placed in the Ark (Ex. 25:16), and only on special occasions were the laws read out to the people. In Deuteronomy the emphasis is on instruction, "impress them upon your children" (Deut. 6:6). Judaism begins to see itself as based on a book.

This act of finding and consecrating as covenant a Torah, a scroll of laws, had repercussions which affected the entire structure of Jewish life. When one thinks visually of Judaism, probably the first symbol that comes to mind is the parchment scroll of the law (Torah) kept in a sanctuary ark. Jews are known as the people of The Book, but as far as we know, before this seventh-century find, there had been no scroll as such. There were lists of laws, possibly on clay or parchment, some incised on stone, some known only to the priests of the various sanctuaries, some kept in the Ark, or later kept sacramentally in the Holy of Holies of the Jerusalem Temple. Deuteronomy consists of a larger and a more consistent collection of *torot* than any heretofore known. Though it is by no means exhaustive, its publication emphasized the existence of a sacred text and public reading emphasized the text's adequacy as a rule for life (4:1 ff.). From now on the Torah would be an available, open, and deliberately publicized book. Every sabbatical year the priest is to read it out to the people (31:10 ff.). Every man is to impress these laws upon his children by regular instruction (6:7). The image which begins to emerge is that of a written constitution. The Torah is no longer simply God's specific word for a specific situation, but His word for all times.

When the Torah is taken from the Ark during worship, the reader often recites a Deuteronomic formula: "This is the Torah which God commanded us through Moses. It is the heritage of the community of Israel." The emphasis is on the collective, the community. Torah law is not a revelation reserved to a priestly caste. As Deuteronomy emphasizes, it is to be read aloud, taught to one's son, and discussed openly. Knowledge is power; knowledge shared empowers the community.

❧❦❧

Josiah renewed the covenant and plunged into the political power struggle which followed Assyria's fall from empire. His hopes were high. With many alliances, his armies were successful for a while. He must have felt confident in his piety. Had he not removed the idols, outlawed fire worship, cleansed the Temple, and proclaimed the covenant? But the shadow of Babylon lay on the horizon, and soon the voice of God announced that these years had been for Judah a short Indian summer; cold, bitter winter began to spread over the land. Josiah's defeat and death raised new questions about God's *ḥesed* and the operation of the convenant.

CHAPTER

↡VIII↟

Judah Is Judged

THE biblical prophets are known as champions of social justice, and activists have often acknowledged the prophets as their models. The words they brought strongly condemned not only the exceptionally greedy and vulgar within their communities, but the community itself, the conspiracy of respectability in which every society engages. "For all, high and low, are out for ill-gotten gain; prophets and priests are frauds, every one of them; they dress my people's wounds, but skin-deep only, with their saying, 'All is well.' All well? Nothing is well" (Jer. 8:10–11). Today someone capable of seeing so clearly the social ills of his country and burdened by the inevitable consequences of injustice—crime, depravity, racial hate, emotional deprivation—would man the barricades or organize a political reform movement. This was not the prophetic way. No prophet raised barricades, preached revolution, or organized Judean youths into a radical underground. Why not? Because the prophets were not the champions of social justice; God was. The words were His, not theirs, and any fundamental changes in the social order would be God's work, not man's.

The paradox of the prophets' energetic decrial of injustice coupled with their political passivity derived from their awareness of their role as messengers of an all-powerful God. The prophets were involved. They preached in the marketplaces and the courts of Jerusalem. They cared about the fate of their nation. The words they spoke dealt with the consequences of the nation's standing under the covenant. Their hope and most serious purpose was to stimulate repentance: "Come back to Me, apostate Israel" (Jer. 3:12). Their words demanded a perfect, active obedience to the covenant of righteousness, for in such obedience lay the nation's hope. "Amend your ways and your doings and I will cause you to dwell in this place" (7:13). Man repents; God delivers.

The prophets' assumption of man's inability to engineer a better social order was both a premise of faith and a precipitate of experience. Faith insisted that all power belonged to God, that man's fiercest exertions were insignificant:

Let not the wise man boast of his wisdom nor the valiant of his valour; let not the rich man boast of his riches; but if any man would boast, let him boast of this, that he understands and knows me for I am the Lord. I show unfailing love, I do justice and right upon the earth; for on these I have set my heart (9:23).

A man lived in the same city, often in the same house, as had his great-grandfather. Most likely he managed his smith or his farm with the same techniques and tools as had his ancestors. This age had no concept of progress. One had only to listen to the poets and storytellers to know that the social order remained much the same from generation to generation. The idea that people could manipulate the social environment so as to eliminate poverty, ignorance, or slavery was beyond their ken. We see the consequences of this lack of sensitivity to the possibility of change in the Israelite attitude toward slavery. Brutality to a slave was strictly prohibited and severely punished, and a Hebrew slave had to be set free at the end of a given period of time—but no prophet denounced the institution of slavery itself. They had no comprehension of the possibility of a nation based on free labor. The prophets attacked cruelty and preached justice, but assumed that until the end of days there would always be slaves in the land.

Eighth-century prophecy had described God's control of history largely, though by no means exclusively, from the perspective of Israel and Judah. The seventh-century prophets Zephaniah, Nahum, Habakkuk, and Jeremiah brought words about Judah and about God's plans for other nations. More and more of the oracles concern other peoples. The larger world had intruded on Israel and Judah. Assyria had destroyed Israel (722 B.C.E.) and for most of the next century had held Judah as a tributary state. Now Assyria's conqueror, the neo-Babylonian empire (605–539), threatened to destroy Judah. Seventh-century prophecy spoke out flatly and unequivocally about God's power over men and nations, and not only applied covenant logic to Judah but assumed that God applied the standard of righteousness to the actions of all the nations: "He will stretch out His hand over the north and destroy Assyria, and make Nineveh desolate, arid as the wilderness" (Zeph. 2:13). Later the rabbis would provide a legal basis for the obligation of the nations to serve God. God had imposed seven prohibitions on the father of all nations, Noah (idolatry, incest, murder, blasphemy, injustice, theft, and cruelty to man or beast), with the clear stipulation that all his descendants would be judged according to these basic requirements.[1] Though there is no biblical tradition of a covenant made with the nations, Jewish thought assumed that there had been one. "I call heaven and earth to witness that whether it be non-Jew or Jew, man or woman, slave or handmaid, according to his deeds will God's spirit rest on him." [2] In Jewish thought no one is wholly outside the law, and consequently no one is wholly without hope.

There were other differences in the prophecies of the seventh century, all of which added to the breadth and complexity of God's word. Isaiah and Amos had brought God's words; Habakkuk and Jeremiah bring God's words and also allow their own thought to appear. The prophet's speech is often cast in the form of a dialogue with God. God had offered to discuss with Isaiah the operation of divine providence (Isa. 1:18). Now the shoe is on the other foot; the prophet challenges God. "You would be right, O Lord, were I to contend with you, yet will I question you" (Jer. 12:1).

Conventional morality had seen life under the covenant as a test of man's will-to-obedience, the power of his faith pitted against lassitude, apathy, and ego. The new prophecy wondered if there were some tragic flaws in human nature which rendered man innately incapable of passing the covenant test. Jeremiah described his neighbors as "sottish children" who cannot grasp the lessons being taught them. "Their ear is dull. They cannot hear" (6:10). Zephaniah described his neighbors as too self-proud "to hear the warning voice, to take the rebuke to heart" (Zeph. 3:2). Pride is the cardinal sin. The prideful hear their own voices, not God's. Increasingly, true believers are identified as the "afflicted and poor" (3:12).

The seventh century has little confidence that there are any who have the humility to hear and the courage to obey. Isaiah had believed that on the day of judgment God would save a remnant, the most saintly men. They would be worthy citizens of a restored Zion. When Zephaniah, Habakkuk, and Jeremiah prophesied about the *dies irae*, they too foresaw a day of redemption and return, but the hope they expressed of a restored Zion is generally cast in the vision of a new Israel different in kind from anything that has been before. God will create a new breed of men. Men of "a new heart" and a "new spirit" will have the law of God written in their inward parts; as if by instinct they will act obediently and righteously (Jer. 31:31). In the new vision redeemed Israel is a kingdom of saints, a new and morally superior breed; which is to say that no one then alive was considered worthy of being listed in the saving remnant.

Such a miraculous transformation of human nature was well within the capacity of a God of unbounded power. But men wondered what kind of God would yoke man to obligations he cannot meet. Prophecy, once an onerous duty, now became a truly tragic burden. To Amos the day of wrath was deserved, and that was the beginning and end of it. To Jeremiah the day of wrath was deserved, and he was racked with anguish. He curses his very existence and damns the day of his birth. Prophecy is now a heartache and the prophets begin to anguish about its purpose. Habakkuk complains, "Why have You forced me to see such misery?" (1:3).

History forced new thoughts. The seventh century had been long and inglorious. The northern kingdom lay in ruins. Its intellectual and upper classes had disappeared, forced into exile. Its poor toiled on the land, leaderless, without any sense of pride or national dignity. In Judah, Manasseh (693–642) and his son Amon (642–640) occupied the shaky throne of a hapless satellite state at the edge of Assyrian power. Having no alternative save national suicide, Manasseh bought survival at any price. When the Assyrian lords ordered their icons set up in the Temple, Manasseh set up the icons. When some of his courtiers sought to curry favor with their masters by aping their ways, Manasseh, the obedient puppet, made no protest; he even used his police to quell the ensuing protest.

Did Judah deserve such misery? Why was rapacious, cruel Assyria wealthy and powerful, while God's people endured as a vassal state burdened with confiscatory annual tribute? The pious answered by listing Manasseh's sins: "And the Lord spoke by His servants the prophets saying: Because Manasseh king of Judah has done these abominable things . . . I will bring disaster upon Jerusalem and Judah, disaster which will ring in the ears of all who hear of it" (II Kings 21:10–12). At the same time a sense of outrage and abuse grew in the nation. Habakkuk asked God directly why He held His peace while enemies swallowed up the nation without distinction between righteous and wicked, as if mankind were no more than a mass of fish trapped willy-nilly in the fisherman's net. Nahum heard God speak a harsh sentence against Assyria and imagined the delight of the nations at her imperial discomfiture: "All who have heard of your fate clap their hands in joy. Are there any whom your ceaseless cruelty has not borne down?" (Nah. 3:19). Nahum's words continually reassure that God "cares for all who seek His protection and brings them safely through the sweeping flood" (1:8), but it is clear that many were not so certain. Assyria's fall, which occurred in 612 B.C.E., satisfied some, but others recognized that though Assyria's defeat could be interpreted as proof of God's power over even the mightiest nation, it did not make clear what God had devised for His people or how God would save Judah from new dangers and make good His word that "the Lord is a sure refuge for those who look to Him in time of distress" (1:7).

Amon was assassinated (640 B.C.E.) and an eight-year-old boy, Josiah, was crowned. It was a time of international upheaval. Assyria was on the skids, and the Babylonian empire was rising on its ruins. Josiah grew into an ambitious and clear-eyed monarch who recognized his diplomatic opportunities, but also recognized that it was first necessary to set things right with God. Of the Deuteronomic reform and the fortunate discovery of a scroll of *torot* in the Temple we have already spoken. Josiah led the ceremonies of covenant renewal. Country shrines were abolished and Manasseh's icons pulled down. Josiah was zealous for the law and confident of God's protection. Correctly judging that Babylonia would be the victor in the power struggle for the vacated Assyrian authority, he hastened to align himself with the new power. There was a moment of glory, but it was brief. An Egyptian Pharaoh crushed Josiah's armies at Megiddo (609 B.C.E.). Now the question was only to which great power would Judah be subservient, Egypt or Babylon? The popular faith might exult that God had had his day over proud Assyria, but the sensitive asked why one tyrant was replaced so soon by another. The conventional answer was that Josiah deserved his fate, but in Josiah's case that answer did not fit. "No king before him had turned to the Lord as he did, with all his heart and soul and strength, following the whole law of Moses . . ." (II Kings 23:25). Josiah had reformed the cult and obeyed the will of God, yet he had been defeated and had died in battle. Pious historians rationalized that Josiah fell victim because God was still angry with Judah over Manasseh's evil deeds (I Kings 23:26), a theme much embellished in rabbinic *aggadah*, where that unhappy king is variously charged with idolatry, incest, murder, and the erasure of the name of God from Scripture.[3] In any event, however black Manasseh's sins, Josiah was not Manasseh. He had turned to God with his whole heart. What more could be asked? If Josiah suffered such a fate, was there any hope for the nation?

The times were tragic. After Josiah's death in battle, Egypt, temporarily in command, placed a subservient prince, Jehoiakim, on Judah's throne. Judah was taxed to provide Egypt with men and supplies, but the armies of Babylonia could not be stayed; Egyptian armies were steadily beaten back. The lines of prophecy were dark with a sense of impending doom and full of foreboding. In 598 B.C.E. Jerusalem was surrounded by the troops of the Babylonian emperor Nebuchadnezzar, and the city surrendered. Eight thousand noblemen and skilled craftsmen were marched off as hostages. The king was replaced by a more pliant younger brother. He, too, began to plot against Babylonia and was summarily deposed, and the third of Josiah's sons, Zedekiah, was elevated to the throne. Zedekiah was irresolute. There were constant plots or rumors of plots. Finally the Babylonians lost patience and Jerusalem was again besieged. This time there was no surrender. The enemy battered down the gates and fired the city. On the ninth of the month of Av, 586 B.C.E., the sacred vessels of the Temple were packed up and carted off, the Temple altar was pulled down, and the whole building was put to the torch. A puppet governor, Gedaliah, was given nominal authority. In short order he was assassinated by revanchist hotheads. Again Babylonian troops appeared on the scene. Hundreds fled, thousands were marched into exile, and Judah was no more.

❦

It was a bitter era, full of fury and dread. It would end in lamentation, but it was a time full of words of God which made clear that these events were not fortuitous. "Shame on the tyrant city, filthy and foul! No warning voice did she heed, she took no rebuke to heart, she did not trust in the Lord or come near to her God" (Zeph. 3:1). Judah was being punished. Soon other nations would be sentenced: those who were now the agents of God's anger would not escape punishment once they had accomplished God's purposes; their deserved punishment would come quickly and would be known as God's vindication (Jer. 51:11). There is a good bit of simple transference of anger and frustration here, with little Judah's helplessness bitterly exposed in graphic images—roofless buildings swarming with vultures and rodents, bloody cities full of carcasses—but there is also a good bit of simple piety. God will show that His power is incomparable. No mortal power can stand against Him. What would be more natural than that God exact vengeance against the imperialists who despoil His earth? God acts in history to prove His power, "for the sake of His name" (Isa. 48:9 passim). As the emphasis on God's power increases, man becomes increasingly a spectator to a divinely produced drama, rather than the actor whose accomplishments under the covenant influence God's decisions. Apocalypse begins to emerge from prophecy.

Zephaniah's dates are uncertain. Assyria is still in power when he begins to prophesy. His words begin in the familiar prophetic vein by ticking off a list of sins, both cultic and moral, which lead to the familiar threat that the popularly expected day of deliverance, the "day of God," will not be the expected day of glory but a "day of wrath" which he describes as a "day of trouble and distress, a day of nastiness and desolation, a day of dark and gloom, a day of clouds and thick darkness, a day of the horn and alarm" (Zeph. 1:14–16). On that day Judah will be invited to a sumptuous banquet only to find that she herself is the intended main course (1:7–9).

This day of wrath is terrible, inevitable, and deserved (1:17). Being deserved, it is proof of God's justice and the faithful can be encouraged by God's dependability: "Seek the Lord, all in the land who live humbly by His laws, seek righteousness, seek a humble heart; it may be you will find shelter in the day of the Lord's anger" (2:3). "It may be"—not much comfort. Experience makes it clear that men are caught by their circumstances. When Abraham pleaded with God to spare the righteous of Sodom, God agreed to spare the city if fifty qualified men, or even forty, thirty, twenty, or ten, could be found among her citizens, but there God stops. An individual is inextricably tied to the fate of his community. Jeremiah did God's bidding faithfully and opposed every policy of Judah's kings, yet he starved with the besieged in Jerusalem and ended his life a displaced person in Egyptian exile. Another question troubled even more: How could God use nations infamous for their belligerence and pride as the agents of Israel's destruction? Why does Judah's chastisement require their triumph? Zephaniah blunted the question by prophesying that their triumph would be short-lived (2:10–11). But was Judah's only comfort to be the vicarious pleasure of being able to watch God's swift vengeance on her enemies? Was there no more positive hope? There will be a day of wrath and another day on which God shall rise up against the nations and turn to those of pure heart. Zion is told to sing and rejoice (3:14), but a close reading suggests that the renewed community is a different community, composed of a different breed of men who are by nature good (3:13). Such a transformation of human nature could easily be imagined of a God in absolute control of history, but the utopian image is both a devastating comment on human incapacity and a challenge to covenant moralizing. Today's men cannot measure up. God no longer waits for proof of man's obedience. He acts on His own and for His own purposes (3:1). Deliverance is certain, but Judah's consequential role in that drama is no longer clear.

⊷§§⊷

Zephaniah's contemporary, Habakkuk, also brought words of doom and vengeance. His style is personal and dialogic, and he puts the embarrassing questions of his confused time directly to God. "Why dost Thou let me see such misery, why countenance wrongdoing? Devastation and violence confront me . . . and so justice comes out perverted" (Hab. 1:3–4). He is answered by a prophecy of vindication—God will raise the Babylonians who will overthrow the hated Assyrians (1:5 ff.). Nahum had come this far, but Habakkuk's prophecy goes one step further. Babylonia would be corrupted by its new-found power and will be punished (1:11). Still the prophet is not fully satisfied. Since by any standard Judah is not as wicked as the murderous Babylonians, how can God use such a savage and impetuous nation as His agent? The question is of paramount significance, and Habakkuk goes into seclusion to await God's answer. However, God does not answer directly; rather He orders Habakkuk to inscribe in large letters on a stone the enigmatic phrase, "He whose soul is not upright in him, shall fail; but the righteous abides in his faith" (2:4), and to set up this inscription where all may see. Clearly it is a promise, but the terms of the promise are clothed in mystery. But then, if retribution were self-evident, where would be the merit of obedience? If righteousness paid off, the shrewdest and most calculating would be first in line to be righteous. Habakkuk admits that there is no full explanation of God's moral government, but urges confidence that the haughty will not long be dominant, and God's justice will soon shine forth for all to see (2:14).

Habakkuk's message states that God has set a time limit to Babylonia's dominance. No reason is given. There is no pretense that the chosen time is related to the nation's conduct. The prophecy is to be written down and published that anyone may read what God proposes (2:1–3). Habakkuk introduces us to the world of apocalypse. He turns our attention from covenant to cosmic drama. There is an appointed time when God will avenge Himself on Israel's enemies. This time has been set by God, and does not appear to be contingent on Judah's righteousness or repentance. It will come. Why? Why then? We are told only that God wills it.

A word of caution: Some Christian discussions of the problem of justification use Habakkuk 2:4, "The righteous lives by his faith," as a doctrinal text, and translate faith as creedal affirmation. Presumably, acceptance of a creed is the key to a God-pleasing life, and correct belief is the distinguishing achievement of those who will be saved. The Hebrew word *emunah*, which is here translated as "faith," cannot mean creed or dogma, but rather signifies steadiness or faithfulness and harkens back to Isaiah's preachment about quietness and trust as the categories which distinguish the faithful. Biblical men searched for and stated what they knew of the way of life acceptable to God. Habakkuk's emphasis was on the way rather than on words, on discipline more than on doctrine.

✌⧌✍

Jeremiah, too, brought God's word to the Judean kings and nation during the last years of their precipitous slide into oblivion. No prophet is more familiar to us. The writings reveal both the sensitivity of his spirit, for the man emerges at times from behind the messenger, and the force and art of his poetic genius. Jeremiah phrased God's word with some of the most compelling verse in biblical literature. These were years of swift and terrible political decisions. Jeremiah's message was black. "I [God] will bring on this place a disaster which shall ring in the ears of all who hear of it" (Jer. 19:3). He was to take an earthen jar and smash it beyond repair, announcing: "Thus will I [God] shatter this people and this city" (19:10).

What was the burden of the message that God sent through Jeremiah in those dark days? "Blow the trumpet . . . for I bring disas-

[133]

ter" (4:5–6). The words were directed at what remained of man's instinctive optimism—to shatter any lingering illusions. There were prophets who still insisted Judah would not experience war or famine; of these God said: "The prophets are prophesying lies in my name" (23:25), "fraudulent visions" (6:13), "their own wishful thinking" (23:16). These seers will themselves be victims of the coming famine and slaughter. Why shatter the hopes men so desperately cling to? Because only a broken heart—Jeremiah called it alternately "a circumcised heart" (9:25) or a "heart of flesh" (36:26)—can truly be sensitive to the radical demand of God's law of righteousness. Before true repentance can begin, the last shred of complacency must be destroyed. Defeat, famine, and exile acquire a positive value, for they shatter the ego and humble men before the imperious will of God. "It is your own wickedness that will punish you, your own apostasy that will condemn you. See for yourselves how bitter a thing it is and how evil, to forsake the Lord your God and revere Me no longer" (2:19).

In Jeremiah and the Bible generally, *musar* means both "punishment" and "moral instruction." *Musar* later was used to describe the whole field of ethics. Much would be said and written about ethical motivation, but in the Jewish conscience ethics never loses touch with its original identification with correction. The anguish of life— illness, death, exile, persecution—is never merely anguish but always the rod of God's anger, the disciplining power of a wise schoolmaster who knows that the animal in man must be broken before the divine in man can emerge. The pain of life was never simply pain, a senseless cruelty, but a learning experience. "Happy the man whom You discipline, O Lord, the man You instruct in Your teaching" (Ps. 94:12).

Judah should have learned from a long series of defeats/punishments/disciplines, but "in vain I struck down your sons, the lesson was not learnt" (Jer. 2:30). Jeremiah proceeds to puncture every remaining hope. Some held that God had made a covenant with David that his house would rule Judah forever, so although God might chastise the nation, He would intervene before the ultimate disaster. Not so, says Jeremiah, the end will be complete, and the king will receive an ass' burial (22:19). Other Judeans held that the Temple was God's dwelling place and Jerusalem His capital, and that God would not allow either to be destroyed. Not so! This city will be smashed beyond repair. Not even the Temple is inviolate. God Himself would take a hand in the work of destruction.

But why? God seems aware that many question the harshness of their punishment; "When you tell this people all these things they will ask you, 'Why has the Lord decreed that this great disaster is to come upon us? What wrong have we done? What sin have we committed against the Lord our God?' You shall answer . . . " (16:10). Jeremiah's answer is straight out of Amos and Isaiah: "Because each of you follows the promptings of his wicked and stubborn heart instead of obeying Me" (16:12). The impending destruction is merited, but the questions persist: Are we so uniquely evil to have deserved punishment after punishment? Jeremiah suggests that Judah's doom does not come solely because of the sins of the present generation. The Judeans are being punished for their own sins and for the sins of their fathers. "You shall answer because your forefathers forsook Me . . . and followed other gods serving them and bowing down to them. They forsook Me and did not keep My law" (16:11). Cumulative guilt is a cruel thought; understandably, one of the hopeful signs of "the days to come" is that "it shall no longer be said, 'The fathers have eaten sour grapes and the children's teeth are set on edge' " (31:29).

Jeremiah spoke God's words of doom, but was not intellectually satisfied that Judah's punishment was wholly just. "You would be right, O Lord, were I to argue with You; Yet will I reason with You: Why do the wicked prosper? Why are those who deal treacherously secure?" (12:1). But there was no answering word—the terrible and fateful question hangs in the air. Jeremiah could only empathize. During those bitter days Jeremiah knew everyman's pain. The pain he bore had no vicarious virtue; it was simply pain. He "heard the whispering of many, terror on every side" (20:10), and he endured pain directly. He was beaten, cursed, sunk in a cistern, imprisoned, and put on trial for his life; he saw his teachings cut up and burned, and ultimately he was dragged off to die in exile. He was truly a man of sorrows, yet a man who knew God's power and found in that knowledge hope.

Covenant language is still here—"Come back to Me, wayward sons. I will make right your backsliding" (3:22)—but Jeremiah's words are heavy with that sense of powerlessness which slowly converted classical prophecy into apocalypse. When Jerusalem had been besieged by Sennacherib, Isaiah had brought words demanding repentance and resistance. Now a hundred years later, when Jerusalem is besieged by Nebuchadnezzar, Jeremiah counsels surrender (21:8–9). God does not promise a last-minute miracle in return for any last-minute repentance; not only is military action futile, but so apparently is spiritual renewal. "I now give all these lands to My servant Nebuchadnezzar, king of Babylon . . . until the destined hour of his own land comes" (27:6–7).

Some have labeled Jeremiah's attitude political quietism. Certainly his prophecies testify to an emerging sense that the scenario of world history has been written and must unfold. Shall little Judea ally herself with the east or the west, since she is too small and impotent to pursue an independent course? Jeremiah's word warns against both alternatives. "Why go to Egypt, to drink the waters of the Nile? Or why go to Assyria, to drink the waters of the River?" (2:18). Jeremiah is not yet an apocalyptic. He still speaks as if spiritual reform were consequential, "Why complain to me? You have rebelled against me" (2:29). But in his thinking, God acts as He wills and for His own reasons.

This may explain Jeremiah's personal anguish. When he received his commission, he was told not to marry or have children. He senses from the first the futility of his mission. "When you tell them this, they will not listen to you; if you call them, they will not answer" (7:27). He is not even allowed to intercede in prayer for his people. No wonder he curses the day that he was born.

Burdened by the recognition that the day of wrath is inevitable, Jeremiah confronted the issue of what lies beyond it. It is the Book of Comfort (chapters 30–32) and other scattered passages of similar import which have made Jeremiah so well loved, for here he spoke of God's indestructible love for His people. This vision lifts his spirits; on this level there is hope. What is the basis of this hope? God's word, His spoken promise, and God's nature, His righteousness. He would not, because He is God, utterly destroy. "I am with you and will save you . . . though I punish you as you deserve, I will not sweep you clean away" (30:11).

God will act out of His grace. He will not wait for hard proof of Judah's righteousness. Thie timetable for deliverance depends not on Judah's repentance, but is an arbitrary time which God has stipulated for His own reasons. "When full seventy years have passed over Babylon, I will take up your cause and fulfill the promise of good things I made you" (29:10). Deliverance comes because God wills it. The date of the return was made known to Judah before the last of the prisoners were marched off into exile.

The just God is also by nature merciful. There is a renewed emphasis on the mercy of God (30:18–20), and there is talk of a new covenant which God will soon announce, "the time is coming" (31:4). The new covenant is a happy but difficult image. It is not clear if it replaces the old or is an addition to it. It is somehow written on the heart of man, rather than in stone and external to him. Being inborn, it need not be taught. Obviously men blessed with such an innate holiness are a new breed born miraculously possessed of natures that are never tempted to sin. "The Lord has created a new thing in earth" (31:22). Will it be the exiled who will be delivered, or their children, or some new species of men called by the familiar name of Judah?

Men eager for the comforting word did not construe these texts too closely; they heard what they wanted to hear. "I will forgive their wrongdoings and remember their sin no more" (31:34). They read the words of forgiveness and comfort as words of simple promise. "When you seek Me, you shall find Me; if you search with all your heart, I will let you find Me . . . I will restore your fortunes and gather you again from all the nations, and all the places to which I have banished you" (29:13–14). Jeremiah's hope is the Zionist hope of a return from exile; but it shades off into an eschatological hope of an end of days when the world will not be as it is now. The new covenant is not only blessed and welcome, but eternal (50:4). Man will no longer sin, so there is no reason to fear another punishment. Jerusalem will be redeemed. The nations will hear and see God's vindication, abandon their idols and idolatrous ways (10:11), and acknowledge God (12:15). Jeremiah here does not talk practically but eschatologically; after the end God promises a brave new beginning. Jeremiah is a man of two traditions. Even as he speaks of the new covenant, he seeks to keep his ties with the old land. During the final siege of Jerusalem he buys from a relative a plot near Anatoth: "Houses, field, and vineyards will again be bought and sold in this land" (32:15). After the disaster, God's song of consolation comes to his mouth. Israel and Judah, their history now seemingly over, are in fact about to begin again their glorious way (31:5–6). He sees the matriarch Rachel weeping for her children. She refuses to be comforted, but God tells her to wipe away her tears. "Your work shall be rewarded. They shall come back. . . . There is hope . . . your children shall come home" (31:15–17).

When the exiles of 597 B.C.E. sent a messenger to Judah to try to promote rebellion, Jeremiah wrote a letter, in the name of God, in which he counseled the exiled not to engage in revolutionary activity, but to seek the peace of the city where He had caused them to be exiled (29:5–9). This letter failed to quiet the hotheads—there was an abortive uprising in Egypt—but as a discrete document it assumed more than passing significance in Jewish history. It seemed to say, on the authority of God, that Jews could live lives acceptable to God outside the Promised Land. Jeremiah had meant no more than to be patient until God in His time ends the captivity. But many Judeans, especially those who grew comfortable in Babylonia, would cite the prophet's letter as proof that they did not have to return, that one could lead a life pleasing to God by the canals of Babylon as well as in Jerusalem. Whether it is a sin under the covenant to live in exile when not compelled to was an issue which would be debated for centuries. It is still being debated today between those who deny the possibility of a full and wholesome Jewish life in the Diaspora and those who believe themselves to be leading precisely such a life.

Jeremiah is the first of the prophets known to have hired a scribe to take down his speeches, and he is the first of the prophets to have edited his writings. These were dangerous years in which men no longer trusted the living book which is man's memory. Moved by an unconscious wisdom, the nation began setting things down, first Deuteronomy, now Jeremiah, moving from the memorized to the written word. They would need their books when the pain of exile dulled their mind.

❧

According to II Kings 14:24, Jonah ben Amittai of Gath-Hapher in Galilee was a court prophet during the reign of Jeroboam (786–746). The book of Jonah often is dated in post-exilic time, labeled legendary, and explained as a fictional illustration of the universality of God's power (a truth which was extensively developed by the exilic prophets), and of God's concern that His word be preached to all nations. It need not be. In substance, the book of Jonah, except for the psalm of thanksgiving which Jonah sings in the belly of the great fish (Jon. 2:3–10), is a legend created by a single author whose central theme is theodicy, a natural choice for a nation whose neck is on the block and whose prophets emphasized the impending disaster. When Amos had pronounced God's word of judgment over Israel, he had added the terrifying phrase "I will grant them no reprieve" (Amos 2:6), and Samaria was no more. Would Judah suffer a similar final catastrophe? Without hope man cannot hold on. Jeremiah and others had dwelt on God's will to save. But where was there proof of such a pardon? Israel had been taught to search history to know the ways of God, yet Israel was no more and now Judah was teetering on the brink. There seemed no relief, no proof.

The author of Jonah pointed to the effective repentance of Nineveh, that great metropolis that had sinned and been warned by God, repented, and been forgiven. Here was proof that God was indeed "gracious and compassionate, long-suffering and ever constant, and always willing to repent of the disaster" (Jon. 4:2). Put in another way, God's words are spoken conditionally. God's words are never idle; they accomplish their purpose, which is not to destroy but to chastise, to shake men awake, to bring men back to God. It was with such hope that these men faced exile, but theirs was no longer the uncomplicated confidence of an earlier age.

CHAPTER

❦ IX ❧

Defeat, Dispersion, and Exile

I<small>N</small> 597 B.C.E. Jerusalem surrendered to Nebuchadnezzar, who packed the king and a few thousand Judean nobles and craftsmen off to Babylon as hostages against Judah's good behavior. They were resettled in central Mesopotamia, near Babylon and Nippur, where they continued to conspire with compatriots back in Judah, a reckless undertaking which led to a second Babylonian campaign against Jerusalem (586 B.C.E.), the razing of the city's walls, the citadel, and the Temple, and a second and more inclusive exile of upper-class Judahites. Still another, though numerically smaller, deportation took place around 582 B.C.E., after ardent revanchists murdered a puppet governor, Gedaliah. In all, perhaps thirty thousand of an estimated two hundred thousand Judeans were forcibly exiled, while an unkown number scattered for safety to Edom, Moab, Samaria, Trans-Jordan, and Egypt. Ezekiel preached among the Babylonian exiles; Jeremiah died in the Egyptian dispersion. Lamentations were composed in conquered Judah.

The neo-Babylonian empire made no attempt to resettle Judah with non-Judeans. Although starvation, execution, and disease must have added their share of misery to the burden of these tragic times

(Lam. 2:11, 19–20; 4), life went on. Those who stayed took over the estates, homes, and businesses of the exiled and self-exiled. Tension between the dispersed and the stay-behinds was inevitable and long-lived. Those who left and saw their property taken over felt that their land had been lawlessly expropriated, and by lower-class people at that. Those who remained feared the return of families who had once been their betters and who might now be backed by the power of the empire. The return of 537 B.C.E. and the much later return under the leadership of Ezra and Nehemiah (mid-5th cent. B.C.E.) essentially represent the reimposition of the authority of the old ruling classes upon groups who had remained in the land, and who opposed the return.

How did the faith survive among those who were not exiled? Uncertainly. The extant literature, from the late words of Jeremiah to the fifth-century additions to Zechariah (Zech. 9–14), contains evidence of syncretism, worship of the Queen of Heaven, intermarriage, and disinterest; there also are indications that improvised sacrifices continued to be offered on the stone which had once been the altar of the Temple (Jer. 41:5), and that memorial days of lamentations and fasting were held in Jerusalem until 516 B.C.E., when a small Temple was reopened on the site of the original structure. Similar memorial vigils may have been observed by the exiles in Babylon, possibly on the annual anniversary of the destruction of the Temple. One suspects that it was against the purely ceremonial preoccupations of some of these memorialists, who fasted religiously but lived unconscionably, that Deutero-Isaiah preached the rousing sermon on true loyalty which to this day Jews read in the synagogue during the morning service of the Day of Atonement:

> Is such the fast I desire,
> A day for men to starve their bodies?
> Is it bowing the head like a bulrush
> And lying in sackcloth and ashes?
> Do you call that a fast,
> A day when the Lord is favorable?
> No, this is the fast I desire:
> To unlock fetters of wickedness,
> And untie the cords of the yoke
> To let the oppressed go free;
> To break off every yoke.
> It is to share your bread with the hungry,
> And to take the wretched poor into your home;

When you see the naked, to clothe him,
And not to ignore your own kin.

Then shall your light burst through like the dawn
And your healing spring up quickly;
Your Vindicator shall march before you,
The Presence of the Lord shall be your rear
   guard.
Then, when you call, the Lord will answer;
When you cry, He will say: Here I am.

(Isa. 58:5–9a)

There were many questions for those who remained in Judah. Would punishment never cease? Would there be one bleeding after another? Was the land still holy? Had God withdrawn His special presence from the land, from the people, or from both? What redemptive rite could replace the sacrificial cult as an acceptable form of service to God and serve as a means of atonement and communion? The literature which survives from these years is sparse, and many textual attributions are uncertain. The best minds, at least the best-educated minds, belonged to the priests and leaders who had been carted off. But there are indications of continuing religious concern: the scroll of Lamentations, some psalms, and a few prophetic passages exude both frustration and tense expectation, which are the ambivalent moods of pained and anxious men.

To their credit, the survivors seem to have faced up to the sweeping dimensions of the disaster. This was a time of national grief. Poets employed the classic dirge or lamentation, a poetic form long familiar in West Asia, where it served as the accompaniment to funerals and grief, to sing the pain of their people. Lamentations comprises five fairly long elegies which represent a distillation of these tears, probably texts chosen to be read at the ceremonies of memorial. These elegies express honest grief. These are days of anguish and affliction (Lam. 1:7). Israel's hands are tied behind her back (1:14). There is none to comfort (1:19). Israel's enemies mock and take delight in her agony (1:21). The poet voices his hate of those who stand off and gloat at Judah's misfortune (1:22), but there is no hate of God. Neither is there any attempt to gloss over God's part in this disaster: "The Lord overwhelmed without pity all the dwellings of Jacob" (2:2). "The Lord played an enemy's part" (2:5), but He is not the enemy. The enemy is Israel's own iniquity and pride (2:14): "It was for the sins of her prophets and for the iniquities of her

[142]

priests" (4:13). The appeal is to God's grace and His love. Seeing Israel's pain, God may now be moved to mercy (3:19). To know God's nature is to be comforted, for though He is all-powerful He is never vindictive or spiteful. "The Lord will not cast his servants off forever. He may punish cruelly, yet He will have compassion" (3:31).

Lamentations is a mood, not a program, yet behind the tears we come upon the same emphasis on patience, fortitude, and faith found in Isaiah and Jeremiah. Patience and steadfastness are the virtues of the faithful: "It is good to wait in patience and sigh for deliverance by the Lord" (3:26). God's providence is assumed, not debated. God is just. The punishment is deserved (1:18); let no one evade his responsibility. Lamentations weeps but never whimpers. No man has any cause to complain against God (3:39). The poet does not whine about a loaded deck or offer any alibi based on a claim of man's impotence in the face of the demonic.

Post-exilic Judaism does not always sustain such honesty. The guilt often seems too much for one man or one generation to bear. Less discouraging explanations will be suggested. The nation had sinned, but this people was not unusually ignoble or weak. The struggle to be righteous is not simply a struggle of will against sloth or of self-discipline against weakness. Hidden forces conspire to lead men to sin. Before the existence of any such identifying term, men recognized the force of the id. The Deuteronomic historian who told the story of David's census—early in his reign David had conducted a census, apparently violating ancient tribal taboos by numbering the people, and traditionalists had blamed him when certain unexpected disasters followed—suggested that God Himself had talked David into carrying out the ill-fated census. "Once again the Israelites felt the Lord's anger, when He incited David against them and gave him orders that Israel and Judah should be counted" (II Sam. 24:1). It is an awkward text, one of a number in which there is language which not only casts doubt on God's goodness but suggests that man's actions are not as freely self-determined as covenant theology assumed. But the implication is clear: mischief is often something other than a conscious decision by a man to do evil. In the Bible there is no talk of compulsion, unconscious motivation, or the irrational, but we now begin to hear that "Sin is the demon at the door, whose urge is toward you," though piety quickly adds, "Yet you can be his master" (Gen. 4:7).

A post-exilic historian actually personified evil in his rehearsal of the story of David and the census. "Now Satan, setting himself against Israel, incited David to count the people" (I Ch. 21:1). Satan became a familiar figure in the exile environment of Babylon, where an advanced and dominant faith (Zoroastrian) taught the myths of a sophisticated dualism. Satan was naturalized by some Jews because he provided a vivid mythic explanation of the origin of evil, which protected the moral integrity of God and quieted the natural fears of the exiled, who must have wondered if they were irredeemable. Pre-exilic man had had only himself to blame for his failings; now there was a tempter, a snake in the garden. Men not only sinned but were enticed to sin. The exiles were not any worse than other men, merely prey to various forces which had conspired against them. The older faith was high-minded and rigorous. It had no room for compulsion, psychoses, and the whole turbulent inner man. The exiles who wrote of a tempter knew nothing of the libido, but they had seen much and had active imaginations. There can be no one so righteous that he does not sin, nor can God hold man to an unyielding, unrealistic standard of performance. The thesis that evil has an independent origin, and may even be a personified spirit, was never adopted normatively, but was certainly popular in late biblical and rabbinic thought. Satan might have developed an even more interesting career than the furtive backstairs role allowed him by normative Judaism if he had not run afoul of the faith's veneration of the one God whose attribute of goodness he had been invited to save. There would be an enduring tension between Judaism's bedrock principle of God's unity and omnipotence and man's existential awareness of the reality of the demonic.

Perhaps we have here a partial explanation of the rapid growth of ritual punctilio in exilic and post-exilic times. This was the great age of food taboos, tithings, and acts of ritual purification. Men sought to know exactly God's prescribed regimen: "Truly by all [Your] precepts I walk straight; I hate every false way" (Ps. 119:128). Judaism sets out a specific way to prepare food, regulate the diet, and cleanse oneself of various bodily discharges and the baby and mother of afterbirth. The object is to *tahor*, clean, to attain *kedushah*, a state of holiness, of purity, in which one can appropriately approach God. Precision of form appeals to those who feel themselves dirty or defiled (and was not the Exile a defilement?) or who feel they face forces which cannot otherwise be controlled. Performing set rituals exactly gives man a sense of control over chaos; he is doing what needs to be done. Becoming clean satisfies his need to prove the purity of his intentions. The anonymous post-exilic prophet who goes by the name Malachi brought words which insisted on a pure and exact ritual form, a demand which has no parallel in pre-exilic prophecy (Mal. 1:6–12). The long and detailed blueprint in Ezekiel 40–48 for a rebuilt Jerusalem Temple shows a similar need for absolute precision in building God's house and following His will. The subject is one for psychologists; for our purposes it suffices that we note that the Exile was a trauma that shook man's confidence not so much in God as in himself. Was man really capable of obeying the covenant? If he could not do it on his own, where could he find help?

All this was, of course, in the future; the writer of Lamentations still sang with a pre-exilic idiom. The disaster was deserved, all was God's work, and so, humbly and steadily, "Let us examine our ways and put them to the test and turn back to the Lord" (Lam. 3:40). God has not yet pardoned, but surely He will: "Therefore I will wait patiently" (Lam. 3:21). Judah's hope is one of national restoration: "Renew our days as in time long past" (Lam. 5:21).

❧⸙❧

The dating of each psalm or separate psalm section is an uncertain enterprise, but there are a number of hymns or parts of hymns which seem to reflect the impatient submission of these bleak first years of the Exile. Psalm 44 can represent many of these. The poet calls to mind God's help in times past. Out of His grace God had favored Israel with the land. But now all is changed—Judah is a defenseless sheep ready for the butcher's knife (12). The nation is mocked and reviled by her neighbors and has touched the depth of shame (14–19), yet, as God can attest, the poet and those for whom he speaks have remained steadfast and loyal (18–19). The poet leaves unsaid but certainly implies that this loyalty should put God under some claim, and he cries out for deliverance (24–27).

Desperation can move men to angry words. Psalm 79 includes the hope that God will quickly discomfit the nation "which has devoured Jacob and desolated his home" (7); and an oracle in Isaiah describes a watchman told to climb a high tower and await the news, obviously glad tidings, that "fallen, fallen is Babylon" (Isa. 21:9). But despite the frustration and occasional anger, the degree of steadiness and calm manifested during this early exilic period is remarkable. There is no deep-throated cursing of God.

⋘⋙

Long before, during the heyday of the monarchy, certain Israelites had established themselves as tradesmen in Syria and Egypt (I Kings 30:24). They were dispersed but could have returned to their native land at any time. Exile begins in 586 B.C.E., when men were driven off in chains and forcibly displaced by conquerors. A measure of the shared sense of being displaced is that, however they left, wherever they went, whether to Babylonia, Egypt, Moab, Amon, Samaria, or Assyria (Isa. 40:11), all used one term, *galut* (exile), to describe their separation from the land.

Galut is a physical place and a psychological state. Implicit in *galut* is the urge to return. *Galut* is also a basic category of biblical thought. Until modern times, Hebrew lacked an appropriate term for voluntary settlement outside of Israel (*tefutzah*), and language thus reveals the prejudices of piety. If over the centuries a Jew wished to speak of life in the scattering of Jewish settlements as legitimate, he had to use a Greek term, "Diaspora."

The Judean expatriates looked upon their existence on alien soil as divine punishment and longed for a return to the homeland. Life in *galut* was basically unhealthy. "The Lord will give you there an anguished heart and eyes that pine and a despondent spirit. The life you face shall be precarious; you shall be in terror night and day with no assurance of survival" (Deut. 28:65–66). Proof of this assertion can be drawn from the history of any community of the Jewish dispersion; Zionist literature over the past century has detailed the psychological carnage of the millennial dispersion. But it would also be impossible not to see the exciting cultures Jews developed in many places, the vitality of many of these communities, and the Diaspora's spiritual and political importance for the homeland when there has been a national home.

Life in Babylonian captivity proved less onerous than life in conquered Judah. Jehoiachim retained the title of king, and when all possibility of further rebellion had faded he was released from prison and given a home, an allowance, and some minor honors at the court in Nineveh (572 B.C.E.). The Judean nobility were treated as befitted captives of their rank. Judean artisans and craftsmen were utilized on Nebuchadnezzar's great building projects in the capital, including the famous Hanging Gardens. Forced labor was required of them, but there is no indication that they were reduced to slavery.

Defeat, Dispersion, and Exile

Much of the captives' time was spent on the business of settling in and making out. Some Jews became farmers, while others engaged in the crafts and in commerce. Ezekiel was free to move about, hold religious meetings, and join the deliberations of a council of elders (Ezek. 14:1; 20:1). Yet, despite the unexpected cultural and commercial opportunities of the captivity, the pious never forgot that Babylon was Babylon and home was home—and they overcame their anxieties by turning their dreams into song:

> By the rivers of Babylon,
>   there we sat,
>   sat and wept,
>   as we thought of Zion.
> There on the poplars
>   we hung up our harps,
>   for our captors asked us there for songs,
>   our tormentors, for amusement,
>   "Sing us one of the songs of Zion."
> How can we sing a song of the Lord
>   on an alien soil?
> If I forget you, Jerusalem,
>   let my right hand wither,
>   let my tongue stick to my palate
>   if I cease to think of you,
>   if I do not keep Jerusalem in memory
>   even at my happiest hour.
>
> (Ps. 137:1–6)

Babylonian captivity was unlike the earlier Egyptian experience. The people were not reduced to slavery, and they retained their sense of cohesion as a community. Out of Babylon came princes and craftsmen, as well as some of the most brilliant prophetic statements of the biblical tradition and a cultic inventiveness which helped to lay the foundations of postbiblical Judaism.

One answer to the many questions posed by the exiles, all of which touched the general theme, "Was God fair to us?," exalted God almost to complete transcendence in order to emphasize that no man can understand or judge His ways. Ezekiel is the prophet of that divine distance. God is *Kavod*, a brilliant, nonhuman glory. Man is the "son of man," or "mere mortal, frail human," not at all like God. No one, least of all Israel, has any claim on God. Israel is a foundling, brought up by God, taken to wife, and unfaithful from the very start (Ezek. 16:1 ff.). Israel is a vine which God planted and tended with care, and which then grew into a weed, useless and wild (15:1 ff.). What God has done, He has done with cause. Again and again God gave Israel another chance. But the nation proved contumacious and continued to sin; indeed, it continues to sin even now.

In reference to God Ezekiel makes much of the term *Kinah*, which suggests divine passion, zeal, and jealousy. God plays for keeps. He is zealous to make His incomparable nature and position clear (8:5), a zeal which leads Him not to remit Judah's sentence (5:13). Genteel readers who prefer to consider God only in the most loving terms are put off by Ezekiel's habit of naming God as zealous and impassioned, or relating the bitter length of the Exile to God's jealousy/zeal to punish the deserving. But the Exile was not gentle, and it was because so many had for so long conceived of God as Father and Protector and not as the zealous/impassioned Lord who demands righteousness that the Exile had been deserved. Moreover, God's jealousy/zeal is not that of a fanatic, but of God, and He will be just as zealous to save as to punish. God's attribute of zeal actually encouraged the exiles: "Now I will restore the fortunes of Jacob and show my affection for all Israel and I will be jealous for my Holy name" (39:25).

The Temple has fallen. The glory of God which had dwelt in the Temple departs for points east (11:22). Was this a protest by an exiled priest-prophet against any attempt to hold unauthorized sacrifice on the old Temple site? Or was this a suggestion that God's presence is now in the Exile and that a Temple-like service in Babylon would be acceptable? The former explanation is the more likely. The exiles seem not to have built a sacrificial altar. The institutional form they developed for their worship cannot be reconstructed. Some say the synagogue had its origins in this exilic community. We can only conjecture. Certainly Jews met. Perhaps they read from Torah scrolls. No doubt they maintained a religious calendar, particularly the Sabbath. But in their hearts they continued to feel that the way of salvation lay through Temple rites. The climax of Ezekiel's message is not his vision of the glory of God flying eastward, but his description of the sanctuary which will be rebuilt on the Temple mount. *Galut* was always a conditional situation for the faith, if not always for the faithful.

Ezekiel spoke words designed to sustain hope. God is a shepherd seeking out the lost sheep (34:11 ff.). In an extended vision, God made Ezekiel see a valley whose floor was littered with dried bones, "and they were very dry." God asked him, "Can these bones live again?" The prophet turned the question. "You alone know" (37:4). God ordered him to prophesy to the bones, in other words, to Israel: "I will put breath into you and you shall live" (37:5). "I will restore you to the land of Israel" (37:13). Words and image promise national renewal. Later Jews, believing what Ezekiel had not believed, in the reality of physical resurrection, read this vision as a promise of rebirth. Freighted with this double meaning, the image of a valley of dry bones which come to life passed over into the *midrash* and into Jewish iconography. A central panel in the third-century C.E. frescoes of the Syrian synagogue of Dura-Europos presents this vision, obviously relating it to the daily liturgy which blessed the God who renews the life of the dead.

Ezekiel's vision of the return is replete with miracles. God will make a covenant of peace with Israel so that even the wild beasts will no longer disturb the land and it will enjoy everlasting tranquillity (34:25). God will purge the people of their uncleanness and the land of its idols. There will be a clean start. "I will take the heart of stone from your body and give you a heart of flesh" (36:26). God will put His spirit in the new man, who will be filled with loathing for the weaknesses of the past (36:27–32). In humanist terms, this might be read: remorse is the high road to repentance and repentance is the essential act of personal and national renewal. But Ezekiel was not a humanist and he spoke of a transforming divine act, not of an ordinary program of self-discipline.

What will cause God to offer Israel this new covenant of peace? Have Israel's sufferings atoned for her past? Will Israel again become a people worthy of God's favor? Ezekiel suggests that it makes little difference what Israel does, since God acts for His own purposes: "It is not for your sake that I act" (36:22). Just as the Exodus had made God's power to save clear to the children of Israel, so now the return would make His power clear to all men. They will see, be awed, and be moved to obey God's law of righteousness. "I will hallow My great name . . . the nations will know that I am the Lord" (36:23–24).

Ezekiel did not jettison the familiar covenant idiom. Indeed, his words insisted on individual moral responsibility under the covenant. God rhetorically asks the meaning of an old proverb: "The fathers have eaten sour grapes, and the children's teeth are set on edge" (18:1), and goes on to say that this maxim no longer applies.

Man will not perish for any but his own sin (18:3). Each man, and he alone, is responsible for his conduct (18:5). Some had complained that God is cruel, punishing men for sins they had not themselves committed. That is not so. "Why would you die, you men of Israel, I have no desire for any man's death" (18:32). Ezekiel had no patience with the idea of cumulative guilt as an explanation of the severity of Judah's sentence. "I will judge every man of you on his deeds" (18:30). How shall men avoid death? "Get yourselves a new heart and a new spirit" (18:31).

For the exiles, this sense of being out from under the burden of inherited guilt must have come as a welcome relief. Later, when belief in retribution beyond the grave became the dominant hope, such passages in Ezekiel were understood to promise each man, woman, or child his special reward, if not in this life, in the next. If a man be just, "and does what is just and right . . . if he conforms to My statutes and loyally observes My laws, he is a *tzaddik* [a just man], he shall live" (18:5–9). The *tzaddik* could expect life eternal, and what had been a simple description, "the *tzaddik* lives faithfully," becomes a promise, "the *tzaddik* will live because of his faithfulness."

Ezekiel also helped the tradition break through earlier thought patterns which had equated kings and the wealthy upper classes with the entire nation. In the Deuteronomic histories the whole nation had been judged by the king's actions. In Ezekiel God no longer speaks of punishing the entire nation for its leaders' sins, but of weeding out the sinner from the midst of the people (14:9). True, a small minority of righteous men cannot save the nation when the majority deserve punishment, but such men will at least save their own souls (14:12–14).

Following this line of reasoning, Ezekiel tied individual retribution to individual repentance. Repentance is not yet a defined regimen. The word *teshuvah*, repentance, occurs as a noun only in postbiblical literature, but the verbal form familiar to Ezekiel implies a turning from evil, a turning to God, a reorientation of goals and priorities. Repentance has about it an element of self-redemption, the achievement of which begins with turning. Another exilic prophet put it this way: "Let the wicked give up his ways, the sinful man his plans; Let him turn back to the Lord, and He will pardon him; To our God, for He freely forgives" (Isa. 55:7). Ezekiel said simply: "It may be that a wicked man gives up his sinful ways and keeps all my laws, doing what is just and right. That man shall live; he shall not die.

Defeat, Dispersion, and Exile

. . . Have I any desire, says the Lord God, for the death of a wicked man? Would I not rather that he should mend his ways and live" (Ezek. 18:21–23). There is a straight way, there is a bent way, and there is the possibility of turning back from one's wanderings to the highway. If God's righteousness is the focus of pre-exilic thought, man's repentance can be said to be the focus of post-exilic teaching. The Day of Atonement becomes post-exilic Judaism's special and most sacred day.

❧⟨⟩☙

About two decades after the Exile began, shortly before the sweeping victories of the Persians over the neo-Babylonian empire, an anonymous prophet spoke the word of God to the exiled Judeans. His words were recorded without attribution, and he has been called Deutero-Isaiah, the second Isaiah, since his words were stitched to the end of Isaiah's scroll. He brought words of good tidings. Babylon will swiftly be punished. Cyrus, the Persian, is the rod of God's vengeance. God will open Babylon's gates to Cyrus (Isa. 45:1) and set him on the imperial throne so that he can issue orders which will insure the rebuilding of the Temple (44:28). God has decreed the return of the Judeans to their home in a Judah which is destined to be a model state alight with the teachings of God, and therefore a compelling example to the nations who will be moved to acknowledge Him. Deutero-Isaiah is the first publicist of *aliyah*. He portrays a safe and easy passage to Judah (40:3–5), and a miraculous renewal of the land (49:22–23). Those who are too comfortable to leave the Exile are alternately badgered and encouraged (52:11–12).

Israel had paid her debt to God, indeed, paid it off doubly (40:2). The past is canceled. God has announced good for Zion and Jerusalem (40:9). In Deutero-Isaiah God is no longer the stern hanging judge but a tender, watchful shepherd who feeds His flock, leads them gently, and cradles the young tenderly in His bosom (4:11).

What assurance is there that God has the power to put Cyrus on the throne and carry out this promise? Deutero-Isaiah insists on God's omnipotence. There are simply no other gods. Deutero-Isaiah engages in a polemic against all forms and manifestations of idolatry. Idols are simply manufactured objects. "If they cry out to it, it does not answer: It cannot save them from their distress" (46:7). God is sharply distinguished from such "gods": "There is no one like Me" (46:9). Idols are helpless; God controls the course of history. God shows His power by revealing those things which have not yet occurred (46:10). The future promise includes not only a triumphant return to Zion (46:13), but the acknowledgment by all nations of God's authority and discipline (42:6–11).

If men want proof of God's power, let them notice the fall of Babylon which the prophets had predicted in God's name. "I am the Lord, that is My name; I will not yield My glory to another, nor My renown to idols. See, the things once predicted have come, and now I foretell new things, announce to you ere they sprout up" (42:8–9). He had revealed all, therefore one can only assume that He caused all to happen. "Long ago I foretold things that happened, from My mouth they issued, and I announced them; suddenly I acted, and they came to pass" (48:3). He had revealed all, therefore those to whom such revelations had been made must appear as His witnesses (43:10–12). Witness has a precise legal implication. God challenges the nations to bring creditable witnesses who might substantiate the claim that their gods or seers ever announced something that eventually happened (43:9). God has; Israel is His witness. Israel can report what the prophets had foretold. Until now the children of Israel have had the single responsibility of serving God obediently. Israel now has a new role. Israel shall witness to the truth of God's prophecies, offering not only verbal confirmation, but the testimony of faithful lives. Israel "shall teach the true way to the nations" (42:1).

Few sections of the Bible exalt God with such powerful imagery or are so full of the promises men delight to hear, but the modern popularity of Deutero-Isaiah rests less on what Deutero-Isaiah said than on what men thought he said. Nineteenth-century Jews, seeking to give meaning to their assimilated existence, developed a concept which they labeled the Mission of Israel, for which they claimed a scriptural warrant in Deutero-Isaiah (42:5–43:11). Israel is to be a "light to the nations" (42:6), and the light that Israel is to bring is the light of social justice, "Opening eyes deprived of light, rescuing prisoners from confinement, from the dungeon those who sit in darkness" (42:7). Such ideas were compelling in the era of liberal reform and many found deliverance through them. But the intention of this exilic prophet was not the same as that of such nineteenth-century reformers. The mission idea as developed by Diaspora Jews was to go out into the cities and fight for child labor laws and every man's civil rights. It was used to justify the continuation of the Diaspora, sometimes even seeming to justify attacks on Zionism: How could Jews residing in a tiny Levantine state be the reformers of Europe? But Deutero-Isaiah had prophesied the return to Zion, an ingathering of the exiles (43:6). Israel, not the Diaspora, is the place where God's people will set the example others will see and copy. Nation building, not social crusading, was his frame of reference.

Some Christians have read the so-called suffering servant portions in Deutero-Isaiah (Isa. 50:4–11; 52:12–53:12), as a prefigurement of Jesus or, at the very least, as foreshadowing his role as a man of sorrows who redeems others through vicarious suffering. In such a view suffering ceases to present a theological problem (Is my suffering merited?) and is transformed into a blessing, the mark of saintliness, a supreme justification for one's life. What had Deutero-Isaiah intended? Actually, these two psalms probably represent interpolations not original to Deutero-Isaiah. They are unique in spirit and cannot be assimilated to his other preachings. That Israel is God's servant is a familiar image, but Israel as a suffering servant whose pain vicariously atones for society's sins is a unique doctrine found only here. Yet, whether by Deutero-Isaiah or not, these speeches are the words of some prophet. What do they mean? In Isaiah 50:4–11 Israel, the nation, is obviously the suffering servant; the image is of a people who suffer in silence, walk humbly yet fearlessly, and hold their ground till righteousness triumphs. It would appear to be a flattering self-portrait by one of the exiles of himself and his community, an encouraging picture of a people who acted with steady courage.

The second poem is a eulogy. There was a man whom the mob beat up and scarred, this man had been something of a pariah, "shunned by men, a man of suffering, familiar with disease" (53:3). "Our suffering he endured . . . he was wounded because of our transgressions, crushed because of our iniquities" (53:5). So far we have a text full of eulogistic hyperbole; but the lament continues: "He bore the chastisement that made us whole, and by his bruises we were healed" (53:5). Obviously this man suffered vicariously. Sin has ceased to be simply human failing and has become a palpable thing, a definable and transferable object.

The images in chapter 53 of Isaiah seem to provide a mythic description of the emotional state of the exiles. They had borne the agonies and suffered the consequences of the sins of earlier generations and consoled themselves that their punishment hastened the time when Israel's account with God would be squared and the return to the homeland might begin. The text is difficult and its role in Western thought far outweighs its literary merit.

Exilic and post-exilic faith slowly lets go of the naturalism of earlier theologies. A Jewish myth is in the making, neither an animistic myth personifying natural phenomena nor a fertility myth, but one dramatizing the struggle within man to be obedient to God's law. Sin is not only an act but a taint, a burden. Atonement is not simply a promise to change one's ways and return to God, but a removal of stain, an unburdening.

This objectification of sin is nowhere better seen than in the post-exilic rite of the Azazel, the scapegoat, on whom the High Priest on the Day of Atonement, following a prescribed ritual, carefully placed the sins of the entire community. The goat was then led out of Jerusalem and dashed from a wilderness cliff, and the community knew itself to be unburdened, cleansed, able to start afresh.

In Deutero-Isaiah, as in Ezekiel, we find language which tends to objectify religious processes. Righteousness is not simply a life of obedience but rather its consequence—acquired merit. A man can pass on righteousness to his children, and no legacy is more precious. How could a generation of no special merit expect God's favors? Fortunately they have inherited what later generations would call "the merits of the fathers" (T. B. Kid. 76b passim). Sin is a burden that can be put on the back of a scapegoat. God places righteousness and sin on the scale of justice and measures a man's worth.

The words of the exilic prophets deal with consolation and deliverance. They dwell on God's mercy and look forward to national repatriation. Deutero-Isaiah is the first Zionist, and his and Ezekiel's texts were regularly read by those who dreamed of the rebuilding of the Holy City and the Holy Temple. There is a new emphasis on the significance of Temple and of Temple ritual, quite different from what other prophets have said on the subject. The way of redemption now requires obedience to covenant law, involvement in a holy community, and participation in the community's redemptive rites. This world is burdened by sin. To be redeemed it needs not only the covenant that defines, but also the altar that atones.

ఇ X ॐ

From the Exile
to Alexander

WHEN Cyrus' successor, Cambyses (537–521), conquered Egypt, all Judeans found themselves subjects of a single imperial power. Some time later the author of the scroll of Esther wrote a fictional history of a remarkable deliverance of the Jews of this vast empire in which he suggested correctly that a decree of extermination issued by a Persian king had the power to eliminate every living Jew. Jewry's dependence on the good will of a single ruler lasted some two hundred years, until Alexander the Great's instant empire proved unstable, unable to preserve its unity through the struggles for succession (322 B.C.E.). Ever since, at least a minority of the Jewish people has lived beyond the reach of even the most extended authority. Widespread dispersion has been a major factor in Jewish survival; no political decree or attack could kill all. But dispersion implied minority status and subordination to another's sovereignty and whim; the Esther story, though fiction, would be read by many a beleaguered Jewish community as a prototypical episode illustrating *galut*, Jewry's apparently unceasing political vulnerability.

Esther bears the stamp of Oriental fiction, although it can also be seen as Israel's first attempt at secular history. It is full of colorful court pageantry, beautiful and wise maidens, crafty intrigue, and ends with an "in the nick of time" deliverance. Esther is neither significant nor profound; the tale reflects a courtier's world that cared much for status and survival, and little for the ideas to which the Jewish community is presumedly loyal. The name of God is not invoked. There is no indication that Mordecai and Esther regulated their lives by Torah law. Esther ate the palace food and Mordecai encouraged her to marry out of the faith. The death sentence is not related to national guilt nor is Ahasuerus' sudden change of mind related in any way to the community's repentance. Mordecai, Esther, and what can only be called good luck are the agents of deliverance. Israel is saved. Nowhere is it explicitly said "God saved."

The villain of the piece, Haman, is introduced as a descendant of Amalek, leader of a nation which had ambushed the tribes of Israel during the wilderness trek (Ex. 17:16). The Exodus story details how Amalek suddenly and without provocation attacked the tribes of Israel as they made their way toward the Promised Land. (For all its covenant talk, even the Torah does not systematically relate every facet of Israel's history to Israel's faithfulness to the covenant. From time to time an Amalek simply appeared.) For his own reasons, "Amalek came and fought with Israel" (Ex. 17:8). Haman had willed Israel's destruction out of pure spite and cupidity. In Jewish thought Amalek-Haman became code names for the spiteful enemy. Judaism recognized the existence of undeserved suffering. "For see, they lie in wait for me; Fierce men are stirred up against me for no offense of mine, O Lord; For no guilt of mine do they rush to array themselves against me" (Ps. 59:4–5). But the grip of covenant teaching on people's minds was never fully dissolved. Even after the Nazi Holocaust there were still Jews who beat their breasts and confessed: "We were guilty of falling away from the traditions of our fathers. God is just." It is a mark of the tough moral core of Israel's faith that radical evil personified in Satan was kept in the shadows, while God, His law, and His promise occupy the spotlight. Satan remains somehow under God's authority. But deep in the psyche of the Jew, the caution "Remember Amalek" reverberated as an emotional counterpart to the confidence "God is truly good to Israel" (Ps. 73:1). After World War II, when a motto was chosen for the stone facade of the Paris memorial to the six million victims of the Nazi Holocaust, it bore the stern warning: "Remember Amalek" (Deut. 25:17).

Persian rule was generally bearable and even at times auspicious for the Judeans. Jews served loyally in the Persian armies. Some of the records of a company of Jewish mercenaries who served the Persian authorities on the island of Elephantine near Assouan in the upper Nile have survived; they indicate that these troops remained loyal to their paymasters throughout the usual quota of local plots and intrigues. Esther suggests that individual Jews had access to the imperial court. The recently discovered business logs of the house of Murashu, a successful Judean merchant clan in Babylon, indicate that by the end of the fifth century some of the exiles had achieved prominence in that commercial world.

When they first came to power the Persians enhanced the peace of their new empire by allowing groups whom the Babylonians had uprooted and resettled to return to their ancestral homes. Since the Judeans were to be included, they took Cyrus' policy as proof of God's power to save, and some were encouraged in the hope that the Temple would soon be reestablished. The oracle read: "Of Cyrus: 'He is My shepherd; He shall fulfill all My purposes.' He shall say to Jerusalem: 'She shall be rebuilt;' and to the Temple: 'You shall be founded again' " (Isa. 44:28). The plan set in motion in 536 B.C.E. was not to recreate an independent Judean state, which the Persians would not have tolerated, but only to establish a national cult center. Despite the oracle and their memories, perhaps because of the modesty of the plans, few Judahites took part in this first opportunity to go home; and the Davidite prince, Sheshbazzar, who led the returnees was not able to bring the project off successfully. He was shortly followed to Judah by an ambitious nephew, Zerubbabel, who, encouraged by fresh messianic oracles spoken by the prophets Haggai and Zechariah (Hag. 2:27, 28), set out not only to reopen the Temple but also to become sovereign in Jerusalem. He was quickly removed by the Persian governor who took effective steps to prevent any further display of Judahite royal ambitions. The house of David disappears as a fact of life, and whatever actual power existed now passed to a priestly hierarchy headed by a High Priest, Joshua ben Jehozadok. In 516 B.C.E. this priest group completed a modest Temple, the core of the sanctuary which was to be the spiritual focus of Jewish life over the next six centuries. "I have come back to Jerusalem with compassion" (Zech. 1:16). Judah gradually became a hierocracy. Priests of Joshua's clan, the family of Zadok, reigned as High Priests and as pliant puppets, cautiously managing the ensuing difficult years and so surviving and slowly extending their power.

When the opportunity of return was granted to the exiles in Babylon, only a few went up, while most stayed. Despite the central importance assigned to the theme of return in biblical theology, there is little reproof spoken of the stay-behinds. No post-exilic prophet brought words condemning them. Indeed, the Jews who returned maintained a warmer relationship with those who stayed in Babylon than with those who had not been carted off and who greeted them coldly on their return home. Access to the imperial court by core-ligionists was of cardinal importance to Jerusalem's security. No one pressed for the emptying out of the Diaspora; the prevailing attitude is best described as spiritual Zionism. Everyone supported the Temple; a head tax for this purpose was collected in every Diaspora community (Neh.11:34), and Temple rites were accepted as efficacious for all Jews. Everyone benefited from the Temple's redemptive ritual, those who participated actively, those who participated vicariously through the recitation of psalms and the celebration of holidays in ways that paralleled Temple worship, and those who simply sent free will offerings and the head tax.

Spiritual authority returned to Jerusalem, while political power remained in the east. Leaders received their mandate from the Persian court. In the fifth century Nehemiah, a layman from the exile community, assumed command in Jerusalem on the authority of "the King's letter" (Neh. 1:9). Imperial authority enabled Nehemiah to build the walls of Jerusalem and make fundamental law; thus he abrogated the ancient rule that creditors could claim as bondsmen the children of defaulting debtors. A short time later a scribe Ezra (ca. 430 B.C.E.), on the basis of a mandate from Artaxerxes' court, promulgated the "book of the Torah" as a national covenant. No Jerusalem-based High Priest could contest the imperial mandate brought by Nehemiah or Ezra, but neither was succeeded by sons or relatives, and at their death domestic authority reverted to the priests. The Persian citadel overlooked and dominated, both architecturally and politically, the Temple compound. The law went out from Jerusalem provided it had Persian agreement.

A later rabbinic saying underscores the importance of the Diaspora for the religious vitality of Israel: In ancient days when Torah was forgotten in Israel, Ezra came up from Babylon and reestablished it; when the Torah again was forgotten in Israel, Hillel came up from Babylon and reestablished it.[1] The impetus to rebuild and beautify the Temple came from Babylon, not from Jerusalem. The exiles of Babylon provided the prophets (Haggai, Zechariah), the leaders (Sheshbazzar, Zerubbabel, Joshua the High Priest, and later Ezra and Nehemiah), the money, and the political support (Ez. 8:28). Local Judeans provided the noisy opposition.

What did the Temple mean to the Diaspora? The Temple was the focus of ritual and the place where atonement was made possible for all Israel. The daily burnt offering, the *tamid*, was seen as the daily and necessary reaffirmation of the covenant and as an act of gratitude for God's special concern for this people. Life was difficult, and men stumbled, sinned, and sent free will gifts as tangible evidence of their contrition and their determination to repair the covenant relationship. God's redemptive power had returned to the Temple, but for those in the Diaspora distance precluded routine attendance, and sometimes even a once in a lifetime visit. For many in the Diaspora a single pilgrimage became the climax of a life of devotion. Psalmists portrayed the indescribable joy of those who have overcome the hazards of the road and rejoice to behold God in Zion (Ps. 84). A head tax paid by all Jews made it possible for everyone to be "near God" and to benefit from the sacrificial worship. The Temple cult kept alive the promise of national redemption. When the second-century B.C.E. Jerusalemite teacher Ben Sira described Temple worship, he used language heavy with redemptive overtones. God "gathers the outcasts of Israel"; "causes a horn to flourish for the house of David"; "casts His fear upon all nations"; "fills Zion with majesty"; is "Shield of Abraham," "Guardian of Israel," and "Redeemer of Israel." [2] Here were concentrated all the nation's hopes. In God's sanctuary the Jew had a glimpse of the grandeur of life for him and for his people in a fully redeemed world.

Ezekiel's precise architectural and ceremonial blueprint of the Temple-to-be (Ezek. 40–48) suggests that he, at least, saw the Temple as an exact microcosm of the heavenly court, and worship there as an earthly mime of man's appearance before God. The movements of priests and worshippers were patterned after the etiquette of the imperial court; what better model of the proper way of approaching royalty—in this case, the King of kings. The Temple was figuratively and literally God's court, and as with an earthly court, a place where tribute was offered, allegiance pledged, petitions tendered, and justice sought.

❧⚓❧

Before we detail the religious ideals of the age, its history should be reviewed. Persia was more important to the Jews than were the Jews to Persia. The Judeans represented a minor millet community and are rarely referred to in the royal archives. The three-quarters of a century that elapsed from the establishment of the Second Temple to the time of Nehemiah (ca. 445–433 B.C.E.) and Ezra (ca. 430 B.C.E.) is for us still so largely a blank that the dates of these two leaders remain uncertain, although the nature of their accomplishment is clear. Nehemiah was a vigorous and dominating man, a political genius. He came west armed with a mandate which established Judea as a separate district within the large Persian province "Beyond the River." He found Jerusalem an unwalled, indefensible city surrounded by smaller agricultural settlements whose citizens fought the elements and their neighbors with equal desperation. His programs sought to give the community self-confidence and a sense of unity. Nehemiah rebuilt Jerusalem by drafting many of the rural folk into an urban work force. He enclosed Jerusalem within a wall, closed the wall with gates, and appointed officers and guards. These acts, together with Judea's new status as a provincial capital, gave the Jerusalemites a modicum of independence, identity, and cohesion.

Ezra was a different kind of leader. Whereas Nehemiah had been escorted by royal cavalry, Ezra came without retinue. Ezra was a scholar-priest, a charismatic figure who lived by the old faith and by his actions witnessed to the God who controls the destiny of men and protects His faithful. Ezra came without military escort because he wanted to show the world the measure of God's protective power (Ez. 8:21–23). Nehemiah had entered Jerusalem with pomp and authority. Ezra entered quietly and went directly to the Temple to offer prayers and sacrifice. A few days later he appeared in one of the plazas, wailing, dressed in sackcloth, pulling at his hair, and carrying out familiar rites of mourning. Suddenly he sat down and through the long day spoke not another word. Naturally, people gathered. That evening Ezra recited a long prayer of confession. He spoke not for God but to God. Ezra was not a prophet-messenger, but the first inspired teacher of the Torah text. He confessed Israel's past guilt and acknowledged that the nation had deserved the pain of the Exile (9:7). Fortunately, God has granted the nation favor in the eyes of the Persian king, who has allowed the Temple to be reestablished (9:9–10). But there is danger that we may miss our opportunity. Even now this land is polluted by our sins (9:11); only God's forgiving nature has delayed our punishment (8:14–15).

Ezra confessed one particular national sin. Against God's will many Judeans had taken wives from "the peoples of the land." In denouncing these marriages, Ezra went beyond the letter of the law.

Torah law prohibited intermarriage specifically with women from the Canaanite nations (Deut. 7:3). For some time there had been no Hittites, Girgashites, Amorites, Canaanites, Perizzites, Hivites, and Jebusites, but when God's work was to be done Ezra was not a strict constructionist. He had other overriding concerns, though we can only conjecture about their nature. His actions had something to do with "blood." In the Babylonian Exile questions of genealogy had assumed new importance. The editor of the post-exilic history we call Chronicles expends much ingenuity in tracing the family trees of the priest leaders and Levitical hierarchy so that they reached back to Aaron or David. Blood lines were matters of great moment to the Persians; the emperor could have many concubines, but he had to take his wife from one of the seven great families and his heir could come only from such a wife. Ezra may simply have brought to Judah a prohibition against exogamous marriages which had developed among Babylonian Jews where it would have served as a defense against cultural and religious assimilation.

Ezra may also have been moved by simple contempt: these men had not married for love, but rather had married women who brought with their dowry the lands which their grandfathers had appropriated at the time of the Exile. Possibly Ezra was concerned with the lax religious habits of locals unfamiliar with the elaborate rules of purity and diet which the Judean priests had brought back from a Diaspora in which ritualism had flourished. Whatever his reasons, Ezra succeeded in his purpose. The foreign wives were divorced, and the readiness of his audience to divorce their wives indicates not only reverence for God, respect for God's law, and fear of His wrath, but recognition of self-interest. The returnees saw the advantages of unquestioned Judean control of the sanctuary, tolls, and pilgrimage business. There was no need to take in a large motley of in-laws.

The issues of blood and birth led at this or a slightly later time to a separation from the Samaritans, who claimed to be descendants of those Israelites not exiled to Assyria in 722 B.C.E. Judean records identified them as descendants of various non-Israelite peoples with whom Nebuchadnezzar had repopulated the land after 586 B.C.E. Probably the Samaritans came of several stocks. They had wanted to participate in the rebuilding of the Temple, but had been spurned (Neh. 6). Shortly after Ezra arrived, their chief's son-in-law, a priest resident in Jerusalem, was expelled. He seems to have fallen out with the local establishment over some ritual discipline. This quarrel lingered and grew into a many-sided religious competition which would last down the long centuries.

The priestly genealogies, the Ezranic legislation, and the Samaritan ostracism brought Judean thinking as close to a racial doctrine as Jewish thought would ever get. Many have read Ezra's order that the Judeans divest themselves of their non-Judean wives as proof that God condemned marriage with anyone not born a Jew. Perhaps Ezra believed it to be so, although his action was in the nature of a limited emergency procedure. But such attitudes had to compete with another and apparently older tradition of openness which remained active even in this parochial and lineage-conscious century. The book of Ruth was either written at this period or gained new prominence now with its message that a daughter of a perennial enemy, Moab, can be of such heroic stuff as to make her worthy of being an ancestress of King David. No aspersions were cast at Esther for marrying a heathen king, nor were the biographies of Moses, Joseph, David, or Solomon altered to eliminate reference to their foreign wives. There was growing interest in proselytism. A large part of the remarkable population growth of the next centuries must have been due to conversions. Concerns of blood and lineage seem to have centered on the legitimacy of various priestly families. Family purity is deemed a category of holiness necessary to their special role and, by extension, an appropriate concern of all Judeans in Jerusalem who felt that closeness and involvement in the shrine gave them a quasi-priestly status. But the heart of a nation can be both open and closed. A half millennium later tannaitic literature indicates that this priestly preoccupation with blood lines continued throughout the very period when the Pharisees were crossing the seas to make converts.

Sometime after the dismissal of the wives, Ezra built a pulpit in the central plaza and assembled the community. For six hours he read out the law of God from a "scroll of the Torah." Aides interpreted his words to the people. At the end of this marathon reading the leaders set their seals to the covenant and the people vowed to obey it. The covenant was deemed ratified (Neh. 10). This is the last reported covenant-making ceremony. There was now a written and rather extensive basic law and, more important, this law was in the possession of the people and imposed on religious leadership the duty to make the people know and understand it. Ezra, the *sofer*, set a personal example of the new role of the religious leader as expositor. The fall thanksgiving holiday, Sukkot, happened to be the first holy day after the covenant reading. Just before that Sukkot, Ezra rose again and read to the people the rules of the festival, to make sure that it was properly observed; this practice of reading the rules of each holiday has continued to this day. The law was an open book. The law imposed a teaching responsibility on religious leaders, and indeed on every man (Deut. 6:7). It would take centuries and much conflict, but the thrust of Jewish life was becoming clear: no caste would be allowed to make the law their private domain and the basis of extraordinary privileges.

A calendar and a specific regimen of Jewish life were set forth in this scroll. Ideas will be reshaped and practices modified, but the idiom and distinctive terms of the constitutive history and law have been set. The Torah becomes the nation's written constitution, and now the voice of God ceases to bring "words" to the land. Later rabbinic tradition dated the cessation of prophecy to the missions of Haggai, Zechariah, and Malachi. The gates of revelation were closed by God Himself in order to protect His word from those who bring false words. It became time to explore what was already known. However, the boundaries that had been drawn were not quite so final as they seem. God's voice was never completely silent. Throughout rabbinic and medieval times men reported hearing a *bat kol*, a divine voice. Minor legal innovations were based on its advice, but the age of revelation had given way to an age of interpretation. Later Judaism would grow through elaboration.

At this great covenant ceremony Ezra read a collection of laws, perhaps part of that collection now called the Priestly Code. The Priestly Code is really not one codex, but several collections of *torot*, drawn together in post-exilic times, which exhibit a special interest in the Temple cult and sacrifices. The last chapters in Exodus describe the Ark, the Tent of Meeting, and the priesthood. The first seven chapters of Leviticus are cultic and include, according to their own table of contents, "the rituals of the burnt offering, the meal offering, the sin offering, the guilt offering, the offering of ordination and the sacrifice of well being, with which the Lord charged Moses on Mount Sinai, when He commanded that the Israelites present their offerings to the Lord, in the wilderness of Sinai" (Lev. 7:37, 38). Leviticus 11–15 is a separate collection which deals with the categories of cleanliness and uncleanliness as applied to land, animals, illness, garments, and persons. Purity and impurity are treated as states of being with their own independent existence. Cleanliness is achieved through confession, cleansings, deodorants, and sacrifice. Leviticus 17–26, often called the Holiness Code, is a varied list of moral and ritual requirements which define holiness (*kedushah*) that is God's nature and way and hence man's obligation. The altar (19:30), land (25:7), people (19:30), and priests (21:1–15) must be holy because such is God's will and His nature (19:12; 21:6). To us many of these laws seem both bizarre and anachronistic, but we must recognize that nothing sustains the powerless more than the feeling that they are fulfilling the will of God precisely, and hence are close to His power.

Holiness is a state of being achieved by living according to God's law. Holiness is the state of being singled out by God or particularly dear to God. It is an aura and a power. Holiness surrounded the priests who ministered at God's altar, and described the God-prescribed rites which they performed. Holiness is not a category of logic. A moral act is not necessarily a holy act; holiness accrues only to an obligation required by God's word. Holiness includes tithing, offering the first-born, the prohibition against sowing diverse seeds in a single field, and "love your neighbor as yourself" (Lev. 19:18). God had declared the sacrificial cult and various rules of diet and ritual purity to be holy. Men concerned with *kedushah* asked "how," not "why." In obeying the holy law and participating in the holy rites, man becomes holy.

The Priestly Code does not suggest that ritual alone is sufficient for salvation. Sacrifice must be accompanied by confession and prayer. Sacrifice is effective, that is, it achieves atonement for the worshipper's sin, only if that sin has not harmed any person and was committed unintentionally. Premeditated acts cannot be atoned for cultically. Atonement for sins committed against others must be preceded by retribution for damages and reconciliation. The very word, *kapparah* (atonement), which became popular, was derived from a pre-exilic usage denoting payment of damages to a victim who has been gored by another's ox.

The cult was holy. The Temple had been planned by God Himself, who had ordered it established so that the burden of sin might be lifted through the agency of its rites. Sacrifices are offered because sacrifices have always been offered, because they facilitate the execution of what a man had already resolved to do, and because they actually atone. Penitence and penance go hand in hand. Religious duty does not begin or end in the sanctuary, but the operation of the sanctuary is redemptive. The Temple is holy. Jerusalem is holy. God had helped David choose the Jebusite city as Judah's capital and the Temple's site. An oracle required that the holy city be religiously closed—"For the uncircumcised and the unclean shall never enter you again" (Isa. 52:1)—but this rule was never enforced. Unlike Mecca, Jerusalem remained open to all, but a sense of holiness inevitably promotes separation. Inscriptions from the later Greek period have been found, warning non-Jewish visitors to the Temple mount not to proceed beyond certain points.

"Priestly" editors now revised the earliest sagas of the people, emphasizing God's control of history and nature. Creation is God's handiwork. There is no such thing as natural law; God's power sustains every moment of every day and every part of the universe. The opening chapter of the Bible, which is assigned by most scholars to a priestly source, is a paean of praise to God's creative might. Creation is a blessing. Life is not to be feared. Man is different in kind from the animal kingdom, and God intends that he have dominion over the beasts. Nowhere else in ancient literature is the status of man so exalted. He has the likeness of God; history is his attempt to live up to that potential.

Man is created in the likeness of God, but not as God. Even as the post-exilic creation saga raised man above the beast, it insisted on an infinite distance between God and man. God is creator, man is creature. God is omnipotent, man has relatively limited powers. Man is not abject, but neither is he divine. Perfection belongs to God; the possibility of becoming holy belongs to man.

The Sabbath seems to have been more strictly observed in post-exilic than in pre-exilic times. The elements of rest and joy were emphasized, formal rules of rest were adopted, and additional sacrifices were offered in the shrine. The Sabbath bound the exiled and the returned. It was defined as a weekly advertisement of God's power to save (Deut. 5:15). The priestly creation epic based the Sabbath on God's own practice. It came frequently enough and was simple enough in its basic rule, rest, to be a tangible bond. It pleased God—had He not rested at creation? In addition, it pleased one's neighbors. The Persian world had no mandatory day of rest, and such a day must have seemed morally desirable to liberal spirits concerned with the abuse of labor. It bound Jews as one people serving God with one distinctive ritual. Not working on the Sabbath allowed a man to feel himself part of the ebb and flow of divine energy. Outside of Jerusalem groups met, the laws were read, scribes commented and taught, and informal worship was offered.

The Sabbath is seen as a celebration of God's creative power and skills. Creation emphasizes regularity, God's majesty, and the omipresence of God's power. The Sabbath is a symbol of Israel's new understanding of the covenant relationship. The covenant of Sinai, with its blessing and curses, remains, but more is made now of a relationship with God which is unbreakable, as eternal as the cycle of the weeks. The Noah story is sharpened and God's abiding promise no more to destroy mankind is underscored. The unconditional covenant with Abraham sealed simply by circumcision is emphasized (Gen. 17). The Temple is the seat of the God who is the "great, mighty, and awesome God who faithfully keeps the covenant" (Neh. 9:32), and worship in the Temple exalts His redemptive power. A broken and exiled people, now miraculously redeemed, have recast their history to obviate their fears and validate their hopes.

Their view of history can be found in a chronicle edited in Jerusalem shortly before Alexander's epochal conquest. In our texts it has been broken into four books, Chronicles I and II, Ezra, and Nehemiah, each a composite of earlier sources, but each showing the peculiar editorial attitudes of the Judean returnees—particularly in matters of caste, pedigree, and political theory.

These books retell the national tradition from Adam to the Exile in the same general terms as the Deuteronomic histories, and provide our only narrative of post-exilic Judean history down to and including the careers of Nehemiah and Ezra. As one would expect of a late biblical book, these scrolls emphasize that God controls the destiny of men and nations and that *kedushah*, holiness, is a critical religious concern. It is assumed that *avodah* (proper worship) gains God's favor. His presence and His promise are assured by careful management of the holy rites. Worship properly takes place only in the Temple in Jerusalem, where it must be properly managed by accredited priests and Levites, whose genealogies are pure and above suspicion. The altar represents the abiding presence of God in the midst of His people. Sacrifices on the altar are necessary to maintain God's favor, establish communion with Him, and free man and the nation of guilt so that the covenant relationship will not be too heavily strained. So it has been since the days of David except for one sad period, the Exile, when the sin of the nation became too grievous and God broke off His favor, signaling the break by having the altar closed down. The returned nation will be a holy people and God's service will be meticulously observed. God had stipulated precisely how He was to be worshipped—in one place, in one way, in a service organized by one caste. Temple worship was effective for all Israel, even though all obviously could not be present. Judeans who did not return knew that the required worship was being offered and that they, by gifts and kinship, shared in its redemptive power.

The chronicler's theology is a blend of Deuteronomy and various attitudes of the pre-exilic prophets. God is transcendent, yet close, steadfast to His promise under the covenant, an honest yet merciful judge. The justice of God's retributive scheme is underlined with a flair for embellishment which can only be called midrashic. Manasseh had flaunted the laws against idolatrous practices, permitting Assyrian totems to be put up in the sanctuary, yet he had lived long and the country had been relatively prosperous. How shall his fortune be accounted for? The chronicler discovers and describes at some length a sudden change of heart, a dramatic conversion, which led Manasseh to repent of past sins and emerge a forgiven man (II Ch. 33:11 ff.). God determines the fate of all men and nations, yet He has a special love for Israel and safeguards her particularly. All this is familiar. What is new are the emphases which shape this history into what might be called a legal brief justifying the takeover of Jerusalem and the Temple by the Judean returnees.

Among the returnees were members of the royal house, priests, Levites, and laymen, all of whom were accepted into the Jerusalem community; only the indigenous population was held in suspicion. No doubts are suggested about the propriety of monarchy or of rule by the house of David. The chronicler omits all reference to Samuel's hesitations over appointing David. David is praised for capturing Jerusalem, bringing the Ark there, appointing the Levites "to minister before the Ark of the Lord, and to celebrate and to thank and praise the Lord, the God of Israel" (I Ch. 16:4), and for deciding that it was inappropriate for the Ark to remain temporarily housed in a tent while the king dwelt in a palace of cedar (I Ch. 17:1). David's line shall never depart from Judah, even though in the chronicler's era a High Priest rather than a king ruled in Jerusalem. David's legitimacy reinforces the rightness of his decision to bring the Ark to Jerusalem; indeed, God Himself had ordered an angel to indicate the proper place for the future altar. God had designed the Temple's plans and given specific and detailed instructions for the operation of the cult. Pre-exilic Judah had been ruled by rulers and priests selected and anointed by God, and it was precisely these

God-chosen families who had been marched off into exile by Nebuchadnezzar. Rule is theirs by right. Non-Judeans are given the back of the historian's hand. The northern kingdom, Israel, is virtually ignored. There is no mention of the pre-exilic prophecies which foretold a reunion of Israel and Judah in a redeemed Zion. Instead, we find references to Israelites who had come to worship in the reopened Temple, acknowledging by their pilgrimage that Jerusalem was the only fully acceptable place for worship.

The chronicler replaced the undifferentiated category of *am* (people) with *kahal* (congregation), specifically a holy congregation, in which proper care would be taken to watch over purity of cult, purity of caste, and the precise organization of religious life. Jerusalem was not just another city-state, but God's city, lived in by a consecrated citizenry fulfilling the commandment, "You shall be unto Me a kingdom of priests and a holy nation" (Ex. 19:6). Writing for and of a returned community, the chronicler knows deliverance has taken place; he wants to safeguard and establish it. The emphasis is on the form of national life, as if to say: we have been delivered, we are again acceptable to God. We do not want anything to occur which will jeopardize that relationship. There is only one religious center, David's Jerusalem; only one group properly appointed to minister there, the descendants of those whom David had appointed; and only one true Israel, the reconstituted Judean community of Jerusalem.

The chronicler uses a different tone when he discusses the pre-exilic community than when he speaks of those who returned to rebuild Jerusalem. The former had been obdurate and stiff-necked, while the latter are sensitive to their duties. It is as if Jeremiah's new heart and new spirit actually had been implanted in Jerusalemite bodies. When Ezra announces the new rule the people weep, repent, and divest themselves of their unacceptable wives. Jerusalem has been purified. The cult is divinely required, dutifully attended, and provides tangible evidence of God's active presence within the community. Let it be a patient, faithful community, steady in the faith that the larger deliverance will come in His time.

❧

These Persian centuries defy easy summation. Commonly they are dismissed as ecclesiastic and narrow, an era when Judaism concentrated on priestly ritual. Ecclesiasticism there was, but that picture must not be overdrawn. Laymen played a major role. Ezra is more scribe than priest. As far as we know he never ministered. He reads the law in a public square, not in the Temple. Nehemiah was a eunuch, disqualified as a priest; a courtier, cupbearer of the king. No priest appears in the book of Esther.

It is a time of contrasts. There were sensitive priests and scandalous priests. One priest committed fratricide to gain his office. Another may have written;

> As long as I said nothing,
>   my limbs wasted away
>   from my anguished roaring all day long.
> For night and day
>   your hand lay heavy on me;
>   my vigor waned
>   as in the summer drought.
> Then I acknowledged my sin to You;
>   I did not cover up my guilt;
>   I resolved, "I will confess to my transgressions to
>   the Lord,"
>   and You forgave the guilt of my sin.
>
> (Ps. 32:3–5)

Men need ritual, the drama which makes the spiritual promises tangible. But there is always the danger that the ritual will become an end in itself. The ritualist whom tradition calls Malachi utters God's word against indifferent and careless priests (Mal. 1:7) and against those who have performed the rites so often that they have become meaningless business, "a weariness" (1:13). Spirituality and superficiality were then and are still in constant tension.

Both doctrines, the special holiness of the sanctuary and God's universal presence, were emphasized in these times. Ezekiel heard the word of God in Babylon, and saw God's glory (*Kavod*) leaving the Temple for the east and hovering over the exiled communities there. This image certainly could have been used as a rationale for the building of a Diaspora temple—a difficult oracle "of wickedness" in Zechariah suggests that the idea was discussed (Zech. 5:5–10)—but as far as we know none was built by or for the exiled priests. Yet Jewish mercenaries at Elephantine in Egypt did build a temple and offer sacrifices there. To complete the confusion, Elephantine Jews regularly sent annual dues to the Jerusalem shrine, obviously believing that its rites of expiation were somehow effective for them. Finally, the choir which attended the rites in the Temple, rites which depended on the faith that this house was God's place, probably sang with conviction "for His presence (*Kavod*) fills the world" (Ps. 72:19).

The period was dominated by those Judeans who went into the Babylonian Diaspora—that is, the old upper class. Many of them settled comfortably into exile. Others of the same class and background created the burning Zionism of the day. Those who opposed them and argued that God was everywhere, hence that Jewish life could go on anywhere, spoke glorious words which appeal to the modern temper. "Thus said the Lord: The heaven is My throne, and the earth is My footstool: Where could you build a house for Me? What place could serve as My abode?" (Isa. 66:1). But were they better Jews or more sensitive to matters spiritual than the nationalists? Broad piety often cloaks narrow self-interests. Those who said to themselves, "I have a good business in Nippur. I don't want to leave," certainly must have found the more universalistic oracles gratifying. The Zionists appealed to memories of "our holy Temple, our pride" (Isa. 64:10) and to God's will that Jerusalem be the place of His service. In their speech Jerusalem was always "God's holy city." Zechariah lauds Jerusalem as "the City of Truth" and the high place of the Temple as "the Holy Mountain" (Zech. 8:3). Use of the adjective "holy" indicates that God had selected this place and that it was dear to Him. Such men were unaware of any contradiction between the idea that God is King over all the earth (14:9) and that "living water shall issue from Jerusalem" (14:8); both convictions could be spoken confidently by the prophet in a single breath.

Because of their concerns for holiness, men were sensitive, perhaps super-sensitive, to the possibility of falling unwittingly into sin. Purification is the technique, forgiveness is the urgency. The people cannot stand much more exile or survive another similar disaster (Neh. 9:32 ff.). The Temple is the promise of divine relief. The priestly blessing is a bowing of one's head to the touch of the hands which impart relief (Num. 6:24–26).

Yom Kippur, which came into its own late in the Persian period, is the annual Atonement Day during which Israel is relieved of the burden of cumulative guilt. This is the day on which the High Priest, as the embodiment of the nation, makes personal, familial, and national expiation through confession, repentance, and prescribed rite. Though he alone performs the rites, the mood of remorse and affliction of one's soul is enhanced by liturgy whose mood makes it clear that the fate of the whole community is at stake. Wearing penitential white, he enters the Holy of Holies to confess his and the people's sins. A measure of the nation's need is the degree of spiritual tension which surrounded the High Priest's entrance into that holy place. He could approach only once each year. His speech had to be precise and faultless, his performance of the rites flawless. When he entered, he would utter God's ineffable name. This is a time of great danger. The power of God surges about and must be most carefully handled. There is great relief when he emerges safely. Afterwards he sacrifices a goat and lays his hands on the shoulder blades of this scapegoat, transferring to the animal his sins and the sins of the nation. The goat is then led out into the wilderness, bearing an invisible but real burden. One can concentrate on the rite and see in it a primitive personification of sin and a mechanical means of expiation, or one can go within the confession and sense God's numinous presence and the honesty and exaltation of the liturgy. Surely Judeans did confess, and some surely were moved to change the pattern of their lives. Note especially that, despite the angelology of the Persian milieu, the post-exilic cult never addressed angels, gods, or semidivine intermediaries; all worship is God-centered. All prayer is for the hearing of the one, holy, creator, just, concerned, terrible, yet merciful, God.

Holiness involves separation, a priestly state, and the putting away of foreign wives. Yet this is the time when Israel first welcomed proselytes:

As regards the foreigners who attach themselves to the Lord . . . I will bring them to my sacred mount and let them rejoice in My house of prayer. Their burnt offerings and sacrifices shall be welcome on My altar; for My house shall be called a house of prayer for all peoples (Isa. 56:7).

Ezra, who forced the Judeans to put away the local women with whom they had intermarried, specifically permitted the resident alien to take part in the Passover sacrifice (Ez. 6:21). An unknown post-exilic prophet predicts that God will gather "all nations and all tongues" and they "shall come and see My glory" (Isa. 66:18). Holiness separates out, puts up signs which read, "Let none but a Jew enter," but since holiness is of God and God is the One universal Lord, Israel's concern with holiness leads naturally to the vision of a holy world in which all men are united in devotion to God. This community was holy, conscious of being set apart, "a people blessed by the Lord" (Isa. 65:23), yet hopeful of the day when "the wolf and the lamb shall graze together . . . in all My sacred mount nothing evil or vile shall be done" (Isa. 65:23–26).

CHAPTER

❧ XI ❧

The Age of Variety

Between 334 and 322 B.C.E., the Macedonian armies of Alexander the Great overran the Middle East and beyond. Rabbinic tradition suggests that the current High Priest, Simon, left Jerusalem to meet Alexander's advancing forces on the coastal plain, where Alexander bent the knee and acknowledged the power of the one God.[1] In Israel's eyes God is always the King of kings. What was in effect an expedient submission probably saved Jerusalem a siege and marked the beginning of a half millennium during which Jewish life carried on within a Hellenized environment, a powerful and exciting presence which necessarily made for major cultural adjustments.

The history of this age needs to be summarized. Before Alexander's death at thirty-two, all the scattered settlements of the Jewish world came under his rule. But the empire so quickly won was almost as swiftly dismembered as rival Macedonian generals fought for rank and wealth. One family, the Ptolemies, ruled Egypt (and most of Palestine until 198 B.C.E.); another, the Seleucid, ruled Syria and Persia (and Palestine from 198 B.C.E.). The dynasts fought repeatedly with each other but remained self-concious about their Greek roots and patrons of Greek cultural interests, so that, despite their intermittent warring, a unified and definable cultural impact was made on the Middle East. A telling indication of their cultural imperialism can be found in the fact that the last of the independent Ptolemies,

The Age of Variety

Cleopatra, the beloved of Anthony, was the first of her line to trouble to master the native language of Egypt.

Hellenism describes that fusion of Greek forms and Asian folkways and faiths which developed in West Asia after Alexander. The noun derives from *hellenistes*, the designation of a non-Greek speaker of Greek, one to whom Greek speech is not native. At its most common Hellenism was no more than a vague blending of Greek habits and Oriental mysteries; Asian men wearing Greek hats (the *petasos*), Asian youth forming sports clubs to participate in Greek games, a Greek king introducing gladiator sports to his Asian subjects. At its best Hellenism was represented by the great Museum in Alexandria, with its academy of scholars and exhaustive collection of manuscripts (every known book was believed to be represented); by the appearance in many Near Eastern cities of amphitheaters where the plays of major dramatists were presented at civic festivals; and by the equally omnipresent *gymnasium* where the sons of the upper class followed a venerable curriculum which, much like England's public schools, provided its graduates with manners, attitudes, and a special universe of discourse which set them apart from the native and lower classes and qualified them for the city's establishment.

To understand the basic forces at work in this age, it is best to look behind culture to commerce, behind tutors and their teachings to the trader and his wide-ranging commerce. Centuries of seafaring and trading had sharpened the mercantile and banking skills of the Greeks, who were quick to apply their sophisticated financial instruments and institutions in the great Asian markets. In West Asia home industry gave way to the factory. The bazaar with its booths and bargaining was partially replaced by state monopolies and fixed prices. Small-scale farming began to give way to large, more efficiently run estates. The Greek rulers were greedy and rapacious, hence conscious of efficiency, particularly of efficient tax collections. National monopolies of silk, salt, and silverware were carefully managed. Duties were efficiently collected and archaic tolls abolished. Fairs, markets, and international trade were encouraged and protected. Persian, Indian, Turkish, Copt, Syrian, and Greek traders mingled in the streets of Seleuceia or Antioch, where they exchanged ideas as well as goods. Alexander's accession became year one of a new calendar which Jews instinctively called *Minyan Shetarot*, "dating according to contracts." This was a commercial age and commerce enticed men from the soil to the city and from city to city. A Greek word, *kosmopolites*, cosmopolitan, described a new man who felt himself citizen not only of his nation, but of the *oikoumene*, the inhabited (Greek-ruled) world.

Traders require cities for ready markets and manufacturers require cities for an adequate labor pool. The Greeks were inveterate builders of new towns and rebuilders of old cities. This was an urban age. Cities in West Asia began to sport the familiar public buildings of a Greek *polis*, often larger and more monumental than their prototypes in Attica. The Greeks transplanted the *polis* to West Asia, but much of the homogeneity and legal autonomy of that city form was lost in the move. The Greek *polis* had been, or had sought to be, a free city-state. The Asian *polis* accepted its place within an empire. The classic emphasis on the citizen and his voluntary and temporary assumption of office did not displace the Asian tradition of a professional bureaucracy. The Greek *polis* had been organized around custom and tradition. The Hellenistic city was regulated by published codes. In Jerusalem, *soferim*, scribe-scholars of the Torah law, self-styled disciples of Ezra, staffed the bureaus and organized the courts. The Torah was the city's constitution.

West Asia's cities became more populous, prosperous, and politically significant than they had been during any preceding era. Large numbers of craftsmen and workers were needed, and the excitement, wages, and color of the city drew men from the land. Populations and slums swelled as the gap between poverty and privilege widened. There was much obvious injustice, yet rags and poverty failed to stimulate a prophetic cry of outrage among the so-called best citizens. Men accepted class enmity as an inevitable fact of life: "What peace is there between a hyena and a dog? And what peace between a rich man and a poor man? Wild asses in the wilderness are the prey of lions; likewise the poor are pastures for the rich." [2] Hellenistic religious and philosophic traditions encouraged fortitude and resignation rather than social activism. Stoicism was the classic distillation of Hellenistic thought; its hope was to instruct gentlemen how to hold themselves aloof, to remain calm and controlled, come what may. Neither religion nor philosophy moved the privileged classes toward social reform, and the masses were faced with an unprofitable choice between bloody revolt, which might overturn a ruler but could not do away with poverty or class structure, or desperate adherence to some promise of miraculous salvation. This world, particularly its masses, looked for saviors.

The Jewish nation had heretofore been composed largely of farmers, vintners, herdsmen, and craftsmen. Throughout the Persian period Jerusalem had remained a rural hill town ruled by a small priestly elite. In the Persian Diaspora most Judeans were simple folk: laborers, farmers, even soldiers.

Jewish demography now changed radically. The new cities required new settlers and Jews were much sought after for this purpose. Ptolemy I forced sizable drafts of Judeans to settle in his new capital, the Nile port of Alexandria. The Seleucids similarly brought Jews to Antioch. Judean farmers, smiths, and craftsmen made good workers and were likely to be grateful for the opportunity; moreover, as new settlers in an alien land and as a minority dependent upon the good will of the rulers, they were unlikely to be involved in local nationalist uprisings. The Greeks recognized the need for a supportive mercantile class; they proved able and willing teachers, and the Jews were quick learners. First in Alexandria and Antioch, and a century or so later in Jerusalem, a sizable Jewish merchant class emerged. Much of the technical vocabulary of Talmudic commercial law, terms which seem so natural to anyone steeped in the later rabbinic traditions, turns out to have been appropriated during this period: *apotropos*, guardian; *prosbul* (*pros boule*), fiat decree; *pinkas* (*pinakes*), register tablet, and so on.

The traditionally suspicious attitude of an agricultural people toward finance and a money economy began to recede, though it still echoes in the more conservative aphorisms of this age: "As a stake is driven firmly into a fissure between stones, so sin is wedged in between selling and buying." [3] The old prejudice against financial manipulation, the use of money to make money, lingered; we find a sage insisting "blessing rests only on a man's handiwork" [4] and that "gold and silver [finance] take a man out of this world and the world to come." [5] But commerce was a fact of life, and the Torah schools now trained their graduates to draw subtle distinctions between interest (*tarbit*), which they declared permissible, and usury (*neshek*), which is specifically prohibited by the Torah; to handle a complicated law of contracts; and to rationalize an extremely subtle logic which in effect discarded various ancient restrictions on loans and interest so that Jews could participate more easily in the fiscal transactions of this trading society.

The Jewish community seems to have enjoyed, or at least endured, a population explosion both in absolute terms and relative to other groups. Tradition had conditioned the Jews to accept large families as the fulfillment of God's express command: "Be fruitful and multiply" (Gen. 1:28). They continued to do so now, despite the diminished economic value of children. On the farm the child is another useful hand; in the city the child is another mouth to feed. In this urban age Jews saw crude forms of birth control widely practiced—infanticide was common, particularly of girls, who were expensive to raise and more expensive to marry off—and were horrified by such unaccustomed practices. To expose a child was simply murder. Jews kept, raised, even romanticized, their children: "Children's children are the crown of the old men" (Prov. 17:6). A second-century B.C.E. Jerusalem school master knew that "the birth of a daughter is a loss" [6] which made the more praiseworthy "a man rejoicing in his children." [7]

Jewish numbers grew. The Jewish population of Judea at the time of Alexander's conquest may have reached one hundred thousand, and an equal number may have been scattered in the Egyptian and Syrian cities. Four hundred years later, when Augustus became the first Caesar, a million Jews may have lived in greater Palestine, and twice that number in Egypt and Syria. Heretofore Jews and Judaism had been largely unnoticed by the outside world; now numbers brought political significance and visibility. Brief notes about Jews and their customs began to appear in Greek sources, particularly among world travelers like Aristotle's pupil, Clearchus, and Ptolemy I's journalist friend, Hecataeus of Abdera. Longer descriptions soon followed, written by men primarily interested in Judaism as a philosophical sect (Theophrastus, Hermippus), but the most extended treatment of Judaism seems to have been stimulated by those who had some anti-Jewish ax to grind, in itself a sign of growing consciousness of the Jewish presence.

The Jewish communities in Antioch and Alexandria participated in the prosperity of those cities, and soon enjoyed advantages which the natives envied. As the locals recovered their voice, they found it advisable not to attack the imperial power directly but to vent their frustration and jealousy on an alien group whom the alien overlord had introduced and protected. The Jews not only provided unwanted competition but enjoyed special privileges. They were excused from emperor worship, from taxes which supported various civic rites because these were devoted to the city's gods, from attendance at the courts on Sabbath, and from army duty because they would not bear arms on the Sabbath—and such privileges provided ready pegs on which the embittered natives could hang their unhappiness. For the first time in Jewish history a self-conscious apologetic literature emerged to "explain" the practices and peculiarities of Judaism.

The Age of Variety

If the development of commerce and urbanization underlies the changes which Hellenism wrought in West Asia, the displacement of Aramaic as the language of diplomacy, commerce, and culture by Greek, or rather by a post-classic Greek vernacular, *Koine*, was its most obvious aspect. Empires come and empires go, but when an empire succeeds in imposing its language on conquered peoples, its cultural impact is destined to be of lasting significance. In the hamlets and on the farms of the Near East the local dialects remained unchanged. But in the cities, particularly the cities of Syria, Palestine, and Egypt, *Koine* became the everyday speech. *Koine* was the speech of traders and street people, not of Athens' classic philosophers, which is to say that the ability to bargain in Greek is no proof that one thought great Greek thoughts. Almost everyone came to know store Greek and perhaps a few well-worn clichés from the treasury of Greek conventional wisdom, but only a miniscule number of intellectuals actually mastered the Greek philosophic or scientific tradition. Among Jews we can name only two men during this long period of over five centuries, Aristobulus (2nd cent. B.C.E.) and Philo (ca. 25 B.C.E.–40 C.E.), whose writings evidence their full control of the classic curriculum, and both are products of Alexandria, the most Hellenized Jewish community of all.

The Greeks allowed the millet communities of West Asia to organize themselves by their ancient customs. In most places Jews were allowed or obliged to organize themselves as a *politeuma*, a self-governing body with corporate responsibility for taxes and public order, and corresponding corporate rights to organize internal affairs according to custom. Torah law regulated these communities. Commercial issues between Jews and questions of personal status were adjusted before Jewish courts according to accepted traditions. The Jew might wear Greek dress, speak Greek to his business associates, and attend the Greek theater, but he paid his annual tax to the Temple in Jerusalem and regulated his life by the Sabbath and the ancient calendar. There was no deliberate attempt to Hellenize the Jew. Harry A. Wolfson, after studying Philo for many years, concluded that sustained intellectual contact between the Jew and others in Alexandria was as infrequent as such contact would be later, during the Middle Ages. A very few intellectuals knew each other's works, but education was parochial and there was no established forum for open discussion.[8]

Education was privately organized. The Greeks had their *gymnasium*. The Jews had their school houses in which Torah was the central curricular element, but Greek was widely spoken and some in the more affluent classes were tutored, generally by other Jews, in various elements of Hellenistic thought. A poet like Ezekiel of Alexandria used the forms of Greek theater to present a drama on the Exodus, but he chose a biblical theme and wrote for a Jewish audience. The poet Philo Epicus (2nd cent. B.C.E.) wrote *On Jerusalem* in Greek hexameters, and his contemporary Theodotes wrote an epic poem, *On the Jews*. Jews borrowed style rather than theme, form more than philosophy. The Wisdom of Solomon includes some of the commonplaces of Hellenistic thought and a number of Greek philosophic terms and forms of debate, but it was ascribed to Solomon and promotes a thoroughly Jewish wisdom replete with attacks on idolatry and proof of God's frequent discomfiture of Israel's enemies and His steadfast protection of His people.[9]

The Wisdom of Solomon may sound like part of Proverbs, but the editor recognizes that some in his audience no longer accept the sober virtues and respected ways. He had heard more than one sophisticate say: "The passing of a shadow . . . such is our life . . . come then, let us enjoy the good things that exist."[10] The creative incoherence of this world obviously has some parallels to the current situation confronting Jewish life. Both worlds are pluralistic. Freedom and the problems of freedom abound. A pietist complains to some young whippersnapper that his "life is a scandal" and upbraids him about "the error of your life,"[11] while a young radical mocks the pretentious moralisms of his father: "We were born by mere chance," "No one will remember our works," and argues the virtue of running barefoot in a spring meadow, "Let no flowers of the spring pass us by. Let us crown ourselves with rosebuds before they wither."[12] Men argued about who is a Jew, worried about the steadiness and dependability of the young and, as we see in the romantic idyll Tobit, even about intermarriage.

The large Jewish community of Alexandria particularly became the focus of a rich, varied literary activity, much influenced by Greek forms and norms, but with a bite and style of its own. The first harvest of this literature was the Septuagint translation of the Torah, and its richest fruition came in the many works of the preacher-philosopher-apologete, Philo. These are the best, but Alexandria's output was many-sided and includes chronicles by Demetrius, Eupolemus, Artapanus, and Jason of Cyrene, The Wisdom of Solomon, The Letter of Aristeas, commentaries by Aristobulus, and possibly the Third Book of the Maccabees.

Greece influenced speech, dress, architecture, and thought, but was not the only influence abroad. This was an age whose intellectual tides took Greek ideas east and brought into the west Oriental mysteries, Persian angelologies, Iranian astrologic computation, and Zoroastrian ideas of cosmic dualism. Goods and ideas moved in many directions. It is not always possible to determine who borrowed what from whom. The author of Ecclesiastes was intrigued by the fact that history seems to repeat itself: "Is there anything of which one can say, 'Look, this is new?' No, it has already existed, long ago before our time" (Ecc. 1:10). Did he take his image of the recurring cycles of nature from popular Stoic teaching or from Indian legends which also describe life as flowing in vast recurring cycles? The idea of the immortality of the individual soul became popular in various Jewish circles. Did it derive from Plato? Perhaps, but no translation of Plato into an Asian vernacular has been found. Should we ascribe it to the influence of Hellenism? W. W. Tarn cautions us that most Hellenistic thought systems reserved immortality to the initiate of a mystery and denied it to the mass of men. Was the concept of the soul's immortality derived from the East? If so, from where? Is it possible that such ideas germinated within the depths of the Jewish tradition itself? We do not know.

We do know that more Jews lived more varied lives, that some read the scrolls of other nations and occasionally talked seriously with men of other countries and philosophies. We also know that commerce and the city encouraged a sharper awareness of self. A trader covered long distances on his own, visited many strange places, and inevitably thought of himself as a self. Men thought for themselves and inevitably their thoughts were disparate. Some began to question the particularism of Jewish practice, and saw it as something of a scandal in the broad world of the *oikoumene*. A number of the religiously indifferent found prohibitions of diet and intermarriage unwarranted and unwanted barriers across their way to profits and position: "Persons who cherish a dislike of the institutions of our fathers and make it their constant study to denounce and decry the laws." [13] Other men were scandalized and frightened by the new world and sought salvation in a defiant withdrawal from the city and its contagion. Many drew back from the confusions of the *oikoumene*. A few undid the mark of circumcision. It was a time of assimilation. Some felt that Judaism had much to teach a decadent and confused world. It was a time of missionaries. We hear not only of converts but of *gerei-tzedek*, righteous neighbors, who join in affirming Judaism's theological teachings but who, for one reason or another, do not allow themselves to be fully bound to the covenant of Abraham. Judaism was both vilified and eulogized. In brief, this was an age of scattering, growing differences, variety, an age in which many men were thinking and others claimed that such thinkers "reasoned but they were led astray." [14] For the first time men like Ben Sira published writings in their own name and a Kohelet, the putative author of Ecclesiastes, sets out to put the accepted virtues to the test of experience.

⌘

Alexander's conquest had stretched thin the available Greek manpower. The far reaches of the conquest could not be maintained. In the course of the third and second centuries B.C.E., first Iran and then the Tigris-Euphrates valleys were retaken by an Asian people, the Parthians. The Babylonian Judean community, which had been close to the seat of power and of consequence throughout the Persian period, found itself, as it were, off the map and unfortunately situated in a recurring war zone involving the superpowers. It would survive, but without any particular distinction. Its exposure to Hellenism remained brief and quite uncreative. Aramaic remained the language of street and school. For more than four centuries no major literary work was to emerge from the Judean communities nestled along the central Mesopotamian irrigation canals. There must have been Babylonian academies, but they can no longer be described. Later, in the first century B.C.E., a Babylonian native, Hillel, appears in Jerusalem sufficiently equipped to gain quick academic recognition; but for these centuries the history of the Babylonian communities remains a blank page.

Hellenistic power and prosperity were centered along the Mediterranean littoral, not in the Persian hinterland. It was in Syria, Palestine, and Egypt that the Greek impact was most evident. Philo preached in Greek in his Alexandrian synagogue, and a rich Judaic civilization developed alongside the Greek. Jerusalem and the western Diaspora come center stage.

As long as the Ptolemies ruled Judea (until 198 B.C.E.), Jerusalem remained an old-fashioned city built according to immemorial West Asian tradition, without *gymnasium* or amphitheater. Throughout the third and second centuries its population grew. Pilgrims and trade brought prosperity and some awareness of the larger world. The book of Wisdom of Joshua Ben Sira, or Ecclesiasticus, was written a century and a half after Alexander's death, but breathes an older spirit, that of an old-fashioned teacher who spent his days instructing, in Aramaic, upper-class students in the ways and habits of respectable Judean gentlemen. In Jerusalem the upper class was largely a priest class; not unexpectedly, the Temple and the sacrificial system are much praised, "give to the most High as He was given and as generously as your hand has found." [15] Within the establishment, learning and cultivation were represented by the scribe-scholar. Ben Sira felt himself one of these, whose involvement in Torah he believed to have the highest spiritual value. A long panegyric [16] contrasts the necessary but mundane skills of farmer, craftsman, smith, and potter with the saving skills of the scribe-scholars who have mastered both the clear and "hidden meanings of law, wisdom, and prophecy," and gained knowledge and character which will enable them to play an effective role as councilors of state and teachers of virtue and truth. They represent an ideal of religious personality and respected authority. One of the virtues of the scribe is that he can be trusted to travel on the city's business and not be seduced by alien ways as "he tests the good and the evil among men." [17]

There was government business to be done in Alexandria and trade to be arranged in the more Hellenized cities on the coast. Men came to Jerusalem on pilgrimage from all over the Diaspora. Among the travelers were some who had not "devoted themselves to the study of the law of the Most High" [18] but who saw clearly the commercial and trade opportunities which Jerusalem could seize if it would adapt its ways to the fiscal and cultural patterns of the *oikoumene*. With the transfer of Judean hegemony from Egypt to the Seleucids, the dam broke. Traditional Syrian markets, Antioch, Damascus, Tyre, and Sidon, were now open to Judean trade. Around 175 B.C.E. a shrewd and ambitious priest, Jason, who seems to have mastered the Greek ways of practical politics, bought the office of High Priest from the crown and then offered the Seleucid court a sizable gift for the right to reconstitute his capital as a *polis*, Antioch-at-Jerusalem (named of course, for the reigning emperor). His petition was granted and this move, in effect, allowed Greek commercial laws and institutions to replace existing Judean customs and institutions. In financial and civic matters Greek ways now had precedence over Torah ways, a new *demos* or citizen's register was drawn up, and a *gymnasium* and *ephebeum* were built as a means of training the youth to think and act Greek so they could mix freely and speak easily with their peers in other cities.

Religious life was not directly affected. Jason's was a priest-sponsored move, and the Temple ritual went on as before. But a direct challenge had been raised to the popular assumption that Torah was an all-embracing way of life and not simply a series of discrete laws. Moreover, the drive among the upper classes was to take advantage of new opportunities. The *gymnasium* began to turn out graduates whose life styles were different and therefore disconcerting. There was a widening cultural gap. Most Jerusalemites, even many priests, kept the old ways, spoke Aramaic, and thought in traditional rather than Greek categories. The sight of naked young men prancing around an athletic field violated everything they had been taught about modesty, homosexuality, and the sin of idolatry. When Jerusalem's athletes went to Tyre, the games in which they participated, like all such contests, were dedicated to that city's gods. The old-fashioned were scandalized while the scribe-scholar class felt directly threatened by a new power group. In this new world would they still "be sought out for the council of the people . . . attain eminence in the public assembly . . . sit in the judge's seat?" [19] What would be the value of Torah mastery?

Jason's direct approach to power unsettled some Jews; more were disturbed when other men bid for the High Priesthood who could not claim descent from the principal priestly dynasty of Zadok. Alliances formed and political demonstrations took place. While political priests fought for power, small groups of the disaffected who felt the cultural and political shock most keenly began to leave Jerusalem for the countryside, where they formed groups of Ḥasidim, men steadfast to the old covenant who wanted to keep the old Torah ways and the old priestly forms. There were ugly incidents. Judea had taken the first step toward civil war. The Hellenists built an *Acra* or citadel from which to rule their *polis*, quarreled among themselves over the distribution of tolls and taxes, and bribed various governors for political advancement. The Ḥasidim took to the streets or the hills, cursed their rulers as "the arrogant," "the mighty," and "the proud," and read apocalyptic visions like Daniel, which assured them that "the few" and "the steadfast" might be cast into the lion's den, but would emerge unscathed, protected by the God who saves, ready to enjoy the discomfiture and defeat of the enemy.

Despite isolated incidents, the Maccabean Revolt (168–164) would not have become a national uprising of critical moment to the future of the Jewish nation if Jerusalem politics had not gotten tangled up in big power politics. It happened this way. In 174–173

Antiochus IV Epiphanes led a Seleucid army against Egypt. He enjoyed some success and seems actually to have crowned himself king of Egypt when Popilius Laenas, Ambassador of the Roman Senate, appeared in his camp at Eleusis near Alexandria and peremptorily ordered his withdrawal. A Seleucid army had been shattered by Rome at Magnesia (190 B.C.E.), and Antiochus lacked the troops for a second round; he had no alternative but to leave Egypt in black anger.

A rumor circulated in Jerusalem that the emperor had died in Egypt, and uprisings against the *polis'* leadership broke out, led by traditionalist bands and ambitious members of the ruling caste who were temporarily out of power. Antiochus was in no mood to be patient with such disturbances. A defeated ruler must stamp out every threat to his authority. On his return from Egypt he entered Jerusalem and ruthlessly suppressed all dissent, an act which only served to widen the rebellion.

There were more incidents. Antiochus' military governor, Apollonius, took repressive measures. He imported foreign mercenaries and their families and made them citizens of the *polis.* Jerusalem ceased to be a homogeneous Judean city. The mercenaries saw no reason why the Torah, with its rules of diet and Sabbath rest, should be enforced on them, or why they could not worship their gods in the *polis'* Temple as they would have in any other city. So they ate what they wished, worked on the Sabbath, and held ceremonies within the sacred precincts. An explosion was inevitable. It came, as is so often the case, in an unexpected quarter, one of the rural towns dependent on Jerusalem, Modin, when Jews obedient to the *Acra* set up a statue of the emperor's patron god and demanded that the appropriate sacrifices be offered. The Hellenists were struck down by a local priest whose family, the sons of Mattathias, took to the hills and began a war of liberation. In retaliation the Seleucids launched a gruesome war of suppression, whose purpose was no longer simply to limit the Torah's domination of Jerusalem's life, but to root out all the parochial elements in this people's law as inimical to public order. Sabbath observance and circumcision were forbidden on pain of death. But it was nearly twilight for Syria's empire; after protracted and bitter fighting the traditionalists won out, captured the Temple mount, and in December 164 B.C.E. celebrated a joyous Ḥannukah or Festival of Dedication. After a further decade of sporadic fighting the Seleucid foreign ministry granted de jure recognition to Judean Jerusalem, then headed by the Hasmoneans, as Mattathias' sons and their descendants were called.

The Maccabean revolt was a critical turning point in the history of Judaism. It resulted in an unexpected victory for the traditionalists. Because of it the Torah remained the uncontested constitution of Jerusalem. The heroes of the revolt, the Hasmoneans, established a dynasty which, by virtue of its origin in a war for religious freedom, was at least nominally bound to the Torah way. Consecrated by the blood of martyrs, the Torah became even more sacred; but time did not stop, Judea was part of the larger world. Torahic law had to be interpreted and expanded. A new understanding of that law began to develop in Judea and to go forth from Zion, and those scholars who could find the possibility of growth and change within the law, rather than outside of it, began to emerge as national leaders. The stage was set for the Pharisees and rabbinic Judaism.

These battles, with their attendant sagas of heroism on the battlefield and the torture rack, provided a new set of powerful legends about faith, courage, and martyrdom. In Daniel we read of unflinching youths who are flung into a fiery furnace and a lion's den, but will not abandon their faith and its practices. In the various histories of the Maccabees we read of undaunted men and women who preferred to die for their faith rather than disobey the will of God. Martyrs are made to utter noble speeches to their tormentors, and their sacrifice is eulogized as a compelling example: "So in this way he died, leaving in his death an example of nobility and a memorial of courage not only to the young but also to the great body of his nation." [20] Martyrdom becomes a consecrated virtue, *Kiddush ha-Shem*, the glorification of God's name, a supreme sacrifice which assures the victim of future blessing. For a while there was even something of a cult of martyrs. What would be their reward? Since it could not be in this life, it must be in the next. Daniel contains both the lion's den and the Bible's earliest explicit affirmation of resurrection.

To live or to die when faced with a choice between disobedience of God's law and death is no easy decision. The Hasidim had had to face such a moment of truth over the issue of Sabbath observance. At the beginning of the rebellion the Syrians learned to track them down on the Sabbath, when the Hasidim lay unresisting in their hideouts. After many deaths and much soul searching the Hasidim determined, despite the laws of Sabbath rest, to fight back if attacked. Torah demands literal obedience, but also suggests that the law is given to man, not man to the law: "Better a live dog than a dead lion" (Ecc. 9:4) and "Choose life" (Deut. 30:19). Men should not needlessly throw their lives away. But there were times when death was to be preferred to disobedience. Better to give up one's life than to take an innocent life, commit rape, or utter blasphemy, if these are the tragic alternatives. Leaders had an added obligation. They must not publicly disgrace God's name. Martyrdom was seen as a witness. The martyr had "sanctified the name of God in public," and in so doing he became a *kadosh*, holy, dear to God, saved. Genesis chapter 18, the story of God's command that Abraham sacrifice his only son as proof of his faith, suggested the many elements in Israel's concept of the martyr. Isaac-Israel is bound on the altar, but he is spared; a ram is caught in the thicket, and its horns become the shofar, which will sound to announce the messianic age. The victim is saved, if not in this life, then in the next.

Rabbinic thought placed restrictions on martyrdom even as it consecrated the act. The controlling text was: "You shall keep My laws and My norms, by the pursuit of which man shall live" (Lev. 18:5). The general principle that emerged held that martyrdom was to be endured if necessary but was never to be courted.[21] Yet the sacrifice and faith of martyrs was much praised. Lists of martyrs were incorporated into the liturgy, where they received the title *Eleh Ezkerah*, "These things will I remember." In reciting these names each generation burdened itself with an obligation of love to those whose lives had been sacrificed for Torah. Had Israel's sense of community and of the meaningfulness of worldly life not been as strong as it was, martyrdom might have become a sought-after way to sainthood and salvation. It never became that. From the Ḥasidim murdered by Syrian soldiers in their caves to the victims of the Nazis, Jews have mourned and revered their martyrs, but insisted that man must be ready to live for God. For Jews there was no urgency to imitate the passion of Christ.

The Hasmonean victory resulted in their becoming a ruling dynasty who remained sovereign for seventy-five years until Pompey imposed the Roman eagle on Jerusalem (63 B.C.E.). The Hasmoneans were not Davidites but priests, and of a minor order at that, not Zadokites of the ancient theocrat ruling line. When Jonathan the Hasmonean invested himself as *Nasi* (head) and High Priest (152 B.C.E.), some traditionalists bitterly but unsuccessfully opposed his act as a usurpation of power and privilege. The Dead Sea community that produced the *Manual of Discipline* and *Habakkuk Commentary* was founded by a Teacher of Righteousness, a priest of legitimacy, who believed that "only the sons of Aaron shall have the authority . . ." and vigorously opposed "the wicked priest" who had "betrayed the covenant for the sake of wealth." [22] He became a martyr to his convictions—and to his impotence. The fallen High Priesthood, like Humpty Dumpty, would never be put back together again; Judea would be ruled by Hasmoneans, then by Roman puppets (Herod, among others), and then directly by Roman procurators.

To support their authority, the Hasmoneans loosely associated themselves with those heirs of the old scribe class who had been loyal and were generally accepted as authentic religious leaders. A council, at times called the Sanhedrin, a quasi-judicial, quasi-legislative group, existed, the members of which included Torah scholars as well as men of rank. Indeed, all its members were assumed to be learned in Torah. Its functions included advising the king and determining the practical implications of Torah for the community. This council existed at the will of the king, and the more powerful Hasmonean monarchs did not suffer rebuke or reproof patiently. Yet something of the mystique which Plato assumed for his philosopher-kings surrounded these men of the council. Learning was the ideal qualification. In fact, many were scribe-scholars, *hachamim*. All were participants in a divinely ordered form of government. Jews knew that God had ordered Moses "to gather seventy men of Israel" who "will bear the burden of the people" (Num. 11:16–17). Were not the judges and councillors of their own day heirs to that God-given authority? The actual history of this council is much debated. It seems to have met erratically. No records survive of its meetings, but it provided an effective symbol of the fact that Judea was a Torah community, bound to the law and burdened with a sense of spiritual continuity. The piety that all its members were under the spirit, and the reality that some were scholars who knew and could interpret the Torah's spirit, provided a new myth of legitimacy: a Jewish community regulated by a scholar class who knew, and in a sense were, the Torah. The crown of David, the throne, and the crown of Aaron, the priesthood, were now complemented by the crown of Torah, the scholars, and in time the third crown would effectively supplant the others.

Even as the Hasmoneans came to power, the long shadow of Rome reached toward Jerusalem and the scattered Diaspora settlements of West Asia. Pompey invested Jerusalem in 63 B.C.E., after which the city had one hundred and thirty-three turbulent years to live before Rome breached its walls, burned its homes, and demolished the Temple. To the Judeans, Roman domination meant the end of a prosperous, expansionist, and exciting era and a reversion to colonial status, a controlled economy, and brutally heavy taxes. Rome's iron boot, greed, and passion for uniformity would first impose quasi-Jewish Idumean governors (Antipater, Herod), then Roman procurators whose rapacity and cruelty ultimately precipitated two courageous but doomed rebellions: 66–72 C.E. and 132–135 C.E. To Diaspora Jews, Rome meant increasing taxes and decreasing privileges. Fearing local mobs, the Greeks had preferred to bring trustworthy alien minorities into their cities; the Romans preferred to rule directly through natives. Rome trusted force. During the first century C.E. in both Antioch and Alexandria, natives contested the hard-won privileges of the local Jewries. Toughs organized anti-Jewish riots. The Jews were accused of being parochial, clannish, and in league with the eastern enemy, Parthia. During Claudius' and Nero's time, charges of disloyalty were brought in Rome against various Jewish communities, particularly in the matter of emperor worship. It was a cruel time, "a time of trouble such as there had never been before" (Dan. 12:1).

In response Jews looked to the old promises and refined their systems of communal welfare. *Torot* requiring that the gleanings and the fallen fruit be left for the poor became the basis of a system of social welfare. In order to provide an adequate food supply during the sabbatical year, the Hasmoneans appointed officials to gather such food and fruit as grew naturally, store it, and ration it to those who had need. What had been a private obligation of the farmer, to allow the poor an opportunity to survive through their own initiative, becomes in this more complex and unsettled age a communal responsibility, public welfare. Each third year the Temple collected an additional tithe to provide food and shelter for the poor.[23] Cities maintained a public kitchen (*tamḥui*) and regular collection boxes (*kupah*).[24] It was not charity. These programs were Torah, one of the clear duties of Jews under God's law of righteousness (*tzedakah*).

By the middle of the second century C.E. the Temple was in ruins, Jerusalem was forbidden territory, and the western Diaspora was beleaguered. Jewish life, simply to survive, had to turn in on itself. An age of openness gave way to an age of consolidation. The Torah now provided not only a way to salvation, but a program for survival. God would take care of His own and the community would take care of its own.

❧❦❧

Despite the Greek environment, Jewish life remained essentially itself. The promise of salvation remained closely tied to the sacredness of the Temple in Jerusalem and to the holiness of the Torah-commanded life. Wherever they lived, Jews faced the Temple during their devotions and sent annual dues for its upkeep and beautification. *Avodah*, the Temple service, was a sacrament in which all Israel vicariously participated. The Temple was constantly being enlarged. Its courts were widened and beautiful bronze doors added. From the time of the High Priest Simon (3rd cent. B.C.E.), "who in his life repaired the house . . . fortified the Temple, laid the foundation for the high double walls . . . quarried out a reservoir . . . ,"[25] through that of Herod, who began in 20 B.C.E. a program which doubled the Temple's size with embankments, flanking walls, and porticoes, the scaffolds were seldom laid aside.

The altar redeemed and the altar atoned. Officiants were divided into twenty-four sections which served in rotation. The whole nation was similarly divided. Representatives from each of the citizen groups served in turn with the priests, but in theory all were present. The daily rites were the rites of the whole nation. Though private sacrifices were offered, it was the twice-daily sacrifice of a yearling lamb on behalf of the nation which was the Temple's central service and of which we have at least two loving descriptions.[26]

Anticult literature was rare, or at least little has survived. Where it does surface—as in Philo's first-century account of the denial by Essenes of the efficacy of the sacrifices—the writer makes clear that these attacks were leveled against the current situation, wicked priests defiling the sanctuary, not against the priestly institution itself, against a polluted Temple which, God willing, would again be purified and properly maintained. Other protesting pietists who were scandalized by the political activities, lack of pedigree, and Greek ways of the current officiants nevertheless continued to send gifts to the shrine. The Dead Sea covenanters had bitter things to say about the Jerusalem priesthood. In their eyes the cult had become so perverted in this "period of wickedness" as to be without efficacy. They did not attend. They called their community God's house, a "Temple built not by hands," and looked on its rites as redemptive. However, they, too, prayed that the fire on God's altar would be rekindled in a renewed Temple and tended by righteous priests.

The Temple was the spiritual capital and visible symbol of the unity of the Jewish nation. Jews believed that the Temple cult made possible Israel's acceptance by God, and that its rites were redemptive. Though the Diaspora had begun centuries before and most Jews lived in scattered millet groups outside of Judea, a sense of

[188]

homelessness spread only after the Temple's destruction in 70 C.E. Only then did the nation add to its liturgy prayers for a return to Zion. Psychologically, Israel had a tremendous investment in the Temple. There was even a popular doctrine that God had designed the Temple's architecture and ceremony as a miniature of the structure and movement of the heavens; thus to understand the secrets of the service was to understand the secrets of the cosmos, and to participate in the service was to participate in God's creative power. The belief that proper understanding of this building and these rituals could provide a sketch of the architectonics of the universe lingered long after the Temple's destruction, and students continued for centuries to study the rules and rituals of a service no one alive had ever seen because these were a key to the mysteries of the universe.

Israel had only one sanctuary, but there were places in the various communities where men met for study, community business, and prayer. The Temple was holy, its rites and structure precisely ordered by God. The protosynagogue was human, a creation of ordinary religious need in the dispersion. Its architecture was as flexible as its forms of service. No Torah law required such extra-Temple meetings. Scholars took pains to make clear that these centers were not surrogate Temples, and reminded their communities of the rules which prohibited the beating of the palm branches on Hoshanah Rabba, the blowing of the shofar on Yom Kippur, and, of course, all sacrifice outside the Temple compound, since these were rites specifically associated with the Temple's redemptive powers.

The Temple was distant and the scattered communities needed an institutional center. We cannot describe the earliest local meeting places, but they were popular. The Greek word *synagoge*, which denotes simply a place of meeting, does not appear in our sources until the middle of the first century B.C.E. The synagogues so far discovered and excavated were built during the Common Era. All that can be said is that religious meetings took place in many places, and that, being of spontaneous growth, they took on a variety of tasks, including elementary Torah education, local town meetings, public Torah reading and explanation, and Sabbath song. Inevitably the calendar and certain basic worship forms including psalms and Torah readings were taken over from the Temple's ceremony.

Although the synagogue's origins were popular, its simplicity and naturalness should not mask its revolutionary thrust. It was of the people, not of the priests. It was flexible and not burdened with an elaborated and consecrated ceremonial. Men read the Torah publicly and prayed, without intercessory sacrifice, directly to God. Here was a first break with Oriental ecclesiasticism, a revolutionary beginning in the development of openness, simplicity, and democracy in religious expression—no intercessors, no sacraments, no authorized hierarchy.

✦

These centuries saw Judaism define its relation to *the* Book. The collating of the various collections of *torot* was completed. The word of God had been heard and set down. There was a Torah scroll. Now the task was to explore the full and many meanings of that revelation. Ezra had set the pattern, reading out of the Scroll of the Law and interpreting it for the people. The Five Books of Moses, the Torah, were the authoritative rule of Jewish life, the covenant between Israel and God, and every reform or elaboration of the Jewish way would hereafter need to validate itself within the terms of this religious compact.

Biblical man knew himself to be bound by a covenant. He knew that salvation lay through obedience, and that he must bend his will and obey the commandments so that he and his nation might deserve redemption. He looked on the various commandments as statements of what he was required to do, but the Torah was more than a law book. It was the word of God—revelation, true on many levels. The Torah was the Jew's manual of discipline, political constitution, and document of truth. Men began to read the Torah not simply as the text of the covenant but as the repository of ultimate metaphysical truths, a guide to right thinking. To abide by the Torah comes to mean not only to obey its stipulations but to understand its cosmology, its description of the nature of things, its teachings about truth.

How did this shift happen? Every language reveals the special values and categories of thought of the group which created it. Since most Diaspora Jews lacked the ability to speak or read Hebrew, and, at least in Egypt, seem to have lost even the ability to speak Aramaic, Hebrew's close cognate, they had to translate the Torah into an understandable idiom. *Tradutorre-traditorre*, to translate is to traduce: a Greek Torah translation was inevitably a Torah different from the Hebrew original.

The closest Greek synonym for Torah was *nomos*. *Nomos* meant "law" and had two major significations in Greek thought. On one hand *nomos* denoted the fundamental law constitutive of a Greek city-state, and on the other hand *nomos* specified the natural law which describes the universe and its operation. Torah, translated as *nomos*, suggested that the Torah was the specific set of commandments and instructions required of Israel, as well as a universal law valid for mankind and a full and accurate description of the nature of things on earth and in the heavens. On the surface the existing Torah was a series of discrete laws and specific historical incidents, but it was easy to assume that proper interpretation of the Torah would uncover these metaphysical truths and permit the student a true and full knowledge of God, man, morals, and the natural order. Torah had been seen as a divine constitution. Now Torah came to be seen as the revelation of "the whole way of knowledge." [27] The long-lived confusion that views the Bible as setting out scientific facts begins here.

The singular use of the term *nomos* would not have precipitated this changed awareness of the Torah if many had not been prepared for it. Torah had long been identified with wisdom, "perfect," "renewing life," "true," "enlightening the eye," "righteous altogether" (Ps. 19:8–10). Torah was law and Torah was wisdom. Being full of wisdom, God's law was more than an arbitrary collection of apodictic rules. Men began to puzzle out the *taamei ha-mitzvot*, the reasons behind God's will, what God had in mind, and to weave the discrete laws into a moral theory. This age reached for analysis and explanation. In Philo particularly, but also in other writings of this period, obedience is deemed to grow out of intellectual assent to the law's propriety as well as humble submission to God's will. God's will is reasonable and necessary, a wholly adequate regimen for those who would lead a virtuous life. The business of the teacher is to provide an interpretation which will adequately express the Torah's good sense. Men began to find in Torah law the Greek categories of virtue.

The Torah was seen as doubly beneficial. On the level of simple observance Torah pleased God and helped to develop virtue; on a higher level Torah provided man wisdom and guided him toward truth. Ideas were conceived to have a force and vitality beyond any power heretofore ascribed to them. As in late Greek thought, noble ideas were held instrumental to nobility of person. If man held right ideas, he would act on them and his life would be righteous. Men began to look on ceremonies and rites not simply as acts pleasing to God but as appropriate reminders of useful and noble ideas. The specifics of apparently arbitrary laws are justified because they remind the participant of various philosophic truths. The Letter of Aristeas (2nd cent. B.C.E.) explains the biblical categories of edible and inedible fowl by noting that the edible birds are all of gentle species distinguished by cleanliness, while the prohibited birds (eagle, vulture, hawk) are predatory types. The law is not simply a rule but

> a symbol that those for whom the legislation was drawn up must practice righteousness in spirit and oppress no one, trusting in their own strength, nor rob anyone of anything but must guide their lives in accordance with justice, just as the gentle creatures among the birds above mentioned consume pulses that grow upon the earth and do not tyrannize to the destruction of their kindred.[28]

Torah known as constitution and as an ultimate repository of metaphysical and theological truth cries out for proper exegesis, and commentators from Aristobulus to Philo, using interpretive forms familiar to Greek literary analysis, set out to elucidate the Torah's infinite yet single truth. To Philo the Torah was law perfect to a degree other laws could only approximate, perfect in the habits it inculcated, in the truths it contained, and in the practice it commanded. Torah was confirmed by history, the well-documented and public revelation at Sinai, and by its unquestioned usefulness. To deny Torah's authority was atheism. But what was Torah to a man who wrote: "It is quite foolish to think that the world was created in six days or in a space of time at all?"[29] For Philo six was not a cosmological fact, but a whole or perfect number used to indicate that the world was created according to a whole and perfect plan. Philo had let go of the Bible's literal meaning. Judaism was no longer an existential fact, in the first instance beyond analysis, but a philosophic exercise conducive to good (acceptable) morals and capable of providing a reasonable (acceptable) metaphysics. Judaism is no longer defined as itself, but by what the environment defines as reasonable. The Greeks identified truth and reason; now a Hellenized Jew identified Torah and reason. But was Torah reasonable? Or itself?

A practical question had to be faced. Torah as *nomos* might imply that these scrolls were full of metaphysical truth, but in fact the Torah was chronicle and law, and nowhere had God's word set out metaphysical demonstrations or conclusions. Moreover, the Torah included material of varying degrees of historical and ethical development. Burning witches and loving one's neighbor are both commanded, though they would seem to be rules from entirely different moral planes. Today those who love the old truths generally content themselves with finding and praising the assumed direction of biblical thought. Their piety thus exceeds their consistency, for if the Bible is God's word no rule can be archaic or ethically inferior. Jews of that age of variety were keenly aware of this logical requirement. The Torah, every word in it, was as eternally valid and significant as its broad implications. To uncover that significance the sages developed the art of *midrash*, an open-ended process of elucidation and commentary which explores, derives, reads into, and gives significance to every aspect and line of biblical teaching.

Midrash was never a conclusion but a process, the process of commenting on and deriving the full consequence of a Torah text. *Midrash*, from *darash*, to search or investigate, became a generic term for all forms of commentary. *Midrash* was the endless search for those meanings that piety required, and since each age accentuated different meanings and virtues, the search, the process of *midrash*, is ceaseless, active as long as there are believers. Almost as soon as there was a Torah scroll we hear of *midrash*. Biblical history tells of a *midrash* by the otherwise unknown prophet Iddo (II Ch. 13:22) and of an anonymous *midrash* to the book of Kings (II Ch. 24:27). In time schools of *midrash* developed. What educational curriculum would be more natural in a Torah-based community than one which sought out the meaning of God's words? Ben Sira apparently ran such a *midrash* academy.[30] The Torah was read and interpreted midrashically in the early synagogue; Philo was a trained Torah commentator and preacher; and we hear that among the sectarians the Torah was read and commented on all day and a third of each night.[31] Citation, elaboration, moralistic commentary, and allegorical interpretation proliferated as men probed and deepened the text, and the forms which were developed became prototypes for centuries of biblical exposition and theological writing. Some of these critical forms were unique to the Jews; others employed interpretive devices borrowed from Greek commentaries on Homer and the classics and from the forms of juridic interpretation devised by Roman lawyers.

Midrash testifies to the force of faith. The nonbeliever has no need of *midrash*. *Midrash* also testifies to a certain tendency toward self-deception among the faithful, for it is in part the process of reading into a text what one wants to find there, what one expects God must have said. Thus, those who reasoned philosophically found in the Torah a full philosophic statement. The most famous such system in

Hellenistic times is Philo's, and the following paragraphs suggest how he "discovered" the Platonic doctrine of ideas in the creation story:

What is the meaning of the words, "And God made every green thing of the field before it came into being on the earth, and every grass before it grew" (Gen. 2:5)?

In these words he alludes to the incorporeal ideas. For the expression, "before it came into being" points to the perfection of every green thing and grass of plants and trees. And as Scripture says that before they grew on earth He made plants and grass and other things; it is evident that He made incorporeal and intelligible ideas in accordance with the intelligible nature which these sense-perceptible things on earth were meant to imitate.[32]

An age of variety produced a widely disparate set of midrashic readings. The simplest form of *midrash* consisted of folkloristic embellishments of the biblical narrative, the search for fuller details, a more effective tale. Some of this literature is pseudepigraphic, the adding of whole incidents or speeches to the biographies of classic heroes, wise men, or prophets. The Letter of Jeremiah, now published as chapter 6 of a large pseudepigraphic work, the book of Baruch, claims to be a copy of the message sent by that prophet to those about to be hauled off into Babylonian Exile. The text heavy handedly mocks various Babylonian idols and idolatrous practices and may be a riposte to some now-forgotten incident in late Seleucid times when the Syrian emperors, for political reasons, began to support the old Babylonian temples, cults, and priests. Whatever it is, it is not by Jeremiah, though it takes as its point of departure Jeremiah's actual letter to the exiles (Jer. 29) and develops its satire on idolatry on the basis of various authentic texts (Jer. 6:7–7:2; 10:1–16). Another apocryphal scroll, Susannah, is a delightful midrashic vignette which pictures Daniel as a male Portia who saves an innocent girl from a malicious charge of adultery by displaying at her trial a truly brilliant technique in the cross-examination of witnesses. In another, the history of Bel and the Dragon, Daniel appears as a Babylonian Hercule Poirot who solves the mystery of the hungry idol, Bel. It seems that the priests of Bel stole back into the temple at night through a secret passage and removed the food which had been placed on the altar table, thus making it appear as if the idol ate each day's offering. By scattering ashes on the floor and getting clear impressions of their footprints, Daniel unmasked this bit of

[194]

priestly chicanery. The extant apocryphal literature also includes a moving litany of thanksgiving, the so-called Song of the Three Children, ascribed to Daniel's friends.

Midrashic supplements were written at this time to many sections of the Bible. Some are simply enthusiastic descriptions of such wonders as Daniel's palace quarters or Sarah's beauty. Others are documents of piety, like the penitential psalm in the Prayer of Manasseh, which is offered as the confession of an Israelite king who late in life repented of his wicked ways and reformed his life. The most extended of these pseudepigraphic *midrashim* is a composite work known as The Testament of the Twelve Patriarchs, which reports words of wisdom and good counsel offered by Jacob's sons as each in his turn feels the approach of death and is moved to justify himself and, when necessary, to warn his descendants against following in his footsteps, and to exhort them to a worthy life. These texts are somewhat pompous but rich in good intentions as the fathers, in fashion immemorial, encourage their sons to avoid wine, women, and indiscretion in favor of reverence for God, Torah, and wisdom.

In the *midrash* the actions of biblical heroes are always edifying. When the reader finds what seems vulgar or wicked the *midrash* takes another look and is able to cast the act in a better light. In The Testament, Joseph heatedly denies that he had been callous in never communicating with his family. As proof he adduces the fact that had he made his identity known to the Ishmaelite slave traders he would have been returned immediately to his father for a handsome ransom. He had refrained "out of respect for them (the brothers)," lest their villainy be immediately revealed. An apocryphon on Genesis, found in the Dead Sea caves, dwells lovingly on Sarah's beauty and Abraham's "reason" for telling Pharaoh that Sarah was his sister. He was not lying, but prudently dissembling: given the Pharaoh's well-known lechery, to lie was the only way to save both their lives and Sarah's honor.

There was apocalyptic *midrash* and philosophic *midrash*. Enoch and II Baruch reinterpret some of the visionary images in Daniel. The Letter of Aristeas and the fragments which remain of the Alexandrian philosopher, Aristobulus, interpret and rationalize various Torah laws. Philo penned both an extended moralistic *midrash* of the Torah law and an extensive philosophic *midrash*, both dependent on Greek techniques in the use of allegory. *Midrash* developed along many lines and used varying techniques. One level was that of probing and search (*derash*), taking the texts to a new depth of meaning.

Another was philological, a search for the exact use of terms and meaning of words. Another involved transposing letters and words into dates for the purpose of messianic predictions. *Midrash* became a full-blown art in the rabbinic period. In this early age many of the rules of the genre were established. One early rule would remain central: However a text was construed, its straightforward meaning could not be dissolved away. *Midrash* could read much into the Bible but could never turn the text into an inconsequential plaything. As a revealed religion, Judaism must somehow justify all innovation as implicit in the revelation; the revelation's idiom, language, content, and even its grammar became significant subjects for theological discussion. The Torah was the source whence all learning flowed.

The period between Alexander's conquests and the fall of the Temple produced the Sanhedrin, a rudimentary juridic council with powers to define the community's Torah obligations. Judaism had a religious calendar, some agreed practices (many practices which are today considered traditional—*kashrut*, the recitation on Passover of the Haggadah, *tefillin*—were intensely developed only during this period), a priesthood, a central shrine, a revealed law, and a growing canon of prophetic and historical writings. What would be called rabbinic Judaism was germinating, but Talmudic style and attitudes were not yet normative. This age featured the broadest possible variation in religious experiences and disciplines. The Temple cult, by its continuing service, said, in effect, that here is the visible presence of God in the midst of His people. Temple sacrifice was deemed quintessential by all Jews, and was quite carefully regulated, but interestingly, the Jerusalem priests never gained doctrinal authority. There is no record of a High Priest actually setting out theologic doctrine in his own right. A panegyric glorifying a third-century High Priest, Simon, describes him as a theocrat who repairs and fortifies the Temple, a governor who improves Jerusalem, and an ecclesiastic whose charismatic authority made the court of the sanctuary glorious during the ritual, but at no time is he pictured as defining Judaism's tenets or setting ceremonial standards outside the confines of the shrine.[33] Scribes, Torah teachers, wisdom teachers, messianic preachers, and charismatic wonderworkers, in ways that are not fully clear, shared a loose authority and organized their own disciplines. No one had a supervening authority—except God.

CHAPTER

ৰ XII ৯৬

A Change in Cultural Style

T
HE literary output of the age of variety was mixed. At least two
scrolls would find their way into the biblical canon: Daniel and Ecclesiastes. Various other books written during this period would be
collected by the Church into two anthologies called, respectively,
Apocrypha and Pseudepigrapha.[1] There was one classic translation
of the Bible into Greek, the Septuagint. Josephus wrote histories.
There were the writings of the Hellenistic Alexandrian renaissance
culminating in the voluminous philosophic commentaries of Philo
and, of course, the recently recovered Dead Sea scrolls.[2] With the
exception of the canonized books, none of this extensive library
would be systematically preserved by rabbinic Judaism. The age of
variety ended in disaster and was supplanted by an age of definition.

What happened to these writings? Rabbinic Judaism turned its
back on them. Josephus had been a traitor. Philo had written in
Greek about systematic problems few of the rabbis ever mastered,
but he was not entirely unknown. The first saying in the largest
midrash collection contains language attributed to R. Oshiah which
reflects Philo's *De Opificio Mundi*.[3] A small number of accurate and a
larger number of inaccurate references to apocryphal materials, particularly Ben Sira, Tobit, and Judith, can be found in the Talmudic

literature. That rabbinic Judaism turned its back on these works implies a lack of interest, not official censorship. Elements from the apocalypse of Enoch surfaced in the mystical literature of the thirteenth century. During Hannukah medieval Jews read the *Megillat Antiochus*, a rousing historical précis drawn largely from I and II Maccabees.

The Septuagint translation of the Pentateuch had been painstakingly done, but Greek translations of other biblical books (the whole set inherited the title Septuagint) were not as faithful to the original. Some scrolls contained gross errors. The process of copying was not rigorously regulated. Even the better copies presented translations which emphasized meanings other than that of the emerging rabbinic consensus. When the Septuagint was enthusiastically seized on by the emerging church, because it offered the Bible in the one language the Greek church understood, Septuagint texts began to appear as Christological proof texts; the Torah schools declared the Septuagint a golden calf and in the third century c.e. initiated in Palestine a new Greek translation by the proselyte Aquila.

No one put the Dead Sea scrolls on an Index. They were used by the covenanters until they were hidden in caves for safekeeping during the Roman rebellion and afterward no one was able or interested enough to reclaim them. Either their existence was unknown to the academies—sectarian literature did not circulate publicly—or, more likely, they had never been part of the Torah curriculum, which dismissed these books as *Sefarim Hitzonim*, extrinsic works. Torah schools busy with the herculean task of making the oral and written laws into a seamless unity simply lacked time, patience, and real interest in accommodating this library of sectarian apocalypse and private musings.

Christian biblical manuals, familiar with the Apocrypha as quasi-biblical texts, are prone to treat these writings as if they represent the sum and substance of creative Jewish output during the last two centuries before the Common Era. To do so is to fail to understand the academic environment of the Torah schools. Learning was entirely oral. Beside the biblical books a vast Jewish library existed in the scholars' minds. Some schools had a live information retrieval system, a professional of infallible memory who repeated on request accepted traditions, customs, and case precedents. It was high praise to name a colleague "a watertight cistern" [4] from whose mind not a drop of the oral tradition escaped. Among the saddest rabbinic stories are those in which a scholar loses his memory. This living library was real, substantial, and constantly enlarged on, and it is to this invisible inheritance, together with the emerging liturgy of the synagogue, the traditions of Aramaic Torah translation and interpretation (the *Targumim*), popular folk and sermonic elaborations of biblical incident and law, and popular apocalyptic expectations that we must turn for much of the Judaism of that day.

For a long time the *soferim*, the scholar-scribes, had been the only ones truly concerned with this invisible library. Control of the body of precedent and rule heightened their importance as religious legitimizers. But, unlike other castes of Oriental schoolmen, they made no attempt to treat the oral legacy as a reserved doctrine: "Let all who are thirsty come and drink" (Isa. 55:1). The prejudice against publishing the oral traditions lingered for centuries, but the attempt to enroll everyone in *Talmud Torah*, the mastery of the teachings, was unflagging. The Torah commanded: "Impress [these instructions] upon your children" (Deut. 6:7). Possession of the Torah was seen as positive proof of God's election of this people. A summary of the program of the scholar class defines three obligatory and redemptive responsibilities: Torah learning (*Torah*); Temple worship (*Avodah*); and empathetic acts (*Gemilut Ḥasadim*).

The *Sefarim Ḥitzonim* deserve serious analysis, not only because they describe attitudes, theologies, and life styles held by Jews during Greco-Roman times (all, incidentally, believed by their adherents to be Torahic), but because the schools out of which rabbinic Judaism developed existed in the same ethos and reflect some of the same cultural pressures. Judaism's salvation drama would be couched in apocalyptic idioms. Greek hermeneutics were useful to Torah interpreters. Hellenistic anthropology, with its familiar duality of body and soul, provided a plausible explanation of the growing certainty that man's soul was or could be immortal. Even those who were most suspicious of Hellenism were not ignorant of its forms. Some of the sharpest attacks on the assimilationists were written in the style of the classic Greek diatribe.

When the Septuagint translators came to the name of God, YHWH, they tended to use the Greek term *Kyrios*. YHWH was both universal creator and a personal God who had led the children of Israel, spoken to patriarch and prophet, and was near to all who called upon Him. *Kyrios* denoted lordship, the creative power, but lacked the implication of a personal God. *Elohim* became *Theos*, a rather denatured and certainly denationalized creative power. *Theos* is pure being, supernal, creative light, the One of whom no imperfection and no limitations may be posited. *Kyrios* and *Theos* adequately expressed God's transcendence, but the immanence of Israel's God and His unique involvement in Israel's history were not reinforced by any of the common meanings of these Greek equivalents. In Alexandria's academies and schools students discussed the logical necessity for positing a universal Creator of whom all local myths were but parochial manifestations, and for assuming that this God was at one and the same time pure existence and pure essence. Traditional assumptions of a special relation between Israel and *Theos* or *Kyrios* began to seem awkward to self-conscious intellectuals, and the Jewish denial of any validity or efficacy to other cults added the unseemly sin of bad form to parochialism. If God is pure being, beyond description, whom men have chosen to imagine in many symbolic ways, how can anyone proscribe all symbols save his own?

Academicians were often skeptical about the traditional pantheons, but not about the idea of God. Plato and Aristotle could be comfortably appropriated to support YHWH as *Kyrios*, particularly since the first cause and the unmoved mover shared the sense of cosmic oneness with the Torah's God. Creation requires a Creator. Monotheism, once a radical postulate of faith, became eminently reasonable in this world which assumed the unity of all being, but a reasonable God is something less than a God of power and mercy. *Kyrios* as the nameless, mythless Creator of the Bible seemed an appropriate idea, but *Kyrios* as Israel's God rather than a philosopher's understanding of divinity was another matter. YHWH walked in the cool of the garden. *Kyrios* was transcendent in the cosmos. YHWH spoke to men. *Kyrios* was the silent intelligence of the spheres. Innocent biblical anthropomorphisms became something of an intellectual scandal to those who required that God be above all attributes. This exaltation and depersonalization of God deeply affected Jewish talk of God. God, once known as "The King of kings," "The Shepherd of Israel," "My Redeemer," becomes "The Most High," "The Righteous One," "Heaven," "The Lord of Days," "The God of Truth." The popular Aramaic translations of Torah, the *Targumim*, whose traditions were now being formed, developed a paraphrastic style which sacrificed vividness for philosophic scruple, but did avoid ascribing human activities to God. Adam and Eve had heard the *memra* (word) of God moving about in the garden. God does not speak to man, rather His will is perceived.

How does a man pattern himself after *Kyrios'* transcendent, nameless, formless, creative power? Obviously, he cannot. Those who, like Philo, felt systematically compelled to conceive of God as creative power, divine intelligence, or pure being no longer used Exodus 34:6–7 or other lists of God's attributes as a basis for a call to *imitatio dei*. In their writings the patriarchs and Moses replace God as patterning heroes. Their virtues are enlarged and incidents unflattering to their character are reinterpreted and somehow given moral significance. Such Jews borrowed and naturalized the technique of hero literature (aretology). Ben Sira is only the first of many who encouraged their audience to praise and emulate famous men.

Moses achieved a new prominence. He became the exemplary Jew and "most perfect of men." [5] Moses is, in Philo's review, "the living law," a fit subject for careful study and emulation.

He set forth himself in his life like a well-painted picture, a supremely beautiful and godlike work, as a model that those who wished might imitate. Thus he became the example for all the people, as the ruler must be. And as he was to be a law giver, he himself, by divine providence, first became the responsible and revealing law. [6]

Moses, much like the Teacher of Righteousness beloved of the Qumran community, certainly stood in the minds of some, if not in the place of God, right beside Him. Moses had devised the alphabet script which the Jews then taught the Phoenicians and the Phoenicians the Greeks (Eupolemus); he had taught Egypt its science (Artapanus); he had brought down to the Jews an esoteric apocalyptic wisdom (IV Ezra). There is only a thin line between such acclaim and actual hero worship, but there is little evidence that Jews crossed that line. Moses was not deified. No statues of him were raised and worshipped. He did not sit at God's right hand to intercede with God for Israel. He was not venerated at any shrine.

The biblical God was exalted, but He remained in touch with man. He had cut a covenant with the patriarchs, given a law to Moses at Sinai, led Israel's armies during the conquest of Canaan, and sent messages through the prophets to castigate the sinners of each age and promise the righteous redemption. YHWH as *Kyrios* was majestic, one and ultimate, the creative power and sustainer, pure being, majestic terms which suggested that for God to be personal, to hear and respond to man's prayer or know man's private needs, was to impose an unsuitable limitation on His nature. Understandably, how to maintain the emphasis on God as pure being, His transcendence, and still affirm the value of the faith enterprise (sacrifice, prayer, confession, judgment) which necessarily assumes that God is immanent and directly involved with man, was a question that had to be faced. An unmoved mover is not likely to be moved by prayers, however urgent or fervent, yet the Torah faith sang daily during Temple worship: "O Lord, hear my prayer . . . when I cry, answer me speedily" (Ps. 102:2-3).

One solution to this dilemma coupled transcendence with the mediating kindliness of any number of lesser celestial beings. The more the theological spirit of the age raised God to the heaven of heavens, the more the folk peopled the lower spheres with angels, spirits, and emanations of the world-soul. What the philosophic spirit threw out the front door, piety brought in the back. In his study a theologian can be satisfied with a God who is silent and unapproachable and can only be contemplated from a great distance; when his child has a raging fever he importunes a God who hears those who cry in distress. The biblical *malachim* (messengers) were transformed into angel-messengers who sped between God and man and were ever ready to do His bidding. Inevitably, some began to look on these angel-messengers as intercessors. In II Enoch God reminds the "watcher-angels," "You should intercede for men, not men for you." [7] Talk of angels and spirits was eminently respectable. The Greeks had their *angeloi*, like Nemesis and Hermes. Plato had talked of "middle creatures" who moved up and down to earth and through the whole heaven with a lightly rushing motion. The Stoics held that God exists as the mind of the world, relating to the world through an infinite number of seminal powers (*logoi spermatikoi*). Angels could be justified at almost any level of superstition or sophistication.

Another more philosophic bridge between transcendence and immanence was suggested in the wisdom literature, where wisdom is described as mediating between God and man. The Spirit of the Lord and Wisdom are equated; [8] the world is of one piece; God's power—wisdom—is immanent throughout. Biblical man had listened for the spoken word of God. Now men sought to open themselves to that wisdom which is imprinted in the universe, the basic truths about life which are valid and necessary as a guide to virtue, as a way of overcoming confusion and uncertainty, and of gaining true freedom—freedom from folly and the futile pursuits folly encourages: "She teaches self-control and prudence, justice and courage . . . she knows things of old and infers things to come." [9] Wisdom becomes identified with the Stoic *sophia*, that attribute of God which is understood as the informing mind of the universe. One is struck by the similarities of such ideas with the Stoic world view, but wisdom-oriented Jews felt that such ideas were not Stoic but Torahic; indeed, some went so far as to suggest that it was Abraham who had first taught *sophia* to the Greeks.

In the first pre-Christian century, an Alexandrian Jew wrote a book, The Wisdom of Solomon, in which he described a program of salvation which emphasized the acquisition of wisdom because "giving heed to [wisdom's] laws is assurance of immortality . . . the desire for wisdom leads to a kingdom." [10] How is wisdom acquired? First there must be a desire to learn, obedience to wisdom's laws, a drawing close to her presence. What is the value of gaining wisdom? Wisdom unravels for men the mysteries of the universe, permits them to foretell the future, brings emotional serenity, and saves her disciples, the righteous, from being ensnared by life or by death. Wisdom is identified with Torah, but wisdom is no longer simply the text of the Five Books of Moses. Torah is *nomos*, the constitutional regulation and unerring knowledge of all that is, of

> the beginning and end and middle of times
> the alternations of the solstices and the changes
>   of the seasons,
> the cycles of the year and the constellations of the stars,
> the natures of animals and the tempers of wild beasts,
> the powers of spirits and the reasonings of men,
> the varieties of plants and the virtues of roots.[11]

Torah is not only a document, but the sum of accessible knowledge. Sinai was no longer a once and only revelation, but nature itself revealing God's teachings: "Send her [wisdom] forth from the holy heavens, and from the throne of thy glory send her, that she may be with me and toil, and that I may learn what is pleasing to thee." [12] One must study not only the words of revelation, but God and God's creation, which "is a reflection of eternal light and an image of His goodness." [13]

The Hellenistic world knew a way of redemption through initiation into the mysteries. The mysteries promised esoteric knowledge which, when mastered, gave man a true understanding of life and of the way to salvation. The idiom of the mysteries appears here. He who takes wisdom unto himself "shall have glory," "life without pain," "pure delight." The believer can be "saved" through a knowledge of "the secret purposes of God." [14] Learning now reaches for the secrets of God possessed by initiates rather than for mastery of the written revelation taught in the schools; the way to immortality, the reward, is no longer a high road anyone can travel. "Who has learned Thy counsel, unless Thou hast given wisdom and sent Thy holy Spirit from on high?" [15]

The concept of wisdom drew to itself various Hellenistic theories of emanation. Simply put, these theories assumed that the transcendent God had somehow extruded or exposed a spirit or intelligence less pure than Himself, as mist sometimes seems to appear out of nowhere. This emanated essence was the active agent of creation, in turn emanating lower, that is, less divine and more physical levels of being—until the world we live in and know had been precipitated. Such theories ascribed personality and intelligence to the highest level of emanation and generally labeled it *logos* (word) or *nous* (mind). Theories of emanation tied the world up in one bundle of life and gave it the look of unity which the Greek world so prized. They explained what Genesis meant when it described man as created in God's image, and provided Jewish mysticism with some of its favorite images: the enlightened soul rising Godward through the spheres, the divine in man (his reason) somehow reaching out through ever more rarified levels of awareness until it touches and couples with a spirit whose divinity is next only to God's. Such theories protected God's unapproachability, yet tied man to divine activity. Still, philosophically, they were as inconsistent as the older and simpler biblical paradoxes which unabashedly affirmed that God had spoken and man had heard. How does pure being extrude contingent being? Moreover, given men's preferences for the concrete over the abstract, many were inclined to worship the approachable intermediary more zealously than the unapproachable God.

Hellenistic Judaism did not resolve the enigma of how pure being becomes contingent being. Plotinus' classic question, "How could all things come from the One who is simple and who shows in its identity no diversity and no duality?" [16] cannot be resolved within the terms of classical logic. Some recognized the difficulty, and Philo, at least, certainly felt he had bridged it with his posited instrumentality, the *logos*. But whatever the proposed solution—a theory of wisdom, a theory of emanation, or a denial of the reality of the problem—it was needed, because the age tended to raise God a bit too high for the simple religious needs of man.

❧❦❧

This age held new ideas about man as well as a new understanding of God. Biblical writers had written honestly of man's complex nature and had cherished few illusions as to his saintliness, but they had lacked the Greek passion for labeling and classification. No biblical writer had parsed the soul into three components (vegetable, animal, rational), but there was nothing essentially un-Jewish in such a psychology. Indeed, Philo naturalized these terms as respective synonyms of the biblical nouns *nefesh*, *neshamah*, and *ruaḥ*, all originally Hebrew synonyms for the soul; and, armed with such definitions, he peacefully read a rather consistent Platonic psychology into the Bible.

But the change in man's self-awareness was more than a matter of semantics. The biblical notion of man as a complex but unitary being is gradually abandoned, and we find in its place an image of man as a composite being comprising body and soul, matter and form, in a lifelong tension. In the Wisdom of Solomon and elsewhere, the soul is seen as preexistent and immortal, placed in the body at birth and chained there until freed by enlightenment or death.[17] The satisfied give thanks that "a good soul fell to my lot" and "because of her I shall have immortality."[18] Philo describes man as in and of the lower, that is, the sensual world, insofar as he is a body, but through his soul possessed of a heavenly form which ties him to the spheres. It becomes man's hope that through God's grace and his own determination he will be able to break through the chains of corporeality—ambition, lust, passion—to free his soul/mind of its envelope of flesh so that it can rise through enlightenment to the pure light. Such dualistic anthropologies tended to encourage both asceticism and a retiring, contemplative life. Men sought to curb their appetites and passions, for these beguiling "needs" drew men to seek that which does not profit and to forsake the service of God, which leads to life eternal.

Men despaired of making over the world, but not of making themselves over. When they used the personal pronoun "I," they did not have in mind a person possessed of will and able freely to match his actions to conscious decision, but the soul or intellect which inhabited an essentially hostile, at best uncooperative, body. To know became a more critical undertaking than to do, since the "I" is rarely free to do. Proper philosophic understanding is a supremely important accomplishment, not simply because the mind influences all that man does, but, so this age believed, because it determines what and whether he feels. The man who "knows" that worldly ambitions are vain truly does not desire power or possessions and can no longer be snared by greed or ambition. It is such knowledge which makes man a free man; without it even an emperor is a slave to his flesh and his fears.

Ecclesiastes (Kohelet) represents an early, perhaps third-century B.C.E., "I" burdened by the need to know, exposed to a world "where all things are wearisome" (Ecc. 1:8) and "what is crooked cannot become straight" (1:15). Ecclesiastes introduced the "I" into biblical writing. Man has become sufficiently conscious of self to weigh his experience against the thrust of tradition, and he finds that life is full of ambiguities. "I applied my mind to study and explore all that is done under heaven" (1:13). He found "in much wisdom is much vexation and the more a man knows, the more he has to suffer" (1:18). Yet, "wisdom excels folly." Despite obvious limitations, wisdom at least prevents us from making utter fools of ourselves (2:19). Hard work is meritorious, but men seem driven more by "rivalry between man and man" (4:4) than by pleasure in a job well done. The puritan philosophy, work for work's sake, is feckless: "Better one hand full and peace of mind, than both fists full and toil that is chasing the wind" (4:6). He finds paradox. Life rests on quicksand and has no implicit purpose. History is cyclical rather than progressive. Talk of duty is pointless. There is no plan of salvation. Let the youth rejoice in his strength, for it is speedily gone. There are no rewards for being virtuous. God is majestic and transcendent, but indifferent (7:13–14). The mood is close to the critical individualism of the Greek philosophic schools. It certainly has little in common with conventional covenant theology except a pious editorial postscript: "This is the end of the matter, you have heard it all. Fear God and obey His commandments for there is no more to man than this" (12:15). Kohelet, however, is a fourth- or third-century B.C.E. Judean individualist, strongly tied to a cultural inheritance whose aphorisms he often quotes. Having denied the long familiar affirmations of God's benevolent providence, Kohelet should have become a cynic and shrugged off all restraints, but he is enough of a Jew to prefer considering sin to wallowing in it—"It is better to be satisfied with what is before your eyes than to give rein to desire" (6:8)—and to find comfort in repeating lines about the merit of covenant obedience—"Whoever obeys the commandments will come to no harm" (8:5).

The biblical ethic was bracing, full of short urgent commands and specific laws: "relieve the oppressed," "judge the fatherless," "plead for the widow," "leave the gleanings." In contrast to the activist moral heroism of an earlier age, wisdom in this age encourages the quiet life, sometimes even a nearly monastic life of vigils and purifications. In all this writing one is hard put to find a vigorous sermon. Apocalypse and philosophy, yes; active commitment, no.

Amos had thundered: "These are the words of the Lord: For crime after crime of Israel I will grant them no reprieve; because they sell the innocent for silver and the destitute for a pair of shoes" (Amos 2:6). In contrast, IV Maccabees begins:

> Thoroughly philosophical is the subject I propose to discuss, namely, whether religious reason is sovereign over the emotions; the theme is essential to everyone as a branch of knowledge, but in addition it embraces a eulogy of the highest virtue—I mean, of course, prudence.[19]

Prudence is, in the first instance, an intellectual virtue, a correct understanding of the nature of life and of man's necessary and proper relationship to life. Prudence represents an intellectual attainment; indeed, prudence and wisdom are sometimes treated as synonymous. The emphasis is on the dianoetic rather than the active virtues. Men shy away from instinct and spontaneity. Thought tended toward quietism, even resignation, and conventional wisdom not only denied man's control of history, but despaired that a man's exertions could markedly alter his private circumstances. Nobility consisted of self-discipline and self-control rather than physical heroism. Life was bruising. History was repetitive, not progressive. Men did not talk of radically restructuring the social order, but of being unruffled by the confusion and temptations of the city. Detachment, escape from worry, *ataraxia*, was the way to happiness. The talk was of withdrawal rather than involvement, of control over passion rather than passionate commitment, of martyrdom rather than social mission. Philo wrote a highly complimentary account of a Judeo-Egyptian cenobitic community, the Therapeutae, under the title *The Contemplative Life*. These monks abandoned occupation and family "without a backward glance" for a life of solitude and vigil which presumedly prepared them to be "initiated into the mysteries of the sanctified life," and Philo, the synagogue preacher, found the whole enterprise eminently praiseworthy.

The author of IV Maccabees used hero figures from recent Jewish history both to glorify martyrdom and to prove the Stoic doctrine that wisdom enables men to rise above ordinary feelings and fears, even pain. He describes how Seleucid officers had tortured various pious rebels, but could not break their spirit: "Your fire is to us cold, your catapults painless, your violence impotent."[20] The martyr knows that he dies to a greater glory, and his wisdom arms him with immunity to pain. Wisdom contains the power to be indifferent to misfortune. Such experiences as illness and pain are inevitable, but they can be transcended by knowing the true value of things. One who is prepared for the swift and changing tides of life will not be swept away by them. There is a way of spiritual awareness, Torah, which teaches man to bring his life into harmony with the cosmos/God, and a program of self-discipline which trains men to be in control of their feelings.

> Reason, the universal gardener, purges and prunes and binds up and waters and irrigates by diverse devices, and so tames the wild growth of inclinations and emotions. For reason is the guide of virtues and of emotions the sovereign.[21]

Such ideas, though they are in a book aglow with national pride and love of Torah, turn biblical ethics inside out. The cardinal virtues become temperance, prudence, fortitude, and justice. Of the four only justice is an active virtue, and in this new context justice suggests sympathy and fairness, the manners of a gentleman. Man's primary aim is to gain "religious reason," wisdom. The commandments are explained as aids in that endeavor. The Torah is seen primarily as a textbook in wisdom. God is acknowledged as the supreme intelligence whom men approach through thoughtful meditation rather than as the commanding voice men tremblingly obey. This side of Judgment Day circumstances may change, but will not improve. Yet man has a role and heavy duties. The soul is free, if only potentially. Wisdom permits man to control his appetites, passions, follies, and ignorance—all that exposes his soul to the coarsening of a hapless existence. Men search for wisdom not as an end in itself but as the key to happiness, defined as the absence of passion. Bodily grace, regular ablutions, the rhythm of worship, memorizations, and ceremony are helpful in tuning the body to the soul and to the universe/God, and in loosening the grip of the flesh. Immortality is to be free of flesh and passion.

For the Stoics, Epicureans, and Cynics, and equally for the Pharisees, Essenes, and early Christians, the message was to turn away from false political hopes and pointless activity to find salvation through introspection, proper faith, and true community. There would be a better world, but only after God's judgment. It was an either/or age. Men did not think in grays. Either lead a life of contemplation and detachment or be enmeshed in vain activities of no profit and much danger to the soul. The armies of light were at war with the armies of darkness. Either turn away and be of the righteous or stay where you are and be sucked down into the morass. For such sectarians as the Essenes and Dead Sea folk there was no salvation outside their ranks, even for their brothers and fathers. Lonely men need tight-knit groups; frightened men need eternal reassurance that theirs is *the* narrow road to salvation. What alternative did they have? Their God was exalted in majesty and in complete command of history. Their lives were determined by imperial decisions of which they were hardly aware. It was a philosophic commonplace that the universe was governed by destiny, a purposeful but inflexible law. Of all the Jewish cenacles, sects, and philosophies of this period of which we have any knowledge, only the conservative Sadducees stoutly denied the existence of fate and "affirmed that God has no influence whatever on man's needs . . . man's will is free to choose between good and evil." [22] The Pharisees tried to adjust old patterns of thought to divine transcendence by insisting on paradox: "Everything is decreed by fate, but they do not deny that man has freedom of action." [23] Philo practically abandoned covenant thinking for the notion of salvation through grace. God alone, he argued, can open the womb of the soul, sow the virtues in it, make it pregnant with noble things, and cause it to give birth to the good.[24] Man's virtue lies in acknowledging that God is the author of all and in control of all. We hear echoes of Jeremiah's "Let not the wise man glory in his wisdom . . . ," but for Jeremiah the goal of the religious enterprise had been a complete opening of oneself to God so as to be totally obedient to God's law of righteousness. Philo's goal began in philosophical demonstration and tended toward a mystical consummation. Judaism was to be reconstructed as a sacred science rather than a consecrated way of life. The Dead Sea covenanters took man's dependence one step further: "Man is not master of his ways and the sons of man cannot direct their steps; for the justification belongs to God and perfect conduct comes from His hand." [25] This proto-Calvinist doctrine of election would not be pursued, but its very existence testifies to the force of the popular emphasis on God's omnipotence and man's impotence and limitation.

Burdened men turn to faith for the promise, a gospel. The old promise had offered national security, good harvest, and rain. Men still longed for these, but more and more they looked to their own needs in this world and the next. Ideas about the immortality of the soul and resurrection of the body (only the Sadducees denied such ideas as nonscriptural) became dominant themes. Popular religions, especially the mystery cults, revealed to their initiates the secrets of a blessed hereafter, and the way there. The accepted description of man as a soul temporarily enveloped in the flesh provided an easily appropriated conceptual base for the promise of immortality. The soul was identified with Plato's concept of form or idea. The soul is the form of the body; consequently, by philosophic definition, the soul is preexistent and immortal, as are all forms. Conventional wisdom affirmed that the immortality of the soul was not only asserted by piety, but proven by what the Greeks delighted to call science. But, however much desired, this promise could not have been adopted by the Jew if his Book had not "taught" immortality. What else had God meant when He promised Moses: "You are soon to lie with your fathers. This people will rise up . . ." (Deut. 31:16)? In context the text meant what it said—"This people will rise up and go astray after foreign gods." In the midrashic scheme where every phrase, indeed every word, had its special meaning, to "rise up" obviously indicated the promise of resurrection. There were other proof-texts. Ezekiel's oracle of a nation which rises out of skeletons strewn around the desolate valley became another classic proof-text for resurrection. Had not God said unto the bones: "I will put breath into you, and you shall live. I will fasten sinews on you, bring flesh upon you, overlay you with skin, and put breath in you, and you shall live" (Ezek. 37:5–6)? The image was of the nation's rebirth, but, no matter, the language was graphic.

Daniel, contains one of two canonized texts, both quite late, which explicitly affirm resurrection. "Many of those who sleep in the dust will wake, some to everlasting life and some to the reproach of everlasting abhorrence" (Dan. 12:2). The other is an apocalypse interpolated into the scroll of Isaiah: "Oh, let your dead revive! Let corpses arise! Awake and shout for joy, you who dwell in the dust!" (Isa. 26:19). Biblical men had been gathered to their fathers. The Maccabean martyrs will be raised up to everlasting life. Life everlasting may involve immortality of soul, resurrection of the body, or both. It has been suggested that the hope of physical resurrection was particularly popular among Palestinian Jews, while the promise of the soul's immortality had particular appeal in the Diaspora. This may be so, but the two themes were commonly intermingled and gained swift, almost universal popularity in Palestine and elsewhere, among scholars and simple folk, among the Hellenized and the loyalists. When a second-century B.C.E. scholar translated the promise of Isaiah 26:19 for the Septuagint, he made sure that no one mistook its import for the older, orthodox theme of national resurrection. "The dead shall be raised up again, even they in the tombs shall be raised up." Immortality and resurrection had become biblical ideas.

⋈

Philo's writings (2 B.C.E.–70 C.E.) brilliantly remind us how reasonable the new awareness was held to be. This well-born Alexandrian gentleman and scholar-contemplative, who occupied himself professionally as a preacher on biblical themes, produced the most extensive surviving body of literature by a single hand from this age. His materials are of several types: personal histories such as *Against Flaccus* and the *Embassy to Gaius;* records of a mission to the Roman emperor consequent on an anti-Jewish pogrom; thematic essays such as *Concerning the Contemplative Life, That Every Good Man is Free, Questions and Answers* to the first two books of the Torah; and two types of allegorical commentaries on the law, one generally labeled "expositions" in which he deals with the teaching of the Torah, more or less moving along with the biblical text: *On the Creation of the Universe, Life of Abraham, Life of Moses, Of Special Laws, Of the Decalogue;* and the other generally called "allegories" in which he focused on a single idea or theme: *Of Cherubim and the Sword of Fire, Of the Progeny of Cain, Of Sobriety, Of Dreams.* Philo was a confessed and proud apologete, but in his writing he described a Judaism which is no longer primarily a national religion of law and covenant but a profound intellectualist metaphysics whose laws and traditions are aids to a redemptive understanding.

Philo offered a set of philosophic ideas which permitted men to accept the broad outline of both the Greek and the biblical world. In so doing, Harry A. Wolfson believes, Philo essentially and originally surveyed and described the field in which most medieval religious philosophers would set their plow. Philo insists that reason is a graceful tool which cannot on its own guide men to an adequate and true knowledge of God. Reason must be aided by revelation, by which Philo meant the record of Sinai as set down in the Bible. The Bible's intrinsic merit is beyond question. The Torah is the perfect book. Revelation, the Bible, makes clear what reason cannot about God, creation, and immortality. The philosopher-commentator's life work was to examine each of the Bible's parts, the law, the lore, and the teachings, and explain how these complement one another so as to form a coherent redemptive understanding of the universe. In Philo's view Torah law and learning are sacred, perfect, and perfecting. Life is redeemed by meditation, metaphysics, moderation, and the mercy of God, by knowledge rather than by *mitzvah*, the deed.

By self-discipline and study, regimen and discipline, men can cut the ties of the flesh and circumstance and rise above their earthbound existence, their souls rising through the various related spheres toward God. Put another way, as Philo says, "to fly from oneself is to flee to God." God "becomes gracious to those who depart with shame from incontinence to self-restraint, and deplore the deeds of their guilty past, abhor the base illusive images which they imprinted on their souls and first earnestly strive to still the storms of the passions, then seek to lead a life of serenity and peace." [26]

Having sanctified religious philosophy, Philo proceeds to show how a Bible-based faith can express itself creditably in philosophic terms. The tendency of the Greek schools had been to speak of God as unknowable, since any attribution of quality to God would imply division within Him. Philo separated God's essence from His existence. God's essence is unknowable. The Torah itself insisted that God was not to be likened to anything known. But the universe, all that man is, sees, and can understand, testifies to God's existence.

Philo's thought seeks to eliminate the necessity of assuming God's total otherness. God's goodness had meant to Plato and the Stoics only that God had created a good world and that His energy sustains its motion. They denied that God knew or concerned Himself with any individual. Philo defends God's active goodness, the presence of will within God's flow of power, by insisting that God's existence as known by man shows that He acts freely and with purpose. Against the Greek assumption of blind power Philo constantly affirms God's concern and His power to save. "To him who is worthy of My grace, I extend all the boons which he is capable of receiving." [27]

The universe was "thought out" by God and His intelligence is imprinted in its every aspect. If all that one can say of God is that He is the source of the ideas which form and inform the world, how does God relate to the physical universe and to man? Did He speak and it was? Not at all. Speech is a human attribute. Philo developed a sophisticated theory of emanations. God's universe is filled with intermediate beings, first among which is the *logos*. God is pure being. The *logos* is the original emanation from this pure being, the unity of ideas, the place of the intelligible world, the fountainhead of all movement, the uppermost reaches of the heaven, God's first-born who carries out His father's will and is senior among all the angelic forms which animate the spheres. Descriptions of *logos* are varied and many, but all assume that within nature there is an intelligent divine energy which is of God, God-like but not God, and through which man comes to God and God to man.

Philo tried to reconcile the notion of God as Greek philosophy generally described deity—omnipotent, transcendent, other—and the biblical record of a God who watches over and cares for individual men. His theory of emanation suggested to him that he could logically hold onto the systematic argument that God is unknowable as well as the biblical record of God's self-revelation in history. "For God, not condescending to come down to the external senses, sends His own words or angels for the sake of giving assistance to those who have virtue." [28] What men see as God's activity is really the activity of the *logos*. One of Philo's favorite texts was Exodus 33:23, "You [Moses] shall see My back; but My face shall not be seen." From this he inferred that God's essence is unknowable, but that His back, the emanations of His power, can be known.[29] Greek astronomy described a universe in which the planets revolved around the earth, and beyond them the fixed stars revolved in the firmament. The animating spirit of each sphere was sometimes called its angel, and each sphere derived its nature, if not its motion, from the supervening circle. Motion/creation/reason passed along and down these circles until it touched the earth; the rational soul could climb back up these circles until it touched the highest heaven, divinity. The purpose of philosophy and faith was to prepare the soul for that journey.

Philo developed those doctrines not as an idiosyncratic theory, but as an adequate and proper interpretation of Judaism. His method was midrashic. He interpreted or expounded a biblical chapter or theme. He approached Judaism almost as if he conceived of it as a particular mystery and of the Torah as containing a special gnosis which, by careful exegesis, might be understood and made to reveal the pattern of being. The Torah, especially the book of Genesis, becomes the subject of a sustained allegory in which the soul burdened with the confusions of life sets out on a spiritual journey that, if properly managed, will permit it to gain truth and immortality. The patriarchs and matriarchs are *nomoi empsychoi*, "fleshed out truths," whose biographies, allegorically interpreted, reveal the basic truths about man, man's nature, and God. Philo explored the full meaning of Torah as *nomos*. *Nomos* on one level was ordinary law, and much of Philo's writing was designed simply to show the deep and valuable insights implicit in the scriptural law which Philo faithfully obeyed. *Nomos* is also a positive or natural law: "The cosmos is in harmony with the law and the law with the world." [30] To understand *nomos*/Torah in this sense is to understand God's purpose for man and to make it possible for man to put himself in harmony with that purpose. To understand *nomos* is to be able to look behind the world of appearances, what men ordinarily mistake for reality, and draw close to God, the only ultimate reality, by a process of reason based on acceptable logical demonstrations.

Philo is literate, learned, subtle, not always consistent, a contemplative, a consummate interpreter of the Septuagint textual tradition, and a passionate defender of the faith. He looms large in the intellectual history of the West, but his own religious tradition hardly acknowledged him. His works were not translated into Hebrew or Aramaic, nor were they directly quoted in rabbinic writings. If the early Church had not found his allegorization of the literal meanings of the various laws suggestive and polemically useful, Philo might have been entirely forgotten. Philo's concept of divine intermediaries fit neatly with the thought behind the Gospel of John. But most of all the Church found itself appealing precisely to the kind of audience for whom Philo had written—one aware of and conditioned by Greek categories of thought. Judaism's scholars, on the other hand, particularly those of Palestine, insofar as Philo's writings were available to them, must have found his commentaries based on a faulty textual tradition and full of well-intentioned but wild allegory. Moreover, he was not by discipline or training one of them—and it was into their hands that circumstance/God would put the future of Jewish life.

CHAPTER

❧ XIII ❧

Torah in the Age
of Variety

In pre-exilic times there were *torot*, divine laws, but no Torah, no single inclusive statement of the will of God. After the Exile various collections of *torot* were edited into such scrolls as "the book of the law of God" (Neh. 8:8), which Ezra read out in the plaza of Jerusalem to a community which bound itself by oath "to obey God's law given by Moses, the servant of God, and to observe and fulfill the commandments of the Lord our God, His rules and His statutes" (Neh. 10:30). Ezra's scroll may not have been identical with the present Pentateuch, but it must have included a good part of the received text. After Ezra the work of authorization and promulgation of the book of the laws of God seems to have been carried on in Jerusalem by scribe-scholars of the priestly caste. By the third century b.c.e., when the Septuagint Torah translation was made, the Five Books of Moses served as the written constitution of the Judean community and were accepted as a faithful record of the revelation at Sinai, and consequently as the substance of the covenant between God and Israel.

Obviously the accuracy of this text was of critical concern. Precision is the first requirement of law, and these scribes sought to establish an authorized text from variant phrasings of the received *torot.* It was reported that the scribes counted every phrase and every letter of the text and discovered that a *vav* in the noun *Gaḥon* in Leviticus 11:42 was the middle letter of the Torah.[1] Such numbering was not an idle game; indeed, one Talmudic etymology derived the title of the scribes, *soferim*, from *safar*, to count.[2] It was all part of their program to establish a standardized text. God's word must be presented accurately, both in phrasing and arrangement. Had not God admonished Israel: "Be careful to observe only that which I enjoin you: neither add to it nor take away from it" (Deut. 13:1)?

The need for an official Torah text was underscored by interminable and bitter debate between the Judeans and the Samaritans. The Samaritans of the hill country to the north of Jerusalem were the spiritual, if not the actual, descendants of those Israelites left behind when the better classes had been exiled to Assyria in 722 B.C.E. They accepted the Five Books of Moses together with the book of Joshua as Torah, but their Torah contained, besides numerous minor orthographic and grammatical deviations from the text the Judeans prized, a significantly different rendering for Deuteronomy 27:4 and Joshua 8:30. When the children of Israel are about to ford the Jordan and cross into the Promised Land, they are told in the received Torah to build their first altar in their new home on Mount Ebal. The Samaritan Torah indicates that this altar was to have been raised on Mount Gerizim, the height above Samaria where, in fact, Israel's high place had flourished. In the fourth century B.C.E. Samaritans began to build a temple on Mount Gerizim as a rival to Jerusalem, claiming that Mount Gerizim had been not only the first center of worship for the children of Israel in the Promised Land, but the site God had designated for His eternal sanctuary. The issue had complex economic and political overtones, but its nub was a disputed reading of the Torah text. It was not an edifying debate, no compromise was possible, and the rupture between these groups, in which each repeatedly involved the Persian authorities, would last for centuries. What the Samaritan schism did show was that the Torah was the rock on which the tides of brotherly dispute would break. Reality, truth, was in the Book, not in nature or experience. Torah study was research into the truth, not simply inspiring reading. Before such study could begin the words of God had to be precisely described. The least scribal error might cause incalculable confusion.

Paradoxically, even as the *torot* were organized into a Torah, the

[216]

concept of Torah was being enlarged beyond the central text. This was the great age of Torah expansion. For the first time Judaism defines itself through a sizable scripture and Jews have a new obligation: to study that literature and make themselves over in light of its teachings. The Five Books of Moses become a canonized anthology of twenty-four works, and the written Torah is supplemented by an oral tradition declared to have been part of the revelation at Mount Sinai.

Various scrolls of prophecy, history, and wisdom were drawn together to form the anthology we call the Bible and the Judeans called *Tanach*. *Tanach* is an acronym composed of the initial letters of the three divisions into which the various books were organized almost from the start—Torah; *Neviim*, the prophets; and *Ketuvim*, hagiographic or holy writings. Torah represented Sinai, the revelation of law and truth. *Neviim* contains the prophetic word and those chronicles which provided a clear description of God's providential care. The *Ketuvim* was an anthology of inspired wisdom. There are obvious differences in form and substance among these scrolls, but it was an article of rabbinic faith that all the scrolls were consistent in spirit and teaching. Like a well-cut jewel, the Bible is the single source which delights the eye with its many brilliances. Psalm 78 begins: "Give ear, O My people, to My teachings." A midrashist used the familiar juxtaposition of "teaching" and "Torah" to make the psalm say, "Give ear . . . to My Torah"; he goes on to argue that this identification is made "that no man should say to you: 'the psalms of David are not Torah'—when in fact they are Torah . . . as the books of the prophets are Torah . . . and not only the revelations, but even the riddles and the parables, they also are Torah." [3]

This was an age of scrolls and scribes, the first bookish age in Jewish history. Motives for putting together the *Tanach* are probably to be located in the need to declare certain works and versions authentic and inspired so that others could be treated simply as literature and judged accordingly. Most manuals describe this century's long process as one of canonization, a term which conjures up an image of bureaucratic process and first appears in fourth-century writings of the Church fathers. Jewish sources have no label for this process, little of which was committee work; but they describe the accepted texts as scrolls "which defile the hands," [4] which means that such books were deemed holy, and to touch them was to receive their holiness into one's hands and to accept a ritual obligation to wash off this holy residue before engaging in any mundane task. In this ceremonial way the divine inspiration of these books was made clear for all to see.

The editing of the *Tanach* was a long process which began even before the Exile, when various individual chronicles and prophetic words were assembled, and was completed only in the second century of the Common Era, when various tannaitic academies held formal sessions at which final decisions were made on the claims to scriptural status of such texts as Ezekiel, Ecclesiastes, and Esther. Here we are not concerned as much with the process of acceptance and rejection—prophetic inspiration was obviously one criterion for inclusion, content another, traditions linking the text to a revered ancestor as author a third—as with the consequences of the promulgation of this vast library as Scripture. Books "which defile the hands" are holy books and must not only be treated with special care and respect—to this day a pious Jew will kiss a *Tanach* if it should accidentally fall to the floor—but must be acknowledged as consistent in teaching, since each work is inspired by a single source, God's wisdom. Such coherence was not always self-evident, and a major thrust of subsequent Jewish thought will be to demonstrate the unity of these texts and in so doing to make plain the consistent teaching which is God's gift to Israel.

In the synagogue a complementary reading (*Haftarah*, conclusion) from the *Neviim* or the *Ketuvim* was added on Sabbaths and feasts to the weekly Torah reading in order to symbolize this unity of spirit and teaching. Much of the cumbersome quality of early *midrash* is due to its formal concern for presenting proof-texts from the three divisions of the *Tanach* in order to expose the Bible's consistency of statement. Often the texts cited hardly seem to bear on a particular point, and rabbinic logic is at its most graceless and formal in some of these expositions; but the drive to create a unity of truth will not be diverted and is a hallmark, perhaps the hallmark, of rabbinic writing. To study Torah was always to confront a coherent truth, ideas which might be in suggestive tension but never in direct contradiction. The men who studied Torah sought to accommodate ideas, not to oppose them. "R. Eliezer and R. Yehoshua sat occupied with Torah . . . joining the Torah to the prophets and the prophets to the holy writings." [5] It is never either/or, but always "both this view and that view are the word of the living God."

Rabbinic works often seem untidy because of the glut of texts and citations which fill almost every page. What the reader faces is not the clutter of an untidy mind, but the almost infinite number of texts which had to be tied together before another detail in the monumental design of God's wisdom could be filled in. The sage faced a gargantuan task. He had to unify twenty-four holy books, each bristling with apparent inconsistencies, as a single teaching, and he could not gloss over or treat offhandedly a single idea or phrase. Judaism paid a price for its books. Their remarkable range and depth was literally a Godsend, providing sweep and wisdom, but faith in their inspired nature burdened the Jew with a problem of synthesis so complicated and vast that he labored for centuries so that these texts would yield the coherent wisdom with which God had inspired them. When I read rabbinic commentary I sometimes long for a simple, personal tale of spiritual quest which would appeal directly to the soul; but I console myself that life is not simple, that simple truths are often dangerously misleading, and that if this welter of commentary is not always neat it is almost always thought provoking.

❧

Some religious traditions insist that God requires a certain attitude toward life, such as joy or empathy, rather than obedience to specific rules. Judaism insists that duty can be precisely defined: "God has told you what is good and what it is the Lord asks of you . . ." (Micah 6:8). For Jews the term Torah represents the service God requires, and by Torah the Jew means the requirements of the revealed covenant, specifically the contents of the Five Books of Moses physically present in a synagogue's ark and all the teachings assumed to be implicit in that scroll. This was to be an age in which the definition of Torah law expanded through need and scholarly analysis.

Torah law is spare; it is anything but complete. What does it mean not to labor on the Sabbath? Cutting wood in the forest is clearly to be classed as labor, but is it labor to take a piece of cut wood and throw it on the fire in your grate, or to have a fire continue burning in your grate over the Sabbath? Various venerable traditions dealt with such contingencies; some of these traditions claimed oracular authority, but others were simply long-standing customs based on broadly accepted interpretations of the written law. The need to reconcile these traditions, to provide order and authority so Israel would know exactly and specifically what God required, was faced up to by a class of scribe-scholars, the *soferim*, who immersed themselves in the Torah, its commentary, and the oral traditions. The questions with which they wrestled were these: What are the full implications of each Torah law for the community? Is a particular law honored by tradition as part of the covenant but not found in the Torah part of the covenant, and, if so, what are its implications? Little is known of the actual work of the *soferim*, but the later tradition suggests their role when it uses such categories as *mikra soferim* (a scribe-authenticated Torah reading), *dikdukei soferim* (scribal details), and *divrei soferim* (scribal teachings).

This process of legal definition and of establishing a coherent covenantal life style continued both formally and informally, and by the second century authority for Torah interpretation and for the systematization of customary practice seems to have been vested in a Torah Council, the *bet din ha-Gadol*, sometimes also called Sanhedrin, which held its sessions in a hall of the Temple. Few issues in Second Temple history are as uncertain as those which involve the composition, authority, and activity of this body. Some historians believe that there was not just one governing council, but two or even three bureaus: one to deal with ceremonial and priestly matters, one political, and one dealing with matters of Torah law. Contemporary references are few and inconsistent.

Because of the New Testament account of Jesus' trials before the Sanhedrin, this council(s) is more widely known as a High Court than as a place of judicial review. However, it is its function in cases that involved the reviewing and establishing of law that primarily concerns us. Under the early Hasmoneans the seventy-one or twenty-three members of the council-court were divided between Sadducees and Pharisees, that is, between men who held divergent interpretive philosophies. The opposition of the Pharisees and the Sadducees is historically famous but was, in fact, remarkably short-lived. During the long reign of John Hyrcanus (135–105), some Pharisees came into open conflict with the king and were summarily dismissed, but after some unrest Queen Alexandra (76–67) reestablished the Pharisaic sages and conceded to them dominance of the *bet din*. In a matter of three generations the Sadducees pretty well played out their string and were almost entirely supplanted by the Pharisees. By the time Jerusalem fell in 70 C.E. the Pharisaic tradition had become dominant and unrivaled there, and it alone effectively survived those catastrophic days.

The Sadducees represent a Torah-devoted traditionalist element, that part of the establishment of Hasmonean Judea which was prepared to spend time and energy dealing with the exigencies of Torah law. Popular histories sometimes confuse the Sadducees with the entire establishment. The extreme Hellenizers were not found among them. Indifferent Jews spent little time with the nuances of *halacha*. Sadducees had fought for the Hasmoneans; otherwise they would not have been allowed to sit on a court under Hasmonean sovereignty. The Sadducees seem like a small legal fraternity—Josephus reports that "their views were received only by a few" [6]—who accepted the written Torah, as it had been traditionally interpreted, and the force of the various oral traditions which formed the customary law, but who denied that such customs were covenant, of divine origin. The Sadducees also accepted the legitimacy of positive law, the prerogative of those in power to promulgate decrees on their own authority. Their reading of Torah simply did not lead them to the notion of an all-embracing Torah. They accepted a fundamental division between constitution and custom, between Torah and tradition. The Sadducees were not fundamentalists who believed that the Torah said it all, and that all the Torah said was readily apparent. Accepting the legitimacy of man-made law, they had no need to declare noncanonized traditions as part of the original revelation. The Sadducees obeyed many such traditions, but they saw them as customary law of great antiquity, valid but not immutable, and refused to declare them Torah.

Louis Finkelstein and others have tried to define the political, social, and economic class interests which Sadducee and Pharisee separately represented and defended. There is no doubt that they represented different interests, the Sadducees perhaps the older, land-based upper class, the Pharisees a growing urban middle class. However, the differences between them cannot be reduced to narrow Marxian terms, for they involved primarily each group's respect for a particular tradition of Torah exegesis. There were priests who were Pharisees and probably commercial types who were Sadducees. No meaningful economic consequence can be drawn from their separate interpretations of such matters as whether metal utensils, like pottery vessels, are subject to the possibility of being rendered religiously impure. It seems more a case of the Sadducees saying, "Such has never been the case," and the Pharisees saying, "It should have been."

When Sadducees debated Pharisees over particular issues, the battles were fought as court battles generally are—at one remove, over the legal theory involved in such apparently nonclass-oriented issues as the dating of Shavuot, the extent of liability incurred by a false witness, and the responsibility of an owner for damages committed by his slave; and over issues where a ruling depended as much upon interpretation of an ambiguous Torah text as on conflicting class interests. One illustration must suffice. The Torah law which establishes the date of the spring harvest festival of Shavuot reads: "From the day after the Sabbath, the day that you bring the sheaf of wave offering, you shall count seven full weeks . . . then you shall bring an offering of new grain to the Lord" (Lev. 23:15). Forty-nine days shall elapse between Passover and Shavuot, that is clear. But when was the community to begin counting? "From the day after the Sabbath." Which Sabbath? The first day of the Passover holiday is by biblical rule a Sabbath, and so is the mandatory weekly day of rest which fell during the Passover holiday week. The matter is not one of little consequence. Correct observance of God's law was a matter of moment. God's pleasure with Israel was at stake. During the second century B.C.E. the Dead Sea covenanters and the devotees of the book of Jubilees broke decisively with the Temple's priesthood over issues involving the calendar. What was involved was a hard and still unclear text—and the unity of the community.

An analysis of recorded decisions by the Sadducees indicates a tendency to favor the venerable prerogatives of the priesthood and customary ritual practices. In the matter of the financing of the daily sacrifice, the Sadducees held that, as in times past, the cost should be borne by individual donors. The Pharisees wanted the cost to be borne by the general treasury so that wealth should have no special privileges before God and all Israel would participate equally in the offering. The Sadducees argued from familiar custom, the Pharisees from social concern. Each buttressed his position by citing various texts which suggested by analogy the validity of their position.

The Sadducees cannot be dismissed as a feudal gentry stolidly defending ancient privileges. Torah, Temple, God's majesty, God's grace, the covenant, and man's covenanted duty were precious values among them. Where they failed was in not recognizing the force of change. A new mood had washed over large sections of the people, a mood which emphasized particularly the promise beyond. The Sadducees stoutly denied physical resurrection and questioned the various claims being made about the afterlife, saying simply, "The soul perishes with the body," insisting, as was in fact the case, that these ideas, however popular, had no Torah base.[7] To make this denial the Sadducees had to repress one of man's basic instincts, his will to live on, his inability to see himself blotted out. Also, they had to speak out against the martyr cult, which by now enshrined the heroes of the Maccabean rebellion and sustained the courage of those who resisted Rome. And they had to oppose a worldwide riptide of salvationist thinking, shared by philosopher and simpleton, Persian and Greek, Diaspora thinkers such as Philo and Palestinian scholar-intellectuals such as Hillel. Only the Sadducees said no. Certainly only a sturdy faith in Torah as it had been known and interpreted for many generations could have made them so dogged.

The Sadducees seem men of robust faith. They could carry on as their fathers had, despite the political shadows, and the darkening mood of Jewish thought. The Sadducees' sturdiness comes through in their attitude toward individual responsibility. In an age when most groups, philosophic and religious, Jewish and non-Jewish, emphasized fate, chance, destiny, and even predestination, the Sadducees emphasized the by now old-fashioned doctrine of individual responsibility. "They do away with Fate, holding that there is no such thing and that human actions are not achieved in accordance with her decree, but that all things lie within our power, so that we ourselves are responsible for our well-being, while we suffer misfortune from our own thoughtlessness." [8]

The Sadducees were not drawn to the folkloristic or mythic explanations of fate available in popular angelology and accepted in most other contemporary Jewish circles. The Torah has its share of anonymous messengers of God's will, but, except in Daniel, these spirits are faceless, without individual identity. There is the accuser in Job, the Cherubim and Seraphim in Isaiah, and the "living creatures" of Ezekiel. But, quantitatively as well as qualitatively, these do not compare with the hosts of angels of different ranks and personalities who populate the apocalyptic writings, or the in-dwelling angels of emanationist philosophers, like Philo, who animate the heavenly spheres. The Sadducees sought to limit this angelic population explosion. The Sadducean position was not, as the New Testament claims, a denial that there is any angel or spirit,[9] but the statement that it was inappropriate to personify the divine messengers or to ascribe to them personal names and distinct personalities. They did not argue that *malachim* or *kedoshim* do not exist—Torah and Psalms mentioned angels—but they refused to name and ascribe to Satan, Gabriel, or Raphael biographies which would endow them in men's minds with a mind and capacity all their own, making them in a sense independent of God. Angel lore is colorful and dramatic, men respond to tales of the evil spirits who trip them up and cause them to sin, they feel relieved of much moral responsibility, but the proto-Sadducee, Ben Sira, certainly spoke truth when he remarked cynically, "When an ungodly man curses Satan, he curses his own soul." [10] The Sadducees insisted that man is free and responsible for his acts, and so, under the covenant, responsible for his destiny. God rules Israel alone, unaided, without Satan or Gabriel or the heavenly host. The Sadducees "disregard fate entirely." [11] The nation had a clear mandate to prove itself to God, but most in the nation wanted more encouragement than this simple realism, and found it in the teachings of the Pharisees.

❦

The Pharisees believed that Torah was the familiar text with its specific teachings, together with its appropriate exegesis, and the body of unwritten *torot* which had circulated authoritatively for centuries, venerable rules consecrated by generations of piety which associated these oral traditions with Sinai, together with its appropriate exegesis. God had chosen Israel to be a holy people. Its laws must be, and are, altogether divine. No mortal, priest or king, has the right to legislate for God's special nation. That power belongs only to God. In any case, there was no need for such legislation. The Torah, written and oral, contains a complete law. God had considered and ruled on every possible contingency. God had described in the twofold Torah an all-embracing regimen. Authority for this catholic theory was the Torah itself. "If you shall diligently keep all [*kol*] this commandment which I command you" (Deut. 11:22). The Torah becomes a *Kol Bo*, an all-inclusive body of revelation which should govern every aspect of Jewish life.

The extracanonical traditions came to be called the *Torah she-be-al Peh*, the oral Torah. Sages described the revelation at Sinai as having been accepted in two different ways. One part, written down immediately, became the familiar Torah text, while the other part had been kept as an oral tradition. Moses had memorized it and passed it on to Joshua, his chosen successor, and so it had passed down the centuries by word of mouth from competent teacher to competent teacher. At all times the oral law had been controlled by reliable authorities. Its authenticity was beyond suspicion.

The Torah is seen as *Torah Shelemah*, a systematic and all-embracing rule and instruction. Torah signified the fullness of the revealed tradition, which is to say, the oral and written stipulations and all the deductions, inferences, and case decisions authoritatively derived from them. There were not two laws, but one: the oral and written laws were of complementary and equal authority, and the task of the scholar was to weave them into the seamless pattern of obedience God required of man. The concerns of American constitutional law offer a rough secular parallel, including as they do a Constitution, naturalized traditions from older legal systems, two centuries of accumulated case decisions, theoretical writing on constitutional issues, and the implicit assumption that a consistent attitude toward the organization of human affairs exists within the law.

The concept of an all-embracing Torah did not emerge full-blown, but how it grew is obscured behind the mists of history. What does it mean when Ezra is called "a scribe learned in the law of Moses" (Ez. 7:4)? The *Mishnah* reports that the men of the Great Assembly advised their disciples "to make a fence for the law." [12] What kind of Torah process was involved? All we know is that the tradition of an all-encompassing Torah goes well back and was not an invention of the Pharisees, who appear only after the Maccabean revolt and are often credited with its origination. It is more likely that the Pharisaic scholars were the first group of Torah scholars to deal conceptually with most of these issues.

The all-embracing law is a compilation of discrete and specific commandments. The Pharisees and their rabbinical successors spent their energies relating these specific mandates one to another, fleshing out the practical implications of each, and speculating on the law's underlying theory of justice and social order. It was taken for granted that these commandments and all the rulings that could be deduced from them were coherent and related parts of a God-mandated, all-embracing legal system. The rabbis would say later that God had made known to Moses on Mount Sinai the law down to its smallest ramification,[13] and the Pharisees would have agreed. But myth was one thing and reality another. In fact, the range of the twofold law was not as catholic as Pharisaic theory assumed. The twofold law was a larger but still finite set of discrete rulings; if Israel was to be fully governed by Torah, authorities could not restrict themselves to mechanical application of *torot*. How the all-embracing law was to be applied to each particular set of circumstances became the primary concern of the Torah scholar. Often he had to derive law from commandments which did not directly relate to a particular issue. His occupation was necessarily one of interpretation and elaboration. Although he would have denied vigorously any implication of invention in his work, and insisted that he was only applying the specifics of Torah or its manifest spirit to a particular case, the Pharisaic Torah scholar in fact made law.

The law was specific. As God's law it was treated with the greatest reverence, but it was a law of many individual parts. Not every law was incumbent on everyone. Children, women, and the retarded had far fewer duties and rights than the adult male. The law was immutable and eternal, but parts of it, such as the laws regulating farming in the Holy Land, could not be obeyed by Diaspora Jews. The law of the Jubilee was not enforced after the Babylonian Exile on the grounds that its provision of land reversion could not be effected without the registers of the original land holdings and these logs were no longer extant. The laws of the Temple cult were suspended when the Temple was destroyed. The revision of Torah law was theoretically impossible, but in reality it was a fact of life.

Though they insisted that God had foreseen every contingency, the Pharisees, inconsistently but wisely, permitted the spirit of the Torah to outweigh its specific statement when such a move seemed necessary for the well-being of the community. A classic example involves the institution of the Prosbul by Hillel. The text of Deuteronomy 15:1–12 stipulates that all loans are canceled by the arrival of a sabbatical year. In this urban and financially sophisticated society the rule of septennial cancellation would have led to a serious slowdown in economic activity during the late years of the sabbatical cycle. Who would lend money if in a few months the loan would be automatically canceled? To obviate this problem, the Pharisaic scholar Hillel late in the first century B.C.E. unabashedly devised a legal subterfuge which had the effect of nullifying the impact of the biblical law. By means of a *takkanah*, or emergency decree, he ruled that such loans could be temporarily made over to the courts, a third party who was not a person and so not specifically covered by the biblical text, which is framed in terms of one man lending to another. Hillel did not repeal Torah or nullify it; he simply set it aside by interpretation. Life took precedence over the letter of the law, for the Torah was "a law of life," a justification which was given a scriptural basis several generations later by a sage who deliberately mistranslated Psalm 119:126, "it is a time for the Lord to work: They have made void the law," to read "at a time of working for the Lord, they broke Thy law." [14]

There were relatively few *takkanot*. The pressure of law on life had to be considerable before the sages would grant relief under cover of a legal fiction and the principle of *darchei shalom*, for the sake of the community's well-being. Unless there was prima facie evidence of gross inequity, the law was adhered to, even when there seemed to be humane reasons to suspend it, as in the case of the rule which required eyewitnesses to a man's death before his wife could be declared a widow and free to remarry. Some day, it was argued, he might return and the holiness of marriage would have been tarnished. God's law was never acknowledged as arbitrary. Even when it was difficult to understand a law's rationale, the law was presumed reasonable; and it was accepted that the source of the difficulty lay with man's limited intellectual capacity.

The Pharisees used the authority of the all-encompassing law to oppose the traditional authority of the priest class. In the distant past the priests had promulgated the oracles of God. For centuries after the Exile priests ruled the community. The second century B.C.E. had seen a two-pronged attack on the priests and their privileges. The Hasmoneans by force majeure simply preempted the authority of the major priestly families and took to themselves the crown of the priesthood as well as the throne. At about the same time a class of nonpriestly scribes and scholars began to challenge the legitimacy of the priestly monopoly of Torah interpretation. Everyone agreed that priests were necessary as Temple functionaries, but why should they have a final voice on Torahic matters? The priests answered that God had given *torot* to the priest in the sanctuary and specifically commanded the priests to staff the courts (Deut. 17:8–13). The Pharisees opposed these assertions with a claim of their own, not to blood rights but to Torah rights. God had given His rule to Moses, Moses to Joshua, Joshua to the elders, the elders to the prophets, and the prophets to the men of the Great Assembly. No priest is mentioned in this chain of authorities who had loved and faithfully preserved the all-embracing law.

Times had changed. This was an urban and commercial age, and the priests no longer had a near-monopoly on literacy. In an older age only those of wealth and privilege really had the opportunity to learn. "The wisdom of the scribe depends on the opportunity of leisure; and he who has little business may become wise." [15] Now literacy was more common, and not limited to those who could afford leisure. The Pharisees based admissions to their academies on merit, not on birth, and they brought a new class of Jews into religious leadership. A surprising number of the great scholars, including Hillel, Meir, and Akiva, were born in the hovels of the poor. The rabbinic tradition not only did not disdain hard manual work, but gloried in it. "Excellent is the study of the Torah together with a worldly occupation for the labor they jointly require puts sin out of mind. All study of Torah without physical labor comes to naught and drags sin in its train." [16] Compare this with the older insight: "How can he become wise who handles the plow . . . whose talk is about bulls . . . so, too, is every craftsman and master workman who labors by night as well as by day." [17] Many in the new scholar class combined Torah with such humble occupations as smith, cobbler, charcoal burner, baker, and tailor. The Torah road to salvation was broad enough for the sons of the poor, and they obviously made the law fit more closely the realities and needs of their existence.

The life of an impecunious scholar was not easy. The more Torah, the fewer hours to earn a living. Anyone who has tried to balance earning a living and a full academic program knows the agonies implicit in a sage's admonition: "Make your study a regular thing." [18] But there were spiritual rewards. The Torah scholar felt that he walked on the road that led to salvation. The very word he chose to describe his legal concerns, *halachah*, expresses the sense of being purposefully on the way. Moreover, he was turning himself not only into a useful functionary, but into a divinely required presence who, like kings and priests, represented God among the people. The scholars often spoke of three crowns: the crown of David, the throne; the crown of Aaron, the priesthood; and the crown of the Torah, equal to the first two and "available to all" who will make the effort.[19] The scholars felt themselves in every way equal to, and in many ways superior to, the old ruling caste. Many of the priests were ignoramuses who had nothing to recommend them except their blue blood. Many priests had disgraced themselves during the heyday of Hellenism, when they had listened to the sirens rather than to Sinai. The Pharisees represent the thrust of a democratic impulse against inherited privilege. To prove that they were not only as learned as the priests, but as pure and holy, the Pharisees required of themselves the same degree of ritual purity, the same schedule of lustrations, and the same rules of diet as priests were required to maintain.

The Pharisees even claimed authority to regulate priestly activity in the Temple, which was, in their view, ultimately regulated by the twofold law of which they, not the priests, were the authentic interpreters. Some of the debates between Pharisees and Sadducees seem to involve the question of whether nonpriests can exert authority over Temple matters. One debate focused on the question whether or not a High Priest should carry a lighted censer into the Holy of Holies. The Pharisees said yes; the Sadducees said no, such was not the custom. There are no clear texts, and the issue seems a specific instance of the broad conflict between Torah interpreters who insist that every aspect of Jewish life, even the ritual of the Temple, must conform to their interpretation of Torah, and men who obeyed a more limited Torah which assumed that priests properly regulated the cult. The Pharisees won out, and their spiritual descendants set down in their law books chapter and verse of an annual pre-Yom Kippur vigil during which sages instructed the High Priest how he must conduct himself that day in the Holy of Holies.[20]

We know of the Pharisees as a specific group largely from two non-Hebrew sources: Josephus and the New Testament. There are a few contemporary Hebrew references to *Perushim*, and the term is often translated as the Pharisees, but *Perushim* may mean simply separatists and may identify various groups who separated themselves from the larger community to organize fellowships or *havurot* in which they lived by stricter rules of diet and ritual purity than the ordinary citizen. There probably were Pharisees in these fellowships, but not all Pharisees belonged to such groups, the common factor of which was ritual rigorism, not a particular understanding of the twofold Torah.

These *havurot* paid particular attention to those Torah rules which dealt with the Sabbath, tithes, and ritual purity. A primary purpose seems to have been apocalyptic: the strict regimen of the *havurah* obviously was pleasing to God and encouraged the rigorist to believe that he would be listed among the saved at the End of Time. Such a regimen must have been emotionally satisfying. Through care with diet and matters of purity one avoided contagion, cleansed one's being, and kept it clean. Such a regimen suggested high religious status. These groups imposed upon themselves rules which, until this time, had been mandatory only for the priesthood. Their belief was that if God had established these rules for those who served at His altar, they were the appropriate rules for all who wished to be holy. Moreover, acceptance of these rigors was part of an attack on the prerogatives of the priesthood who justified their special rights by their special purity and holiness. If others attained holiness, did they not merit similar consideration?

[229]

Farmers were in the habit of separating from their harvest the biblically required annual tithe, but few bothered about other prescribed agricultural dues—the heave offering, the second tithe (which was given four times every seven years), and the poor man's tithe (which was to be given on the third and sixth years of the seven-year cycle)—since only priests were prohibited from eating food which had not been fully tithed. The *havurot* took this restriction upon themselves. They would not eat grain from which all the various dues might not have been separated, holding such food to be ritually unclean and capable of rendering unclean anyone who touched it.

There appear to have been many *havurot* and little uniformity in *havurah* practice. Some required one degree of purity, others another; some groups required assurances that the food had not touched the hands of anyone who was careless in matters of tithing; but all the groups shared an overriding concern with "clean" and "unclean" as elemental categories. Ritual cleanliness should not be confused with physical cleanliness. It was a question of taboo, of those things which a society arbitrarily assumes to be unclean and for which various lustrations and purification rites are prescribed on religious, not hygienic, grounds. Insofar as these men rationalized their acts, they probably maintained that duty shapes the man. Constant concern with purity, the making of fences about the law, help to separate man from the noisome vulgarities of the everyday world. A man is what he thinks, and he thinks as he lives. The more he concerns himself with fulfilling God's will, the more he fulfills that will on all levels. Since the Torah made no distinction between ethical and ceremonial duties, the communitarians, like every Torah-bound Jew, accepted as axiomatic that moral and ritual commandments must be obeyed with equal care. One obeyed God in all He required.

How does an individual know that he has not fallen short? By doing more and more of what the law commands, by going beyond the strict measure of the law. Why this sudden interest in such things as ritual purification? The Magi and other religious orders in the East had popularized similar ritualist categories throughout Asia Minor. Men warmly welcomed rigid standards because such rituals made it possible to know when one was living a life which pleased God. There is a certain superficial logic to the theory that a man is what he eats, that if a man's body is clean so is his soul, and that evil is a tangible taint which can be purified or washed away. One of the most characteristic unconscious acts of those burdened by guilt is a constant mime of washing hands and face. Here is a clearly defined way to "wash yourselves clean, put your evil doings away from My sight" (Isa. 1:16). However rigorous the ritual, there is satisfaction in knowing that you have carried it out and a joyous sense of fraternity with those who have been equally rigorous.

Ḥavurot were open to anyone who would undertake their discipline: lay and priest, son and parent, slave and master. On the other hand, *ḥavurot* raised barriers to neighborliness and social contact between the initiate and the ordinary Jew, sometimes even to normal relationships within a family. A son who followed the strict disciplines could not eat in his father's house if his father was not scrupulous in these matters. There was a growing sense of separation between the scrupulous and the ordinary Jew, and some of the scrupulous had little empathy for the courage required by ordinary men trying to live out their lives and provide for their families in extraordinarily hard times.

Communalism weakened the sense of belonging to a religious nation; the son of the poor who was an initiate in a *ḥavurah* looked down on the less ritually rigorous, but no less poor, plebeian Jew. "An *am ha-aretz* cannot be a *ḥasid*." [21] Some groups even established grades and ranks among novice, initiate, and leader within their fellowship. Each *ḥavurah* came increasingly to assume that only they, "the elect," "the righteous," would enjoy the fullness of God's salvation. Attempts by some historians to paint the Pharisees and/or *Perushim* as the first complete religious democrats emphasize only the antipriest side of their lives and thought.

A ramified code of discipline developed in these *ḥavurot* to protect the scrupulous from even accidental contagion, and clear rules set out the steps of purification from acquired impurity. Voluntary assumption of the full burden of these rules separated the initiate from the teeming mob. He lived largely in and among men of like practice, protected from the vulgarity of the city and isolated from its barrage of dirt, sights, sounds, and allurements. There was psychological benefit to the individual in undertaking such a regimen. Religion became tangible. One knew he was fulfilling God's will and felt more confident of salvation. The initiate knew that he was as obedient as the most scrupulous priest. He might have been saying, "I am in all things a priest. I study the law. I accept the same rules of ritual purity. He has no personal disciplines that are not mine. He has no unique claim on salvation which is not mine."

The twentieth century has rediscovered the elemental human need for community. In our urban sprawl men seek the companionship of small groups where they will be known as individuals and whose way of life will set them apart emotionally from the noise of the mob and the grind of the city. To justify being apart, the group develops a private regimen and a strong conviction that it has something unique to offer those who join. Some of the communalists looked upon ritual concerns as ends in themselves. The *Talmud* tells of "shoulder-*Perushim*" who display their deeds high on their shoulders, of "just a moment *Perushim*" who say "wait a moment, and I shall do a good deed," and "pestle *Perushim*" whose heads are always bowed in mock humility.[22] Ritual was ultimately significant to them, but the ethical reach of the *Perushim* was often quite saintly and their moral theology of a sophisticated order. The Pharisee scholar Hillel, at least for certain periods of his life, seems to have been a member of such a *havurah*, and no gentler or more noble figure emerges in Jewish history. Those who were ethically sensitive certainly were not coarsened by their demanding way of life.

Alongside such *havurot*, fellowships of Torah scholars sprang up which took pains not only with the rituals of purity but with the ritual of study. When rabbis looked back on these groups several centuries later, it seemed appropriate to say: "The *haverim* [the fellows] are none other than the scholars." [23] Torah study was required of all male members. These were the first Jews to declare study, *Talmud Torah*, an essential religious discipline. The Torah, they said, stipulated *Talmud Torah*. "Impress them upon your children, recite them when you stay at home and when you are away" (Deut. 6:7). This rule was confirmed in the historical books: "This book of the law must ever be on your lips; you must keep it in mind day and night" (Josh. 1:7). Torah study pleased God, deepened one's knowledge of the law, and offered a broad wisdom/truth. The emphasis on study may also reflect the program to displace the priestly elite, who, in the age of the *soferim*, had taken upon themselves sole responsibility for instruction in the law. Ezra, a priest, had instructed his generation in the law; the *soferim* were mainly priests; but now *Talmud Torah* became a universal male obligation, and the scholar was looked upon as performing an activity essential to the faith's salvational power. Study comes to be called *avodah*, the holy service of God, the very term which had been used to describe sacrifice upon the Temple altar. *Talmud Torah* is seen as a redemptive act. Torah was God's immanent presence as well as His truth. Through study men learned His will, gained understanding of the structure of creation, and drew as close as man can to the divine intelligence; Torah was a way to salvation and mystical union.

Talmud Torah grew from within, but precisely because it seems so natural to Judaism its encouragement by the environment must not be discounted. This age revered and needed philosophers and scholars. The urbanization of a once largely rural population required new insights and a new self-understanding. Semimonastic communities of Stoic, Cynic, Epicurean, and neo-Pythagorean thinkers were common throughout Asia Minor. Study was both profession and a path to enlightenment. It prepared a man to govern others and to govern himself. Study was also a mystical occupation. In study the divine part of the soul/intellect rose above the body and became one with the divine intelligence. Study was a way of enlightenment and of mystic union with the Godhead.

The Jewish scholar-fellowship differed from the Greek largely in this: Whereas Zeno and Plotinus centered their concerns on metaphysics and philosophy, Hillel, Shammai, Yoḥanan ben Zakkai, and Akiva centered their concern on Torah, particularly on its specific implications for everyday life—that is, on Judaism's way of obedience. The Greek philosophers used logic and the various sciences to understand the nature of being. Jewish scholars turned to the Torah and used the tools of exegesis to find not only the requirements of obedience, but an understanding of the nature of being. In the opening chapters of Genesis God had revealed the nature of creation. In the vision of the chariot which opens Ezekiel and in chapter 10 of that scroll, God had suggested the nature of His being. The researches of Gershom Scholem have made it clear that cosmology and theosophy were discussed in Pharisaic circles, and that "it was apparently considered inadvisable to make public these discussions." [24] The scholars studied these texts and talked of metaphysical matters, but never in print or openly or outside their intimate circle. How shall we explain why the scholars maintained silence about what the Greeks published openly? The answer lies less where explanations have generally been located—in Judaism's presumed incapacity for systematic thought—and more in the fact that the Torah itself dealt with these issues, unsystematically and cryptically. Then, too, Jewish thought developed within a religious system; in a redemptive system thought is never merely thought but always a powerful instrument. To understand God's mysteries was to understand His power and presumably to be able to appropriate and use that power. Publication of their esoteric tradition would have seemed to

Pharisaic scholars much like publishing a book of magic, a do-it-yourself manual on the appropriation and use of divine power which could easily fall into the wrong hands.

The Torah was the immanent face God offered to man. Torah was explained in many ways: as a preexistent cosmic blueprint, as a *logos*, as a remarkable and redeeming revelation. The images are not as important as their emotional valence. They suggest that those who studied Torah did not do so simply to master law and to read classic literature, but to meet God and participate in His power. They said *Torah orah*, which translates prosaically as "the Torah is light," but which they translated spiritually to mean the Torah not only enlightened the mind, but was numinous, gave off a holy radiance, and was divine, and that study of the divine word was the most appropriate way to take divinity unto oneself.

Hillel the Elder (ca. 30 B.C.E.–10 C.E.) stands as the classic figure of a Pharisee scholar. He is significant not only for what he accomplished as an academician but for the force of his religious presence, which irradiates the many legends piety wove about his life. As little is known with certainty about his life as about the life of his near contemporary, Jesus, whose saintly silhouette suggests similar qualities of sensitivity and wisdom. Hillel lived in a world where, for the first time, the crown of Torah was available to anyone who could fit it on his head. Torah was an open road, and Hillel's achievement became the proof-text of this openness. According to the accepted tradition, he was born abysmally poor, of nonpriestly lineage, in Babylon. He became the leading scholar of his century in Jerusalem. His story was the Abraham Lincoln epic of the day. One even senses in him some of the same brooding, but intensely human, melancholy.

Hillel vaulted into prominence after a discussion in one of the Torah schools in Jerusalem on an issue which, in import, was trivial: Can the paschal lamb be sacrificed if the eve of Passover happened to fall on a Sabbath? The issue was whether or not the law of Sabbath rest precluded the offering of this sacrifice. Hillel argued that the sacrifice could be offered. His arguments were incisive and his talent won him fame and a semiofficial position in the scholarly hierarchy. Why all this fuss? The event is not all that clear, but what seems to have happened is that Hillel offered several interpretive ways (analogy, deduction from a general case to the specific) to arrive at a decision, and then showed that in each case logical interpretation led to a confirmation of current and accepted practice. In effect he "proved" that the oral tradition and the written law were one. Whereas earlier scholars ruled simply on the basis of precedent, Hillel established and validated seven *middot*, or rules of inference and deduction, as bona fide interpretive techniques which, if properly used when commenting on Torah law, could be depended on to yield Torahic conclusions. Armed with these rules, scholars could handle Torah far more flexibly and confidently and apply Torah law far more easily to the complex problems of society.

Hillel's rules allowed the law to be interpreted more extensively than ever before, but they also created new problems. Once you prove that an interpretive technique permits you to justify what you believe are the aims of the tradition, for example, to establish equality before the law, you may find that these same techniques lead in other cases to unwanted conclusions. This problem has no formal solution. A living law must constantly be interpreted. The only solution is to trust the jurist, who can never be merely a technician. The Torah scholar must really be "a living Torah" who can be trusted to expose the true spirit of the constitution, whatever legal reasoning he adopts. Mental acumen alone was never an adequate qualification for a Torah master. Like Hillel, he had to be what he taught.

In the tradition of many exciting teachers, Hillel founded a school named for him, *Bet Hillel,* and uniquely a dynasty which gained for itself a remarkable suasive authority over the Jews of Palestine. For several centuries descendants of Hillel held authority over Palestinian Jewry as patriarch, and through them the spirit of his juridical approach came to dominate Palestinian Judaism. Hillel is described as pious as well as learned, a teacher as well as a scribe, a mystic, a man of retreats and silence, and a sensitive man who knew well the anguish of the poor. Sages such as he were not merely careerist lawyers. Analysis of Hillel's few surviving decisions reveal a special concern for the common folk, women, and the outcast. To be sure, the search for the historical Hillel is almost as difficult as the much more famous search for his contemporary, Jesus. Our texts are late recensions which include much that is legendary and sometimes contradictory evidence. Scholars have pointed out enough parallels between the Hillel stories and the tales told by Cynics and Stoics about Socrates and Diogenes to make us wonder if any part of the received biography is true. But, at the least, the legends reflect the measure

of the man. Among his Jewish contemporaries Hillel alone is gar-
landed.

Hillel set character above ceremonial punctilio. In those days
moral concern was directed into calmness and sympathetic help
rather than social activism. "Be of the disciples of Aaron, loving
peace and pursuing peace." [25] He lived by a code of infinite patience, and was deeply concerned for another's feelings: "Do not appear standing among those who sit or seated among those who
stand." He set human relations over possessions and learning above
all attainments: "The more flesh, the more worms; the more possessions, the more worry," and "The more Torah, the more life; the
more study and contemplation, the more wisdom; the more counsel,
the more discernment; the more charity, the more peace." [26]

Hillel's theology is submissive. "Blessed be the Lord, day by day,
He bears our burden." [27] "My humiliation is my exaltation. My exaltation is my humiliation." [28] The way of virtue was the way of
Torah and Torah study. "The uneducated man knows not the fear
of sin." [29] "He who has knowledge of the Torah has life in the
World to Come." Torah was a way of "gaining life in this world and
life in the World to Come." [30] In learning Torah one mastered the
lore of nature, learned what life was all about, and became truly
free. The Torah was both knowledge and commandment. By properly obeying the Torah, the Jew aligned his life with God's overarch-
ing plan. He was no longer at odds with himself, God's world, or
God, but united with Him. Harmony had entered his soul and the
world.

To recreate the gestalt of the best of the Pharisees, remembering
that all *Perushim* were not scholars and not all Torah scholars *Perushim*, is to pull together ideas scattered about in the later literature.
These scholars and *ḥavurot* left no systematic theology. Indeed, their
various and disparate careers must give pause to anyone who seeks a
consensus. Certainly this can be said: Their God was the God of
Israel, supreme, One, Creator, omnipresent, one who hears prayer,
a judge who rewards the steadfast and punishes the wicked in this
world and the World to Come. God was exalted above men's
prayers, ineffable, beyond description. They spoke of God, not as
YHWH or even *Adonai*, but as "Might," "the Place," "Ruler of the
Universe," "King of kings," "The Holy One, praised be He," who
ruled the world according to His will and wisdom. Man was free
largely in the sense that his spirit was his. The circumstances of his
society, however, were largely beyond his control.

Torah in the Age of Variety

There was a way that man should go, Torah; an understanding that man should have, Torah; and an exact technique to master that law and that understanding, *Talmud Torah*. He who observed Torah merited salvation, a spiritual blessing in this world and in the World to Come, but the final decision was God's and His alone. The gate was narrow, but God was nigh to all who called honestly and close to man wherever and whenever he was in need. The Temple was a fitting place for worship; the synagogue, which could be located in any place, was appropriate for prayer and meeting. Study, the central virtue, belonged in the school and was that discipline which brought man before God and allowed him to confront the whole Torah. Josephus describes the life of the Torah scholars as simple, unadorned, tradition-bound, respectful of elders, strict, and truly communitarian in spirit.[31] Decency was written large, and so was an otherworldly and eschatological hope to which they were not loath to convert others.

What was the self-image of the Jew in an age of variety? There was not one image, but many. The Essenes and some other contemplatives prided themselves on being adept at divination. At the same time, other Jews felt themselves superior to such foolishness.

> . . . They do not think of the course of the sun and moon
> Nor of the dreadful things under the earth,
> Nor of the depths of the sparkling seas,
> Nor of the signs of the convulsions of the body,
> Nor of the prophetic flight of birds,
> Nor of fortune telling, magicians and sorcerers.[32]

Josephus spoke of "a spirit of brotherhood that prevails among us, our deeds of benevolence, our love of work, our patience to endure the decrees against us." [33] Yet the century-long guerrilla war of the Zealots against Roman rule hardly reveals the Judeans as a patient or quietistic people, and the bitter quarrels between the sects went far beyond the exchange of academic barbs and failed to set an example of generosity of spirit. Nor did every Jew feel himself equally close to all parts of his people. There were high walls between the fellowships and sharp divisions within the community. A nephew of that gentle apologete, Philo, led a Roman legion against Jerusalem during the siege of 70 C.E.

Such unity as existed in Jewish life was, in the first instance, fraternal and formal. Jews affirmed God, Torah, and the Temple. The

Torah gave shape, color, a calendar, structure, a diet, and a holy idiom to Jewish life. Torah imposed upon the Jew his stubbornness and helped set him apart from an easy conviviality with the larger world. Torah imposed distinctness and humanity. It affirmed election and taught that all men have one Father. The exposure of children, common in Greece, was forbidden, as were homosexuality, sodomy, and adultery. Nakedness in public games was looked upon as immodest. Had not the Torah required priests to wear undergarments when they mounted the steps for the ritual? The Torah encouraged universal education. A faith which depends upon a book must be able to read and interpret that book. In time *Talmud Torah* became a redemptive virtue. The book men turned to was no longer in heaven, but on earth, and its teachings promised salvation to those who found God in schoolhouse, worship, and irenic acts of reconciliation.

The illustrations on the first six pages demonstrate what is known of the development of Jewish symbols. The seven branched *menorah*, first in time of the artifacts that survive, bespoke the cosmos, the tree of life, and particularly the redemptive power of the Temple cult. After the Temple's destruction, the *menorah* and representations of the Temple's façade promised its restoration and the coming of messianic times. With the destruction of the Temple (70 C.E.) its power was attached visually to the synagogue by placing pictures of Temple apparatus in it: namely, *lulav*, *ethrog*, *shofar*, and incense shovel. The redemptive authority of the synagogue was uniquely expressed by the Ark of the Covenant as repository of Torah scrolls. In the aniconic ethos of Muslim times, the Torah word itself became an art form and a powerful symbol.

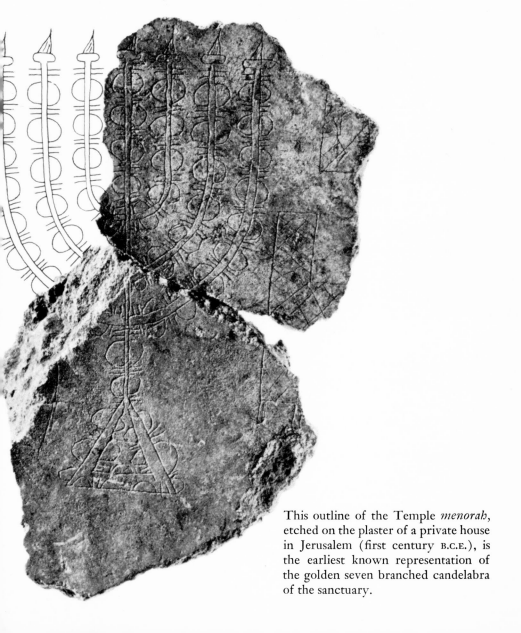

This outline of the Temple *menorah*, etched on the plaster of a private house in Jerusalem (first century B.C.E.), is the earliest known representation of the golden seven branched candelabra of the sanctuary.

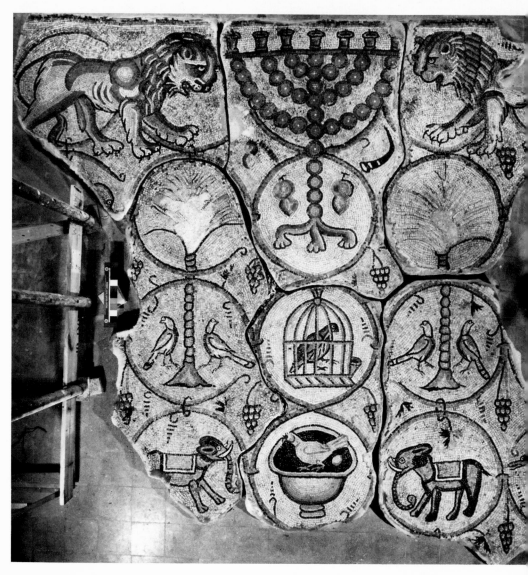

A detail of the mosaic floor of the synagogue at Maon (fifth–sixth century C.E.), which features a *menorah*, *shofar*, lions, and a vine whose tendrils form medallions containing various animals.

TOP: A silver tetradrachm that was minted during the Bar Kochba rebellion (132–135 c.e.) showing the Temple façade and inscribed "Simon" (Bar Kochba).

BOTTOM: Two pieces of gold glass (fourth century c.e.), probably from the catacombs in Rome. The promise of redemption is implicit in the lighted *menorah* and the open Ark of the Law.

A bronze oil lamp (fourth century c.e.), probably of Egyptian origin, decorated with *lulav, ethrog, shofar,* and *menorah.* Such oil lamps were used for light, as gifts for synagogues, and as funeral offerings.

A mosaic floor of the synagogue of Bet Shean (sixth century C.E.). Again we see the important symbols—the Ark of the Law (with drawn curtains), bracketed by *menorah*, *shofar*, and incense shovel.

A carpet page from the Second Leningrad Bible, which was inscribed in Fustat, Egypt (1008–1010). The quotations urge study and meditation of Torah and have both decorative and symbolic force.

The pictures on the last six pages of this section illustrate Judaism's sense of sanctuary as it evolved from shrine to Temple and from Temple to synagogue.

The Holy of Holies from the Israelite Temple in Arad (ninth century B.C.E.). Two incense altars stand at the top of the three steps that lead from the main sanctuary.

TOP: A frontal model of the First Temple (after R. P. Roland de Vaux, O.P.), showing the twin pillars of Boaz and Jachin. The door leads into the vestibule, behind which were the main sanctuary and the Holy of Holies.

BOTTOM: A reconstruction of the Second Temple as it appeared after the reign of Herod. The steps lead to Nicanor's Gate and the inner court, where the main altar and laver stood. Behind these rise the tall doors that lead to the porch, sanctuary, and Holy of Holies.

TOP: A column from The Thanksgiving Scroll, which contains the hymns of the community of Qumran (first century B.C.E.–first century C.E.).

BOTTOM: The eastern view of the excavations of Qumran.

The large, central medallion of the mosaic floor from Bet Alpha Synagogue (sixth century C.E.). Helios driving the horses of the sun is shown in the center, surrounded by the twelve signs of the zodiac, with Hebrew-Aramaic identifications. The four seasons are pictured in the corners.

A general view of the sixth century C.E. synagogue at Kirbet Susiya, south of Hebron. The seats were around the wall of the inner room, which held a Torah niche.

Maimonides certainly passed through these carved pine doors from the Ben Ezra Synagogue in Fustat, Egypt (late twelfth century C.E.). The lintel was added to the synagogue in the thirteenth century and bears a Hebrew memorial inscription.

CHAPTER

ᥰᥰ XIV ᥰᥰ

Angels, Devils, and Judgment Day

I SAW in my sleep what I will now say with a tongue of flesh. . . . Behold in the vision clouds invited me and a mist summoned me, and the course of the stars and the lightnings sped and hastened me, and the winds in the vision caused me to fly and lifted me upward and bore me into heaven." [1] Translated to heaven, Enoch, the pseudonymous hero of this text, saw a great house all of crystal. A flaming fire surrounded its walls; in the innermost room stood a lofty throne enshrined in fire. Here God sat, known as the Great Glory, so awesome that no angel dared approach. God offers Enoch special protection, assures him that he has nothing to fear, and speaks to him of events on earth, of the everyday evils which occur and which will not cease until "the great day of judgment" when this aeon will be consummated so that another may begin.

I Enoch is an apocalypse, a literary genre which appeared for the first time after the Exile and blossomed during Hellenistic times. Apocalypse claims to present revelation, often, as here, in the form of God's speech to a mortal who has ascended to heaven; at other times God's words are made known in dreams or visions. Generally the focus of the revelation is eschatological and concerns the course of history, the timing and nature of the End of Days, the final judg-

[239]

ment, and the ultimate salvation of the loyal and the righteous. It may explain other mysteries: the secrets of creation, the names and functions of angels, or something of the nature of God. Infrequently the revelation concerns halachic matters, a required calendar or regimen.

Apocalypse comes from the Greek *apokalupsis*, which means "unveiling" or "uncovering." As etymology suggests, the purpose of this literature is to disclose hitherto hidden knowledge, mysteries otherwise beyond man's research. The most extended biblical example of apocalypse is the book of Daniel, but fragments of the genre are to be found in various prophetic scrolls, such as Isaiah 24–27, Ezekiel 38–39, and Zechariah 12–14.

Beyond this there are any number of pseudepigraphic works which are in whole or in part of this genre; examples are I Enoch, Baruch, IV Ezra, The Assumption of Moses, and The Ascension of Isaiah. Much of the library of the Dead Sea covenanters is apocalyptic in nature and particularly significant because it comes to us together with a fairly complete picture of the mood, beliefs, and practices of an apocalyptic-ascetic cenacle which formed around a particular teacher's knowledge of the mysteries. These materials afford us a glimpse of the tight discipline, the lustrations, purifications, long night vigils, and communal meals which such groups practiced in the belief that they were qualifying themselves as the "elect," the "righteous," the "saints," the "wise," the "poor," the "silent"—they called themselves by many names—who would enjoy life beyond the cataclysm.

Zechariah 14 offers an early skeletal example. The Day of God is near. It will be a time of bloody national defeat, but God will not permit Israel's total annihilation. In the nick of time He will rise up and fight against the enemy. His victory will mean not only Judahite independence but a miraculous change in the terms of the nation's life. God will refashion Jerusalem's geography and climate. A rocky and arid section of hill land will become a fertile and well-watered plain.

The last chapters of Daniel (10–12) present apocalypse in fuller bloom. A word, "and the word was true" (10:1), is brought by Michael, guardian angel of the Judean exiles, to Daniel, and the word purports to be "what is written in the Book of Truth" (10:21). This writing and these words describe the future: "I have come to explain to you what will happen to your people in days to come" (10:14). Daniel is awestruck. He falls prostrate, but Michael touches his lips and tells him not to fear. Michael's message suggests, albeit in a cryptic and coded way, the fate of various rulers and the occurrence of a series of portentous events which will occur between Daniel's day and "the end of time" (11:40), "a time of distress such as has never been" (12:1), darkness, the End. But out of darkness, light: "Your people will be delivered." Who will be saved? Those "who shall be found written in the book" (12:1), not the whole nation but its "best" part, "the wise leaders" (12:3). The promise is literally one of new life: "Many of those who sleep in the dust will awake, some to everlasting life and some to the reproach of eternal abhorrence" (12:2). The apocalypse ends with a warning: This knowledge is made known to you, Daniel, but "keep the word secret and seal the book till the time of the end" (12:4).

Apocalypse purports to make known the course of history before it happens. History is finite and linear. There will be "an End of Days," Judgment Day, and a new beginning, "The World to Come." The key secret in these writings concerns the actual date of the End. Generally it is said to be quite near and its coming cannot be delayed or changed by prayer or repentance.

Apocalypse is both a style and a statement. Its signature is a unique and fascinating use of strange and bizarre figures as coded illustrations of its prophecies and teachings. Various, often incredible, animals stand in for the kings and nations whose fate is described; coded numbers purport to reveal God's timetable for the time of tribulations and the final Judgment Day. These disjointed images we recognize as the stuff of the unconscious, and they remind us that though many of these visions were ascribed to long-dead heroes, they were not necessarily self-conscious literary inventions. Of course some elements were consciously added, but at least the core of apocalypse seems to have been genuine. These writers knew the spirit "which transports and makes me to tremble" [2] and the vision "which fell upon me." [3]

Apocalypse developed two biblical themes: the Day of God (*Yom YHWH*) and the End of Days (*Aharit ha-Yamim*). When the faith was young the "Day of God" had designated God's triumph over enemy nations. The pre-exilic prophets had turned these expectations into a nightmare image. Because of Israel's sins the Day of God would be a day of darkness, a day of wrath, trouble, distress, and ruin which is "a swift and terrible end" (Zeph. 1:18). After the Exile apocalypse retained the shiver, but omitted the prophetic charge that doomsday was deserved. Doomsday is assumed, but it will come because it will come, not because the nation's sinfulness forces God's hand. All peoples are doomed. The covenant equation is no longer at the center of things. Mankind's fate is prepared, and man has no alternative but to prepare himself for judgment.

The "End of Days" image underwent a parallel development. In earlier theologies it described the more generous time when Israel would be secure in the land and all her dreams would be realized. "After that they will again seek the Lord their God and David their king, and turn anxiously to the Lord for His bounty in the end of days" (Hos. 3:5). It was a happy dream, emotionally satisfying and spiritually necessary, and the dream became bolder as exile lengthened and the few who managed to return found their lives insecure and endangered. Gradually the End of Days became a vision not merely of a happy and secure nation, but of a miraculous transformation of the natural order (Isa. 2:2–4; 30:26). Man's soul will be of a piece, wholly good. Nature will no longer be violent or predatory. The lion will lie down with the lamb. The poetic symbolism of Isaiah 2, in which the child will put his hand without danger on the basilisk's den and no one shall any longer hurt or destroy in all God's holy mountain, becomes, in apocalypse, specific, if rather pedantic, prose:

Wolves and lambs together shall crop grass upon the mountains and leopards shall feed with kids, prowling bears shall lie down with calves, and the carnivorous lion shall eat in the manger like the ox, and the tiniest infant shall lead them in bonds, for He shall make the beasts upon the earth incapable of harm.[4]

The End of Days becomes Arcady. The quietly feeding sheep are not only Israel, but every man and nation. They graze contentedly and securely, for there is none to make them afraid. The world has been converted.

During the political convulsion of the last pre-Christian centuries, the scheduled arrival of the End of Days was moved up. The patient hope "and it shall come to pass in the end of days" gave way to more immediate expectations. Judgment Day and the Kingdom of God were at hand. Relief from Syrian or Roman tyranny was needed now. Men began to see signs of the End all about them: earthquakes, storms, eclipses, worldwide plague, and bloody war warned of impending disaster. Apocalypse was a projection of profound political and social fears, but equally apocalypse projected man's will to live.

"Be prepared; make ready . . . hold yourselves in reserve" (Ezek. 38:7). Beyond the time of tribulation and the Day of God there is a new beginning; beyond death there is resurrection, but the new life will come, as life always arrives, only after hard labor pains, the so-called birth pangs of the Messiah. The Day of God will be a time of convulsion, but God is just and the Day of God will also be a time of judgment. Those who are judged worthy, the righteous, and only the righteous, will enjoy the blessings of the new age.

The spirit of apocalypse dovetailed with a popular fatalism. In the Hellenistic world determinism was personified as *Moira*, Destiny, Fate. In Persia Fate ruled the cosmos and all creatures inexorably, without feeling or sympathy. This was a doomed world in which man knew himself to be prisoner of his instincts, his history, his time and place, his star, and sometimes even of contending cosmic forces struggling to dominate his soul and the world. There was a widely circulated conceit that the world had been programmed before creation to pass through five, six, seven, or ten different and separate ages, and no more. The final age had been entered and was nearing its close. "The world had lost its youth . . . the times began to wax old. . . ." [5] When the End comes the world will revert to its pristine nature or be replaced by a better model, for, using the popular Platonic definitions with which many apocalyptic circles were familiar, this world was only one form of "world." With the death of this world another and better world would be formed. *Midrash* wove this theme into the creation saga. Each day of creation represented one earth aeon; the Sabbath represented the End of Days, when the ideal world would be formed.

Some have described apocalypse as a child of prophecy, for, like prophecy, apocalypse purports to bring God's word to man. It is fairer to describe apocalypse as prophecy's bastard—there are recognizable similarities, but also marked differences of uncertain origin. The lore and lure of astrology, the popular folklore of angels and demons, the Eastern myths with their forceful tales of the struggle between the forces of light and darkness, the activities and intrigues of guardian angels, the images of the fires of Hell and the gardens of Heaven, are perceptions which shimmer off the surface of Persian dualism in its then contemporary Zervanite form and sometimes find their way into Jewish apocalypse. So does something of the emphasis on initiation, secrets, and the saving knowledge of the Greek mysteries. The prophetic word is clear; the apocalyptic word is enigmatic. God had spoken directly to the prophets; in apocalypse an intermediary often mediates the word of God. Both apocalypse and prophecy castigate men for their sins, but in apocalypse the sins are largely those of cult and religious regimen and there is no cause and effect relation between the nation's conduct and its destiny. Covenant language is often used, but it is not primary. "And what was and what will be, he saw in a vision of his sleep, as it will happen to the children of men throughout the generations of men until the Day of Judgment. He saw and understood everything, and wrote his testimonies." [6]

Prophecy dealt with the fate of separate nations, apocalypse deals with the fate of the world. The prophetic words of comfort spoke to the restoration of the nation after the Exile. The apocalyptic hope speaks of the restoration of the saved, the few, in the World to Come. Prophecy had been addressed openly to the nation; apocalypse was presented secretively, its truth reserved for a small coterie of the faithful. The prophetic word tied promise to repentance. The apocalyptic word tied promise to God's plans for the World to Come. The promise reads, "then all who have fallen asleep in hope of Him shall rise again." [7] Mankind's fate is sealed, but the pious follower of a particular teaching can, through fasting, vigils, and pieties, qualify as one of the few whom God will save and revive.

Apocalypse speaks to a world of the emotionally and politically beleaguered, to the desperate loyalists persecuted by Antiochus, Herod, and Rome. Daniel is a paragon of faithfulness whose commitments are severely tried but never broken. He and his friends will not eat prohibited food even though the alternative may be starvation. He risks high office at court, and indeed his very life, to defy a royal ban on God's worship. He is thrown into the lion's den, his friends are cast into the fiery furnace. There is never a whimper or doubt, and they are saved.

Apocalypse speaks to a world which had faith in pneumatics and holy men. The pseudonymous heroes of these scrolls are men of infinite faithfulness and special powers. Daniel was a Judahite Merlin. Enoch had "walked with God." Moses had talked with God face to face. Qumran's Teacher of Righteousness had visited Heaven. Messianic imagery first blossomed in the legends which surrounded these holy men.

As Antiochus and then Rome shadowed this world, the conviction grew that the last epoch was well advanced. Time was short and the usual prudent concerns about retirement, marriage, or children were simply irrelevant.

[244]

Now, therefore, set in order your house and reprove
   your people,
Comfort the lowly among them, and instruct those
   that are wise.
Renounce the life that is corruptible,
   Let go from the cares of mortality;
Cast away the burdens of man, put off now
   the weak nature
Lay aside your burdensome cares, and hasten to
   remove from these time. . . .
For already the eagle is hastening to come which
   you saw in vision.[8]

Apocalypse dates the End, and it is all too near. Why does God reveal his plans? So that man, forewarned, will not be trapped in and by this world. Only those who have renounced the world can escape its death. The apocalyptic world was a world of antimonies. Worldliness/spirituality; this world/the World to Come; the doomed/the saved. Apocalypse deals in black/white; death/life; either/or—rigid polarities. What is demanded is total conversion/renunciation/commitment. Apocalyptic anthropology pictured man in terms derived from the familiar Greek body/soul dualism. Only the soul can be saved. The body is of the world and must be renounced. Virtue begins in self-denial. The cenacle of Qumran was abstemious, confined to one light meal a day, communist, and celibate. Philo says of the Essenes that they looked upon sexual intercourse as a form of defilement. Apocalyptic writings often combine the Persian myth of a battle between cosmic forces, light/darkness, with Greek ideas which described body and soul as antagonistic elements. The reader marvels at the battle of the children of light against the children of darkness—cosmic darkness/body/flesh against cosmic light/soul/spirit—and the tension is high, but in the end God will have His way and those who have kept the faith loyally and broken free of darkness/body/flesh can confidently expect to be saved.

Jewish apocalyptic interest flourished between the third century B.C.E. and the bloody defeat of the Bar Kochba revolt against Rome in 135 C.E. These were difficult years; a time of marching armies, grinding taxes, and, for many, grinding poverty; years when desperate attempts to retain national independence were continually beaten down. The iron maw of Rome, "the eagle that is hastening," crushed all that fell to it. The terrors and loneliness of those days made palpable a sense of ultimate despair even to the point of suggesting that hope itself was a danger: "When they abandon hope, then the time will awake." [9]

Apocalypse is theological drama, with God as both playwright and director. God is all-powerful and transcendent, majestic, and omniscient. Man, like the angels, exists only to serve God. All control is in God's hands: "According to Thy name everything comes to pass, and without Thee, nothing is done." [10] There are no happenings; history develops according to a scenario long since written by God. God is at His most majestic and transcendent seated in Heaven on His throne of glory. Why does God act as He does? God does what He does to sanctify His great name, which has till now been profaned among the nations. "I do not do this for your sake, O House of Israel, but for My Holy Name" (Ezek. 36:22). God is glory (*Kavod*). Creation and Judgment are mighty acts "done for His Glory." God wills to be known, acknowledged as God, and vindicated. We might say that God acts to defend His honor, lest anyone read history as a record of human achievements or fail to see the awesome hand of God behind all phenomena and events.

The term *Kavod*, God's glory, seems innocent enough as a divine attribute. In much apocalyptic material, however, it refers not simply to God's majesty, but to a specific cosmic power, an emanation or materialization of the divine essence, the visible glory of the King of kings upon His celestial throne. Ezekiel had seen "the likeness of the *Kavod* of God" (Ezek. 1:28) in the chariot leaving the destroyed Temple. Since this age conceived of God as *Kyrios*, transcendent, beyond image, some presence had to fill the void and provide man's imagination with something to consider beyond otherness. Philo had described various emanations which arrange themselves in neat concentric circles and touch and animate each other but never break the harmony of the spheres. What the philosophers handled systematically writers of apocalypse handled mythically. *Kavod* became the brilliant majesty of the King of kings, seated on a glittering throne in a glorious heavenly palace. Those who are summoned enter the reception hall with downcast eyes and many prostrations. They cannot see God. The throne is behind a veil, but they have approached the Presence. For the next fifteen centuries Jewish mysticism would use these images of king, throne, veil, and palace to describe what the souls of the righteous perceive as they approach God in moments of mystical communion. That body of writing produced during the first millennium C.E. which describes how man can ascend the heavens to appear before the divine throne became known as the *heichalot* ("palaces") books. In the Jewish unconscious the King of kings ruled a heavenly court, and man knew himself as the most humble of petitioners who presented himself at the gate.

God does not sit in solitary splendor. Apocalypse mixed Hellenistic theories of emanation with Eastern angelologies, and the emanations were fleshed out and became independent spirits, with specific names and duties. These spirits or heavenly beings have many names, such as Gabriel, Michael, Metatron, and Satan, and many functions. They are angels, spirits, guardians of various nations— Raphael is "over the spirits of men," Michael is over "the best part of mankind and chaos," Uriel is "over the world and over Tartarus." [11] Angels animate the forces of nature or rebel against God and are cast down on earth where they tempt men and do great mischief. As these angels and spirits act and interact, myth is reintroduced into Judaism. Michael, Israel's guardian angel, wields his sword in her defense. There are fallen angels who had rebelled against God and now war against God and man, causing illness, suffering, bad luck, folly, seeding evil. There is Satan, now a proper noun and a proper devil; Belial, Prince of Deceit; and Azazel, who teaches mankind unrighteousness. [12]

There is much talk of battle, including gory sketches of heavenly wars which remind one of the cosmic struggle of the Zoroastrian gods of light and darkness, Ahriman and Ormuzd, full of trumpets, marches, flashing swords, and mythic gore, sketches written, we should remind ourselves, by pious men of faith, some of them monastics. No happier evocation of the torments of the damned exist this side of Dante. Apocalypse is a canvas by Bosch beside a sunlit landscape by Monet, a nightmare painted over a daydream. One recognizes popular folk explanations of evil, a fictionalizing of man's sense of evil's separate personality and powerful grip. Folklore, pagan myth, animism, and the symbolic presentation of philosophic ideas, particularly those which deal with theories of emanations and the reality of evil, meet here, and are somehow accommodated to monotheism by the statement that these spirits are all creations of God who, for His own reasons, had appointed them to their distinct missions. Satan is God's creation and remains God's creature. God has set a time limit to the activity of the evil spirits and at the proper time will reassert His majesty. But Satan is such a bold and dramatic fellow and man's nature so perverse and unmanageable that much in the later literature reveals man's fascination with satanic personality.

To those who long for and fear the End, particularly those who have set aside ordinary duties and pleasures for an extraordinary and rigorous discipline, the certainty of God's absolute sovereignty is comforting. Bound to a world they cannot change, men who feel impotent escape total frustration by making a virtue of humility and dependence. Rarely in Jewish thought has God been so transcendently acclaimed and man so consistently demeaned as in these apocalyptic circles. Covenant writings accepted as reality that man cannot change his world, but insisted that he can change himself from a human beast into a human being, from a creature of passion and lust into an obedient servant of God, and that God in His mercy will take his conduct into account. Apocalypse raised doubts on this score. A myth of original sin appears. Adam was burdened with an "evil heart" and "the infirmity became inveterate." [13] But most apocalyptics were still too Jewish, too covenant–bound, to accept such a thesis, and it was directly answered:

Though Adam first sinned and brought untimely death upon all, yet, of those who were born from him each one has prepared for his own soul torment to come, or has chosen for himself glories to come. Adam is, therefore, not the cause save only for his own soul. But each of us has been the Adam of his own soul. [14]

Man had at least this choice: to remain with the godless and the blind or to join the elect and be saved. Sin is not ordinary evildoing so much as blindness to the signs of impending judgment and tardiness in joining the community of the saved. There will be no salvation for any outside this circle. Preaching becomes an announcement of the millennium. Repentance is a turning away from ordinary cares and activities in favor of a rigorous world-denying preparation. The call is to abandon the city for the wilderness and civilization for a cenobitic discipline of poverty, prayer, and purification. Those who made this choice felt cleansed and made over "from the impurity of man and the sin of the children of men." [15] They found purity in the silent, blistering heat which hangs over the shores of the Dead Sea. Sin, they believed, had polluted the cities. In the wilderness ascetic temperaments found the privation their souls required, privacy, and a dryness and heat which burned passion and fatness from their flesh. Here was the fiery furnace where their faith would be tested, proven and rewarded.

A new figure begins to appear in the eschatological drama—the *Mashiah*, the Messiah, God's anointed. Originally the term described anyone anointed ceremonially for some consecrated task, such as a king or a priest. When the Babylonian exiles had looked forward to their return to Judea, some had talked of their future as organized around one of God's anointed, and had endowed this king or priest with flattering virtues.

The early simple scenario of deliverance became increasingly laced with elements of miracle as men recognized the enormity of the power ranged against them. Israel's drama of redemption grew ever more mythic. Men drew into the promise "I will deliver" a plethora of images and incidents which satisfied their need for concrete and conceivable reassurance. Without abandoning the older, purely human image of the Messiah, various miraculous potencies were added to his person, and his role in the eschatological drama became a more supernatural one.

In the Psalms of Solomon (1st cent. B.C.E.) the term *Mashiaḥ Adonai*, the Messiah of God, describes a mortal being, descendant of the house of David, graced by God with special talents of heart and head which will enable him to rule Israel successfully and righteously so that they and he will remain pure of sin and always merit God's favor.[16] With God's support he will scatter Israel's enemies, permanently secure the nation's borders, and gather the dispersed into a Torah-obedient Judea which is to be the center of God's kingdom on earth. As life under Rome became more desperate, idealization shaded off into apotheosis. The Messiah, bearing many titles—"the man," "the son of man," "the elect one," "the righteous one"—became a power-laden presence, a supernatural being, angelic in form, immortal, first among the hosts of the Lord, master of the secrets of the universe, God's advance agent in the business of salvation, Israel's heavenly intercessor. Such images abound in the later sections of I Enoch (37–71), II Ezra, and II Enoch, but they seem to have been limited to certain apocalyptic circles and were neither popular nor widespread until well into Talmudic times. Until the terrible disasters of the first and second centuries C.E. most Jews seem to have retained the older human image of the messianic leader, the successful liberator and ideal king. They were confident that in His love for Israel and through the agency of such a messianic leader and successful general, God would restore Jerusalem to glory and the Jewish people to their land. Josephus reports that when the guerrilla leader, Judah the Galilean, raised a revolt after Herod's death (4 B.C.E.), there were those who proclaimed him Messiah,[17] and that Judah's son and heir presumptive was murdered in the Temple while clothed in robes of royal purple, robes which proclaimed his messianic pretensions.[18] There is a tradition that the great *tanna* Akiva acclaimed Simon bar Kochba as Messiah when his troops entered Jerusalem during the second revolt against Rome (132–135).

A heady blend of apocalypse and messianism made plausible what would otherwise have been inconceivable—an active hope for an end to Roman oppression. The forces of evil, the armies of darkness were identified with Rome, and some read the oracles of a final Judgment and the End of Days as a summons to enlist in the armies of the Lord. Apocalyptic expectations certainly encouraged the Maccabeans, Judah the Galilean, the Zealots, the rebels of 60–70, the defenders of Bethar, and the forces of Bar Kochba as they warred in the name of God against the forces of Edom/Rome. There was an intimate connection between apocalypse and rebellion, which the Romans fully appreciated. When, after the fall of Jerusalem, a Jewish weaver in Cyrene led his followers into the wilderness to "see signs and portents," they were quickly rounded up by the authorities. Josephus, the Roman stooge, mocked such apocalyptic activity, but he details what happened.

There were such men as deceived and deluded the people under the pretense of divine inspiration, but were for procuring innovations and changes of the government; and these prevailed with multitudes to act like madmen, and went before them into the wilderness, as pretending that God would show them the signals of liberty; but Felix [52–60] thought the procedure was to be the beginnings of a revolt. . . .[19]

In the difficult and tense years of the first century the apocalyptic mood was infectious; men saw the predicted signs. Josephus reports that in 62 C.E. a mysterious light illumined the altar and war chariots and soldiers were seen in the sky. In the Temple the priests heard an invisible chorus of many voices saying: "We are departing hence." The paradox of an activist apocalypse depends on the blending of two themes—the Return to Zion and the End of Days— in the Jewish heart.

Apocalypse need not be read as a summons to enlist in the armies of the Lord. Since God is in absolute control of every aspect of history, there is equal logic to counsels of patience: sit and wait for His day, and by prayer, repentance, pious acts, and renunciations prepare yourself to be declared righteous and numbered among the saved. Why fight when the future is set? Many who went into the wilderness to establish cenobitic orders like the monastery at Qumran were certain the End was near, and that only a regimen of prayer, lustrations, study, and simple work would qualify them for a new and better age, when only the righteous of their fellowship "will be renewed with all that is or shall be and with them that know, in a common rejoicing." [20]

The decision of Yoḥanan ben Zakkai to flee from the Roman siege of Jerusalem in 70 C.E. and submit himself to Vespasian in return for the privilege of opening a Torah academy at Javneh has been seen by many historians as evidence of the Pharisaic position that Jews required complete freedom to obey the Torah, but that the Torah did not require that Jews enjoy national sovereignty. Yoḥanan's activities may be explained equally well as a reflex of a faith, shared by many Pharisees and various quietistic apocalyptic circles, that the fate of the nations was settled. There was simply no point in political or military activity. God would have His way in His good time. What was important was to live in such a way as to be prepared for God's time. To the Dead Sea circle and Pharisees of Yoḥanan's stamp, Zealot activists must have appeared not so much as patriots but as men of little faith, their activism an indication of an unwillingness to trust God fully.

This paradox has still another face. The apocalyptic scroll, *The Wars of the Sons of Light and the Sons of Darkness*, which was cherished by the Dead Sea covenanters, describes at length a cosmic battle between supernatural hosts. It is clear that these monastics and ascetics were prepared to fight alongside God's heavenly cohorts; indeed, took some real delight in imagining themselves decked out in the swords and armor they would wear when they fulfilled the duty "of carrying out God's judgments on that awesome day." [21] Monastics they might be, but they were also feral creatures, and we are not surprised to learn that men of Qumran died fighting the Romans.

With the exception of the book of Daniel, which was, of course, canonized, the Jewish community made no effort to preserve its library of apocalyptic writing. It was the Church which copied, translated, expanded, and treasured most of these Hebrew and Aramaic scrolls. But Judaism's rejection of apocalypse was not simply a question of putting aside anything picked up by the Church. It must not be forgotten that these prophecies did not turn out to be true. God's kingdom remained stillborn and the afterbirth could be seen in the ruins of Jerusalem, where hardly one stone was left upon another by vengeful Roman legions. To plan for further wars of the Sons of

Light against the Sons of Darkness was suicidal. Discouraged by such failures, Israel was warned not to calculate the End.

Another reason why the apocalyptic writings were rejected has to do with the character of Judaism as a Torah-based faith. Apocalypse was new Torah. Inevitably, each cenacle looked on its eschatological books as divinely inspired. Enoch or Ezra had heard new teachings in heaven, but the original Torah had stipulated that its text was immutable and warned against "the prophet who presumed to speak in My name an oracle which I did not command him to utter" (Deut. 18:20). Against the normative tradition that prophecy and revelation had ceased with Haggai, Zechariah, and Malachi, apocalypse asserted that there was knowledge in the heavens beyond what heretofore had been vouchsafed to man. Conscious of the heresy of innovation, Jewish apocalypse tried to minimize the impact of the new revelation on the old. It was said that these books were part of the original revelation, but had been hidden by the faithful of each generation lest their secrets and powers be abused.[22] But those who accepted Torah as an all-embracing teaching had no need for new scrolls and new words. The *Tanach* itself was a complete apocalypse. All secrets and dates were there. What hope did one need beyond that which was already in these scrolls?

The apocalyptic scrolls were put away. There were no new scrolls in heaven, but there was a divine scroll on earth, the Torah; since the eschatological themes of the apocalypse were originally prophetic terms—the wars of Gog and Magog, the End of Days, the World to Come—the sages were able to discover almost all of them in the Torah text itself. This discovery had two consequences. First, the exuberant symbols of the apocalypse were interwoven with the messianic themes found in the Scripture, and so passed as authentic tradition. Second, the secrets of the eschaton were located in the Torah text, and Torah scholarship now had an eschatological face. A special interpretive tradition developed which taught men how to decode the Torah's deepest secrets. The breaking open of biblical texts and images by a variety of artificial techniques in order to predict the Day of Judgment and the date of the coming of the Messiah formed the basis of a long, often urgent, unbroken, mystical enterprise within normative Judaism which even today has its occasional devotee.

How did Torah men discover the date of the End? One technique was to put new values on prophetic numbers. Jeremiah had brought God's word that seventy years would pass between the destruction of Jerusalem and Judah's return from Babylonian captivity (Jer. 25:11–22). Daniel related Jeremiah's prophecy to the Day of Judgment by transposing the seventy years into seventy weeks of years (7 × 70 = 490; cf. Dan. 7:25; 9:12; 24–27), which suggested to a second-century reader that the End was near (597 − 490 = 107 B.C.E.), only a very brief "time, times, and half a time" lay between now and the Day. The author of I Enoch had a different explanation. Jeremiah's seventy years referred not to seventy weeks of years but to seventy rulers. The End of Time was near because the seventieth ruler was even now on the throne.[23] Almost any text was available for messianic computation. Hebrew lacks a separate numerical system and uses its alphabet for numeration: Aleph = 1, Bet = 2, and so on, so every word represents both a meaning and a sum. *Gematria* is the name of the hermeneutic rule which governs the process which reads Torah words as numbers and either translates those numbers into dates and relates these dates to the coming of the Messiah, or relates them midrashically to other words which have the same numerical value. Such calculations were not seen as either trivial or specious. The Torah represented the word of God and could be assumed to contain all truth. Popular Hellenistic philosophies, particularly those associated with the disciples of Pythagoras, had developed the notion that numbers represent the ultimate form of all things, and that words, numbers, and reality are interchangeable; men who turned letters into dates and read these dates as prophecies found nothing incongruous in such intellectual gymnastics. Many found the practice of calculating the coming of the Messiah by ciphering biblical texts so seductive that, despite repeated warnings by those who recognized the high probability of human error and the great danger of frequent disappointment "that he who calculates the coming of the Messiah forfeits his own share in the future," [24] such calculations were made in every generation.

Rabbinic Judaism turned apocalypse into apocalyptic *midrash* and, by putting aside other scrolls, preserved the centrality of the Torah and made apocalypse Jewish. Apocalyptic *midrash* saw itself as drawing out the full meaning of revelation. Its imagery is highly imaginative, often providing incredibly bizarre incidents to fill out some biblical event. Genesis 1–2 provided the central texts on the basis of which various cosmologies and cosmogonies called *maaseh bereshit* (work of creation) were developed. Ezekiel 1 and 10 became the *locus classicus* for various descriptions of God's visible presence (*Kavod*) and of the soul's ascent to the divine throne. These themes were labeled *maaseh merkabah* (work of the chariot) and represent traditions and images of mystic translation from earth into God's presence. Messianism and apocalypticism, the political and eschatological hope so variously and creatively developed in this era, entered the mainstream of rabbinic Judaism as a series of imaginatively entangled ideas destined to remain vigorous and unsystematically commingled.

Rabbinic Judaism never let go of redemption as a purely political category. "There is no difference between this world and the World to Come except the end of our political subjugation." [25] But the image of redemption was rich, and that wealth of image was the gift to rabbinic Judaism of the apocalyptics. Apocalypse knew redemption in time and beyond time. The End of Days is meant literally, and beyond there is a new aeon and a new world. To man's understanding of sacred history apocalypse added a description of the End: the notion of the birth pangs of the Messiah, the strictness of the final judgment, and the utopian hope of the world that is to come.

These themes were treated with the respect for ambiguity which hope deserves. The Jewish hope was neither romantic nor naive. It does not deny evil, Satan, violence, or human pathology; indeed, apocalypse is primarily and paradoxically a threat, a dismal teaching. The Day of God is a terrible time. The birth pains of the Messiah are brutal. Both man and man's world are doomed. Only in the World to Come is there blessedness and rest. If apocalypse drained the day of all beauty and possibility it must be faulted, because there is beauty, love, a sunset, a moment of quiet, some political hope. Such promises were provided by the older messianic theme which spoke of hope here and now, restoration on one's own land, freedom, and peace. The messianic age and the World to Come are intertwined ideas, but not the same idea. The one is hope in this life, and the other light at the end of the tunnel.

The Jewish hope was as complex and as confused as life, and as necessary to life as breath.

CHAPTER

❧ XV ❧

After the Fall

I N 71 of the Common Era the Roman emperor Vespasian issued coins bearing the inscription, "Judea Capta," to signal that Judea had been recaptured from troublesome rebels who, incredibly, had held the capital city of Jerusalem for almost three years. For the defeated Jews the dark night of *galut* settled on their world. Their Temple had been destroyed. Their capital had been fired, and tens of thousands had died or been sold into slavery. *Galut* means "exile," but in the language of rabbinic thought it took on a broader meaning; it signified not only defeat and life in exile, but life in an alien world, an unnatural existence, the amputation of Israel's ability to walk confidently before men and God.

Galut does not describe the elimination of all Jews from the Promised Land. Although the defeat was total, and terrible punishment was exacted by an angry emperor bent on teaching fractious subjects a bitter lesson, major elements of the Jewish community continued to live there, particularly in the Galilee. Indeed, there was never to be a generation in which the Land of Israel would be without some children of Israel. *Galut* describes Jewish life under unnatural conditions. *Galut* began with the destruction of the Temple, when Jews felt that the familiar road to redemption had been blocked off. Rabbi Yehoshua (late first century) was in *galut*, although he lived in Palestine and spoke from a promontory overlooking the Temple mount where now no Jew could set foot: "Woe unto us, that this place where the iniquities of Israel were atoned for is laid waste." [1]

[255]

Sacrifices could no longer be offered on the Temple altar. The annual half-shekel duty paid by every Jew, whether in Palestine or the Diaspora, toward the Temple's upkeep was diverted into a Roman tax, the *Fiscus Judaicus*, whose income provided for the upkeep of a temple in Rome dedicated to Jupiter. The redemptive pattern of Jewish life lay in shreds. A Pharisaic sage, Yoḥanan ben Zakkai, surrendered to Vespasian in order to establish a Torah school outside besieged Jerusalem. He was a man who looked to the future, but when he heard that the Temple had been razed "he tore his clothing and his students tore their clothing, and they wept crying aloud and mourning." [2]

The community went into deep mourning for its lost glory:

Large numbers in Israel became ascetics, binding themselves neither to eat meat nor drink wine. R. Yehoshua got into a conversation with them and said to them: "My sons, why do you not eat meat?" They replied "Shall we eat flesh, which used to be brought daily as an offering on the altar, now that the altar is in abeyance?" [3]

We hear of suicide, vows of celibacy, and spiritual lassitude, all familiar reactions to deep shock and grief. One of the first tasks of the surviving leadership was to set limits to the cult of mourning which, if it had been allowed to wax unchecked, might have eroded the people's will to live. The same Yehoshua is reported to have admonished those who burdened their lives with excessive privations:

If that is so, we should not eat bread either, because the meal offerings have ceased. . . . We should not eat fruits either because there is no longer an offering of first fruits. To this they could find no answer, so he said to them: My sons, come and listen to me, not to mourn at all is impossible, because the blow has fallen. To mourn overmuch is also impossible, because we do not impose on a community a hardship which the majority cannot endure. [4]

A series of memorial fasts were promulgated so that life on other days could go on. The day of the Temple's destruction, the ninth of Av, *Tishah be-av*, which by one of those haunting coincidences was also the anniversary of the destruction of the First Temple in 586 B.C.E., became the principal fast day. On this day the community read from the scroll of Lamentations and observed all the usual rites of mourning. A group of customs known as *zecher le-ḥurban* (memorials of the destruction) became part of the life of this people: a newly plastered house was to have one corner left unfinished, a dinner was to have one course omitted, women were to leave off one piece of jewelry from their costumes. These customs suggested the crippled condition of Jewish life and would be continued over the centuries, thus keeping the sense of loss palpable and the hope of return to Zion alive even for those who hardly knew any history. *Galut* began as a historical calamity. It became the condition of Jewish life and in time thinkers recognized that *galut*, alienation, was the condition of every man's life. After all, who and where is the secure man?

Before we suggest how Yoḥanan and other Torah scholars reknit the spiritual fabric of Judean life, a brief look at the long, slow decline of the various Jewries under Roman authority is in order. The social, economic, political, and eschatological pressures which had precipitated the revolt of 66 C.E. did not cease with its suppression. Roman taxes remained oppressive. Apocalyptic teachings about an approaching Judgment Day continued to circulate. Parthia, which limited Roman expansion to the east, occasionally moved her troops westward and usually sent ahead Jewish agents to find support among this unhappy and restive minority. Between 112 and 115 the Diaspora communities of Cyrene (Libya), Egypt, and Cyprus became fractious, and their unrest was summarily and cruelly put down. By the middle of the second century the great Diaspora communities of Alexandria and Antioch had ceased to be creative intellectual centers, and Jews in such places found themselves caught between suspicious and greedy Roman overlords and ambitious and greedy natives who sensed a chance to take over Jewish prerogatives. In 132 C.E. Judea again took up arms under the banner of Bar Kochba, but by 135 C.E. Jerusalem lay in ruins, every town in Judea was razed, and Judaism lay under the ban. Torah teaching was forbidden, Sabbath observance proscribed, and circumcision listed as a capital offense. Thousands were sold into slavery. Jerusalem was rebuilt as Aelia Capitolina and no Jew was allowed within the city's gates. The reign of terror which followed the defeat of Bar Kochba was ended by Antoninus Pius (ca. 139 C.E.), and under the Severides conditions eased a bit, but this was still *galut*. A rule forbidding adult circumcision was retained as a deliberate brake to Jewish missionary activity. Jews retained the right to organize themselves as a self-governing community, but they now lived in Palestine (land of the Philistines), a label deliberately chosen by Rome to symbolize that, officially, this land was no longer considered Judea—that is, belonging by historic claim to the Jews. It was a time of constant frustration and growing alienation. Politically and numerically Jewish life slid slowly, but steadily, downhill.

It was a time of defeat and renewal. Judaism did not jettison the long-familiar way of salvation which centered on the Temple; it could not be abandoned, since it was prescribed in the Torah, the revelation, and was eternally valid. A few brave souls stole to the Temple mount to offer surreptitious sacrifices. Some priests tried to live as if the Temple still functioned. Each morning and late afternoon a scholar-priest, Tarfon, collected food specifically and properly tithed and explained to anyone who cared to ask: "In this way I offer the *Shaharit* and *Minha* sacrifice." [5] In the messianic era the Temple would be reestablished; until then scholars would continue to study the laws dealing with the ritual and architecture of the Temple and keep careful watch over the genealogical register of the priests. God was just. God's promise was certain. Israel would be prepared.

Judaism faced an ultimate test: Could the Jewish people survive the amputation of the central redemptive apparatus of their national life and yet remain a self-conscious and vigorous community? Why not? Had not Judaism survived the destruction of its First Temple? Hindsight makes the transition seem natural, if not inevitable, but it was not easily accomplished. The Babylonian captives had barely survived as a cohesive community. After a mere fifty years of exile only a minority of the expatriates had been willing to return, and of the settlements of those who remained in Babylon we know only that they lingered in spiritual somnolence and intellectual sterility. How many survived? How much attrition through assimilation was there? These questions cannot now be answered.

Fortunately, an alternate religious place, the protosynagogue, had been in existence for centuries, both in the Diaspora and in Judea. These early synagogues were little more than popular assemblies where men prayed and preached. Their leaders were the community elders. There was no ecclesiastical hierarchy, no resident priests. Someone presided over the community's business. Perhaps the same man, perhaps a more learned man, read from the Torah and discussed its meaning. The synagogue was of the people and would never be dominated by a blooded or professional hierarchy; indeed, the synagogue was destined to be the prototype of all congregationalist groupings which have been so important to Christianity and Islam as well as to Judaism.

These assemblies adapted Temple forms for their worship. Their calendar was that of the Temple, their hymns the Temple's psalms, and the schedule of Torah readings followed Temple practice. After 70 C.E. the popular mind instinctively transferred the faith's promise of salvation to these assemblies. The synagogue, which had been town hall, place of public instruction in Torah, and house of prayer, now became a sanctuary. The Temple had been the *bet ha-Mikdash*, the Holy House. Yohanan's generation was the first to call the synagogue a *mikdash meat*, a miniature holy place. Yohanan ben Zakkai authoritatively attached the Temple's special power of benediction to the synagogue. Yohanan ruled that the shofar could be sounded in the synagogue on a New Year's Day which fell on the Sabbath, a ritual which had been the sole prerogative of the Temple, and that the ceremony of handling the lulav on Sukkot could be celebrated in the synagogue on each of the seven days of the festival, again a privilege which had been reserved to the Temple. These were minor ritual changes, to be sure, but each was a recognizable signal to the Jewish public that a transference of spiritual authority had been effected.

Several mosaic floors of Palestinian synagogues of the third and fourth centuries have been found which depict the seven-branched menorah, the ram's horn, the lulav and ethrog, and the incense shovel, the most public advertisement possible that these objects once associated specifically with Temple ceremonies are now associated here. A priest, descendant of those who had served at the altar, was the first to be called up to read the Torah scroll. A priest blessed the congregation each day from a high platform, as his ancestors had done in the Temple. The hopes of Israel were attached to the synagogue service, which was now called *avodah*, just as the sacrificial service had been called *avodah*. The synagogue, which had long complemented the central sanctuary, now temporarily substituted for it. "These things Yohanan ben Zakkai brought to pass in the world when the Temple was destroyed and when it will be rebuilt, these matters will return to their original condition." [6]

The synagogue was not a blank canvas on which the sages could print an exact replica of Temple practice. The early assemblies had developed a schedule of three daily moments of prayer and there were scriptural texts to back up this custom. Daniel had prayed "three times a day" (Dan. 6:11). A psalmist had called upon God "evening, morning and at noonday" (Ps. 55:18). Some sages felt that there ought now to be only two daily services, to conform to the Temple's schedule, but the scholar's council was not willing to undo popular habits and could not argue against the cited texts. They could do no more than name the first two daily services *Shaharit* and *Minhah*, after the sacrifices customary at those hours (the third service was called *Arvit* or *Maariv*—simply evening), and the additional Sabbath service *Musaf*, again a corresponding term. In every way they could the sages made the synagogue into a Temple surrogate. In Talmudic times sections of *Mishnah* which described the ritual of sacrifice (*Korbanot*) would be introduced into the daily liturgy. By reciting these paragraphs the worshipper participated vicariously in the cult and drew to himself its redemptive power: "Whenever they will read the section dealing with the sacrifices, I will reckon it as if they were bringing Me an offering, and forgive all their iniquities." [7] If the cult was temporarily shut down, its power was still alive and could be tapped by surrogate acts. Just as the Jew had looked to the Temple altar for atonement, so now he looked to synagogue worship for those redemptive moments and acts which would free him of the burden of sin and win for him God's favor.

The Temple had a carefully orchestrated and formal order of procedure. Men needed to find in the synagogue liturgy certainty and order similar to that they had experienced and trusted in the Temple. The *tannaim* did not create liturgy so much as organize, elaborate, and formalize old traditions. We hear that Gamaliel II, Yohanan's successor, had his council collect the more popular formulas of petition and organize them into a fixed litany of praise and expectation, the *Tefillah*, which became a central element in every service. The thrust of a revealed faith is always toward order, God's order; synagogue worship was now given structure and shape.

The synagogue service began to seem Temple-like. As the Temple had had a special court for the women, so, too, women began to be segregated to the court of the synagogue. There had been signs at each of the Temple's gates forbidding entrance to heathens. Gamaliel's court composed a malediction against the *Minim* (heretics) which effectively excluded nonbelievers from services. [8] God's love for Israel had been confirmed each year on Yom Kippur when the High Priest entered the Holy of Holies and asked God's forgiveness for himself, his household, and the nation. This had been the high moment of renewal. Its spirit was kept alive by a lengthy reading each Yom Kippur which detailed those famous rites. On Yom Kippur each Jew dressed himself in priestly white and chanted the High Priest's confession and plea. In the synagogue each man was a priest seeking God's favor not only for the nation but for himself.

After the Fall

The altar had been the agency of atonement. Now Yom Kippur atoned. The constant rehearsal of Temple practice kept its power of atonement visible; but the way of atonement was more private than it had ever been. After the defeat of Bar Kochba, men abandoned any real hope for a quick reversal of their political situation and looked to Yom Kippur for relief from their private sense of alienation from God. Although defeated, they could, through *teshuvah*, national repentance, hasten national renewal; but it was the possibility of *teshuvah* as a means of private deliverance which was emphasized. Though the Jew could not extricate himself from *galut*, he had a chance to set himself right with God through repentance, worship, and good works and thus qualify for blessing in this life and in the life to come. "*Teshuvah* and irenic acts (*maasim tovim*) provide a shield against punishment." [9] Repentance was an act of contrition and an active redemptive force, hope with a capital "H." "The gates of prayer are sometimes open and sometimes closed. The gates of *teshuvah* are always open." [10] *Teshuvah* is the way man proves himself to God and the redemptive road that he must take. A thousand, perhaps ten thousand, sermons during these centuries cited such classic *teshuvah* texts as Hosea's: "Return, O Israel, to the Lord your God, for you have stumbled in your evil courses" (Hos. 14:2), and answered such questions as these: How does one turn, who permits "turning," and what gives it significance?

Christians insisted that Christ's atoning death had introduced the possibility of salvation into a world heretofore consigned to a state of unforgiveness. The rabbis rejected this understanding. *Teshuvah* had been created before Day One. The possibility of moral regeneration is implicit in creation, and constantly manifests itself in man's ability to take hold of his life and change it. *Teshuvah* implied that one could and must bring oneself into line with a well-defined pattern of duty and an undefined pattern of saintliness. Needless to say, *teshuvah* is a full-time undertaking, but it was, after all, the way to life eternal, though not a guarantee of it. Salvation belongs to God alone; those who are saved are saved through God's grace. Jews prefaced their hopes with the phrase *im yirtzeh ha-Shem*, "God willing," which was a shorthand way of saying: "If you are worthy, I will hasten it, if you are not worthy, all in its time." [11]

Teshuvah was both concept and rite. Various rituals of confession became part of the liturgy, but the process of return could not be completed with words. At times the *tannaim* catalogued various categories of sins and suggested graded rituals of contrition, but we misunderstand their sensitivity and seriousness if we assume that they looked on obedience to the will of God as a hard-headed and calculated trade. The *Mishnah* reports that on fast days an elder arose in each congregation to remind everyone that the rite of fasting was not an end in itself, that only a life of righteousness validated the ritual.[12] Hypocritical ceremonialism was anathema. "If a man says: 'I will sin and I will do *teshuvah* again,' he is not given a chance to do *teshuvah*." [13]

Teshuvah was the promise and the way. Yom Kippur was *Yoma*, The Day, *galut* Jewry's high spiritual moment. It focused the guilt of exile and every man's personal burden of guilt, the need to confess, the relief of confession, and the promise of reacceptance, atonement. The day was powerful, but its promise was never automatic. "[If a man says] 'I will sin and the Day of Atonement will do *teshuvah*'; then the Day of Atonement does not effect *teshuvah*. For transgressions that are between man and God the Day of Atonement effects *teshuvah*, but for transgressions that are between a man and his fellow the Day of Atonement effects atonement only if he has appeased his fellows." [14]

The transfer of the saving power of the Temple to the synagogue was the popular part of a program which helped sustain Israel's trust in the vitality of God's power to save. The *tannaim*, however, were not primarily synagogue men, but rather schoolmen for whom the way of learning, *Talmud Torah*, complemented and went beyond the way of *teshuvah*, the way of good deeds and of obedience. Study of Torah was a commandment whose fulfillment was pleasing to God as evidence of man's loyalty. Through study God's rule became explicit and clear. Through study men came to see the real world behind the world of semblance. The way of study offered a wisdom which could clear up all philosophic confusion, resolve all moral doubt, and, by dissolving doubt, so disencumber man's will that he could marshal the power to control his passions and his life. Torah study was also a mystical enterprise which permitted men to draw closer to God, for God was somehow in the revelation.

Beside the rather non-specific text of Deuteronomy 6:7, "Impress them (these words) upon your children," the Torah text does not mention schools or learning. However, the *tannaim* found innumerable proof texts confirming the redemptive value of *Talmud Torah* in the wisdom literature. Wisdom and Torah were one; so "get wisdom" implied "study Torah." The blessings that wisdom promised the devotee were transferred to *Talmud Torah*. The texts they cited are revealing: "She is a tree of life to those who take hold of her; fortunate are they who can hold her fast" (Prov. 3:18). "She offers long life with her right hand and with her left hand riches and honor" (Prov. 3:16). Therefore, life is given to those who study Torah "in this world and in the World to Come." [15] Torah study was the key to a long life. As long as a man studied Torah the angel of death had no power over him. A man who studied Torah built up merits which would stand him in good stead in this world and in the World to Come. The prayer *Ahava Rabba* was added to the various readings which comprise the *Shema* in the daily service, for it appropriately asked God's help to "put into our hearts to understand and to discern, to mark, learn and teach, to heed and to fulfill in love all the words of instruction in Thy Torah," for he who has learned "will never be put to shame." [16] *Talmud Torah* becomes a way of salvation.

By Torah study the scholars described a competent course in Torah law, now the twofold law, and much more. Knowledge of Torah was a necessary step in man's private spiritual growth as well as functionally required for the proper organization of the community: "A teacher introduces a man to the study of the Five Books of Moses. Such study leads one to a study of the whole law, which study leads to right action and ultimately to reverence of the Lord." [17] Torah study did not simply fill the mind, it changed the mind and the person. "It [Torah] fits him to become just, pious, upright and faithful. It keeps him far from sin and brings him nearer virtue . . . and he becomes modest, long suffering and forgiving of insults." [18] Of course, these claims were a trifle excessive. The scholars remained men. Tarfon was irascible, Meir was footloose, and Akiva was a strident debater. "Warm yourself by the fire of the sages, but beware of their glowing coals, for their bite is the bite of the fox and their sting is the scorpion's sting and their hiss is the serpent's hiss, and their words are like coals of fire." [19] Yet, whatever their human failings, these men knew that Torah study had given them insight and competence, had changed their lives, and given them new confidence and power.

The law was divine and the man of Torah drew to himself some of its supernatural force. Inevitably these followers of Torah came to be seen as holy men. Yoḥanan had gained Vespasian's favor by predicting that the general would become emperor. His student, Ḥaninah ben Dosa, was a faith healer and intercessor who claimed to know which of those he prayed for would live and which would die. These were holy men in an age when holy men healed, divined, exorcised evil spirits, wrote amulets, called down the rain, and cast the evil eye. There was an unpublished esoteric curriculum in the schools which enabled scholars to tap the Torah's latent and awesome power, for it took them behind the literal meaning of Torah to its mysteries—the secret names of God, the mysterious nature of the universe, the date of the End of Time. These scholars would have denied emphatically that they ever practiced magic. Torah provided the power to save, but not the power to tamper with God's plans. If God willed death or a drought, no amulet or prayer could be effective. If God chose to act through a simple, perhaps illiterate, faith healer or rainmaker rather than through a scholar, so be it. Of one itinerant rainmaker, a sage commented that he would willingly put him under a ban: "But what shall I do? You importune God and He performs your will." [20]

The new emphasis on learning seemed to imply that a simple man could not serve God as adequately as a student, and hence was less likely to merit salvation. *Talmud Torah* talk does reflect the intellectual bias and self-esteem of the schools, but the best of the sages were conscious of the danger of elitism. "If you have learned a great deal of Torah do not claim credit for yourself, for thereunto were you created." [21] Since formal study was beyond the ability or schedule of the average man, paragraphs from each of the major sections of the Bible were added to the liturgy in order that everyone would read each day sufficient text to satisfy the commandment of study and thus earn merit toward entry into the World to Come. The sages taught and most believed that "It matters not whether much or little [is read] provided man directs his heart to heaven." [22]

Torah scholars were not, at this early period at least, tenured academics. They earned their living as artisans, physicians, scribes, tradesmen, and bailiffs. To have accepted pay for obeying God's will would have been to prostitute their love of God and of His Torah. The *tannaim* were not philosopher kings, but working folk who knew that God required study, worship, and good deeds. The more pretentious among them may have encouraged the instinctive awe of the unlettered for the sage; certainly they spun myths which told how the world depended on their learning. But other sages circulated the legend of the unknown righteous, thirty-six simple folk, who are the guarantors of the existence of each generation. Early in the second century Rabbi Joshua forcibly reminded his fellow scholars of their limitations and their total dependence on God: "When the Temple was destroyed, the sages began to be like school teachers, and the school teachers like synagogue servants, and the synagogue servants like people of the land, and the people of the land waxed feeble and there was none to seek and none to supplicate. On whom can we stay ourselves? On our Father in heaven." [23] There was no getting around the fact that the discipline of *Talmud Torah* required literacy, and that something of a scholar's cult was developing. However, the consecration of learning had one democratic consequence. By the middle of the second century the Jewish communities of Palestine had organized a relatively effective program of universal male elementary education. "He has spurned the word of the Lord" (Num. 15:31) was taken to refer to one who studies Torah, but does not teach it to others. Obedient always, the sages set out to "Impress them [these teachings] upon your children" (Deut. 6:7) and popularized the Torah by preaching at engagements, weddings, and funerals, and on the Sabbath. Whereas other intellectual castes sought to build high walls around their class, the sages tried to turn every boy and man into a scholar.

The *tannaim* worked diligently to make their life style and values universal among Jews. There was to be no special class of the religious. " 'You shall faithfully observe all the instruction': Lest you say these teachings are solely for the scholars or the elite or the prophets. Scripture says 'you shall . . .' to make it clear that all are equal in their duty before the law." [24] It would nevertheless not be correct to say that the community of sages was a democratic and open society. Learning is a matter of talent. Genealogy remained a vital subject. Jews were accustomed to the prerogatives of blood. Yohanan's successor, Gamaliel II, a grandson of the most famous of all the scholar/jurists, Hillel, who could also claim to be scion of a collateral line descended from King David, was empowered by Rome with the title of patriarch, and such was the thrust of blood and lineage that his heirs would hold this authority without contest for ten generations.

After the fall the Romans allowed Yohanan ben Zakkai, who was not of priestly or Davidic descent and therefore not a political threat, to set up an advanced Torah school at Yavneh near modern Ashdod. Other Torah scholars joined him there, and this group formed a scholar's court or *bet din* which could provide overall direction to Jewish life. Although at first the scholars and their courts had no criminal jurisdiction and could not even levy fines in civil cases without Roman authorization, they considered that their council was the successor to the Sanhedrin. They felt capable of dealing with all issues arising out of the Torah law and rendered decisions in terms of that law as if their powers were untrammeled.

These men faced two practical urgencies: how to take control of the routines of community life which had once been the prerogative of the Sanhedrin or the Temple priests (the right of ordination, collection of Temple dues, authority to promulgate the calendar, and so on), and how to make the people understand and obey the commandments of God as the teachers of the written and oral law understood them. These challenging and demanding tasks had to be carried out in difficult times. There was not a generation without revolt, the rumblings of revolt, rumors of Parthian advance, or the reality of Roman exaction: the *bet din* was driven hither and yon, from Yavneh to Usha, from Usha to Sepphoris, from Sepphoris to Tiberias. There were periods when its meetings were prohibited. We hear of meetings on the roof of a member's home. A number of arresting figures emerged—Akiva, Ishmael, Meir, Yehudah ha-Nasi—and during this period such men laid down the main outlines of the interpretive tradition which was to control the future development of rabbinic Judaism.

The problem was to relate Torah to the times. Every line in the literature of rabbinic jurisprudence testifies to the inevitable tension between the changing needs of the time and the unchangeable text of revelation. No Torah phrase or text could be taken lightly. Every word was God's word, and it was an article of faith that the *peshat* or literal meaning of a text was never to be dissolved by hermeneutical devices. Still, it was possible to interpret certain texts so that their consequences fit changed needs and new cultural attitudes.

The Torah prescribed capital punishment in a wide variety of cases. Tannaitic rules continued to list the various categories of capital crime and the applicable method of execution, but these sages also developed a code of trial procedure which ruled out circumstantial evidence in capital cases and required not only two eyewitnesses to the crime, but also the rendering of a specific warning to the accused before the crime was committed. The effect was to make the death sentence a rare occurrence and to set in motion a strong anti-capital punishment tradition which, if occasionally overlooked, as in some medieval Spanish *aljamans*, nevertheless informed subsequent rabbinic practice as it does the law of the State of Israel today. The Bible requires capital punishment, but the *Mishnah* comments: "A Sanhedrin that carried out an execution once in seven years is branded a murderous Sanhedrin" and R. Eliezer ben Azariah adds, "Once in seventy years." [25]

Many of the sabbatical laws caused severe hardship. We have already noted that Hillel abrogated the sabbatical cancellation of debts by seizing on the peculiar language of the biblical law, which was phrased in such a way that it could be construed as applying to persons, but not institutions. No similar textual opportunity existed which would have allowed the rabbis to mitigate the rule requiring that all land in Israel lie fallow every seventh year, yet relief was desperately needed. Rome exacted heavy taxes every year whether or not the farmer harvested a cash crop. The patriarch who was responsible to Rome for these taxes sought to set the sabbatical rule aside, but a majority of the scholars would not consent. The Torah was explicit, but the rule applied only to the Promised Land, so the *tannaim* defined the land's boundaries as narrowly as possible. What was the Promised Land? All of Palestine? Part of it? Which part? Rather than void the law, the scholars circumscribed its effective authority, but, as this instance makes clear, Torah took precedence over private advantage, except in the case of dire need. If the Torah text precluded certain changes, they were not made. The law's justification lay in its divinity rather than its humanity.

Such adjustment of the law to life required professional mastery of law, and the intellectual effort required in mastering Torah must have been prodigious. Scholars had to memorize the basic texts, and generally not only the Torah but the proper exegesis by which a law was derived from a Torah text, and, of course, the oral tradition. The oral law was just that—a vast deposit of material which existed only in the scholar's mind. The presence of many mnemonics and acronyms in the texts which subsequently emerged points to the vastness of the task. The sparse, discrete style of these texts was an aid to memorization, but increased the difficulty of interpretation, and today their gnarled style discourages any but the most determined. The *tannaim* were heirs to an oral tradition complete with all manner of taboos against publishing. When these taboos were broken and the first law books were published, they appeared as the distillate of law rather than extensive discussions of legal practice and theory. Later rabbis rarely treated such compilations as completed works. Each generation added paragraphs, citations, even extended sections, and no one was loath to amend or correct a text if he believed he had a better recension.

Glancing at the writings of the *tannaim*, one would hardly suspect that their first order of business had been to bring coherence into Jewish life. The age of variety had tolerated laxity in standards and confusion in practice as well as in theology, and it had ended in convulsion. The sages were certain that there was a right way, a clear way, a clearly described way, the Torah way. The episodic quality of this literature must not mask for us its steady purpose. Through teaching, regimen, and private example the scholar-jurists sought to weave their clearly defined way and their clear understanding of the Torah into the pattern of a community's life.

Perhaps the most characteristic form of literature in this period is the *midrash halachah*, which presents the derivation of law and juridic principles from the Torah text. Two commentaries to the legal portions of Exodus, the *Mechilta* of R. Ishmael and the so-called *Mechilta d'Rabbi Simon bar Yohai*, two similar commentaries to Leviticus (*Sifra de-vei Rav* and *Sifra Zuta*), and a composite exegesis of Numbers and Deuteronomy (*Sifre de-vei Rav*) contain in the main such commentary. *Mechilta* means "measure"; *Sifra de-vei Rav* means "The Book of the Schools." Each book was edited by several hands, and until quite late in the Talmudic or Gaonic period it was considered permissible to add discrete rabbinic traditions or to reedit particular sayings. Recently Ben Zion Wacholder has challenged the tannaitic dating of the *Mechilta*, and inferentially the early dating of all these works. He believes that they are Gaonic (8–10 cent.). The mere existence of the debate testifies to the process of textual accretion and the lack of apparent change in rabbinic method, approach, and conclusion over many centuries.

Anyone who enjoys scholarly puzzles can have a field day with the many questions raised by nearly every citation. Is a text authentic to the man in whose name it is cited? There are invented incidents and speeches. What is the text's proper wording? A teaching may be repeated in several places and with significant changes. These academicians cultivated a scholarly shorthand and used a host of allusions, some of which cannot now be deciphered. They had a penchant for a cryptic, almost enigmatic style, and quite often our ability to understand them depends on our being able to place a statement in context. One illustration must suffice. Tarfon and Akiva are recorded as having debated: Which is the primary virtue, learning or the deed?

Tarfon said, "Practice is greater." Akiva said, "Study is greater because it leads to practice." [26] Was Tarfon downgrading the scholar in his ivory tower? Was Akiva faulting the hothead who chafes for action for action's sake? This story has been so interpreted. But one source tells us that this debate did not take place in the calm surroundings of a seminar room, but on a locked and barricaded roof during a time of Roman repression. Such a setting hardly suggests a theoretical debate. If this was indeed the situation, the issue was survival—whether the sages ought to keep on with study, the business of interpreting and enlarging the law, or ought to throw this "intellectualism" to the winds and concentrate on the practical needs of the people.

No more puzzling literature exists. The style is terse and meanings often are elusive. An identical quotation may be ascribed to two different teachers or to opposing arguments by the same teacher. Some of the material and sayings are original to the man in whose name they are cited, while other material is pseudepigraphic or invented. The precise meaning of many idioms is uncertain and allusive. We are told, for instance, that four of the more famous scholars of the early second century (Akiva, Ben Zoma, Ben Azzai, and Elisha ben Abuyah) entered Pardes, a Hebraized form of the Greek *paradeisos*, garden (from which the word paradise was derived). The word is used here presumedly to mean the realm of mystical experiences and theosophical speculation. Only Akiva emerged safely; Elisha ben Abuyah was led into heterodoxy, Ben Zoma into madness, and Ben Azzai to his death.[27] But what were they seeking? What questions did they raise? What mysteries maddened them? How did Akiva escape? Are we to understand that speculation with the mysteries literally leads to death and madness? Our secular training says, "Of course not." Then we find a cryptic passage in the *Sifre* to Deuteronomy which has Akiva offer his companions a magical formula which will get them safely past the gates of paradise. Someone believed in the actual dangers of the mystical experience, and that failure to use the proper cipher spelled death.

Jewish life lacked serenity and rarely permitted the Jew a happy sense of accomplishment. Life was endured rather than mastered. Not surprisingly, the *midrash halachah* reflects this incompleteness. It tends to offer snatches of insight rather than the steady light of finished reason. It is anything but self-confident, drawing its coherence not from any attempt to synthesize the texts, but from the fact that each text comes from a single source, Torah-God. The *midrash halachah* is commentary rather than original creation. The Torah was revelation and the scholar's task was to draw out its truth, to uncover rather than discover, to relate Torah to the many and various situations in which men found themselves, rather than to sift experiences and arrange perceptions into a coherent philosophy of life. What we have are anthologies of exegesis and law, writings which make up in variety what they lack in style and systematic arrangement, perception rather than philosophy.

Tannaitic *midrash* is compressed and complex, much like the gnomic speech that many persecuted peoples have adopted in order to shield their thoughts from the prying eyes and ears of authority. No attempt was made to develop a chapter-long logical argument or even to deal with ideas on similar levels of sophistication or profundity: theology, eschatology, etymology, apologetics, jurisprudence, psychology, and just plain wordplay tumble over each other. In the nonlegal paragraphs there is little evidence of editing for consistency of form or content. These men intuitively recognized that after the destruction of the Temple God's providence could no longer be rationalized to man. Yet, as one studies these disjointed comments and commentaries—and study one must, for they cannot simply be read—they seem, like the moving shapes of a light sculpture, able to form various appealing images, but also able to suggest that their illumination radiates from a fixed light source. Indeed, the *tannaim* used just such an image. They likened *midrash* to the sparks given off when the hammer of the mind strikes the iron of a Torah text.

The difficulties and possibilities of halachic *midrash* are more easily understood when confronted directly than when described. A section in the *Mechilta*, known as *Masechta de-Shabbata* (the portion on the Sabbath—Exodus 31:12–17), offers a typical illustration of the jumble of insights and mixture of themes, all of which somehow relate to the central ideas and promises of rabbinic Judaism.

And the Lord spoke unto Moses. Directly and not through the medium of an angel or a messenger.

Verily, Ye Shall Keep My Sabbaths. Why is this said? Because it says: "Thou shalt not do any manner of work" (Ex. 20:10), from which I know only about activities that can be regarded as labor. But how about activities that can be regarded as merely detracting from the restfulness of the Sabbath? Scripture says here: "Verily, ye shall keep My Sabbaths," thus prohibiting even such activities as only detract from the restfulness of the day.

Once R. Ishmael, R. Eleazar b. Azariah, and R. Akiva were walking along the road followed by Levi the netmaker and Ishmael the son of R. Eleazar b. Azariah. And the following question was discussed by them: Whence do we know that the duty of saving life supersedes the Sabbath laws? R. Ishmael, answering the question, said: Behold it says: "If a thief be found breaking in," etc. (Ex. 22:1). Now of what case does the law speak? Of a case when there is a doubt whether the burglar came merely to steal or even to kill. Now, by using the method of *kal vahomer*, it is to be reasoned: Even shedding of blood, which defiles the land and causes the Shekinah to remove, is to supersede the laws of the Sabbath if it is to be done in protection of one's life. How much more should the duty of saving life supersede the Sabbath laws! R. Eleazer b. Azariah, answering the question, said: If in performing the ceremony of circumcision, which affects only one member of the body, one is to disregard the Sabbath laws, how much more should one do so for the whole body when it is in danger! The sages however said to him: From the instance cited by you it would also follow that just as there the Sabbath is to be disregarded only in a case of certainty, so also here the Sabbath is to be disregarded only in a case of certainty. R. Akiva says: If punishment for murder sets aside even the Temple service, which in turn supersedes the Sabbath, how much more should the duty of saving life supersede the Sabbath laws! R. Jose the Galilean says: When it says: "But My Sabbath ye shall keep," the word "but" (*ak*) implies a distinction. There are Sabbaths on which you must rest and there are Sabbaths on which you should not rest. R. Simon b. Menasiah says: Behold it says: "And ye shall keep the Sabbath for it is holy unto you" (v. 14). This means: The Sabbath is given to you but you are not surrendered to the Sabbath.

Wherefore the children of Israel shall keep the Sabbath to observe the Sabbath throughout their generation (v. 16). This implies that we should disregard one Sabbath for the sake of saving the life of a person so that that person may be able to observe many Sabbaths.

For It Is a Sign between Me and You. But not between Me and the nations of the world.

Throughout Their Generations. This law should obtain throughout the generations.

That Ye May Know. Why is this said? Because it says: "Wherefore the children of Israel shall keep the Sabbath" (ibid.), from which I might understand that the deaf and dumb, the insane and the minor are also included in this commandment. Therefore it says here: "That ye may know." So I must interpret it as speaking only of such persons as have understanding.

That I Am the Lord Who Sanctifies You. In the future world, which is characterized by the kind of holiness possessed by the Sabbath of this world. We thus learn that the Sabbath possesses a holiness like that of the future world. And thus it says: "A Psalm; a Song of the Sabbath day"

(Ps. 92:1), referring to the world in which there is Sabbath all the time.

And Ye Shall Keep the Sabbath for It Is Holy unto You. This is the verse which R. Simon the son of Menasiah interpreted as saying: The Sabbath is given to you but you are not surrendered to the Sabbath.

For It Is Holy unto You. This tells that the Sabbath adds holiness to Israel. Why is the shop of so-and-so closed? Because he keeps the Sabbath. Why does so-and-so abstain from work? Because he keeps the Sabbath. He thus bears witness to Him by whose word the world came into being that He created His world in six days and rested on the seventh. And thus it says: "Therefore ye are My witnesses, saith the Lord, and I am God" (Isa. 43:13).[28]

It remains to be indicated that there were two broad interpretive traditions named after preeminent scholars of the second century, Ishmael and Akiva (Appendix III). The difference is one of interpretive techniques. Ishmael refined Hillel's seven rather straightforward rules of logical inference, involving such categories as linguistic analogy, inference, association, and deduction, into thirteen logically understandable hermeneutic rules. His emphasis was on rational explanation, the relationship and implication of details, etymology, logical analysis, exoteric meaning, and sophisticated but straightforward exegesis. His operative assumption was that the "Torah speaks as men do."[29] Language has implicit meaning and exegesis cannot violate the clear import of a text. Ishmael's methodology had the virtue of being faithful to a text, but in practice it proved restrictive. There are obvious limits to how much could be coaxed out of a given statement. But his rules made good sense and seemed self-evident. The rabbis impressed Ishmael's rules on the average person by including their recitation in the daily morning liturgy.

Akiva was a brilliant, intense, mystical genius, and his interpretative theories reflect all of these qualities. He accepted the familiar straightforward meaning, but insisted that the Torah was not limited by the categories of logical coherence. Individual words, phrases, idioms, every definite article was the word of God and had been spoken for a purpose. The word of God was special, unique. Words have meaning in and out of context. Sentences and phrases have import in and out of sequence. Following Akiva's system, rabbinic Judaism developed a complex, quite special eisegesis which associated rabbinic law to biblical texts which at first glance did not suggest such association. Many old traditions that were felt to be biblical were thereby authorized, but the dangers are clear, and in time eisegesis had to be severely limited to "accepted" interpretations.

Akiva's system emphasized the search for the deeper mystery and a radical distrust of such common sense categories as grammar, construction, and chronology; it insisted on the divine meaning of every preposition and letter in the Torah. Akiva approached the Bible with awe and found awesome secrets. His system was infinitely flexible, but raised the specter of an interpretation which knows no bounds. Later Torah scholars wrote that Akiva based mountains of law on every dot in the Torah text, and a rabbinic legend described a visit by Moses to one of Akiva's lectures. Moses sat there stupefied and bemused; the man was brilliant, but he was finding things in his (Moses') law of which Moses had not been aware.

The *tannaim* edited another kind of literature, *Mishnah* (teaching), code law. *Mishnah* is law set out without its justifying biblical text. *Mishnah* detached legal decisions from legal commentary, and in time gave the oral law an independent existence that allowed it to become the basic text of the rabbinic curriculum. *Mishnah* lists rules, procedures, and decisions, even at times minority opinions, generally without exegetic commentary. Spare as a skeleton, it requires the wires of commentary to hold it together.

For the most part the *Mishnah* is in Hebrew, which makes it today a rather accessible text; but in the second century C.E. Hebrew was a scholar's language (*Leshon ha-Hachamim*), and this code was an academic work prepared for academics. It makes no attempt at felicity of style or emotional appeal. The text assumes that the reader is familiar not only with such mundane matters as coinage rates, weights, and acreage measurements, to which it frequently refers, but with a highly complex and ramified legal system whose terms it suggests, but does not always detail.

It was one thing to proclaim the oral tradition Torah, but quite another to define and delimit that law. The purpose of the *Mishnah* was not to publish a complete code of Torah laws, but to state the law, particularly where there were inconsistent or conflicting traditions, so that these issues could be dealt with in the Torah academies and where possible resolved. One senses a painstaking effort to collect the traditions, examine them carefully for precise language, ascertain that they had been stated by creditable authority, and cite relevant precedent. What can be resolved is resolved, but conclusion is not the *Mishnah's* major purpose. Many issues are simply left open.

Rather, the *Mishnah's* purpose seems to have been to organize and set out the oral tradition so it could be studied and discussed in the various Torah academies.

A wholesaler must clean his measures every thirty days, and the house-holder once every twelve months. Rabban Shimeon ben Gamaliel said: The reverse is the case, the shopkeeper must clean out his measures twice a week, rub up his weights once a week, and clean off his scales before each and every weighing.[30]

R. Eliezer said: A man is required to eat fourteen meals in the Sukkah, one during the day and one each night. The sages said: There is no prescribed number, but he must eat in the Sukkah on the first evening of the festival. R. Eliezer also said: If a man has not eaten in the Sukkah on the first evening of the festival, he must fulfill the *mitzvah* on the last evening of the festival. The sages said: You cannot speak of compensating for the missed *mitzvah*, for it is written: "That which is crooked cannot be made straight, and that which is lacking cannot be counted" (Ecc. 1:15).[31]

The *Mishnah* is not a code which precedes systematically from general rule to particular consequences, although it sometimes gives that appearance, nor is it a statement of discrete laws set out in such a way that general principles of jurisprudence can be inferred. One who seeks to read the *Mishnah* will find himself in a welter of detail, vaguely disturbed that no one makes the effort to relate the laws to each other or to reduce the mass of facts to broad, simply grasped ideas. The *Mishnah* is the oral law drawn up to permit academic discussion. In editing the *Mishnah*, Yehudah ha-Nasi and his council had a practical rather than an analytic purpose in mind. The oral law was scattered; it needed to be drawn together and systematized. The oral tradition contained conflicting traditions, and these texts needed to be examined, authenticated, and reconciled. Here were tasks for the Torah schools sufficient for the generations. Yehudah's task was to provide a competent and accurate resource book, as specific and as precise as he could make it.

Scholars still debate the *Mishnah's* origin. The mishnaic form is old; there is evidence that it had been used in the schools of the Pharisees long before the whole was reduced to writing. The citation of discrete laws may have developed to obviate the cumbersome and not always compelling process of justifying every inherited ruling with a scriptural proof-text, or simply because the shortened form was all most jurists could master. Various collections of these discrete rules circulated throughout the first and second centuries, generally grouped about specific concerns of the law (torts, damages, Sabbath rules). These were enlarged and rearranged several times until about 200 C.E., when the patriarch, Yehudah ha-Nasi, headed a group of sages who worked over an edition of Meir's, who had taken over a schematization of Akiva's, who had depended on earlier collections. This group of sages authorized and published a *Mishnah* collection which gained general approval.

The *Mishnah* sets out the oral law almost defiantly, as if to say, "The era of debate is over, the authority of these rules is beyond question." Typically, the betrothal laws (*Kiddushin*) begin with bald law, oral law: "A woman can be acquired in three separate ways and she acquires her freedom in three ways: She is acquired by money, by writ, or by intercourse. . . ." [32] Similarly, the book of marriage laws begins: "A virgin should be married on a Wednesday and a widow on a Thursday since the courts convene twice each week, on Mondays and on Thursdays; thus should the husband need to lodge a virginity suit he would be able to go immediately the next morning to the court." [33]

Yehudah ha-Nasi's *Mishnah* was divided into six major divisions, each subdivided into treatises, sixty-three in all (Appendix IV). The six tractates are more or less self-explanatory groupings: agricultural laws, festivals, family law, civil and criminal law, cult law, and ritual purity. Each treatise collects the laws dealing with a specific theme, such as tithes or Rosh Hashanah; a particular category such as family regulation (divorce, inheritance) or due process (oaths, testimonies), or cult, and divides the relevant law into chapters which are subsequently subdivided into single-theme paragraphs. The *Mishnah* was designed for research and reference rather than as a piece of literature. It was convenient, with its laws grouped as they were considered in the schools. The *Mishnah* organized the laws into meaningful categories and the rabbis were able to work out procedure, precedent, and legal theory far more effectively than before.

The *Mishnah* is the classic collection of the oral law, the text which the Talmudic schools would provide with endless commentary, but it was not the only such anthology. Possibly in the fourth century a Palestinian Torah school published a larger collection of discrete laws, the *Tosefta* (addition), arranged according to the same tractates as the *Mishnah*, though certain treatises, *Avot*, *Tamid*, *Middot*, and *Kinnim*, are missing. The *Tosefta* includes mishnaic law, many rules not found there, and others differing in phrasing or even in substance. Rabbinic literature has a special word, *Baraita*, to describe a tannaitic decision not found in the *Mishnah* but found in the *Tosefta*, in the halachic *midrashim,* or in the text of the *Talmud* itself. The lack of systematic completeness on the part of the *Mishnah* and *Tosefta* editors, deliberate or not, introduced a degree of flexibility into rabbinic law which would prove remarkably healthy, although it was theoretically impossible to admit that the Torah was anything but complete and whole.

What began as a teaching aid became the constitutive text of rabbinic Judaism. More and more the schools established the *Mishnah* rather than the Torah as the basic curricular text. To do so avoided much tedious, and sometimes dubious, scriptural exegesis. Traditions developed resolving apparent contradictions. The authority of rabbinic law was assumed rather than argued. The *Mishnah* accomplished its purpose: the old questions about the differences between written and oral law fade from memory. The *Mishnah* replaced the Bible as the core curriculum of continuing education.

❦

Not all who survived the various defeats were content to seek salvation through a life of worship, study, and quiet obedience. The teachers of apocalypse made one last appeal: "And the Lord said unto me. This city shall be delivered up for a time, the people shall be chastened during a time, and the world will not be given over to oblivion." [34] In IV Ezra, II Baruch, and elsewhere, visionaries offered their by now shopworn eschatological hopes, but the apocalypse of the second century was not as innocently confident as its progenitors. Defeat had finally shaken these visionaries. Even as IV Ezra restated the promise, he suggested that "the age was full of sadness and infirmities," perhaps unworthy of redemption, and he raised the tormenting question of theodicy. Jerusalem is razed. Rome stands. Are the Romans really better than the Jews? Of course the answer is no. [35] What then? The conventional answer is offered: God's ways are inscrutable, but such a nonexplanation no longer satisfies the pious author; as if transfixed, IV Ezra returned to this issue again and again, and by way of answer spun for himself ingenuities remarkably close to the Christian doctrine of original sin. Somehow Adam's fall had condemned the world to anguish and pain: "When Adam transgressed My statutes then that which had been made was judged, and then the ways of the world became narrow and sorrowful and painful . . . and full of perils coupled with great toils." [36] Doubt cut like a knife into his confidence:

[276]

After the Fall

Let the human race lament, but the beasts of the field are glad, for it is far better with them than with us, for they have no judgment to look for, neither do they know of any torture or of any salvation promised to them after death. For what doth it profit us that we shall be preserved alive, but yet suffer great torment? For all the earthborn are defiled with iniquities, full of sins, laden with offenses and if, after death, we were not to come into judgment it might perchance have been far better for us.[37]

Apocalypse faltered. To justify God it began to damn man, suggesting that man was constitutionally incapable of obeying God.

As always, apocalypse was intoxicating drink to restless men. With its promise of a near Judgment Day it fanned the flames of rebellion, but after the second bloody defeat—that of Bar Kochba—the Jewish community could not afford another Zealot bid for national independence. What was needed was steadiness, community solidarity, and unflinching patience. The schools consciously put apocalypse aside, although its spirit and themes were not totally forgotten. Apocalypse went underground, only to reemerge several centuries later in so-called palace (*heichalot*) mysticism. *Heichalot Rabbati* speaks of an End Time which is near at hand, of angel intercessors, of divine secrets. But such works emphasize personal transcendence, the soul's visit to God's court, the *via mystica* as much as messianic expectation. It is assumed that men, at least the pure and saintly, can make the dangerous but exciting trip into the heavens to commune with God and gain some knowledge of divine secrets. A sense of the proximity of the Judgment Day led men to adopt a life of strict discipline in order to prepare themselves for mystic translation. The natural question of the uninitiated as to who can know the secret of the throne is answered: Those who are pure of idolatry, sexual offenses, bloodshed, slander, vain oaths, profanation of the Name, impertinence, and unjustified enmity. Many heard and gave up, thinking there are none who are that pure. The mystic literature equated initiation with purity and provided secret formulas and sacred songs to aid the initiate. Apocalypse was transformed into a mystic literature which alternated between suggesting gnosis, the secret redemptive knowledge, and making calculations about the Messiah's arrival.

Apocalyptic writing which foreshortened history and encouraged men to believe that redemption was breathing down their necks served only to embitter and deepen the mood of national frustration. In order to survive, it became necessary to accept the nation's fate for what it was, a long sentence to *galut*, and to anticipate God's deliverance in God's good time. One heard again counsels of patience and quiet courage: "If you have a sapling in your hand and it is said to you, behold there is the Messiah—go on with your planting and afterwards turn and receive him." [38] Various preachers put cautionary words in God's mouth. God said to Israel: "You built the Temple and it has been destroyed, so do not build it again until you hear a voice from heaven," which is really a paraphrase of Zechariah's admonition: "Not by power nor by might, but by My Spirit, saith the Lord" (4:6). We have seen that many would not accept the full import of these climactic events. Scholars continued to pledge offerings to the Temple, to be paid when it would be rebuilt. A great effort was made to retain the various practices associated with ritual purity. But Jewish life had embarked on a new dimension of existence. The way of Torah offered the familiar national hope, and the expanded Torah offered a way of redemption to each individual, both in this world and in the next. This hope was desperately needed. Literally, in *galut*, "It [The Torah] is our life and length of days to us."

As Akiva and his disciples disembarked at a port near Rome, his disciples began to weep. Akiva, however, seemed untroubled. His companions were puzzled at his behavior. Akiva turned their behavior on them. "Why do you cry?" "Should we not cry? These, our conquerors, worship idols and live in security and abundance while the Temple of our God has been consumed by fire and has become a lair for wild beasts!" "That, precisely, is why I am untroubled. If they who offend God are doing this well, how much better will those fare who obey him." [39]

During the Bar Kochba revolt Akiva died a martyr's death, full of confidence in his God.

CHAPTER

❧ XVI ❧

Talmudic Judaism

T̶HE *Talmud* defines Mishnaic Judaism, or, rather, two *Talmuds* define it. One presents the teachings of various Galilean academies between the publishing of *Mishnah* (ca. 200 C.E.) and the end of significant and organized Jewish life in the Galilee (ca. 480) and is called the *Palestinian* or *Jerusalem Talmud*. The other, which became authoritative, is the *Babylonian Talmud*, compiled in schools located in such Mesopotamian places as Pumbedita, Sura, Nehardea, Mehoza, and Nersh between 200 C.E. and the Arab conquest (ca. 640). In both *Talmuds* each line or paragraph of *Mishnah* has its own clump of commentary. The men who held these discussions and provided notes, legal theories, variant texts, cases, and exegesis are known as *amoraim* (seekers or interpreters). The *Palestinian Talmud* reached its "finished" form with their work. *Savoraim* (expositors) edited the available records of the Babylonian academies and left us their encyclopedic commentary to the *Mishnah* in its "finished" form.

Talmud means teaching. Specifically, *Talmud* describes the sixty-three tractates of the *Mishnah*, plus *Gemara* (completion), which is the sediment, more or less edited, of legal discussions; academic notes; case citations; exegesis deriving law from biblical text; biographical notes establishing law on the basis of the habits of great scholars, complex and subtle analysis, and determined reconciliation of disparate tannaitic traditions (the law had to speak with one voice); as well as scraps of history, etymology, folklore, astronomy and astrol-

[279]

ogy, medicine, homiletic parable, and discrete theological comment, all bound in one fashion or another to a *Mishnah* text (Appendix IV). No *Gemara* exists to twenty-six and one-half *Mishnah* tractates in the *Babylonian Talmud* and to twenty-four tractates in the *Palestinian Talmud*, most of which deal with areas of law which were no longer active, such as tithing and the sacrificial cult. The *Talmud* is a lawbook and much more. The lawbook sets out *halachah*, the way. The much more is *aggadah*, discussion, lexicography, history, theology, messianic expectations, biblical interpretation, allegory, liturgy, bits of travel journal, the stuff of life.

Each term an academy would select a *Mishnah* tractate and carefully analyze each successive statement. The *Gemara* is a report of the salient points made. When it came time for that tractate to be studied again, the *Mishnah* was reported together with existing *Gemara*, and after review and further discussion a cumulative report was made. So *Gemara* grew, discussion by discussion, and it was only natural that these academic notes should be kept in the actual speech of the classroom: Eastern Aramaic in Babylon, Western Aramaic in the Galilee.

These notes were never intended to be read as literature. Any competent editor would have thrown up his hands if either *Talmud* had been submitted for publication. The sheer size of the record is overwhelming. The *Babylonian Talmud* contains over two and a half million words, a majority of them set out in terse and grammatically incomplete sentences. Except for the quality of compactness, the *Talmud* is without style; even a cursory study reveals that such art as the text manifests derives from concern for the difficulties of memorization rather than for literary form. There was a long-lived taboo against publishing the oral law. Incredibly, *Gemara* was carried about in the scholar's head, which helps account for its terseness, the presence of many mnemonics, an occasional admission that no one understands a received tradition, and an utter lack of care about language and effect. Inconsistencies, omissions, and duplications abound.

The *Talmud* is a nonbook. No one set out to write a *Talmud*. The *savoraim* who drew these blocks of commentary together and put an end to the laying of layer upon layer were determined to safeguard rather than to edit this record of significant *Mishnah* commentary. Lack of style and continuity, together with the *Talmud's* language, a long-dead Aramaic dialect, and its graceless legalese combine to keep the *Gemara* a closed book to almost anyone outside the rabbinic field.

Even fluency in Hebrew does not qualify you to read *Gemara*. Despite it all, to Jews this was *the* book. For fifteen hundred years going to school meant studying *Talmud*. There were compensations. The *Talmud's* sweep was broad, including bits and pieces from most of the fields of human knowledge. Talmudic logic is sharp and tested the subtlest intellect. There were also drawbacks. No field outside Jewish law is treated systematically. Such sciences as mathematics and astronomy are introduced only when they are necessary to the sacred science, law.

Each basic block of *Gemara* is a *sugyah* or thematic unit. A *sugyah* has no classic form, but appears as an accumulation and distillation of texts and citations, cases and refinements, relevant legal theory, and classroom questions and answers which had been brought together during study of a particular *Mishnah*. Various *sugyot* may deal with the same theme; if so, there will be differences in the citation of authorities and cases or even in the statement of the law. There is no fine writing, although legal terminology is handled with precision. The purpose of a *sugyah* was less to state law than to define a law's ramifications and reconcile it with other rules in the oral tradition. It was axiomatic that God's words were consistent. Argument proceeds from analysis to accommodation rather than from analysis to a clear choice between alternatives. Nothing is ever cut away; instead, in the process of reconciliation and accommodation much is added.

The *Mishnah* assertively set out the traditions of the oral law; the *Gemara* self-consciously related these laws, ideas, and values to the written Torah and to each other. Talmudic argument follows its own rules of logic, mixing in questions of equity, manifest justice, and appropriate legal theory, but, ultimately and finally, the law derives from the revelation. Many a *sugyah* begins: "What is the scriptural source of this rule?" The suggested source is at times logical and at times, to an outsider, surprising, but biblical citations are always available. It is difficult to find two successive *Gemara* paragraphs in which a *Tanach* text is not cited. However, the *Talmud* rarely gives the impression of harried scholars urgently in search of a proof-text. Even when they admitted that a particular body of rules is like a mountain suspended by a hair, the rabbis knew that the Torah was the context of all rabbinic law. Their search was less to tie law to Torah than to place a particular text in a new light and vary its association so as to extricate new meaning.

The *Talmud*—to medieval Jewry this meant the *Babylonian*

Talmud—is an unkempt text. There are broad principles of organization: *Gemara* commentary follows regularly each *Mishnah* paragraph, but within each section there are loose ends and loose connections; most, but not all, material is related to what precedes. Sometimes the connection is only that two successive sentences are quotations by the same teacher or contain an identical phrase or word. The categories of rabbinic analysis, although at times related to Greek logic and Roman law, are *sui generis*. The sages called the *Talmud* a sea. The modern student is constantly aware of the swelling power of its ideas, but also that, like the sea, it is without fixed limits, beyond being controlled. Just when you think you have exhausted an issue, a new question is raised. This encyclopedic commentary on the *Mishnah* would provide challenges and puzzles sufficient to occupy scholars for the next millennium. The modern reader searches for conclusions and finds none except Torah.

There are depths and currents in the *Talmud*, but a curious lack of progression. The clash of opinion is muted by the drive to accommodate all differences as only apparent divisions. We prize fresh ideas; they prized the familiar and the certain. Law and ethical principles had been clearly and finally stated by God and were valid at all times and all places. On forty different occasions in the Torah God had described His law as "a law for all time" (Ex. 28:43, etc.). God's law can be deepened, but not changed. "You shall not add anything to what I command you or take anything away from it" (Deut. 4:2). Waves rise and whitecaps form, but the sea ultimately settles back. Judaism's forms and rules, its religious and ethical mandates, and its affirmations, are assumed throughout to be fixed and immutable, and this sense of certainty is not without profound emotional appeal.

There might be discussion and debate, but the Torah remained unchanged. Inevitably there were shifts of emphasis and even ritual and legal innovations, but "the Torah was one" and each generation's Torah was believed identical with that of Moses. Amoraic thought is associational rather than dialectic. Rabina in the sixth century did not observe exactly as Hillel had observed in the first, nor did he think as Hillel had thought; but he thought he did. Each obeyed the revelation at Sinai, followed the *halachah*, studied and taught Torah, and maintained the regimen of diet, holy day, and Sabbath. Rabina knew that he differed from Hillel in matters of *minhag* (custom), but *minhag* represented local color, minor variations, rather than substantial modification of the Torah way.

Talmudic Judaism

Knowing that a student will pick up the *Gemara* and be puzzled by its legal terms, and that if he masters these—a good piece of work—he will seek underlying philosophic norms and be frustrated, a writer is tempted toward apologetics—a few paragraphs which would draw out the sensitivity and humanness behind, for example, the *Gemara's* treatment of children or slaves, and let it go at that. Such manuals exist and are valuable for those who have been raised with the Christian condemnation of the *Talmud* as a frightful monument to legalism, but they are untrue to the *Gemara*. The *Gemara* is often sympathetic and humane in its judgments, but humanity is not its final or operative standard. This standard remains the judgment as to whether a position is consistent with Torah. The *Gemara* is exactly as humane as the oral and written law, no more and no less.

No one reads the *Talmud*. It can only be studied, patiently. At first it was studied orally. There were professional memorizers in each school who were expected to know by heart the received *sugyot* and to recite them on command. These living books were essential to a school's operation, although a good memory did not a scholar make: "The memorizer repeats and does not know what he is saying." [1] At the opening of the class session a *Mishnah* text was spoken out together with known related *baraitot*. Then the master and senior scholars contributed what they had heard on the subject from their masters or colleagues. Interesting or relevant cases were cited. Students asked questions and were answered. Relevant biblical exegesis was suggested, and then the student was left with the incredible task of fixing in his memory law, authority, citations, case, and prooftext. During the Talmudic period there was no published *Talmud*. A student carried home after graduation a few notes and his memory. Scattered in the *Talmud* we hear the sighs of these students: "The Torah can be acquired only with the aid of mnemonic devices"; [2] they worked hard and some broke down from overwork.

Who were the *amoraim?* What were their academies for and like? Did ordinary folk accept Talmudic law? Like their immediate predecessors the *tannaim*, the *amoraim* were Torah scholars, students of the Torah defined as the oral law. The *amoraim* were the first rabbis of rabbinic Judaism. Rabbi, literally "my teacher" or "my mentor," appears as a title, apparently largely honorific, in second-century Palestine; in time it became the familiar title granted to those whom the masters deemed qualified to administer and interpret the oral law, what they called Torah. To appreciate the rabbi's role we must discard all modern associations which identify a rabbi and a congregation. The rabbi was a schoolman, not a synagogue person. He did not officiate at synagogue worship or even necessarily teach or preach there. Often he did not have a major say in synagogue administration. There were sages, powerful men of first rank, who lived in communities whose synagogues contained floor mosaics depicting human or animal figures, designs that so offended them that they refused to prostrate themselves, claiming that these images violated the second commandment. However, they were not influential enough to get the offending images removed or covered.

The rabbis were members of a scholars' caste for which they qualified themselves by mastering Torah law to the satisfaction of their teachers. They also had to satisfy their masters as to their character and style of life. Structurally, the community of scholars was not unlike a medieval university, a corporate body of masters and students with special rules and rights and even a special uniform. The scholar's dress was a white cape. He wore phylacteries and was scrupulous in matters of ritual purity and diet. He enjoyed special privileges by virtue of his caste, including exclusion from the poll tax and the right to trial before a court of his peers. The academy had its punctilio and special ceremonies and rigidly regulated the behavior of students toward masters.

The atmosphere was authoritarian. A student rose when the master entered and served his master's most menial bidding. The masters demanded humble discipleship. They saw themselves not simply as schoolmasters or intellectuals, but as living Torahs. By mastering Torah they had made themselves over in its spirit, and that spirit was reflected in their every act. They insisted that the same reverence shown to the Torah be offered to them. The *Talmud* often describes how and what a master ate, how he dressed, what words and lore he used in his speech, even how he relieved himself in the privy. The master's life was a holy model from which a student could learn how Torah could be lived on the most intimate and domestic level. The scholar's life style was the audiovisual component of Torah education.

The rabbis were a distinct caste, but not one that was hereditary. Admission was open to any male who qualified academically. Nor were the rabbis a parasitical class. Although they were excused from the poll tax, they did not live off alms or public funds; each supported himself as best he could. The academies were scholarly corporations, not dormitory communities. The scholars had their own homes, lives, and wives, and were free to travel when and where they wished. The rabbis were in no sense monastics. They were distinguished not by ascetic practices but by the vigil of study. They worshipped as other men did, but their role was not as men of prayer. Sometimes the sages even absented themselves from public prayer. "R. Yitzḥak asked R. Naḥman, 'Why does the master not come to the synagogue in order to pray?' 'I can not.' 'Why not then gather a *minyan* and pray at home?' 'It is too much trouble.' " [3]

These schools were male societies. There were no women colleagues. The Torah does not specifically require sexual segregation, but every line of *Talmud* reflects a growing commitment to what would be called today an agenda of male chauvinism. Grammar came to the aid of their maleness. Since the written law used masculine pronouns and case endings, it was possible to exclude women from many rights and duties. Torah was construed so that women could not offer testimony. Women were praised in their place—if they looked well to the ways of their household, provided their husbands with sons, and set their sons on the way of learning if the husband would not or could not—but their place was not in the academy or in the synagogue. A woman could not be counted as a person in order to complete the congregation of ten required for public worship. *Gemara* discussion assumed and established the maleness of a rabbinic life style whose full-fledged citizens, all men, would each morning bless a kind God "who has not made me a woman." [4] The rabbinic attitude was tempered by respect for a woman's special qualities within the terms of traditional sex-role differentiation, and an implacable opposition to homosexuality. Marriage was mandatory. Preferably marriage should take place at an early age, but marriage was for procreation, not companionship.

Why did young men go to study at these schools? Study had social utility. The Jewish community was subservient to Roman or Sassanian authority but was generally allowed to regulate its own domestic affairs, and the oral law provided the norms and forms of such government. Like the leaders of other ethnic and religious groups within the society, the patriarch in Roman Palestine and the exilarch in Sassanian Babylon were accepted by the Jews, accredited by the imperial court, and given responsibility for taxes, law and order, and the creation of a communal infrastructure which would not only carry out the government's wishes, but effectively, that is, peacefully, organize life according to the Jewish nation's accustomed ways. The imperial government expected such leaders to enforce its decisions. The Jews looked to their headman to present their special needs to the government, and because both patriarch and exilarch were chosen from families which claimed Davidic ancestry, the community found in their authority encouraging evidence of the continued existence of the Jewish nation and the ongoing validity of its messianic hope.

Obviously, decisions had to be religiously appropriate, hence the rabbi as Torah officer. The patriarch and exilarch looked to the rabbis to staff their bureaus and the community's courts, particularly to organize properly matters of personal status (marriage, divorce, inheritance, adoption, genealogy) and the transfer of property, and to administer the law in the several settlements. The law which the rabbis mastered enabled them to maintain registries, act as law experts in the courts, supervise markets and fairs, manage bureaus of weights and measures, organize equity and small claims courts, and the like. The rabbi's willingness to work for the exilarchate said to the ordinary Jew, "The exilarch's rule is legitimate. Our lives are organized as they should be, according to God's word, by men who understand these words." The presence of these Torah men validated the whole system.

The rabbis cooperated with the exilarch or patriarch because he alone could provide them access to authority and a chance to fashion Jewish life according to the norms of their oral law tradition. Just as it was their fixed purpose to pattern their lives after their holy masters, so as a religious class they hoped to encourage every Jew to make normative the rabbinic pattern of obedience. In this, in time, they were remarkably successful. The rabbis' central role in the courts and administration, their obvious learning, and their claim to derive their ways from God's will, which they were uniquely qualified to understand, led many to accept their word and follow their example. What began as the unique life style of a scholar class was destined to become the way of life of an entire people.

Study had obvious ethical value. The Torah was God's law and the only appropriate guide to the good life. The more a student studied, the more he gained in ethical understanding and reach. The master became a living Torah. His every action presumedly reflected the profoundest understanding of divine wisdom. Study was redemptive, *the* act of obedience. In an earlier generation *teshuvah*, a return to covenant faithfulness, was seen as the appropriate signal to a just God that Israel was ready for redemption. Now we find the suggestion that "all the exiles will be gathered in only through the merit of *Mishnah* study." [5] On a private level study was a *mitzvah*, an ordained duty whose fulfillment was pleasing to God, a necessary credit when the scholar appeared before the heavenly tribunal. Late at night, eyes tired and mind exhausted, a scholar reviewed the cost of his hard-won learning and found it acceptable: "Be pleased, my soul, it is for your sake that I have studied *Tanach*, for you I have studied *Mishnah*." [6]

Study was not only the way to a useful profession, ethical awareness, and heaven and immortality, but a power-laden enterprise full of cosmic significance. "He who busies himself with the law for its own sake brings harmony into the universe [causes peace in the upper and lower families]. He is as if he had built the upper and lower palaces; he protects the whole world. He brings near redemption." [7] The rabbi's world was divided between the heavens above and the earth beneath; God was in the heavens and Torah was the presence of divine power on earth. Being of the heavens, Torah gives off the harmonies of God. If a man wants to be in tune with the divine he has only to tune his life to Torah. In the scholars' awareness, Torah was not simply a scroll or even the book of truth, but *Torat Ḥayyim*, a life-giving teaching, a fountain of living waters, the source through which divine energy and blessing flow to man. Water was a favorite metaphor for Torah. Without water the land cannot be fertile and man becomes parched and weak, unable to wash off the dust and grime of everyday. Water, which revives the earth and man, is a code word for resurrection and immortality.[8] The sages studied to learn, to serve, and to be saved.

The Torah is an active agent of divinity, the vital presence of God's word and will in the community of Israel. Such was the power of Torah that, like a radioactive element, it had to be handled with care; and those who successfully and routinely handled it inevitably had ascribed to them some of the Torah's redemptive and creative power. *Talmud* scholars participated in the holiness of the revelation and came to be acknowledged as holy men, healers, wizards, possessors of theurgic wisdom, even occasionally as intercessors for man before God. Like the Magi among their Zoroastrian neighbors, the rabbis looked upon themselves and were seen by many folk as religious virtuosi whose mastery of matters divine gave them power to pray effectively, cure the sick, bring the rain, exorcise demons, and communicate with the dead. A rabbi's prayer and learning had exceptional power. There were a hundred stories such as that of R. Huna, who had left in a dilapidated house some wine casks which he later wanted to retrieve. He asked R. Adda ben Ahavah to come with him and study until all the casks had been removed. When Adda stopped studying, the house fell down.[9]

It seemed plausible to many folk that a man who had mastered the Torah, through which God had created the world, could, like God, create a man out of clay. Certainly he knew power-laden formulas.[10] Ordinary men and women turned to the rabbi for advice, for amulets to protect mothers during childbirth and children from the plague, for rain during seasons of drought, for interpretation of dreams and omens, and for an incantation or sign which would protect them from the evil eye. The rabbis fulfilled such requests, but still did not look on themselves as wizards. They disapproved of magic and said so often and publicly. What they possessed, they said, was not magic, but Torah. Magic evoked a twilight world of shades and demons. The Torah was of God, a gift of His grace, light not darkness, a power He clearly intended to be used for Israel's benefit. One finds side by side in the *Talmud* careful and precise legal formulation, evidence of sober and realistic minds, and what seem incredible reports of miracle cures, exorcisms, and rainmaking. The power of God which the rabbis and the people acknowledged was full and overwhelming, and they made no effort to civilize that power. God was real, not a God-idea. God's revelation was powerful and offered man salvation. As long as this cultural world remained in being, the rabbi was more than a teacher and judicial functionary. Eighteenth-century Polish rabbis were still writing amulets to ward off disease or the dangers of childbirth. But although the rabbi had about him an aura of divine power, he never laid claim to divinity; such "nonsense" was left to Christians. There were no rabbinic Elishas who were translated alive to heaven.

The rabbis not only believed in the revelation at Sinai, but looked on Torah as both a divine teaching and a divine power come to earth which could be tapped by faithful study and faithful obedience. There were secrets in the Torah—the secret of God's names, the date of Judgment Day. There were mysteries in the Torah—a description of the cosmos, physical and metaphysical truths, truths about the nature of God. There was power in the Torah—no illness or accident could befall one who engaged in study. These secrets, mysteries, and powers were discussed privately, not in the classroom; they were taught cryptically, not openly. Not every scholar applied himself to esoteric matters, and no master showed patience to any would-be magician who wanted to master the Torah's secrets but had no desire to accept the commandments: "If one learns the law without the intention of fulfilling the law, it would have been better if he had never been born." [11] Because of rabbinic restrictions against the public disclosure of mystical and theosophic matters, the *Talmud* only suggests these speculations, and it is difficult fully to reconstruct them. A few patently esoteric volumes such as the *Alphabet of Rabbi Akiva* took form in these centuries, as did at least one rather unabashed book of magic, the *Sefer ha-Razim* (*Book of Secrets*), discovered by Margalioth just a few years ago. But the *Talmud* was not of this genre. Talmudic *aggadah* reflects the beliefs and credulities of a believing world, but the *Talmud* was a lawbook and as such retained significance long after the rabbinic world began to read as pure metaphor amoraic statements of the Torah's power to redeem and save.

The rabbis were interested in all that interested God. Their *Gemara*, with its practical and analytic juridical concerns, its medical axioms, astronomical calculations, ethnological observations, bits and pieces of an intense and highly imaginative esoteric tradition, moralistic parables, homiletic reflections on life, gnomic statements about the nature of God and man, textual commentary, cosmetic advice, dream interpretation, and speculation on the Messianic age and the World to Come reveals the breadth of God's world and theirs. God's world, the cosmos, was vast and could not be exhaustively visited or explored, but God's word described that universe. The *midrash* described the Torah as a cosmic blueprint and suggested that God Himself had consulted the Torah during creation. The universe was the macrocosm, vast and overwhelming. Torah was the microcosm, an outline of the universe on a scale men could assimilate. The student, by assiduous examination of Torah, was not simply commenting on the text; he was doing physics, extending the frontiers of knowledge, and developing a metaphysical understanding, hence philosophy. Extending the range of knowledge was as difficult and rare then as it is today. Oral law was a thicket of ideas, often so densely packed as to seem impenetrable. What was needed was study and review and then more study and review until a student began to see the shape of the forest and some of its natural paths. "This may be compared to an impenetrable thicket of reeds. What did a clever man do? He cut a path and entered, cut some more and penetrated further. In time he entered the clearing and all began to enter by following his path." [12]

The rabbis dealt with a sacred, not a humanist, legal system. The

Torah included socially necessary and patently beneficial laws such as those prohibiting murder, adultery, and incest, but these rules had no greater claim on man than commandments which today seem antique, if not superstitious, and defy functional explanation, for example, the prohibition of mixing fibers in a garment. Each had its purpose; the *Talmud* did not exaggerate one class of laws and demean another, but required full obedience to God's will.

As Torah scholars, the rabbis primarily worked to clear up remaining uncertainties about the specifics of God's rules and legislation and to understand their application to specific situations rather than to organize ethical categories which could be defended philosophically. In their language, *mitzvah*, commandment, covered the category we call good deed. Their Torah was a discrete and limited set of instructions from which the *amoraim* set out to establish an all-embracing godly style of life.

Antinomian children of an antinomian age, we imagine that an all-encompassing law must be suffocating. We may or may not be right. In our rapidly changing world, law is often identified with repression. To the rabbis in their rather static and sombre world, law meant redemption. The rabbis welcomed the law as the kindest gift of a kind God; without it life would be hapless and hopeless. Torah gave direction through everyday confusions. Torah provided encouragement which was proof against ceaseless political and social frustration. Patterning one's life according to the law gave it meaning in one's own eyes and merit in the eyes of God. *Halachah* taught the way a man should go, what was required of him, and by whom. Without knowledge of the way, existence remained mean and confusing. A sense of accomplishment was available only to those who obeyed God; they walked straight while others stumbled: "As fish live in the sea and perish when they leave it, so man lives in Torah and would perish should he abandon it." [13]

Pauline Christianity offered men an antinomian faith and praised an ethic whose advantage presumably lay in its insistence that men should be moved by the spirit, not by the law. Christianity was not without its appeal to Jews and there are indications of apostasy, but Judaism, when allowed to, won its share of converts. Talmudic life was not a timid submission to divine tyranny, but a way of life which freed the best in the human soul. Obedience was a devotion. The rabbis applauded the virtue of saintly deeds which transcend legal obligation. They had a special label for such actions, *Middat*

Ḥassidut (the way of the saintly), but they rejected both systematically and instinctively any way to the kingdom which was based purely on spirit, spontaneity, or impulsive piety. "Greater is he who feels commanded." [14] The Christians rejoiced that they had broken the yoke, while Jews reminded themselves and their neighbors that only a yoked pair can pull the cart.

At Sinai the commandment had been engraved (*ḥerut*) and, lovers of word games that they were, the rabbis pointed out that *ḥerut* also means freedom. Divine law frees men to their higher selves. Paul saw the commandments as a "dispensation of condemnation," a burden which only increased man's sense of guilt: "If it had not been for the law, I should not have known sin." [15] The rabbis, on the contrary, looked on the law (not all law) as proof of God's will to redeem. Through law man purified himself, sublimated his aggressive nature, organized his distinctive community, and made himself pleasing to God and man. Because of Torah law the Jew did not have to suffer an identity crisis; he knew what was required of him and did not feel compelled to spend his days desperately praying for God's unpredictable gift of grace. By clarifying duty, "Commandment Judaism" lightened the psychological burdens of an anxious existence. The Jew was reassured by his every act of obedience that he was doing God's will. He walked lightly because he walked with purpose; when he looked at the counciliar Church of the fourth or fifth century, with its myriad rules and regulations, he noted that Paul's antinomian teachings had not stood the test of institutional or human need.

Israel was in *galut*. The way of redemption lay in fulfilling the will of God. The rabbis lived such a life and were determined to make their practice normative, since, so they taught, the Messiah would come when the whole people properly observed even a single law or Sabbath. Their mission was to make all Israel a kingdom of priests (rabbis), which would, ipso facto, make them a holy nation to whom the Messiah might be sent. One might call the rabbis domestic missionaries. Their tactics were suasive (the organization of mass education, preaching, and personal example), political (control of the courts), and mythic (the image of the rabbinic way as the glory road). An obedient generation could expect salvation. No foreign overlord would long rule over an obedient Israel. Law, ethics, and redemption were one. R. Yehudah said: "He who would like to be truly faithful to God, let him carry out scrupulously the law of damages." [16]

❦

The centers of Talmudic activity in Roman Galilee and Sassanian Babylonia, despite intermittent Roman-Persian war, were in constant contact and shared one overriding purpose: to rabbinize Jewish life. We hear of students and masters traveling both east to west and west to east. The *Mishnah* was one, despite minor textual differences in the various recensions, and most schools were aware of what other schools were teaching. Nevertheless, inevitably there developed significant differences in style, emphasis, use of *aggadah*, treatment of folk attitudes, and the formalities of local jurisdiction due to differing political and social circumstances.

The *Babylonian Talmud* seems to relate to a more advanced commerical economy than the *Palestinian Talmud*. Louis Ginzberg, who carried out pioneering research in the *Palestinian Talmud*, cites, among other evidence, a decision that a moneylender who has a reputation for exacting excessive interest may not testify in a financial dispute, on the grounds that his evidence would be colored by his greed. In a similar case the *Babylonian Talmud* disqualifies both lender and borrower. Presumedly, in a more highly developed economy the borrower at high interest rates does so less out of need than out of greed for something like a quick killing on the stock market, and so by the *Mishnah's* original logic he too ought to be disqualified. On the other hand, the *Palestinian Talmud* seems to reflect a less credulous society. It regulates far more carefully than the *Babylonian Talmud* the sciences of the East, astrology, magic, faith healing, amulets, and "secret" things, and is less prone to describe the rabbi's role as that of a power-laden wizard.

Oral and written law were part of a single truth, consistent in teaching and requirement, but in effect it was the oral law which determined the content and practice of rabbinic Judaism. The Torah, now called *Mikra* (the reading), remained the pulsating center of the tradition. A boy began reading the Torah at the age of five or six. Torah and *Haftarah* were read in the synagogue on Sabbath, holidays, and market days. Torah texts were used sermonically both to underscore rabbinic rulings and to encourage and to edify the people. Its familiar themes, such as Creation, the Flood, the Exodus, and Sinai, provided the central themes of the nation's carefully nourished collective unconscious. As God had redeemed Israel from Egypt, so would He redeem their communities from tyranny. The

Torah was particularly useful in guiding and teaching the young. The great midrashic collections of biblical comment and text-related sermon outlines (*Midrash Rabbah, Pesikta, Pesikta Rabbati*) were begun in this period and were essentially aggadic or instructional in nature, full of legend, lore, illustration, ethical advice, poetry, pithy proverb, intellectual dainties, and historical embellishment (Appendix III).

The Torah was read through annually in the Babylonian synagogues and triennially in Palestine. Its role as a holy thing is suggested by several dozen rules requiring its special care. A Torah had to be written according to a rigid scribal tradition, on special parchment with a special quill, using a specially prepared ink. A little scroll of rules, *Masechet Sefer Torah*, condenses these rules, and the rabbis dealt with them at length in a volume, *Soferim*, which is added today to most editions of the *Babylonian Talmud*. When the Torah scroll was taken from its ark the congregation rose. A scroll which was somewhat faded could no longer be used in worship, but neither could it be tossed aside. It had to be buried or stored. The Torah was rarely read without being translated, generally into the Aramaic vernacular, and these translations followed strict forms.

Torah gave its name to and lay at the heart of the oral tradition, but it was a rabbinic Torah which was acclaimed. The young child was given Torah to read, by age ten he was introduced to the *Mishnah*, and thereafter his studies were of the oral law.[17] Rabbinic learning always overlay the biblical text, giving the twenty-four books an internal coherence and fitting them into a unified tradition. The Bible required an eye for an eye (Ex. 21:24); rabbinic tradition permitted only monetary compensation. Was there a contradiction? Not really. The verse in the book of Exodus which precedes its statement of *lex talionis* required monetary compensation for physical injuries done by animals. A formal hermeneutic rule stipulated that successive laws in the Torah shared a common factor. Here the common factor is monetary compensation. Such associations were accepted as self-evident. In short, there was a rabbinic Bible which was the same as ours and at the same time quite different. They were less aware of geography and chronology and far more aware of legal consequences. Each sentence, each phrase, each juxtaposition was significant, holy, requiring explanation. A half-sentence in Daniel (6:11b) reads that after the king had signed an edict requiring emperor worship of all citizens, Daniel "went into his house—now the windows were open in his upper chamber toward Jerusalem—and he kneeled upon his knees three times a day and prayed and gave thanks before his God, as he did aforetime." The modern reader discovers here a simple description of a pious man in an hour of trial. The rabbis found a complete liturgical rule, and the rule is venerable, "as he did aforetime." There are to be three daily services, to be held at separate times. In prayer one should face Jerusalem, kneel, and couple petition with praise.[18]

In the schools the rabbinic consensus might become determinative even against the clear biblical intent. Biblical law had ordered the remission of all debts every sabbatical year. Hillel, as we have seen, had counteracted the effect of this rule with a legal fiction. No one had any doubts as to the purely economic purpose of Hillel's *takkanah*. The most famous scholar of the first generation of *amoraim*, Samuel, said: "If I am ever in a position to abolish it [Hillel's ruling], I will abolish it." [19] He never did, although he knew that he could set the Bible's explicit statement against Hillel's innovation. The rabbinic consensus was determinative and the rule was that the authorities of one generation could not, in the normal course of events, abolish or annul the decisions of their predecessors unless they should convene a court superior to the earlier tribunal in learning and number.

The oral law was authoritative. Legend suggested that even God could not be appealed to against the law. Once upon a time a determined sage found himself a minority of one in his academy. He appealed to God. A heavenly voice was heard saying: "This man is right!" Another vote was taken; not one of his colleagues changed his mind. [20] In a world where some sages were rainmakers and faith healers while others talked with the dead or provided incantations against fever, it is all the more remarkable that a *bat kol*, a heavenly voice, was not authoritative. But the rule remained, "One does not rest his case upon a miracle." [21] Torah was the linchpin, fidelity to Torah the unifying theme, the Torah way the way of salvation. In the schools the Torah was *the* curriculum. In the synagogue the architectural focus was the Torah niche and the liturgical focus was Torah reading. No one might talk while a Torah was open. One was not to handle the Torah unnecessarily or roll it to the next reading in the presence of the congregation. The rabbis firmly believed that their fate, their people's fate, and the fate of the world depended on proper observance of Torah—and that they were the only accredited interpreters.

Talmudic Judaism

❦

Did the rabbis succeed in bringing Torah to the people?

Inevitably, the semiliterate plebeian or farmer fell short in his studies. Lacking time and opportunity, he must have felt inadequate and sometimes angry at the special privileges granted the Torah elite. Sometimes the elite mocked him. Talmudic *midrash*, carefully cultivated by rabbis, described in loving detail the special honors that must be paid to the scholar and insisted on economic privileges for them, such as exemption from taxation. The best spirits in the scholar class rose above such pretensions, though few voluntarily surrendered their privileges, but the drive for special status among these intellectuals introduced a long-lived class division between scholar and folk which at times became quite bitter. Understandably, later protest and reform movements against Rabbinism, like Karaism and Ḥasidism, were tinged with anti-intellectualism and taught that the way to God was a way of devotion and deed rather than a way of study.

The folk had for centuries accepted the Five Books of Moses. The rabbis used this legacy of faith to encourage their way of obedience. They preached on the weekend or holiday, using the biblical portion of the day to draw out the Torah's practical and ethical values and to show how Torah encouraged and certified the rabbinic way. Synagogue lectures were usually held after the *Maariv* service on Fridays, or after the Torah reading Sabbath morning, or on Sabbath afternoon. Preaching was textually based and popular, heard both in the synagogue and out, a familiar event at engagements, weddings, and funerals, and often a feature of the visit of the scholar-jurist to the small towns of his circuit. Preachers spoke seated rather than standing, as did the Roman rhetors. One *midrash* tells us that when Rabbi Akiva "sat and spoke the congregation dozed." [22] A speaker's words were said in a normal tone and picked up and repeated by men skilled in forensics who, with raised voices, repeated and sometimes embellished the thought. Preaching was exegetical. Various accepted forms developed, and skillful elaboration of these forms was a much-praised art. In one form, the *yelammedenu*, the speaker began with a question of law or custom. Using a filigree of texts drawn from the three accepted divisions of Scripture (Torah, Prophets, and Hagiographa), he elaborated his point of law and the scheduled Torah portion, subsequently tying it all together with a message of hope and consolation. In another form he related prophetic and hagiographic writings to the week's Torah portion so as to produce an edifying homily. The formal rules which governed rabbinic rhetoric concerned how texts were selected from various parts of Scripture. The connections made between these texts are conventional—for example, the presence of a similar word or phrase in each—rather than logical. One test of a preacher was the ingenuity of his use of texts; among the literate, form was critically judged.

How did the Jew read or hear Scripture? He turned to it for instruction in the art of living, he read for pleasure, but most of all he read for the promise of redemption and deliverance. Perhaps two-thirds of all *midrash* deal with the final judgment, resurrection, the end of time, immortality, and retribution. Typically, the first section of *Pesikta Rabbati*, a collection of sermons on the holy days and festivals generally ascribed to a fifth-century scholar, Tanḥuma, but certainly by several hands, begins with a question about the acceptability of a blessing over the new moon which had been recited incorrectly and ends with a question of far more immediate interest to the audience: "How long until the Messiah comes?" The whole is held together by certain concerns about the calendar which, of course, was lunar, and by a text (Isa. 66:23) which indicates that the monthly ceremony of the new moon will be observed even in the messianic age. Along the complicated journey from the minor ritual point to the major spiritual idea, any number of texts were cited and commented on. There is no final statement of the Messiah's time of arrival—forty years is suggested, then six hundred, then one thousand. Such issues necessarily were left open. That the Messiah would come was, however, a matter of firm conviction. No issue was explored as often as that of redemption. In this *midrash* alone the rabbis discussed the time of the coming, the signs which herald the Messiah's arrival, the particular advantages which will accrue to those who live or have lived in Israel, and the nature of the merit through which Israel qualifies for the Messiah and resurrection. Torah, as interpreted through preaching, lightened the way because it certified the light at the end of the tunnel. Many pretty pictures were painted, based on many prophetic texts; the *midrash* is varied and sometimes wild, its only common denominator the certainty of hope and a rather quietist attitude toward politics. These men sealed their minds to political Zionism. The activist "let's help God along" messianism of Bar Kochba had been disastrous. Men are warned not to hasten the End. The Messiah will come in God's good time. Until then, let men hope and qualify themselves and their society for God's favor. "The matter now depends on repentance and good deeds." [23]

The *aggadah*, for reasons which are not yet clear, flourished particularly in the Palestinian environment, perhaps because rabbis there were familiar with the serious homiletical efforts of the Church fathers. Then, too, the Palestinian Jew, who was constantly being offered another gospel of salvation by Christian missionaries, backed by all the power of the zealous Byzantine Caesars, had a particular need for vivid encouragement and effective argument. Whatever the reasons, *aggadah* described and delighted in Israel's redemptive promise. Many lived more in the prospect of those anticipated joys than in the poverty of their everyday lives.

◆§◈§◈

Rabbinic literature constantly returned to the promise that encouraged and comforted. Obviously, Jews had many doubts and a great need for reassurance. These were difficult, unredeemed years. The Palestinian community pulled itself together slowly after two bloody defeats, and for a time was even granted a measure of self-government under the patriarchs. However, there was never again to be security. There were constant exactions and stringent limitations upon the community's self-rule. Though these Jews lived in the Holy Land, they lived in *galut*. Only on the ninth of Av, the anniversary of the destruction of the Temples, were they allowed to enter Jerusalem, and then only to be reminded of Roman might and Christian ascendancy. A church, St. James, rose above the ruins of the Temple mount. In 312 Christianity became the Imperial Church, and the incessant preoccupation of the early Church fathers with the faith which their fathers had rejected spilled over into persecution and became enshrined in the anti-Jewish legislation of the Theodosian and Justinian codes. In that literature the Jewish community was seen as the enemy and a danger, Judaism as a pernicious doctrine, and Jews as blind to the grace of Christ. Jews could not hold public office lest they influence Christians. Jews could not build their synagogues higher than the local church. Jews could not hire Christian servants lest they entice them to the despised faith. I have already indicated how in 429, under pressure of his bishops, the Byzantine emperor closed down the patriarch's office, the last vestige of Jewish national dignity in Palestine.

[297]

Life was a bit easier in Mesopotamia, but not much. The Sassanian empire, which in 226 C.E. replaced the Parthian government, had been helped to power by the political activities of the fire-worshipping Magi, and at first gave that priest class great power. The Jewish community had been useful to the Parthians in their incessant warfare with Rome and had been granted favored status. Now they found themselves barely tolerated by a regime which cared little for their good will. During the first years of Sassanian rule, especially under the founder emperor Ardashir (226–241), many Jews were killed. Moreover, as the Jewish communities were concentrated on the Persian empire's contested western boundary with Rome, the Jews found themselves exposed to dangers on all sides. In 261 the great academic center of Nehardea was razed by an invading Palmyrene army. However, a period of relaxation followed and the Jews were allowed restricted self-government under their exilarch. The fate of this community fluctuated. The fourth century was more peaceful than the fifth, but in better times or worse this was exile and there was no ultimate security. Again and again there were sharp, if generally brief, persecutions. It was clear to all that the Messiah was unduly delayed. The test of faith became the test of a long and steady perseverance. At the gates of heaven, the rabbis said, each Jew would be asked: "Did you confidently await redemption?" Atheism was not the statement "There is no God," but the statement "There is no Judge and there is no divine justice."

❧❧❧

The writing out and compilation of the two *Talmuds* can be briefly told. The *Palestinian Talmud* is the shorter, the more repetitious, and the more embarrassed with contradictions—that is, the less edited. It consists of two sections. The first is a concise and predominantly halachic commentary to the three first tractates of the order *Nezikin* (Damages), apparently compiled in Caesarea some time before 359. Since these tractates deal primarily with civil law, it has been suggested that this portion may have been prepared as a practical handbook for unqualified judges who had been empowered by Roman, rather than Jewish, authorities and who perforce had to use rabbinic law in deciding cases involving Jews, which came before their courts. The rest of the *Palestinian Talmud* has the aspect of a hastily compiled compendium of discussions of functional tractates of the *Mishnah*, the whole apparently edited at the academy of Tiberias during the last decades of the fourth century. This was a time of severe Byzantine suppression when harsh legal restrictions were imposed on Jewish life by the Eastern emperors, urged on by officers of an increasingly arrogant state church who were intoxicated by their new power. Jewish unhappiness, fed by messianic hopes and false conclusions about Byzantine weakness, led to revolt, defeat, and worse suppression. The academies were closed (ca. 351), and although they were allowed to reopen a few years later under tightened controls, the sages were all too aware that the reprieve was temporary. A dominant Christianity was eager to eliminate the validating structures of Jewish life and pressed the imperial government to deprive Palestinian Jewry of the last vestiges of self-government. The *Gemara*, as developed in Sepphoris, Lydda, Caesarea, and Tiberias, was hastily accumulated and edited. It was none too soon, for within a few years the Patriarchate was abolished by Emperor Theodosius II, and centrally organized Jewish life in Palestine came to an end.

The *Babylonian Talmud* grew over a longer period. After the initial period of danger, the Sassanian academies enjoyed relative security for about a century and a half under an agreement arranged with the imperial court by the academic master Samuel (ca. 200–260), who in return for domestic autonomy pledged the community's loyalty to the Persian empire and accepted the legitimacy and primacy of imperial law, so long as that law did not require abrogation of Torah. During the third and fourth centuries there seems to have been a steady migration of Jews from west to east. But in the fifth century imperial authority weakened and Magi influence in government grew. All non-Persian faiths suffered, the Jews at first less than others, but an ill-advised revolt in 468 (inspired by messianic expectations) led to serious repression and the recognition by the academies that the time to draw their traditions together had arrived. Tradition ascribes a first effort to Ashi (5th cent.) and various successors in the schools of Sura and Pumbedita, and a second effort to Rabina (6th cent.). Modern research suggests that the process was less formal and more gradual, but confirms the effort and its impulse. During the fifth and sixth centuries the *savoraim* continued to study *Mishnah* and edit *Gemara*. However, the rabbinic drive had slackened, and Jewish life remained relatively limp until its energies were galvanized in the seventh century by the swift appearance of the Arabs and Islam.

CHAPTER

৩ XVII ৯

The Rabbinic Mind

In *galut* time became as unjointed as life itself. History, which describes the progression of events in linear relationship, ceased to be a central interest. In previous eras Jews had produced the Deuteronomic (Judges, Samuel, Kings) and the priestly historians (Chronicles, Ezra, Nehemiah), the authors of I and II Maccabees, and Josephus. In the first century Jews were still writing biographies (Philo's *Life of Moses*) and publishing journals of their personal involvement in affairs of state (Philo's *Legation to Caius*, Josephus' *Against Apion* and *Vita*); but with the disastrous revolts of the first and second centuries, annals and biographical memoirs cease to appear. When, early in the second century, the patriarch Gamaliel II, together with such scholar-associates as Akiva, Yehoshua, and Eleazar ben Azariah, went on a high-level diplomatic mission to Rome, not unlike Philo's a century earlier, to place before the emperor a Jewish plea, no record of their mission was prepared. The *midrash* records a number of legendary incidents associated with their visit, but of the actual negotiations no one wrote a word. No participant prepared a connected history of the Talmudic period or, as far as we know, kept a journal; at least none has survived except one bare chronology, *Seder Olam Rabbah*, which lists in a few pages significant events from Adam to Akiva. Beyond this skeleton, historical writing in the Talmudic period consists of an occasional paragraph or two setting out a chain of tradition, offered to prove that the oral law had

[300]

been transmitted faithfully by an unbroken line of competent authorities.

Galut was limbo, a dreary weariness between a glorious past and a glorious future. The Jew relished the biblical chronicles and messianic prophecies. He lived in the swirl of the real world and did not deny it, but at the same time he drew little encouragement or pride from it. His essence as a Jew preceded his existence as a particular man. Rabbi Yose is reported to have said: "I observe the law of the King of kings who told me at Sinai: 'I am the Lord your God.' " [1] On the Passover every Jew considered himself among those God had delivered from Egypt. David's harp still could be heard playing in the quiet of the night. Elijah was the kind face in the crowd at the city gates. To live with his biblical ancestors was to share with tall men in the most significant of all adventures, and thus escape the dreariness of *galut*.

Such indifference to history was not primarily the result of the trauma of national disaster, although the numbing pain of defeat certainly deadened Jewish interest in the "game" of power. Rather, it was an emotional numbness born of impotence, an awareness by the Jew that he was a political prisoner serving an indefinite sentence. History deals with power and change. History is a function of a society's sense of expectancy. Confined for life, a prisoner has no reason to keep records since no day has any particular distinction. In his cell memories of the days before his incarceration take on added poignancy, and his mind dwells on the possibility of a miraculous escape or unexpected pardon. In *galut* each Jew was born into chains, as was his father before him. But his imagination could not be shackled. He could relish the grand imperial days of David and Solomon, when a free Israel bestrode the world, and sense what life would be when a son of David again sat on Judah's throne. Every Passover he recited the hymn of triumph first sung by the shores of the Red Sea and felt as though he were there. He sang God's praise, knowing these words would again be on his lips on the day of final redemption.

History disappears and is replaced by a time tunnel in which the rabbinic Jew rode forward or back at will. In the *midrash*, tenses and references points become confused; that which has been is that which is. The Bible tells of Jacob "who dwells in tents" and of Esau, the cunning hunter, the man of the wilds, and of their rivalry; and, somehow, Jacob is Israel and Esau is Rome. The oracle pronounced at the twins' birth (Gen. 25:23–27) becomes an existential comment,

"One people [Esau/Rome] shall be stronger than another [Jacob/Israel]," and a delicious promise, "the elder [Esau/Rome] shall serve the younger [Jacob/Israel]." Eliding past with present, Israel witnessed God's power to save. Eliding the future with the present, Israel acknowledged that God's mighty hand is active and thrusting; though the capital lay in ruins, God was at work. The Jew prayed to a God "who restores His powerful presence to Zion," [2] and thanked the Lord "who rebuilds Jerusalem." [3] Without intending to do so, the Jew tested and proved the Stoic doctrine that the context of one's inner life is the true reality: If I cannot change my world, *galut*, for the better, it is also true that *galut* cannot change me, or beat me down, or destroy my dignity.

Biblical events suggested the grand themes of the faith. The Exodus was a paradigm for God's power to save; Sinai represented election, covenant, and revelation. The forty years of hard wandering presented the struggle every generation must expect and the possibility that only their children may reach the Promised Land. The style of rabbinic theology was illustrative rather than analytic, tales well and often told. Not all *midrash* had philosophic pretensions; many stories simply illustrated folk wisdom or presented an imaginative elaboration of a biblical episode or text. Each biblical story was handled so that it exposed various facets of the human drama. The story of Cain and Abel was not simply a sad tale of fratricide. Each man was an archetype; Cain represented all farmers, Abel, the shepherds. It was only to be expected that Cain would be the aggressor. Farmers seek to enclose the pasture. The shepherd is content with open spaces. Moreover, farming is brutal work; and since the makers of the *midrash* were city folk they mistook the farmers' illiteracy for dullness, and assumed that in his weariness and ignorance a farmer, like Cain, would think with his fists. In further elaboration *midrash* emphasized the blinding fury of anger. At first the brothers had determined to part amicably, with each taking his share. Cain, the farmer, took the land, and Abel, the flock, but Cain could not let the matter rest. Next morning, when the flocks set off for the field, Cain barred the way: "Your sheep cannot pasture on my land." Aroused, Abel demanded Cain's cloak—after all, it was woven of wool from his flocks—and the fight began. The rabbis hoped to teach a lesson in accommodation.

The Bible had presented the stubborn individuality of its major figures. The rabbis explored the biblical narrative, its particular language, form, and even grammar, to delineate human nature in its fascinating complexity. In Genesis man's appearance on earth is simply described, "The Lord God formed man" (Gen. 2:7). The letter *Yod* unexpectedly appears twice in the verb "formed," which suggested to a writer of *midrash* that each man contained two *yetzarim*—two innate drives, one active and passionate, the other reflective and compassionate. These drives coexist turbulently in every soul, where they compete for supremacy. It became a commonplace to speak of two innate instincts, one a thrust toward goodness, *yetzer tov*, the other the thrust of passion, *yetzer ha-ra*.

Life and the rabbis taught that rivalry, passion, and appetite, all the forces that comprise the *yetzer ha-ra*, cannot be completely suppressed; indeed, they have a rightful place in our lives, since they provide the energy, presumably through sublimation, that builds cities and leads men to accept the restrictions, burdens, and duties of marriage and family. Rabbinic thought does not despair of life or of man. The physical is not necessarily evil. The law is *Torat Ḥayyim*, a law of life, for this life. Torah law does not enjoin a regimen of celibacy or ascetic denial. The rabbinic Jew was not conditioned to curse the human condition or to become so morose or apprehensive that he despaired of life and devoted himself to a search for Nirvana. Some sages undertook minor forms of ascetic discipline, but none, as far as we know, courted self-mortification. Suicide was a sin, and so were unnecessary acts of fasting and denial.[4] Marriage was a duty, as were many joys: "Rejoicing on a festival is a *mitzvah*."[5] Life was a gift of God, who had pronounced it very good, but obviously the *yetzer tov* must become dominant. How could this come about?

The rabbis assumed that life was a time of strenuous testing during which the wish to obey God struggled with indulgence and appetite. They spoke of the yoke of the commandments—yoke here symbolized patient submission—and acknowledged that young oxen are not easily trained to accept the halter. They did not press the ox/yoke analogy too far, for man was not an animal, but they asked the question: What can induce man to accept the yoke of the commandments? and answered this question simply: the fear and love of God. Only the man who trembles in love and fear before God will obey quietly and happily the commands of his Master.

A life of obedience depends on a submission of will, and no man gives up worldly pleasures unless he is clearly aware of how much depends on his acceptance. What is at stake? No less than salvation, long life here and the renewal of life beyond the grave. Even with so much at stake submission does not come easily. Man is a restless creature of many appetites, but the rabbis suggest that an hour or two of Torah lessons, like a cold shower, can dampen the raging fires. "Let a man pit his good *yetzer* against his *yetzer ha-ra;* if the good *yetzer* wins, well and good; if not, let him engage in the study of Torah." [6] The benefit lay not so much in the lesson as in what was learned. He who studies Torah clarifies his understanding of the will of God and begins to remove the clog of doubt and confusion which normally blocks the channels through which man's vital energy needs to flow. Doubt paralyzes the spirit; Torah study dispels doubt.

The rabbis did not glorify man and would not have described him as a noble primitive whose natural goodness is distorted by a vicious social order. They accepted man's complex nature as inherent, and they believed in the necessity of social and legal restraints to curb excess and selfishness. The rabbis were great believers in law and order. Without government, men would eat each other alive. Since, to the rabbis, law and order meant Torah law and order, justice was an implied category of authority. A Torah-governed community would restrain the powerful from abusing the weak and create an environment in which men would appreciate the justice of God's law and abide it willingly. The question of how Israel ought to live so as to be assured of God's approval was given a tripartite answer. "Accept the yoke of the kingdom of Heaven, subdue each other in the fear of Heaven, and deal generously with each other." [7] No one should settle in a community without good laws and effective government. The steady rise of urban crime in our day would not have surprised them. Leviticus 26:37, "They shall stumble over one another," suggested a domino theory involving sin; one man's sin tends to open the door for his neighbor's crime. Conversely, a community under strict Torah enforcement restricts the opportunity of its weaker members to fall from grace. Rabbinic thought emphasized the primary category of community. Radical freedom belonged only in the jungle, which was not a fit place for human habitation.

Man, unlike the beast, possessed a soul, a spark of divine light, an intelligence which can hear and understand duty and then perform it. The statement in Genesis that God had created man in His own image was interpreted to mean that God had placed in man's soul the capacity to understand God's will. The primary motivation for Torah study was a normative one. He who studies Torah and makes Torah his own transforms himself from beast into human being.

Uncivilized, un-Torahized, man was a beast; beware. Asked "Who is the most despicable person in the world?" a sage might have named Haman or Nero or some other tyrant from the Jewish past. One *tanna* answered instead: "He who denies his creator." Why? "Because a man does not violate any commandment . . . until he denies the fundamental truth." [8] It was good to love God, but love is a sometime feeling. Life was an unremitting test. There was an annual Judgment Day on which God determined who shall live and who shall die. The disinterested love of God was the ultimate devotion, but men were not abashed that they also feared Him. It seemed natural and right to pray: "Impose Thy dread upon all that Thou hast created . . . that all creatures prostrate themselves before Thee, that they may all form a single band to do Thy will with perfect heart." [9]

❧❦❧

Preaching flourished in this age of testing. The synagogue, with its regimen of liturgy and Torah reading, offered preachers a regular audience in an effective setting. Preaching was both popular and academic: simple thoughts and illustrations for the spiritual sustenance of the folk and, for academic audiences, complex thoughts and juridic tours de force, sometimes of a high order of subtlety and sophistication. No one spoke *ex cathedra*. The prophets had brought God's word. Preachers offered their learning and their sense of drama. It was no longer "Thus says the Lord," but "R. Akiva used to say." Preaching was textual and often highly stylized. Its purpose was to educate, not to offer spontaneous witness. There is no indication that synagogue preachers ever spoke under the hypnotic force of inspiration.

A good deal of folk legend and pure fable is caught up in the précis and notes of such sermons as have survived. Preachers often used or adapted familiar materials to make their point. The foxes, storks, and wise fish familiar to us from the *Panchatantra* and Aesop make their appearance with suitable biblical credentials. One possible translation of a verse in Job reads: "He teaches us through the beasts of the earth and makes us wise through the fowl of heaven" (35:11). Solomon, wisest of men, who had understood the language of birds and animals, becomes the teller of many of these stories. Some are pure fancy, and some fancifully teach Judaism. A fox, enticed by a succulent garden, manages to squeeze through a narrow opening in the wall and gorges himself, only to find that in his bloated condition he cannot escape. To get free he must starve himself amidst plenty. This image is a compelling judgment on life which could effectively be tied to Job's profession: "Naked came I out of my mother's womb, and naked I shall return there" (1:21).

Deuteronomy 4:9, "But take utmost care and watch yourself scrupulously," was a favorite preaching text for those who wanted to emphasize how narrowly and severely man is tested. The test was demanding and the stakes were high, a fact often developed through the parable of a king who caught a bird and gave it for safekeeping to a servant, with the caution to guard the bird carefully or else forfeit his life. Naturally the king emphasized his warning with a biblical text: "For this is not a trifling thing for you . . . it is your very life" (Deut. 33:47).[10]

Popular preaching coupled bracing admonition with consoling promise. God ruled the world in righteousness, but, knowing man's limited capacity, tempered justice with mercy. This alternation of moods and need led to a tendency to reduce God's attributes to two: *middat ha-din*, His quality of justice, and *middat ha-rahamim*, His grace. Exegesis made every line of the Torah reveal God's twin nature. There are two common biblical names of God. Whenever *Elohim* appeared, Torah referred to God's justice; whenever *Adonai* appeared, Torah suggested His attribute of mercy. Israel's watchword read: "Hear O Israel: The Lord (*Adonai*) our God (*Elohenu*) is one God" (Deut. 6:6), which clearly meant not only that God is and is one, but that He is just and merciful.

Men feared God's judgment but not God. God was not a creature of caprice or whim, but God, righteous and just in all His ways. They trembled before His judgment because each knew his frailties. To fear God was to fear one's own inconsistency, to accept the urgency of a higher obedience. The prophet had said: "The fear of the Lord is man's treasure" (Isa. 32:6). How is that so? Because fear compels men toward a self-energizing level of duty where the commandment is obeyed for its own sake. It was only natural to fear one's day in court: Job "had feared God" (Job 1:1) and so had Abraham (Gen. 22:12). Yet it was hoped that men would transcend fear and act out of love of God; that is, that they would do the good disinterestedly, *lishmah*. To those who wondered if man can act purely out of love, the answer was a simple and unequivocal yes. Many a man has begun study or some civic task for an ulterior reason, such as status, and ended by doing the good for its own sake.

Virtue's definition was never exhausted by the phrase "obedience to the law." The righteous man went beyond the law's requirements. When Yehoshua ben Levi boasted that he obeyed the law always and in every respect, Elijah appeared and challenged his smugness: "Yes, but is that the way of the saintly?" [11] The way of the saintly led "above and beyond the requirements of the law." The *ḥasid*, the thoroughly obedient, obeyed the law and fulfilled those obligations which are left to personal discretion (*devarim ha-musarim la-lev*)—care for the sick, encouragement of the anxious, time-consuming acts of loving kindness.[12] Rabbinic ethical theory was both narrowly specific and broadly exhortatory.

As an instructional exercise the rabbis could—and often did—reduce the whole field of Torah law to some single broad mandate, such as "You shall love the Lord your God" (Deut. 6:5) or "Love your neighbor as yourself" (Lev. 19:18), but reductionism and generalization were not their style. Meticulous analysis was. The sages were primarily concerned with the application of specific rules in concrete situations. Generally, they avoided high-flown sentiment and emphasized realizable goals, with special concern for the consequences of an act. An old Pharisaic motto that an *am ha-aretz* (a peasant) cannot be a *ḥasid* (one who is scrupulous) was reinterpreted to mean that a simpleton can never be a saint. Why not? Because impulsive generosity, however well intentioned, is not aware of the consequences of the impulse, and can at times cause more harm than good.

⋙⋘

Rabbinic thought operated within a definable field of religious ideas. In His transcendent glory God was the world's august Creator, majestic in power and wisdom. God was invoked as "the King of kings" or "the Holy One, Praised be He," never directly by His special name, YHWH. To name God was to limit Him. The Tetragrammaton carried such awesome power that it must not be spoken. But, in His familiar immanence, God was careful and caring, generous and long-suffering. Men felt encouraged to do the will of their Father in heaven, who watched over them with parental care.

Life was uncertain, but not absurd. God had created life and declared it good. The created universe revealed in its operation God's cosmic purposes and His loving care for each created being. Life was confusing, but not meaningless. God managed history and imposed His providential rule over all. Though men were not privy to God's counsel, nothing happened purely by chance. When visits of consolation were made, those who came were advised to sit in silence and not to try to explain God's ways to men, for His ways are beyond human understanding.

The biblical record provided encouraging evidence of God's saving power. God had redeemed the slaves from Egypt and, through Cyrus, the exiles from Babylon. God was "mighty forever," "powerful to save." He "supports the falling, heals the sick, frees the captives," "revives the dead" and "makes salvation flourish." [13] God's attributes were drawn from His redemptive acts. Rabbinic *midrash* can be read as an endless, unsystematic, historical romance with a single theme: God's saving acts in behalf of His people. *Midrash* finds proof of God's saving concern and power everywhere. Creation is not an accident or an impulsive act, but a carefully designed achievement. God had made and destroyed many worlds before He declared Himself satisfied with this one. God had fashioned the world according to the teachings of the Torah, a teaching of hope, and then had given man the Torah so that he might know precisely how to live successfully in this world—that is, how to please God and merit salvation.

Suffering is not accidental or vindictive, but part of God's plan. Suffering can be instructive. Suffering helps to destroy egotism. Suffering offers men an opportunity to prove their worth by rising above self-pity. Israel was sometimes compared to oil. God had addressed His beloved, "Your name is as oil poured forth" (Cant. 1:3), which led to the analogy that oil is refined from dates which are ground and pressed, so Israel is refined by the grinding pressures of exile. As oil is improved by beating, so man is made sensitive to repentance by suffering. The great and worthwhile gifts—the Torah, the Promised Land, and the World to Come—are gained only through suffering.[14] Suffering exists so that a good man is purged here and now of minor sins, that he may enter immediately into Paradise. Suffering hastens the Messiah. Sufferings are precious, not pernicious.

Dwelling as it did on the hope of redemption, *midrash* necessarily emphasized the immanence, even the humanness, of God. In the *midrash* God lives, hears prayer, performs miracles, heals the sick, and delivers. His *Shechinah*, His immanent presence, is with Israel when men gather for prayer, when scholars sit and study Torah, and when a husband and wife manage their home harmoniously. God is not an idea, but an intimate. *Midrash* often pictures God as one of the folk. God participates in the exile, cries over Israel's anguish, bends down to hear prayer, rejoices with a bride at her wedding, puts on *tefillin* and joins in public prayer. The *midrash* innocently and happily speaks of God as father, friend, shepherd, lover, and avenger. One episode may picture God as guardian protecting Israel, another as sage teaching Torah, still another as shepherd shielding his flock; but a restriction will be inserted, *kiveyachol* (as if one could say); for in fact God is neither sage nor shepherd and these are not several gods, but one. In *midrash* formal theology was subordinated to communication, the god-idea to God, and the perception of the folk to the formal conceptions of theologians.

God alone has power, but Israel has an essential role in the scheme of things. "When you are My witness, I am God, and when you are not My witness, I am, as it were, not God." [15] Mutual need binds Israel and God. Each strengthens the other. The theologian seeks to prove that God is; the believer knows that God is and seeks to draw close to Him. To the theologian God is everywhere, always. To the believer God is nearer when he chants his prayers in the synagogue than when he walks in the street. To the theologian God reveals Himself. The believer knows that God needs human agents to make His name great and His rule known, and that such service is Israel's dignity and purpose. Abraham, the first monotheist, is made to say: "Before I made God known to His creatures, He was the God of Heaven. Now that I have made Him known to man, He is the God of the earth." [16] Recall the metaphor of Israel and oil. As oil brings light to the world, so Israel brings light to the world. Proof? Isaiah 60:3: "And nations shall walk by your light, kings by your shining radiance." [17]

Logic is objective. Logically, the God who brought creation into being is the father of all and loves all equally. *Midrash* is personal and can make logically scandalous statements which express and sustain a people's faith. God loves Israel more than the angels. God needs Israel as much as Israel needs God. The *midrash* gave Israel the dignity and self-esteem which history denied. The world was created for the sake of Israel. Israel's steadfast loyalty sustains the world. Were it not for Israel's steadfastness, God would have every reason to destroy the world and start over again.

To attempt to synthesize the *midrash* is to impose an order and unity which the *midrash* consciously rejects. More often than not, the *midrash* flows from a biblical text and simply comments on whatever ideas the text throws up; theology, grammar, legend, epistemology tumble over each other. *Midrash* makes no claim to consistency, nor can its thoughts be made to fit any systematic interpretation of rabbinic Judaism. Judaism was one, a faith consistent with the will of God, but no man fully comprehends this unity; so the rabbis could and did say that conflicting points of view can be the words of the living God.

Midrash offers a series of impressionistic insights into the meaning of Torah. It represents the interplay of imagination and tradition, a deliberate decision not to submit flights of imagination to the restrictions of consensus or logical constraint. As long as the Jewish community walked the halachic way, the rabbis were happy to allow such thoughts free rein. To make a point the preacher might deliberately mistranslate or abuse a biblical text. It was a game. Everyone knew he cherished the text—and who knew how the mysteries of the universe might be revealed?

Much aggadic material is popular theology translated into story form. Genesis 1:26 reads, "Let *us* make man in our image. . . ." Is Scripture suggesting plural gods? The rules of grammar would label "us" a plural of majesty, but *midrash* eschewed style for story. The plural pronoun implied that God had consulted His advisers, the angels. God knew what He would do, but He had accorded His courtiers the courtesy of asking their counsel, and in so doing set us a good example. No one should feel so confident of his judgment, so arrogant, that he does not seek advice even of less talented folk. Another preacher invented dialogue for the various angels whom God consulted. The angel of love favored man's creation, believing man would be affectionate and sympathetic. The angel of truth voted against it, fearing that man would be devious and full of lies. Justice favored man because he would establish courts, while Peace opposed man's creation because he would make war. Here we have a fascinating anthropology and a damning, if gently spoken, critique of man. But there is more to this story than innocent fancy. The image of God's courteous but perfunctory consultation with the angels was deliberately enlarged, as Louis Ginzberg has shown, to demonstrate Judaism's disagreement with a popular gnostic view which taught that man had been created, not by God, but by evil and lower powers. "In the beginning God created," God alone.

Rabbinic literature was always open. Rabbinic inventiveness was not exhausted by this scenario of a delightful heavenly debate. Someone tied this story to a biblical text and a familiar legend about disobedient angels whom God cast out of heaven. Apparently, after

His consultation, God cast down the angel of truth to invalidate the force of his objection, and when the other angels complained about this act God said simply, "Truth springs out of the earth" (Ps. 85:11). A familiar myth about a fallen angel has been turned inside out. The fallen angel is not Satan, but Truth, and he is cast out of heaven not to do his worst among men, but to do his best. All this was fascinating, inconclusive, revealing, and far too much for a rabbinic conservative who felt compelled to pencil in the obvious objection that all this is sheer fancy.[18]

Many legends grew to account for anomalies in the biblical text. God had warned Adam and Eve that if they ate of the forbidden fruit, "in the day you eat of it you shall die" (Gen. 2:17). Adam ate and, although he was exiled from Eden, he lived for many more years. Someone asked a preacher why God had not made good this threat. What the folk asked their preacher, the preacher had the angels ask God. God answered: I said he would die in the day. I did not specify your twenty-four hour day, but a heavenly day which lasts a thousand years. An answer? To men and women conditioned to belief, this was a sufficient answer. Moreover, Adam did die that day. How so? A sinner, even if alive, is considered dead. Why? Because he has forfeited his claim to eternal life. An answer? We may not be satisfied, but to men conditioned to a particular piety, it was an answer.

❦

Popular preachers and the teachers of the folk could indulge themselves in legend and theological extravagance because they knew that the liturgy stated unequivocally the central teachings and remained within the definite limits of rabbinic Judaism. The liturgy became the Jew's catechism. It was spoken thrice daily, and since there were no prayerbooks, prayer was assimilated by repetition, known by heart; thus the prayers provided the idiom and ideology which average folk understood to be Judaism. The liturgy was deliberately phrased and self-consciously cautious in theological matters, precisely where the *midrash* was uninhibited. None of the legends of the *midrash* were repeated in the liturgy, and few, if any, esoteric fancies appear there, at least not this early. Though rabbis did not officiate in the synagogue, its liturgy was created largely under their impress and highlights their view of faith. A preacher could describe exuberantly a whole host of angels and celestial beings, some singing

God's praises, some carrying His messages, some arranging happy marriages. The liturgy made it clear that, in fact, only God answered prayers. "Do Your will, O God, in the heaven above and bestow tranquillity of spirit on those who fear You below, and what is good in Your own sight do. Blessed be You, O Lord, who hears prayer." [19] The formulas by which the Jew evoked God were precisely written. The invocation of any save God was specifically prohibited. "When he is in trouble a man must not invoke Michael or Gabriel, but God alone, He will hear him." [20] A benediction which did not precisely name God was unacceptable.

Theological caution extended to the language of the liturgy. Worship was generally conducted in Hebrew, the language of Torah and psalm, rather than in Aramaic, although legally the vernacular was permitted. The use of Hebrew derived from the frequent use of psalms in the liturgy and from the attempt to equate the hour of synagogue worship to the worship of the Temple. The Levites had sung their Temple hymns in Hebrew. This preference for Hebrew tended to limit liturgical creativity to the learned, those least likely to voice superstitious belief or carelessly invoke demons or guardian angels. In time Aramaic paragraphs and phrases were included, but when the *amoraim* wrote liturgy, they generally put aside the Aramaic idiom of the academy for the holy tongue. One fortunate result of this deliberate adoption of a precious language was that the liturgy remained independent of geography and time. A Jew could travel from Rome to Sassanian Sura and participate in public worship. The Roman Jew did not need to know Pahlavi, nor the Persian Jew, Greek. Another fortunate result was that even the barely educated retained some familiarity with the language of the Scriptures. The routine of worship introduced all Jews to the rudiments of the Bible's idiom. Through the patterning of liturgical texts they "knew" that their Bible and their worship were one in language and promise.

Ordinary folk knew the Bible largely through liturgy, and thus knew God primarily as a merciful Father who had bound Israel to the covenant and who was certain to support, deliver, and save the righteous. Each weekday worship began with one or all of the six concluding psalms in the Psalter (145–150), psalms of heartfelt and open praise which invoked a God who is majestic, splendid, full of creative power, but named primarily as "gracious and merciful, slow to anger and of great loving kindness," "good to all, His tender mercies are over all His work," "loving in all His works," "near to all who call upon Him." The folk's Bible was simple, straightforward, and full of the certain promise of God's support and deliverance.

The liturgy taught the Jew what he needed to know of Judaism's theology. The *Shema*, "Hear O Israel the Lord is our God, the Lord alone" (Deut. 6:4), had been said for centuries by each Jew twice a day, and had become Israel's capsule creed. It affirms that God is (thus atheism is denounced) and that God is active (against all doctrines of passivity and pantheism). God is one; dualism, trinitarianism, polytheisms of all varieties are misbegotten. The Lord is our God; God is not distant and uninvolved, but near to all who call upon Him, and particularly near to Israel. To recite the *Shema* in public was a required act of commitment whose value was emphatically reinforced by scribal tradition. When the *Shema* is written in a Torah scroll the last letter of the first word, *Shema*, "hear," an *ayin*, and the last letter of the last word, *ehad*, "one," a *daled*, are written large to suggest another word, *ed*, which means witness. By professing the *Shema* a worshipper witnesses to his faith in the one and only God.

The *Shema* developed from a single rubric into a selection of three Torah readings (Deut. 6:4–9; Deut. 11:13–21; Num. 15:37–41). These portions explain what it means to love and obey God, the rewards of love, and the punishments for disobedience. To love God with "all your heart" is to open your spirit to God. To love God with "all your soul" is to love God more than anything else in life, if necessary more than life itself. To love God with "all your might" is to devote your substance to God's service. He who loves God in these three ways has accepted the yoke of the Kingdom of God, citizenship in God's community.

The subsequent paragraphs deal with duty and to speak them is to accept a second yoke, the yoke of the commandments, the specific obligations of citizenship in the Kingdom of God. One should obey God in all things, joyously, and engage in the primary obligation of group survival, which is to indoctrinate the next generation to understand, accept, and obey. Those who bear the yoke of the commandments can confidently expect God's protection. Reward is certain for an obedient people. "If, then, you will obey the commandments . . . I will grant the rain of your land in season" (Deut. 11:13–14). Rain, so precious to these people, was a symbol of many blessings in this world and a code name for resurrection in the World to Come. A caution is coupled to this promise. "Take care not to be lured away to serve other gods . . . for the Lord's anger will flare up against you and He will shut up the skies" (Deut. 11:16–17). Finally, the promise and the warning are concluded and confirmed by the God who brought you out of the land of Egypt and is ready to deliver you once again.

During rabbinic times these biblical paragraphs were provided with a liturgical commentary that underscored Israel's special relationship with God: God is "our sheltering rock, our protective fortress." God "chose Israel in love." God's love and protection are wondrous and unmerited. We might have stumbled through life, but You offered us "the laws of life, truths established and enduring, right and faithful, beloved and precious, desirable and pleasant, revered and mighty, well ordered and acceptable, good and beautiful." [21] For Israel, God's covenant meant certainty, the obligation of obedience, an end to confusion, and the promise of salvation; and the *Shema* expressed all the covenant themes.

The *Shema* is a liturgical creation, and therefore also a statement of need. What is needed? Determination: "The will to study Your Torah, to keep its words and to teach its precepts." Insight: "Enlighten our eyes in Your Torah," "open our hearts to your commandments." Quietness of spirit: "Trust in God," trust in God's justice and the ultimate fulfillment of His promise. Trust (*bittaḥon*) implies patient but confident waiting. For the man of trust Torah is life giving, in this world and in the next. It is the faith that as God had redeemed us from Egypt, "so does He now." The Exodus was history and paradigm; a deliverance which had been, is, and will be. But the night was long, the exile often brutal. Confidence in God's promise had to be reinforced. The liturgy, the holidays, the preaching, constantly restated the hope, as if by sheer repetition it became more certain. But there was no minimizing the cost and difficulty of obeying God at all times. As if wryly commenting on their trials, the rabbis seized on the qualifying clause in Amos 5:15, " 'Hate evil, love good; enthrone justice in the courts; *it may be* that the Lord, the God of hosts, will be gracious'—such obligations; all this and only 'it may be.' " [22]

Those men knew a God who hears prayers and redeems Israel. Prayer was not meditation or introspection, but a statement of need. A properly addressed prayer reached a source of effective power. The believing Jew spoke his prayer in full confidence that worthy prayers are answered, but he reminded himself that God alone knows what is truly for our good. "Do Your will, O God . . . what is right in Your own sight do, blessed are You, O Lord, who hears prayer." Pray expectantly, but do not be calculating about prayer.

"He who draws out his prayers and relies on an answer ends disappointed." [23]

❦

In the formal *Tefillah* it was not "I" but "we" who petitioned God. What was asked for? There were nineteen formal requests, and they deal with deliverance from the universal fears—death, incapacity, aimlessness, ignorance—and deliverance from Israel's existential fate—exile, persecution, arbitrary abuse. "Favor man with knowledge," "Restore us in perfect repentance," "Forgive our sins," "Take up our cause . . . redeem us speedily," "Heal us," "Bless this year and its harvest," "Sound the great horn of freedom and gather us from the four corners of the earth," "Restore our judges . . . remove from us sorrows and sighing," "Cast down and humble the arrogant," "Let not the righteous and the pious be put to shame," "Return to Jerusalem in compassion," "Cause the scion of David to flourish," "Accept our prayer in mercy and favor," "Revive the dead." [24] Jews did not pray for power, physical prowess, or beauty, but for knowledge, a sense of being free of the burden of sin, the nearness of God, repentance and forgiveness, and a happy portion in this life and in the World to Come. The community did not seek dominion or affluence, but freedom, an end to *galut*, the rebuilding of the Temple, and the reestablishment of a normal, full, and close relationship with God.

Public worship was formal rather than spontaneous. The liturgy was daily and repetitive. Worshippers did not depend for their prayers on the spirit moving within them, but on preselected passages and verses. There was room for improvisation, since liturgy was *minhag*, custom, and not law, but the worship hour had structure and gave off a sense of timeless form and truth. Even if a paragraph was only a generation old, it used the venerable language, Hebrew, and the Torah's familiar idiom.

The use of Hebrew and of a structured ritual reflects a consistent if perhaps unconscious decision to transform prayer into worship, spontaneous private expression into artful and carefully devised public affirmation. Spontaneous prayer is a measure of man's anxiety. Liturgy is a measure of man's commitment. The former begins in the overheated heart, the latter in the questing soul. To accept order rather than to glorify the spontaneity of spiritual impulse is to turn prayer into worship and to change the synagogue occasion from an

[315]

undirected moment into a controlled experience. The Jew had to learn certain texts in order to participate in prayer. He was taught that there was a proper way to pray and certain appropriate postures for prayer, and reminded that the ideas and phrases of the liturgy expressed and defined the realities of his spiritual life.

Worship was artifice, consciously designed not only to stimulate and express natural piety, but also to educate the people to think Torah, to sing Torah, to live in the Torah world, to believe Torah, and to practice Torah. No one challenged the validity of a formal liturgy and a fixed calendar. Far from being questionable, as it might be today, formalized worship had the weight of religious authenticity. The rabbinic mental attitude assumed that truth was not out there waiting to be discovered, but in the Ark, needing only to be taken up, heard, and pondered. Furthermore, being authentic and prescribed, these phrases were fraught with power. In worship one participated in significant activity. A great deal more attention was placed on words, posture, and form than we may imagine. Worship was an awesome moment to which the congregation and God both responded. There was a proper way of approaching God, including bowing, prostration, and precise formulas for presenting one's case, even as there were proper ways of approaching the emperor. No one came barging into the royal audience chamber, that is, if he valued his life. To appear carelessly before the King of kings, to fail to watch one's words, was to court disaster. As a courtier called attention to himself when he appeared with his petition, so the worshipper by his prayer drew God's attention to him. A careless word could cost the petitioner dearly; God might discover on examination that, far from being abused, the petitioner had been treated with undeserved generosity. The hour of worship was fraught with opportunity and danger.

Although they emphasized form and structure, the rabbis were on their guard against the perfunctory statement, hypocritical repetition, or a prayer discipline which had no impact upon a person's life. There was room for freedom within the fixed order. "A new prayer should be said every day." [25] Worship required *kavannah*, immersion in, awareness of, reflection upon the text. Rote or careless worship was no worship. "A man should test his mental set before prayer; if he can concentrate, let him pray; if he cannot, let him not pray." [26]

Sensitive men were concerned that the liturgy might be used as a mechanical contrivance to gain God's favor. Any number of sermons caution the worshipper against *iyyun tefillah*, calculation in prayer. Yes, God answered prayer, at least those prayers which asked for blessings that were actually for man's good, but it was unseemly to use prayer to try to force God's hand. A sage named Rava overheard a man praying that a particular girl become his wife, and he admonished the impatient suitor; "Be still, if she is for you, you will not lose her; and, if she is not for you, you will have challenged Providence. . . ." [27] The prayers were couched in language designed to avoid the presumption that the worshipper knew better than God how the world ought to run. Men did not say "give me" but "May it be Your will," or "Do Your will, Lord, in the heavens above and bestow a calm spirit on those who fear You below; What is good in Your sight do. Blessed art You, O Lord, who hears prayers." [28] Israel's liturgical forms limited man's tendency to assault God's ears with endless requests by organizing inclusive prayers—for redemption, resurrection, abundance, long life, return to the Holy Land, and so on—in whose general terms the worshipper could silently insert his special plea, always recognizing the dependence of his fate on the fate of others.

The Jew prayed, as his father had prayed, for deliverance. His liturgy was rich in phrases which promise salvation and deliverance, especially those appropriate to an exiled people—may we return to our land, may the Temple be rebuilt, may appropriate fire be restored upon its altar—together with the expectation of immortality, resurrection, and the messianic coming. In some of the early synagogues at places like Dura-Europos, the promissory biblical texts were not only chanted but present in fresco paintings on the walls. In later synagogues the paintings disappear, but the salvationary themes continue to be conspicuously displayed.

The Jew had need of God's power to save. In the Song of Songs, as interpreted by the rabbis, Israel sings of her loneliness: "Night after night on my bed I have sought my true love" (3:1). A commentator elaborated: "The Israelites said to God: 'Lord of the universe, at one time You granted us a brief interval between one night and another—between Egypt and Babylon; between Babylon and Persia; between Persia and Greece; between Greece and Rome—but now night follows night uninterruptedly.' " [29]

❦

Christianity helped to darken the night. Christianity had become the Roman state-church under Constantine, and Constantinople was both the governmental capital and a center of the Near Eastern churches whose monks and bishops exerted a growing influence over state policy, almost all deleterious insofar as it related to Jews. During the third and fourth centuries various Church Fathers and councils put together the basic themes of what Jules Isaac has called "the teaching of contempt." Judaism was depicted as a narrow legalism and scandalous superstition; Jews were deicides, and the destruction of the Temple was proof of God's anger against them. To keep Jews a people apart and deprived was to fulfill God's will; to bring them to the light of the true faith was an act of kindness, even if conversion must be done forcibly. The Christian attack was pressed on both a popular and a governmental level. Monks preached inflammatory sermons and led mobs who burned local synagogues. Then high churchmen brought pressure on various governmental agencies to deny the Jews rebuilding permits. Various edicts of fourth-century church councils closed all public office to Jews. In 429 the patriarch's office was abolished, and a few years later the code of Theodosius II drew together the existing laws about Jews into what amounted to a rule of apartheid. Finally, under Justinian, the right of the Jews to govern themselves in domestic matters was abolished. Judaism was branded a heresy; as heretics, Jews were dismissed from all tasks of any responsibility. Plans were set in motion to make the Jews more receptive of proselytism. Scripture could be read in the synagogue only from the Church-authorized Septuagint translation. Teaching or preaching by the sages was prohibited, as was recitation of the *Shema*, which was seen as a denial of the trinity, and the *Tefillah*, which asked for the restoration of the nation and the coming of a Messiah who had already come.

A contemporary sage equated Israel with dust, using as his text Genesis 28:14: "Your descendants shall be as the dust of the earth." "As the dust of the earth is trodden down by all, so shall thy children be trodden down by all, but as the dust of the earth wears down vessels of metal and itself lasts forever, so shall thy children wear down the nations of the earth and make themselves last forever." [30] The results of such persecutions were predictable: more intense loyalty among the abused and increased use of the liturgy as a polemical instrument. A benediction was added after the reading of the *haftarah* which made it clear that the Messiah had not yet come. "Gladden us, O Lord our God, with Elijah the prophet, Thy servant, and with the kingdom of the house of David, Thine anointed. Soon may he come and rejoice our hearts. Suffer not a stranger to sit upon his throne, nor let others any longer inherit his glory. . . ." [31] When non-Jewish authorities ruled that the *Shema* could not be recited, it was introduced piecemeal into other paragraphs; when that particular prohibition was abolished, the prayer was retained in both places as a reminder of sufferings past. Many of the monks spoke Aramaic, while few spoke Hebrew, so the Jews revived the holy language as a subversive tongue. The *piyyut*, or Hebrew liturgical hymn, seems to have had its origin during these bitter centuries. Unable to teach Torah openly, the rabbis fashioned messianic hope and rabbinic teaching into Hebrew verse, including in these poems innumerable coded comments on their enemies.

The *piyyut* style was later to become an intellectual pastime, as heavy with erudition and scholarly allusion as a poem by T. S. Eliot, but its early purpose was to teach a persecuted people its traditions and to encourage faith and hope: "Remember the bird within your house/seek out the silent dove/summon it with a shofar blast/call it with a ringing voice" (Yose ben Yose). In a hundred poems the King of kings was asked to take sovereignty from the nations and restore dominion to Himself. In the seventh century the persecutors fell before the Arabs, and there was a collective sigh of relief: God redeems.

CHAPTER

·&XVIII&·

Judaism and Islam

H ISTORY records few events more dramatic than the Arab conquests of the seventh century. In a few decades the armies of the early caliphs carried the authority of Islam from the Hejaz to the gates of Constantinople, the approaches of India, and the shores of the Western Ocean. Almost every Jewish community save a few in Byzantium had to adjust to a different and vigorous cultural mix. Subservience to fire and icon worshippers was ended. The Muslims were strict aniconic unitarians. Greek and Aramaic were gradually but finally replaced by Arabic. The new state-church was guided by jurist-scholars and structurally similar to rabbinic Judaism; in that fact lay new opportunities and new perils.

Islam is based on a spoken revelation. The Koran represents God's "great and long speech." Like the Torah, its text was treasured by the faithful as God's gift of truth to man. Among orthodox Muslim theologians the Koran was equated with the uncreated and eternal word of God. The wisdom of wise men came through commentary and interpretation, for the Koran contained the whole truth.

God is one, creator, omnipotent, and omniscient in His relation with creation; and in His relations with man, sustainer, lawgiver, judge, and restorer of life. God is unique. He has no sons or heirs. Like Moses and unlike Christ, Mohammed is a messenger and a man first, last, and always.

History is seen as linear rather than cyclical, as moving from Creation and the Garden of Eden through the confusions of the present to a final Judgment Day, and beyond to a new life in the World to Come. Each day man is sorely tested. The burdens of life are so overwhelming and the decisions so confusing that life would be hopeless had not God in His grace given mankind a saving teaching. Acceptance of God's immutable law offers man hope of victory over himself, and of salvation. Life remains threatening, the winds howl, and the pious are betimes and properly warned to repent and submit themselves. Salvation, gained through obedient service to God, consists of blessing in this life and rich reward in the life to come. Whatever the joys of this world, they cannot compare with those of the next.

These elements are familiar to anyone conversant with rabbinic Judaism although they were somewhat differently balanced. The duty of missionarizing by the sword as well as by the spirit, *Djihād*, occupies a place in imperial Islam without parallel in Judaism. There was a tendency in Islam to see man not only as a servant of God, but as His slave. God is one, omnipotent, at times heedless of man, even of men of quality. "Allah destroys whom He wills and saves whom He wills." [1] "These to heaven and I care not; these to Hell and I care not." [2] Orthodox Islam tends toward a fatalism which not only denies that there is any effective power but God's, but suggests that man can do little but throw himself upon God's mercy in the hope that God will be gracious. Islam means submission, surrendering one's self. There was, in the Muslim world, a sharp sense of impending judgment. Preaching was evangelical, passionate, full of hellfire and damnation rhetoric. The tortures of the damned and the glories of paradise were lingered over and elaborated, often in generous detail. Islam was otherworldly in its promise, resigned to the burdens of this world and happy to dwell on the bliss that awaits. Talmudic Judaism had looked on this world as an antechamber to the World to Come. Under Islamic influence the *midrash* became even more graphic, the images of heaven more compelling and those of Judgment Day starker.

Neither rabbinic Judaism nor medieval Islam treated its rituals as sacraments. Neither invested an hereditary caste with ecclesiastical power. Religious authority in both derived from study and was exerted in the courtroom and the community rather than in a sanctuary. Jew and Muslim washed their hands and feet before worship and chanted their prayers in a holy tongue, facing a holy city. Islam's five daily liturgies (compared to Judaism's three) were performed congregationally, following set and familiar forms and without a priest-mediator. At worship in both faiths men bowed the head, bent the knee, and fell prostrate as they chanted their praise according to set formulas and spoke a capsule credo—the *Shahada* (word of witness) or the *Shema*. One finds in both literatures innumerable admonitions to prepare oneself properly for worship, to dress for one's audience with God as carefully as one would when entering the court of a ruler, and to look upon worship as a recurring opportunity to refresh oneself in the sweet cool waters of truth.

Distance allows us to see similarities to which the average Muslim and Jew certainly were blind. For the Muslim Allah was Allah, their God. The Koran was in Arabic, their language, and offered to them a unique promise. The mosque did not allow non-Muslims to enter during worship. Islam did not consider itself a daughter faith, but a unique revelation. Only those of the true faith could expect the blessings that await the righteous in the World to Come. And Jews did not accept the Koran as either a welcome complement or necessary supplement to the Torah.

Christians had claimed that Jesus' mission had been foretold by biblical prophecy, and had backed their claims with various proof-texts. Islam took a different tack. Mohammed's message had come from the same heavenly scroll which had been opened for the earlier prophets, but his report was the only authentic one. Mohammed had been instructed by God Himself in the book's original language, Arabic. Jewish and Christian prophets had seen the words in uncertain visions or heard them in awkward translation, and had transmitted inaccurately what they had seen and heard. Consequently, the *Tanach* and the New Testament bear little resemblance to God's book. Only the Koran was a faithful and accurate copy. Medieval Islam never bothered to translate the Bible into Arabic. Muslim mythmakers never bothered to create legends about Mohammed's career which would make it fit more closely the biblical paradigm of a prophet. Christians had shaped Jesus' career after Elijah. Muslims allowed Mohammed's career to follow its own course.

European Jew and European Christian often battled over texts. In the Arab world the Muslim had his Koran, the Jew his *Tanach*. Neither Arab nor Jew paid much attention to the other's scripture, but since each had a scripture they shared an unflagging interest in the techniques of exegesis and in any science which could improve the art of commentary, e.g., linguistics, philology, and grammar. However, since they fought on different battlefields, Muslim-Jewish polemic did not develop as a literary form; debate tended toward broad-gauged denunciation and diatribe, as unedifying as they were futile.

Muslim and Jew did business together and sometimes mixed socially, although neighborliness was severely inhibited by their separate dietary regulations. This was still an age of hermetic religious communities. Each had a distinct religious code which governed not only where and when one worshipped, but what one ate and drank, how one married and whom one could marry, where one went to court, and how one's case was tried. All schooling was parochial. Each believed that membership in his community brought him into the community of the faithful for whom God had a special love.

Muslim and Jew accepted each other as unitarians. Early in the eighth century Arab authorities, in a paroxysm of racist emotion, banished Jews from Arabia proper, but the general theory was that the Jews were *ahl ah-kitab*, a people of scripture who could be tolerated as residents within the Muslim world without being required to convert. Conversely, the Jew acknowledged the Muslim as a monotheist to whom the rules of *avodah zarah*, the prohibition of all contact with idolatry and the idolatrous, did not apply.

Orthodox Islam not only insisted that God is one, but that God was absolutely beyond description. Mohammed had kept the black stone in the Kaaba, but the *Shahada* insisted "there is no God but the one God," and this was interpreted by the orthodox to require not only the repudiation of all forms of polytheism, but as a strict prohibition against any representation of God. Representational art was prohibited in the mosque, and generally even in the palace. The alphabet replaced the human body as a basic art form. The embellishment of Arabic writing, particularly of Koranic verses, emphasized the beauty of the script and suggested the many levels of beauty in these teachings. In this environment Jews felt compelled to apply the second commandment with rigor. The mosaic floors of Palestinian synagogues, with their florilegium, legendary animals, and zodiac circles, were covered up. No painter of the seventh century would have dared to duplicate the frescoes of the synagogue of Dura-Europos. New synagogues were bare of design except for intricate biblical texts in stucco or low relief proclaiming God's oneness and promise. Manuscripts began to be treated with great artistry. The scribe became something of an artist as various hands and styles were much praised or criticized. Folio texts were embellished with marginal commentaries which not only sharpened their meaning but pleased the eye, as they were set out in arresting designs and forms. Minuscule illumination of biblical folios begins at this time under Muslim influence.

In short, each faith community acknowledged that the other was civilized, but the dominant mood was assertively parochial. Each community felt the singularity of its truth. Imperial Islam particularly felt the need to bring the unbeliever to the light. Parochialism was a logical extension of the Islamic belief that truth was not in the world of experience which could be shared, but in the singular revelation treasured by the faithful. Muslims spoke of the Koran's inimitability, Jews of *Torat Emet*, the Torah of Truth. Each faith had its special program of salvation, its own way of obedience which the other did not follow (*shariah-halachah*), and a venerable truth the other did not acknowledge. The sense of election and closeness, hence of mission, runs strong in both camps. Each community was organized to defend its faith and governed by a leader whose authority derived, theoretically, from his role as protector of the faith and the faithful.

The first Jews to face the Arab armies outside of Arabia were those of Palestine and Syria, who had suffered long and often under the Christian Caesars of Byzantium. Preferring the unknown policies of the new conquerors to well-known Byzantine contempt, most Jewish communities of West Asia welcomed the Muslim conquerors. But they soon discovered that Islam, like Christianity, was energetically and effectively missionary. There was the allure of a successful, almost miraculous, conquest. There were economic and social advantages for the convert: the possibility of government service, and release from certain taxes and from embarrassing dress restrictions. In each century some Jews willingly converted. Some were forcibly converted. But Jewish communities survived and even flourished. For their part, Muslim rulers did not find Jews a particular source of danger. Unlike the Christians, Jews had no ties to a state-church outside Islam's borders; unlike Christianity, Judaism had ceased to be an active missionary faith. Nor were the Jews led by political activists. Rabbinic messianism emphasized Torah and repentance as the way to redemption, and that the Messiah would come to a spiritually fit people in God's good time.

The first imperial caliphs (the Ummayads, 650–750) were faced with the task of governing an instant empire without adequate Arab manpower. Necessity, if not Providence, prompted them to maintain the long-established Near Eastern patterns of minority self-government. Jews continued to be ruled by a court-appointed official named from certain families who claimed descent from David. An exilarch once again collected taxes, guaranteed law and order, and served as Jewish ambassador to the court and effective head of organized Jewish communal life. His person and prerogatives symbolized the fact that all Jewish communities within the empire were united and governed by a single law, the *halachah*, and a single hope. Though his rank and regalia were more glamorous than substantial, his court reminded all that the scepter had not departed completely from the house of David.

During the eighth and ninth centuries the exilarchs' powers were broader, more efficiently organized, and farther reaching than those of their predecessors under the Sassanians. As before, the exilarch was supported in the government of the Jewish community by rabbinic academies and their graduates, and their relationship was an effective one. Only two academies, preeminently Sura but also Pumbedita, were centrally empowered. With the rise in the eighth century of the Abbasid caliphs whose imperial seat was in Baghdad, this city became the seat not only of the exilarch but also of the above two academies, which moved in from the countryside. Each academy had a head, a Gaon (eminence or excellency), who was chosen from the more scholarly scions of certain privileged families. Only graduates of these two academies were accredited to administer the halachic system without running a monetary risk for possible legal error. As in the earlier academies, the *Talmud* provided the basis of study. In addition, two months each year, Adar and Elul, were given over to convocations, *Kallot*, during which scholars came from all the Jewish communities to examine the practical consequences of the most recently studied tractate, conduct the examination of would-be scholars, and discuss and provide authoritative answers to legal questions sent in from all over the empire. At each *Kallah* seventy senior scholars empowered themselves as a Sanhedrin, patterned after the administrative councils of Second Temple days, and by discussion and vote established law, which was then set down in letter form, signed by the *Kallah*'s leading officials, and dispatched to the inquiring community.

Talmudic law did not change so much as increase its effective range. Sura and Pumbedita flourished in the shade of the capital, and during the early Arab centuries inevitably participated in its imperial power. Cases, questions, students, funds, and legacies came from Jewish communities all over the Abbasid empire. The judgments of these schools were sent throughout the Diaspora. Accredited graduates were sent or found their way throughout the Mideast and North Africa. Businessmen who had commerce in Baghdad visited the academies during *Kallah* sessions and carried away tales of their ceremony and authority, immeasurably enhancing the *Kallah*'s influence and consequently helping to validate its judgments. Centralization was the order of the day. A Gaon's authority within his college was final, so much so that decisions were given in his name alone. We no longer hear, as in the *Gemara*, the determined voices of minority opinions or the echoes of intrarabbinic debate. A question is asked of Sura, and only one answer is given. With few exceptions, scholars who were not Geonim remain anonymous.

These academies were clearly centers of power, part of the governing apparatus. Men came to the schools to qualify as law officers and returned to their communities to enforce rabbinic law. During the first two centuries of Islam there is no record of a new academy being organized spontaneously. To be sure, in various places men studied *Talmud* with a local *dayyan* or scholar, but decision on the law was left to the administrative centers. Efficiency was gained, but so was enmity. Sura and Pumbedita represented a privileged establishment manned by scholar-bureaucrats, not holy men. Their research helped to organize and unify Jewish life, but their position was politically calculated, and they no longer enjoyed in the public mind the charisma of earlier sages.

The business of the academy was law. The literary remains of the academies are in a new form, *Sheelot u-Teshuvot* (questions and answers), responses of varying length and comprehensiveness to cases and legal problems which had been submitted to the Geonim. The drive is to provide clear and systematic statements of various branches of law, legal theory, and practice. Responsa are succinct statements of law designed to be read by men with responsibility in their communities. Some questions dealt with actual cases, often appeals from local court decisions. Others sought guidance in the application of legal theory, an explanation of a Talmudic passage, or the proper form of a contract or will. Hundreds of questions were dealt with at each *Kallah*. During the ninth and tenth centuries Gaonic responsa tended to become essays, and some of these monographs are historically significant, especially those which set out to organize Talmudic law on a given legal subject. One such Gaonic monograph provided a Spanish community and, incidentally, all Jewry, with an approved outline for the liturgy, the first to be authoritatively set down (Amram, d. 874). Sherira Gaon (d. 998) provided Kairouan in

North Africa with a brief chronology of the academies and a dictionary of key halachic terms and their special use in Talmudic debate. One responsum presented, in effect, a compact dictionary of the *Talmud* (Semaḥ ben Paltoi, d. 890), while another set out the mathematical computations necessary for establishing the Jewish calendar (Naḥshon, d. 880).

The *Babylonian Talmud* was readied for the first time for circulation outside the academies whose administrators supervised the production and distribution of the folios. Since these Babylonian schools circulated only the *Babylonian Talmud*, it inevitably became *the Talmud;* and, although folios were rare and costly, they soon displaced entirely the Palestinian version, which became a supplementary research text studied, if at all, only by the advanced scholar.

Today few except halachic researchers read the writings signed by the Geonim, but they are important as the first phase in what was to be a millennial interpretive process which sought to explain the *Talmud*, relate its decisions to the ever-changing conditions of life, and discover the legal and theological theories which inform it. The Gaonic schools prepared and circulated dictionaries of halachic terms; handbooks analyzing Talmudic methodology; lists of scholars organized by their generation to establish primacy and, therefore, preeminence; explanations of mnemonic devices and acronyms that appear in the text; shorthand rules indicating which Talmudic master was authoritative on a particular issue; and comprehensive line-by-line commentaries on the books of the *Mishnah* and the treatises of the *Gemara*.

Another line of effort was directed toward editing summaries of complex Talmudic discussions to highlight the operative rulings. An early Gaon, Yehudah ben Naḥman (8th cent.) prepared such a list of effective laws, the *Halachot Pesukot* (Decided Laws), by simply copying out from the *Gemara* the law without the surrounding discussion. Three-quarters of a century later a Persian scholar, Simon Kayyara, compiled a somewhat larger codelike anthology, *Halachot Gedolot* (Substantial Laws), and the literature includes mention of other compilations. They were wrestling with the problem of preparing a functional index of the law. The *Mishnah* was arranged according to academic conventions rather than as a working jurist's reference book; there was need for a system which was better organized for everyday use, particularly for those who had not studied in the academies.

A Persian scholar, Ḥefetz ben Yatzliaḥ, broke new ground in his

Book of Precepts by assembling the various laws under the particular biblical commandment from which they were traditionally derived. Ḥefetz chose to arrange his code in this way in order to emphasize the oral law's authenticity. This creedal assumption of rabbinic Judaism had gone unchallenged for centuries, but now Karaite sectarians claimed that the rabbis had substituted the *Talmud* for the Bible, manmade law for God's law. What better way of underscoring the oral law's complete legitimacy than to fit it all neatly under one or another biblical commandment? But this structure was artificial and cumbersome. Scholars were reaching for a functional system, but the pressures of tradition and curriculum were hard to shake. It would be another two hundred years before Maimonides would publish a purely topical organization of the law, Judaism's first.

The Book of Precepts was intended for a new type of community leader. The spread of Jewish life in the burgeoning cities of the Muslim empire and the restriction of advanced Talmudic training to two major schools reduced the percentage of trained scholars in the population. In the outlying centers a new class of business and civic leaders arose who were literate in Arabic but not in Hebrew or in Aramaic and who knew only a smattering of *Talmud*. Ḥefetz edited his code in Arabic, the language commonly understood. The *Gemara* had become a book in an alien tongue and there was an urgent need to maintain the communities' ability to handle and use Talmudic law.

A rabbinic tradition counted six hundred and thirteen commands in the Torah and taught that the law was derived from these rules except for those extraordinary or emergency *takkanot* that various courts had introduced. That same tradition broke down these six hundred and thirteen rules into three hundred and sixty-five "you shall nots" (equivalent to the days of the year) and two hundred and forty-eight "you shalls" (assumed to be the number of bones and muscles in the body), leading to the obvious sermonic conclusion that the Torah law is to be observed every day of the year with every energy a man possesses. Since the biblical text is unsystematic and repetitive, there was no agreement on the list of six hundred and thirteen laws, much less the three hundred and sixty-five "you shall nots" and two hundred and forty-eight "you shalls." A long-lived academic debate developed among proponents of various lists. Minor poet-scholars waged hymnic war over which list was the proper one, each enshrining his selection in a *piyyut* or liturgical poem for the Shavuot festival, which celebrates the giving of the law at Sinai.

Long lists of rabbinic rules make awkward poetry, but these songs drove home the rabbinic insistence that the *Talmud* had only drawn out the full meaning of Torah, and that each rabbinic law was implicit in the holy text.

The scholars developed synagogue liturgy as a teaching device. The *tannaim* had established the liturgy's basic form; now poet-scholars interpolated *piyyutim*, Hebrew language prayer poems, which not only added length and variety to the service, but taught history, theology, doctrine, and the essentials of the faith. These poems are highly stylized, delight in alliteration, acrostics, and wordplay, use Arabic meters and stress, and assume a high degree of familiarity with the Bible, midrashic lore, and the law. Thousands of such prayer poems were written, mostly for the festivals, fast days, and the Sabbath.

The use of biblical texts and references in such liturgical poetry is only one indication of a significant revival of interest in the Bible. Many explanations have been offered: environmental, the host culture was ardently scriptural; sociological, the growth of a literate leadership class who had neither time nor opportunity to study *Talmud;* psychological, the full-bodied spirit of the Bible appealed to a full-blooded age. Despite these changes, the academies did not change their Talmudic curriculum. We know on no less authority than the ninth-century Gaon, Natronai (d. 863), that the academies neglected the systematic study of Torah on the questionable theory that Scripture would be learned *pari passu*, "relying on the saying, 'all rivers run to the sea,' that is Scripture, *mishnah* and *midrash*." [3] This error of judgment was to prove nearly fatal to rabbinic Judaism.

As Arabic slowly but inexorably became a native tongue to Jews, fluency in Aramaic, including the ability to read the *Talmud*, was restricted to the rabbinic class. Despite strong opposition from the conservative academies, many communities dropped the habit of following the customary Torah readings in the synagogue with the *Targum* or Aramaic translation, since it was no longer a helpful enterprise but simply a pedantic exercise in a "dead" tongue. In Kairouan, Antioch, and Granada well-educated men emerged who, like the Jews of first-century Alexandria, read much, but not necessarily the traditional curriculum. The *Talmud* was for them a closed book, and they were probably dependent on hearsay, sermons, *piyyutim*, the admonitions of the local *dayyan*, and custom for such rabbinic knowledge as they possessed. The displacement of Aramaic separated the community from the *Talmud*, with its labyrinthine vastness and special language, and, paradoxically, increased its dependence on those scholars who could handle the complex Aramaic-Hebrew texts of rabbinic law. Talmudic knowledge remained essential. The *Talmud* was still the governing legal text. Every business arrangement had to be certified according to prescribed halachic terms. Every court decision had to be couched in appropriate Talmudic formulas. Everyone knew some Talmudic phrases, but not every educated Jew had mastered the texts. More and more Jews looked on the *Talmud* simply as the professional library of their lawyers, rather than an encyclopedia of divine truths. For truth such Jews turned to the Torah, in much the way a Muslim neighbor turned to God's speech, the Koran. The Torah was read regularly in the synagogue and used as the text and context for innumerable sermons. The Torah was open to all, in Hebrew or in translation, and universally credited. Students began again to study Bible intensively as a primary text, to examine it carefully and minutely for its exact and full meaning, what Arabs called *tafsir*, and to interpret it systematically and develop from it a consistent theology, what the Arabs called *ta'wil*. The wise man's task was to discover as exactly and completely as he could what Scripture said. The Bible held the truth a man should know.

Men took a fresh and sustained look at the Bible. What did a text mean? What truths did it enclose? Commentaries, grammars, lexicons, translations, paraphrases, lengthy introductions, and dictionaries, many of high order, were written between the eighth and thirteenth centuries. Indeed, until the advent of modern scientific criticism, textual analysis hardly progressed beyond the sharp analytic introductions of the Gaon Saadiah (10th cent.), the careful grammatical analysis of Jonah ibn Janaḥ (early 11th cent.), and the linguistic exegesis of Moses ha Kohen ibn Gikatilla and Abraham ibn Ezra (11th cent.). These works were careful, controlled, and scholarly. They lack the warmth and hortatory enthusiasm of such medieval European commentaries as the popular writings of Solomon ben Isaac of Troyes (Rashi, 1040–1105), but for sheer acumen and precision they are unrivaled in the Jewish exegetical tradition. These studies owe much to Arab learning, and would have been impossible without that stimulus. The special love of the Muslim for the Koran and for Arabic had stimulated their scholars to make some remarkable linguistic advances which proved transferable from Arabic to other Semitic languages, including Hebrew.

Muslim grammarians recognized that most Arabic words were

formed by adding or subtracting various formal elements to a root composed of three letters. Jewish scholars soon recognized that Hebrew, too, was based on such triradical roots. This seemingly simple discovery, which had eluded the grammarians of the Semitic languages for well over a thousand years, permitted a more careful and precise grammar than heretofore, and proved to be an invaluable tool in etymological research. Carefully worked-out rules of conjugation and declension could now be systematized. A new and sophisticated system of sublinear vocalization and punctuation evolved, and the meter and rhyme of poetry became subject to close examination. The immediate result was a far more precise understanding of the structure of biblical language than had been possible.

To a modern student, grammar seems a pedantic concern with minutiae. In that day grammar was fraught with religious significance. It is hard to recapture the sense of piety and even danger which must have accompanied it. A false or unnecessary vowel, a scribal error, a misplaced conjunction, or an incorrect verbal or nominal suffix might give a text a totally different meaning, and thus change the record of God's revelation. To offer one biblical example, the last line of the book of Psalms (150:6) reads: "Let everything that has breath praise [*tehallel*] God." Make a single slip with your pen in one letter and this verse would read "Let everything that has breath revile [*tehallel*] God." Grammarians were not dealing with just any author, but with God's words. The *Talmud* had warned the scribes to be careful, "yours is sacred work; by leaving out or adding a single letter you can destroy the whole world." [4]

Internecine religious controversy inevitably focused on rival claims by various sects, each insisting it held fast to the true meaning of Scripture. Orthodox and sectarian, Rabbinite and Karaite, battled vigorously over interpretation, but shared a consuming interest in establishing an accurate Torah text. This common concern with an accurate text led to some remarkable editorial efforts carried out with truly praiseworthy critical detachment by the Masoretes. Bible scholars of varying theologies, both Karaite and rabbinic researchers, cooperated in this holy task.

The Masoretes came at the end of a long and scholarly textual tradition stretching back through the Talmudic academies to the *soferim* of the Second Temple. Indeed, *Masorah* means to hand on, hence, tradition. Particularly in this Arabic period, and particularly in the schools of Tiberias, scholars patiently collected already venerable scribal traditions dealing with the orthography, spelling, punctuation, and vocalization of the *Tanach*. In the process they formulated a methodological system which enabled them to establish norms of vocalization, cantillation, and spelling. They labored to present a vocalized, collated, and standardized text and a phrase-by-phrase commentary explaining their decisions and providing cross-references to similar phrases elsewhere in Scripture, examples of differing translations of the same word, and lists of similar idiomatic usage. These notes were set out in the margins of school folios and took two basic forms. One was the *Masorah Magna* (the larger tradition), an explanation of forms, vocalizations, and punctuation together with discussion of appropriate rules and other linguistic excursuses, usually written in the open space at the top and bottom of the folio page. The other was the *Masorah Parva*, a series of specific comments to words and phrases, usually written in the side margin next to the word or sentence being commented on. In addition, these scholars produced separate short treatises dealing with such matters as the crowning of letters (*Sefer Tagim*), the differences among various codices (*Sefer Hillufim*), and guidance for cantillation (*Dikdukei ha-Teamim*).

For all intents and purposes this textual work was completed by the middle of the tenth century. Several carefully punctuated and vocalized folios, particularly those set by Aaron ben Asher of Tiberias (ca. 930), became authoritative. These books, embodying the Masoretic tradition, have remained to this day the accredited text of the synagogue. For rabbinic Judaism the biblical text was fixed.

Launched as an aide to the exegesis of the Koran, grammar developed into an independent field of inquiry whose critical standards affected all writing and literary criticism. The development of a branch of knowledge useful to religious learning into a distinct branch of research was typical of these times. This remained a religious world, believing that truth was in the revealed book, but its economy encouraged urbanization, internationalism, and bourgeois caution. These habits of mind in turn led men to trust what their eyes saw and their ears heard. The need to verify all that could be known of the life of Mohammed, and the process of authenticating tradition through an *isnad* or chain of trustworthy reporters, led to historical study and in time to an independent interest in history. Similarly, the need to fix the calendar for religious purposes stimulated the sciences of astronomy and mathematics, but the natural sciences were pursued by relatively small circles. Reason was encouraged to do its specific work within a religiocultural frame, but since the revealed word was all-encompassing, thoughtful men were faced constantly with the difficult task of adjusting the results of experimental study to their revelation's omnicompetence. Thoughtful men knew that reason and revelation often seemed to be in tension, but most believed that the tension could be resolved by logic or explanation. Such a resolution became a major task of religious philosophy.

❦

Muslims, following the lead of Mohammed, called Jews "the people of the Book." Possession of that Book defined the Jew's legal status, and its study, paralleling Koran study, offered the way to truth/salvation through knowledge. Talmudic learning was no longer the only learning, and had in effect become a separate professional discipline. The *dayyan* was necessary, but he was also resented as a representative of the exilarch and of the Gaonate whose distance, hauteur, and power to tax and to excommunicate made many enemies. Some Jews began to question the basis of established authority, and, because Gaonic authority obviously rested on the requirements of Talmudic law, the validity of the *Talmud* itself. Chief among these dissenters were the Karaites (Champions of Scripture or Callers). This name begins to be used during the ninth century to designate various groups who asserted what we might label today a Protestant theology—the right of each person to confront Scripture directly, without the mediation of tradition, and to interpret it according to his own understanding, thus, in effect, denying the accepted interpretive tradition as embodied in the *Talmud* and effectively by-passing that rabbinic class which based its claims to authority on control of the oral law.

Those who came to be called Karaites shared almost all the familiar rabbinic theological attitudes. They believed in the One God, the revelation of Sinai, reward and punishment, man's special role in God's universe, immortality, the chosenness of Israel, the return to Zion, and the messianic promise. They broke with the tradition over the reliability of the oral law and the legitimacy of rabbinic authority. The rabbis, they claimed, had misrepresented Scripture and imposed their own rules by misconstruing the Torah for their own purposes. The laws establishing Sabbath boundaries (*eruvim*), which permitted certain activity within a village on that day, had multiplied until they filled a whole Talmudic tractate; the Karaites insisted, and correctly, that the whole procedure had no clear scriptural base. According to the Karaites, no legitimate reading of the Torah permitted the various exceptions by which the Talmudic schools had mitigated the Sabbath's severity. In interpreting Exodus 35:3, "You shall kindle no fire throughout your settlements on the Sabbath day," the rabbis had emphasized the act of kindling and ruled that a fire lit before the Sabbath began might be allowed to burn during the twenty-four hour period. In his *Book of Precepts*, Anan ben David (d. 780), the man most Karaite groups placed first in their histories, insisted that a proper exegesis of "You shall kindle no fires" required that any fire must be extinguished before the Sabbath begins.

Anan's reading is not logically inevitable and it suggests what is, in fact, true, that the Karaite scholars were anything but simple and determined rationalists, scrupulously applying common sense rules of inference to the Bible in contrast to the tortured hermeneutic procedures of the rabbis. These men were not biblical commonsensers. Karaite law is, if anything, more rigorous than Talmudic practice. Karaite exegesis is as complex and artificial. Karaite scholars accepted the thirteen hermeneutic rules which Ishmael had promulgated centuries before and which had provided rabbinic Judaism with its interpretive structure, as well as other interpretive devices, such as *hekesh*, a rule of analogy which paired similar phrases, words, or letters to establish a relationship between otherwise unrelated sentences. Their approach is illustrated by Anan's reasoning on the matter of the Sabbath lights.

It is written: "You shall kindle no fire on the Sabbath day." One might perhaps say that it is only the kindling of fire on the Sabbath which is forbidden, and that if the fire had been kindled on the preceding weekday it is to be considered lawful to let it remain over the Sabbath. Now the Merciful One has written here: "You shall kindle no fire," and elsewhere: "You shall not do work," (Ex. 20:10) and both prohibitions begin with the letter *tav*. In the case of labor, of which it is written, "You shall not do any work," it is evident that even if work was begun on a weekday, before the arrival of the Sabbath, it is necessary to desist from it with the arrival of the Sabbath. The same rule must therefore apply also to the kindling of the fire, of which it is written "You shall not kindle," meaning that even if the fire has been kindled on a weekday prior to the arrival of the Sabbath it must be extinguished.[5]

Anan appeared in Baghdad during the uncertain days before the Abbasid caliphs consolidated their authority. A perhaps apocryphal history portrays Anan as a nephew of the reigning exilarch who had hoped to succeed to that office, but was passed over in favor of a brother. The disappointed pretender protested and was imprisoned. In the immemorial tradition of prisoners, Anan used his jail term to write an apologia and a manifesto which raised his personal complaint to the level of political protest. In this pamphlet Anan openly challenged the root principle of rabbinism that the oral law was an authentic part of the Sinai revelation. There had been no second revelation. The written Torah was all. The Bible is God's word, and the *Talmud* is no more than a catchall of interpretations often palpably at variance with the Torah's clear intent. Anan advocated a direct personal approach to Scripture: "Search well in the Torah and do not rely upon my opinion." Anan's manifesto was an appeal for the disestablishment of rabbinic authority.

The rabbis justified their authority on the basis of their competence as interpreters of Israel's twofold revelation; Anan insisted their claim was unfounded. What they interpreted was not the Torah, but an oral law of human manufacture. To prove his point Anan compared the biblical rule which required the months be announced on the basis of direct visual observation of the new moon with the rabbinic practice of publishing a calendar based on mathematical calculations. The rabbis clearly had set aside biblical tradition; moreover, since the Muslim calendar, like the biblical calendar, was lunar, and Muslim holidays were proclaimed on the basis of direct observation, Anan's point had cultural reinforcement and was clearly designed to appeal to Muslim authorities, who, he hoped, would accredit Karaism as the true Judaism.

Anan's followers settled mostly in Egypt. During the eighth century similar groups appeared in Ukbara near Baghdad, in Ramleh and Jerusalem in Palestine, and in Iran. Those various communities were united only in their opposition to rabbinic authority. As the tenth-century Karaite historian and scholar Jacob Al-Kirkisani observed, and as Protestant leaders would rediscover almost a thousand years later, "Reason can lead to various results." Each Karaite group was a law unto itself. Consolidation as a sect called the Karaites came later, and was largely the result of heavy and unremitting rabbinic political pressure. Leadership in unifying these separate communities is ascribed to the scholar Benjamin ben Moses Al-Nahawandi (9th cent.), who insisted on the unity of purpose and community of all who asserted the right of independent biblical analysis. Gradually a sense of community emerged, and in time consensus evolved an interpretive tradition, the so-called yoke of inheritance, which allowed Karaites to organize their own courts and congregations and to move from one city to another.

Like rabbinic Judaism and Islam, and unlike modern Reform Judaism, to which it is sometimes carelessly compared, Karaism remained a law-oriented faith. Karaism took biblical law with utmost seriousness. For the guidance of his disciples Anan compiled in Aramaic his aforementioned *Book of Precepts*, in which he set out the law as he understood it. He arranged the law topically: criminal law, liturgy, diet, Sabbath, incest, and so on. In those days a charismatic teacher, a few theological affirmations, and a new service liturgy did not a faith make. Faith had to have form and rules to govern its organized life.

Karaism was not only a protest against an establishment's privileges, but also against its passivity, its tacit surrender of political messianism. Since the days when Yoḥanan ben Zakkai had made his peace with Vespasian, the rabbis had encouraged Jews to accept *galut* patiently. The Messiah would come in God's own time; in the meantime lead a life of joyous trust, full obedience, study, and generous acts, and be confident of resurrection in the World to Come. No one should force God's hand.

But empires had fallen and great events shaken the world, and there were those who recognized in all this the birth pains of the Messiah. Karaism drew many who could not or would not passively endure *galut*. At first there were a few messianically motivated rebels, but in its maturity Karaism abandoned militancy for a program of *aliyah* and piety designed not to overthrow the caliph but to move God to mercy. Karaites organized pilgrimages to the Promised Land; groups of Karaites settled in Jerusalem, where they formed small congregations and occupied themselves as Mourners of Zion. "The Lord Himself has commanded the men of the exile to come to Jerusalem and to stand within it at all times before Him, mourning, fasting, weeping and wailing, wearing sackcloth and bitterness." [6] In exile there could be no truly meaningful life. The tumult of the Diaspora struggle for survival is joyless. Until redemption, "therefore, it is incumbent upon you who fear the Lord to come to Jerusalem and dwell in it in order to hold vigils before the Lord until the day when Jerusalem shall be restored as it is written: 'and give Him no rest'" (Isa. 62:7). [7] These exhortations by a Karaite scholar, Daniel Al-Kumisi (9th–10th cent.), who had made *aliyah*, can be duplicated in many works. They form a part of the immemo-

[336]

rial Zionist longing of the Jewish people, and at the same time reflect a sharp protest against a rabbinism which prayed for redemption but had effectively made its peace with *galut*. Karaism was restless, burdened by the sense of exile, eager to move God to have mercy on His people. The Karaites' favorite invocation of God was as *ha-Rahaman*, the Merciful One. Daniel Al-Kumisi identified those who tolerated *galut* with the sodden inebriates of Joel 1:5: " 'Wake up, you drunkards!' [These are] Our brethren in Israel who are heedless or asleep or lazy. Wake up and weep over the House of Israel." [8] As if to illustrate this Karaite-Rabbinite difference, at the same time that Daniel Al-Kumisi left Babylon for Jerusalem and a life of vigil, the doughty anti-Karaite polemicist, the future Gaon Saadiah, left Palestine for Babylon and a life of power.

Karaism emphasized the pulsating heart of the biblical promise of salvation and deliverance. Anan developed for his followers a liturgy made up entirely of biblical verses. The rabbinic *Tefillah* asked for restoration; Anan wanted the worship hour itself to be restorative. The hour of worship was a chance for the Jew to be whole, to leave his alienated condition and worship as his forefathers had worshipped when they were free men. The Jew's union with God had been ruptured by the exile. The Karaites tried to heal that rift by reintroducing the forms of worship Israel had used as a free nation. Whenever possible Temple language and routines were reintroduced. Only a priest could read the Torah. Only such hymns as had been used in the Temple were sung. The number of prayers was equal to the number of sacrifices. The synagogue was divided into sections corresponding to the courts of the Temple. Here was Judaism before Talmudic law had distorted it. Here was a foretaste of the messianic age, when the long exile would be ended, Israel pardoned, and the Temple restored.

Who were the Karaites? Their attitudes first appear in the eighth century among Jews who had migrated from the old rabbinic centers near Baghdad into the border regions of Armenia and Persia. Here they were far from the exilarch's authority and part of a restive political situation. These areas were never fully subjugated by the Abbasid armies and were endemic centers of Arab messianic nationalism and ascetic mysticism.

Some were merchants and physicians, literate men who knew the Bible, spoke Arabic but not Aramaic, and for whom, therefore, the *Talmud* was a closed book. No capable man likes to be dependent on another's knowledge. Karaite piety drew on native Jewish sources, but was reinforced by the atmosphere of pious intensity, messianic expectation, and ascetic mysticism which developed among various sects of Islam, particularly Shiite fundamentalists and Sufi mystics, groups which reacted with strong distaste to the worldliness and imperial glory of the Arab empire. The writings of Benjamin ben Moses Al-Nahawandi, after Anan the next scholar of Karaite fame, emphasize redemptive-messianic pieties. He encourages fasting, turns the holidays into austere memorials, mutes the joy possible in daily life, and argues against acquiescence in *galut*. The only light lay at the end of the tunnel, when Jerusalem would be restored. Karaite attitudes were culturally reinforced by an environment which suggested that orthodoxy lay in loyalty to Scripture rather than to an interpretive consensus. In Armenia and Persia, the early centers of Karaism, various Shiite groups similarly rejected the *Sunna* or oral tradition and based their way of life on the Koran as interpreted for them by a trusted *imam* (teacher).

Other Karaites came from the scholar class and had received a Talmudic education. These people probably had some economic or personal argument with the establishment and found it comforting to raise a private quarrel into a public cause against a distant and wealthy exilarch (the fourth official in rank, according to court protocol) and a Gaonic administration which was often high-handed and demanding and which was guaranteed personal exemption from the otherwise universal poll tax. By the tenth century Karaism could claim the allegiance of some extremely competent Talmudists. Jacob Al-Kirkisani and Japeth ben Ali ha-Levi were so well versed in the *Gemara* that Karaite historians boasted that their scholarship was unrivaled. Such claims were exaggerated, but such of Kirkisani's work as survives reveals a first-rate mind, well trained in rabbinics as well as other branches of learning.

Karaite biblicism necessarily led to an affirmation of "reason." The conventional definition of reason among Muslims and Jews was an interpretive one which found it reasonable to reject all literal implications of the anthropomorphic descriptions of God which are to be found in Scripture. However, there was more to reason than the rejection of biblical anthropomorphisms. Reason denoted a scholastic interpretation of Scripture, using the categories and definitions which were the legacy of Greek philosophy to this Arab world. Reason thus suggested that Scripture offered a coherent philosophic system. It is in this sense that Kirkisani called his colleagues "the disciples of pure wisdom" and for such an end that he set out to draw together the biblical texts which established God's existence, the inseparability of His essence from His existence, God's unity and justice, etc. Kirkisani and others attempted what might be called a systematic *midrash* or biblical theology. In this task they found they could profitably adapt many of the arguments of the earliest Muslim scholastics, the Mutazilites, who had interpreted metaphorically all descriptions of God in the Koran save His unity and justice, and had integrated God's omniscience and man's freedom, God's unity and His immanence, into a single coherent theology. God is one, thus all dualistic and trinitarian claims are false. God is just, hence man must be free to obey God's law or to fail in this, the ultimate test. Sin is man's failing and not to be excused as predestined. Retribution is certain and just.

Systematic theology was not native to either Islam or Judaism. It was a Greek legacy. During the Byzantine years Syrian churchmen had translated the major Greek thinkers, and now, particularly during the eighth century, Galen, Hippocrates, Plato, Aristotle, Plotinus, and the rest were translated or paraphrased from Syriac into Arabic. Reason, defined as the use of Greek categories and interest in Greek intellectualism, spread rapidly through the upper reaches of Arab culture. Its categories became conventional and carried an implicit assumption of truth; its conclusions were identified with the revealed teachings.

Greek philosophy had not been a single coherent statement, but a single-minded drive to comprehend all reality based on the conviction that philosophic knowledge was the highest form of knowledge. Greek thought tended to be intellectualist in both metaphysics and psychology. Greek reason must not be confused with empiricism. The way of reason was the way of logical demonstration, not laboratory research. Among the literate it was a commonplace to conceive of God as pure thought, the divine intelligence animating the spheres; and man's intelligence as that capacity which makes him uniquely human and potentially divine. The spark of the divine in man is the potential of his rational mind. To activate the mind is to open oneself to God and to know truly what life is all about, to concentrate the powers of the mind on a single objective so that sufficient psychic energy, will power, is available to overcome lassitude, fear, and irresolution.

Man stands in constant need of a wisdom that would regulate his conduct and behavior. . . . Principally that consists in this particular instance in his exercising control over his impulses and having complete mastery over his likes and dislikes. . . . Any person who follows this course of giving his cognitive faculty dominion over his appetites and impulses is disciplined "by the discipline of the wise" (Prov. 15:33).[9]

What man knows to be right, true, and necessary, he wills to do and can do.

As a scholastic Kirkisani operated with two assumptions: that reason, the Greek apparatus, is reliable, and that revelation, the Bible, is truth. He assumed further that reasonably understood reason and revelation yield a unified and clear understanding of God, man, and the universe. The scholastic drive was to press Scripture to make it yield what the Arab philosopher, Al-Ghazali, called knowledge of the form of the natural order. Why did men need to know all that could be known of God, the cosmos, and man? Because such knowledge was the key to salvation. The aim of reason, the systematic organization of thought, was to get behind the confusing world of appearances, separate demonstrable truth from conventional wisdom, and attain knowledge of the Master and mastery of oneself. Man's distinction from the beasts—and this distinction was insisted on—lies in his possession of a spark of the divine, defined as his intellectual potential. An animal's soul/mind lacked such a cognitive faculty. As man activates that intellect, he becomes a human being. If he does not activate it he remains an animal and can be treated as such. Salvation begins in knowing. What man knows about the true nature of life clarifies for him the true ends of life. The mind that is free of confusion will direct the mind's powerful energies toward truly useful ends. If these scholastics had been asked, "Why not simply memorize and repeat the approved dogmatic formulas?" they would have answered, "What is memorized but not understood remains on the top of the mind; true knowledge informs our whole being and we are transformed by it."

At least until the tenth century, Karaism and rabbinism coexisted despite ritual and communal differences. The Karaites were few, rabbinic authority pervasive. After the tenth century Karaite growth and rabbinic political pressures led to a widening of the gap. Excommunications were freely pronounced. Intermarriage was prohibited. Karaite writings were systematically destroyed by their powerful and ultimately victorious rabbinic opponents, so that we know more about what was said against their claims than what Karaite scholars wrote in their own defense. The rabbis accused the Karaites of treason, "of being rebels against the decision of the courts," [10] of being self-seeking, heretics, liars, Sadducees, and worse. Karaite communities would linger in Palestine and Egypt, later in Constantinople, and even later in the Crimea, Russia, and the Baltic states, where they could still be found in the twentieth century.

❧

Karaism was born in and clearly reflected the Muslim environment. Rabbinism did not escape the same pressures. Nowhere can this be more clearly illustrated than in the career of the foremost anti-Karaite polemicist, the Egyptian-born Gaon of Sura, Saadiah ben Joseph ha-Fayyum (889–942). A child of his age, Saadiah reflects its interest in Scripture. Saadiah prepared the first and what was to be the best known Arabic translation of the *Tanach*, together with a popular commentary on the text. He, too, had read the Muslim scholastics, and, much like Kirkisani, he sought to express Judaism in scholastic categories. Again like the Karaites, he approached *halachah* thematically, even though he and they disagreed radically on the basis of legal authority. Saadiah spoke Arabic and was familiar with Arabic culture, particularly linguistics, poetry, astronomy, and medicine; like the Karaites, he knew he had to popularize his view to an Arabic-speaking polity. Saadiah presented most of his *halachah* as well as his outline of the liturgy in the vernacular. Yet Saadiah was a bull dog when it came to attacking Karaism; debate is never as sharp or acrimonious as when the debaters understand each other.

Saadiah provides a convenient *terminus ad quem* for a discussion of Gaonic Judaism. Within a hundred years of his death the Babylonian academies to which he brought leadership and luster would cease to be international institutions and survive only as parochial rabbinic centers. Their supremacy had grown with imperial Islam, depended on its power, and disappeared with the weakening and destruction of the caliphate's hegemony.

The decline and fall of the Baghdad caliphate is a long history which relates to the inevitable encroachment of regionalism and feudalism on imperial authority. Spain declared her independence in the mid-eighth century. The Berber Fatamids took over North Africa and Egypt in the tenth. At about the same time Persia came under semi-independent rulers. By the late tenth century the Abbasids could no longer maintain security even in the capital city, a fact reflected in Jewish history by a substantial exodus of Jews from the old Talmudic heartland near Baghdad to places of greater opportunity, particularly in North Africa and Spain. The Seljuks plundered Baghdad in 1055, which is as good a year as any in which to date the effective end of the Gaonate. Palestine, Egypt, North Africa, Spain, and areas within each necessarily developed local academic resources, and arrogated to themselves increasing autonomy. Legal appeals previously sent to Baghdad were now sent by Palestinian Jews to Acre and Alexandria, by Egyptians to Fustat, by North Africans to Kairouan and Fez, and by Spanish Jews to Lucena or Toledo. New patterns of religious authority evolved, based on local academies empowered by the presence of famed scholars. From the age of centralized Gaonic authority we move into an age of decentralized rabbinic authority, vested *ad personam* rather than inherent in any school.

True, for perhaps three generations after Saadiah, men of some stature ruled in Sura (Shemuel ben Ḥofini, d. 1013) and in Pumbedita (Sherira, d. 1002, and Ḥai, d. 1032), and, interestingly, perhaps half of the extant Gaonic literature is signed by these men. But this was an afterglow. Gaonic powers were failing, academic revenues were diminishing, and the scholars were relocating.

Saadiah transcended the formal powers of his office. He was incredibly versatile, a Talmudic genius, master of the basic Arabic sciences, thought, and literature, a mathematician, grammarian, poet, and linguist. In his unrelenting polemic against the Karaites, his classic translation of the Bible into Arabic, and his systematic introductions to many of the biblical books, Saadiah represents the traditional Gaon confronting the written revelation, explaining Scripture according to accepted rabbinic perspectives. To this exegesis, and it is this that makes it valuable, Saadiah brought a sound academic knowledge of grammar and lexicography, evidenced by impressive linguistic and philologic monographs, including *The Book of Hebrew Song*, the first book of Hebrew lexicography, and *The Book on Language*, the first critical biblical grammar to be written in Hebrew. Saadiah possessed a well-organized analytic mind. His biblical commentaries are models of careful organization and clear analysis. Saadiah generally avoided *derash*, homiletic commentary, for a scholarly search for exact meaning. Only in cases where a literal reading might mislead or suggest a nontraditional interpretation did he offer a figurative or metaphorical explanation, and then always on the authority of accredited rabbinic commentators. Karaism had made everyone conscious of the text's literal meaning and Saadiah was eager to establish a text's exact meaning and to show that the rabbinic tradition was faithful to it.

In this scripturalist age there were a few free thinkers. One, a Persian Jew, Ḥiwi Al Balchi, published some two hundred *sheelot* (questions) which were in reality not questions at all, but citations of contradictory Torah texts, or texts which ascribed unworthy or inexplicable actions to God. Ḥiwi popularized the very questions which would be raised with such delight and pleasure in their inventiveness by Voltaire and his friends at the beginning of the Enlightenment. How could God not know where Adam had hidden himself in the Garden? What kind of God would harden the heart of Pharaoh so that he would refuse exit permits to the children of Israel? God's law requires the death penalty for murder, yet God did not kill Cain. It could be said that God is susceptible to a bribe. In Genesis 12 God promised Abraham and Sarah a son after His messengers had eaten a full and, incidentally, nonkosher meal at which both milk and meat had been served them by Abraham. To an orthodox sage like Saadiah, Ḥiwi's list simply reinforced the importance of accepting the rabbinic claim of an inspired and unbroken tradition of interpretation. As Saadiah saw it, literalism in biblical exegesis not only led to folly but was unworthy of so profound a text. Not content to make his points in books most Jews might never read, Saadiah capsuled his explanations in *piyyutim* so that, through liturgical repetition, the people might learn by heart the time-honored rabbinic understandings and truly appreciate their Torah.

Saadiah was not an enemy of reason. As a scholastic he believed that reason and revelation were the obverse and reverse of a single coin, complementary rather than conflicting statements of the truth. His preface to the translation of the Torah concludes with disarming confidence. "This is a simple, explanatory translation written with an eye to reason (*aql*) and tradition (*naql*)." If the men of reason can be described as those who were confident that the doctrines of faith can be logically systematized and argued, Saadiah was certainly one of them.

Indeed, Saadiah's devotion to reason seems daring when it is placed beside that of his Muslim contemporary, Al-Ashari, the founder of what was to be the dominant scholastic school in orthodox Islam. Al-Ashari argued that one must accept the Koran without knowing how certain phrases are to be interpreted. In case of doubt it was better not to hazard an explanation. Saadiah was not so passive. If the common sense interpretation of a text seemed to violate reason, he argued that a figurative interpretation was intended. His example is instructive. "For the Lord your God is a devouring fire, a jealous God" (Deut. 4:24). "Fire," he explains, "is something created and defective, for it is subject to extinction. Hence it is logically inadmissible that God resemble it. We must, therefore, impute to this statement the meaning that God's punishment is like a consuming fire." [11] In interpreting "fire" metaphorically, Saadiah certainly did not believe that he was subordinating revelation to reason. He was being true to Torah, which teaches that God is incorporeal and beyond representation.

Saadiah's *Tafsir*, which is both a biblical translation and popular commentary, helped to make Scripture intelligible and intellectually acceptable to an Arabic-speaking Jewish community, and to establish the legitimacy of the rabbinic understanding of biblical law. All anthropomorphic phrases were blunted; all actions that seemed anomalous to God were circumlocuted. Most important, the *Tafsir* was readable and immensely popular. Through it, Jews who could not understand Hebrew knew their Bible and learned that reason and revelation are one.

Saadiah was first and foremost a Talmudist. He wrote a methodological introduction to the *Talmud* and a systematic commentary on the hermeneutic rules, as well as extended digests on the law in such areas as inheritance, testimony and deeds, sales and gifts, and pledges. These monographs are models of clear organization. Each has a careful introduction defining its area of law, and then numbered sections and paragraphs outlining details and Talmudic proofs. Saadiah, of course, championed the Talmudic tradition enforced by the Babylonian academies. Various Palestinian schools had kept alive old theories about the primacy of the schools of the Promised Land. By Saadiah's day Baghdad was no longer the uncontested center of power and a Palestinian schoolman, Aaron ben Meir, tried to reassert the long-dormant authority of the Palestinian scholars to determine the calendar. The texts were on ben Meir's side, although custom was not. The Bible requires direct visual observation of the new moon, but for centuries the calendar had been set by computation in the Babylonian schools. Vigorously defending that practice, Saadiah blocked Aaron's bid for power. However, he was the last of the self-confident representatives of Babylonian spiritual and legal hegemony who had established the primacy of the *Babylonian Talmud* and the decisions of the Babylonian Gaonate.

[344]

Intellectual currents do not stop at religious dikes. Saadiah was part of a world in which Talmudists read Plato in Arabic paraphrase and Al-Kindi in the original, asked about the purpose of religion as well as its practice, and discussed men's doubts as well as their duties. Arab theology had confronted, and quite early, the question of human freedom. The Koran's poetry suggested a doctrine of submission, which many interpreted to mean that man's fate was predestined. The Mutazilites had challenged this emphasis on fate because another Koranic doctrine, that of retribution, logically required that man be free to obey or disobey, or else the rewards and punishments which the Koran promised were purely arbitrary and God's justice was brought into question. The Mutazilites were unable to establish human freedom as a fully accepted dogma. The dominant Asharite school held views close to determinism. Conditioned by covenant theology, Jewish scholastics rejected determinism, but the issue had been raised, and Judaism, which spoke of God as all-knowing and yet a righteous judge, had to review the issue of man's responsibility. The *aggadah* had proposed various formulations of free will which affirmed both that God is all-powerful and all-knowing and that man, in respect to the *mitzvot*, is free. Discrete aggadic statements were no longer fully satisfying. The age credited only systematic thought, so theologians like Saadiah dealt systematically with the issue, achieving, one must say, little more than a reaffirmation of Akiva's antimony, "all is foreseen, but freedom is given." [12] Thus Saadiah: "If men were predestined, God could have had no purpose in revealing the law. We must assume that all God's actions are meaningful; therefore, man is free in relation to obedience. Again, if man is not free, the existence of a system of rewards and punishments, the fact that some will be resurrected and others not, would make of God an arbitrary autocrat. He is not. He is a righteous judge." Saadiah even offered empirical evidence: "I find that a human being feels conscious of his own ability either to speak or to remain silent, or to take hold of things or to desist from them while, at the same time, he is not conscious of the existence of any other power that might at all prevent him from carrying out his will." [13]

Saadiah was, of course, not a Mutazilite, but their approach and the structure of their argument inform his basic philosophy of Judaism. The largely neo-Platonic strand of the Greek philosophic inheritance in which they had been trained encouraged them to see God as the source of all knowledge and faith as participation in the intellectual nature of God, a saving knowledge. Man's distinction from the beast was defined by his capacity to know; salvation lay in "the way of knowing," for knowledge gave man control of his instincts and passions and led to the love of God and a life acceptable to God. In a similar vein Saadiah considered Torah to be the repository of all truth, and thought of Judaism within a similar intellectualist context: "Afterward . . . we inquired into what it could have been that distinguished man, and we found that his distinction above the rest of creation was due to the wisdom with which God had endowed him and which He had taught him." [14] Right knowing precedes right doing: "If man's Reason rules over his nature he is truly human. If it is the other way around, his actions are like that of beasts. Though Nature comes first in the building up and in disposition, it is Reason which decrees what to do and then man does it; if it decides something should be left, then man does not do it." [15] Metaphysical knowledge, it was assumed, gave man control of himself, presumedly of his instincts as well as his actions, and permitted him to lead a fully worthy life.

The similarities of Muslim and Jewish apologetics are striking, but Saadiah and other Jewish theologians did not simply copy Muslim arguments. As the *aggadah* makes abundantly clear, such issues as the apparent conflict between the dogmas of God's omniscience and human freedom had been debated for centuries. Saadiah was defending the Jewish "given," using definitions and demonstrations which had contemporary cultural acceptance.

Scholastic metaphysics, both Arab and Jewish, argued from stock school propositions that the universe must have had a beginning in time, hence a creator, God, who, by an act of free will, had brought the world into being. These philosophers were not trying to prove the existence of God to a skeptical age; few denied God the creator. Rather, they sought to prove the unity of creation, and to show that the soul is of God and somehow participates in His intellectuality. These scholastics debated vigorously with those who denied "beginning," followers of Aristotle who insisted that *hyle*, primal matter, is eternal, thus seemingly denying that divine intelligence is the basic stuff of all that truly is; and with materialists who saw change simply as change, who, like the *Dahriya* in Islam, argued that God had created all out of some external preexistent substance which cannot be analyzed by the intellect, thus denying the existence of a beneficent divine purpose and casting radical doubt on the whole scholastic enterprise, particularly its claim that salvation accrued to man through his mastery of knowledge. Those who denied the fundamental claim of the whole intellectualist apparatus that reality (God) can be known, and that knowledge of God is both the highest bliss and the means of gaining control of one's soul and will, were few, but they were the enemies, the atheists of this believing scholastic world.

Saadiah dealt with all these themes within a special Jewish context. His *Kitab al-Amanat wal I'Tiḥadat* (*Book of Beliefs and Opinions*; Heb., *Sefer ha-Emunot veha-Deot*) is a systematic apologetic work which seeks to support revelation by reason. Truth is one. Revelation (Sinai) is proof of God's love for man and the place where man can find the saving truth. Reason properly handled can demonstrate and help organize these truths. Why did God provide man with both reason and Sinai? Wouldn't reason have been enough? God did not want any person, even the simple-minded, to be without the truth, and He wanted to provide the philosophers with a check for their demonstrations and conclusions. To put it scholastically, there are three natural sources of knowledge: sensation, intuition, and logical inference. Unless handled with great skill, these sources can give confusing evidence, and so must be complemented and confirmed by "authentic tradition which verifies for us the validity of the intuition of reason," "confirms for us the validity of knowledge inferred by logical necessity," and "informs us that all sciences are [ultimately] based on what we grasp with our rational sense." [16] The acquiring of truth through careful reasoning is a religious duty which, properly handled, confirms Torah and confirms man's soul in its control of the body.

Here is a partial explanation of the major role played by the question of attributes in medieval scholasticism. Scholasticism begins with the assumption that reason and revelation are complementary. Scholastics do not question God's word, God forbid; but God's word speaks of such positive attributes as thought, sight, and speech, and often describes God anthropomorphically. If these attributions are literally accepted, God is something less than omniscient and omnipotent; if they are not accepted literally, then the revelation is somehow deficient. The scholastics had to justify the living, relating God of the revelation with the unmoved mover or the first cause of the philosophers, for otherwise the unity and identity of the two thought systems could not be maintained.

Scholastic philosophy necessarily tended to take the form of philosophic *midrash*, line-by-line exegesis of those passages of Torah in which anthropomorphisms and positive attributes appear. One solution was to raise God above relationship, to deny that God was immanent in history or intimate in His relation to man. This was the position of the unorthodox Muslim *Dahriya* (naturalists or materialists), but it failed to appeal broadly, for both Koran and Torah insisted that God heard prayer, performed miracles, sent messengers, and controlled history. To resolve the dilemma, scholastics tried to affirm the special virtue of certain attributes described in Scripture, particularly life, power, and wisdom, and to insist that these did not imply any plurality in God, but were necessary statements about God which took their particular form because of the unavoidable limitations of language. The scholastics insisted on the essential identity of these attributes with God's essence. This seemed logical, but on closer examination it raised a semantic problem of what, if anything, such terms then meant.

Saadiah and the Mutazilites posited two further attributes of God, unity and justice, with, of course, the caveat that these did not imply any division in God or diminution of His perfection. *Yihud*, God's oneness, was a denial of dualism, trinitarianism, and polytheism, as well as a positive statement about a single creative will vitalizing creation and, implicitly, a claim for the organic unity of all that is and the necessary tie between Torah and Greek wisdom.

Scholastic Muslim and Jewish theology necessarily denied to evil any independent power, and insisted that evil was a privation, that God had not created evil. To the question, "Can God commit an injustice?" the theoretical answer is yes. God is omnipotent, but, the theologian quickly adds, in fact, He does not violate His nature, which is wholly just. Then where does evil come from? Generally, the scholastics blamed evil on man, calling it the result of man's inconstancy. Why do men sin? Because they lack the will to overcome passion and temptation. Why do they lack sufficient will power? Because their thoughts are confused.

At other times the scholastics labeled evil as edifying and argued in almost Puritan fashion that suffering was character building and thus to be welcomed. Sometimes they spoke of the spiritual value of suffering: it teaches sympathy and humility. They also suggested the purgative value of suffering: the good are punished now for their few sins so that they may enjoy fully the blessings to come. Not surprisingly, Saadiah's most philosophic commentary was to the book of Job; no scriptural book was the subject of more constant review and debate.

The age's monistic emphasis led scholastics generally to deny mystical and gnostic doctrines about possession, demons, and so on. They believed themselves above superstition. Orthodox Islam and rabbinic Judaism admitted no rites of exorcism. Fear of the omnipotent God and of His judgment replaced fear of one's lower self as the primary inhibiting emotion. Scholastic psychology is as intellectualist as scholastic philosophy. The man of reason need not fear that he is a prisoner of instinct or passion. The soul which animates the body wholly determines its actions. The rational man, that is, the man whose soul is alive with truth, can control the lower and more animal drives by accepting the higher truth and guiding the will to act. The conduct of the body depends upon the soul, and it is the soul's rational faculty which has the determinative say. Reason is subtler and stronger than the other faculties; it was self-evident to Saadiah that the soul's other perceptions were subject to its management.

Saadiah did not present a consistent intellectualist philosophy. He saw creation as a free act of God's grace, and not an act of necessity. God proposed to bless His creatures by providing them an opportunity, through obedience of His commandments, to gain "complete happiness and perfect bliss," [17] which is to say blessing in this world and life in the World to Come. Saadiah's proof was Psalm 16:11: "You will teach me the path of life. In Your presence is perfect joy; delights are ever in Your right hand."

Saadiah proceeded to bring reason to bear on the law, and did so by dividing the commandments between laws which can be sociologically or politically justified by their manifest social utility since they protect life and property or enhance human dignity (*mitzvot sichliyot*), and rules which are beyond explanation but are required by the revelation (*mitzvot shimmiyot*). As a man of reason Saadiah did not leave matters here: "One cannot help noting, upon deeper reflection, that they (*mitzvot shimmiyot*) have some partial uses as well as a certain slight justification from the point of view of reason." [18] The festivals provide relaxation from backbreaking labor and leisure for social intercourse. The laws of purity lead men to think of cleanliness and of the necessity of curbing passion, and to recognize as holy those places like the sanctuary which cannot be entered while defiled. In all cases obedience to the laws witnesses to our submission to God.

The man of reason tries to explain even what he claims cannot be explained. The virtue of the commandments lies ultimately in their usefulness. God did not issue any commandment for man *simply* to test his obedience. The rationality of life is preserved. Man is free to obey or sin. Otherwise the gift of the law would have been pointless, and this cannot be, for all God's actions have meaning. Moreover, God's goodness demands that man be given the opportunity to earn God's reward. What then can be said about God's omniscience? One philosophic solution argued that God's knowledge extended to universals, the species, but not to particulars, a man. But the liturgy spoke of a God who knows man's innermost thoughts before he utters them. Saadiah argued that God knows what man's decision will be, but that His knowledge is not causative and does not limit man's freedom. Man is free. How does man choose? His soul contains a reasoning faculty which somehow participates in the divine intelligence, has a latent capacity for metaphysical knowledge, and moves him to obey God's will. The equation reads: the more man understands Torah/God/creation/truth, the more he will free his soul of confusion, rise to a level where sin, the flesh, no longer tempts him, and merit salvation.

The major portion of *The Book of Beliefs and Opinions* provides rational arguments for the rabbinic agenda: the commandments, theodicy, free will, redemption, and resurrection. The clear assumption that informs the whole is that such knowledge is a tree of life to all who will lay hold of it. Saadiah and his successors approached reason in the firm conviction that reason would provide rational proof of what was already known through revelation. The virtue of their attempts lay in the intellectual pilgrimage, not in the discovery of unexpected truth.

Saadiah is caught between two worlds and is brilliantly inconsistent in dealing with them. God is one. His attributes and His essence are essentially identical, but creation as we know it would be impossible unless life, power and wisdom, unity and justice, are attributed to God. Saadiah holds contradictory opinions here; God's attributes are identical with His essence, which would mean that these attributes indicate no substantial quality, yet God is alive and active, has power and is wise. Saadiah believed in the God of history and prayed to a personal God, all the while philosophizing about the God who is pure being. The God of action, who is in tension with history and man, somehow blends into a divine intelligence, who does not rush to man's side but has man come to Him through awareness and understanding. Saadiah seems not to have been troubled by any sense of inconsistency; indeed, he was supremely confident of his intellectual powers. God is self-sufficient. God's self-sufficiency proves that all God does is good, hence wise. God acts in history, listens to prayers, and performs miracles. God had spoken at Sinai (revelation is an objective phenomenon), the multitudes had heard and affirmed, and the leaders had preserved the revelation faithfully; all these claims pressed vigorously against arguments by Muslim, Gnostic, and Christian detractors who challenged the Torah's authenticity. Child of a polemical age, Saadiah was always ready to cross swords and to set Judaism's wisdom above all other claims. If the faithful believer insisted that his Jesus or Mohammed had performed miracles, so be it. Miracles may have taken place, but they do not validate the authenticity of Christian or Muslim teaching. "The reason for our believing in him [Moses], and in every other prophet, is the fact that he first called upon us to do what is proper . . . if we had felt that the appeal he made at the beginning was not proper, we would not have demanded any miracles from him, because miracles are of no account in supporting the unacceptable." [19]

The major part of Saadiah's work is a reasoned statement of the traditional rabbinic affirmations of God's activities. When he deals with God's unity he is an intellectualist. When he deals with God's justice, God's relations to man and mankind, he is an intellectual rabbi. Saadiah added a final chapter, offering a few ethical first principles based on a moral philosophy he derived from Ecclesiastes and Aristotle's Golden Mean: Nothing in excess and all life's actions will somehow blend into a harmonious whole. Certainly Saadiah believed that he presented his readers with such a harmonious and graceful teaching.

Scholastic *piyyutim* found their way into public worship, and ordinary men began to chant scholastic syllogisms. If many did not understand fully what they sang, they nevertheless began to accept Judaism as a way of thought as well as a way of life. With the popularization of such rationalist presuppositions, Judaism embarked on its first self-conscious shift into systematic theology, a journey which takes us to the works of the Spanish-Jewish thinkers of the next three centuries, particularly those who flourished in Spain itself.

CHAPTER

❧ XIX ❧

Dar al Islam—West

W HEN the wave of Muslim expansion swept over Spain early in the eighth century, the conquerors found small, scattered, and bedeviled Jewish enclaves ready to welcome almost any rule after the repressive, often brutal, policies of fanatically Catholic Visigoth kings.

Although Spain was conquered in the name of the Umayyad caliph, his navy failed to sweep the seas of Byzantine and other enemy fleets; communication between Asia Minor and Spain was necessarily by coastal traffic or by the long overland route from Egypt along the North African coastal plain to Gibraltar. The markets and ports along this African land route soon developed a sizable settlement of Jews; some few had lived here since Roman times, while others were attracted from Egypt and the East by new opportunities.

At first these communities remained spiritually and legally dependent on the Gaonate; many of the extant *sheelot* (queries) addressed to Sura and Pumbedita came from judges and courts in Ifriquia (North Africa) and Al Andalus (Spain). Late in the eighth century a number of qualified scholars and certified copies of the *Babylonian Talmud* found their way west. Such men and this authoritative text now made rabbinic study feasible outside the traditional centers, and by the ninth century the larger communities had their own rabbinic academies which could train their own *dayyanim*. Gaonic authority was essentially coextensive with caliphal power, and when the West acknowledged the Umayyads of Cordova rather than the Abbasids of Damascus there was no longer any reason for Spanish or North African Jews to submit to the Baghdad academies.

In the West Talmudic competence would remain an exceptional accomplishment. Spain had no inherited tradition of Talmudic scholarship and was far from any center where Aramaic was spoken. The language of the *Talmud* had to be deliberately mastered. Of necessity, western communities sought to ease the difficulty of halachic study, to arrange the literature for easy reference, to translate Aramaisms if not into Arabic at least into Hebrew, in brief, to turn the *Talmud* from a comprehensive religious library into a functional law code. The *Talmud* continued to provide the law by which the Jewish communities organized their domestic affairs, and was consequently treated as a law library, but it was no longer every man's full and complete academic curriculum. In school or from tutors, young Spanish Jews learned Bible, some Hebrew, the liturgy, details of the *halachah* which affected their daily lives, and mathematics, astronomy, medicine, rhetoric, physics, poetry, grammar, and logic—all that passed for knowledge among the literate classes of their world.

These "Greek" studies—called Greek because the standard texts were often translations of Greek classics—were similarly mastered by young Muslims. Control of this learning provided men of different faith communities with at least a common idiom and a shared field of discourse. This was not, however, an open society. Those Jews who studied non-Talmudic disciplines did so as Jews, as students whose citizenship and regimen were set by the rabbinic practice of their communities. Outwardly nothing seemed to have changed. Men brought cases involving contracts, inheritance, and divorce to a rabbinic court and deferred to its opinion. But the cultural climate was different; the oral law defined the Jew's life style, but no longer fully circumscribed his learning. A new breed of Jews debated Aristotle's Golden Mean, discussed Galen on healing, and cited Socrates on the meaning of language. To equate the truths of the new learning with the truths of God's word again became a pressing problem.

Rabbinic scholars and scholarship continued to be essential to the organized Jewish communities, but neither of the central Babylonian institutions, the Gaonate or the exilarchate, was reproduced in the West. Decentralization was the order of the day. There was no official representative of the Jews at the Cordova court. The Jewish legal system operated by sufferance, the Muslim government choosing not to intervene rather than to empower a Jewish bureaucracy as an official arm of the state. Rabbinic authority was suasive rather than established. No Spanish *Talmud* school ever achieved unquestioned authority or was supported by massive feudal land grants. Those who wanted to learn went to famed scholars, wherever they happened to be. In turn, Kairouan, Fez, Lucena, and Toledo attained prominence. Power and homage went to that man or family who for the moment held the caliph's ear and the people's hearts— and went elsewhere when that moment was over.

The special spirit of this western Islamic-Jewish world first emerged in North Africa. In 907 a Berber dynasty, newly converted to Shiite Islam, overthrew the governor sent out from Cordova and founded the Fatamid dynasty, a long-lived house which was to rule in North Africa and then in Egypt and Palestine for several centuries. Their capital at Al-Mahdiyah ("city of the hidden *mahdi*") was forbidden to the non-Muslim. The closest open city was Kairouan, just south of Tunis, and it was here that Jewish life and thought would flourish. At first these communities depended on the learning and authority of the Geonim. Medieval European scholars would acquire their considerable knowledge about the Geonim largely from responsa preserved in the compendia of Kairouan scholars such as Ḥananel ben Ḥushiel (d. 1056) and Nissim ben Jacob (11th cent.). But if these men quoted the academies, they also wrote legal opinions on their own authority, and their work indicates that by the eleventh century provincial scholars were breaking away from judicial dependence on the eastern academies. Ḥananel wrote competent commentaries on the first three orders of the *Talmud*. Nissim's original work includes a Talmudic cross-reference, the *Sefer ha-Mafteaḥ* (*Book of Introductory Suggestions*), a discursive explanation of terms in Talmudic literature and the *midrash;* commentaries to various *Talmud* tractates, particularly those sections which deal with the holidays; *Sefer Mekabble Torah* (*The Book of Those who Receive Torah*), a treatise on the history of the rabbinic traditions; and a volume of scholastic explanations of various *aggadot* of which only portions survive. The thematic thrust of their commentaries, and of Nissim's legal monograph on Talmudic methodology and traditions, indicates a concern for organizing the vastness and diffuseness of the *Talmud* into more manageable form. Their choice of language for their commentaries—Ḥananel used Hebrew, Nissim Arabic—indicates that the Aramaic vocabulary of the Gaonic schools in which

[354]

both men were fluent no longer was understood by a large segment of the western literate classes to whom these works were addressed.

Kairouan was sacked by mountain tribesmen in 1057, forcing the student who was to be its academy's most famous graduate, Isaac Alfasi (1013–1103), to move farther west to Fez, where he taught until another political upheaval again forced him, at the age of seventy-five, to flee, this time to Spain where, at an academy in Lucena, he completed his chef-d'oeuvre, an abridgement of the *Talmud*, the *Sefer ha-Halachot* (*The Book of the Laws*). Alfasi's practical aim, which was substantially the aim of all these men, was to transform *Talmud* from a curriculum into a code, from an overwhelming intellectual exercise in a now little-understood language into a manageable legal text for those charged with the domestic governance of their communities. One need was for indices, another for digests and précis of lengthy and involved Talmudic debates, and another for the separation of theoretical and practical Talmudic material. These needs had been felt in the Geonic academies, but Alfasi went much further than any Gaon had been willing to go. He left out those sections of the *Talmud* which dealt with inoperative laws, summarized the operative law, removed repetitions and extraneous matters, indicated accepted halachic rulings, compressed lengthy discussions, inserted terms which cleared up difficult phrases, and placed otherwise scattered material in appropriate context.

Alfasi's digest was a useful book which reduced a vast Talmudic library into a long but ready reference. It was willingly used by generations of students; indeed, rabbinic study in Spain was often based on this abridged version rather than on the full text of the *Talmud*. Alfasi had not changed the feel of the *Talmud*; he kept the original style, idiom, and organization. Teachers said "how useful" rather than "how novel," but its very acceptability to the professors was proof of its innate conservatism. Alfasi cleared some of the underbrush, but left the material organized loosely in Talmudic categories rather than systematically and expressed in the original Aramaic rather than in Arabic or Hebrew. Alfasi had not provided the fully functional manual many cried out for. This work had to await the pupil of Alfasi's most famous pupil, Joseph ben Meir ha-Levi Ibn Migash, the celebrated Moses ben Maimon (1135–1204), whose classic *Mishneh Torah* uprooted the law from its Talmudic bed and reorganized it into a neatly arranged and clearly indexed frame: fourteen topical volumes, each subdivided into carefully categorized topical sections, the whole translated into a graceful Hebrew.

Tenth-century Kairouan on the eve of this rabbinic renaissance could claim men of broad, if not necessarily Talmudic, learning. The physician philosopher Isaac ben Solomon Israeli (d. 932?) came here from Egypt and became physician in residence of the first Fatamid caliph. Studies of Israeli's surviving works have shown that he had read Galen, Hippocrates, and the other classic physicians necessarily familiar to any medieval doctor, Plotinus' *Enneads*, the neo-Platonic work which circulated under the title *Theology of Aristotle*, the pseudo-Empedoclean *Book of the Five Substances*, *The Epistles of the Sincere Brethren* (*Iḥwan As-safa*), and the systematic works of the Muslim philosophers Al-Kindi and Al-Musadi.

Israeli's *Chapter on the Elements* begins: "Aristotle, the philosopher and master of the wisdom of the Greeks, said: 'the beginning of all roots is two simple substances. . . ,' " [1] and it ends: "Thus we have said here what we intended to explain of the words of the philosopher [Aristotle] by way of arguments and proofs and where he finished his words, by what other philosophers have mentioned, with the help of the Creator, Whose Name he blessed and Whose Rememberance he exalted." [2] The intervening eight paragraphs are a carefully reasoned, logical demonstration of the nature of intellect and of the various intellectual emanations which comprise the spheres. Neither Torah nor *Talmud* is cited. A contemporary Arab thinker might have written these pages—they are, of course, in Arabic—as easily as a Jew. Israeli was doing philosophy, and one did philosophy with the aid of Aristotle's logic rather than biblical proof-texts.

Israeli undoubtedly obeyed rabbinic law and believed that the teachings of the Bible and of philosophy lead to similar conclusions. One brief excursus, now generally titled *The Book of Spirit and Soul*, is a filigree of scholastical propositions dealing with life, death, and how to gain immortality, tied together with appropriate biblical quotations. Despite the biblical proofs, there can be no doubt that philosophic ideas, particularly those of the neo-Platonic tradition, not only provided categories for Israeli's thought, but determined his understanding of the way to personal salvation.

His was a neo-Platonic universe in which the focal point is creation, not Sinai, and the focus of interest is the nature of the universe rather than exegesis of a particular revelation. Creation is conceived not in terms of the familiar myth of Genesis but as an emanationist process in which all that is, besides God, is connected by descent from the highest and first element in God's creation, intellect. Israeli argued that God is absolutely one and unchangeable. God cannot be known. Only His creation is known, and since the world manifests intelligence and wisdom throughout, we must infer that intellect emanates somehow from a source directly beside the One. From that source intelligence flows or descends into the world. This active and all-pervasive intelligence was often symbolized as light. Light shines into the darkness and produces brightness, but as a light decreases in brightness the further it gets from its source, so, too, intellect permeates the spheres with decreasing intensity until it reaches the earth, the furthest point from its source, where nothing participates in intellect save man—or, more accurately, where all is material, dark, save a single spark, the potential of man's rational soul.

None of this was original with Israeli. The theory of emanations reached back behind Plotinus (204–269) to Philo, and had been appropriated long before by thinkers of all three scripturalist faiths as a feasible solution to the logical dilemma of affirming a God who is pure being without change or imperfection, yet creator of a material universe, and as the basis of an elaborate mystical doctrine. Like the ladder in Jacob's dream, the downward path of intellect from God could also be an upward path along which the activated intellect/soul raises itself from its earthbound condition toward the source and destiny of all life, God. This path is open to the soul, "which is inclined to the highest excellence which can be reached by wisdom." Such a soul "is the most noble of things, and is with the angels above the spheres." [3] How do we know this? Israeli cited the prophet Zechariah: "If you will conform to My ways and carry out your duties . . . I grant you the right to come and go among those in attendance here" (Zech. 3:7).

To free that part of the soul which participates in intellect so that it can take the upward path, a man must activate its latent powers of knowing. Insofar as it is enlightened, freed of heavy, earthbound thoughts, immersed in thoughts divine, purified by holy fasts and rites, the soul can rise through the spheres toward God and enjoy *devekut*, the moment of blessed communion. Christian versions of this neo-Platonic tradition at times suggested that an enlightened soul lost its distinctiveness at the moment of union with God, and became one with God. Jewish neo-Platonists shied away from the possibility of complete apotheosis. The enlightened soul has the capacity to enter God's court, but not to become one with God Himself. A century after Israeli, the Spanish philosopher-poet Solomon ibn Gabirol described the soul's ascent through the spheres toward the supernal light and ultimate mystery of God in a poem, *Keter Malchut (The Kingly Crown)*, which came to be one of the most beloved parts of the Yom Kippur liturgy:

> Who can come to Thy dwelling place, when Thou
>   didst raise up above the sphere of intelligence
>   the throne of glory in which is the abode of
>   mystery and majesty
> In which is the secret and the foundation,
>   to which the intelligence reaches—and
>   then stops short?
> And above it Thou art raised up and exalted
>   on the throne of Thy might,
> And none shall come up with Thee.[4]

Typically, Ibn Gabirol denies the possibility of apotheosis. However successful his ascent, the mystic remains earthbound, a man who, after his moment of ecstasy and closeness, must descend the ladder and reenter this world—although he has now had a foretaste of the heaven which awaits the righteous, "The abode of the pure souls, that are bound in the bundle of life. . . . This is the repose and the inheritance."[5]

The upward way is a way of learning and knowing; it is also a way of withdrawal from the material and worldly. The soul must be freed of earthly concerns, ambition, appetite, and passion; to go this way requires obedience, knowledge, and a regimen of self-denial and abstemiousness, study, vigil, fasting, and meditation. Man must break the bars of the body in order to free the soul imprisoned within. To a degree not hitherto so pronounced, Jewish thought emphasized an ascetic regimen designed to loosen the hold of desire and passion over the soul. However, it did not prescribe mortification of the flesh. The Bible's earthiness and monistic anthropology discouraged rabbinic Judaism from viewing the physical as evil. God is the creator of all. He endows all with spirit and life. There are not two opposing worlds—one spiritual and one material—but one world, God's. There are not two distinct elements in man—one the soul, the other flesh—but rather body and soul bound together, each bearing in its way the image of God. The writers generally offered a version of Aristotle's Golden Mean weighted toward austerity, but avoided demanding total self-denial. What is essential is that the soul be freed of the turbulence of appetite and passion. Once free, the soul's inherent intelligence becomes active and permits man to recognize the transiency and superficiality of his ordinary human preoccupation, the vanity of the worldly. Psalm 39:13 was a favorite text of Israeli's: "For I am a stranger with Thee as were my fathers," which he interpreted to mean that there is no security and no solid happiness for man in the everyday world, that man is a wanderer here below who can find peace only when his soul ascends to the heavens, its original home and its eternal resting place.

Men like Israeli were involved in an essentially nonmessianic vision of deliverance, a private way of illumination and salvation which changed the focus of religious life without breaking formally with the *halachah*, the way of duty, or with the community's messianic hope. Halachic obedience was not gainsaid, but was only a first step on the ladder. Talmudic learning was approved, but again such learning was only a beginning. Joy and the pleasures of the flesh were not completely denied, but "A wise man is satisfied with a little of this world rather than very much of it; may God make us one of the pious." [6] Israeli seems not to have been a landmark figure to his contemporaries, but although his was not a pivotal literature he expressed most of what would be the functional concerns of this intellectualist world: God's absolute oneness, the soul as an emanation of the world soul, the downward and upward path, the significance of enlightenment and denial, suspicion of worldiness and ambition, and the goal of communion with God. Thinking men looked on this world as a temporary abode, their aim was to transcend the world and avoid being trapped by and in it.

Jewish mystics, influenced by neo-Platonic categories, may have sought the heavens, but their bodies were in Spain, then a generous and pleasing land of wheat, vines, and dates, green with a fertility that the goat and human carelessness had not yet blighted. The eye of the poet delighted in "the purling of the brook/the thrushes' song/the couch of flowers more brilliant than the weave of Persia's looms/the myrtle's shade." [7] Heretofore underpopulated and underdeveloped, Spain thrived under the Arabs, who brought the necessary energy and skill for its commercial and cultural expansion. Cities grew and flourished; commerce and industry multiplied. The Jews of Spain—a few settlements dated back to Roman days, and many others emigrated now from North Africa and the Middle East—prospered in measure with their country.

Jews organized their lives somewhat differently in Al Andalus than they had in the Arab Middle East. In Spain Islam did not convert the majority of the conquered. Muslim rule was that of a feudal hierarchy dominating a restive, sometimes rebellious native population who never abandoned their revanchist hopes or the old gods. Arab armies never subjugated the far reaches of Leon and Navarre. Within a half century of the Arab conquest Barcelona was again a Christian-ruled city. Unremitting Christian pressure finally broke the authority of the Cordova caliphate in 1034. Thereafter Muslim Spain was little more than an agglomeration of small emirates, autonomous city-states known as *taifas* which fought among themselves as often as they fought Castile and Aragon. The central tier of these cities fell to Christian armies in the eleventh and twelfth centuries: Toledo in 1085, Saragossa in 1118, Lisbon and Calatrava in 1147, Tortosa in 1148. At the same time the more southern cities were overrun by a new wave of Muslim invaders, North African Berbers, the Almovarides in 1086, and then the bloody and religiously fanatic Almohades in 1146, but these African kingdoms proved short-lived. Castile again took the offensive against Islam. Cordova fell in 1236 and from then until the fall of Granada in 1492 only a small Muslim toehold remained in the southernmost part of the peninsula.

When the Arabs arrived in Spain early in the eighth century they brought with them vigor, the skills of a literate people, an urban economy, and an advanced agriculture. Under Arab guidance the Spanish economy flourished, and many Jews benefited. But war was never far away. There was little security. Again and again, using the language and incident of the Bible as Muslim poets used the language and idiom of the Koran, Hebrew poets lamented the fate of their people, caught between the upper millstone, Edom (Christendom), and the lower, Ishmael (the Arabs). "My friend, the days of my affliction have compelled me to dwell in the scorpion's and the viper's company." [8] Praised indeed were those shepherds who protected the defenseless lamb, Israel, with their vigilance. There were many images of danger, and a single hope: "Be ready for the End, even if it delays; For I have not put another nation in your place." [9]

We know little of the organization of the Jewish community during the first two centuries of the Cordova Caliphate. The first dominant personality to emerge is a court Jew, Ḥasdai ben Isaac ibn

Shaprut (915–970), minister and physician to Abd Er-Rahman III. High-handed and arrogant, conscious of living on the edge of power, fully capable of dismissing men from his academic retinue as whimsically as he might be dismissed from the caliph's court, Ḥasdai exerted authority on the basis of his usefulness to his master. His family had no claim to Davidic blood, so, unlike the Babylonian exilarch, he and his heirs played no role in the people's messianic imagination. Ḥasdai was a well-read man and linguist, and his pleasure, like that of his king, was to be a patron to scholars and poets. A scholarly court was a measure of the wisdom and wealth of the master. To prove his worth Ḥasdai enticed to Spain men of proven Talmudic learning and provided them the necessary libraries and texts. Legends told how he amassed a library of four hundred thousand volumes. In effect, he bought first-rate Talmudic minds, a most profitable investment, for they proceeded to lay the foundations of a substantial rabbinic culture for Spanish Jewry.

The great political power he exercised at the height of the Arab imperium, and his awareness that he was still in *galut*, an alienated man, have made Ḥasdai one of the romantic figures in Jewish history. His name is forever linked with that of a Turkic people of the South Russian steppes of whom he heard in the course of his diplomatic correspondence. What attracted Ḥasdai to the Khazars was the report that they were Jews. Who were these Jews? Were they descendants of the lost ten tribes? Copies of a reported exchange of letters between Ḥasdai and Joseph, King of the Khazars, circulated during the Middle Ages. Ḥasdai writes: Is there truly a place where Israel enjoys sovereignty? If there is I would willingly abandon office and position, leave my family, and go to see Israel's king. If you have information about the ultimate miracle, the Messiah whom we have so long awaited as we have wandered from place to place in *galut*, pray tell us—for we are taunted: every people has a kingdom, but we have none. The king answered that his people had been converted to Judaism and that they, too, awaited the Messiah. Ḥasdai remained in Spain, and Spanish Jews continued to wonder about these romantic confreres far to the east.[10]

Shortly after Ḥasdai, Christian pressures and Arab feudalism led to the collapse of all but the symbolic authority of the Cordova court. In the several *taifas* Jews were organized as a separate community and led by someone who, for the moment, had a special relationship to the court and was accepted there as de facto representative of the Jews. *Dayyanim*, local scholar-judges and administrators of Talmudic matters, existed in most of the larger communities, but they were rarely leading figures in intellectual or political life. Communal power rested with the wealthy courtier and was as unstable as royal favor.

Samuel ha-Nagid (992–1055) was a vigorous Jewish intellectual who combined in his person political success, Talmudic and secular learning, poetic talent, cultivated elegance, and, of all things, military genius. All the incongruities of this world are wrapped up in his person. Samuel was not a run-of-the-mill scholar, but a recognized rabbinic authority, author of a well-conceived Talmudic methodology, *Mevo ha-Talmud*, which is still printed in standard editions of that work, a compilation of *halachah* (*Sefer Hilchata Gavrata*), and of incisive commentaries to several Talmudic tractates. He was a Talmudist trained in various Arabic sciences, particularly calligraphy, philology, and poetry; author of a scientifically organized and voluminous biblical dictionary, *Kitab al-Istighna* (*The Treasure Book*), and of three poetic anthologies modeled, as was the convention, on the style and form of specific biblical books—poems of personal anxiety and need based on the psalms (*Ben Tehillim*), moralistic couplets based on Proverbs (*Ben Mishle*), and musings on life and its vicissitudes based on Ecclesiastes (*Ben Kohelet*). All the while he was also vizier, minister of foreign affairs, and general of the army to one Habbus, King of Granada, and to his son and successor, Badis. Samuel's piety was sturdy rather than subtle, and his poetry stylish rather than original, but obviously sincere, even in revealing a Jewish hidalgo's vanity and pride of family and a general's love of action and bravery. Samuel saw himself in various heroic, even messianic, poses: "I am David of my day, protector of my people, sweet singer of Zion, learned in science, sacred and profane, somehow God's chosen tool in His drama of salvation, humble before God, proud before man." [11]

Men like Samuel had at least a gentleman's understanding and patron's appreciation of what passed in Spain for Greek wisdom: mathematics, medicine, physics, astronomy, astrology, rhetoric, and philosophy. Theirs was a renaissance world in which a small upper class lived well when they were in favor. Their inner life was as inconsistent as their political condition. Worldliness alternated with fits of piety, and the study of Torah alternated with a rich philosophic and scientific diet of Galen, Hippocrates, Plato, Aristotle, and Plotinus. Samuel's renaissance world emphasized not only the Greek classics— "Occupy yourself diligently with secular books, they are useful for public life" [12]—but the Hebrew classics as standards of style and beauty. There was a deliberate use of Hebrew for poetry and chronicle, and a renewed emphasis on the history, poetry, and belletristic aspects of Scripture. Men again read the Song of Songs as poetry of passion, David's eulogy of Jonathan as a tribute to friendship, and Deborah's war chant as a rousing martial song. The Bible was read as law, truth, and with an eye to its greatness as literature—almost every phrase of Spanish Jewish poetry cites, alludes to, or takes off from a biblical phrase. Panegyrics and eulogies compare their subjects to biblical heroes, who come to personify a long list of noble virtues, particularly friendship, magnanimity, courtly bearing, noblesse oblige, and pride of family. Moses, our teacher, became Moses, our leader, the tall, strong, steady, royal leader of men. This renewal of interest in biblical man as heroic model suggests that these men could envision Moses, David, and Ezra in their place—in places of power, danger, and dignity, where loyalty and courage are constantly tested.

Leading Jews were now not only scholars and leaders in the domestic affairs of a minority community, but part of the action of their times. There was, however, one insurmountable, unavoidable difference between a Spanish Jew and the heroes of the past. The ancestors had been free men, whereas their power was now contingent and conditional. Even at the height of his power a Samuel ha-Nagid knew that a sword hung precariously over his head. The pain of exile, the indignity of dependence, the anguish of national impotence seared their souls. Even as those few who were fortunate enough to do so wielded power and built palaces, they longed desperately for an end to their servitude, for the Messiah, and Israel's return to Zion. The same Samuel who wrote poems in which he prayed for victory over other Moorish armies wrote psalms in which he asked God to allow him to serve as a Levite in the restored Temple in Jerusalem. Such men found their challenge in Spain and their comfort in Zion.

Zionist messianism, the hope of national redemption, burned brightly in their souls, and no private mystical program of salvation ever fully displaced it. Solomon ibn Gabirol, who wrote *The Fountain of Life*, in which he described a way of obedience, knowing, and denial which could lead any philosophically minded monotheist to that ultimate moment of communion—a book so universalist in tone that for centuries it circulated in Europe as an Arab or Christian work—also wrote of Israel: "Wait, O suffering one!/It will not be long/Soon I will send my messenger/He will prepare the way,/And on Mt. Zion I will anoint My king." [13]

For some time after the Arab conquest the pressures of circumstances led to a relatively close Jewish-Muslim relationship; each needed the other. The Muslims were short on manpower and required Jews to staff the professions and bureaucracy. They did not trust the local Christians, whose brothers in the north had taken up sword and cross in a crusade of reconquest. In the ninth and tenth centuries Jewish integration into the upper reaches of the urban Muslim world went further than it ever went in the Muslim east. We hear of Jewish viziers, treasurers, physicians-in-residence to various courts, of large Jewish landowners, estate managers, and viniculturists, of Jews who wrote Arabic texts in astronomy, medicine, logic, poetry, and comparative Semitic grammar, and whose books were read by a general public. Popular histories label this age in Spain a golden one for the Jews.

The truth is that some Jews enjoyed power and wealth; some, not all or even most. Most were ordinary folk—poor shoemakers, weavers, and tailors. Poetry, philosophy, and science were the attainments and interests of a small elite who looked down on the hoi polloi; genealogy and attainment were significant to this small upper class, and their literature is rich in contempt for the cloddish masses. An elite, particularly one whose perch is precarious, tends to take its pleasure while it may. The *Diwan* or collected poetry of a Samuel ha-Nagid portrays the pleasures of war, women, and wine; but, as youth became age, as impulse gave way to wisdom, the poets sang less of their pounding blood and more of the snares of passion and the impermanence of feeling. Guilt shadowed every pleasure. They lived for the moment and knew how quickly the axe could fall; wealth and poverty crowded each other in the street, and both faith and reason taught men to acknowledge the vanity of possessions and physical pleasures. The dominant tension of the age lay in a field of force which ran between the pole of reason (which taught the vanity of worldliness) and nature (delight in the attractions of love and a beautiful spring day), between wisdom and passion, between this world and the World to Come. The dominant conclusion of the wise was that the sensate world was, if not an illusion, a mask which hid life's true face.

❧

Quite early, in the court which Ḥasdai ibn Shaprut maintained, a group of scholars took up grammar where Saadiah had left off. They laid the foundation of the systematic study of Hebrew as a language, thus giving Hebrew the flexibility to become again a vehicle of song. In no era was song so warm or so close to the surface. Sensitive men sang of their zest for life, of spring, of the many charms of an inamorata, of the hardships of life, and of the inconstancies of companions, as well as of the illusion that is life, of the incomparable majesty of God, His special mercies toward Israel and the bliss that awaits.

Hebrew poetry went Arabic in style and imagery as well as in form and meter. Stylized panegyrics, wine songs, wedding verse of indifferent quality, poured from a hundred agile brains. A new figure, the wandering poet, emerges in the Jewish community, sometimes expressing delight in being unencumbered, more often bemoaning a piece of malicious gossip which has alienated his most recent patron, sometimes seeking adventure or truth, sometimes simply fleeing unsettled times, willing to sing for his supper, equally capable of ribald verse or inspired hymns.

These men put to quick use the new grammatical science being developed by a growing band of first-rate philologists and linguists. There was Menahem Jacob ibn Saruk, Hasdai's scribe, whose *Mahberet* was the first Bible dictionary along scientific linguistic lines; Dunash ben Labrat, Menahem's archenemy and bitter critic and the first man ever to write Hebrew verse according to the rules of Arab meter; Menahem's pupil Judah ben David Hayyuj, discoverer of the triradical base of all Hebrew verbs and of the rules of conjugation and declension; and Judah's pupil, Jonah ibn Jannah, whose Arabic *Kitab al Tankih* (*Book of Minute Research*) was for a time the classic investigation of language.

The widespread use of Hebrew in poetry must not lead us to exaggerate the age's fluency. Hebrew fluency was the accomplishment and proof of scholarship of a certain class. Arabic was the common language, Hebrew a mark of cultivation. Until the twelfth century Jews rarely wrote scientific texts or philosophy in Hebrew. Rather they wrote in Arabic using the Hebrew alphabet; even grammars of the Hebrew language were written in Arabic. Only poetry was generally written in Hebrew, partially because Arabs knew from the Koran that God spoke in Arabic verse and did not take kindly to nonbelievers who wrote verse in God's own speech. There were other reasons. These Jews, for all their sense of class and occasional real wealth, were marginal to their society. The sense of *galut*, of alienation, was sharp. Hebrew was the language of the Messiah, of a redeemed people. Hebrew allowed the poets to tap the rich lode of allusions and idiom in Scripture. On a more practical level, only

Hebrew could bridge the language gap between the separate Jewries under Muslim and Christian rule. When the wandering poets went north into Christian Europe they entered communities which knew no Arabic. Hebrew poetry alone was a convertible currency which could earn bed and board in Barcelona or London as readily as in Narbonne and Marseilles.

Grammar and linguistics held a special fascination for the Jews. After Judah ben David Ḥayyuj analyzed the various transpositions which occur in regular and irregular verbs and published the first systematic Hebrew grammar based on specific rules for vowel change and other grammatical forms, a whole rash of style books, lexicons, compendia, dictionaries, and concordances were edited. By the eleventh century Hebrew was taught with a sophistication which would do credit to a modern university, and critics were as arch about a writer's style as any English don. The gap between high literature and folk literature widened (incidentally, we still know all too little of Spanish-Jewish folk literature). Because poetry was a class phenomenon, this Hebrew renaissance proved short-lived, but its scholars provided Hebrew with the grammar and an extended vocabulary which would allow the holy tongue to be revived in the twentieth century as a living language.

Although its flower was poetry, both profane and profound, the serious study of language was undertaken not to encourage the muse but to understand the message of Scripture. It was axiomatic that "one can only understand Torah if one has a firm knowledge of the language in which it is written." [14] Muslim and Karaite polemicists challenged familiar rabbinic interpretations as grammatically or linguistically improbable. Attacked on many sides, the traditional homiletic exegesis (*derash*) fell into disrepute and was considered fit only for elementary school children. The emphasis was on *peshat*, literal exegesis based on rigorous grammatic and philological analysis. *Peshat* here means careful and sophisticated philology, not popular explanations of the Bible in simple words. The most famous Spanish biblical commentator, Abraham ibn Ezra (1089–1164), is so terse and cryptic that deciphering his phrases remains hard work even for the scholar. To these men commentary was a science, not sermonics, the object of which was the correct statement of the word of God.

This school of critical interpreters found its first major expression in the Arabic commentaries of Moses ibn Gikatilla (11th cent.), who had prepared himself by translating Ḥayyuj's principal studies into Hebrew. Because Moses' commentary was not translated into Hebrew, European Jews came to know the results of this school's rigorous grammatical and etymological approach largely through the Hebrew exegesis of Abraham ibn Ezra. Gikatilla and Ibn Ezra's commentaries struck a new note. They sought literal accuracy wherever possible, and introduced a sense of time into the understanding of a text. Historiography, when and where a statement had been made, became a matter of critical interest. For a thousand years Jews had accepted the nonhistorical thesis that chronology is not to be considered in interpreting Scripture. Living in the limbo of *galut*, Jews had encouraged history to pass them by. Now Jews were again living in time, and commentators became conscious of chronological anachronisms in the biblical narrative. If the children of Israel had not yet crossed into Canaan, how could the Torah refer to lands east of the Jordan as "on the other side of the Jordan" (Deut. 1:1)? Deuteronomy 31:9 reads, "Moses wrote down this Teaching." Does "this" suggest that he wrote the teachings that follow, and not the whole five books? Had Isaiah lived for over two hundred years or were the poems in the book of Isaiah which specifically refer to the sixth-century B.C.E. Persian emperor Cyrus by a later hand? Do not some of the psalms patently refer to post-exilic events?

Ibn Ezra sprinkled his commentary with a number of such questions, many apparently borrowed from Gikatilla. Generally, he drew no conclusion beyond "the wise will understand." Scholars have debated for centuries the implications of these references. Did Ibn Ezra foresee a theory of the composite authorship of the Pentateuch? Half a millennium later Spinoza referred to Ibn Ezra's marginalia in his *Tractatus Theologico-Politicus*, where he laid the groundwork for the modern documentary hypothesis that the Torah is a much-edited book. In all probability neither Gikatilla nor Ibn Ezra doubted the fact or the substance of the revelation at Sinai. They asked a few questions of detail, but accepted Sinai as a historical event and frequently insisted that the Torah had been given publicly, had been passed on faithfully, and was to be observed scrupulously. Ibn Ezra was inquisitive for a medieval man, but he remained a medieval man.

Gikatilla's and Ibn Ezra's commentaries are Spanish and Arabic in yet another respect. They assume the peculiar rationalism or intellectualism of that world as formulated by their circle of Jewish neo-Platonists. Assumptions about the active intelligence, emanations, form and matter, and immortality as the reunification of the rational soul with the world soul underlie their commentary, as if these men found such philosophic assumptions so natural as to seem inevitable. The highest good is the knowledge of God and His work.

Two other members of this school of rationalist grammarians need to be mentioned: Judah ben Samuel ibn Balam (late 11th. cent.) and David Kimḥi (1160–1235). Their textual work followed familiar forms, but their comments are novel in that they include elements of an anti-Christian polemic. Judah wrote his commentaries on the prophets with a particular eye to refuting Christian claims that various prophecies had been fulfilled in Jesus. As Judah proved, biblical language and history made it clear that the prophetic messages dealt with specific events in their day, were meant for a particular audience, and in some cases were clearly *post eventum*, poetic descriptions of occurrences which had already taken place. Twelfth-century Spanish Jews still spoke Arabic, and their thought was conditioned by that of the Muslim world, but the reconquest had moved south and Christianity impinged on their lives and that of their coreligionists with increasing force. Sections of Kimḥi's popular line-by-line commentary frequently begin: "The Christians thus interpret this psalm; but you must object. . . ."

Nineteenth-century Jewish historians, in particular, waxed rhapsodic over the openness and unabashed cultivation of this world, apparently so different from the parochial existence from which they had just emerged. They saw the Spanish-Jewish world as full-bodied rather than cramped; as receptive to, rather than suspicious of, rational investigation. They asked their readers to look at Maimonides, the consummate medieval champion of rationalism—physician, logician, mathematician, philosopher, and rabbi; at the poets who sang openly of wine and of the physical charms of women, free of any puritanism or prudery; at Samuel ha-Nagid, Talmudic authority and Granada's Minister of State, patron of all the arts, and patriotic poet glorifying his army's exploits; and to find in these men the necessary models for a many-sided modern and confident Jewish spirit. Spanish-Jewish history provided the paradigm of the full, many-faceted, pious but never parochial life for which these historians, émigrés from Europe's ghettos, longed. In their need they exaggerated its openness and modernity and built moorish-style synagogues in which to worship as modern hidalgos.

Some Spanish Jews did sing unabashedly of the delights of the table and bed, and the best of them did so with fresh feeling rather than with the tired, conventional phrases of oriental wedding songs. Such a man was Moses ibn Ezra of Granada (1070–1139), a happy son of privilege whose young eyes never wearied of a lithe form or a sparkling eye: "Beautiful is the loved one/As she sways in the dance/Like a bough of the myrtle/Her unbound tresses/Billowing about her." [15] These lines make no pretense at being symbolic or allegorical.

The loved one is a real person; in other poems we hear more of her dark hair, flashing eyes, and full breasts, and we discover that, denied her charms, the poet took to the open road, an unhappy, frustrated swain who still had eyes to see the beauties of nature:

> I went out into the garden in the morning dusk
> when sorrow enveloped me like a cloud
> and the breeze brought to my nostril the odor of spices
> as a balm of healing for the sick soul
> Then a sudden dawn flamed in the sky, like lightning
> and its thunder surged like the cry of a woman that gives birth. [16]

Moses' sensitive essay on poetic forms, *Kitab al-Muhadarah wal-Mudhakarah* (*The Songs of Israel*), reveals him as well-read in the classic works on aesthetics, especially Plato and Aristotle, and as insistent as any modern critic on integrity of feeling and form. But Moses is not a lake poet or an *homme naturel*. He is a child of a religiously inhibited age which cannot for long free itself of the conviction that feeling and passion are enticing, but dangerous, emotions. Even as they sang of wine and love the poets were dark with guilt, constantly admonishing themselves "to turn aside from the five senses" (Ha Levi) to "sell the preciousness of today and buy the goodness of tomorrow" (Harizi). Moses ibn Ezra himself came to repent his early passion and joy of life, "In sin and folly I passed my youth/I am ashamed; and my life arrears/now strive to pay." [17]

Youth, high blood, passion, and lust for adventure entered this world, but never without being shadowed by guilt. Revivalist preachers commanded large audiences for whom they rang all the doomsday bells.

Unto you, O men, I call. Remember the awesome God. Awake, you whose mind is asleep and put away your wine, you who are smitten with error, who sell life eternal for the life of the moment. Know that this is not the resting-place. Therefore, prepare for the day of departure. Depart, descend from the hill. Arise, go forth into the valley, the dwelling place of your fathers and the land of your sojournings, and prepare provision for departure for the destined cities. Do you know that you are strangers and sojourners in the land which devours her inhabitants and hates those that love her, and puts far off those kin to her? Bitter is her taste and her wells slime pits, and a cup of foaming wine is in her hand. From terror of it, all flesh shudders and every heart burns. They call her "World" but she is as her name—"Pollution." Her beginning is mourning and her end is pang and throe. She lures you with her ornaments. She seduces you with her beauty. Her pains she barters with you for her finery. She appears as a bride that adorns herself with her jewels.

Her crown is destruction, treachery is her robe, stumblings are her skirt, and the entanglements of vicissitudes are her cord. The chambers of Sheol are her palaces and the blood of her virginity is the blood of the innocent slain. Every day she divorces her husband and slays all who come unto her. Her dawns are darkness and her luminaries are extinguished. Her men of understanding are confused and her kings are humiliated. Her merrymakers weep. Her gardens are tangled thorns and her wines are mingled with wormwood. She dethrones her kings and destroys her princes—a swift dromedary entangling her ways. Her goodness is rooted out and her sickness is incurable. Her hope betrays. Her cup intoxicates and her reproach remains from generation to generation.

Awake, you drunkards: and wail, you mighty ones. What have you to do with the love of this accursed world? Why do you suck barren breasts? You seize her but she flees from you. You approach her but she repulses you. Know you not that her foundation and secret is upon nothingness. Her havoc and disaster forestall you. Her flames and calamities scorch your hearts. Her festivals and lovers deal falsely with you. Wormwood and ruin you suck from the milk of her breasts.

Treachery is her cloak and rebellion is her veil. She is snares and her heart nets and her hands bands. She is a luxuriant tree whose precious fruit is death. And if you seek to know the foundation from whence you were hewn, my brothers, where you do come from, lo! You were formed from nothingness, and from naught you were begotten. Though you beget children and children's children and grow old, death will devour what you have begotten and your own carcasses!

Therefore, awake. Bestir yourselves. Cleanse and purify yourselves. Pray and perhaps your entreaty will be granted. Then on the day of the wrath of the Lord's anger, you may be concealed. From those ancients who have passed away before you, you may be instructed.[18]

Youth and zest may temporarily free a soul of such conditioning, but it catches up as age and bruising disabuse a man. Conventional wisdom insisted that worldliness is a snare, passion folly, worldly ambition vain; that passion and desires keep the soul entangled in the body, heavy, lifeless; and that wisdom taught men to see the pretense on which most lives were based. The learned shared these assumptions with the simple. The simple prayed simply for strength, while the learned developed intellectualist theories about the redemptive power of knowledge, of an acquired awareness which could free the soul of its passion for worldliness. Moses ibn Ezra knew that he was mistaken to desire life: "Blind are they, bemused with worldly pride, who think to flourish on earth always." [19] Knowledge alone could remove that blindfold. "My desire is to fill my bowl/At the gate of instruction/and to dwell with the wise . . . in them is the delight of my eyes and heart." [20] Men acknowledged passion and craved rescue from its turbulence.

❧

Wisdom was a universally praised attainment. Muslim and Jewish leaders were empowered by their learning. Grandees and merchants coveted the status of being known as learned. Every city had its schools, most had academies, and many had fine libraries. Enlightened rulers were patrons of learning. Wisdom is automatically praised, but wisdom here had its medieval meaning, knowledge of God and His teaching, rather than the modern meaning of knowledge acquired through empirical research. Knowledge was a many-branched attainment. Knowledge meant competence in the written and oral law, and a reputation as one learned in Torah was both religiously meritorious and a coveted mark of honor. Knowledge meant an understanding of the reality of being as taught by Greek science and metaphysics, and of what lies beyond the semblance of things. Knowledge is awareness and movement toward God. Knowledge was recollection of the divine truths which the soul forgot at birth, and awareness of the divine truths which God had offered when he gave man the Torah—His word. Whatever its content, knowledge, or rather the gaining of knowledge, was the most prized attainment. Knowledge opened men's eyes to the distinction between the vain and the substantive. Knowledge freed man from confusion, hence it enabled him to rise above his passion, be worthy, and merit reward.

A special anthropology helped establish knowledge as the key to salvation in this world and the next:

The definition of man, which conveys his essence, is the "rational animal." "Animal" in this definition refers to the body which grows, develops and eventually perishes. "Rational" refers to the power to reason logically, to differentiate between good and evil and to recognize wisdom and reason. It is wisdom and reason which distinguish man from the animals and this is conveyed by the word "rational," the rest of the definition being common to animals.[21]

The soul is the locus of man's power to reason, and hence of man's distinction. The soul is not part of man's inherited physical equipment, but a gift of God's grace. That part of the soul which makes man unique, its rational element, is made of the divine stuff itself. "Oh soul, do not be like a dumb horse or mule without understanding/or as a drunk or a fool/for you were made of the stuff of understanding/and taken from a holy place/from a heavenly city/from God/from the heavens." [22]

Generally, following Plato's doctrine of recollection, men see knowledge as a process of activating what is latent in the soul/mind; that is why we can think at all about the divine. Recollection, study, and meditation bring knowledge from a dormant to an active state and permit the soul to unfold, redeem itself, become clear, gain control over the body, and provide man a foretaste of the bliss that awaits. The first evidence of enlightenment is a growing contempt for physical pleasures and material possessions; its ripe fruit is a wisdom which knows life for what it is and sees that the only true joy lies in escaping the trammels of existence and finding oneself with God. A soul enlightened by wisdom can control all of a man's actions. There are, to be sure, instincts and simple physical needs. These were explained by the long-familiar, originally Greek, four-part division of the soul into vegetable, animal, sensible, and rational components, but it was man's distinction that when his soul was activated it could and did govern his actions. And since the soul activates itself through "knowing," the emphasis of ethical discussion, even in some halachic statements, was first on knowing, then on doing. What you "knew" determined what you "did." No one found it unusual when law codes, Muslim and Jewish alike, were prefaced, like Maimonides' *Mishneh Torah*, by a "Book of Knowledge" (*Sefer ha-Madda*) which outlined the substance of what the soul of man should know. Presumably, only the man who understood these first principles could obey the law with unremitting energy. He knew why, and so he knew how.

Since their salvation road was intellectual, a way of knowing, many of these men come across as intellectual snobs, always talking about us, "the choice," and them, "the mass." The ordinary religious way of piety, laws, and rituals is adequate for ordinary folk but for us only a beginning. Above law is learning, an academic discipline whose virtue, at least in part, would seem to be that it could be undertaken only by the small inner circle with higher intelligence. Writers deliberately cultivated an enigmatic style, claiming it would not do to mislead the ordinary man, while the wise would understand their coded allusions. There were the clear-eyed and the blind, the select and the simple.

We use knowledge to describe information and its use. Intellectualist philosophers used knowledge to describe awareness of a premise which assumed that the ultimate stuff of the universe was not a physical property, but intellectual energy. God's active intelligence rather than atomic structure or magnetic force was believed to compose the basic substructure of all that is. Intellect was the first of God's creations. In decreasing concentrations, intellect permeates all creation—the heavens, the earth, man. In man this intellectual-divine element is the soul, or at least is in the soul. Insofar as man awakens the latent knowledge contained in the rational soul, he can see truly and therefore can govern his actions wisely. What we call today unconscious motivation these men called folly.

The knowledge of which these men spoke was not a precipitate of research or common sense, but awareness of the nature of God; it was apprehension through logical inference of the nature of creator and creation. Some "knew" through study of the tradition, others "knew" through philosophy and logical analysis, but always their knowledge has a special context. To know God's majesty and His creative plan was to see behind the world of semblance, to instruct the soul so that it was no longer confused by illusion and could act wisely and well. "Notice the hidden way of the soul/analyze it, and be refreshed thereby/He will make you wise and you will find freedom/for you are a captive/and the world is a prison." [23]

Life is a masquerade; behind the mask is ugliness, under the bouquet a scorpion: Life is a dream and death is the reality. To remind themselves of this, rich men placed death grottoes in their palaces. The duty of wisdom is to strip life bare and reveal its nakedness. If death is the beginning of philosophy, what is its end? To know God's being and power and unity—that is, to see and rejoice in the supernal light which alone truly lightens the darkness. Again and again these poets sing God's praises because God has not left man to stumble in blindness, but in His mercy provided wisdom and the capacity to know.

[373]

The philosopher Solomon ibn Gabirol described in clear, calm terms in *The Fountain of Life* the theory of wisdom and the way to wisdom. His poetry reveals how emotionally strenuous that ascent really was. The youth is already at war with the warming sun, his hot blood and the dragons of materialism, sensuality, hypocrisy, insensitivity, all that is not pure and good. In the way of an adolescent he is self-consciously wise beyond his years: "Sixteen though I am, Yet my wisdom excels/The wisdom of one of fourscore years." "My soul opened wide for me the doors of sorrow/and firmly closed behind me the gates of youth." "Life has, like a snake, bitten my heels." [24] Friends advised him to enjoy life and cautioned him not to weary himself seeking what cannot be found. He answered with the hauteur and arrogance of sixteen, "No, my friend. . . . How I would despise myself if I were to forget wisdom and, like an insignificant worm, crawl after earthly desires and slavishly enjoy life." The routines of life, society, business, and politics were vulgar distractions. "Do not think my friend that we purchase wisdom for small change in the noisy regions of life." [25] Wisdom is not making out or high professional skill or taking life in stride, but knowledge of the higher things: God, truth, the nature of the universe. Such wisdom enlightens, but, like the sun, its light is too bright to be looked at directly. In his intensity Ibn Gabirol suffered what Erik Erikson would probably identify as an adolescent identity crisis. He gives himself over to morbidity and expresses excessive disgust at life.

> We children of earth all tremble in this accursed net
> We all carry the sinner's stamp on our brow
> We all reflect its terrible image. [26]

Ibn Gabirol perseveres. Though black with despair, he still wishes to gain the light of wisdom. He takes his bitterness out in iron song, sharp, cold, satiric denunciation of those who seem careless or carefree, pompous windbags, spendthrift wastrels, pious frauds. Even while his body wandered in the depths, his soul began to gain strength, even to soar. The imagery becomes one of depths and heights, of bondage and freedom, of shadowed valleys and high peaks, of descent and flight.

Ibn Gabirol's anthropology is heavy with images of the body's weakness and baseness. What is man but "a carcass fouled and trodden, a noxious creature brimming with deceit . . . he rolls in mud

[374]

and lies, insanely fouls the clean and spoils the fine, proud, defiant, a trickster, vile, abhorred." [27] Fortunately, man is more than physical. He possesses a soul which strives toward the height. "Call you she [the soul] must, she cannot be still." "Strive further upward, my spirit, toward the light." [28] What is light? A falling away of the accidental, the mundane, the corporeal, the recognition that light/God is reality, truth, inspiration, and understanding. The contrast here is between darkness/light; blindness/sight; ignorance/understanding; the soul, inert and blind/the soul, alive and clearly seeing. The drive is away from tension and opposition to the peace of being all of a piece, enlightened, no longer confused; obedient to God's will, no longer unpredictable; controlled, no longer tortured by appetite and passion. Peace enters his troubled soul. He finds God the supreme light, the God whose unity resolves all the apparent conflicts of life. Ibn Gabirol's poetry picks up many of the images of ascent to the heavenly palace and of God's throne, which were the staples of the *heichalot midrashim*. God is the source of life, unapproachable behind the veil. The divine will is the presence of light in that heavenly place, the first emanation through which the stream of being comes from the seeming void. Through knowledge of God a man releases his soul from leaden earthly preoccupation, so that it begins to ascend higher and higher toward the heavenly court, where the soul will find the pleasure of God's nearness and enjoy a foretaste of immortality.

Turbulent souls such as Ibn Gabirol's, surfeited by the glamour of the world, find the clarity and quiet they seek in the harmony of the spheres. Man's life is cluttered; God's world is spare and orderly, every movement measured. In God's world there is no noise, only repose.

Ibn Gabirol's restlessness subsided as his soul contemplated the divine order, nature's harmonies. Perhaps it was inevitable that his popular book of moral instruction, *Tikkun Middot ha-Nefesh (The Improvement of the Moral Qualities)*, should suggest that man's emotional life can be as harmonious and balanced as nature. God's cosmos is his model, the macrocosm. Man is the microcosm; with judgment he can arrange his drives and passions as harmoniously as God has ordered the heavens. Like the universe, man consists of four natures or humors corresponding to the four elements of air, water, earth, and fire. The test is to use one's senses wisely so as to balance these humors appropriately in each area of one's life. The poet turns out to be a mechanic who measures out proportions exactly and who has reduced "nothing in excess" to precise formulas. Men who trembled at the thought of God's judgment are not likely to be carefree children who delight in being impulsive. "Set the Most High before you/know that every thought/and every secret impulse/is known to Him. Tremble before the day of trial/before the existential moment/during which there is no help or support for any man." [29]

The eleventh and twelfth centuries were creative years, but obviously not free and untrammeled. This world is characterized not so much by the open expression of emotion and ideas as by spiritual tension. The Jew was torn between love of the newfound luxuries of a comparatively abundant urban and urbane life in which indulgence, sensitivity, and a taste for art and beauty were cultivated, and an ominous, pervasive fear of sudden political reversal and the Judgment Day when each man must render account to God for his folly and indiscretion, for worldliness and ambition:

> Deaf are they that from instruction turn—
> Watchmen who cannot see and will not learn;
> Who deem ye bide in safety, while ye haste
> down the pitward path. Ye have ears, indeed,
> But hear not; neither will you heed.
> Go! leave the thronged heights
> of sensuous delights,
> And meditate within the lonely waste! [30]

Again and again, in the midst of temporary good fortune, men reminded themselves that the only lasting joys are spiritual and otherworldly. Those who sang of wine and love, even the new breed of wandering poets, progenitors of Europe's troubadours and minnesingers, turn out to have had rabbinic educations, to have sung only at the feasts and weddings of Jewish patrons, and to have longed for the end of the weary and bloody exile. The *aljamans* were organized according to Talmudic law, which was faithfully and rigidly enforced. Theirs was a separate and distinct Jewish world and a turbulent, insecure place.

There are moments pleasant to the senses. They are tempting and beguiling, but evanescent. The wise man follows the light of reason, a sharp, clear, unflattering light which exposes all the wrinkles of anxiety and age, describes this life realistically as short, bruising, and a trial, and points the way to the only true joy—knowledge of God and obedience to His law. Knowledge is desired for the perspective in which it places everyday appetites and attitudes. *Mivḥar ha-Peninim*, an eleventh-century book of proverbs compiled by the poet-philosopher Solomon ibn Gabirol, suggests how such "knowledge" was parceled out to the average man.

Men search the world only for wealth and ease and honor; but one who searches the world [for these things] cannot attain them, whereas he who separates from it will derive glory through abandoning the quest of anything from men. He is likewise rich through rejoicing in his portion, restful in his body by banishing this world from his heart, and he reaches his goal without trouble or labor.

Seek for that which is necessary and abandon what is unnecessary; for by abandoning the unnecessary, thou mayest secure what is necessary.

Who loves life, let him be lowly.

Who does not accept the decrees of the Creator, his heart is grieved over the world; and he who imagines that the only good that the Creator can grant him is food and raiment is brutish. Who looks upon another's possessions prolongs his grief, and it is impossible to provide a cure for his vexation.

What advantage the poor man has over the rich! For thou never findest anybody rebel against the Creator for the purpose of being reduced to poverty, but only to enrich himself.

Whose soul is precious in his estimation, the world is small in his estimation.[31]

Among a number of mystically oriented circles, particularly in northern Spain, ascetic considerations played a significant role. The rabbinic outlook, which assumed the naturalness of marriage and of feeling and saw life as the gift of a kind God, began to give way before a deliberate denigration of feeling, the senses, and even life itself; some considered life inherently inadequate, if not evil, and the cause of human suffering and confusion. A twelfth-century philosopher who lived most of his life in Christian Barcelona and was a transitional figure between the Islamic-Jewish culture and the European world, Abraham bar Ḥiyya, advocated in effect what some twentieth-century preachers would call a "dying unto life."

So you will see that he who despises the world and removes himself from its preoccupations draws closer to the ways of God and deserves a good life.

As one of them said, "If you change life to love of life you will acquire life" or, in other words, despise the world for the glory of the Lord of the world and you will rule the world. You see from here that a man can acquire the world for very little and it is easy to do and involves no effort; it is a question of suppressing your desires so that you should hate the vain pleasures of this world, which cause exertion and sorrow. In this way you will free yourself from the burden of this world, and go out from Exile and attain salvation and the Kingdom of God. He who considers the good and desirable things of this world will find many corresponding loathsome evils. He will not enjoy the good, except for the object of removing the evil. He will eat and drink only to remove hunger and thirst, and if out of greed he partakes of more than is essential, he brings evil and sickness to his body. That is why the individuals separated unto God eat whatever is to hand, not for the sake of its taste, but to prevent hunger, and they wear clothes so as not to be harmed by the cold, and it makes no difference whether they are of wool or linen; and those who follow their path, will attain their superiority.[32]

Bar Ḥiyya went further than most, but denial was in the air. The various circles of Spanish-Jewish mystics did not actually mortify the flesh, but they came as close to the practice of rigorous asceticism as any group of Jews since the desert conventicles of the Essenes.

Inevitably men began to write devotional guidebooks, detailing the upward path of the soul seeking communion with God. Perhaps the most popular was written around 1180 by a poet-pietist of Saragossa, Baḥya ben Joseph ibn Pakuda. *Kitab al Hidayah ila Faraidi al-Kulub* was quickly translated, both in full and in abridgment, into Hebrew as *Ḥovot ha-Levavot* (*The Duties of the Heart*). Baḥya divided man's duties into those which are active and outer directed, the duties of the limbs, and those which are introspective and involve the clarification of the mind, the duties of the heart. The "you shall" and "you shall not" imperatives of the law are duties of the limbs. Belief in God, our attitudes toward divine providence and judgment, and the beliefs which motivate our actions involve duties of the heart. Since there were halachic manuals dealing with all the active commandments, Baḥya set out to write a manual for the duties of the heart.

Baḥya's book might be called "The Development of the Soul's Potential." The soul is of divine origin, but the trauma of being put into a body shocks it into forgetfulness. Through reason which refines the impression of the senses, the soul's knowledge of heaven and God is revived. Baḥya likens the process to a man of science who found a hunk of blackened and rusted metal of no apparent value buried in the yard of a friend. The scientist took salt and vinegar and cleaned a spot or two, revealing the metal's luster; it turned out to be silver, so he told his friend to go and clean the rest. In the same way knowledge, Torah, cleans a few places, but then each man must use his effort and mind to clean the rest and reveal its true value and luster.

Reason allows us to see behind nature to its marvelous structure, to marvel at God's wisdom as evidenced by every created thing and the majestic, harmonious whole which is the cosmos. Reason here leads to a knowledge of God and gratitude for His blessings. Knowledge and gratitude lead to trust, and the more a man trusts in God, the more he will turn away from worldly preoccupations and be able to serve God. As reason recollects the orderliness of God's cosmos, the soul becomes orderly and tranquil. Man accepts his circumstances as they are, for they are of God. Baḥya delighted in homely parables. A pietist in a preliminary stage of his training traveled on business to another country, where a heathen priest asked him, "Whom do you serve?" "I serve the One, omnipotent God who cares for all His creatures." "Why, then, have you taken this long and dangerous journey. If God provides will He not provide for you in one place as well as another?" The budding pietist returned home.

Trust leads to the joy of service. Wherever he is, whatever God has decreed as his lot and station, the man of trust accepts his appointed place and seeks to serve God in all the ways open to him. Reason leads him to accept a morality which transcends the common sense rules of prudence. He begins to scorn this world and all its works, escaping in his soul and body to God, recognizing the shoddiness of this world compared to the beauties of the World to Come. As he concentrates his reason, now trained through study, humility, trust, honest repentance, constant self-examination, denial, and love of God, he reaches communion when "he will see without eyes, hear without ears . . . become insensible to his own needs, merging his preferences with those of His creator, binding his own will to that of His master, and his love to divine love . . . of him the sage said . . . 'For he who found Me found life' (Prov. 8:35)." [33]

Enlightenment of the soul is the means by which the soul casts off worldliness and begins its ascent. Righteous living, abstinence (*perishut*), and sincere worship must precede the soul's enlightenment. As it gains in knowledge the soul becomes active, powerful; when it has become fully enlightened it rules the body. Only an active concern with the duties of the heart can inspire the soul so that man's obedience is full rather than partial, wholehearted rather than distracted. Despite his concentration on the duties of the heart rather than the *mitzvot*, Baḥya did not doubt for a moment that Torah and philosophy dealt with a single truth. Even as he used various elements of neo-Platonism in describing the steps to *devekut*, Baḥya prayed to God to guide him in the paths of His adoration and quoted Psalm 15:11, "You make me to know the path of life; in your presence is fullness of joy, in your right hand bliss for evermore." Baḥya found *the* way not in Plotinus' *Theology* or the *Enneads*, but in the Torah. He did not cite texts as afterthoughts, as proof-texts, but as the natural complement, the obvious source of his religious understanding. Had not God said, "Those who love Me I love, those who search for Me find Me" (Prov. 8:17)?

This world is essentially a place of testing. Baḥya strikes again the ascetic note. In Gate 9 of his work he describes a necessary regimen of abstinence. His is an austere spirit, insisting that man must rise above passion and appetite, be detached from ambition, lust, the captivating emotions, so that his soul can find the peace and quiet in which to discover and recollect God. Man must rigorously examine his conscience to see that his soul has "only God as its goal and not pride of physical health, leisure, honors, glory, riches or the possession of the evanescent human splendor." [34] Baḥya sets a high value on denial and discipline, but he does not deem the body contemptible. It is, after all, God's creation. Nor does Baḥya preach celibacy or immurement, for God's law specifically proscribes such extreme forms of denial. His ideal man wants for nothing but the nearness of God as he lives out his appointed role within the social order. "We must never go beyond the limits set by the law so that we mortify ourselves during the Sabbath and the holidays or become celibate and fail to fulfill God's law 'be fruitful and multiply.' " [35] Spain was a land of sharp contrast, of riches and poverty, of the green and the blasted, of hospitality and violence. Its soul was aware of and never fully resolved the tensions between passion and piety, nature and reason. This tension can be put in another, particularly Jewish, way. Spain is home, but also the farthest reaches of *galut;* beyond there is the ocean and the end of the earth. The Jew is in Spain, but not of Spain, as he is in the world but not of the world. His true home is far to the east, beyond the sea.

Men of reason shared a high valuation of austerity and a basic suspicion of emotion and of worldly pleasures, but not all shared the intellectualist assumptions which led so many intellectuals to teach that it was primarily through knowledge that men attained salvation. Judah ha Levi (ca. 1085–1140) stands apart in that at the age of fifty, after having accepted these assumptions for almost a lifetime, he set them aside and began to question the premises with which this world operated. He did so not as an outsider, but as a central figure in a small, brilliant Cordovan circle where intellectualism and rationalism were the accepted world view, and whose members included Abraham and Moses ibn Ezra, Joseph ibn Zaddik, Isaac ben Judah ibn Ghayyat, and Joseph ibn Migash, the leading Jewish intellectuals of that time and place.

Ha Levi was an erudite physician-poet-philosopher as well as a highly trained Talmudist, having been a student of the finest rabbinic scholar of his day, Isaac Alfasi. Ha Levi did not make a virtue of ignorance, nor did he glorify contrived simplicity or mindless passion, nor was he a fundamentalist who saw all speculation as a threat. Indeed, it was his intellectual training and critical spirit which allowed him to expose philosophy's claim to provide a saving truth. He saw the intellectuals' blind spot, the fact of their continuing disagreements. Despite all their grandiose talk about philosophy leading the soul to truth, philosophers disagreed with each other on almost every point, and agreed only in heaping contempt on those who did not subscribe to their particular system. "Ask the philosophers and you will find they do not agree on one action or one principle." [36] Ha Levi argued that a confused science cannot lead men to certain truth. Why were there these fundamental divisions? Because philosophic conclusions are not experimentally verifiable. "They rely on theories." [37] Philosophy is brilliant, but not conclusive. Philosophy momentarily satisfies the mind, but the soul needs a more substantial diet.

Ha Levi did not attack conventional assumptions about the underlying identity of reason and revelation, but he insisted that reason and revelation relate to different levels of reality. Reason can provide useful data in the practical sciences, but falters as a metaphysical tool. The various philosophic schools claim to prove the existence of a creator from the nature of creation, yet they differ over which proofs are valid. Moreover, by philosophy's own admission, some metaphysical problems cannot be solved by logic, particularly the question of whether the world was created *de novo*, in time, or out of some preexistent matter. Certainty eludes philosophy; thus the assumption that philosophy provides the saving truth is sheer arrogance. Had it not been for Sinai and prophecy, men would still not know with certainty any truth about God, God's nature, God's commandments for man, and the future hope.

Ha Levi applied the test of experience to the whole medieval intellectual edifice and found it unstable. The men of reason dealt with theory, he dealt in history; they dealt in logical demonstration, he dealt in human experience. Sinai represents not only the giving of words/truth but an overwhelming experience in which a whole people were awed and humbled by the will of God become manifest. Sinai was a national experience which compelled and compels submission and obedience. Reason concentrated on God's transcendence; Ha Levi glorified God's immanence. Truth begins in the manifest evidence of God's special care—the public revelation at Sinai, the recorded experience of the prophets who felt the inrush of God's words, and the continuing experience of those who have felt His presence and communed with His will. Reason rests on insecure logic; revelation rests on incontrovertible evidence.

For Ha Levi it is religious experience rather than religious knowledge that compels obedience to God's word and an unceasing love of His being. The men of reason emphasized the transformation of personality which occurs as man activates his intellect and doubt gives way to certainty. Ha Levi emphasized the changes of spirit and will, hence of character, which occur when man assents to the manifest evidence of God's power—when he responds to a religious experience. The poet-philosopher found no evidence that philosophy changes men; at best it commands intellectual assent, a moment's pleasure in a well-argued proposition. Acceptance of a theological proposition fully proven rarely affects the intensity of one's love of God or the humility with which one seeks to obey His will. Despite their pretensions, philosophers were not known for their saintliness. Philosophers had waxed poetic about the rational mind which alone, of all man's parts, participates in God's nature and which could, when trained, enter into communion with God. Ha Levi rejected on historical grounds the theory that one communed with God by learning philosophy. The prophets had not been philosophers. Amos was not a scholar, but a dresser of sycamore trees. God's words came to the simple and pious as well as to the learned. The argument that men can deliberately prepare for and assure themselves of intellectual communion is rejected as unverified. God draws near to whom He will.

Judaism is not a series of ideas about God, but a way of life organized around a nation's experience with God. It is Sinai, prophecy, and the personal response of every Jew to God's recurring self-revelation. In Ha Levi's chef-d'oeuvre he does not seek to prove God's existence, but offers instead historical evidence of God's actions. Ha Levi's God is the "God who . . . led the Israelites out of Egypt with signs and miracles," [38] who guides and directs the universe, enters into special relationships with man and men, especially with Israel, who receives prayers, judges deeds, and confirms men's hopes—the God of Abraham.

I believe in the God of Abraham, Isaac and Israel, who led the children of Israel out of Egypt with songs and miracles; who fed them in the desert and gave them the land, after having made them traverse the sea and the Jordan in a miraculous way; who sent Moses with His law, and subsequently thousands of prophets, who confirmed His law by promises to the observant, and threats to the disobedient. Our belief is comprised in the Torah—a very large domain. [39]

Ha Levi's God is the God of Abraham, not the God of Aristotle who sustains all by His being, the creator God whose activity is limited to His informing of the universe, of whom men know only that He is. Ha Levi elaborated this existential approach in an original and defiant dialogue, *Kitab al-Hujjah wal Dalil fi Nusr al-din al-Dhalil* (*The Book of Argument and Proof in Defense of the Despised Faith*), familiarly known by his fellow Jews as *The Kuzari* after the dialogue's protagonist, the king of the Khazars.

By the twelfth century legend had richly embellished the conversion to Judaism of the Khazars. According to a popular version of this event, the Khazar headman decided to choose a religion for himself and his people, summoned various religious leaders, examined their assertions, and declared that the rabbi had won the day. *The Kuzari* tells the story this way: An angel appears to the king and admonishes him: "Your intention [thought] is pleasing, but your way of acting is not pleasing." Already Ha Levi suggests his conclusion, for, by accepted intellectualist standards, if one's intention (thought) is pleasing to God, it necessarily follows that one's actions must be. Apparently there is a right way which good will, common sense, and reason cannot clarify for man. Seeking that right way, the pagan king summons a scholastic philosopher, a Christian, and a Muslim to present their respective claims. Each is a stick figure and quickly disposed of. The philosopher offers intellectual enlightenment. The king already knows this way to be inadequate. "I know that my soul is pure," yet "I am told my acts are not acceptable." The Christian claims a marvelous gospel whose very uniqueness is its mandate, but "here is no logical conclusion." The Muslim claims a wondrous teaching, but one in which others have no share; such narrowness troubles the king. He had not thought to summon a Jew, but since both Christian and Muslim had referred to the Bible as validating their scripture, a rabbi is called.

The king seeks a religious discipline which is directly and immediately pleasing to God. The rabbi offers him the biblical way and proves its authenticity by the undisputed fact of Sinai. Alone among the revelations affirmed by the world's faiths, Sinai is admitted by all. It occurred publicly, openly; no one can doubt that here is God's word.

It is a gladsome service of joyous obedience the rabbi prescribes to the king, not bovine submission or dour denial. Ha Levi has little patience with the ascetic emphasis of the neo-Platonic intellectualist circles. "The Torah imposes no asceticism on us, but desires that we should keep a middle way and allow every mental and physical faculty its due." [40] The flesh does not impede enlightenment; indeed, it is only with his body that a man can obey the *mitzvot*. Ha Levi emphasized Deuteronomy 26:11—"You shall rejoice in every good thing"—as evidence that God wishes man to find pleasure in all that sustains. Almost alone among the poets, Ha Levi's love songs and joyous evocations of nature remained uncomplicated by guilt.

Spiritual peace comes through trust, love of God, and joyous obedience, not, as the philosophers keep insisting, through classroom studies and austere regimens. "O God, Thy name! I will exalt Thee. And Thy righteousness I will not conceal. I have given ear and I have trusted; I will not question. I will not prove: For how should a vessel of clay say unto its moulder, What doest Thou?" [41] One does not need to understand Aristotle to know God. The prophets had been closest of all men to God, and none was philosopher or metaphysician. The capacity for experiencing God requires as a prerequisite spiritual sensitivity rather than academic training. "Happy is the man who is quick to perceive the strength of His great deeds!" Prophecy, the ultimate in religious intimacy, is God's free gift to man. It comes when and where God wills. One cannot train to be a prophet. [42]

Ha Levi goes on to suggest the distinction between God talk and life with God, between verbal constructs about God and the reality of belief.

Al-Khazari: Now I understand the difference between *Elohim* and *Adonai*, and I see how far the God of Abraham is different from that of Aristotle. Man yearns for *Adonai* as a matter of love, taste and conviction; while attachment to *Elohim* is the result of speculation. A feeling of the former kind invites its votaries to give their life for His sake, and to prefer death to His absence. Speculation, however, makes veneration only a necessity as long as it entails no harm, but bears no pain for its sake.[43]

God is alive. The meeting with God is specific, real, and overpowering. God talk leads only to academic religious interests.

Ha Levi does not defend religion, but he zealously defends Judaism, sometimes so vigorously that the reader is tempted to discount him as an unconscionable chauvinist. Only Judaism's revelation is authentic. Jews possess a special religious faculty. True prophets arose only among the Jews, and only in the Holy Land. Judaism is the only authentic bearer of revelation's truth and prescribes the only regimen truly satisfying to God. Ha Levi was playing with new ideas, and he did not know how to qualify them, nor did he feel much need to. Much of his assertiveness is a direct riposte to the aggressive polemics being pushed by Arabs, Orthodox and Almohade, and by Christians. *The Kuzari* is part philosophy, part polemic—the first angry Jewish polemic to surface in the West, forerunner of many to follow, evidence of an increasingly unhappy religious confrontation in which the Jew was always of the minority, the victim. But Ha Levi is not simply a child repeating "My faith is better than your faith." He looks at religious life rather than religious ideas, and seeks to explain empirical data as best he can. Sinai is the only revelation acknowledged by all three major faiths. Jews have been extraordinarily precocious in matters religious. That prophecy acknowledged by all three faiths occurred only in the Holy Land. How else to explain these facts except by saying that Jews must be congenitally religious and that the Holy Land's climate must be especially salubrious for religious innovation?

Historians of philosophy say that Ha Levi introduced into Judaism the sophisticated anti-intellectualist attitudes popularized in Islam a generation before by Al-Ghazali, who insisted that philosophy is not a religious enterprise at all and emphasized the religious moment rather than religious ideas. Ha Levi knew of Al-Ghazali, but he knew rabbinic Judaism better. His work can be seen as a reassertion of traditional affirmations of the freedom of God's will, the primacy of God's command, and the immediacy of God's relation to man's life, against a theology which equated God's law with order and stability in nature and subordinated *mitzvah* to metaphysics. Ha Levi attacked intellectual elitism and offered again a way of salvation open to all. His faith was not only personally warm and encouraging, but full of the national hope. As *The Kuzari* ends the rabbi proposes to leave for Jerusalem, where he will add his prayers and tears to those of others who seek to expiate the sins that caused God to drive Israel into exile. May Zion soon be redeemed. Ha Levi genuinely anguished in exile and actually made the long dangerous pilgrimage to the Holy Land, where he died, so pious legend has it, pierced by an Arab lance as he bent to kiss the soil at the foot of the Temple mount. His pilgrimage was a long-remembered symbol of the nation's longing for redemption from the darkening shadow of the age.

❦

Despite *The Kuzari*, reason continued to be the focus of interest of Spanish-Jewish intellectuals who cherished Ha Levi more as poet and martyr than as the philosopher who had exposed the structural fallacy of their cultural world. A few years after the writing of *The Kuzari* Ha Levi's fellow townsman and friend, Joseph ibn Zaddik (d. 1149), wrote a closely reasoned scholastic philosophy, and it was as if *The Kuzari* had never been penned. *Sefer ha-Olam ha-Katan (Microcosm)* baldly reasserted the claims of reason and the identity of reason and revelation. Ibn Zaddik did not even pause to argue with Ha Levi. Reason precedes revelation in time; revelation's purpose was to confirm true reason and to assert the uniqueness of God, a proposition at which reason cannot arrive. The soul is man's essence and distinction, the divine element within man, and being divine, the soul recapitulates in miniature God's nature. The rational soul is a microcosm of the world soul. It is by introspection that man comes to understand creation and creator. Reason is abstract rather than experiential. That which can be grasped by intellect is alone real and good, the wisdom of wisdom. Knowledge which derives from the senses is of limited value and often misleading.

Ibn Zaddik's philosophy follows the well-worn path of Israeli, Ibn Gabirol, and Bahya, but it is somewhat less quietist. He seems to be responding to criticism of philosophy as an end in itself. To know is man's first duty, but one learns in order to do; knowledge leads to actions which are pleasing to God and valid in themselves. Ibn Zaddik drove home this point by a subtle discussion of the question of divine attributes. We know of God only through His actions. Our conclusions about God's power, wisdom, and so on, obviously are only figurative statements dependent on our perception of His acts; thus, we say God is wise because we are awed by the perfection of creation. We base our statement that God is wise on the manifest evidence that such a creator cannot be ignorant. Every negative assertion about God has a positive correlative. Thus Ibn Zaddik resurrected man's ability to posit, at least figuratively, certain attributes of God, and in so doing he gave men a positive model for the familiar obligation of *imitatio dei*, the emulation of God's actions. Reason leads to a knowledge of God which has major ethical implications, and not simply to the possibility of communion with Him.

Microcosm is an incredibly dull and pompous book with an awkward central image. But the book is important because it indicates that Ibn Zaddik worried that philosophy might become a religion of its own, a special way of salvation which was essentially apart from the historic faith enterprise. The literature of the day makes it clear that there were already a few who studied a little science and a little faith and lacked the capacity to hold the twin candles of faith and philosophy steady in their hands. As one reporter observed: "All too often when the light of philosophy is lit the light of faith goes out." [44]

This observer, the historian and thinker Abraham ibn Daud (1110–1180), knew Ha Levi, but composed his philosophy as if Ha Levi had not written. The problem was not reason, but the use of inadequate reasons. Ibn Daud abandoned the neo-Platonic assumptions of his predecessors, although not their intellectualism, and used a more or less Aristotelian logic recently popularized in scholastic Muslim circles by the pioneering works of Avicenna. The soul ceases to be an emanation of the world soul and is described as the form of the body. The soul's rational capacity is activated not by recollection (meditation, concentration, vigils, as well as learning) but by abstraction, demonstrative logic, and concern with the makeup and structure of the universe. The purpose of activating the intellect is to comprehend the suprasensual world, and the very act of knowing is man's blessing and happiness.

Ibn Daud began his scholastic apologia *Kitab al-Akidah al-Rafiyah* (*The Exalted Faith*) by citing rabbinic precedent for studying Greek wisdom. His argument was against those who maintained that such learning sowed doubt, was confusing at best, and was guilty of bringing alien fruit into Jacob's tents. To establish his religious credentials Ibn Daud attacked theologians like Ibn Gabirol, who had dealt with faith as a universal phenomenon, an upward path, a discipline of learning and living presumably available to any man of intelligence, whatever his formal practice. Such defenders do not defend, but bring the entire Torah into question. The upward path must begin in halachic obedience. Judaism is the starting point.

According to Ibn Daud, reason and revelation are one, in Saddiah's sense that they teach identical truths, but revelation provided the Jewish people with life saving truths long before demonstration could have discovered them. Moreover, the Torah includes not only the universal truths about God's unity and justice which men like Ibn Gabirol had emphasized, but also "practical truths," the specific commands necessary for the proper organization of society and disciplining of the soul. The Torah's commandments create an environment which permits the intellect to mature, an environment whose rules and forms reason could not have discovered on her own.

Ibn Daud was a well-trained, observant, and believing rabbinic Jew. A late child of his time, a period of increasing trouble, Ibn Daud saw the entire Jewry of his native Cordova uprooted and scattered to the winds by Almohade fanaticism; he was to die a martyr in Christian Toledo. He took the Torah as literal truth and did not allegorize its specific requirements. His philosophy is sprinkled with biblical and rabbinic citations and sometimes seems more like commentary than logical argument. Ibn Daud sought to comprehend in one system an intellectualist metaphysics based largely on the *Organon* of Aristotle, as understood by Avicenna, and on the rabbinic-biblical pieties which nurtured his soul. As a philosopher he believed that metaphysical demonstrations of God's being and unity should precede specific discussion of the Jewish tradition, and that the supreme goal is knowledge of things divine, the intellectual love of God. As a rabbi he spoke of the ultimate goal as an ethical one—"The goal of philosophy is right action" [45]—forgetting that in Aristotle, whose methodology he claimed to employ, ethics belong to the science of apparent truths. In Ibn Daud one has the sense of a system at war with itself. Following Aristotle, the soul is the form of the body, its entelechy, rather than a separate substance or entity. Not being separate, it is not immortal; rather, immortality accrues to it when and if its latent intellectual capabilities are actualized. Presumedly only the illumined possess immortal souls, yet Ibn Daud also insists that the obedient and the good who are not philosophers gain immortality, and goes to great lengths to prove this thesis. What he proves is the gap between his theological game and his active beliefs. With similar inconsistency, prophecy is described as an ultimate in-

tellectual achievement and as somehow limited to the childen of
Israel and to the land of Israel.

The gap between "the men of speculation" and "the men of faith"
widened as philosophy became a more sophisticated and self-conscious enterprise and men systematically drew out its implications.
Philosophy dealt with the blessed orderliness of the universe. Judaism dealt with creation as a manifestation of God's irrepressible
power and will; God spoke and it was. Philosophy delighted in the
regularity with which forms entered and defined matter; the Bible
spoke of miracles, God's intrusion upon order. Philosophy dealt with
truth as an achievement of the rational soul, while the Bible spoke of
prophecy as the gift of His word. Philosophy speculated whether
God's omniscience extended to particular individuals or only to the
species; the liturgy spoke of God as consciously aware of man's most
private thoughts. Philosophy suggested that immortality was an
achievement of the soul which has activated its full potential for
knowing; the Bible spoke of immortality as a reward for obedience.
Reason tended to restrict God's free and untrammeled activity behind a curtain of words, much as that world shut its women behind
seraglio screens, proclaiming all the while that this was done out of
love, to protect their purity from the gaze and appreciation of the
vulgar.

Despite all these precious intellectual efforts of the elite, faith was
sustained more by simple hope than by the subtlest reason. Ibn
Daud wrote the first systematic and certainly the most famous early
medieval history, *Sefer ha Kabbalah (The Book of Traditions)*, in
which he set out to prove that the biblical-rabbinic tradition had
been preserved faithfully and without change against the various
challenges to its reliability raised by Arab, Christian, and Karaite.
Ibn Daud's history was destined to remain popular and influential,
while his philosophy was not. The sense of continuity under God's
care which provides the leitmotif of his history was a familiar and
welcome comfort to a people crushed between Almohade and Catholic crusaders, living among those nurtured on the teachings of contempt, continuing testimony "to the God who prepares the remedy
before the affliction." [46] Scratch any of these men of reason and you
will find a Jew praying for the Messiah, and probably calculating the
date of his coming.

[389]

CHAPTER

⟨ XX ⟩

The Other Moses

URING the eleventh century the Catholic reconquest of
Spain made steady headway. Alphonso VI of Castile captured Toledo in 1085 and the continuing military pressure of the Catholics on
the disunited Arab cities in the South was more than they could
bear. In desperation they sought help from a rather primitive but
vigorous Berber North African empire, the Murabits. These mountain folk, called by the Spanish Al-Murabitun (Almovarides), crossed
over to the Peninsula, checked the Christian armies, and took for
themselves what was left of Muslim Spain. At first the Jewries were
not severely affected, but Christian pressures proved unremitting,
and, as political frustration mounted, so did Arab religious fanaticism. In the early 1100s there are many reports of forced conversions, special dress codes, forcibly closed synagogues, and expul-
sions. Worse was in store. A second Berber group, known to the
Spanish as Al-Muwahhidun (Almohades) for their fervent and rigid
unitarian doctrines, toppled the Murabits. The Almohades modeled
themselves after the warriors of Mohammed, and out of devotion to
Allah declared that infidels had to convert, depart, or be killed.
They spread terror through North Africa and Spain, as this first
hand account makes clear:

Years of war, evil decrees and persecutions overtook the Jews who were
compelled to wander from their homes, "such as were for death, to death;

[390]

and such as were for the sword to the sword; and such as were for the famine to the famine; and such as were for the captivity, to captivity." To Jeremiah's prophecy (15:2) there was now added "such as were (destined) to leave the faith." This happened in the wake of the sword of ibn Tumart (the *Mahdi* of the Almohades) . . . when he decreed apostasy on the Jews saying: "Come let us cut them off from being a nation; that the name of Israel may be no more in rememberance." Thus, he wiped out every last "name and remnant" of them from all of his empire from the city of Silves at the end of the world (in Portugal) until the city of Al-Mahdiya.[1]

The rebels against the Berber kingdom (of the Almovarides) crossed the sea to Spain after having wiped out every remnant of Jews from Tangiers to Al-Mahdiya. . . . They tried to do the same thing in all of the cities of the Ishmaelite kingdom in Spain. . . . When the Jews had heard the report that the rebels were advancing upon them to drive them away from the Lord, God of Israel, those who feared the Lord's word fled for their lives, and "fathers" almost failed to look back to their children for feebleness of hands. Some were taken captive by the Christians to whom they willingly indentured themselves on condition that they be rescued from Moslem territory. Others fled on foot, naked and barefoot, their feet stumbling upon the mountains of twilight, with "the young children asking bread, and none to break it to them" (Lam. 4:4).[2]

By 1180 the Jewries of Muslim Spain were no more. Some Jews had converted. Most, like Ibn Daud, the author of this chronicle, fled north to Christian lands, where they were tolerated for a time as a useful entrepreneurial and artisan class. In Christian Spain these refugees would enjoy a brief Indian Summer of relative wealth and culture, but the Church Militant was as imperial as the militant Almohades. The Church's aim in respect to the Jews was conversion; failing that, at the very least, complete religious apartheid. The Jew was pictured as a pariah, an outcast, who must be kept apart, damned as a deicide and self-condemned for having denied the saving teaching of the Christ. The Church prohibited Christians from offering hospitality to Jews, hiring themselves as domestics in Jewish homes, appointing a Jew to public office, even from seeking the help of a Jewish physician. There was the Jew badge. Conciliar decrees were not always or even generally enforced and malicious sermons were not always believed, but the image of the perfidious, alien Jew was consistently and deliberately cultivated until it grew into an unquestioned cultural theme. As soon as Spain's economy no longer required the skill of these Jews, their properties were expropriated, and they were exiled (1391, 1492).

These bitter years were dominated by the personality of Moses Maimonides (1135–1204). He was *ha-Rav*, the master, an authentic genius who had command of every aspect of Jewish thought and of most of the science and high culture of his day. His fame was as far-flung as the Jewish world. "Moses was a faithful messenger [of God]. He regulated scrupulously all matters of faith. His pen took the place of [Moses'] staff with which he performed miracles." [3] Those who came after had to take into account what he had said.

Maimonides signed his correspondence *ha-Sepharadi*, the Spaniard. He was a proud son of the *aljamans* of Muslim Spain, a child of its old age. Maimonides was twelve when his family fled his native Cordova which had been captured by the Almohades. In the language of formal modesty which oriental writers formally cultivate, Maimonides told a correspondent about these times:

> Although I studied the ordinances of the Lord, I did not attain to the learning of my forebears, for evil days and hard times overtook us; we did not abide in tranquillity. We labored and had no rest. How could we study the Law when we were being exiled from city to city and from country to country. . . . Only recently have I found a home. [4]

Unlike the Jews who fled north to the Spanish cities their parents and grandparents had known, the family of Maimonides, for reasons still unclear, chose the longer and more dangerous road eastward, a road which led them to Fez in the heart of Almohade country. Persistent rumors would follow the family that they had managed to stay in Fez only by passing as Muslim. It may be so. In any event, their goal was Fustat, old Cairo, capital of Fatamid Egypt. Under this dynasty, which had ruled for two centuries, Jews had known a relative security that had been seriously broken only once by a sharp series of persecutions under the so-called mad caliph Al Hakim (996–1020). But the Fatamids had proven themselves irresolute and ineffective against the Crusaders, and their years of power were numbered. A new dynasty was asserting itself in West Asia and Egypt, the Ayyubids, led by Salah-al-din, famed throughout Europe as Saladin, Richard the Lionheart's noble enemy. Maimonides' family arrived in Egypt at about the time these princes of Turkish extraction came to power. It was a fortunate coincidence, for, although the Ayyubids were fundamental in their faith, they left their Jewries as they had been, and the Ayyub governor chose the brilliant young Spanish-Jewish doctor as his court physician. This appointment as well as his personal attainments established Maimonides as the leading Jew of Egypt.

His Egypt was prosperous and his Jewry relatively secure; but, again, this was an Indian Summer. Saladin made no provision for a successor, and at his death his empire fell apart in fratricidal war. Mercenary troops, Turkish and Circassian, saw their opportunity and seized it. By 1250 the Mamelukes, or slave troops, ruled Syria and Egypt, ruled cruelly and greedily and with utter contempt for all infidels including, of course, Jews. After 1250 Near Eastern Jewry entered a long winter of cultural and spiritual hibernation during which survival demanded every bit of its energy. The Mamelukes ruled in the East. The Mongols poured off the steppes into Persia. Jewish life in late medieval Islam was a world of small, insecure, desperate communities completely set apart, sustained by a fervent messianism, occasionally inspired to moments of ascetic piety and rife with superstition. The intellectual vitality of the ninth and tenth centuries disappears. Men and women cherished amulets, visited the graves of saints, and listened to *ḥachamim*, dedicated teachers who kept the faith and taught the faith as best they could, simply and reassuringly. It was a world for which Maimonides was the heroic ancestor, the noble Jew, the rabbi whose books stood alongside the Torah in the Ark; men agreed that his like would not be seen soon again.

Maimonides' works climax a truly remarkable Jewish cultural achievement and, to a large degree, write finis to that age. His encyclopedic writings—the *Talmud* commentary, the law code, the classic philosophy—would be seen as the summation and repository of the best that this world had offered. Maimonides' work is so monumental that men forcibly had to remind themselves that he was a man, not a cultural monument; that he wrote and taught as a Jew who knew from experience the existential anguish of his people; and that he had had need of divine reassurance as much as they.

As his faith preceded his philosophy, let us look at it first. Shortly after his arrival in Egypt Maimonides received a letter from Jacob ben Nathaniel al Fayumi telling of various dangers facing the Jews of Yemen: mob violence; a messianic pretender who urged everyone to convert to Islam; a rebel sheik who forced all Jews under his authority to convert or be killed; an active missionary who based his appeal on the practical argument that since Islam and Judaism were essentially similar, Jews need no longer bear the now unnecessary burdens of minority existence; and a Jewish convert to Islam who proclaimed that the coming of Mohammed was foretold in the Bible. Jacob asked for guidance. Maimonides responded with traditional understanding. He quoted Amos 7:5: "Then said I, O Lord, God, cease I beseech you: how shall Jacob stand? For he is small." Maimonides admonished the Yemenites to be strong and steady in their faith. Evil times are upon you, but such times are bound to pass. Study history and note the fate of every tyrant who sought to destroy us: "Amalek, Sisera, Sennacherib, Nebuchadnezzar, Titus, Hadrian, may their bones be ground to dust and others like them." "Our nation speaks with pride of the virulent oppression it has suffered and the sore tribulations it has endured. For the bearing of these hardships is a source of glory and a great achievement in the sight of God." His letter closed with this prayer:

> May God, who created the world with the attributes of mercy, grant us the privilege to behold the return of the exiles to the portion of His inheritance, to contemplate the graciousness of the Lord, and to visit early in His Temple. May He take us out from the Valley of the Shadow of Death wherein He put us. May He remove darkness from our eyes and gloom from our hearts.[5]

But Maimonides was not simply another preacher. The advice in his letter was practical and hard-headed. It began with an appeal to community discipline. "It behooves you to hearten one another, the elders to guide the youth, and the leaders to direct the masses." [6] Do what must be done to survive. If there is no choice but exile, take that road.

> When a man finds it difficult to gain a livelihood in one place he emigrates to another. All the more is it incumbent upon a Jew who is restricted in the practice of his religion to depart to another place. If he finds it impossible to leave for the time being he must not become careless and indulge with abandon in the desecration of the Sabbath and the dietary laws on the assumption that he is exempt from all the *mitzvot*. It is the eternal, ever present duty of everyone who belongs to the stock of Jacob to abide by the Law.[7]

Maimonides was not content to feed his fellow Jews fanciful descriptions of the messianic age and the World to Come and let matters rest there. He believed in strong community discipline. He proudly asserted Judaism's claim to be a saving truth. He was convinced that Jews would remain loyal as long as they were convinced of the ultimate significance of obeying God's will. "Remember, that ours is the true and authentic divine religion, revealed to us through Moses . . . by means of which God has distinguished us from the rest of mankind. . . ." Judaism is unique, the truth, the only way:

Give your assent to the truth that is immutable and unchangeable, and to the following postulates of a religion that shall never fail. God is one in a unique sense of the term, and Moses is His prophet and spokesman, and the greatest and most perfect of the seers. To him was vouchsafed by God what has never been vouchsafed to any prophet before him, nor will it be in the future. The entire Torah was divinely revealed to Moses of whom it was said, "with him do I speak mouth to mouth" (Num. 12:8). It will neither be abrogated nor superseded, neither supplemented nor abridged. Never shall it be supplanted by another divine revelation containing positive and negative duties.

Keep well in mind the revelation on Sinai in accordance with the divine precept to perpetuate the memory of this occasion and not to allow it to fall into oblivion. Furthermore, we were enjoined to impress this event upon the minds of our children, as it is written, "Only take heed to yourself, and keep your soul diligently, lest you forget the things which your eyes saw, and lest they depart from your heart all the days of your life; but make them known unto your children and your children's children" (Deut. 4:9).

It is imperative, my fellow Jews, that you make this great spectacle of the revelation appeal to the imagination of your children. Proclaim at public gatherings its momentousness. For this event is the pivot of our religion, and the proof which demonstrates its veracity. Evaluate this phenomenon at its true importance for Scripture has pointed out its significance in the verse, "For ask now of the days past, which were before you, since the day that God created man upon the earth, and from the one end of heaven unto the other, whether there has been any such thing as this great thing is, or has been heard like it?" (Deut. 4:32).[8]

In this letter and on frequent occasions, Maimonides concentrated on expressing Judaism as Truth on the grounds that what a man knows to be valid, he will not contravene. His life's work was to lay open to intellectual inspection the truths contained in the incomparable revelation at Sinai. What the mind has affirmed, it will not let go. Yes, Maimonides believed in the Messiah and the World to Come; but these were God's mysteries. Instead of conflating the promise, he kept it simple. Believe in resurrection, but

Know that, as the blind man cannot image colors, as the deaf cannot experience sound and as the eunuch cannot feel sexual desire, so bodies cannot attain spiritual delights. Like fish who do not know what the element of fire is, because they live upon its opposite, the element of water, so are the delights of the spiritual world unknown in the temporal world.[9]

The messianic age, yes, may it come speedily, but

Let no one think that in the days of the King Messiah any of the laws of nature will be set aside, or any innovation will be introduced into creation. The world will follow its normal course. . . . No one should occupy himself with the legendary themes or spend much time on midrashic statements bearing on this or like subjects. He should not deem them of prime importance since they lead neither to the fear of God nor to the love of Him. Nor should one calculate the end. . . . One should wait (for his coming) and accept in principle this article of faith.[10]

Maimonides fought with his head and his pen to make the requirements of the law clear to everyone and to establish with certainty the meaning of the revelation at Sinai. His practical program of survival resisted the temptation to live in happy dreams of a future reward. In another age his authority would be invoked against tendencies in the Kabbalah and Ḥasidic thought which encouraged men to dream of the future bliss, and he would have approved.

Maimonides had no official position among Egyptian Jews, although as physician to the governor he was in a sense a court Jew. His authority among Jews did not come primarily from the court, but from his omnicompetence as a rabbinic authority, head of his own school, a busy legal correspondent, and an appeals justice for *dayyanim* throughout Egypt and Palestine. I emphasize Maimonides the Talmudist and rabbi because his incredible halachic learning established Maimonides as a learned Jew; therefore, among Jews, Maimonides the philosopher could be trusted even when he seemed to be saying scandalous things. His contemporary, the historian Abraham ibn Daud, like Maimonides wrote in Arabic a brilliant scholastic apologetic in the new Aristotelian manner, but Ibn Daud lacked rabbinic credentials and so for more than a century no one moved to translate this text into Hebrew. His voice was that of one man, not of the tradition. Maimonides was the tradition incarnate. The first of the three volumes of Maimonides' philosophy was being translated before the second and third had been completed.

Maimonides is outsized, but magnificent. By the age of sixteen he had compiled a creditable *Treatise on Logic*, a lexicon of the logical terms and philosophic concepts basic to Aristotelian speculation (*Ma-*

kalah fi Sinai At al Mantik; Heb., *Millot ha-Higgayon*). As a physician he was doctor in attendance to the Egyptian court, and a medical theoretician and writer of note. As a Talmudic scholar he completed, in his early thirties, a brilliant and incisive gloss commentary on the *Mishnah, The Book of Light* (*Kitab al Siraj;* Heb., *Sefer ha-Maor*). As a rabbinic jurist he was consulted from far and wide; his responsa ran into the thousands. In his forties he put together the first truly original codification of the entire corpus of Jewish law, the *Mishneh Torah,* together with *A Book of Commandments* to explain his arrangement of these laws according to their biblical source (*Kitab al' Faraid;* Heb., *Sefer ha-Mitzvot*). Finally, as a philosopher-apologete, he wrote in the decade before his death what was to be the best-known and, by all standards, the most original and systematic of Jewish scholastic texts, *The Guide of the Perplexed* (*Kitab Dalalat al' Ha-irin;* Heb., *Moreh Nevuchim*); it was to become the major rabbinic work to crack the curtain of the Christian chauvinism which, until the mid-twentieth century, defined civilization as that which was produced in ancient Judea, Greece, Rome, and Christian Europe.

If Maimonides had not suffered from a tin ear and been without talent at poetry, he would have been the complete medieval Jew. As it is, he is the most famous, and his influence on Jewish life was certainly the most profound and lasting. For centuries Jews, learned and simple, were convinced that Maimonides had proved that their theology and tradition were intellectually creditable and philosophically valid. Saadiah had insisted that reason and revelation were the obverse and reverse of a single coin; Maimonides had proved the point. He had taken the most advanced of all philosophic traditions, the Aristotelian, and naturalized it. He had explained the social and individual purpose of the various Torah laws. He had fit the entire corpus of rabbinic law into a functional code and brilliantly analyzed its underlying structure. He had attacked superstition in all its forms. He had formed Jewish theology into carefully stated articles of faith and defended these formulas with arguments based on seemingly irrefutable logic.

Maimonides was brilliant and encyclopedic where others were merely trained and competent. His codification of rabbinic legislation became the *Mishneh Torah,* a second Torah. Contemporaries stood in awe of its sweep and used it even as they accused him of handling certain texts cavalierly, of having failed to cite a law in the name of its original proponent or with its Talmudic source, and of having omitted various singular opinions. Coreligionists turned his creedal formulations into a hymn and added it to the liturgy even as they argued that Judaism was a way of duty, not a dogmatic faith. Fellow theologians read the *Guide* avidly, even though they claimed that Maimonides had shifted the emphasis of Jewish life from *halachah* to a way of contemplative meditation, and had turned the God of Abraham into the God idea of Aristotle. Controversy swirled around all his works and served only to prove their overriding importance.

⁓ঌৡ⁓

Maimonides brought his unique genius for system and organization to bear on every aspect of rabbinic thought. He made complex ideas appear crystal clear and complex areas of the law understandable. He wrote easily as if his prodigious learning had come easily. It had not. Learning was a matter of endless hours of study and memorization. Commenting on the last *mishnah* in the *Sayings of the Fathers*, Maimonides wrote:

Ben He He said: According to the suffering is the reward.
And Ben He He said, your recompense shall be according to what you will suffer in the (study of the) Torah. They said: The only segment of wisdom that will endure is what you will learn through travail, toil and awe of the teacher. However, studying for enjoyment and pleasure has no durability nor is there benefit in it. They said through interpretation of this statement, . . . also (*af*) my wisdom remained with me, the wisdom that I learned through (the) wrath (*b'af*) (of my teacher) remained with me. Therefore, he counselled to cast solemnity upon the students, and they said: Project awe into the students.[11]

Maimonides was as strict and stern with himself as he must have been with others. For all the authority and power that came to him late in life, he lived lean and never slackened the pace of his work. When his translator asked permission to visit, Maimonides demurred:

But with respect to your wish to come here to me, I cannot but say how greatly your visit would delight me, for I truly long to commune with you, and would anticipate our meeting with even greater joy than you. Yet I must advise you not to expose yourself to the perils of the voyage, for beyond seeing me, and my doing all I could to honour you, you would not derive any advantage from your visit. Do not expect to be able to confer with me on any scientific subject for even one hour, either by day or by night, for the following is my daily occupation: I dwell in Mizr (Fustat), and the Sultan resides at Kahira (Cairo); these two places are two Sabbath days' journeys distant from each other.

My duties to the Sultan are very heavy. I am obliged to visit him every day, early in the morning; and when he or any of his children, or any of the inmates of his harem, are indisposed, I dare not quit Kahira, but must stay during the greater part of the day in the palace. It also frequently happens that one or two of the royal officers fall sick, and I must attend to their healing.

Hence, as a rule, I repair to Kahira very early in the day and even if nothing unusual happens, I do not return to Mizr until the afternoon. Then I am almost dying with hunger . . . I find the antechambers filled with people, both Jews and Gentiles, nobles and common people, judges and bailiffs, friends and foes—a mixed multitude, who await the time of my return.

I dismount from my animal, wash my hands, go forth to my patients, and entreat them to bear with me while I partake of some slight refreshment, the only meal I take in the twenty-four hours. Then I go forth to attend to my patients, write prescriptions and directions for their several ailments. Patients go in and out until nightfall, and sometimes even, I solemnly assure you, until two hours and more in the night. I converse with and prescribe for them while lying down from sheer fatigue; and when night falls, I am so exhausted, that I can scarcely speak.

In consequence of this, no Israelite can have any private interview with me, except on the Sabbath. On that day, the whole congregation, or, at least, the majority of the members, come unto me after the morning service, when I instruct them as to their proceedings during the whole week; we study together a little until noon, when they depart. Some of them return, and read with me after the afternoon service until evening prayers. In this manner I spend that day. I have here related to you only a part of what you would see, if you were to visit me.[12]

His pleasures were intellectual, a successfully demonstrated argument or a neatly arranged analysis of some area of law. His mind drove toward synthesis, and his writings reflect its power of organization. The *Mishneh Torah* pours into numbered paragraphs and chapters the principles, procedures, and details of the entire far flung body of Jewish law, including, when necessary, biblical citation and historical precedent. To appreciate his accomplishment, at least a chapter should be read. I have chosen one, not too complicated or heavy with terminology and procedure, which is a rather nice example of the mixture of petty detail and broad principle characteristic of halachic jurisprudence. In this case the principle is to use a ritual so that men will constantly be reminded that God, not chance, rules the world.

LAWS CONCERNING FAST DAYS
INVOLVING ONE POSITIVE COMMANDMENT

TO WIT

To Cry out before the Lord whenever great trouble befalls the community.

CHAPTER I

1. A positive Scriptural commandment prescribes prayer and the sounding of an alarm with trumpets whenever trouble befalls the community. For when Scripture says, "Against the adversary that oppresseth you, then ye shall sound an alarm with the trumpets" (Num. 10:9), the meaning is: Cry out in prayer and sound an alarm against whatsoever is oppressing you, be it famine, pestilence, locusts, or the like.

2. This procedure is one of the roads to repentance, for as the community cries out in prayer and sounds an alarm when overtaken by trouble, everyone is bound to realize that evil has come upon them as a consequence of their own evil deeds, as it is written, "Your iniquities have turned away these things, and your sins have withholden good from you" (Jer. 5:25), and that their repentance will cause the trouble to be removed from them.

3. If, on the other hand, the people do not cry out in prayer and do not sound an alarm, but merely say that it is the way of the world for such a thing to happen to them, and that their trouble is a matter of pure chance, they have chosen a cruel path which will cause them to persevere in their evil deeds and thus bring additional troubles upon them. For when Scripture says, "But walk contrary unto Me; then I will walk contrary unto you in fury" (Lev. 26:27–28), the meaning is: If, when I bring trouble upon you in order to cause you to repent, you say that the trouble is purely accidental, then I will add to your trouble the fury appropriate to such an "accident."

4. On the authority of the Scribes, fasting is required whenever trouble befalls the community, until mercy is vouchsafed to it from heaven. During such fasts people should cry out in prayer and supplication and should sound an alarm, but with trumpets only. In the Temple, they used to sound the alarm with both trumpets and ram's horn, a short blast from the ram's horn and a long blast from the trumpets, since the commandment concerning the day specified only trumpets. It was only in the Temple that both trumpets and ram's horn were sounded, in accordance with the verse, "With trumpets and sound of the horn shout ye before the King, the Lord" (Ps. 98:6).

5. Such fasts, imposed because of trouble which has befallen the community, should not be observed on consecutive days, seeing that the majority of the community would be unable to endure so great a strain. Initially fasts should be appointed on Monday, the following Thursday, and the Monday after that, and the same sequence of Monday-Thursday-Monday should be repeated until mercy is obtained.

6. Communal fasts may not be imposed on Sabbaths or festivals. Similarly, neither ram's horn nor trumpets may be sounded on those days, nor may there be any crying out in supplication and prayer, unless a town is surrounded by a heathen enemy or by a river in flood, or a ship is storm-tossed at sea, or even a single individual is pursued by heathens, bandits, or an evil spirit. In such cases it is permissible to fast on the Sabbath and to cry out in prayer and supplication, but not to sound trumpets or ram's horn, except for the purpose of summoning people to assist in the rescue.

7. Similarly, a fast day should not be appointed initially on new moons, on Hanukkah, on Purim, or on the intermediate days of festivals. If, however, even one fast day has already been observed because of some misfortune, and a subsequent fast day coincides with one of the days just mentioned, the whole of that day may be observed as a fast day.

8. Expectant and nursing mothers and minors are not required to fast on fast days observed because of some misfortune. It is also permissible to eat during the preceeding night, even though the next day will be spent in fasting. Fasts for rain, however, are exceptions to this rule, as will be explained. Whenever it is permissible to eat during the night preceding a communal or private fast day, it is permissible to eat and drink until dawn, provided that one does not fall asleep. If one has gone to sleep, he may not eat thereafter.

9. Just as a community should fast when in trouble, so should an individual fast when in trouble. Thus, if a dear one is ill, or if one is lost in the wilderness or is confined in prison, it is his duty to fast on this account and to solicit God's mercy by reciting the prayer beginning, "Answer us, O Lord," etc., during each of the daily services. However, one should not fast on Sabbaths, festivals, new moons, Hanukkah, or Purim.

10. If an individual does not undertake to fast on the preceding day, the subsequent fast is not effective. How does one undertake to fast? When he has finished the afternoon prayer he should say, "Tomorrow I shall observe a fast day," and should resolve to fast on the morrow. Even if he eats during the following night, he in no way detracts from the fast. Similarly, if he resolves and undertakes to fast for three or four consecutive days, he does not detract from his fast if he eats on each intervening night. Nor need he express his intention for each of the several days on each preceding day.

11. If one undertakes during the day to fast on the morrow only, and does so fast on the next day, and then during the night decides to fast on the following day as well, the second day's fast is not effective, even if he

does not break his fast during the preceding night; for this latter fast was not undertaken during the preceding day. Needless to say, if one eats and drinks during the night and then decides early in the morning to fast, such a fast is not at all effective.

12. If one has a bad dream, he should fast on the next day, so that he might look searchingly into his conduct and repent. He should observe such a fast even if the next day is a Sabbath, and should during each service recite the prayer beginning, "Answer us, O Lord," notwithstanding that his fast was not undertaken during the preceding day. If one fasts on a Sabbath after a bad dream, he must afterward observe another day of fasting in penance for having failed to make the Sabbath a delight.

13. One may fast for a number of hours only, that is, by eating nothing at all for the remainder of the day. Thus, if one is so preoccupied with attending to his affairs and needs that he does not eat before noon or before the ninth daylight hour, and then decides to fast for the remaining hours of that day, he may fast during these hours and recite the prayer beginning with "Answer us, O Lord," for he had arrived at his decision to fast before the period of the fast began. Similarly, if one has already eaten and drunk, and then begins to fast for the rest of the day, this is regarded as a fast for a number of hours.

14. If one is fasting—whether because he himself is in trouble or has had a bad dream, or because he is participating in a communal fast observed because of a common calamity—he should not pamper himself, nor act frivolously, nor be joyful and glad of heart, but should fret and mourn after the manner indicated in the verse, "How mournful should a living man be, a strong man because of his sins?" (Lam. 3:39).

One is permitted to taste of cooked food, even as much as a quarter "log" of it, provided that the mouthful is not swallowed, but is savored and expelled. If one forgets and eats on a fast day, he may nevertheless complete his fast.

15. If while an individual is fasting his dear one recovers his health or his trouble passes away, he must nevertheless complete his fast. If one goes from a place where a fast is being observed to a place where there is no fast, he himself must continue his fast to its completion. If one goes from a place where there is no fast to a place where a fast day is being observed, he must join in the fast. If he forgets and eats and drinks, he should not let himself be seen, nor should he pamper himself.

16. If a community observes a fast day because it needs rain, and rain begins to fall, the rule is as follows: If the rain falls before noon, the fast day need not be completed, rather everyone should eat and drink, and then assemble to recite the Great Hallel. For the Great Hallel may be recited only after one's hunger has been satisfied and one's stomach is full. If the rain falls in the afternoon, the fast day must be completed, seeing that most of the day has already been spent in a state of holiness.

[402]

The same rule applies to a fast day observed because of some trouble, if the trouble has passed away, or because of some oppressive decree, if the decree has been withdrawn. If it is still before noon, the fast need not be completed; if it is afternoon, it must be completed.

17. On each fast day undertaken by a community beset by troubles, the court and the elders should remain in session at the synagogue from the end of the morning service until midday, to examine into the conduct of the citizens and to remove the obstacles to righteous living provided by transgressions. They should carefully search and inquire after those guilty of extortion and similar crimes, in order to set them apart, and those who act high-handedly, in order to humble them, and after other such matters. From midday until evening should be spent as follows: For the third quarter of the day, the Scriptural blessings and imprecations should be read, in accordance with the verse, "My son, despise not the chastening of the Lord, neither spurn thou His correction" (Prov. 3:11), with the lesson from the Prophets consisting of admonitions having reference to the particular trouble involved. During the last quarter of the day, the afternoon service should be held and everyone, to the best of his ability, should recite supplications, cry out in prayer, and confess his sins.[13]

The *Mishneh Torah* was completed in 1180 and constantly revised and corrected until Maimonides' death. Maimonides offered several explanations of this code. At times he claimed to have written it for his own private use to obviate the time-consuming necessity of checking references and sources in the handling of his legal correspondence. This is doubtful. Maimonides had a photographic memory which, by his own testimony, rarely left him in the lurch. The *Mishneh Torah's* Introduction offers a more credible explanation. Halachic terms are difficult and confused. Old patterns of study have been broken. Given the pace of life, few today have the leisure or opportunity to assimilate the bulk of rabbinic material. Access, brevity, and correct determination are elementary communal necessities; therefore, this book becomes essential.

Wherein lies the code's commanding force? In part the *Mishneh Torah's* fame rests on usefulness and scope. Maimonides paid scant heed to many hoary conventions. He broke new ground with his topical organization of the law. He translated the *Gemara's* formulation of positive law from Aramaic into Hebrew. In the overwhelming majority of cases he cited only one opinion, dropping minority or variant decisions. He stated the law without indication of its source. In these fourteen volumes a reader will find the entirety of the oral and written tradition neatly arranged for ease of reference. This was no pedant's feat requiring only patience, scissors, and paste. As we have noted, rabbinic law had ramified largely by scholarly excursus and specific case decision. The volume of such material was fantastic. Rules were scattered in the unindexed, multi-folioed *Talmudim*, in the responsa, in the excursuses and compendia of the Geonim, and in numerous other writings. There existed, in addition, an extensive library of variant teachings, texts, and traditions. All these materials had to be mined, for the most part, without library aids or indices. No wonder a contemporary poet sang: "Moses arose and delivered them. He winnowed the *Talmud* as flour in a sieve. He took from it the choice fine flour. He prepared it specially for those who busied themselves with the needs of time—well-prepared food, full of sweetness and fatness—and the children of Israel ate the manna for which they did not have to toil." [14]

Maimonides brought the whole scheme off magnificently and provided the long-desired indexed and readable code, but his originality and disdain of old forms aroused a hornet's nest of protest. There were good and valid reasons for taking issue with certain aspects of the *Mishneh Torah*. In their new Hebrew dress, some laws suggested unexpected meanings. The laws were stated with a finality which reduced the lawyer's freedom of interpretation and so made equity difficult and change hard to achieve. The publication of halachic debate and minority opinions had provided a basis for legal development in much the same way as do dissenting opinions issued by justices of our Supreme Court. Tradition and a concern for equity, judicial prerogative, and future need required that the law have elbow room. Maimonides had structured the law. Many of his critics feared he had also strait-jacketed it. Nevertheless, the *Mishneh Torah* was universally used and cited.

The *Mishneh Torah* was, from its inception, a many-sided force as well as a legal tour de force. It had been traditional to keep law separate from *aggadah* and dogmatics. *Halachah* was a precisely detailed study, *aggadah* a deliberately nonprecise area where the broadest freedom was tolerated. Law commanded absolute obedience. The *aggadah* was suggestive rather than prescriptive. Along came Maimonides, and in the first volume of his code, the *Sefer ha-Madda*, he set forth briskly and unequivocally what he considered the uncontestable theological and metaphysical principles of faith. To be sure, Maimonides set down little that could not be found in the tradition, but his terse formulation and the unavoidable implication that assent to these exact formulas was a religious duty on a par with obedience to the practical law startled many, particularly scholars who lived in the vastly different cultural environment of Christian Europe. Until Maimonides published the *Mishneh Torah* no Jewish legal text had ever begun, "The basic principle of all basic principles and the pillar of all sciences is to realize that there is a First Being who brought every existing thing into being. All existing things, whether celestial, terrestrial or belonging to an intermediate class exist only through His true existence." [15] The affirmation of God's creative power is essential to Judaism, but to treat a philosophic statement of the attribute of divine power as dogma was not.

Maimonides called such formulas "true beliefs" and held that, without accepting them, "No right action and no correct opinion can be achieved." This was a logical position for a teacher who believed that obedience to God's law and, consequently, salvation depend on the clarity with which a man perceives truth. Similar doctrinal treatises prefaced a number of contemporary Muslim codes. In this literary milieu it was almost axiomatic that only a clear grasp of metaphysical truth could free the mind of indecision and error, and that only an enlightened mind could govern the body so that a man would be truly obedient to God. The average man acknowledged religious law and tried to obey God's commands; but his actions were inconstant. Why? Because such a man obeyed the law as an animal might its master. The law was not yet part of him, instinctive. Could it ever be? Maimonides believed man could become a living law, and that he became so when he understood the terms in which God's law was framed and learned to see reality as God saw it. When the mind perceives truly, which to Maimonides meant simply when it accepts reality to be what philosophy conceives it, the mind will naturally and inevitably make righteous and wise decisions.

Maimonides proposed in his *Commentary on the Mishnah* a thirteen-plank catechism of basic truths which he offered, not as the fullness of wisdom, but as the beginning of wisdom, a first step designed to help men gain knowledge, overcome their blindness, and recognize the ideas they must think about. According to the philosopher, these thirteen articles of faith are: 1) the existence of a God, perfect and sufficient and the Creator of all that is; 2) God's incomparable unity; 3) God's incorporeality and freedom from all the accidents which occur to corporeal beings; 4) God's eternity; 5) God alone is to be worshipped, and no other; 6) the reality of historic prophecy; 7) the incomparability of Moses as prophet; 8) the revelation of the Torah through Moses; 9) the unalterability of that revelation which will never be superseded or abrogated; 10) God's omniscience and His knowledge of man's deeds and thoughts; 11) God's justice, for He rewards the righteous and punishes the wicked; 12) the arrival of the Messiah when God determines his coming appropriate; 13) the resurrection of the dead. His creed became part of the liturgy when Daniel ben Judah of Rome (13th–14th cent.) transformed Maimonides' ideas into a hymn, the *Yigdal*, which is still sung as part of the daily worship. Maimonides would readily agree that a creed carelessly recited was meaningless; but he would have insisted that to understand these fundamental principles of the faith was to understand the nature of God, and to know reality as opposed to appearances.

Know, thou who studiest this my Treatise, that belief is not the notion that is uttered, but the notion that is represented in the soul when it has been averred of it that it is in fact just as it has been represented. If you belong to those who are satisfied with expressing in speech the opinions that are correct or that you deem to be correct, without representing them to yourself and believing them, and still less without seeking certain knowledge regarding them, you take a very easy road. In accordance with this, you will find many stupid people holding to beliefs to which, in their representation, they do not attach any meaning whatever. If, however, you belong to those whose aspirations are directed towards ascending to that high rank which is the rank of speculation, and to gaining certain knowledge with regard to God's being One by virtue of a true Oneness, so that no composition whatever is to be found in Him and no possibility of division in any way whatever—then you must know that He, may He be exalted, has in no way and in no mode any essential attribute, and that just as it is impossible that He should be a body, it is also impossible that He should possess an essential attribute. If, however, someone believes that He is one, but possesses a certain number of essential attributes, he says in his words that He is one, but believes Him in his thought to be many. This resembles what the Christians say: namely, that He is one but also three, and that the three are one. Similar to this is the assertion of him who says that He is one but possesses many attributes and that He and His attributes are one, while he denies at the same time His being corporeal and believes in His absolute simplicity; as if what we aimed at and investigated were what we should say and not what we should believe. For there is no belief except after a representation; belief is the affirmation that what has been represented is outside the mind just as it has been represented in the mind. If, together with this belief, one realizes that a belief different from it is in no way possible and that no starting point can be found in the mind for a rejection of this belief or for the supposition that a different belief is possible, there is certainty. . . . . Then you shall be one of those who represent to themselves the unity of the name and not one of those who merely proclaim it with their mouth without representing to themselves that it has a meaning. With regard to men of this category, it is said: "Thou art near in their mouth, and far from their reins" (Jer. 12:2). But men ought rather to belong to the category of those who represent the truth to themselves and apprehend it, even if they do not utter it, as the virtuous are commanded to do—for they are told: "Commune with your own heart upon your bed, and be still" (Ps. 4:5).[16]

By making doctrine precise, Maimonides simply drew out the logical consequences of medieval scholasticism, but at the same time he was imposing a theological rigidity on Judaism that was alien to its development. The rabbis had thought of theology as insight rather than systematics and had let their thoughts flash out from the comments and illustrations of the *midrash*. When medieval thinkers began to write extended philosophies of Judaism, they offered these as apologetics, not as creedal statements. By adding the *Sefer ha-Madda* to his halachic code, Maimonides turned speculation into dogma; he not only froze theological perception at a particular cultural point, but also required a particular theological perception of the faithful. Had Maimonides been followed in this regard, Judaism might have become a confessional community. He was not. The current of Judaism continued to flow within halachic rather than theological banks; and, however much scholastics were attracted to creedal statements, the faithful continued to accept, indeed to encourage, theological flexibility.

⋙⋘

The *Mishneh Torah* was the accomplishment of a master codifier; for all its bulk, hardly a word is superfluous and the whole is entirely original in scheme. Maimonides' introductions to the various Talmudic tractates were the work of a mature rabbinic scholar, comprehensive, incisive, original. His religious philosophy was no less special and significant.

This Talmudist had mastered philosophy; he had not simply appropriated some of its idiom. Listen as Maimonides advises a correspondent on a philosophic curriculum.

Be careful not to study the works of Aristotle except by the help of his commentators, the commentary of Alexander, Aphrodisius, Themistius, or Averroes (ibn Roschd). Among the works which you mention as being in

[407]

your possession you name *De Pomo* and the *Golden House*. These two treatises are spurious, and entirely valueless: they are among those which are ascribed to Aristotle, but which are not genuine. The work on theology composed by Alrasi is genuine, but it is without value, as Alrasi was a mere physician. It is true I have not seen the *Microcosmos*, which Rabbi Joseph Saddiq has written, but I know the author and his method of philosophy, and I am acquainted with his worth, and the worth of his book; for no doubt he has followed in that treatise the system of those who ascribe attributes to the Deity. As a general rule I may tell you, study only the works on Logic. . . . The writings of Aristotle are the foundations upon which all these philosophical works are based, and, as I have said above, they can only be understood by help of their commentaries—the Commentary of Alexander, or Themistius, or Averroes. But other works, besides those here enumerated . . . it is not right to waste time upon them. He, Aristotle, indeed arrived at the highest summit of knowledge to which a man can ascend, unless the emanation of the Divine Spirit be vouchsafed to him, so that he attains the stage of prophecy, above which there is no higher stage. And the works of Avicenna, although they contain searching investigations and subtle thought, do not come up to the writings of Abunazr Al-Farabi. Still they are useful, and it is right that you should study them diligently.[17]

Maimonides had mastered the ocean of rabbinic literature and the sea of Greek wisdom as none before him. His mind sailed serenely over the restless, teeming waters, and his writings made many feel that they had nothing to fear from the deep. He believed implicitly in the Torah as incomparable and immutable, and that "the works of Aristotle are the roots and foundations of all works on the sciences"[18] and that his own thought and careful demonstration had woven reason and revelation into a seamless unity. Many who read him agreed.

Maimonides' philosophic chef d'oeuvre, *The Guide of the Perplexed,* which was to become the most significant text of rabbinic apologetics ever written, is a work best taken on its own terms as a syllabus or study guide to the meaning of Scripture for those who have been exposed to the more advanced forms of philosophic speculation and who find their biblical faith challenged and unsettled by some of its assumptions.

It should be read as a justification of faith for intellectuals who turn to the Bible with minds conditioned by some of the presuppositions of Greek thought and who consequently are led to question the validity of some of the Bible's apparent meanings. Philo and Christian commentary had gotten around this problem by treating the whole of Scripture allegorically. Maimonides eschewed allegory because it eliminates the specific obligation of each biblical law by reducing the commandments to symbolic acts or techniques for gaining some supposedly higher spiritual or social end. In line with the rabbinic tradition Maimonides insisted that each *mitzvah* was an end in itself and its observance had an absolute value. But, if you insist on the Bible's literal meaning, what are you to do with its anthropomorphic vocabulary? Religious philosophy of the twelfth century insisted on the principle of *Yiḥud*, God's oneness, and was scandalized by language which spoke of a God who talks, walks, and changes His mind. The commentaries had developed an extensive set of midrashic explanations and the *Targumim* had an elaborate series of circumlocutions for these phrases; but to Maimonides' orderly mind these seemed to evade the central issue of biblical meaning because they were based on subjective rather than objective criteria.

Most of Part I of the *Guide* is a systematic examination of all the biblical terms which are, or seem to be, anthropomorphic, suggesting in each case their "true" meaning based not on metaphor or on *derash* but on the laws of language and meaning. His comments to Exodus 33:12–23 are typical and will serve to indicate his approach. In that chapter Moses asks God for a fuller revelation of His nature: "Let me know Your ways, that I may know You." "Let me behold Your presence." God refuses the immediate request, but allows Moses to sense His power. "You cannot see My face, for man shall not see Me and live. . . . See, there is a place near Me. Station yourself on the rock and, as My presence passes by, I will put you in a cleft of the rock and shield you with My hand until I have passed by. Then I will take My hand away and you shall see My back; but My face must not be seen."

The problem in the first instance rests with the Torah's language, which refers to God's "hand," "back," and "face." Maimonides will not allow himself to dismiss such nouns as poetic imagery. They are in the revelation. They must be appropriate designations, appropriate but not anatomical. In his systematic way, Maimonides proceeds to analyze every biblical use of these words and their cognates, and groups them according to use. In the process he discovers that "face" was sometimes used to specify that part of our anatomy and other times as a homonym to specify apprehension of God's essence; and that "back" was sometimes used specifically as back and other times to specify apprehension of God's action. Clearly then, when the Torah speaks of God's hand covering Moses' eyes, it may mean that

God has so created the rational soul that it can apprehend God's back, His actions, but not His face, His essence.[19] Verses 22–23 mean, therefore: Man is constitutionally incapable of knowing God's essence, but he can appreciate God's actions.

> Moses demanded a certain apprehension—namely, that which . . . is named "the seeing of the face"—and was promised an apprehension inferior to that which he had demanded. It is this later apprehension which is called "the seeing of the back." . . . Scripture accordingly says in this passage that God . . . hid from him the apprehension called that "of the face" and made him pass over to something different; I mean the knowledge of the acts ascribed to Him. . . . When I say He hid from him, I intend to signify that this apprehension is hidden and inaccessible in its very nature.[20]

By a careful analysis of language Maimonides locates in a seemingly mythic chapter precise metaphysical statements about the limits of human comprehension and reason's capacity—in short, a theory of knowledge—and he did so, he believed, without resort to allegory.

The Torah is God's word, written in such a way that those of simple faith—children, women, and the uneducated, to use a favorite rabbinic triad—are taught and encouraged; while an understanding reader will sense the deeper meaning and perceive there the substance of knowledge. Maimonides knew Torah as a revelation of infinite depth and bemoaned the fact that some otherwise intelligent people had been misled, by lack of training in Torah study or by superficial philosophic training, about the Torah's actual meaning.

> The human intellect having drawn him on and led him to dwell within its province, he must have felt distressed by the externals of the law and by the meaning of . . . equivocal, derivative or amphibolous terms . . . hence he would remain in a state of perplexity and confusion as to whether he should follow his intellect, renounce what he knew concerning the terms in question, and consequently consider that he has renounced the foundations of the law. . . . Or should he hold fast to his understanding of those terms and not let himself be drawn on together with his intellect, rather turning his back on it and moving away from it, while at the same time perceiving that he had brought loss to himself and harm to his religion.[21]

In the *Guide* he sought to provide a key by means of which the philosophically trained might unlock the Torah's deeper meaning. But Maimonides feared that the unprepared might drown in such deep waters so he sometimes veiled his thought even to the point of placing in the work deliberate inconsistencies. He tried to write a book which, like the Bible, could be read at many levels of sophistication, and in the end this most orderly of men scattered only confusion; the reader sees, but through a veil darkly. However much he is stimulated he is not sure he fully understands.

Maimonides did not write the *Guide* as an exercise in abstract scholarship. It was in his eyes a religious tract. Right knowledge is the way a man must take if he seeks to become holy and merit God's reward, if he seeks to be saved. Since, in Maimonides' thought, right actions derive from right knowledge, actions pleasing to God can flow only from a full and appropriate knowledge of God. "My purpose," he wrote, "in this was that the truth should be established in your mind according to the proper methods and that certainty should not come to you by accident." [22] Why truth? Why certainty? Maimonides accepted Aristotle's view of knowledge as man's ultimate happiness and cast it in a particular religious frame by insisting that it is through knowledge (what Spinoza would call the intellectual love of God) that man attains that ultimate happiness. Once man's intellect has been activated, it can participate in the active intellect, the animating intelligence of the spheres, and insofar as it "knows" so it is enabled to participate in the divine truth whence it was born. The soul is insubstantial, a form. Immortality is not given, but acquired, and the way of knowledge is the only way to acquire such reward.

Maimonides startles us when he argues that God's providence attaches only to those who have activated their intellect, yet this is a necessary corollary to his metaphysical system. "Divine Providence does not watch in an equal manner over all the individuals of the human species, but providence is graded as their human perfection is graded." [23] For popular consumption he made his elitist concept of immortality sound conventional. "The resurrection of the dead is one of the cardinal principles established by Moses, our Teacher. A person who does not believe in this principle has no real religion, certainly not Judaism. However, resurrection is only for the righteous. This is the meaning of the statement in *Genesis Rabbah* which says: 'The creative power of rain is for both the righteous and the wicked, but the resurrection of the dead is only for the righteous alone.' " [24] However, in his private vocabulary, righteous meant more than a good and pious Jew; it described the good and pious Jew who had cultivated his soul, become enlightened, and so developed the potential for immortality which lies within the soul. Immortality is reserved for those whose intellect has been so trained that it never ceases to be occupied with God.

Maimonides obviously preferred not to set down the unavoidable conclusion of his argument that ordinary folk who cannot philosophize fail to make themselves the object of God's providence, and consequently do not acquire immortality—but this heresy lies at the center of his vaunted "secrets." Only the rational mind distinguishes man from the beast; in the fool and the uneducated the rational mind lies undeveloped, rusted over. Maimonides had an icy contempt for fools and simpletons, whom he categorized as human beasts, beyond the purview of God's providence and useful only to support the activities of better folk. The best that can be said for them is that in the messianic age their minds will be strengthened. I suspect that Maimonides sometimes empathized with the mystic teacher, Simeon bar Yohai, of whom the *Talmud* says that when he looked about he found few men qualified to enter Paradise. "If there are three, my son Eleazer and I are among them. If there are two they are my son and I. If there is only one I am he." [25]

Maimonides was a learned and observant Jew. The path of knowing was not meant to cancel the path of duty. But his assumption that the path of knowing went higher than the path of duty led him to sometimes unsettling conclusions about the traditional practices. This is made particularly clear in his discussion of *avodah* (worship), which he describes as a sociologically conditioned set of devotional acts rather than as a set of God ordained and immutable requirements. Sacrifices, he wrote, were ordered by God because, since time immemorial, they had been associated with worship, and man, according to his nature, is not capable of suddenly abandoning forms to which he has become accustomed. That is, Jews could not have survived the leap from idols, sacrifices, and an ecclesiastical cult to the nonecclesiastic, aniconic worship of the synagogue without an intermediate stop, the Temple with its sacrifices and priests. [26] Such an analysis was radical enough for a people who accepted each Torah law, including the various sacrificial laws, as a clear statement of God's will; but Maimonides went on to suggest that contemporary worship, the practice of the synagogue, might not be an ultimate and inviolate form of devotion, but still another intermediate step. Prayer and public worship, he suggests, are closer to an ideal service than sacrifices; but they do not center on the intellectual love of God, and he leaves the reader with the tantalizing image of a prophet who even now might come and say: "God has given you a Law forbidding you to pray to Him, to fast, to call upon Him in misfortune. Your worship should consist solely in meditation without any works at all." [27] God has not sent such a prophet, but we cannot doubt that Maimonides would not have been shocked by his message.

Maimonides certainly attended public worship, but his way of holiness was the intellectual love of God, an essentially private way. Maimonides was horrified by the conventional superstitions and follies, especially those of so-called intelligent people. He was one of a handful of medieval thinkers to wage war against astrology, which then, as now, claimed scientific credibility. He was an elitist. He had no patience with the inconstancies of the heart or the inadequacies of ordinary folk. He wrote the *Guide* for a single competent pupil, and his seminars rarely had more than two or three students. Maimonides' way is a way few could walk, since its demands were too high, yet many in subsequent generations read Maimonides with appreciation. He stands as a symbol of the spiritual reach and rational respectability of Judaism.

Had he said that theology requires training in basic reasoning and the sciences, no one would have objected. But Maimonides was not interested in doing theology, but in drawing close through knowledge to the source of all knowledge. He sought an authentic and full religious experience through reason. The way of reason is the preeminent way. Maimonides suggested that there were various grades of perfection in men. The lowest people are those who possess only the perfection of wealth, next are those who possess physical health, and then come the virtuous whom he describes as those who are obedient to the law. He goes on to say: "The true human perfection consists in the acquisition of the rational virtues—I refer to the conception of the intelligibles, which teach true opinions concerning the divine things. This is the true reality, the ultimate end . . . through it man is man" [28] and gains immortality. God-meeting, as Maimonides pictured it, had academic prerequisites, and only the trained could expect to enjoy intellectual communion or the full development of their spiritual capacities.

Maimonides operated within a thoroughgoing intellectualist scheme, but he was not a thoroughgoing rationalist. Revelation is more significant than reason. Reason cannot reach to the nature of God. Maimonides' answer to Ha Levi's or Al-Ghazali's insistence that reason cannot remove doubt about God's nature was to admit this limitation; indeed, he found it stated clearly in Scripture: "Do not do otherwise, why should you die before your time?" (Ecc. 7:16–18). Reason requires that "you should let your intellect move about only within the domain of things that man is able to grasp." [29] Yet the power of the intellect is such that it can use reason to look behind the world of appearances and so understand the nature of the universe. The intellect can study revelation to look beyond reason's reach to what God has revealed about Himself.

Maimonides saw God's unity (*Yihud*) as the unifying truth that validated his *via intellectualis*. *Yihud* certified the axiom that truth is one, that reason and revelation refract a single truth, and that their wisdom is capable of being systematized. The apprehension of God as one is bedrock Judaism. That God's "oneness" implies "otherness" was at least as old as Deutero-Isaiah's question, "To whom can you liken God?" (Isa. 40:18). The systematics of this otherness, especially as regards divine attributes, had been developed centuries before by Saadiah. What distinguished Maimonides' formulation was his hypostasizing of the principle of otherness. God is a necessary being whose existence follows from its essence; any denial or compromise with this position puts one under suspicion of heterodoxy. God's otherness is not a sensible assumption, but an essential formula for arriving at a certain and complete understanding of the nature of life and of the universe. In nonphilosophical language, the universe is of God, but not responsive to any whim of God's. What seems erratic only seems so. Prayer, faith, healing, prophecy, and immortality are implicit in the nature of the universe and are not powers which God occasionally wields.

The emphasis on God's simplicity tends to circumscribe those religious assumptions that depend on God's spontaneity. Prophecy becomes more an intellectual accomplishment than an occasional message from a merciful and concerned God. Miracles are subtleties implicit in God's orderly control of nature, rather than unexpected, inexplicable acts. Immortality is earned by the wise man. The messianic age is like this age except that violence and political subjugation will disappear.

A diamond shines brilliantly, but the crystal is cold. Urbane Jewish sophisticates in the Arab world, dissatisfied with the intellectual content of their faith as they understood it, were delighted with the *Guide*'s clean-cut brightness. Those to whom Judaism was warm and intimate noticed the coldness and elitism of this system. The God who delivers had become simply the God who sustains. The God who hears prayer had become the God whom men contemplate in

[414]

philosophic meditation. Maimonides said God is alive, but the ordinary man asked: "What is God's life to me, if He does not answer my prayer?"

❧§❧

They had become Jews, these people of whom Maimonides was born and whose law and philosophy he had developed so brilliantly. They were possessors of a special heritage of divine commandments and divine assurances that confirmed their lives. They lived according to the *Mishneh Torah*, which is to say rabbinic law. They worshipped a God who answered prayer, who promised immortality and resurrection to the righteous, who would send the Messiah to redeem Israel from exile, and who would return His people to the Promised Land, where they would live in freedom under His unceasing protection. They saw their heritage not as folkways or customs, but as commandment. Their hope was not a projection of need, but a confirmed and true report of God's oft-repeated word. The Jew saw himself as citizen of a holy nation which God had chosen, whose rules God Himself had set, and whose destiny God particularly vouchsafed.

From Moses to Moses much had changed. A land had been won and lost. A Temple had been built and destroyed. A priesthood had been enshrined and abandoned. Prophets had spoken and gone unheeded. This people's history had had its sunlight and its shadows, and for centuries it had endured *galut*. But the Torah had always brought them God's word. God's way was clear, as was His covenant. What had been—freedom—would be again. Until then they would bear exile; although the Messiah was delayed, the promise of redemption was real. If we mean by religion the power of a people's hopes to sustain life and dignity, Judaism had not failed this people.

They had carried their traditions and hopes into the far places of the world. They were now a homeless people. Everywhere they went they met other ways of thinking. If Maimonides is the classic Jew, then we must say that the Jew was never single-minded—the art of accommodating differing philosophies was his genius, while the constant in his life and in his people's life, was the way, the *halachah*. The law bound Jews to themselves and to the covenant God. Each week had its Sabbath, each year its cycle of holidays, each day its dietary regimen, its public prayers, the putting on of *tefillin*. The law bound Jews to their past. Learning bound Jews to the revelation of God, the God-inspired teachings of their ancestors, and the cultural and philosophic attitudes of their times. The present was always breaking in on the past. The medieval Jew somehow bound law and learning in one person, and whenever he doubted that these two worlds could be synthesized, he remembered Maimonides.

APPENDIX

⸱⸱ I ⸱⸱

Books of the Apocrypha and the Pseudepigrapha

THE books of the Apocrypha are defined as those noncanonical books included in the Septuagint: III Ezra, Tobit, Judith, Additions to Esther, Wisdom of Joshua ben Sira (Ecclesiasticus), Baruch with The Letter of Jeremiah, The Prayer of Azariah and The Song of The Three Young Men, Susanna, Bel and The Dragon, I and II Maccabees. Some Christian sources define Apocrypha as those Jewish books not in the *Tanach* but published in the Latin Vulgate edition, and add IV Ezra to the above list.

The books of the Pseudepigrapha are defined as those other Jewish works which were accepted into the scriptural canon of the Oriental Christian churches: The Letter of Aristeas, The Book of Jubilees, The Martyrdom and Ascension of Isaiah, The Psalms of Solomon, III Maccabees, IV Maccabees, * The Sybylline Oracles, * The Ethiopic Book of Enoch, * The Slavonic Book of Enoch, * The Assumption of Moses, IV Ezra, * The Syriac Apocalypse of Baruch, * The Greek Apocalypse of Baruch, * The Testament of the Twelve Patriarchs, * The Life of Adam and Eve (* titles include interpolations by Christian hands).

APPENDIX

೮ᵓ II ᵓ₃

The Dead Sea Scrolls

THE Dead Sea Scrolls include: Wars of the Sons of Light and the Sons of Darkness; Thanksgiving Hymns (*Hodayot*); Manual of Discipline; Genesis Apocryphon; Order of the Community; The Copper (or Treasure) Scroll; Blessings (*Divrei Berachot*); The Angelic Liturgy (*Seresh Shirot Olat ha-Shabbat*); The Book of Mysteries; and fragments of the Damascus (or Zadokite) Document; besides copies or fragments of all the biblical books except Esther.

The most important commentary (*pesher*) is the Commentary on Habbakuk. Fragmentary commentaries exist to Genesis, Isaiah, Hosea, Micah, Nahum, and Psalms. There are no commentaries to any noncanonical book. Biblical and apocryphal texts have also been found, and fragments of a number of other apocalyptic, astronomic, and midrashic works.

APPENDIX

❧ III ❧

Chronology of *Midrashim*

ERA	AGGADIC WORKS	MIDRASHIC COMMENTARIES
The Age of Variety 300 B.C.E.– 70 C.E.		
After the Fall 70 C.E.–500 C.E.		*(Ishmael)* * Mechilta (Ex.) * Sifre (Num.) * Mechilta (Deut.) *(Akiva)* * Mechilta (of R. Simeon ben Yoḥai (Ex.) * Sifra de-vei Rav (Lev.) * Sifrei Zuta (Num.) * Sifrei (Deut.)
Rabbinic Judaism 400 C.E.–640 C.E.		Genesis Rabbah *Leviticus Rabbah* Lamentations Rabbah

ERA	AGGADIC WORKS	MIDRASHIC COMMENTARIES
		Esther Rabbah I
		Pesikta de-rav Kahana
		Song of Songs Rabbah
		Ruth Rabbah
Islamic 640–1000	Megillat Antiochus (on Hanukkah)	Targum Sheni
	Midrash Petirat Moshe	Midrash Esfah
	Tanna de-vei Eliyahu (Seder Eliyahu)	Midrash Mishle
	Pirkei de R. Eliezer	
	Midrash Agur (on Prov. 30)	Ecclesiastes Rabbah
	Midrash Yonah	Midrasn Haserot vi-Yterot (on Masorah)
	Midrash Petirat Aharon	*Tanhuma Midrash (Yelammedenu)*
	Divrei ha-Yamim Shel Moshe	
	Otiyyot de-R. Akiva	*Deuteronomy Rabbah*
		Tanhuma (Buber)
	Midrash Shelosha ve-Arbaah	*Numbers Rabbah* II
	Midrash va-Yissau	*Pesikta Rabbati*
		Exodus Rabbah II
		Va-Yehi Rabbah
Byzantine 400–1000	Thrones and Hippodrones of Solomon	*Midrash Samuel*
		Midrash Tehillim
		Exodus Rabbah I
	Midrashei Yehudith (Judith)	*Aggadat Bereshit*
	Midrash Hallel	
	Midrash Tadshe	Aggadat Shir-ha Shirim Zuta
		Ruth Zuta
		Ecclesiastes Zuta
		Lamentations Zuta
Early European 1000–1200	Midrash Aseret ha Dibberot	Midreshei Hanukkah
	Midrash Konen	Midrash Shir-ha Shirim
	Midrash Avkir	Abba Guryon
	Alphabet of Ben Sira	Esther Rabbah
	Midrash va-Yosha (on Ex. 15)	Midrash Tehillim II
	Sefer ha Yashar	
	Pesikta Hadta (on Festivals)	Panim Aherim Le-Esther

ERA	AGGADIC WORKS	MIDRASHIC COMMENTARIES
	Midrash Temurah	
		Moshe ha Darshan
		Midrash Aggadah
		Genesis Rabbati
		Numbers Rabbah I
Late Anthologies		Yalkut Shimoni (13th cent.)
		Midrash ha-Gadol (14th cent.)
		Yemenite
		Yalkut Machri (14th cent.)
		Ein Yaakov (15th–16th cent.)
		Haggadot ha-Talmud (15th–16th cent.)

Based in part on *Encyclopedia Judaica* (Jerusalem: Keter, 1971). Vol. 11, pp. 1511–1512.

* Midrash Halacha.

Italics: Homiletical *midrashim*. Each chapter contains sayings on one topic which appear to be the skeleton of a homily rather than discrete and variegated comments on individual verses as in exegetical *midrashim* (roman type).

Most collections contain earlier material.

APPENDIX

ఆ IV ఊ

The *Talmud*

THE *Mishnah* is divided into six divisions, each of which is composed of several tractates. There is *Tosefta* to all *Mishnah* tractates except *Avot, Tamid, Middot, Kinnim*.

	BABYLONIAN TALMUD	PALESTINIAN TALMUD
1. *Zeraim* (Seeds)		
Berachot—Benedictions	x	x
Peah—Gleanings (Lev. 19:9–10)		x
Demai—Produce questionably tithed		x
Kilayim—Diverse kinds (Deut. 22:9–11)		x
Sheviit—Sabbatical year (Ex. 23:10–11)		x
Terumot—Heave offering (Lev. 22:10–14)		x
Maaserot—Tithes (Num. 18:21)		x
Maaser Sheni—Second tithe (Deut. 14:22 ff.)		x
Ḥallah—Dough offering (Num. 15:17–21)		x
Orlah—Fruit of young trees (Lev. 19:23–25)		x

	BABYLONIAN TALMUD	PALESTINIAN TALMUD
Bikkurim—First fruits (Lev. 26:1–11)		x
2. *Moed* (Feasts)		
Shabbat—Sabbath	x	x
Eruvin—Sabbath limits	x	x
Pesaḥim—Passover	x	x
Shekalim—Shekel offerings		x
Yoma—Day of Atonement	x	x
Sukkah—Tabernacles	x	x
Bezah—Festival laws	x	x
Rosh ha Shanah—New Year's Day	x	x
Taanit—Fast days	x	x
Megillah—Purim	x	x
Moed Katan—Intermediate days of festivals	x	x
Ḥagigah—Festival offering (Deut. 16:16–19)	x	x
3. *Nashim* (Family Law)		
Yevamot—Levirate marriage (Deut. 25:5–10)	x	x
Ketuvot—Marriage contracts	x	x
Nedarim—Vows (Num. 30)	x	x
Nazir—The Nazarite (Num. 6)	x	x
Sotah—The accused adulteress (Num. 5:11 f.)	x	x
Gittin—Divorce	x	x
Kiddushin—Marriage	x	x
4. *Nezikin* (Civil and Criminal Law)		
Bava Kamma—Torts	x	x
Bava Metzia—Civil law	x	x
Bava Batra—Property law	x	x
Sanhedrin—Courts	x	x
Makkot—Flagellation (Deut. 25:2)	x	x
Shevuot—Oaths	x	x
Eduyot—Testimonies		

	BABYLONIAN TALMUD	PALESTINIAN TALMUD
Avodah Zarah—Idolatry	x	x
Avot—Sayings of the Fathers		
Horayot—Erroneous judicial rulings (Lev. 4:22 ff.)	x	x
5. *Kodashim* (Cultic Laws)		
Zevahim—Animal offerings	x	
Menahot—Meal offerings	x	
Hullin—Slaughter for food	x	
Bechorot—Firstlings (Deut. 15:19 ff.)	x	
Arachin—Temple vows of valuation (Lev. 27:1–8)	x	
Temurah—The substituted offering (Lev. 27:10)	x	
Keritot—Extirpation (Lev. 18:29)		
Meilah—Sacrilege (Lev. 5:15–16)	x	
Tamid—The daily holocaust (Num. 28:3–4)		
Middot—Temple measurements		
Kinnim—Bird offerings		
6. *Toharot* (Ritual Purity)		
Kelim—Vessels		
Ohalot—Uncleanness through overshadowing (Num. 19:14–15)		
Negaim—Leprosy (Lev. 13:14)		
Parah—The Red Heifer (Num. 19)		
Toharot—Ritual purity		
Mikvaot—Ritual immersion		
Niddah—Menstrual purity	x	x
Machshirin—Liquids that predispose to uncleanness (Lev. 11:37–38)		
Zavim—Those who suffer a flux (Lev. 15)		

	BABYLONIAN TALMUD	PALESTINIAN TALMUD

Tevul Yom—Uncleanness after immersion
(Lev. 22:6–7)
Yadayim—Uncleanness of hand
Uktzin—Uncleanness of plants

Minor Tractates (Geonic Times)
    Avot de-rabbi Nathan (ethical commentary to M. Avot)
    Soferim—Scribes
    Semaḥot—Mourning
    Kallah—Bride
    Kallah Rabbati—Larger tractate on a bride
    Derech Eretz Rabbah—Larger tractate on correct behavior
    Derech Eretz Zuta—Short tractate on correct behavior
    Perek Hashshalom—Peace
    Gerim—Proselytes
    Kuthim—Samaritans
    Avadim—Slaves
    Sefer Torah—Torah scroll
    Tefillin—Phylacteries
    Tzitzit—Fringes
    Mezuzah—Doorpost sign

The *Mishnah* is available in a translation by H. Danby (London: Clarendon Press, 1933). The *Babylonian Talmud* has been translated by a group of English scholars under the direction of I. Epstein, 35 vols. (London: Soncino Press, 1935–1948) and *The Minor Tractates of the Talmud* has been translated by the same group under A. Cohen, ed., 2 vols. (London: Soncino Press, 1965). There is a French translation of the *Palestinian Talmud* (Paris: Librarie Orientale et Americaine, 1932).

For those who would like to dip their toes in the sea of the *Talmud*, A. Steinsalz has begun an attractive and ambitious program of presenting text, translation, and a popular, but far-ranging, interpretation, including illustrations and charts. Parts of T. B. *Berachot* and *Kiddushin* are available (Jerusalem: El Am, 1968).

APPENDIX

❧ V ❧

Tables of Abbreviations

Abbreviations of Biblical Books

Genesis	Gen.	Zephaniah	Zeph.
Exodus	Ex.	Haggai	Hag.
Leviticus	Lev.	Zechariah	Zech.
Numbers	Num.	Malachai	Mal.
Deuteronomy	Deut.	Psalms	Ps.
Joshua	Josh.	Proverbs	Prov.
Judges	Jud.	Song of Songs	Cant.
I Samuel	I Sam.	Lamentations	Lam.
II Samuel	II Sam.	Ecclesiastes	Ecc.
Isaiah	Isa.	Daniel	Dan.
Jeremiah	Jer.	Ezra	Ez.
Ezekiel	Ezek.	Nehemiah	Neh.
Hosea	Hos.	I Chronicles	I Ch.
Obadiah	Ob.	II Chronicles	II Ch.
Habbakuk	Hab.		

Translations from the Bible are from *The Torah, Isaiah,* and *Psalms* (Philadelphia: Jewish Publication Society, 1967; 1973; 1972) and from *The New English Bible* (New York: Cambridge University Press, 1970), although a number have been translated by the author.

Appendix V

Abbreviations of Apocryphal and Pseudepigraphic Books

II Baruch	II Bar.	I Maccabees	I Mac.
I Ezra	I Ez.	II Maccabees	II Mac.
II Ezra	II Ez.	IV Maccabees	IV Mac.
Jubilees	Jub.	Sybilline Oracle	Syb. Or.
The Wisdom of		I Enoch	I En.
Solomon	Wis. Sol.	Assumption of	
The Wisdom of		Moses	Moses
Ben Sira	Wis. Sir.	Psalm of Solomon	Ps. Sol.
Letter of Aristeas	Let. Aris.		

Abbreviations of Talmudic and Rabbinic Literature

Avot de-Rabbi		*Palestinian Talmud*	P.T.
Nathan	A.R.N.	*Song of Songs*	
Babylonian Talmud	T.B.	*Rabbah*	Cant. R.
Derech Eretz Rabbah	D.E.R.	*Siddur*	Sid.
Deuteronomy Rabbah	Deut. R.	*Sifra* on Leviticus	Sif.
Genesis Rabbah	Gen. R.	*Sifrei* on Deu-	
Exodus Rabbah	Ex. R.	teronomy	Sif. Deut.
Leviticus Rabbah	Lev. R.	*Sifrei* on Numbers	Sif. Num.
Mishnah	M.	*Tanna de-vei Eliahu*	Tan.d.b.El.
Mechilta	Mech.	*Teshuvot ha Geonim*	T.G.
Midrash Tehillim	Mid. Teh.	*Tosafot*	Tos.
Mishneh Torah	M.T.	*Tosefta*	Tosef.

Abbreviations of Mishnah and Talmud

Avodah Zarah	A.Z.	*Pesahim*	Pes.
Berachot	Ber.	*Shabbat*	Sab.
Bava Batra	B.B.	*Sanhedrin*	San.
Bava Metzia	B.M.	*Semahot*	Sem.
Eruvin	Erv.	*Sotah*	Sot.
Gittin	Git.	*Sukkah*	Suk.
Hagigah	Hag.	*Temurah*	Tem.
Ketuvot	Ket.	*Terumot*	Ter.
Kiddushin	Kid.	*Yadayim*	Yad.
Makkot	Mak.	*Yevamot*	Yev.
Megillah	Meg.	*Yoma*	Yom.
Moed Katan	M.K.		

Abbreviations of Dead Sea Covenant Materials

Hodayot (Thanksgiving Psalms)	IQH
Manual of Discipline	IQMD
Habbakuk Commentary	IQHC
The Psalms of Qumran	TPOQ

Abbreviations of Classical Materials

Josephus, *Jewish Antiquities*	*Ant.*
Josephus, *Against Apion*	*Apion*
Josephus, *The Jewish War*	*War*
Philo, *De Confusione Linguarum* (On the Confusion of Tongues)	*Conf.*
Philo, *De Somniis* (On Dreams)	*De. Som.*
Philo, *Legum Allegoria* (Allegorical Interpretations of Genesis)	*Leg. All.*
Philo, *De Praemiis et Poenis* (On Rewards and Punishment)	*Praem.*
Philo, *De Specialibus Legibus* (On Special Laws)	*Spec.*
Philo, *Questiones et Solutiones in Genesin* (Questions and Answers on Genesis)	*Ques. Gen.*
Philo, *De Vita Moyesis* (The Life of Moses)	*Vita M.*
Philo, *De Opificio Mundi* (On the Creation of the World)	*Or. Mun.*

NOTES*

I The Fathers and Their Way

1. J. B. Pritchard, ed., *Ancient Near Eastern Texts* (Princeton: Princeton University Press, 1950), p. 19.

2. Ibid., p. 165.

3. Ibid., p. 90.

II The Covenant Relationship

1. Herodotus *Histories* 2:36.

III God's Freedom and God's Bondage

1. J. B. Pritchard, ed., *Ancient Near Eastern Texts* (Princeton: Princeton University Press, 1950), p. 378.

2. Ibid., p. 165.

IV Land

1. J. B. Pritchard, ed., *Ancient Near Eastern Texts* (Princeton: Princeton University Press, 1950), p. 153.

2. Ibid.

V Power

1. M. San. 2:2–5.

VI The Way and the Wayward

1. H. B. Huffmon, "Prophecy in the Mari Letters," *The Biblical Archeologist* 31 (1968): 101–124.

2. J. B. Pritchard, ed., *Ancient Near Eastern Texts* (Princeton: Princeton University Press, 1950), p. 26.

* Abbreviations used in the Notes are contained in Appendix V.

Notes

VII This Was Believed

1. J. B. Pritchard, ed., *Ancient Near Eastern Texts* (Princeton: Princeton University Press, 1950), pp. 421–424.

2. Ibid., p. 434.

VIII Judah Is Judged

1. Gen. R. 34:8.
2. Tan. d. b. El. 48.

3. T.B. San. 103b.

X From the Exile to Alexander

1. T.B. Suk. 20a.

2. Wis. Sir. 51:2, 6, 8, 10; 36:2, 14.

XI The Age of Variety

1. T.B. Yoma 69a.
2. Wis. Sir. 13:18–19.
3. Wis. Sir. 27:2.
4. Tosef., Ber. 7:8.
5. Sif. Num. 119:39b.
6. Wis. Sir. 22:3.
7. Wis. Sir. 25:7.
8. H. A. Wolfson, *Philo*, vol. 1 (Cambridge: Harvard University Press, 1947), pp. 78 f.
9. Wis. Sol. 19:22.
10. Wis. Sol. 2:5–6.
11. Wis. Sol. 1:11–12.
12. Wis. Sol. 2:2, 4, 8.
13. Philo *Conf.* 2:1.
14. Wis. Sol. 2:21.
15. Wis. Sir. 35:10.
16. Wis. Sir. 38:24–39:11.
17. Wis. Sir. 39:4.
18. Wis. Sir. 39:4.
19. Wis. Sir. 38:33.
20. II Macc. 6:31.
21. T.B. Yoma 85 a–b.
22. IQHC 8:12–13.
23. M. Peah 8:5.
24. M. Peah 8:7.
25. Wis. Sir. 50:1, 3.
26. Wis. Sir. 50; Let. Aris. 96 ff.
27. II Bar. 3:36.
28. Let. Aris. 144 ff.
29. Philo *Leg. All.* 1:2:2.
30. Wis. Sir. 51:23.
31. IQMD 6:6.
32. Philo *Quest. Gen.* 1:2.
33. Wis. Sir. 50.

XII A Change in Cultural Style

1. Works included in these collections are listed in Appendix I.
2. Known works are listed in Appendix 2.
3. Gen. R. 1:1.
4. M. Avot 2:10.
5. Philo *Vita M.* 1:1.
6. Philo *Vita M.* 1:160–162.
7. II Enoch 15:2.
8. Wis. Sol. 1:6 ff.
9. Wis. Sol. 8:7–8.
10. Wis. Sol. 6:18–20.
11. Wis. Sol. 7:18–20.
12. Wis. Sol. 9:10.
13. Wis. Sol. 7:26.
14. Wis. Sol. 5:13, 8:16–17.
15. Wis. Sol. 9:17.

16. *Enneads* 5:2:1.
17. Wis. Sol. 3:1–5; cf. Philo *Or. Mun.* 46.
18. Wis. Sol. 8:20, 13.
19. IV Macc. 1:1–3.
20. IV Macc. 11:26.
21. IV Macc. 1:29–30.
22. Josephus *War* 2:8–14.
23. Josephus *Ant.* 18:3.

24. Philo *Leg. All.* 3:180.
25. IQMD 11:10–11.
26. Philo *Praem.* 19:116.
27. Philo *Spec.* 1:18:43.
28. Philo *De. Som.* 1:190.
29. Philo *Spec.* 1:8:45 ff.
30. Philo *Or. Mun.* 1:3.

XIII Torah in the Age of Variety

1. T.B. Kid. 30a.
2. Ibid.
3. Mid. Teh. 78:1.
4. M. Yad. 3:5.
5. P.T. Hag. 2:1:77.
6. Josephus *Ant.* 18:1:5.
7. Josephus *War* 2:8:18.
8. Josephus *Ant.* 13:9.
9. Acts 23:8.
10. Wis. Sir. 21:27.
11. Josephus *War* 2:8:14.
12. M. Avot 1:1.
13. T.B. Ber. 21b.
14. T.B. Tem. 14b.
15. Wis. Sir. 28:24.
16. M. Avot 2:2.
17. Wis. Sir. 38:25–26.
18. M. Avot 1:15.

19. Sif. Num. 119:114a.
20. M. Yoma 1:3.
21. M. Avot 2:5.
22. P.T. Sot. 5:5:20c.
23. T.B. B.B. 75a.
24. Gershom S. Scholem, *Major Trends in Jewish Mysticism* (Jerusalem: Schocken, 1941), p. 41.
25. M. Avot 1:12.
26. Tosef. Ber. 2:24; M. Avot 2:8.
27. T.B. Betzah 16a.
28. Lev. R. 1:5.
29. M. Avot 2:5.
30. M. Avot 2:8.
31. Josephus *Ant.* 18:1:3.
32. Syb. Or. 3:218.
33. Josephus *Apion* 2:39.

XIV Angels, Devils, and Judgment Day

1. I En. 14:2, 8–9.
2. I En. 68:2.
3. I En. 13:4.
4. Syb. Or. 3:788–93.
5. IV Ezra 14:20.
6. Jub. 4:18–19.
7. II Baruch 30:2.
8. IV Ezra 14:13–17.
9. II Baruch 25:4.
10. IQH 1:20.
11. I En. 20:2 ff.
12. I En. 9:6.
13. IV Ezra 3:20–22.

14. II Baruch 54:15, 17.
15. IQS 11:A.
16. Ps. Sol. 17:36.
17. Josephus *Ant.* 17:71–76; *War* 2:50.
18. Josephus *War* 2:44–48.
19. Ibid., 11:13:4.
20. IQH 5:14.
21. IQH 1:12.
22. Moses 1:16–18.
23. I En. 85–90.
24. Tosef. *Derech Eretz* 6:13.
25. T.B. San. 91b.

XV After the Fall

1. A.R.N. 4:5.
2. A.R.N. 4:6.
3. T.B. B.B. 6ob.
4. Ibid.
5. Sif. Zuta. 293.
6. Tosef. R. H. 4:3.
7. T.B. Meg. 31b.
8. T.B. Ber. 28b.
9. M. Avot 4:15.
10. Deut. R. 2:7.
11. P.T. Taanit 63d.
12. M. Taanit 2:1.
13. M. Yoma 8:9.
14. Ibid.
15. M. Avot 6:7.
16. Siddur, pp. 115–117.
17. Sif. Deut. 17:16.
18. M. Avot 6:1.
19. M. Avot 2:15.
20. M. Taanit 3:8.
21. M. Avot 2:9.
22. T.B. Ber. 17a.
23. M. Sot. 9:15.
24. Sif. Deut. 8:1.
25. M. Mak. 1:10.
26. Sif. Deut. 41.
27. T.B. Hag. 14b.
28. Mech. Shabbata 1.
29. P.T. Yev. 8:8d.
30. M. B.B., 5:10.
31. M. Suk. 2:6.
32. M. Kid. 1:1.
33. M. Ket. 1:1.
34. II Baruch 4:1.
35. II Baruch 4:14 ff.
36. II Baruch 7:11–12.
37. II Baruch 7:65–69.
38. A.R.N. 31 (Text B).
39. Sif. Deut. 43.

XVI Talmudic Judaism

1. T.B. Sot. 22a.
2. T.B. Eru. 54b.
3. T.B. Ber. 7b.
4. Siddur, p. 21.
5. Lev. R. 7:3.
6. T.B. San. 7a.
7. T.B. San. 99b.
8. Sif. Deut. 11:22.
9. T.B. Taanit 20b.
10. T.B. San. 65b.
11. Lev. R. 35:7.
12. Gen. R. 12:1.
13. T.B. A.Z. 3b.
14. T.B. Kid. 31a.
15. Romans 7:7.
16. T.B. B.K. 30a.
17. P.T. Maas. 3:50d.
18. P.T. Ber. 7a.
19. T.B. Git. 36b.
20. T.B. B.M. 59a.
21. T.B. Pes. 64b.
22. Gen. R. 58:3.
23. T.B. San. 97b.

XVII The Rabbinic Mind

1. P.T. San. 4:21b.
2. Siddur, p. 151.
3. Ibid., p. 147.
4. M. Taanit 4:1.
5. T.B. Pes. 68b.
6. T.B. Ber. 5a.
7. Sif. Deut. 32:39.
8. Tosef. Sab. 3:6.
9. Siddur, p. 849.
10. Sif. Deut. 11:16.
11. P.T. Ber. 2:46c.
12. Sifra, Behar 41:30.
13. Siddur, p. 135.
14. T.B. San. 101a.
15. Sif. 144a.
16. Gen R. 59:8.

Notes

17. Cant. R. 1:21.
18. Gen. R. 8:8.
19. T.B. Ber. 2b.
20. P.T. Ber. 13a.
21. Siddur, p. 127.
22. T.B. Hag. 4b.
23. T.B. Ber. 32b.
24. Siddur, pp. 133 ff.

25. P.T. Ber. 4:3.
26. T.B. Ber. 30b.
27. T.B. M.K. 18b.
28. T.B. Ber. 29b.
29. Cant. R. 3:1.
30. Mid. Teh. 119:12.
31. Siddur, p. 497.

XVIII   Judaism and Islam

1. Koran 74:34.
2. G. E. von Grunebaum, *Islam* (Menasha: The American Anthropological Association, 1955) p. 82.
3. T.G. 90.
4. T.B. Er. 13a.
5. Leon Nemoy, *Karaite Anthology* (New Haven: Yale University Press, 1952) pp. 17–18.
6. Ibid., p. 36.
7. Ibid., p. 37.
8. Ibid., p. 35.
9. Saadiah Gaon, *The Book of Beliefs and Opinions* (New Haven: Yale University Press, 1948) p. 361 [10:2].

10. M. San. 11:1.
11. Saadiah, *The Book of Beliefs and Opinions*, p. 266 [7:2].
12. M. Avot 3:15.
13. Saadiah, *The Book of Beliefs and Opinions*, p. 188 [4:4].
14. Ibid., pp. 181–182 [4:1].
15. Tafsir, Prov., Intro.
16. Saadiah, *The Book of Beliefs and Opinions*, p. 31 [Intro:6].
17. Ibid., p. 135 [3:1].
18. Ibid., p. 141 [3:1].
19. Ibid., p. 163 [3:8].

XIX   Dar al Islam—West

1. A. Altmann and S. M. Stern, *Isaac Israeli—His Works Translated with Comments* (London: Oxford University Press, 1958), p. 119 (*Elements:* 1).
2. Ibid., pp. 126–127 (*Elements:* 9).
3. Ibid., p. 110 (*Spirit and Soul:* 8).
4. B. Lewis, trans., *The Kingly Crown* (London: Valentine-Mitchell, 1961), p. 47.
5. Ibid., pp. 47–48.
6. Altmann and Stern, *Isaac Israeli*, p. 114 (*Spirit and Soul:* 15).
7. S. Solis-Cohen, trans., and H. Brody, ed., *Selected Poems of Moses ibn Ezra* (Philadelphia: The Jewish Publication Society of America, 1934), p. 76.
8. D. Goldstein, trans., *Hebrew Poets from Spain* (New York: Schocken Books, 1966), p. 91 (Judah ha Levi).
9. Ibid., p. 92.
10. J. Mann, *Texts and Studies in Jewish History and Literature* (Cincinnati: Hebrew Union College Press, 1931), vol. I, pp. 12–14.
11. D. S. Sassoon, ed., *Diwan of Shemuel Hannaghid* (London: Oxford University Press, 1934), *Ben Tehillim* p. 143.
12. B. Martin, trans., *A History of Jewish Literature of Israel Zinberg* (Cleveland: The Press of Case Western Reserve University, 1972), vol. 1, p. 26.
13. Solomon ibn Gabirol, "Geulah" for the first Sabbath after Passover.
14. Jonah ibn Jannah, Kitab al Tankih (Berlin: Wissenschaft des Judentums, 1930).
15. Solis-Cohen and Brody, *Selected Poems of Moses ibn Ezra*, p. 75.
16. Ibid., p. 77.
17. Moses ibn Ezra, "Zeman Havli."
18. V. E. Reichert, *The Tahkemoni of Judah al-Harizi* (Jerusalem: Raphael Haim Cohen's Press, 1965), vol. I, pp. 60–63.

Notes

19. Solis-Cohen and Brody, *Selected Poems of Moses ibn Ezra*, p. 158.

20. Goldstein, *Hebrew Poets from Spain*, p. 80.

21. G. Wigoder, trans., *The Meditation of the Sad Soul of Abraham bar Ḥayya* (New York: Schocken Books, 1969), p. 38.

22. Bahya ibn Pakuda, "Barechi Nafshi."

23. Judah ha Levi, "Mi Chamocha Amukot Goleh."

24. Solomon ibn Gabirol, "Nigdeah Keren Adinah," "Lu Haitah Nafshi," and "Keshoresh Etz."

25. Solomon ibn Gabirol, "Behar Mehahabi."

26. H. N. Bialik and Y. H. Rawnitzky, eds., *Poems of S. ibn Gabirol* (Heb.) (Tel Aviv: Devir, 1924), pp. 1, 137.

27. I. Zangwill, trans., and I. Davidson, ed., *Selected Religious Poems of Solomon ibn Gabirol* (Philadelphia: The Jewish Publication Society, 1923), p. 52.

28. Solomon ibn Gabirol, "Nefesh Asher Alu Shonehah."

29. Zangwill and Davidson, *Selected Religious Poems*, p. 55.

30. Solis-Cohen and Brody, *Selected Poems of Moses ibn Ezra*, p. 158.

31. A. Cohen, *Solomon ibn Gabirol's Choice of Pearls* (New York: Bloch Publishing Company, 1925), pp. 105–107 (Nos. 498, 500, 501, 503, 504, 506).

32. Wigoder, *Meditation of the Sad Soul*, p. 147.

33. M. Hyamson, *Duties of the Heart by Bachya ben Joseph ibn Paquda* (New York: Bloch Publishing Company, 1943), 4:2.

34. Ibid., 9:5.

35. Ibid., 9:1.

36. I. Heinemmann, ed., *Jehudah Halevi, Kuzari* (Oxford: East and West Library, 1947), p. 34 (1:13).

37. Ibid., p. 34 (1:13).

38. Ibid., p. 33 (1:1).

39. Ibid.

40. Ibid., p. 77 (2:50).

41. N. Salaman and H. Brody, *Selected Poems of Jehudah Halevi* (Philadelphia: The Jewish Publication Society, 1924), p. 127.

42. Ibid., p. 128.

43. Heinemmann, *Jehudah Halevi, Kuzari*, p. 118.

44. A. ibn Daud's *Emunah Ramah* has not yet been translated into English.

45. Ibid., Introduction.

46. G. D. Cohen, *The Book of Tradition by Abraham ibn Daud* (Philadelphia: The Jewish Publication Society, 1967), p. 97.

XX   The Other Moses

1. G. D. Cohen, *The Book of Tradition by Abraham ibn Daud* (Philadelphia: Jewish Publication Society, 1967), pp. 87–88.

2. Ibid., pp. 96–97.

3. D. J. Silver, *Maimonidean Criticism and the Maimonidean Controversy* (Leiden: Brill, 1965), p. 20.

4. A. Halkin, ed., and B. Cohen, trans., *Epistle to Yemen (Iggeret Teman)* (New York: American Academy for Jewish Research, 1952), p. ii.

5. Ibid., p. xx.

6. Ibid., p. vi.

7. Ibid., p. viii.

8. Ibid., p. vi.

9. A. J. Wolf, trans., "Maimonides on Immortality and the Principles of Judaism," *Judaism*, 15 (1966): 211, from *Helek Sanhedrin*, Chap. 10.

10. A. M. Hershman, trans., *The Code of Maimonides—The Book of Judges* (New Haven: Yale University Press, 1949), pp. 240–241, from *M. T. Melochim* 12:1.

11. A. David, trans., *The Commentary to Mishnah Aboth* (New York: Bloch, 1968), p. 122.

12. H. Adler, *Miscellany of Hebrew Literature* (London, 1872), p. 223.

13. S. Gandz and H. Klein, trans., *The Code of Maimonides—The Book of Seasons* (New Haven: Yale University Press, 1961), pp. 431–435. *M. T. Taanit* 1:1–17.

14. Silver, *Maimonidean Criticism*, p. 176.

15. *M. T. Madda* 1:1.

Notes

16. S. Pines, trans., *The Guide of the Perplexed* (Chicago: University of Chicago Press, 1963), pp. 111–112 (1:50).

17. A. Marx, trans., "Texts by and about Maimonides," *Jewish Quarterly Review*, 35 (1935): 378.

18. Ibid.

19. Pines, *The Guide of the Perplexed*, pp. 48–49 (1:21).

20. Ibid., p. 50 (1:21).

21. Ibid., p. 5 (Intro. part I).

22. Ibid., p. 4 (Dedication).

23. Ibid., p. 475 (3:18).

24. Wolf, "Maimonides on Immortality," p. 214.

25. T.B. San. 53b.

26. Pines, *The Guide of the Perplexed*, p. 526 (3:32).

27. Ibid., p. 526 (3:32).

28. Ibid., p. 635 (3:54).

29. Ibid., p. 69 (1:32).

GLOSSARY OF HEBREW TERMS

Aggadah: The nonlegal part of the postbiblical oral Torah, consisting of narratives, legends, parables, allegories, poems, prayers, theological, and philosophical reflections.

Akedah: The biblical account of Abraham's trial of faith when he is ordered to sacrifice his son (Gen. 22). In rabbinic times a paradigm of the test and of the reward of loyalty.

Aliyah: Literally "going up." Jerusalem was in the Judean hills and pilgrimage there was an ascent. The term came to designate all immigration from the Diaspora to Israel.

Am ha-Aretz: Literally "people of the land." Originally farmers who could not be trusted to tithe their produce, then a synonym for illiterate or boor.

Amora: (pl. Amoraim) The title given to the Jewish scholars of Palestine and especially of Babylonia in the third to the sixth centuries whose work and thought is recorded in the *Gemara*.

Apikoros: A Hebraized form of Epicurus, used by the sages to designate a cynic or hedonist.

Arvit: The public evening service celebrated after sunset. Today it is better known as *Maariv*.

Avodah Zarah: The collective term for idolatry and paganism. By law the Jew must separate himself from contact with all religious forms so defined.

Baraita: A name for those oral law traditions which derive from tannaitic times and were not included in the *Mishnah*.

Berit: Literally "covenant." Israel's relationship with God is bound by a formal compact (Sinai). By extension, the term came to describe the act of enrollment, the circumcision (*berit milah*) of a male on the eighth day after his birth.

Bet ha-Knesset: Literally "a place of meeting." The synagogue which

[436]

in rabbinic times served as meeting house, popular assembly, hotel, and school as well as sanctuary.

Bet ha-Midrash: A school for higher rabbinic learning. In the post-Talmudic age most synagogues had a Bet ha-Midrash or were themselves called by the term, since they were centers of study as well as prayer.

Bet ha-Mikdash: Literally "The Holy Place." The Temple in Jerusalem which served until 70 C.E. as the ceremonial center of the Jewish people and, according to rabbinic Judaism, will do so again in messianic times.

Bittaḥon: The virtue of trust, faithful confidence in God's promise, untroubled reliance on God.

Dayyan: A judge in a rabbinical court who is competent to decide on cases involving financial liability and civil law as well as questions of a religious or ritual character.

Derash: Homiletical interpretation of Scripture.

Devekut: The ultimate goal of the mystical enterprise consisting of a cleaving to or communion with the *Shechinah*, God's immanent presence.

Ethrog: A citrus fruit (citron), one of the four species (Lev. 23:40) blessed during Sukkot festivities as symbol "of the fruit of goodly trees."

Galut: Literally "exile." The term describes a condition of Jewish life which does not have its center in a free Zion, and the abnormality of life as a minority in the various places of actual dispersion.

Gaon: (pl. Geonim) The spiritual and intellectual leaders of Babylonian Jewry in the post-Talmudic period, from the sixth through the eleventh centuries. The head of each of the two major academies of Babylonia, at Sura and Pumbedita, held the title Gaon.

Gemara: The second basic strand of the *Talmud*, consisting of a commentary on, and supplement to, the *Mishnah*.

Gematria: A system of exegesis based on the interpretation of a word or words according to the numerical value of the constituent Hebrew letters.

Genizah: A depository for used and damaged sacred books, manuscripts, religious utensils, and so on. The most widely known *genizah* was discovered in modern times in a synagogue of Fustat (Old Cairo) which had been built in 882 C.E.

Haftarah: A section from the Prophets or Writings read after the synagogue reading from the Torah. A *haftarah* portion is usually thematically consistent with the Torah selection.

Halachah: The prescriptions of the oral law, in contrast to *aggadah*, the nonlegal elements.

Hanukkah: The annual eight-day celebration (25 Kislev) of the rededication of the Temple by the Maccabees (167 B.C.E.).

Hasid: (pl. Hasidim) Strict Sabbath observers who fought against the Hellenization of Jerusalem (2nd cent. B.C.E.). Also a rabbinic term for one who not only obeys the law, but does so in a spirit of loving devotion, who is willing to go beyond the law's letter. Such a "saint" built up credits with God, and so was sometimes turned to as a rainmaker or holy man.

Kaddish: The best-known doxology in the Jewish liturgy. Originally recited at the conclusion of an exposition in a house of study, it eventually became the special prayer for mourners.

Kallah: (pl. Kallot) Semiannual month-long academic and administrative conferences of scholars in the Geonic academies.

Kavannah: The term describes joyous involvement in one's duties to God; intention as opposed to rote or careless repetition.

Lulav: A palm branch to which myrtle and willow sprigs are bound which is raised during the Sukkoth Festival in association with the hope of rain.

Maaseh Bereshit: Literally "work of creation." Cosmological speculation based on the first chapter of Genesis, one of the primary interests of early Jewish mysticism.

Maaseh Merkavah: Literally "work of the chariot." Theosophical speculation based on the first chapter of Ezekiel, to which the mystics turned for various descriptions of the nature of God.

Masorah: The scholarly tradition which determined the text, punctuation, vocalization, spelling, and so on, of the Hebrew Bible.

Mazzal Tov: Literally "a good star." A greeting: good luck.

Midrash: (pl. Midrashim) The discovery of new meanings besides literal ones in the Bible. The term is used to designate collections of Scriptural exposition.

Minhag: A well-established practice which, though not specifically required by the oral law, still is considered binding. Synagogue liturgy is a case in point.

Minhah: The daily cereal offering. This term was used by the rabbis to describe the daily public service scheduled in the afternoon before sunset.

[438]

Glossary of Hebrew Terms

Mishnah: The legal codification containing the core of the post-biblical oral Torah, compiled and edited by Judah ha-Nasi at the beginning of the third century C.E.

Mitzvah: (pl. Mitzvot) Any of the discrete commandments of the law. The term was also broadly applied to good deeds and irenic acts not specifically stipulated, thus the colloquial expression to "do a *mitzvah*."

Musaf: Originally the additional sacrifice offered on the Sabbath, new moons, and festivals, then the title of the additional service added to the liturgy on those occasions.

Olam ha-Ba: Literally "the World to Come." In the apocalyptic texts a term for life after Judgment Day, the world which will be created after this world is destroyed. In rabbinic times it describes the time of resurrection.

Pesaḥ: Passover, the week-long celebration of the deliverance of the children of Israel from Egyptian bondage. The ritual features a ceremonial meal (*Seder*) at which each family recites a liturgy which relives the freedom march (*Haggadah*).

Peshat: A straightforward or exoteric explanation of Scripture, as opposed to a homiletic or mystical interpretation.

Piyyut: (pl. Piyyutim) A Hebrew liturgical poem. The practice of writing such poems began in Palestine, probably around the fifth century C.E., and continued for centuries.

Purim: An annual celebration of the deliverance of the Jews of Persia (14 Adar) from the genocidal plans of Haman (see book of Esther). Also a general name for local celebrations of deliverance from various dangers.

Rosh ha-Shanah: A High Holy day, New Year's Day (1 Tishri), whose theme is God's judgment of each individual and man's concern with his standing before the Heavenly Tribunal.

Sanhedrin: A Hebrew word of Greek origin which appears in rabbinic literature, as a designation for an assembly of scholars who serve both as the supreme court and the legislature of Judaism.

Savoraim: Babylonian scholars of the sixth and seventh century who organized the *Gemara*, added some explanations and ended the growth of the *Babylonian Talmud*.

Shaḥarit: Literally "dawn." Originally the morning sacrifice, then adopted as the title of the daily morning service of the synagogue.

Shechinah: A term used to designate the presence of God in the world, in the midst of Israel, or with individuals. In contrast to the principle of divine transcendence, Shechinah represents the principle of divine immanence.

Shema: The first word of Deuteronomy 6:4, "Hear O Israel, the Lord our God, the Lord is One." Originally a simple watchword, then a sizable section of the daily liturgy comprised of three Torah readings, (Deut. 6:4–9, Deut. 11:13:21, Num. 15:37–41), together with special benedictions. The *Shema* states the central affirmations of the faith.

Siddur: The order of public worship for daily and Sabbath worship. The first such order was published by the Gaon Amram in the ninth century.

Sofer: (pl. Soferim) Scribes and teachers who participated in the promulgation of the Torah and the administration of Judean life from the fifth to the third centuries B.C.E.

Sugyah: (pl. Sugyot) Title for a unit of *Gemara* commenting on a particular *Mishnah*.

Takkanah: A regulation supplementing the law of the Torah.

Talmud: The title applied to the two great compilations, distinguished as the *Babylonian Talmud* and the *Palestinian Talmud*, in which the records of academic discussion about postbiblical Jewish law are assembled. Both *Talmuds* also contain *aggadah* or nonlegal material.

Tanach: The Hebrew acronym which designates the three major sections of the canonized Bible: Torah (*Pentateuch*), *Neviim* (prophets), and *Ketuvim* (writings).

Tanna: (pl. Tannaim) A teacher mentioned in the *Mishnah*, or in literature contemporaneous with the *Mishnah*, i.e., the first two centuries C.E.

Targum: An Aramaic translation of the Bible.

Tefillin: Two black leather boxes fastened to leather straps worn on the arm and head by an adult male Jew, especially during the weekday morning prayer. The boxes contain four portions of the Pentateuch written on parchment (Ex. 13:1–10, 11–16, Deut. 6:4–9, 11:13–20).

Teshuvah: The term describes the turning of one's life toward God and God's word, most commonly translated "repentence."

Tishah Be-Av: An annual fast day (9 Av) which memorializes the destruction of the First and Second Temples.

Torah: In its narrowest meaning, the Pentateuch. In a broader meaning, Torah comprises all the written as well as the oral law. In its widest meaning Torah signifies Jewish learning.

Tzitzit: Threads intertwined with blue cords, the wearing of which on the corners of garments is ordained by biblical law (Num. 15:37–41).

Yetzer ha-Ra: The evil inclination, passion, the worldly drive.

Yetzer Tov: The good inclination, discipline, conscience.

Yom Kippur: A solemn fast day (10 Tishri) when the High Priest sought divine atonement for Israel's sins. In rabbinic times the fast became a twenty-four hour vigil of confession and petition during which the worshipper sought God's forgiveness and promised a renewal of his spiritual undertaking.

Zohar: The chief work of the Spanish Kabbalah, traditionally ascribed to Simeon bar Yoḥai (second century) but probably written by the Spanish Kabbalist Moses de Leon at the end of the thirteenth century.

BIBLIOGRAPHY

RATHER than offer yet another alphabetical list of reference works, we propose to mention and briefly comment on studies which a nonprofessional may find useful. Assuming that those who read Hebrew, Greek, or Arabic, not to speak of German and French, already know or can easily acquaint themselves with the multilingual technical literature, we have limited references to works available in English.

By way of general information, there are three multivolumed Jewish encyclopedias in English: *The Jewish Encyclopedia* (New York: Funk and Wagnalls Co., 1901), which has classic essays on Hellenistic and rabbinic theological ideas; *The Universal Jewish Encyclopedia* (New York: The Universal Jewish Encyclopedia, Inc., 1939), which is shorter and spotty; and the *Encyclopedia Judaica* (Jerusalem: Keter Publishing House, 1971), which brings the archeological and historical material up to date and has a particularly brilliant section on mysticism and Kabbalah organized and largely written by the master, Gershon Scholem. There is a handy one-volume work, *The Encyclopedia of the Jewish Religion*, edited by R. J. Z. Werblowsky and G. Wigoder (New York: Holt, Rinehart and Winston, 1966), which presents concise articles on major concepts and the realia of Judaism.

Critical history is less than a century and a half old among Jews. The granddaddy of such works is Heinrich Graetz's six-volume *History of the Jews* (Philadelphia: The Jewish Publication Society, 1891). Graetz occupies about the same place in Jewish historiography as Gibbon in Roman. He is fun to read, brilliant, caustic, opinionated, and completely outdated. Simon Dubnow's five-volume *History of the Jews* has been translated by Moshe Spiegel from the Russian (South Brunswick: Thomas Yoseloff, 1967–1972). The original was completed during the 1920s and is oriented to political and social matters. Dubnow's approach to the biblical era is that of a freethinking socialist historian to whom the mass of archeological research of the last half century was simply not available. He is superb on the European experience. Salo W. Baron's fifteen volume *A Social and Religious*

[442]

Bibliography

History of the Jews, 2nd ed. rev. and enlarged (New York: Columbia University Press, 1952–1972) hardly pauses over the biblical material but is extensive, one might almost say exhaustive, on the periods he treats (down to 1650 C.E.). His style is verbose and often murky, but everything is there. To anyone without access to a card catalogue, Baron's comprehensive notes open every field and issue. He lists all the relevant monographic literature to the date of publication. Rutgers has begun publishing a translation from the Hebrew of a multivolume *World History of the Jewish People* (Jerusalem: Jewish History Publications Ltd., 1966–1972) of which the following have appeared: vol. 1, *At the Dawn of Civilization*, ed. E. A. Speiser; vol. 2, *Patriarchs* and vol. 3, *Judges*, both ed. B. Mazaar; vol. 6, *The Hellenistic Age*, ed. A. Schalit; and vol. 11, *The Dark Ages*, ed. C. Roth. This series presents the thinking of some of the best Israeli scholars of the last generation; when completed its various essays will provide a mass of useful information, although a beginner may find it difficult to sort out the main themes from the profusion of detail.

Of one-volume histories there are a plethora. Two deserve special mention. They are Cecil Roth, *A Short History of the Jewish People*, 2nd ed. newly rev. (London: East and West Library, 1969), a readable and accurate political history by a fine scholar and stylist; and the older and reliable M. Margolis and A. Marx, *History of the Jewish People* (Philadelphia: Jewish Publication Society, 1927) which is full to the brim with one fact after another. Unless you have a taste for fiction, avoid M. I. Dimont, *Jews, God and History* (New York: Simon and Schuster, 1962) which is popular because it invents what every Jew would like to believe his history had been.

Developmental histories of the religious culture of the Jews are rare. Edited by Louis Finkelstein, *The Jews, Their History, Culture and Religion* 3rd ed., 2 vols. (Philadelphia: Jewish Publication Society, 1960) offers significant essays by leading American scholars under four general rubrics: "The History of Judaism and the Jews," "The Role of Judaism in Civilization," "The Sociology and Demography of the Jews," and "The Jewish Religion." Each essay is followed by a short bibliography. *Great Ages and Ideas of the Jewish People* (New York: Random House, 1956), edited by L. W. Schwartz, is an excellent companion to any standard history, providing as it does a chronologically arranged series of introductory essays. *Great Ages* concludes with a bibliography not unlike this one in spirit, but the reader is warned that a number of titles available only in Hebrew are cited as if they were available in English. J. B. Agus, *The Meaning of*

Bibliography

Jewish History (New York: Abelard-Schuman, 1963) seeks to define the Jewish experience so as to make Jewish history teach certain "truths" to which he is committed, particularly "the high potential of freedom in human affairs and . . . the melancholy consequences of its [Judaism's] failure to utilize its opportunities" (p. 484). It is a brief against both contemporary Orthodoxy and Zionism, but it stands as a pioneering attempt to treat the history of Judaism as well as the history of Jews. Agus, *The Evolution of Jewish Thought, From Biblical Times to the Opening of the Modern Era* (New York: Abelard-Schuman, 1959), evidences the same predispositions and manages to devote one quarter of a one hundred and fifty-eight page text detailing the first twenty-five hundred years of Jewish thought to "the secession of Christianity." B. J. Bamberger, *The Story of Judaism* (New York: Union of American Hebrew Congregations, 1957) is far more than the secondary school text which was commissioned. Succinct, eminently readable, informed with sound scholarship, perhaps too confident of the future of Jewish liberalism, it is the book besides this one I would give to anyone who has the time or the inclination to read a single volume on the evolution of Jewish thought.

There are any number of one-volume analyses of Judaism, each, of course, reflecting its time and the preconceptions as well as the scholarship of its author. Everything is neatly and confidently blocked out in K. Kohler, *Jewish Theology* (New York: The Macmillan Co., 1918) but M. Joseph, *Judaism as Creed and Life* (London: George Routledge and Sons Ltd., 1903) and S. Schechter, *Some Aspect of Rabbinic Theology* (New York: The Macmillan Co., 1909) are more discursive, rabbinically oriented, and readable. The novelist H. Wouk's *This Is My God* (Garden City: Doubleday, 1959) is an orthodox layman's existential view of what he has been taught Judaism is, and a delightful plate from which to taste rabbinic Judaism as the people relished it. G. Abraham, *The Jewish Mind* (Boston: Beacon Press, 1962), offers an arresting contrast to Wouk, for this book, too, is a personal appreciation, but from an English and more legal than literary perspective. A more scholarly and poetic appreciation of that same tradition can be found in A. Heschel, *Man Is Not Alone, A Philosophy of Judaism* (New York: Farrar, Straus and Young, 1951) and *God in Search of Man, A Philosophy of Judaism* (Philadelphia: Jewish Publication Society, 1956).

A. H. Silver, *Where Judaism Differed, An Inquiry into the Distinctiveness of Judaism* (New York: The Macmillan Co., 1956) is just that, a suggestive attempt to isolate the major Judaic attitudes and treat

[444]

them in terms of comparative religious systems. B. Z. Bokser, *Judaism and the Christian Predicament* (New York: Knopf, 1967) takes the comparative approach from a somewhat narrower perspective.

There are cultural predispositions. Systematic philosophy developed naturally among the Greeks and as an acquired taste among the Jews. The reason for this escapes us. It has something to do with spiritual conditioning and perhaps a good bit to do with language. Greek is highly inflected, rich in abstractions, capable of expressing the shadings of meaning. Hebrew, on the other hand, expresses action and emotion feelingly and is disposed to the concrete and the visual. In two sentences a full story can be told. The Bible obviously contains philosophical and theological ideas, but these are not analytically expressed. The struggle to formulate Judaism systematically can be followed in two readable books, J. Blau, *The Story of Jewish Philosophy* (New York: Random House, 1962) and the more complete J. Guttmann, *Philosophies of Judaism* (New York: Holt, Rinehart and Winston, 1964). Please do not be tempted by Z. Cahn, *The Philosophy of Judaism* (New York: The Macmillan Co., 1962).

Histories of the ritual and calendar of Judaism reveal much about its conceptual development. L. Yarden, *The Tree of Life, A Study of the Menorah* (Ithaca: Cornell University Press, 1971) illustrates what can be done when a single ritual object is traced through texts and remaining physical records. H. Schauss, *The Jewish Festivals* (Cincinnati: Union of American Hebrew Congregations, 1938) was a Yiddish classic before translation, a first serious attempt to treat the holidays developmentally. T. H. Gaster, *Festivals of the Jewish Year* (New York: Sloane, 1953) adds a good bit of anthropology and liturgy and is eminently readable. Before anyone rushes out to speak at the local church on Jesus and the Last Supper, he ought to read J. B. Segal, *The Hebrew Passover, From the Earliest Times to A.D.* 70 (London: Oxford University Press, 1963). L. Jacobs, *A Guide to Yom Kippur* and *A Guide to Rosh ha-Shanah* (London: Jewish Chronicle Publications, 1957, 1959) are brief and useful. N. Barack, *The History of the Sabbath* (New York: Jonathan David, 1965) and A. E. Millgram, *Sabbath, The Day of Delight* (Philadelphia: Jewish Publication Society, 1944) are more complete and systematic than A. J. Heschel, *The Sabbath: Its Meaning for Modern Man* (New York: Farrar, Straus and Young, 1951) presents the Sabbath in a telling and poignant way.

Postbiblical Jewish material is not readily accessible. A number of anthologies have been edited, of which the following are varied enough to be of some use: Curt Leviant, ed., *Masterpieces of Hebrew*

[445]

Bibliography

Literature (New York: Ktav, 1969) and N. M. Glatzer, *Judaic Tradition* (Boston: Beacon Press, 1969).

I The Fathers and Their Way

H. Orlinsky, *Ancient Israel* (Ithaca: Cornell University Press, 1960) is a useful syllabus which provides a clear introduction to biblical history. W. F. Albright's short *The Biblical Period from Abraham to Ezra* (New York: Harper Torchbooks, 1965) revises his article in Finkelstein, *The Jews*, and is a good place to begin study of the work of the dean of American biblical scholars and archeologists. His earlier works, *From the Stone Age to Christianity* (Baltimore: Johns Hopkins Press, 1940) and *Archeology and the Religion of Israel* (Baltimore: Johns Hopkins Press, 1942) are harder going, but are seminal classics in what has proved to be a significant revision of an earlier scholarship that had used the texts but not the evidence from the tells. Anything by Albright can be read with profit. M. Noth, *The History of Israel* (New York: Harper and Brothers, 1960) and J. Bright, *A History of Israel* (Philadelphia: Westminster Press, 1972) are reliable accounts which are often and wisely assigned as required readings in courses on the Bible.

There are a plethora of modern Bible translations. I have found *The New English Bible* (New York: Cambridge University Press, 1969) the most satisfying when I want to enjoy the sweep of a passage, and *The Torah* (Philadelphia: Jewish Publication Society, 1967) and *The Holy Scriptures According to the Massoretic Text* (Philadelphia: Jewish Publication Society, 1917) to be best when I want a rather faithful rendering of the Jewish meaning. Among the commentaries *The Interpreters' Bible*, 12 vols. (New York: Abingdon Press, 1956) is a standard for Protestant divinity schools. It contains much information clothed in liberal Christianity's conscious and unconscious biases. The still incomplete *The Anchor Bible* (Garden City: Doubleday, 1960 to date) is self-consciously ecumenical. Each volume provides a new translation, line-by-line notes, and longer comments on each section. Quality varies with the author. For those who want the original Hebrew text along with traditional rabbinic commentary, *The Soncino Books of the Bible*, 16 vols. (London: Soncino Press, 1956) provides the text, the Jewish Publication Society 1917 translation, and a conventional selection from midrashic and medieval commentaries. If you want a single bedside companion for your study of the Bible, *Peake's*

[446]

Commentary on the Bible (New York: Thomas Nelson, 1962) will serve the purpose.

For those who want a guidebook into the highways and detours of biblical analysis, Otto Eissfeldt, *The Old Testament, An Introduction* (New York: Harper and Row, 1965) contains most everything including material on the Apocrypha and Pseudepigrapha arranged with Germanic precision. Each section is preceded with a bibliography of all significant literature through the 1950s. If you just want a simple introduction, J. K. West, *Introduction to the Old Testament* (New York: The Macmillan Co., 1971) was written as a college text and offers an adequate presentation of the current interpretive consensus. J. A. Bewer, *The Literature of the Old Testament*, 3rd ed. rev. by E. G. Kraeling (New York: Columbia University Press, 1962) is a long familiar and useful standby.

Nahum M. Sarna has written a solid popular commentary to the sagas, *Understanding Genesis* (New York: Jewish Theological Seminary of America, 1966) and E. A. Speiser a model critical commentary, *Genesis* (Garden City: Doubleday, 1964). J. M. Holt, *The Patriarchs of Israel* (Nashville: Vanderbilt University Press, 1964) and A. Parrot, *Abraham and His Times* (Philadelphia: Fortress Press, 1962) attempt to draw together what has been learned.

For those who would consult comparative literatures, James Pritchard, ed., *Ancient Near Eastern Texts*, 3rd ed. (Princeton: Princeton University Press, 1964) is the anthology. If you are not worried about precision and want simply to enjoy the various myths, T. H. Gaster, *The Oldest Stories in the World* (New York: Viking Press, 1952) provides a swift-paced and unpretentious retelling.

Questions as to the nature of the Hebrews' God are best left to the experts, but if you will not leave the matter alone, A. Alt's discussion, "The God of the Fathers" in his *Essays on Old Testament History and Religion* (Garden City: Doubleday, 1967) is useful.

II The Covenant Relationship

Three works lay out with scholarly thoroughness the covenant base of biblical religion: G. Mendenhall, *Law and Covenant in Israel and the Ancient Near East* (New York: Biblical Colloquium, 1955); W. Eichrodt, *Theology of the Old Testament*, 6th ed. (Philadelphia: The Westminster Press, 1967), and A. Alt's previously cited *Essays on Old Testament History and Religion*. G. von Rad, *Old Testament Theology*

(New York: Harper and Row, 1962) broadens the perspectives of biblical thought and is required reading for anyone really interested in biblical religion.

The study of biblical theology is still in its infancy, since it is always easier to deal with linguistic analysis than cultural synthesis, but several studies can be mentioned: N. Snaith, *Distinctive Ideas in the Old Testament* (London: Epworth, 1947); H. H. Rowley, *The Faith of Israel* (London: SCM Press, 1957); W. A. Irwin, *The Old Testament: Keystone of Human Culture* (New York: H. Schuman, 1952); and G. E. Wright, *The Old Testament Against Its Background* (New York: Harper and Row, 1969). B. Albrektson, *History and the Gods* (Lund: Gleerup, 1967), reminds those who are mesmerized by the Bible's uniqueness that neither the covenant theme nor the concept of a God who acts in history was original to Israel.

Readable studies in biblical law are rare. D. Daube, *Studies in Biblical Laws* (Cambridge: Cambridge University Press, 1947), and M. Noth, *The Laws in the Pentateuch and Other Studies* (Philadelphia: Fortress Press, 1967) are heavy with facts. Several monographs may be of greater use: S. E. Loewenstamm, "Law," in the previously cited vol. 3 of *World History of the Jewish People*; A. Alt, "The Origins of Israelite Law," in his *Essays*, 1967; and W. Harrelson, "Law in the Old Testament," in *The Interpreter's Bible*, vol. 3, 1956.

III   God's Freedom and God's Bondage

G. von Rad, *Moses* (New York: Association Press, 1960), and M. Buber, *Moses* (Oxford: East and West Library, 1947), are interpretive biographies of first rank which analyze *inter alia* such issues as the reliability of the biblical evidence, the influence of Akhenaton's monistic theology of Aton, and the date of the Exodus. A. Neher, *Moses, and the Vocation of the Jewish People* (London: Longmans, 1959) provides a brief life and an occasionally suggestive discourse on the impact of the Mosaic legacy on Jewish life and thought. Teachers who believe in "relevance" sometimes assign S. Freud's *Moses and Monotheism* (New York: Knopf, 1939), about which the kindest thing that can be said is that however psychologically imaginative his theme, it is historically worthless.

Since our focus is not only on events but on their influence, Book I of L. Baeck's *This People Israel; The Meaning of Jewish Existence* (New York: Holt, Rinehart and Winston, 1964), might well be read at this point. Written in a German concentration camp with only his memory for reference, these chapters distill brilliantly and feelingly what Covenant, Exodus, Sinai, Wilderness, and Land have meant to Jews over the long centuries.

IV   Land

K. M. Kenyon, the excavator of Jericho and second millennium Jerusalem, presents the culture of Canaan and Israel's other neighbors in *Archaeology in the Holy Land* (New York: Praeger, 1970), a book which has the added advantage of a bibliography arranged according to the various excavated sites. M. Noth, *The Old Testament World* (Philadelphia: Fortress Press, 1966) is arranged topically rather than chronologically and provides clear, if tightly compressed, information on all phases of West Asian life during the second and first millennia. Y. Aharoni, *The Land of the Bible* (Philadelphia: Westminster Press, 1967) is a standard manual of biblical geography, and Y. Aharoni and M. Avi Yonah, *The MacMillan Bible Atlas* (New York: Macmillan Co., 1968) allows you to follow the movements of tribes, armies, and boundaries with ease and precision. Interestingly, the four-volume *Interpreter's Dictionary of the Bible* (New York: Abingdon, 1962) does not include an entry under "Land," "Promised Land," or "Holy Land," mute testimony of the unconscious way in which Christian scholarship has imposed Christian theological categories on biblical thought.

On the practice of war, the two-volume work of the general-archeologist Y. Yadin, *The Art of Warfare in Biblical Lands* (New York: McGraw-Hill, 1963) tells more than you may wish to know about a violent art, but the text is well written and the illustrations are magnificent and, what is not always true in books on antiquity, useful. G. von Rad's monograph, "Deuteronomy and the Holy War," in his *Studies in Deuteronomy* (London: SCM Press, 1953), deals with the all too rarely explored theme of the theory and theology of war in Israelite thought.

V   Power

This is as good a place as any to recommend a popular history, *The Jews in Their Land*, edited by D. Ben Gurion (Garden City: Doubleday and Co., 1966), a profusely illustrated, well-mapped book of essays by Israeli scholars on the successive periods of Jewish settlement in their land.

Biblical political theory is a relatively uncharted area. R. de Vaux, *Ancient Israel: Its Life and Institutions* (New York: McGraw-Hill, 1961) provides a thorough and succinct statement of the operations of the tribal federation, judgeship, and the person and office of the king, as well as a complete and authoritative description of the religious forms of biblical Israel, which makes information retireval on any particular subject simple. For those who want to sample the rarified arguments of scholars who see Israel's kings as sacred cultic figures, A. R. Johnson, *Sacral Kingship in Ancient Israel* (Mystic: Verry Press, 1967), is a short review of this group's main arguments.

VI   The Way and the Wayward

J. Lindblom, *Prophecy in Ancient Israel* (Philadelphia: Muhlenberg Press, 1962), a translation of a 1934 work, remains a valid manual. For those who seek meaning as well as critical analysis, two Jewish scholars have written sensitive studies of the prophetic movement: M. Buber, *The Prophetic Faith* (New York: The Macmillan Co., 1949), and A. J. Heschel, *The Prophets* (New York: Harper and Row, 1962). J. P. Hyatt, *Prophetic Religion* (New York: Abingdon Press, 1947) and H. H. Rowley, *Men of God* (London: Thomas Nelson and Sons, 1963) are valuable studies by Protestant scholars. If you want to understand prophecy in an hour, try S. H. Blank, *Understanding the Prophets* (New York: Harper and Row, 1969). Better yet, if you are not put off by a religious school text, try H. G. Goodman, *The Story of Prophecy* (New York: Behrman House, 1965).

Naviism is delineated in W. F. Albright, *Archaeology and the Religion of Israel* (Baltimore: Johns Hopkins Press, 1942) and in his "Samuel and the Beginnings of the Prophetic Movement," in *Interpreting the Prophetic Tradition* (Cincinnati: Hebrew Union College Press, 1969). Analyses of individual literary prophets can be found in any of the standard commentaries.

VII   This Was Believed

Wisdom literature is easier going than the prophets, so there is a correspondingly greater number of synthesizing works. J. C. Rylaarsdam's essay in the cited *Peake's Commentary* provides an excellent overview, as does G. von Rad in *Wisdom In Israel* (Nashville: Abingdon Press, 1972). O. S. Rankin, *Israel's Wisdom Literature* (Edinburgh: T. Clarke, 1954) is a generation older, but a familiar and useful guide. R. B. Y. Scott's commentary in the Anchor Bible series, *Proverbs—Ecclesiastes* (Garden City: Doubleday and Co., 1965) has excellent notes and a careful translation. Add, if you have a chance, "The Social Background of Wisdom Literature," in R. Gordis, *Poets, Prophets and Sages* (Bloomington: Indiana University Press, 1971).

I was weaned on M. Buttenwieser, *The Psalms: Chronologically Treated with a New Translation* (Chicago: University of Chicago Press, 1938), a brilliant tour de force of the "let's rearrange the text" school. S. Mowinckel, *The Psalms in Israel's Worship* (Nashville: Abingdon Press, 1962) insists on their cultic use and meaning. H. Ringgren, *The Faith of the Psalmists* (Philadelphia: Fortress Press, 1963) is a more modest and moderate introduction. Since the psalms are piety, they are sometimes best understood within one's religious conditioning. For those who want Christian spirit as well as scholarship, see J. Paterson, *The Praises of Israel* (New York: Scribner, 1950) and for those who want Jewish spirit as well as scholarship, see S. B. Freehof, *The Book of Psalms* (Cincinnati: Union of American Hebrew Congregations, 1938).

Job is the most written about book of the Bible and, paradoxically, one of the least studied. Its text is incredibly difficult. Two commentaries are particularly useful, M. H. Pope, *Job* (Garden City: Doubleday and Co., 1965) and N. H. Tur-Sinai, *The Book of Job* (Jerusalem: Kiryath-Sepher, 1957). S. B. Freehof, *Book of Job* (Cincinnati: Union of American Hebrew Congregations, 1958), is a pleasing introductory statement.

G. von Rad's commentary *Deuteronomy* (Philadelphia: The Westminster Press, 1966), is laden with scholarship, and G. E. Wright's commentary in *The Interpreter's Bible* is readable. Two fine, thorough studies have recently appeared: E. W. Nicholson, *Deuteronomy and Tradition* (Philadelphia: Fortress Press, 1967) and M. Weinfeld, *Deuteronomy and the Deuteronomic School* (New York: Oxford University Press, 1972).

VIII   Judah Is Judged

Besides the general books on prophecy already suggested, many of which offer extended analysis of the pre-exile prophets, the following have been useful: A. D. Haldar, *Studies in the Book of Nahum*

(Uppsala: Lindequist, 1947); A. C. Welch, *Jeremiah, His Time and Work* (Oxford: Oxford University Press, 1951); and in the Anchor series, J. Bright, *Jeremiah* (Garden City: Doubleday and Co., 1965).

Elias Bickerman insists that Jonah, along with Daniel, Ecclesiastes, and Esther, was written in Greek times. Perhaps, but his study of Jonah in *Four Strange Books of the Bible* (New York: Shocken Books, 1967) is certainly a most thoughtful and fascinating study, proof that scholarship can be fun. His work deserves reading.

IX   Defeat, Dispersion, and Exile

The standard histories deal adequately with the Exile. I would particularly recommend the translation by C. W. Efroymson of the pertinent sections of Y. Kaufmann, *The Religion of Israel* published as *The Babylonian Captivity and Deutero-Isaiah* (New York: Union of American Hebrew Congregations, 1970). D. R. Hiller, *Lamentations* (Garden City: Doubleday and Co., 1972) for the Anchor series, is an excellent commentary. On the norms of the poetic art the best introduction is S. Gevirtz, *Patterns in the Early Poetry of Israel* (Chicago: University of Chicago Press, 1963). H. H. Rowley, *The Book of Ezekiel in Modern Study* (Manchester: Manchester University Press, 1953), can be recommended, as well as G. A. F. Knight, *Deutero-Isaiah* (Nashville: Abingdon Press, 1965), and J. D. Smart, *History and Theology in Second Isaiah* (Philadelphia: Westminster Press, 1965).

X   From the Exile to Alexander

Debate rages on the sequence of events during the restoration. J. M. Myers' commentary on *Ezra-Nehemiah* (Garden City: Doubleday and Co., 1965) presents the issues and places them against the general background of this period. M. Smith, *Palestinian Parties and Politics That Shaped the Old Testament* (New York: Columbia University Press, 1971) insists that previous reconstructions have overestimated the spread of the biblical faith among the folk, although not necessarily the spread of a syncretistic Judaism. Nehemiah rather than Ezra becomes the effective champion of the Torah faith, and in an unexpected way. A conventional tyrant, he controls the Temple and has a power base at the Persian court that allows him to impose upon Judea the traditions of the "Yahweh-Alone Party," whose traditions the Bible refracts. The merits of the argument aside, Smith's book proves that there is still room for creative scholarship in the biblical field.

The Elephantine material is thoroughly explicated in B. Porten, *Archives from Elephantine; The Life of an Ancient Jewish Military Colony* (Berkeley: University of California Press, 1968).

XI   The Age of Variety

The Hellenistic Age, vol. 6 of *World History of the Jewish People*, 1972, is the best introduction to this age's history, although, after the introductory chapters, its focus is limited to Jewish life in Palestine before Pompey's invasion. S. Lieberman, *Greek in Jewish Palestine* and *Hellenism in Jewish Palestine* (New York: Jewish Theological Seminary of America, 1942, 1950) are anthologies of the author's pioneering work in this difficult but essential field. V. Tcherikover, *Hellenistic Civilization and the Jews* (Philadelphia: Jewish Publication Society, 1959) is excellent on demographic and political history, but regrettably lacking in extended discussion of cultural and philosophic matters.

With the events in modern Israel, the military history of the Maccabees and the political history of the Hasmonean state have recently received more than their share of attention. E. Bickerman's little volume, *The Maccabees* (New York: Schocken, 1947) is a classic of research and interpretation. S. Zeitlin's two-volume *The Rise and Fall of the Jewish State* (Philadelphia: Jewish Publication Society, 1962–1967) provides a terse social, political, and cultural history from Alexander to the first Jewish rebellion, 66 C.E., which exhibits all the power and certainty of this great scholar's mind.

More histories have been written of this period than almost any other because of Christianity's obvious interests; indeed, it is often called "intertestamental." The standard work was E. Schürer, *A History of the Jewish People in the Time of Jesus Christ* (New York: Schocken Books, 1961). The field has been plowed by Jews and Christians from this essentially Christian perspective innumerable times. M. Simon, *Jewish Sects at the Time of Jesus* (Philadelphia: Fortress, 1967) provides a short, eminently readable manual which concentrates on the messianic and apocalyptic sects, Qumran and the Essenes, and people like Philo, areas where the parallels to primitive Christianity are the most obvious. The result is to give these groups significance which they certainly did not enjoy. J. Bonsirven, *Palestinian Judaism*

[453]

in the Time of Jesus Christ (New York: Holt, Rinehart and Winston, 1964) reveals another element in the hidden agendas of many books: "Judaism's instinctive tendencies proved to be most unfortunate in the field of ethics . . . legalistic tendencies clothed ethics with a judicial aspect . . . the inevitable result was a formalism which was interested only in the outward fulfillment of the commandments . . . this is the harder line of hypocrisy" (p. 25), and we must add of that cultural blindness which has led Christianity to "put down" rabbinic Judaism rather than to understand it. F. C. Grant, *Ancient Judaism and the New Testament* (New York: The Macmillan Co., 1959) sets out to rectify the prejudice that leads the Bonsirvens "to treat Judaism as merely a foil, with the intention of showing only the superiority of Christianity, with the consequence that every shadow has been painted black, every bright light dimmed and only a caricature of that religion has survived in the imagination of most readers" (p. 14).

There are no good books about the origins of the synagogue because there are no facts, only conjecture. All that can be said was clearly laid out in S. Zeitlin, "The Origin of the Synagogue," in *Proceedings* (New York: American Academy of Jewish Research, 1951). Those interested in the development of the synagogue in rabbinic times can find the relevant facts in I. Levy, *The Synagogue, Its History and Function* (London: Vallentine, Mitchell and Co., 1963).

XII   A Change in Cultural Style

Since the texts are difficult and this world complex, it is perhaps best to begin studying the age of variety by understanding its milieu. M. Hadas, *Hellenistic Culture, Fusion and Diffusion* (New York: Columbia University Press, 1959) is a delightful guide and has the advantage of being the work of a man particularly interested in the Jewish component. F. E. Peters, *The Harvest of Hellenism* (New York: Simon and Schuster, 1970) also places the Jewish experience in the larger context.

Oxford has published the *Apocrypha of the Old Testament* (London: Oxford University Press, 1965) in an attractive format. *The New English Bible, Apocrypha* (London: Oxford University Press, 1971) is readable, but without notes. B. M. Metzger, *An Introduction to the Apocrypha* (New York: Oxford University Press, 1957) has the virtue of being the only one-volume manual available. The individual texts, translations, and commentaries in The Dropsie College series are attractive and recommended: *I. Maccabees*, and *II. Maccabees*, ed. S. Tedesche and S. Zeitlin; *III. and IV. Mac.*, ed. M. Hadas; *Aristeas to Philocrates*, ed. M. Hadas; *Tobit*, ed. F. Zimmerman; *The Book of Wisdom*, ed. J. Reider; and *Judith*, ed. S. Zeitlin (New York: Harper and Brothers, 1950–1972). Most other pseudepigraphic works are available only in R. H. Charles, *The Apocrypha and Pseudepigrapha of the Old Testament in English* (Oxford: The Clarendon Press, 1913). Philo's writings have been edited by F. H. Colson and G. H. Whitaker in the Loeb Classical Library, 10 vols. (Cambridge: Harvard University Press, 1932–1971) and are made understandable in the master's masterly analysis, H. A. Wolfson, *Philo* (Cambridge: Harvard University Press, 1947).

Morris Jastrow, Jr., knew how to write, and his *A Gentle Cynic* (Philadelphia: J. B. Lippincott Co., 1919) is a pleasant introduction to Ecclesiastes and a good sampler for anyone who wants to know how biblical studies were done a half century ago. R. Gordis, *Koheleth, The Man and His World* (New York: Jewish Publication Society, 1951), is thorough, critical, and contains both the author's translation and an extensive commentary.

XIII   Torah in the Age of Variety

Everyone knows the Pharisees, but no one knows much about them. J. Neusner, *Fellowship in Judaism, the First Century and Today* (London: Vallentine, Mitchell and Co., 1963) and *From Politics to Piety* (Englewood Cliffs, N. J.: Prentice-Hall, 1973) presents a lucid picture of the various communitarian sects and the available data on the sages. Utmost caution should be taken when reading any standard manual on the Jewish "sects." Either rabbinism is read back into this period or positive delight is taken in contrasting Pharisaic "legalism and apartheid"; the terms are those of *The International Dictionary of the Bible*, with Christian freedom and love. R. Travers Herford, *The Pharisees* (Boston: Beacon Press, 1962); L. Baeck, *The Pharisees and Other Essays* (New York: Schocken Books, 1947); and L. Finkelstein, *The Pharisees, the Sociological Background of Their Faith* (Philadelphia: Jewish Publication Society, 1962), shed helpful light on the developing rabbinic spirit without solving the riddle of the Pharisees. A. Guttmann, *Rabbinic Judaism in the Making* (Detroit: Wayne State University Press, 1970) is a rather narrow analysis of texts, as its subtitle

Bibliography

indicates: "A Chapter in the History of the Halakhah from Ezra to Judah I." N. N. Glatzer, *Hillel the Elder, the Emergence of Classical Judaism* (New York: B'nai B'rith Hillel Foundations, 1956) offers a quick and poignant visit into that world; the only trouble is that he has written the biography of a man whom legend so envelops that the mists cannot really be parted.

XIV Angels, Devils, and Judgment Day

A thorough descriptive manual on the apocalyptic literature has been provided by D. S. Russell, *The Method and Message of Jewish Apocalyptic* (Philadelphia: The Westminster Press, 1964). J. Bloch's monograph "On the Apocalyptic in Judaism," in *The Jewish Quarterly Review*, 1952, is based on the author's experience as an editor of The Dropsie Apocrypha Series. H. H. Rowley, *The Relevance of the Apocalyptic* (New York: Harper and Row, 1963) attempts to answer a probably unanswerable question.

Believe it or not, there is a *Dictionary of Angels*. The second chapter of G. Scholem, *Major Trends in Jewish Mysticism* (New York: Schocken Books, 1963) deals with angels and apocalypse and, hopefully, will lead you to read through this pathfinding study. Scholem's essay, "Towards an Understanding of the Messianic Idea in Judaism," in *The Messianic Idea in Judaism* (New York: Schocken Books, 1971) has it all. For detail, text, and historical references see J. Klausner, *The Messianic Idea in Judaism from Its Beginning to the Completion of the Mishnah* (New York: The Macmillan Co., 1955) and A. H. Silver, *A History of Messianic Speculation in Israel from the First Through the Seventeenth Centuries* (New York: The Macmillan Co., 1927). J. H. Greenstone, *The Messiah Idea in Jewish History* (Philadelphia: Jewish Publication Society, 1948) offers a brief historical overview.

There is an overabundance of literature on Qumran and the Dead Sea Scrolls. G. R. Driver, *The Judean Scrolls* (New York: Schocken Books, 1965), is typically thorough, but before tackling such a formidable work I would read H. Ringgren's brief but well-devised *The Faith of Qumran* (Philadelphia: The Fortress Press, 1961), together with G. Vermes, *Dead Sea Scrolls in English* (Baltimore: Penguin, 1962), where their literature can be tastefully sampled and a basic understanding of the community's organization, beliefs, and history gained. Generally, the Qumranites are associated with the Essenes. Alternate views are offered by C. Rabin in *Qumran Studies* (Oxford:

[456]

Oxford University Press, 1957), who connects this community with the Pharisees, and C. Roth, *The Dead Sea Scrolls: A New Historical Approach* (New York: W. W. Norton, 1965), where they are connected to the Zealots.

XV   After the Fall

J. Neusner, *A Life of Yohanan b. Zakkai* (Leiden: Brill, 1962) is more than a biography. Its real purpose is to describe the response of Pharisaism to the Temple's destruction. L. Finkelstein's two-volume biography and critical analysis of *Akiba: Scholar, Saint and Martyr* (New York: Covici Friede, 1936) is a full, if rather dense, economics- and class-oriented explanation of the work of the dominant *tanna* of the Bar Kochba period. For those who simply want to grasp the spirit and life style of the sages I can recommend a remarkably authentic historical novel, *As a Driven Leaf* (Indianapolis: Bobbs-Merrill Co., 1939) written by a scholar, rabbi, and man of letters, Milton Steinberg.

H. Danby's translation of *The Mishnah* (Oxford: Clarendon Press, 1933) is the standard. If you want only to browse and get a taste of its many parts, E. J. Lipman has published an appetizer, *The Mishnah, Oral Teachings of Judaism* (New York: Norton, 1970), which is not too taxing and has the advantage of an excellent glossary of concepts and terms. The one purely ethical treatise in the *Mishnah*, *Pirke Avot*, has been translated repeatedly and can be found bound into most *siddurim*.

The *Mekilta de Rabbi Ishmael* is the only readily available tannaitic *midrash*. There is J. Z. Lauterbach's excellent three-volume translation (Philadelphia: Jewish Publication Society, 1949) and two extended commentaries to parts of the work: J. Goldin, *The Song at the Sea* (New Haven: Yale University Press, 1971) to *Shirata* (Ex. 15) and M. Kadushin, *A Conceptual Approach to the Mekilta* (New York: J. David, 1969) to selections from *Pisha* (Ex. 12). The former is a straight midrashic evaluation and a new translation, an absolute delight to read. The latter uses the Lauterbach text as a proving ground for various theories about the existence of patterns of meaning clustered around specific rabbinic terms, a theory which the author developed more systematically, but no less heavily, in *Organic Thinking, A Study in Rabbinic Thought* (New York: Jewish Theological Seminary, 1938) and his simplified and more readable sequel, *The Rabbinic*

Bibliography

Mind (New York: Blaisdell Publishing Co., 1965). Despite his style, Kadushin makes his point. Anyone who wants to confront rabbinic thought must understand the special rabbinic value concepts which do not translate readily from Hebrew (for example, *Kedushah, Malchut Shamayim*), but express its essence.

There is a thoroughly inadequate and much excerpted translation by P. Levertoff of *Sifre* (Num.), *Midrash Sifre on Numbers* (New York: The Macmillan Co., 1926).

To appreciate the Palestinian rabbinic spirit, G. F. Moore's three-volume *Judaism in the First Centuries of the Common Era* (Cambridge: Harvard University Press, 1946) is a carefully arranged and complete classic. His achievement is proof to Jews that a non-Jew who takes the time to master texts and spirit can understand Talmudic Judaism. S. Belkin, *In His Image, The Jewish Philosophy of Man as Expressed in Rabbinic Tradition* (New York: Abelard-Schuman, 1960), depends heavily on European materials, but I know of no happier introduction to this area of thought. R. A. Stewart, *Rabbinic Theology* (Edinburgh: Oliver and Boyd, 1961) represents an interesting, rather popular approach to this material by a contemporary non-Jewish writer.

A half-century ago, G. C. Montefiore and H. Loewe published a topical, useful, if somewhat apologetically selected source book, *A Rabbinic Anthology* (Philadelphia: Jewish Publication Society, 1960) of Palestinian and Babylonian materials which has long been a standard resource for those who want a rabbinic proof text.

XVI Talmudic Judaism

The Talmudic world is difficult to understand unless you learn the idiom, and that is a major undertaking. M. Adler, *The World of the Talmud* (Washington: B'nai B'rith Hillel Foundation, 1958) is a short discussion intended to give college students the illusion of understanding. The manuals include Z. H. Chajes' mid-nineteenth-century handbook, a critical classic in its day now translated by J. Schachter as *The Student's Guide Through the Talmud* (London: East and West Library, 1952). Obviously it is dated, but it has material on language and *aggadah* not otherwise available. Useful handbooks are few, dry, and necessary. H. L. Strack, *Introduction to the Talmud* (Philadelphia: Jewish Publication Society, 1959) is a reprint of another nineteenth-century staple, this one by a leading Christian academic, and M. Mielziner, *Introduction to the Talmud* (New York: Bloch Publishing, 1925) can be recommended.

The *Babylonian Talmud* has been translated in thirty-six volumes (London: Soncino Press, 1935–1948) under the editorship of I. Epstein. An extra volume provides a topical index. More recently the same press, under the editorship of A. Cohen, added *The Minor Tractates of the Talmud* (1965). A. Cohen, *Everyman's Talmud* (London: J. M. Dent, 1949) is a terse and clear introduction that sets out the nonesoteric elements of Talmudic teaching under eleven rubrics: "The Doctrine of God," "God and the Universe," "The Doctrine of Man," "Revelation," "Domestic Life," "Social Life," "The Moral Life," "The Physical Life," "Folklore," "Jurisprudence," and "The Hereafter." Cohen's admittedly cursory treatment of what, after all, lies at the heart of the *Talmud*, the law, should be supplemented by such analyses as G. Horowitz, *The Spirit of Jewish Law* (New York: Central Book Co., 1953) and I. Herzog, *The Main Institutions of Jewish Law* (London: Soncino Press, 1936).

Perhaps the best way to capture the spirit of Talmudic law is to read one of several studies of special issues with immediate relevance. D. Daube's short *Collaboration with Tyranny in Rabbinic Law* (Oxford: Oxford University Press, 1965) is particularly interesting in light of the pressures of the Holocaust period. A. Kirschenbaum, *Self Incrimination in Jewish Law* (New York: Burning Book Press, 1970) deals with the question of confessions. L. M. Epstein, *Marriage Laws in the Bible and the Talmud* (Cambridge: Harvard University Press, 1942) and D. M. Feldman, *Birth Control in Jewish Law* (New York: New York University Press, 1968) are self-descriptive. Those interested in the relationship between the *Talmud* and other legal systems, particularly the Roman, will benefit from R. Yaron, *Gifts in Contemplation of Death* (Oxford: The Clarendon Press, 1960) and B. Cohen's essays in the field of *Jewish and Roman Law* (New York: Jewish Theological Seminary, 1966). To catch the spirit of Talmudic ethics there is a wonderful translation of a wonderful commentary on the *Mishnah*'s tractate *Avot*: J. Goldin, *The Fathers According to Rabbi Nathan* (New Haven: Yale University Press, 1955).

The relationship of Jews to the Eastern Byzantine emperors and their Church is dealt with in the plethora of books on anti-Semitism, particularly H. J. Schoeps, *The Jewish-Christian Argument: A History of Theologies in Conflict* (New York: Holt, Rinehart and Winston, 1963) and E. Flannery, *The Anguish of the Jews* (New York: The Macmillan Co., 1965). The history of the Balkan Byzantine Jewish community has to a degree been overlooked; A. Sharf's recent *Byzantine Jewry, From Justinian to the Fourth Crusade* (New York: Schocken Books, 1971) draws together what we do know.

XVII   The Rabbinic Mind

Midrash is more fun to read than to read about, and formal criticism of midrashic materials is in its infancy. L. Ginsberg, *Legends of the Jews*, 7 vols. (Philadelphia: Jewish Publication Society, 1938) is the classic compilation of rabbinic *midrash* written as a consecutive narration of the biblical story. Its three volumes of notes are a treasure lode of suggestions which this generation is just beginning to mine. Two long pieces by H. Slonimsky in *Essays* (Cincinnati: Hebrew Union College Press, 1967), "On Reading the *Midrash*" and "The Philosophy Implicit in the *Midrash*," are the best and most thoughtful introductions to the literature. A popular handbook on *midrash*, S. M. Lehrman, *The World of the Midrash* (New York: Thomas Yoseloff, 1961) serves only to show the wealth of the material and the paucity of our critical control of such matters as dates, recensions, literary forms, and method of compilation. A. W. Miller, *Understanding the Midrash* (New York: J. David, 1965) is a mistitled text. It is not a handbook, but a collection of *aggadot* from many sources and centuries.

Translations are available of the following midrashic collections: *Midrash Rabbah*, by A. Freedman and M. Simon, 10 vols. (London: Soncino Press, 1939); *The Midrash on Psalms* (*Midrash Tehillim*) and *Pesikta Rabbati*, by W. G. Braude (New Haven: Yale University Press, 1959, 1968); and *Pirke De Rabbi Eliezer*, by G. Friedlander (New York: Hermon Press, 1965). For those who can afford only fifteen minutes, N. N. Glatzer, *Hammer on the Rock, A Short Midrash Reader* (New York: Schocken Books, 1948) fulfills the title's promise.

A. Millgram, *Jewish Worship* (Philadelphia: Jewish Publication Society, 1971) is the most readable introductory text in a field where A. Z. Idelsohn, *Jewish Liturgy* (New York: H. Holt and Co., 1932) is the classic. For a sense of the deeper meaning and spiritual beauty of the Jewish service, B. Martin, *Prayer in Judaism* (New York: Basic Books, 1968) is a must. Millgram's bibliography is extensive and topically organized. On a nontechnical level I have found useful: S. B. Freehof, *The Small Sanctuary; Judaism of the Prayer Book* (Cincinnati: Union of American Hebrew Congregation, 1942); L. Jacobs,

Bibliography

Jewish Prayer (London: Jewish Chronicle, 1962); and S. Greenberg, *The Jewish Prayer Book; Its Ideals and Values* (New York: Jewish Theological Seminary, 1942).

On the early structure of the liturgy see S. Baron's chapter "Worship, Unity Amidst Diversity," in *A Social and Religious History of the Jews*, vol. 7; B. Cohen, "Liturgic Literature," in *The Jewish People, Past and Present* (New York: Jewish Encyclopedic Handbooks, 1946–1955), vol. 3, 1952; and a much continued article by S. Zeitlin, "An Historical Study of the First Canonization of the Hebrew Liturgy," in *Jewish Quarterly Review*, vols. 36, 38, and 54.

On preaching consult I. Bettan, *Studies in Jewish Preaching* (Cincinnati: Hebrew Union College Press, 1939) and J. Mann, *The Bible as Read and Preached in the Old Synagogue* (Cincinnati: Privately printed, 1966). There is room for a fuller appreciation of this basic cultural form.

XVIII   Judaism and Islam

S. D. Goitein, *Jews and Arabs: Their Contacts Through the Ages* (New York: Schocken Books, 1955), is an excellent starting place. A. I. Katsh, *Judaism in Islam* (New York: New York University Press, 1954) attempts to analyze the influence of Judaism on sections of the Koran.

More specialized histories include W. J. Fischel, *The Jews in the Economic and Political Life of Medieval Islam* (London: Royal Asiatic Society, 1937) and J. Mann, *The Jews in Egypt and in Palestine Under the Fatamid Caliphs* (London: Oxford University Press, 1920–1922).

S. Assaf's article on "Gaon" in *Encyclopedia Judaica*, vol. 7, 1971 is a succinct description of this office. S. B. Freehof, *The Responsa* (Philadelphia: Jewish Publication Society, 1955) and his numerous popular works in this field present material on this genre.

L. Nemoy, ed., *A Karaite Anthology* (New Haven: Yale University Press, 1952) is a source book provided with an excellent introduction. Z. Cahn, *The Rise of the Karaite Sect* (New York: M. Tausner Publishing Co., 1937) and the essays in P. Birnbaum, ed., *Karaite Studies* (New York: Herman Press, 1971) suggest the standard problems in this field. Z. Ankori, *Karaites in Byzantium* (New York: Columbia University Press, 1959) is a thorough study of these groups during a later stage of their development.

Saadiah Gaon's philosophic statement has been translated by S.

Bibliography

Rosenblatt, *The Book of Belief and Opinions* (New Haven: Yale University Press, 1948). H. Malter, *Saadia Gaon, His Life and Work* (Philadelphia: Jewish Publication Society, 1921) is an adequate biography. Much more on this giant can be gained from the essays in A. A. Neuman and S. Zeitlin, eds., *Saadia Studies* (Philadelphia: Dropsie College, 1943); E. J. Rosenthal, ed., *Saadia Studies* (Manchester: Manchester University Press, 1943); and *Saadia Anniversary Volume* (New York: American Academy for Jewish Research, 1948).

In addition to the general philosophic studies mentioned in the first section of this bibliography, I. Husik, *A History of Medieval Jewish Philosophy* (Philadelphia: Jewish Publication Society, 1958) thoroughly outlines the work of the major medieval figures.

XIX   Dar al Islam—West

There are two extensive histories of Spanish Jewry: A. A. Neuman, *The Jews in Spain* (Philadelphia: Jewish Publication Society, 1948) and Y. F. Baer, *History of the Jews in Christian Spain* (Philadelphia: Jewish Publication Society, 1961). The major philosophic works so far translated include: S. ibn Gabirol, *Tikkun Middot ha Nefesh* as *The Improvement of Moral Qualities*, translated by S. S. Wise (New York: Columbia University Press, 1901); S. ibn Gabirol, *Mivḥar ha-Peninim* as the *Choice of Pearls, A Collection of Ethical Sentences, Maxims, etc.*, translated by A. Cohen (New York: Bloch Publishing House, 1925); J. ha Levi, *Kuzari*, translated by H. Hirshfeld (London: Cailin Gold, 1905), however, the abridged *Kuzari, The Book of Proof and Argument* (Oxford: East and West Library, 1947) with notes and introduction by I. Heinemann, is technically preferable; B. ibn Paquda, *Ḥovot ha Levavot* as *The Duties of the Heart*, translated by M. Hyamson (New York: Bloch Publishing Co., 1947); A. b. Ḥiyya, *Hegyon ha-Nefesh ha-Azuvah* as *Meditation of the Sad Soul*, translated by G. Wigodor (New York: Schocken, 1969).

The difficulty of translating medieval Hebrew poetry has led to a paucity of good materials in English. There is nothing in English to compare with the important Hebrew studies and anthologies of J. Schirmann and I. Davidson. As introductions, S. Spiegel, "On Medieval Hebrew Poetry," in L. Finkelstein, ed., *The Jews* and J. Schirmann, "The Function of the Hebrew Poet in Medieval Spain," *Jewish Social Studies*, vol. 16, 1954, are worthwhile. Available translations of varying merit include: *Selected Religious Poetry of Solomon ibn Ga-*

birol, translated by I. Zangwill (Philadelphia: Jewish Publication Society, 1923); *The Kingly Crown, Keter Malchut of Solomon ibn Gabirol*, translated by B. Lewis (London: Vallentine, Mitchell Ltd., 1961); *Selected Poems of Moses ibn Ezra*, translated by S. Solis-Cohen (Philadelphia: Jewish Publication Society, 1934); and *Selected Poems of Jehudah Halevi*, translated by N. Salaman (Philadelphia: Jewish Publication Society, 1924); and *Hebrew Poems From Spain*, translated by D. Goldstein (New York: Shockon Books, 1966), which is a choice selection in good English.

On belles lettres V. Reichart has translated the first sixteen gates of *The Taḥkemoni of Judah al Ḥarizi* (Jerusalem: Raphael Haim Cohen Press, 1965) and the rest should not be far behind. An earlier translation by M. Hadas of Joseph b. Meir Zabara, *Sefer Shaashuim* as *The Book of Delight* (New York: Columbia University Press, 1932) is eminently readable. M. Epstein, *Tales of Sendebar* (Philadelphia: Jewish Publication Society, 1967) and M. Hadas' translation of Berechyah ha Nakdan, *Mishle Shualim, Fables of a Jewish Aesop* (New York: Columbia University Press, 1967) complete the available literature of romances and fables. Benjamin of Tudela's travel journal is available as *The Itinerary of Benjamin of Tudela*, translated by M. N. Adler (New York: Philipp Feldheim, 1907). If you want to sample the various literary and intellectual forms, see A. E. Millgram, *An Anthology of Medieval Hebrew Literature* (New York: Abelard-Schuman, 1961).

There is as yet no good English translation of Jossipon, but G. D. Cohen has translated and fully explained A. ibn Daud, *Sefer ha Qabbahal* as *The Book of Tradition* (Philadelphia: Jewish Publication Society, 1967).

XX   The Other Moses

Most of Maimonides' works are available in English and are listed in the bibliography of a model introductory reader, I. Twersky, ed., *A Maimonides Reader* (New York: Behrman House, 1972), which has been outfitted with an excellent introduction and notes. There are two translations of the *Guide*, M. Friedlander, a popular rendering (London: G. Routledge and Co., 1910) and S. Pines, a somewhat more precise version (Chicago: University of Chicago Press, 1963); but if you want to grasp the nature of Maimonides' approach rather than do a thorough study, C. Rabin, trans., with an introduction by

Bibliography

J. Guttman, *The Guide to the Perplexed*, (London: East and West Library, 1952) is a successful and functional abridgment.

S. Zeitlin, *Maimonides, A Biography* (New York: Bloch Publishing, 1935) lays out the basic facts of his life and an unusual theory to explain the *Mishneh Torah*. An older biography, D. Yellin and I. Abrahams, *Maimonides* (Philadelphia: Jewish Publication Society, 1903) is usable. F. G. Bratton, *Maimonides, Medieval Modernist* (Boston: Beacon Press, 1967) is concise, but shows a surprising disinterest in the nonphilosophic, nonmedical sides of *ha-rav*.

Because of the Cairo Genizah it is now possible to reconstruct in great detail Egyptian Jewish life during the Maimonidean age, and S. D. Gotein's two-volume *A Mediterranean Society* (Berkeley: University of California Press, 1967–1971) (third volume in press), provides a truly remarkable reconstruction of the demography, sociology, political organization, and educational system of this community.

An original and incisive exposition of Judaism has been written by L. Jacobs on the basis of a historic and theological examination of Maimonides' thirteen point creed, *Principles of the Jewish Faith, An Analytic Study* (New York: Basic Books, 1964). This book is not for neophytes, but by now anyone who has read the works listed in this bibliography will find Jacob's volume an excellent preparation for the second volume of our *A History of Judaism*.

INDEX

Aaron, 69, 161, 185, 186, 236
Aaron ben Asher, 332
Aaron ben Meir, 344
Abbasid caliphs, 325, 334, 336, 341, 353
Abd Er-Rahman III, 361
Abel, 302
Abir, 15
Abraham, 4, 5, 6, 8, 9, 13, 14, 15, 20, 21, 24, 26, 29, 50, 51, 131, 166, 185, 195, 203, 309, 343, 383
Absalom, 46, 57, 109
Academies, 279, 299, 325–327, 329, 342, 352, 354–355
Acra, 182, 183
Adam, 60, 166, 200, 248, 276, 300, 311, 343
Adda ben Ahavah, 288
Adonai, as name of God, 236, 306
Adoption, 286
Adultery, 238, 290
Aelia Capitolina, 257
Aesop, 305
Aggadah, 130, 280, 289, 292, 297, 310, 345, 346, 354, 404
Agur, 109
Ahab, 64, 78, 81, 85, 87, 91–93
Ahasuerus, 156
Ahava Rabba, 263
Ahitophel, 46, 109
Ah-mose I, 35
Ahriman, 247
Ai, 52
Akiva, 228, 233, 250, 263, 266, 268–269, 271, 272–273, 275, 278, 289, 295, 300, 305, 345
Akkadian texts, 118
Alalakh, 12
Albright, W. F., 90
Alexander (philosopher), 407, 408
Alexander the Great, 155, 166, 172, 173, 176, 180, 181, 196
Alexandra, 220
Alexandria, 173, 175, 176, 177, 178, 181, 187, 197, 257, 329, 342
Alfasi, Isaac, 355, 381
Aliyah, 58, 151, 336
Aljamans, 266, 376, 392
Allah, 321, 322, 390
Allegories, 211, 214

Almohades, 360, 385, 388, 389, 390, 392
Almovarides, 360, 390–391
Alphabet, 61, 63, 201, 253, 323, 365
Alphonso VI, 390
Am, 168
Amalek, 50, 156, 394
Amaziah, 57, 96–97
Amen-Em-Opet, 109
Amnon, 65
Amon (king), 128, 129
Amoraim, 282, 294, 299, 312
Amorite people, 50
Amos, 57, 62, 79, 87, 90, 94–98, 99, 105, 108, 120, 127, 128, 135, 138, 207, 382
Amos (book), 29, 57, 62, 68, 69, 86, 94–98, 314, 394
Amram, 326
Amulets, 288, 292
Anan ben David, 334–335, 336, 338
Anath, 16
Angels, 171, 179, 202, 213, 223–224, 240, 243, 247, 310–311
Animal fables, 305–306
Animism, 247
Annals, writing of, 300
Anthony, 173
Anthropology, 310, 371–372, 374–375
Anti-intellectualism, 295
Antioch, 175, 176, 181, 187, 257
Antiochus IV, 22, 183, 244
Antipater, 187
Antoninus Pius, 257
Aphrodisius, 407
Apocalypse, 239–254, 257, 276–278
Apocalypse of Enoch, 198
Apocrypha, 197, 198, 239–254, 417
Apollonius, 183
Apologetic literature, 176, 211, 346
Apostasy, 290
Aquila, 198
Arabic language, 320, 322, 323, 328, 329, 330–331, 337, 341, 342, 345, 364, 365, 368
Arab world, 299, 319, 320–351
Aram, 103
Aramaic language, 177, 180, 181, 182, 190, 199, 200, 280, 293, 312, 319, 320, 329, 337, 353

Index

Ararat, 10
Architecture of temples, 189
Ardashir, 298
Arel, 22, 54
Aristobulus, 177, 178, 192, 195
Aristotle, 200, 339, 346, 351, 353, 356, 358, 362, 369, 383, 388, 396, 397, 407, 408, 411
Ark of the Covenant *(Aron ha-Berit)*, 24, 53, 70, 71, 89, 109, 123, 124, 163, 167
Armenia, 337, 338
Art, 323
Artapanus, 178, 201
Artaxerxes, 158
Asaph, 114
Ashari, Al-, 343, 345
Asher, 15
Asherah, 15, 78
Asheroth, 94
Ashi, 299
Assyria, 98, 100–101, 103, 107, 124, 126–129, 131, 136, 146, 167
Astrology, 9, 179, 243, 292, 362
Astronomy, 213, 281, 332, 353, 362, 364
Ataraxia, 207
Atonement for sins, 164
Augustine, 113
Averroes, 407, 408
Avicenna, 387, 388, 408
Avodah, 188, 199, 232, 259, 412
Avot, 3, 4–8, 275, 422
Ayyubid dynasty, 392
Azazel, 247
Azazel (scapegoat), 154

Baal, 64, 65, 92, 93, 94
Baalam, 42, 78, 109, 122
Babel, tower of, 9
Babylonian empire, 9, 10, 16, 91, 106, 109, 151, 152
Babylonian exile, 19, 42, 70, 93, 113, 133, 136, 138, 157–158, 161–162, 194, 249, 292, 308
Babylonian Talmud, 279, 280, 281–282, 292–293, 299, 327, 344, 352, 422–424
Badis, 362
Baghdad, 325, 326, 334, 341, 342, 343, 353
Bahya ben Joseph ibn Pakuda, 378–380, 386
Baltic states, 341
Baraitot, 275–276, 283
Barcelona, 360, 361
Bar Ḥiyya, Abraham, 377–378
Bar Kochba revolt, 245, 250, 257, 261, 277, 278
II Baruch, 194, 195, 276
Bathsheba, 74, 81, 87
Bat kol, 163
Bel and the Dragon, 194–195, 417
Belial, 247

Ben Azzai, 269
Bet din (scholar's court), 265–266
Benei Yisrael (tribes of Israel), 4–6, 34–39, 69–76, 107
Benjamin (tribe), 53
Benjamin ben Moses Al-Nahawandi, 335, 338
Ben Sira, 159, 180, 181, 193, 197, 201, 224
Ben Zoma, 269
Berbers, 341, 354, 360, 390
Berit, 24
Berit milah, 23
Bethar, 250
Beth-el (shrine), 94, 96–97
Bethlehem, 40
Betrothal laws, 275
Bezalel, 109
Bible: grammatical study of, 330–331; Mesopotamian legends and stories in, 9, 10–11; Spanish Jewry and, 360, 363. *See also specific books of the Bible*
Biographical memoirs, 300
Birth control, infanticide as, 176
Bittaḥon, 68
Book of Comfort, 136–137
Book of the Covenant, 11
Book of the Dead, 39
Bosch, Hieronymus, 247
Buber, Martin, 97
Buddha, 40
Burial customs, 38–39, 57

Cain, 302, 343
Caleb (tribe), 53
Calendars, 9, 16, 163, 173, 189, 196, 222, 266, 296, 316, 327, 332
Caliphs, 324–325, 334, 336, 341, 342, 352, 353, 354, 360
Calvin, John, 113, 209
Cambyses, 155
Canaan, 6, 7–9, 31, 35, 41, 45, 50–51, 56, 58–59, 60, 61–66, 107, 367
Capital punishment, 266–267
Census of David, 143–144
Children, 175–176, 226, 238, 283
Christ, 261, 320
I Chronicles, 63, 144, 166, 167, 300
II Chronicles, 166, 167, 193, 300
Church, 40, 198, 214, 251–252, 276, 299, 322, 351; fathers of, 86, 217, 318; Paul in, 290, 291; persecution by, 317–319; salvation in, 208, 261; in Spain, 352, 360, 361, 364, 368, 385, 389
Circumcision, 20–23, 179, 183, 257
Classic prophets, 79, 87, 88, 94, 103
Claudius, 187
Clearchus, 176
Cleopatra, 173

Index

Commerce, 173–175, 179, 181
Congregation, 168
Constantine, 317
Constantinople, 317, 341
Contrition, rituals of, 261–262
Conversions, 23, 162, 171, 290, 324
Cordova, 353, 360, 361, 388, 392
Councils, Church, 318
Court prophets, 9, 88, 106, 138
Covenant, 68–69, 80, 149, 190, 206, 312; Deuteronomy and, 121–122, 123; early Hebrews and, 19–33; with Ezra, 162–163; Israel's founding and, 50, 51; Josiah's renewal of, 124, 129; Judah's punishment and, 61, 134, 135; psalms and, 115–116
Creation stories, 9, 60, 194, 240, 243, 246, 253, 292, 304, 310, 356–357
Crimea, 341
Cult prophets, 69
Cynic philosophy, 208, 233, 235
Cyrene, 257
Cyrus, 151, 155, 157, 308, 367

Dagon, 78
Dahriya, 346, 348
Daniel, 109, 120, 194–195, 210, 240–241, 244, 259, 293–294
Daniel (book), 182, 184, 197, 210, 223, 240–241, 251, 293–294
Daniel ben Judah, 406–407
Dante, 247
Dar al Islam, 352–389
David, 24, 46, 50, 70, 71, 72, 74, 76, 81, 85, 87, 91, 109, 143–144, 161, 162, 165, 166, 167, 168, 265, 301, 363
David, house of, 70, 73, 81, 91, 134, 157, 167, 249, 265, 301, 318, 361
Day of Atonement (Yom Kippur), 48, 141–142, 154, 170–171, 189, 229, 260–261, 262, 358
Day of God *(Yom YHWH)* theme, 241–242
Dayyanim, 326, 333, 352, 361–362, 396
Dead Sea (Qumran) community, 185, 188, 198, 201, 209, 222, 244, 245, 251
Dead Sea scrolls, 195, 197, 198, 240, 418
Deborah, 363
Decalogue (Ten Commandments), 11–12, 26, 27–28, 48, 123, 291
Deification of leaders, 75–76, 201
Demetrius, 178
Derash, 195, 342, 366
Determinism, 243, 345
Deutero-Isaiah, 76, 141, 151–154, 414
Deuteronomy, 5, 8, 28, 32, 36, 37, 39, 42, 43, 46, 53, 56–57, 59, 62, 63, 65–66, 69, 73–74, 81, 93–94, 108, 121–124, 129, 138, 145, 150, 156, 160, 162, 165, 166, 167, 185, 269, 300, 313

Devarim, 27, 31, 75, 76, 80
Diaspora, 93, 146, 152–153, 158, 170, 175, 180, 186–188, 210, 223, 226, 257, 258, 325, 336
Dietary rules, 179, 183, 229, 284, 323, 415
Diogenes, 235
Diviners, 79, 106
Divorce, 33, 275, 286
Djihād, 54, 321
Drama, 173, 178
Dunash ben Labrat, 365
Dura-Europos, 149, 323

Ea, 10
Ebenezer, 24
Ecclesiastes, 39, 179, 180, 197, 218, 351, 362
Ecstatics, 79, 90
Eden, 9, 10–11, 321, 343
Edom, 20, 51, 140, 250, 360
Education in *gymnasium,* 173, 177, 180, 181, 182
Egypt, 7, 75, 98, 136, 155, 172, 352, 393; circumcision in, 20, 21; exile and, 141, 146; Exodus and, 39–42, 51, 104, 301, 308; Hellenistic, 180; Islamic, 354; Judah and, 129, 130; Roman, 183; Solomon and, 91; tribes of Israel under, 35–39, 147, 201; wisdom literature in, 109, 110
Ehyeh-Asher-Ehyeh, 47–48
El, 14–15, 16, 47
Eldad, 69
Elders, 227
Eleazar ben Azariah, 300
Eleh Ezekerah, 185
El Elyon, 14, 15, 47
Elephantine, 157, 169
Eliezer, R., 218
Eliezer ben Azariah, 267
Elihu, 119
Elijah, 21, 40, 78, 81, 87, 89, 90, 92–93, 105, 301, 307, 318, 322
Eliot, T. S., 319
Elisha, 57, 78, 82, 87, 88, 93, 105
Elisha ben Abuyah, 269
Elohim, as name of God, 199–200, 306
El Olam, 14
El Roi, 14
El Shaddai, 14, 47
Embalming, 38
Empiricism, 339
Emunah, 133
End of Days (*Aharit ha-Yamim*) theme, 241–250, 252, 254
Enlightenment, 343
Enoch, 239, 244, 252
I Enoch, 195, 239, 249, 253
II Enoch, 249

Index

Enoch, Apocalypse of, 198
Ephraim, 72
Epicurean philosophy, 208, 233
Eruvim, 333–334
Esau, 4, 34–35, 301–302
Eshnunna, 11
Essenes, 188, 208, 209, 245
Esther, 155–156, 157, 162
Esther (book), 169, 218
Ethics, 134
Ethrog, 259
Eupolemus, 178, 201
Eve, 200, 311
Excommunication, 340
Exilarchs, 286, 298, 325, 335, 353, 361
Exile *(galut)*, 140–154, 155, 166, 255–257, 261,
    277, 278, 291, 297, 300–302, 315, 336, 361,
    363, 367, 380, 415
Exodus, 8, 39–49, 69, 121, 156, 178, 292, 302
Exodus (book), 11, 13, 22, 24, 28, 32, 36, 37,
    41, 42, 43–45, 46, 47, 49, 65, 121, 123, 156,
    168, 268, 293
Exorcism, 349
Ezekiel, 6, 79, 86, 140, 147, 148–149, 151, 154,
    159, 210, 246
Ezekiel (book), 6, 84, 86, 120, 145, 146,
    147–151, 154, 158–159, 160, 218, 233, 240,
    253
Ezekiel of Alexandria, 178
Ezra, 158, 160–163, 166, 168–169, 171, 174,
    190, 215, 225, 232, 252, 363
Ezra (book), 166, 171, 300
II Ezra, 249
IV Ezra, 201, 276, 417

Fables, 108, 109–110, 305–306
Faith healing, 292
Family, 175–176, 275
Farabi, Abunazr Al-, 408
Farming, 226, 229, 267
Fasting, 141, 256–257, 262, 303, 400–403
Fatamid dynasty, 341, 354, 356, 392
Fathers, Church, 86, 217, 318
Fathers, law and, 107
Fellowships *(ḥavurot)*, 229–234, 236
Finkelstein, Louis, 221
Fiscus Judaicus, 256
Five Books of Moses (Pentateuch), 43, 49, 80,
    190, 203, 215, 216, 217, 219, 263, 295, 367
Flood story, 9, 10–11, 292
Folk legends, 305
Fortitude, 208
Free will, 345, 350
Funerary rites, 38–39

Gabriel, 223, 247, 312
Gad (prophet), 87

Gad (tribe), 5, 52
Galen, 339, 353, 356, 362
Galilee, 255, 279, 292
Galut (exile), 140–154, 155, 166, 255–257, 261,
    277, 278, 291, 297, 300–302, 315, 336, 361,
    363, 367, 380, 415
Gamaliel II, 260, 265
Gaonic Judaism, 325, 326, 327, 338, 341–342,
    352, 353, 355
Garden of Eden, 9, 10–11, 321, 343
Gedaliah, 130, 140
Gemara, 279–283, 285, 289, 299, 326, 327, 328,
    338, 403
Gematria, 253
Gemilut Ḥasadim, 199
Genealogy, 161–162, 265, 286
Genesis, 3, 4–5, 6, 7, 8, 11, 12, 13, 14, 15, 29,
    34–35, 38, 45, 50, 51, 53, 56, 57, 70, 107,
    143, 166, 175, 194, 204, 253, 303, 304,
    418
Gerei-tzedek, 179–180
Germany, 42
Ghazali, Al-, 340, 385, 413
Gideon, 64, 68
Gikatilla, Moses ibn, 330, 366, 367
Gilgamesh epic, 10, 17
Ginzberg, Louis, 292, 310
Glory of God *(kavod)*, 169, 170, 246, 253
Gog, 252
Golden Mean of Aristotle, 351, 353, 358
Gomer, 100
Gospel of John, 214
Grammar, 285, 330–331, 332, 342, 353, 364,
    365–368
Granada, 360, 362, 368
Greece, 172–182, 187, 193, 238, 282, 353;
    language in, 199, 312, 320; mysteries in,
    203–204, 243; philosophy in, 86, 110, 205,
    206, 211, 212–213, 233, 245, 247, 269, 338,
    339, 345, 356, 387
Guide of the Perplexed, The (Maimonides), 397,
    408–409, 411, 413, 414
Guilt, 230–231
Gymnasium, 173, 177, 180, 181, 182

Habakkuk, 126, 127, 128, 129, 132–133
Habakkuk (book), 132–133
Habbus, 362
Ḥachamim (scribe-scholars), 186
Hadad, 16
Hadrian, 22, 394
Haftarah, 218, 292
Haggadah, 44, 196
Haggai, 157, 158, 163, 252
Haggai (book), 157
Hai, 342
Hakim, Al, 392

Halachah, 228, 240, 280, 282, 290, 310, 325, 327, 341, 353, 359, 362, 396, 398, 404, 407, 415

Ha Levi, Judah, 369, 381–386, 387, 413

Hallel Psalms, 44

Haman, 156, 305

Hammurabi, 11, 13, 43

Ḥananel ben Ḥushiel, 354

Hanging Gardens, Nineveh, 146

Ḥaninah ben Dosa, 263–264

Hannaniah, 88

Ḥannukah, 183, 198, 401

Ha-Raḥaman, 337

Ḥasdai ben Isaac ibn Shaprut, 360–361, 364, 365

Ḥasidim, 182, 184–185, 295

Hasmonean dynasty, 183–184, 185, 186, 187, 220, 227

Ḥavurot (fellowships), 229–234, 236

Heaven, 243

Hebrew language, 312, 315, 319, 342–343, 353, 354, 355, 363, 364–366

Hebrews, in ancient Near East, 3–18

Hecataeus of Abdera, 176

Ḥefetz ben Yatzliah, 327–328

Hell, 243, 321

Hellenism. *See* Greece

Ḥerem, 55, 90

Heresy, 260, 318

Hermes, 202

Hermippus, 176

Herod, 186, 187, 188, 244, 249

Herodotus, 20

Hero literature, 201, 207

Ḥesed, 84, 120, 124

Hezekiah, 101, 110

High Priest, 170–171, 186, 260

Hilkiah, 27, 121

Hillel, 158, 180, 223, 226, 228, 233, 234–236, 265, 272, 282, 294

Hippocrates, 339, 356, 362

Hiram, 61

Historical writing, 300–301, 320–321, 367

Hittite empire, 6, 25, 50

Ḥiwi Al Balchi, 343

Ḥochmah, 109

Holiness (*kedushah*), 144, 164, 166

Holiness Code, 164

Holy of Holies, 48, 124, 170–171, 229, 260

Holy war, 54

Homer, 193

Homosexuality, 182, 238

Hosea, 73, 81, 84, 87, 98–100, 261

Hosea (book), 65, 84, 98–100, 418

Hoshanah Rabba, 189

Huna, R., 288

Hurrian culture, 4

Husbands, law and, 65

Hyksos, 35–36

Hymns, 115, 319, 337

Hyrcanus, John, 220

Ibn Daud, Abraham, 387–389, 391, 396

Ibn Ezra, Abraham, 330, 366, 367, 381

Ibn Gabirol, Solomon, 357–358, 363, 374–376, 377, 386, 387, 388

Ibn Jannaḥ, Jonah, 330, 365

Ibn Migash, Joseph ben Meir, 355, 381

Ibn Zaddik, Joseph, 381, 386

Iddo, 87, 193

Idolatry, 151–152, 167, 182, 323

Imam, 338

Immortality of soul, 179, 205, 210–211, 333

Incense shovel, 259

Incest, 290

Indo-European peoples, 7

Infanticide, 176

Inheritance laws, 275

Instructions of Amen-Em-Opet, 109

Interest on loans, 175

Intermarriage, 65, 141, 160–162, 171, 179, 340

Iran, 179, 335

Isaac, 4, 8, 14, 15, 185

Isaac ben Judah ibn Ghayyat, 381

Isaac, Jules, 318

Isaiah, 73, 80, 87, 101–103, 108, 120, 127, 135, 143, 367. *See also* Deutero-Isaiah

Isaiah (book), 42, 58, 61, 67, 69, 80, 81, 91, 100–103, 105, 141–142, 145, 150, 151–153, 157, 165, 170, 171, 210, 240, 367, 418

Ishmael, 4

Ishmael, Rabbi, 266, 268, 272, 334

Ishmael (tribe), 20, 360

Islam, 54, 299, 320–351

Israel (kingdom): covenant with, 115–116; devastation of, 106, 107; Egyptian bondage of, 35–49; etymology of name, 34–35; power and monarchy in, 67–76; in Promised land, 50–66; prophets in, 77–105

Israel (modern state), 42

Israeli, Isaac ben Solomon, 356–357, 386, 395

Ivri, Hebrew name from, 5

Jacob, 4, 8, 29, 34–35, 50, 53, 96, 107, 195, 301–302, 357

Jacob ben Nathaniel al Fayumi, 393–394

Japeth ben Ali ha-Levi, 338

Jason, 181–182

Jason of Cyrene, 178

Jebusites, 50

Jehoash, 110

Jehoiakim, 73, 74, 130, 146

Jehovah, as name of God, 48–49

Jeremiah, 73–74, 81–83, 84, 88, 90, 105, 126, 127, 128, 133–138, 140, 141, 143, 168, 194, 209, 253

Index

Jeremiah (book), 20, 23, 38, 67, 71, 80, 81, 83, 84, 85, 86, 109, 125, 126, 127, 128, 131, 133–138, 141

Jeremiah, Letter of, 194

Jericho, 50, 52, 107

Jeroboam, 72, 97

Jerusalem, 24, 135, 160, 180, 336; Greek power over, 181–182; Judah's punishment and, 134, 135; Maccabean Revolt and, 182–184; monarchy and, 71, 91, 121; Persian rule of, 157, 160, 174–175; prophecy of destruction of, 82, 104, 128, 252–253; rebuilding of, 154; Rome and, 185, 186, 220, 250, 251, 257; Solomon and, 71, 76

Jesus, 220, 234, 235, 261, 322

Jethro, 47

Jezebel, 78, 81, 87, 90, 91–93

Job, 116–120

Job (book), 116–120, 305, 348

Joel, 39

John, Gospel of, 214

Jonah, 77, 82

Jonah ben Amittai, 138–139

Jonah ibn Jannah, 330, 365

Jonathan, 363

Jonathan the Hasmonean, 185

Joseph, 4, 36, 96, 162, 195

Joseph, King of the Khazars, 361

Josephus, 197, 221, 229, 237, 249, 250, 300

Joshua, 19, 21, 27, 41, 51, 70, 93, 224, 227

Joshua, Rabbi, 265

Joshua (book), 5, 21, 27, 28, 51, 52, 65, 93, 108, 216

Joshua ben Jehozadok, 157, 158

Josiah, 74, 121, 124, 129–130

Jothan, 109

Jubilee, laws on, 226

Jubilees, 222

Judah, 12

Judah (kingdom), 13, 111; Assyria and, 100, 102; fall of, 76, 103–104, 106, 107; Israel and, 95; judgment of, 125–139; monarchy in, 70, 72–74, 91

Judah ben David Ḥayyuj, 365, 366

Judah ben Samuel ibn Balam, 368

Judah the Galilean, 249, 250

Judea, 160, 216

Judges (book), 52, 65, 68, 76, 93, 94, 109, 110, 300

Judgment Day, 239–254, 257, 277, 288, 305, 376

Judith (book), 197, 417

Jupiter, 256

Justice, 208

Justinian, 297, 318

Kaaba, 323

Kadesh Barnea, 19, 28, 41

Kadosh, 185

Kahal, 168

Kairouan, 326–327, 342, 354, 355, 356

Kallot, 325, 326–327

Kapparah, 164

Karaism, 295, 328, 333–341, 342, 366, 389

Kashrut, 196

Kavod, 169, 170, 246, 253

Kayyara, Simon, 327

Kedushah, 144, 164, 166

Ketuvim, 217, 218

Khazars, 361, 383–386

Kiddush ha-Shem, 184

Kimḥi, David, 368

Kindi, Al-, 345, 356

Kings of Israel, 50, 75–76, 109, 150

I Kings, 64, 66, 71, 72, 92, 93, 94, 110, 130, 300

II Kings, 57, 58, 66, 93, 110, 129, 300

Kinnim, 275, 422

Kinship gods, 14–15

Kirkisani, Jacob Al-, 335, 338, 340, 341

Kittum, 12, 13

Knowledge, 372–373

Kohelet, 180, 206

Koine, 177

Korah, 46, 69

Koran, 320, 322, 323, 324, 330, 333, 339, 345, 348, 360, 365

Kumisi, Daniel Al-, 336, 337

Kyrios, as name of God, 199–200, 201, 246

Laban, 4

Lamentations (book), 141, 142–143, 145

Laws: anti-Jewish, 297; commercial, 175; Deuteronomy and, 121–122; embalming under, 38; Ezra and, 162–166; fathers under, 107; Justinian, 318; Mesopotamian parallels to, 11–13; midrash halachah and, 268–273; Mishnah and, 273–276; Muslim, 354; nomos concept and, 190–193; process of definition of, 219–220; study of, 262–265; takkanah and, 226–227. See also Torah

Lemuel, 109

Letter of Aristeas, 178, 192, 195, 417

Letter of Jeremiah, 194, 417

Levites, 161, 167, 312

Leviticus (book), 24, 25, 36, 37, 39, 55, 56, 63, 64, 65, 163–164, 185, 268, 304

Lexicography, 342

Lipit-Ishtar, 11

Literature, 178, 188, 268–273, 326. See also specific forms of literature

Liturgy, 311–317, 326

Loans, 226, 292

Logic, 282, 309, 353, 364

Index

Logos, 204, 212–213, 234
Lot, 9, 20
Lulav, 259

Maccabean Revolt, 182–184, 210, 223, 225
I Maccabees, 300, 417
II Maccabees, 300, 417
III Maccabees, 178
Macedonia, 172
Magi, 230, 287, 298, 299
Magic, 289, 292
Magog, 252
Mahdi, 391
Maimonides, Moses, 368, 372, 392–415
Malachai (book), 84, 169
Malachi, 77, 145, 163, 169, 252
Malachim, 202
Mamelukes, 393
Man, ideas about, 204–211
Manahem Jacob ibn Saruk, 365
Manasseh (king), 128, 129, 130
Manasseh (tribe), 52, 167
Manasseh, Prayer of, 195
Manuscript decoration, 323–324
Marduk, 12, 13, 43
Margalioth, 289
Mari Tablets, 78
Marriage, 65, 275, 286, 303, 323, 370
Martyrs, 184–185, 207–208, 223
Masechta de-Shabbata, 270–272
Masorah Magna, 332
Masorah Parva, 332
Masoretes, 331–332
Mathematics, 281, 327, 332, 353, 362
Matriarchs, 213
Mattathias, 183, 184
Mazzal tov, 9
Mecca, 40, 165
Mechilta (Ishmael), 268, 270–272
Medad, 69
Medicine, 353, 356, 362, 364
Medieval times, 198, 211, 281
Megiddo, battle at, 129
Megillat Antiochus, 198
Mehoza school, 279
Meir, 228, 263, 266
Melchizedek, 75
Melkart, prophets of, 78, 90, 92
Menorah, 259
Merchant class, 175
Mer-ne-Ptah, 35
Mesopotamia, 9–11, 31, 36–37, 38, 45, 75, 110, 298
Messiah tradition, 70, 93, 243, 248–251, 253, 254, 296–297, 298, 301, 308, 318, 333, 336, 361, 363, 389, 395–396
Metaphysics, 346, 385

Metatron, 247
Micah, 80, 83, 84, 87, 103
Micah (book), 31, 32, 104–105, 418
Michael, 240, 241, 247, 312
Middat Hassidut, 290
Middle Ages, 177
Middot, 275, 422
Midian, 47, 64, 68
Midrash, 20, 122, 193–196, 197, 218, 243, 253, 289, 295, 296, 300–303, 308–310, 311, 321, 329, 339, 347, 354, 407, 419–421
Midrash halachah, 268–273
Midrash Rabbah, 293
Mikra, 292
Milhemet hovah, 54
Minha sacrifice, 258
Minim, 260
Miracles, 351, 389
Mishnah, 225, 260, 262, 267, 273–276, 279–283, 287, 292, 293, 299, 327, 329, 398, 422
Mishneh Torah (Maimonides), 355, 372, 397, 399–405, 407, 414
Mission of Israel, 152
Mithraism, 23
Mitzvah, 30, 212, 287, 290, 303, 385, 409
Moab, 20, 51, 52, 78, 122, 141, 146, 162
Mohammed, 40, 320, 322, 323, 390
Moira, 243
Monarchy, 70–76, 167–168
Monet, Claude, 247
Money, 175, 226, 292
Mongols, 393
Monotheism, 13–15, 60, 200, 247, 309, 323
Mordecai, 156
Moses, 11, 14, 19, 22, 50, 69–70, 120, 162, 186, 213, 273, 282, 300, 320, 351, 363, 404, 411; covenant with, 11, 26, 27–28, 47, 48, 163, 210, 224, 225, 227, 244, 383, 395; Deuteronomy and, 122–123, 124; Exodus and, 8, 37, 40, 41, 43–44, 49, 51; as hero, 201, 363
Moses ibn Ezra, 368–371, 381
Mount Ebal, 216
Mount Gerizim, 216
Mount Horeb, 40
Mourners of Zion, 336
Mourning cult, 256
Murabits, 390
Murashu, house of, 157
Murder, 290, 302, 343
Musadi, Al-, 356
Musar, 134
Music, 110
Muslim world, 320–351
Mutazilites, 339, 345, 348
Mysteries, Hellenistic, 203–204, 210, 243
Mysticism, Jewish, 204, 246, 277, 359
Myths, 15–16, 247

Index

Naaman, 57
Naboth, 92–93
Nahor, 5
Naḥshon, 327
Nahum, 126, 129
Nahum (book), 129, 418
Nathan, 72, 74, 78, 81, 87, 89, 105
Natronai, 329
Natural sciences, 332
Nature, 59–61
Naviism, 79, 87, 88–89, 90, 93–94
Nazism, 156, 185
Nazirites, 66
Nebuchadnezzar, 109, 130, 135–136, 140, 146, 161, 168, 394
Nehardea school, 279, 298
Nehemiah, 141, 158, 160, 166, 169
Nehemiah (book), 28, 158, 161, 162, 166, 170, 300
Nemesis, 202
Neo-Assyrian empire, 25
Neo-Babylonian empire, 127, 140
Neo-Platonism, 356, 357, 359, 367, 380, 384, 387
Neo-Pythagorean philosophy, 233
Nero, 187, 305
Nersh school, 279
Neshek, 175
Neviim, 217, 218
New Testament, 220, 222, 229, 322
New Year's Day (Rosh Hashanah), 259
Nineveh, 82, 127, 139, 146
Nissim ben Jacob, 354
Noah, 10–11, 26, 120, 127, 166
Nomos (law), 190–193, 203, 214
North Africa, 341, 342, 352, 354, 360
Nous, 204
Numbers (book), 30, 43, 46, 50, 51, 52, 54, 56, 69, 109, 170, 186, 313
Numbers, prophetic, 252–253
Nun, 70
Nuzi archives, 4, 12

Oaths, 275
Obedience, 290, 303–304
Oikoumene, 174, 179, 181
Oil, as metaphor for Israel, 308, 309
Omri dynasty, 87
Oral tradition, 198–199, 224–225, 267, 273, 274, 275, 281, 283, 289, 292–294, 333, 335
Oriental mysteries, 179
Original sin, 248, 276
Origin myths, 5
Ormuzd, 247
Oshiah, R., 197

Paḥad, 15
Pahlavi, 312
Palace mysticism, 277
Palestine, use of term, 257. *See also* Hebrews; Israel
Palestinian Talmud, 279, 280, 292, 293, 298–299, 327, 422–424
Panchatantra, 305
Pardes, 269
Paris memorial to Holocaust, 156
Parthia, 180, 187, 298
Passover, 40, 41, 42, 44, 63, 131, 196, 234, 301
Patriarchs: abolition of, 297, 299, 318; early Hebrew, 3, 4–8, 14–15, 201, 213; Roman, 265, 267, 285–286
Paul, 113, 290, 291
Pentateuch (Five Books of Moses), 43, 49, 80, 190, 203, 215, 216, 217, 219, 263, 295, 367
Persia, 110, 151, 156–160, 165, 172, 174–175, 179, 216, 243, 245, 292, 337, 338, 341, 393
Perushim, 229, 231–232, 236
Pesaḥ, 62–63
Peshat, 366
Peskita, 292
Peskita Rabbati, 293, 296
Pharaohs, 75, 195, 343
Pharisees, 162, 184, 208, 209, 220, 221–222, 224–229, 236, 251, 274, 307
Philistines, 24, 70–71, 89, 90
Philo, 177, 178, 180, 188, 191–195, 197, 201, 204, 205, 207, 209, 211–214, 223, 237, 245, 300, 357
Philo Epicus, 178
Phoenicia, 51, 201
Phylacteries, 284
Physics, 353, 362
Pilgrimage holidays, 62
Piyyutim, 319, 328–329, 343, 351
Plato, 179, 186, 194, 200, 202, 205, 210, 212, 339, 362, 369, 372
Plotinus, 204, 233, 339, 356, 357, 362, 380
Poetry, 319, 328, 329, 353, 358–369
Poland, 42, 288
Polis, 174, 182, 185
Politeuma, 177
Poll taxes, 284, 338
Polytheism, 14–15
Pompey, 185, 186
Poor, tithes for, 187
Popilius Laenas, 183
Pork, dietary laws on, 33
Prayer, 311–317, 347
Prayer of Manasseh, 195
Preaching, 295–296, 305–307, 321
Priestly Code, 163–164
Priests, 13, 69, 105, 112, 123, 161–162, 163, 164, 167, 169, 181, 227–229, 258, 266

Index

Promised Land, 8, 50–66, 302, 308
Prophets and prophecy, 19, 42, 69, 108, 123, 168, 227, 322, 381, 382, 388–389, 415; apocalypse compared with, 243–244; cessation of, 163; Judah's downfall and, 126–139; numbers and, 252–253; social justice and, 125–126; will of God and, 77–105, 305
Protosynagogues, 189, 258–259
Proverbs (book), 68, 108–113, 176, 178, 362
Prudence, 207, 208
Psalms, 31, 41, 42, 45, 57, 60, 67, 68, 75, 76, 113–116, 117, 134–135, 144, 145, 146, 153, 156, 159, 169, 170, 191, 217, 312, 331, 349, 362, 419
Psalms of Solomon, 249
Pseudepigrapha, 197, 417
Ptolemy I, 175, 176
Ptolemy dynasty, 172–173, 180
Pumbedita school, 279, 299, 325, 326, 342, 352
Punishment, 30–31, 37, 60–61, 107–108, 134–135, 266–267
Purim, 401
Purity rituals, 170, 229–231, 278, 284
Pythagoras, 253

Qumran (Dead Sea) community, 185, 188, 198, 201, 209, 222, 244, 245, 251

Rabbinic Judaism, 184, 214, 218–219, 253, 254, 295, 321, 353; Apocrypha in, 197–198; beginning of, 196; interpretive tradition of, 266, 272–273; Karaism and, 333, 335, 337, 340–341
Rabbis, 44, 286; amoraim as first, 283; preaching by, 295–296, 305–307, 321
Rabina, 282, 299
Rachel, 4, 137
Raphael, 223, 247
Rashi, 330
Ras Shamra tablets, 60, 62
Rava, 317
Reason, 338–339, 343–344, 347, 349, 350
Rechabites, 66
Redemption themes, 254
Red Sea, 41, 301
Reform Judaism, 336
Rehoboam, 72
Repentance (teshuvah), 99, 150–151, 261–262, 286–287
Resurrection belief, 210–211, 222
Retarded, laws on, 226
Reuben, 52
Rhetoric, 353, 362
Richard the Lionheart, 392
Roman empire, 23, 292; galut (exile) and, 255–257; Israel ruled by, 185–187, 198, 199, 237, 242, 244, 245, 251, 300, 301–302; legal influence of, 193, 282; Maccabean Revolt against, 183–184, 223; Messiah theme and, 249–250, 251; self-government under, 285, 286; Spain and, 352, 359
Rosh Hashanah, 259, 275
Russia, 341
Ruth (book), 65, 162

Saadiah ben Joseph ha-Fayyum, 330, 337, 341–351, 354
Sabbath, 37, 148, 176, 243, 260, 401; boundaries (eruvim) on, 333–334; Ḥasidim and, 184–185; laws on observation of, 33, 183, 219, 234, 267, 275; Mechilta on, 270–272; New Year's Day on, 259; post-exilic observance of, 165–166; synagogue readings on, 218, 292–293
Sacrifices, 62–63, 112, 141, 164, 166, 185, 188, 189, 234, 256, 258, 260
Saddiq, Joseph, 408
Sadducees, 209, 220–224, 229, 341
St. James Church, Jerusalem, 297
Salah-al-din, 392
Salvation beliefs, 16–17, 209, 223, 261, 303–304, 321
Samaria, 138, 141, 146
Samaritans, 161–162, 216
Samson, 109
Samuel (amora), 294, 299
Samuel (prophet), 27, 70, 71, 72, 79, 87, 88, 89–91, 105, 167
I Samuel, 24, 27, 38, 45, 46, 54, 66, 72–73, 74, 76, 90, 93, 300
II Samuel, 46, 57, 65, 66, 70, 71, 72, 85, 93, 109, 143, 300
Samuel ha-Nagid, 362–363, 364, 368
Sanhedrin, 186, 196, 220, 266, 267, 325
Sarah, 4, 8, 195, 343
Sargon, 9, 98, 100
Sassanian empire, 285–286, 292, 298, 299, 325
Satan, 144, 223, 224, 247, 311
Saul, 50, 70, 75, 79, 90, 91
Savoraim, 279, 280, 283–291
Scapegoat, 154, 171
Scholars, 227–228, 295; hachamim, 181, 182, 186; soferim, 163, 174, 199, 216, 219–220, 232, 331
Scholar's Council, 259–260
Scholasticism, 347–348
Scholem, Gershom, 233
Scribe-scholars, 293, 331; hachamim, 181, 182, 186; soferim, 163, 174, 199, 216, 219–220, 232, 331
Seder, 40, 44
Sefarim Hitzonim, 198–199

Index

Sefer ha-Razim, 289
Seleucid dynasty, 172, 175, 181, 183, 194, 207
Seljuks, 342
Semaḥ ben Paltoi, 327
Semitic tribes, 35–36
Sennacherib, 101, 103, 135, 394
Septuagint translation, 178, 197, 198, 211, 215, 318
Severides, 257
Shaddai, 16
Shahada, 322, 323
Shaḥarit sacrifice, 258, 260
Shakespeare, William, 10
Shamash, 12
Shammai, 233
Shavuot, 8, 62, 63, 64, 222, 328
Shechem, covenant at, 27, 28
Shechinah, 308
Shema, 263, 313–314, 318–319, 322
Shemuel ben Hofini, 342
Sheol, 17, 38
Sherira, 342
Sherira Gaon, 326
Sheshbazzar, 157, 158
Shiite Islam, 338, 354
Shiloh, 89
Shimeon ben Gamaliel, 274
Shofar, 189, 259
Simeon bar Yoḥai, 412
Simon, 172, 188, 196
Simon bar Kochba, 250, 257, 261, 296
Simon Kayyara, 327
Sin, 154, 170–171, 244, 247, 261–262, 276
Sinai covenant, 26, 27–28, 49, 120, 163, 166, 192, 203, 211, 215, 224, 225, 288, 291, 292, 301, 302, 328, 333, 347, 356, 381–385, 395, 396
Sinhue, 7
Sisera, 394
Slavery, 36–37, 126, 283
Socrates, 235, 353
Sodom, 131
Soferim (scribe-scholars), 163, 174, 199, 216, 219–220, 232, 331
Soferim (volume of rules), 293
Solomon, 24, 52, 61, 62, 71–72, 76, 81, 91, 109, 110, 162, 178, 301, 305
Solomon, Wisdom of, 203, 205
Solomon ben Isaac, 330
Song of Songs, 317, 363
Song of the Three Children, 195
Sons, law and, 107
Sophia, 202–203
Soul, 245, 277, 304, 372, 388; immortality of, 179, 205, 210–211, 222; upward path of, 357–359
Soviet Union, 42
Spain, 266, 341, 342, 352–389, 391
Speiser, E. A., 75

Spinoza, 367, 411
Stoicism, 174, 179, 202–203, 208, 212, 233, 235, 302
Suffering, 308
Suffering servant portions in Deutero-Isaiah, 153
Sugyot, 281, 283
Suicide, 303
Sukkot, 6, 62, 64, 163, 259
Sumer, 9
Sunna, 338
Sura academy, 279, 299, 325, 326, 342, 352
Susannah (apocryphal scroll), 194–195, 417
Synagogues, 284, 318, 337; design in, 323; liturgy of, 311–317; origins of, 148, 189–190, 258–262; Torah reading in, 292–293
Syncretism, 141
Syria, 9, 172, 180, 183, 242, 324, 393

Taifas, 360, 361
Takkanah, 226–227, 294
Tale of Aqhat, 56
Talmud, 175, 279–299, 344; *Babylonian*, 279, 280, 281–282, 292–293, 299, 327, 344, 352, 422–424; Karaism and, 333–334; *Palestinian*, 279, 280, 292, 293, 298–299, 327; study of, 325, 326; writings on, 355, 356
Talmud Torah, 199, 232–233, 237–238, 262–265
Tamar, 12
Tamid, 275, 422
Tanach, 217–218, 281, 287, 322, 332, 341, 342
Tanḥuma, 296
Tannaim, 162, 266–268, 283, 305, 329; *midrash halachah* of, 268–273; sins and contrition and, 261–262; study and, 262–265
Tanuch, 252
Tarbit, 175
Tarfon, 258, 263, 268–269
Targumim, 199, 200
Tarn, W. W., 179
Taxes, 295; Muslim, 324, 325; poll, 284, 338; Roman, 256, 257, 267
Teacher of Righteousness, 185, 201, 244
Tefillah, 315, 318, 337
Tefillin, 196, 415
Tefutzah, 146
Temperance, 208
Temple (Jerusalem), 61, 115, 121, 124, 128, 157, 160, 170, 187, 220; anniversary of destruction of, 297; as center of Jewish nation during Greek times, 187–189; destruction of, 130, 134, 140, 148, 189, 196, 255, 256, 258, 318; Diaspora and, 152, 158, 159; duty for upkeep of, 256, 266; fasts in memorial to destruction of, 256–257; God's

Index

planning of, 164–165; Mount Gerizim Temple as rival to, 216; Pharisees and, 228–229; prophecy on razing of, 104; rebuilding of, 79, 145, 151, 154, 315; Solomon and, 71; synagogues and rituals of, 258–262; worship in, 166, 168, 202

Ten Commandments (decalogue), 11–12, 26, 27–28, 48, 123, 291
Tent of Meeting, 163
Terah, 5
Teshuvah, 99, 150–151, 261–262, 286–287
Testament of the Twelve Patriarchs, 195
Testimonies, 275
Themistius, 407
Theodosius II, 297, 299, 318
Theodotes, 178
Theophrastus, 176
Theos, as name of God, 199–200
Therapeutae, 207
Tiamat, 16
Tiberias, schools at, 331
Tiglath-Pileser III, 98
Tithes, 187, 229, 230, 275
Titus, 394
Tobit (book), 197, 417
Torah, 36, 62, 65, 76, 95, 163, 177, 185, 252, 257, 306, 346, 356; as active agent of divinity, 287–288; canonization of, 217; clan law replaced by, 107; covenant and, 25, 26, 41; Deuteronomy and, 123–124; etymology of, 27; *galut* and, 148, 278; God's gift of, 308, 371; as Jerusalem's constitution, 174; law of God within, 13; Maccabean Revolt and domination of, 183, 184; *midrash* to, see *Midrash*; *Mishnah* and, 273–276; as national covenant, 158; need for official text of, 215–219; as *nomos* (law), 190–193, 203, 214; Pharisees and, 224–229; Philo's writings on, 211, 212, 213; prophecy and, 80, 252–253; rabbis as officers of, 286; rules on use of, 293; Sadducees and, 220–224; *Shema* and, 313–314; social restrictions within, 68–69; study of, 262–265, 294, 304, 319, 362; as sum of accessible knowledge, 203; *torot* organized into, 215–216; translations of, 178, 197–200, 210–211, 403; worship and, 190, 316; writing of, 293
Torah Council, 220
Torah Shelemah, 224–225
Torat Emet, 324
Torat Ḥayyim, 287, 303
Torot, 27, 121, 123–124, 129, 187, 190, 215–216, 224, 225, 227
Tosefta, 275–276, 422
Tower of Babel, 9
Trade, in Greek world, 173–175, 179, 181
Trans-Jordan, 52, 140
Translations, 178, 197–200, 210–211, 293, 403

Tribes of Israel, 4, 5–6, 34–39, 69–76, 107
Tzaddik, 150
Tzedakah, 187
Tzitzit, 64

Ugarit, 12, 113
Ummayad caliphs, 324–325, 352, 353
Ur, 9
Uriah, 87, 90
Uriel, 247
Usury, 175
Utnapishtim, 10

Vespasian, 251, 255, 256, 263, 336
Virginity suits, 275
Virtue, 207–208, 307
Visigoths, 352
Voltaire, 343

Wacholder, Ben Zion, 268
Wars of the Sons of Light and the Sons of Darkness, The, 251, 418
Washing rituals for guilt, 230–231
Wen-Amon, 78
West Semitic culture, 4
Wisdom literature, 108–113, 116, 178, 202, 206–208, 262
Wisdom of Solomon, 178, 203, 205
Wives, rights of, 65
Wolfson, Harry A., 177, 211
Women, 235; divorce by, 33; in Hellenistic times, 176; laws regarding, 226, 275; synagogue and, 260; Torah study and, 285
Worship, 311–317, 321–322

Yehoshua, Rabbi, 218, 255, 256, 300
Yehoshua ben Levi, 307
Yehudah, R., 291
Yehudah ben Naḥman, 317
Yehudah ha-Nasi, 266, 274, 275
Yelammedenu, 295–296
Yetzer ha-ra, 303, 304
Yetzer tov, 303, 304
Yetziat mitzrayim (Exodus), 8, 39–49, 69, 121, 156, 178, 292, 302
YHWH, 14, 47–49, 199–200, 201, 236, 307
Yiḥud, 348, 409, 414
Yoḥanan ben Zakkai, 233, 251, 256, 257, 259, 260, 263, 265, 336
Yom Kippur (Day of Atonement), 48, 141–142, 154, 170–171, 189, 229, 260–261, 262, 358

Index

Yose, Rabbi, 301
Yose ben Yose, 319

Zadok family, 157, 182, 185
Zealots, 237, 250, 251, 277
Zechariah, 141, 157, 158, 163, 252, 278, 357
Zechariah (book), 68, 141, 157, 169, 170, 240
Zecher Le-ḥurban, 256–257
Zedekiah, 73, 82, 130

Zeno, 233
Zephaniah, 126, 127, 128, 131–132
Zephaniah (book), 127, 130, 131, 132
Zerubbabel, 157, 158
Zervanites, 243
Ziggurats, 9
Zimri-lin, 78
Zion, 112, 151, 250, 333, 337, 363
Zipporah, 22
Zoroastrianism, 144, 179, 247, 287

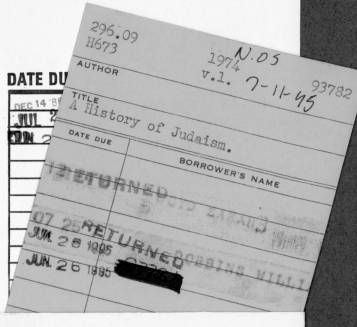